The Role of Innovation and Entrepreneurship in Economic Growth

A National Bureau of Economic Research

Conference Report

NATIONAL BUREAU of ECONOMIC RESEARCH

The Role of Innovation and Entrepreneurship in Economic Growth

Edited by **Michael J. Andrews, Aaron K. Chatterji, Josh Lerner, and Scott Stern**

The University of Chicago Press

Chicago and London

The University of Chicago Press, Chicago 60637
The University of Chicago Press, Ltd., London
© 2022 by the National Bureau of Economic Research
Published 2022
Printed in the United States of America

31 30 29 28 27 26 25 24 23 22   1 2 3 4 5

ISBN-13: 978-0-226-81078-2 (cloth)
ISBN-13: 978-0-226-81064-5 (e-book)

DOI: https://doi.org/10.7208/chicago/9780226810645.001.0001

Library of Congress Cataloging-in-Publication Data

Names: Andrews, Michael J., editor. | Chatterji, Aaron, 1978–, editor. |
    Lerner, Josh, 1978–, editor. | Stern, Scott, editor.
Title: The role of innovation and entrepreneurship in economic growth /
    edited by Michael J. Andrews, Aaron K. Chatterji, Josh Lerner, and
    Scott Stern.
Other titles: National Bureau of Economic Research conference report.
Description: Chicago : University of Chicago Press, 2022. | Series:
    National Bureau of Economic Research conference report | Includes
    index.
Identifiers: LCCN 2021043214 | ISBN 9780226810782 (cloth) |
    ISBN 9780226810645 (ebook)
Subjects: LCSH: Economic development. | Technological innovations. |
    Entrepreneurship.
Classification: LCC HD82 .R6595 2022 | DDC 338.9—dc23
LC record available at https://lccn.loc.gov/2021043214

♾ This paper meets the requirements of ANSI/NISO Z39.48-1992
(Permanence of Paper).

Relation of the Directors to the Work and Publications of the NBER

1. The object of the NBER is to ascertain and present to the economics profession, and to the public more generally, important economic facts and their interpretation in a scientific manner without policy recommendations. The Board of Directors is charged with the responsibility of ensuring that the work of the NBER is carried on in strict conformity with this object.

2. The President shall establish an internal review process to ensure that book manuscripts proposed for publication DO NOT contain policy recommendations. This shall apply both to the proceedings of conferences and to manuscripts by a single author or by one or more co-authors but shall not apply to authors of comments at NBER conferences who are not NBER affiliates.

3. No book manuscript reporting research shall be published by the NBER until the President has sent to each member of the Board a notice that a manuscript is recommended for publication and that in the President's opinion it is suitable for publication in accordance with the above principles of the NBER. Such notification will include a table of contents and an abstract or summary of the manuscript's content, a list of contributors if applicable, and a response form for use by Directors who desire a copy of the manuscript for review. Each manuscript shall contain a summary drawing attention to the nature and treatment of the problem studied and the main conclusions reached.

4. No volume shall be published until forty-five days have elapsed from the above notification of intention to publish it. During this period a copy shall be sent to any Director requesting it, and if any Director objects to publication on the grounds that the manuscript contains policy recommendations, the objection will be presented to the author(s) or editor(s). In case of dispute, all members of the Board shall be notified, and the President shall appoint an ad hoc committee of the Board to decide the matter; thirty days additional shall be granted for this purpose.

5. The President shall present annually to the Board a report describing the internal manuscript review process, any objections made by Directors before publication or by anyone after publication, any disputes about such matters, and how they were handled.

6. Publications of the NBER issued for informational purposes concerning the work of the Bureau, or issued to inform the public of the activities at the Bureau, including but not limited to the NBER Digest and Reporter, shall be consistent with the object stated in paragraph 1. They shall contain a specific disclaimer noting that they have not passed through the review procedures required in this resolution. The Executive Committee of the Board is charged with the review of all such publications from time to time.

7. NBER working papers and manuscripts distributed on the Bureau's web site are not deemed to be publications for the purpose of this resolution, but they shall be consistent with the object stated in paragraph 1. Working papers shall contain a specific disclaimer noting that they have not passed through the review procedures required in this resolution. The NBER's web site shall contain a similar disclaimer. The President shall establish an internal review process to ensure that the working papers and the web site do not contain policy recommendations, and shall report annually to the Board on this process and any concerns raised in connection with it.

8. Unless otherwise determined by the Board or exempted by the terms of paragraphs 6 and 7, a copy of this resolution shall be printed in each NBER publication as described in paragraph 2 above.

Contents

Acknowledgments

We are grateful for the generous support of the Ewing Marion Kauffman Foundation, which made this volume possible. The Foundation has been a critical source of support for the NBER's research activities on entrepreneurship and innovation for nearly two decades.

Many individuals deserve a great deal of thanks for the success of this endeavor. First, we thank NBER President James Poterba and the NBER Productivity, Innovation, and Entrepreneurship Program Directors Josh Lerner and Nick Bloom for helping to shape the direction and themes of the conference. The NBER conference department, and especially Rob Shannon, provided invaluable logistical support, as did the staff at the Computer History Museum and Natalia Kalas of MIT. We also thank Helena Fitz-Patrick of the NBER Publications Department, and the two external reviewers who provided very helpful comments that improved both the individual chapters and the Introduction.

Introduction
Beyond 140 Characters

Michael J. Andrews, Aaron K. Chatterji, and Scott Stern

Are technological innovations and new business starts driving economic growth? Prominent innovators and entrepreneurs express differing views. In 2011, Peter Thiel lamented that "we wanted flying cars, instead we got 140 characters" (Thiel 2011). That same year, Marc Andreessen took the opposite view, arguing that "software was eating the world," a trend that made him "optimistic about the future growth of the U.S. and global economies" (Andreessen 2011). The ensuing decade has provided evidence to support both the optimistic and pessimistic views of the role of innovation and entrepreneurship in economic growth.

The academic literature is likewise divided. Several authors have documented recent sluggish productivity growth rates (Bloom et al. 2020; Gordon 2000) and declines in business dynamism (Decker et al. 2014). Some scholars go even further than Thiel and believe that not only has innovation underperformed over the past several decades, but that it will be difficult or impossible to achieve high levels of growth in the future (Cowan 2011; Gordon 2012, 2016, 2018). Another group disagrees with these bleak forecasts for the future, identifying high levels of entrepreneurial growth potential

Michael J. Andrews is an assistant professor of economics at the University of Maryland, Baltimore County. He was previously a postdoctoral fellow in innovation policy at the National Bureau of Economic Research.

Aaron K. Chatterji is the Mark Burgess and Lisa Benson-Burgess Distinguished Professor at Duke University's Fuqua School of Business, professor at the Sanford School of Public Policy, and a research associate of the National Bureau of Economic Research. He is currently on leave from Duke and the NBER as chief economist of the United States Department of Commerce.

Scott Stern is the David Sarnoff Professor of Management and chair of the Technological Innovation, Entrepreneurship, and Strategic Management Group at the MIT Sloan School of Management. He is a research associate, and the past director of the Innovation Policy Working Group, at the National Bureau of Economic Research.

For acknowledgments, sources of research support, and disclosure of the authors' material financial relationships, if any, please see https://www.nber.org/books-and-chapters/role -innovation-and-entrepreneurship-economic-growth/introduction-beyond-140-characters.

(Guzman and Stern 2020) and pointing to the almost unimaginable possibilities arising from technologies such as artificial intelligence, advanced genetic engineering, financial technology, and clean energy—technologies for which the economic impact has yet to be fully realized (Mokyr 2018). In fact, some are concerned that future innovation will be sufficiently rapid to cause unemployment and lower wages, for instance as a result of artificial intelligence or robots (e.g., Acemoglu and Restrepo 2020). Scholars with a historical perspective dismiss the technological pessimists and note how often past predictions of long-term stagnation have proven wrong (Mokyr, Vickers, and Ziebarth 2015). Reviewing the literature, it truly can seem that we are living in both the best of times and the worst of times.

In short, we live in an era in which innovation and entrepreneurship seem ubiquitous, particularly in regions like Silicon Valley, Boston, and North Carolina's Research Triangle Park, yet many metrics of economic growth have been at best modest over recent years. At the time of this writing, we are in a pandemic that has consistently challenged our ability to create and scale innovative solutions to pressing problems. While economists have long posited a relationship between innovation, entrepreneurship, productivity growth, and economic output (Abramowitz 1956; Schumpeter 1942; Solow 1956, 1957), the conflicting observations above led us to question just how much we actually know about the role of innovation and entrepreneurship in driving economic growth. This lack of consensus is particularly problematic given the extent to which private and public resources are increasingly being targeted toward programs and policies whose objective is to leverage innovation and entrepreneurship as a source of growth.

Thiel's memorable expression gives one clue as to why both the optimistic and pessimistic views can coexist: we expected dramatic innovations in fields like transportation to dramatically change our physical lives, but instead we have seen far more innovation in information technology (IT) as our lives move online. Though not well understood, this heterogeneity is critical. By construction, the impact of innovation and entrepreneurship on overall economic performance reflects the cumulative impact of innovation and entrepreneurship across sectors. Given the wide variation across sectors, understanding the potential for growth in the aggregate economy depends on understanding the potential for growth in each individual sector.

This insight motivates the work in this volume, where we leverage industry studies to identify specific examples of productivity improvements enabled by innovation and entrepreneurship, whether via new production technologies, increased competition, new organizational forms, or other means. Taken together, we can then understand whether the contribution of innovation and entrepreneurship to economic growth is likely to be concentrated in a few sectors or more widespread. More specifically, we sought to answer the following questions:

- What is the relationship between innovation/entrepreneurship and economic growth in specific industrial sectors?
- How has the relationship between innovation/entrepreneurship and economic growth changed over time?
- How much do policies, programs, and specialized institutions (such as venture capital) meant to encourage innovation/entrepreneurship ultimately spur economic growth?
- Does innovation/entrepreneurship affect economic performance and social progress through channels other than measured productivity and economic growth, and if so, how can these effects be measured?

We commissioned studies from experts on 12 different industries: manufacturing, IT, agriculture, energy, transportation, retail, services, the creative sector, government, health care, housing, and education. While innovation and entrepreneurship in some of these sectors have been well studied by economists (e.g., energy, health, IT), others have been less examined (education, housing). In this introduction, we draw out some of the lessons learned by comparing across these very different types of industries.

The ideas in each of these industry studies were discussed and refined at a pre-conference held in July 2019 in Cambridge, MA. Fittingly for a collection of studies on the role of innovation and entrepreneurship, formal presentations and discussions were held at the Computer History Museum in Mountain View, CA, in January 2020. In addition to the 12 industry studies, the conference included a panel of academic and government economists on the role of public policy in promoting innovation and entrepreneurship and a keynote address, as well as three fireside chats and two panels of practitioners consisting of entrepreneurs, venture capitalists, and policymakers.

Below, we first describe each of the twelve industry studies, highlighting similarities and differences across sectors, as well as the conclusions of the policy panel. Next, we give a broad overview of the practitioner comments. We then draw out common themes. Finally, we close by addressing the extent to which our conclusions from this conference have been altered or reinforced in light of the 2020 COVID-19 pandemic and the resulting economic situation.

Outline of Chapters

In this volume, we organize the industry studies into three groups: "productivity driver" sectors, which include manufacturing, IT, agriculture, and energy; the "on-demand" sectors, comprising transportation, retail, professional services, and the creative sectors; and the "cost disease" sectors, which consist of government, health care, housing, and education.

As a preview of these industry studies described below, we first summarize key metrics for each sector in table I.1. Ben Jones revisits many of these metrics in his concluding chapter. For this table, we define a "sector" using two-digit North American Industry Classification System (NAICS) codes, although as the detailed industry studies make clear, it is often far from obvious where the boundaries of one sector end and another begin, especially when trying to account for innovative activities. In the first two columns of table I.1, we present metrics that give a sense of the importance of each sector: each sector's share of gross domestic product (GDP) from the Bureau of Economic Analysis and each sector's share of employment from the Bureau of Labor Statistics Quarterly Census of Employment and Wages. In all, the sectors studied in this volume cover more than 75 percent of US GDP and almost 80 percent of employment.

The next two columns present common measures of innovativeness. The first of these measures is the patenting rate, defined as the number of patents issued to firms in each sector per 1,000 employees. The patenting rate is a measure of each sector's innovative output. Data on patenting are from the US Patent and Trademark Office (USPTO); we link patents to sectors using a crosswalk developed in Goldschlag, Lybbert, and Zolas (2020) that maps USPTO-assigned patent classifications to NAICS codes. Over all the sectors studied, firms produce just under one patent for every 1,000 employees. The second measure is research and development (R&D) intensity, defined as the amount of R&D spending per employee; this is a measure of innovative input. Data on R&D spending come from the Census Bureau and National Science Foundation's Business R&D and Innovation Survey (BRDIS). While BRDIS does not collect R&D data for all sectors, over the six sectors for which we have data, firms spend about $21 on R&D for every employee.

The final column presents a measure of the level of entrepreneurship in each sector, the establishment entry rate. This is calculated by dividing the number of new establishments in each sector by the average number of establishments in that sector. Data on establishment entry rates are from the Census Bureau's Business Dynamics Statistics. While these data are not available for the agricultural or government sectors, for the other 10 sectors, the establishment entry rate is 0.10.

Table I.1 reveals extreme heterogeneity across sectors for these measures of innovation and entrepreneurship. The sectoral patenting rate varies by more than two orders of magnitude. The R&D intensity exhibits a similar range across sectors. The most dynamic sectors have an establishment entry rate more than twice as high as that of the least dynamic sectors, although establishment dynamics appear to be weakly negatively correlated with our measures of innovativeness.

While informative, these statistics can provide only the roughest of sketches about the state of innovation and entrepreneurship in each sector. Each of the next 12 chapters in this volume contains a detailed industry study that puts these numbers into context.

Table I.1   Key metrics for the 12 sectors discussed in this volume

Sector	Share of GDP (1)	Share of employment (2)	Patents per thousand employees (3)	R&D spending per employee (2015 $US) (4)	Establishment entry rate (5)
Productivity Driver Sectors					
1 Manufacturing	.12	.088	5.648	23.262	.066
2 IT	.047	.021	2.394	33.222	.107
3 Agriculture	.01	.009	1.927	—	—
4 Energy	.034	.011	.455	6.685	.084
On-demand sectors					
5 Transportation	.03	.04	.503	.488	.139
6 Retail	.059	.113	.117	—	.079
7 Services	.072	.063	.884	24.263	.122
8 Creative	.01	.018	.284	—	.125
Cost disease sectors					
9 Government	.13	.052	.101	—	—
10 Health	.072	.145	.065	—	.092
11 Housing	.041	.063	.435	4.778	.127
12 Education	.011	.088	.016	—	.108
All sectors	.767	.794	.924	20.928	.100

Notes: All statistics are calculated at the sectoral level using 2-digit North American Industry Classification System (NAICS) codes. Column 1 presents data on each sector's share of total value added from the Bureau of Economic Analysis "All GDP-by-industry" data (https://apps.bea.gov/iTable/iTable.cfm?isuri =1&reqid=151&step=1). Column 2 presents data on each sector's annual average share of total employment from the Bureau of Labor Statistics Quarterly Census of Employment and Wages (BLS QCEW) (https://www.bls.gov/cew/downloadable-data-files.htm). Column 3 presents data on the rate of patenting, calculated as the number of patents in each sector divided by employment (in thousands) from the BLS QCEW. Patent data are from the USPTO's Patents-View database (https://patentsview.org/download/data-download-tables). Each patent is matched to a NAICS code using the probabilistic crosswalk from Goldschlag et al. (2019). Column 4 presents data on R&D intensity. R&D data is from the Business R&D and Innovation Survey (BRDIS) conducted by the US Census Bureau and the National Center for Science and Engineering Statistics within the National Science Foundation (https://ncses.nsf.gov/pubs /nsf18313/#general-notes&data-tables). R&D intensity is calculated by dividing each sector's total domestic R&D dollars by total employment from firms surveyed by BRDIS in that sector. Column 5 presents data on the establishment entry rate from the Census Bureau Business Dynamics Statistics (https:// www.census.gov/programs-surveys/bds/data.html). Each row lists these statistics for one of the studied sectors. The final row presents combined results for all sectors studied in this volume. All data are from 2015, as this is the last year for which we can map patents to the full set of sectors.

Productivity Drivers

We begin by examining four "productivity driver" sectors. These are sectors that have undergone substantial innovation-driven change to increase measured productivity. Additionally, each of these sectors represents a general-purpose technology (Bresnahan 2010) and thus facilitates innovations in other sectors, including the on-demand sectors we describe below.

First, Erica Fuchs, Christophe Combemale, Kate Whitefoot, and Britta Glennon present results on the manufacturing sector, which has experienced dramatic innovation, particularly in the form of widespread mechanization. While manufacturing looks different in the US today than it did half a century ago, the economic statistics are underwhelming. Manufacturing accounts for 66 percent of US R&D but only 12.5 percent of value added. The authors argue that this is largely because manufacturing R&D investments made in the US are increasingly realized overseas. Most of the largest manufacturing firms operate internationally, and the increasing offshoring of supply chains raises numerous questions about the calculation of national innovation and productivity statistics. The authors also emphasize the importance of heterogeneity across the manufacturing sector, as manufacturing statistics include industries as diverse as automobile manufacturing, pharmaceuticals, and animal slaughtering. Not surprisingly, the amount of R&D conducted and value added varies dramatically across sectors. In her discussion at the conference, Kathryn Shaw emphasized the firm dynamics that underlie the observed patterns of R&D and productivity in manufacturing, as increasingly low productivity firms are exiting, leaving the high-productivity and high R&D firms, which also tend to be multinationals. Shaw also noted that much of the R&D conducted by traditional manufacturing firms, such as IBM, are in fields only tangentially related to manufacturing, such as artificial intelligence, making it difficult to know what to classify as manufacturing.

Perhaps the most obvious sector when discussing innovation-driven productivity growth is IT. This sector is examined by Chris Forman and Avi Goldfarb in chapter 2. IT holds a special place, because improvements in IT are often behind innovation and entrepreneurship in other sectors. For example, in the on-demand sectors examined below, IT has already revolutionized firms to dramatically reduce frictions, in some cases facilitating nearly instantaneous fulfillment of consumer needs. The successes in the IT sector over the past half century have been well documented, in particular, massive improvements in computing power and the networking of computers through the Internet. And more recently, these successes have revolutionized business models, such as software as a service, and they have changed connections across industries through the Internet of Things. While IT has rightly been held up as the model of dynamism, Chris Forman and Avi Goldfarb argue in chapter 2 that the IT sector is increasingly showing signs of becoming mature and less dynamic. With a deep dive into patent data, they show that the IT sector has become increasingly geographically concentrated in Silicon Valley, patents increasingly come from a smaller number of firms, and those firms increasingly tend to be incumbents. In his conference discussion, Erik Brynjolfsson reminded us that patents are an imperfect measure of innovation, and this may be particularly true for software. Nevertheless, Brynjolfsson highlighted several other metrics that tell a similar story to that of Forman and Goldfarb. Namely, high-IT industries are more concentrated using various measures, and the often-intangible assets that are complementary to IT are increasingly found in superstar firms.

In chapter 3, Julian Alston and Phil Pardey examine the agriculture sector. Agriculture is a sector that has already undergone many of the massive productivity changes currently occurring in the manufacturing and IT sectors and thus provides a useful case study for thinking about the future of innovation and entrepreneurship. Alston and Pardey survey the many labor-saving technologies in agriculture implemented over the past century, and consequently the dramatic decline in labor working in agriculture, the small decline in land used for agriculture, and the increase in agricultural inputs (e.g., pesticides and herbicides) and capital (farm machinery). In many respects, the transition in US agriculture over the twentieth century resembles the manufacturing sector in recent decades, with large increases in mechanization and productivity, the sector increasingly filled with workers having low human capital, and much of the low value-added production shifting overseas. One unique feature of the agricultural sector is that the government has kept detailed statistics on agricultural output and R&D inputs for a much longer time than it has in most other sectors, making it possible to construct detailed estimates of the return to R&D. These estimated returns are massive, with estimated median internal rates of return ranging across studies from 12 to 41 percent per year, and benefit-cost ratios ranging from 7 to 12. Notably, these estimated returns are calculated over many years, and it can take decades for R&D to manifest itself in the productivity statistics. Alston and Pardey also review adoption lags for numerous agricultural technologies, and likewise find 30–50 years between when a technology is introduced and when it is widely adopted; hybrid corn as studied by Griliches (1957) and, more recently, genetically engineered crops are the rare exceptions that were adopted remarkably quickly. The authors also analyze numerous more recent technologies, including precision agriculture, variable rate seeding and fertilizer, the use of satellite imaging, auto-steering on tractors, and more, and they find much slower adoption rates. In his comment on chapter 3, included in this volume, Brian Wright elaborates on many of the facts documented by Alston and Pardey, particularly emphasizing the influences behind US public support of agricultural research and innovation. Wright also speculates that, over time, farmers have realized that they appropriate a relatively small share of the returns to public research in agriculture, and they have instead turned their attention to lobbying for market-distorting policies that favor their interests. Such a hypothesis is consistent with the slowdown in the increase of corn yields following the adoption of biofuel mandates in the early 2000s.

The energy sector, analyzed by David Popp, Jacquelyn Pless, Ivan Haščič, and Nick Johnstone in chapter 4, is another sector in which innovations are best viewed over long time scales. The energy industry is characterized by high fixed costs, and so most of the major actors are large incumbent firms. The industry is undergoing a structural transformation, however, and so both of those patterns, the gradual pace of change and the dominance of established firms, may be changing. In particular, costs of renewable energy production have been falling rapidly, with the cost of a kilowatt hour of electricity from solar power in 2017 being only about 30 percent of what it was in 2010, and several sources of renewable energy are now nearly competitive with fossil fuels on price. While it has taken decades for the costs of these new technologies to become close to competitive with conventional sources, progress has not been steady, with most innovations (as measured by patents) occurring when conventional energy prices are high. Green energy thus provides perhaps the cleanest example of induced innovation. Clean energy technologies do have some drawbacks relative to conventional sources, such as their intermittency, which highlights the importance of energy storage and transportation as well as grid management technologies. The latter in particular relies on improvements in IT and, as the authors show using venture capital data, has opened the door for small, young, entrepreneurial firms to become important players in the energy sector. In his conference discussion, Hunt Allcott compared the recent rise of fracking and clean energy technologies to historical cycles in the energy market, especially the 1970s oil shock, documenting similar patterns of increasing innovation as energy prices rise. Building on this historical perspective, Allcott then asked several important questions: First, how predictable are energy-sector policies, such as cap and trade? And second, are researchers currently too focused on policies that reduce static distortions at the expense of policies that could reduce dynamic disincentives to innovate?

The On-Demand Economy

We next examine the on-demand economy. These are sectors in which general purpose technologies from the productivity driver sectors, often information and communication technologies (ICTs), have changed how sectors deliver their products, dramatically reducing the speed at which consumers can acquire a product or increasing the geographic scope over which transactions can occur.

Perhaps the most obvious on-demand sector is transportation. Transportation is also one of Thiel's (2011) primary examples illustrating the innovation slowdowns in recent decades: since the retirement of the Concorde supersonic jet, "the travel time across the Atlantic Ocean . . . for the first time since the Industrial Revolution, is getting longer rather than shorter." Derrick Choe, Alex Oettl, and Rob Seamans describe the innovations that have occurred in the transportation sector. While passenger travel times for transoceanic travel have been nearly constant over the past several decades, the transportation sector as a whole has made major strides incorporating sensors and other IT technologies. Choe, Oettl, and Seamans focus on warehousing, one part of the transportation sector in particular that has been transformed by these technologies. The importance of delivering goods to consumers has not diminished in importance in recent decades. Last mile delivery services account for an increasing share of employment in the transportation sector, and the use of logistics technologies and autonomous vehicles inside warehouses have allowed firms to sharply decrease delivery times. The authors also review several other recent technologies that would have been impossible without underlying IT innovations, most notably ride sharing apps and self-driving cars. Many (although certainly not all) of the remaining hurdles to widespread adoption of self-driving cars are not technological but rather legal and regulatory, hurdles that ride sharing apps were able to sidestep initially but with which they are increasingly forced to reconcile. In his comment on chapter 5, included in this volume, Gilles Duranton takes a step back to examine the broader transportation sector. Duranton identifies four features that make the transportation sector unique and affect how innovation occurs in that sector: the presence of externalities, especially congestion, accidents, and pollution; the fundamental role of publicly provided goods, namely, infrastructure; the durability of assets; and the fact that transportation affects nearly all other sectors of the economy. While Choe, Oettl, and Seamans document substantial innovation in warehousing and passenger transport, the features identified by Duranton tend to slow the rate of innovation in the broader transportation sector.

Innovations in the transportation sector that have changed how goods are delivered to consumers have consequently ushered in massive changes in the retail sector as well. Francine Lafontaine and Jagadeesh Sivadasan investigate retail in depth. The "retail apocalypse" has been well publicized, with massive closures of retail establishments and drops in retail employment since the late 1990s. The authors show, first, that some of these losses in traditional retail have been regained, particularly in employment. Much of this is driven by "big box" stores, which accounted for a growing share of retail sales until about 2009, when they plateaued or experienced a modest decline. In contrast, e-commerce continues to account for a growing share of all retail sales, although by 2017 this share was still less than 7 percent. But the more important trend is the rise of restaurants. The number of restaurant establishments and restaurant employment has increased dramatically since the early 2000s, more than offsetting losses in retail. While Americans have been eating a growing share of meals away from the home for decades, the recent growth in restaurants is enough to radically change the commercial landscape, with the explosion of restaurants occurring in all types of locations and across all restaurant categories. In her comment, included in this volume, Emek Basker focuses on how retail has been classified in administrative data, how this classification has changed over time, and how it affects how we view the patterns documented by Lafontaine and Sivadasan, especially in light of the rise of online retail. Basker also further dives into the heterogeneity in the retail apocalypse. While Lafontaine and Sivadasan highlight the rise of restaurants, Basker points out that other customer-facing establishments, such as gyms and nail salons, have also experienced dramatic growth over the past decade.

As many traditional retail establishments close and the manufacturing sector shrinks as a share of employment, numerous authors have documented the growth in the service sector (Fuchs 1980; Buera and Kaboski 2012; Eckert, Ganapati, and Walsh 2019; Delgado and Mills 2020). One might expect this to be a sector of the economy beset by Baumol's cost disease; after all, how much more productive is a barber or hairdresser today relative to 50 years ago? But Mercedes Delgado, Daniel Kim, and Karen Mills show in chapter 7 that the services sector is indeed innovative. They identify one subset of the services sector that has been growing especially rapidly, which they call "supply chain traded services." These are services sold to businesses or government in the process of producing a separate final product and include such fields as programming, design, and logistics. The key insight is that many of the jobs that make our high-tech and IT-intensive economy what it is, which allow firms to scale rapidly and serve disparate customers, are themselves service jobs. While these jobs are relatively new, the firms that perform the jobs tend to be incumbents. In fact, many are firms that used to mainly be manufacturing firms (for instance, IBM used to be known for manufacturing mainframes but now is primarily a consulting and data analysis firm) and manufacturing incumbents now have almost a third of their employees and 40 percent of their payroll in supply chain traded services. In his comment, included in this volume, Sharat Ganapati focuses on the spatial aspects of servicification. A large non-tradable local service sector limits the extent to which industries can cluster in one location; as services become more tradable, this may be expected to unleash larger agglomeration economies. At the same time, Ganapati notes that wage growth in the supply chain traded services sector has been growing faster than employment, suggesting that the labor force for this sector may still be fairly immobile.

Next, in chapter 8, Joel Waldfogel discusses the arts, media, and the creative sector. Ironically, this is the sector that Baumol and Bowen (1966) described when they introduced the concept of the cost disease: for example, a Beethoven string quartet takes the same amount of labor to perform today as it did in the early nineteenth century. While this may be true, thanks to improvements in recording and streaming technologies, a much larger audience can now listen to any given performance. Decreasing costs of production and distribution of media content are valuable for at least two reasons. First, there is now "infinite shelf space," facilitating a long tail of content that appeals to consumers with niche tastes. Second and more importantly, when the appeal of new content is unknown at the time of production, increasing the amount of new content makes it more likely that hits will be discovered. Consider the success of independently published books such as *Fifty Shades of Gray* (James 2011) or music by artists like Ed Sheeren (Davis 2019), both of which would have been unlikely to find a large audience without distribution platforms like Amazon or YouTube, respectively. Waldfogel refers to this second benefit as "the random long tail." Building on the analysis of Aguiar and Waldfogel (2018), which examined the benefits of digitization in the recorded music industry, Waldfogel estimates that digitization has increased sales by about 10 percent in the movie industry, 50 percent in television, and 10 percent in books and, moreover, that the benefits of the random long tail are four to thirteen times larger than the benefits of the "conventional" long tail. Waldfogel also examines the creative labor market and finds that total earnings of creative workers are rising while average earnings per worker are falling, consistent with a larger number of part-time or hobbyist creatives who are now able to sell their content. In his comment on chapter 8, included in this volume, Gustavo Manso builds on these observations of the creative labor market, noting that lower average earnings for artists is consistent with experimentation: individuals can more easily enter the creative market; learn whether they are likely to succeed; and if not, exit to other types of employment. Thus digitization may paradoxically be associated with both lower average earnings and higher lifetime earnings for artists; Manso (2016) documents similar findings in entrepreneurship more broadly.

The Cost Disease Sectors

Finally, we examine the sectors afflicted by Baumol's cost disease (Baumol 1967; Baumol and Bowen 1966), defined as those sectors in which it has been difficult to increase labor productivity. In contrast to the on-demand sectors, the cost disease sectors have so far been largely unable to leverage IT or other general purpose technologies to improve productivity at scale.

In chapter 9, Joshua Bruce and John de Figueiredo examine perhaps the ultimate cost disease sector: the government. While the federal government is a massive funder of innovation, innovation within government itself—that is, organizational, regulatory, and policy innovation—is much harder to measure. In terms of the innovation funded by the federal government, more than 40 percent of R&D dollars go to the Department of Defense, 27 percent go to Health and Human Services, and 12 percent goes to the Department of Energy. That leaves only about 10 percent of federal R&D

to go to all other programs, including NASA, the National Science Foundation (NSF), and agricultural research. The distribution of federal scientists and federally funded patents is similar. What is striking is how little federal research is conducted in such areas as education, housing, and the social sciences, not just as a share of the overall federal research budget, but in absolute terms as well, even though these areas concern major federal policies. In his comment, included in this volume, Manuel Trajtenberg steps away from the analysis of direct federal funding of intramural research to discuss how the federal government has adopted information and communication technologies to function more effectively; these types of innovations, as noted by Bruce and de Figueiredo, are difficult to capture in official statistics. Nevertheless, Trajtenberg sketches several case studies, including the government's use of digital technologies in the health and transportation sectors, highlighting the crucial role of the government in affecting innovation in several other sectors outlined in this volume.

One sector that has received massive amounts of research spending from both the federal government and private sources is the health sector. But this research tends to overwhelmingly be directed toward new drugs, with a relatively small share of research directed toward health services. In chapter 10, Amitabh Chandra, Cirrus Foroughi, and Lauren Mostrom investigate the health sector, with a particular focus on venture capital–led entrepreneurship. They report that 60 percent of venture capital (VC) investment in health is directed to firms working on pharmaceuticals, 20 percent to firms working on medical devices, and only 20 percent to firms working on all aspects of health-care delivery and infrastructure. In contrast to the government sector, in which it is difficult to measure innovation, in the health sector, numerous measures of innovation inputs and outputs are available: Chandra, Foroughi, and Molstrom make use of data on patenting, academic publications, and public research spending, in addition to the aforementioned VC investment. Overall, the authors conclude that it is likely more difficult to find economically attractive projects in the health sector than in other sectors: VC funding tends to grow more slowly and is directed at earlier-stage firms in health than in other sectors. The geographic concentration of health innovations is increasing over time, measured both by patents and publications. The authors present suggestive evidence that many useful innovations that are created away from "health innovation hubs" like Boston and San Francisco are not developed, because venture capitalists and other potential funders do not know about them. Given the challenges that the private sector faces in identifying and funding attractive projects, does the public sector fill the gap? The National Institutes of Health (NIH) allocates a larger share of funding to basic science than does private industry, a necessary condition for efficient expenditure of public funds. But when it comes to translational research that is directly linked to a disease, the distribution of NIH funding is indistinguishable from private funding. Additionally, the NIH allocates a larger share of funding to pharmaceuticals, and less to health-care delivery, than does the private sector. Together, these facts raise the possibility that public funding is not working to resolve market failures in the health-care sector. At the conference, Heidi Williams discussed some of the inferential difficulties in determining whether health innovation is becoming more inefficient. She also placed the increasing concentration of health innovation in context by comparing it to other sectors, including computing (as also highlighted by Forman and Goldfarb in chapter 2 of this volume), biology/chemistry, and semiconductors.

In chapter 11, Ed Kung investigates the housing sector. This sector is also one that has seen little R&D spending or measurable innovation. While there has been little change in how housing units are constructed, numerous real estate technology firms have appeared, either tools to use the Internet for housing searches like Zillow or online home-sharing platforms like AirBnB. While these new firms do not increase the productivity of housing construction, they do increase the match quality between home buyers and sellers, and Kung argues that this can represent substantial gains to consumer surplus. Kung also considers potential explanations for the lack of innovation in the construction of new housing units. In particular, note his survey of the literature on policy's role in restricting innovations in housing. Land-use regulation can stifle the supply of new housing and depress incentives to innovate in the sector; Hsieh and Moretti (2019), for instance, conclude that land use restrictions have reduced the GDP growth rate by as much as one third. In her comment on chapter 11, included in this volume, Jessie Handbury notes that while higher match quality between home buyers and sellers increases welfare, this is reflected in higher sale prices and hence exacerbates issues related to housing affordability. The solution is an expansion in the housing supply, but both Kung and Handbury note that innovation in the production of housing stock is unlikely without policy reforms, such as a reform of the aforementioned zoning and land use regulations.

In the final sector study, Barbara Biasi, Dave Deming, and Petra Moser discuss the education sector. They overview the expansive literature documenting the importance of human capital for promoting innovation and entrepreneurship. But in spite of the massive importance of the education sector, as well as the large share of the economy it encompasses, there is very little formal R&D devoted to education. In fact, the Congressional Research Service reports that the Department of Education has the smallest R&D budget of any federal agency in fiscal years 2018–2020, about 1/3 of 1 percent of the R&D budget allocated to the Department of Defense (Congressional Research Service 2019). When researchers have studied the use of new technologies in the education sector, such as the use of computers in classrooms, the results have been uninspiring at best (Chatterji 2018). Instead of technological innovations, most innovation in the education sector over the past 150 years has been institutional or pedagogical in nature. For instance, universal primary school and high school and the expansion of colleges has sought to close the "leaky pipeline" and provide skills to potential innovators and entrepreneurs. Meanwhile, programs like gifted and talented programs and an expanding menu of college majors seek to improve match quality between students' interests and abilities and the skills that are taught. In her comment on chapter 12, included in this volume, Eleanor Dillon highlights some difficulties that anyone attempting to improve the education sector's ability to produce innovators will face. In particular, most innovators come from a small number of elite colleges; it is not clear that expanding access to college at non-elite institutions will lead to much of an increase in patenting. Dillon sees more hope in bringing programs that develop entrepreneurial skills to a wider set of colleges. She highlights in particular the role that vocational education could play in developing innovative skills in sectors outside the high-tech sectors in which universities typically patent.

Remarks by Panelists

In addition to the industry-specific studies, we also conducted a panel made up of innovation scholars with experience in the policy space to offer their cross-sectoral perspectives and insights into how policy affects innovation and entrepreneurship. Remarks by these panelists are included as chapters in this volume.

Karen Mills and Annie Dang provide a brief survey of the different kinds of government policies to promote innovation and entrepreneurship. Many government policies are designed to aid small firms, but of course, not all small firms promote economic growth equally. Mills and Dang discuss "smart" policy to promote innovation and entrepreneurship that is targeted specifically to the high-growth small firms. These policies frequently look different from policies designed to help other kinds of small firms, which they classify as "main street" firms, like restaurants and coffee shops; "supplier" firms that primarily act as vendors to large firms or the government; and non-employer firms. In particular, high-growth firms will be affected by different policies that affect access to capital (e.g., policies that affect venture capital and R&D tax credits instead of bank loan guarantees), different policies for advice and education (e.g., startup academies instead of small business development centers), and different policies that affect the local ecosystem (e.g., accelerators and incubators instead of Main Street associations).

In her panel remarks, Lucia Foster focuses on the role of government agencies in producing the innovation and entrepreneurship data used by researchers and policymakers to design the kinds of smart policies that Mills and Dang describe. Foster discusses three approaches that the Census Bureau takes toward measurement. First, the Census Bureau has multiple large-scale projects to produce innovation and entrepreneurship statistics from administrative data, which are data collected by government agencies for nonstatistical reasons. Second, the Census Bureau conducts numerous surveys designed explicitly to elicit information on innovative and entrepreneurship activities. While survey data is less comprehensive than administrative data, there is greater flexibility to ask different questions as technologies and the structure of the economy change. Finally, the Census Bureau applies indirect inference to document changes in innovation and entrepreneurship; in other words, the Bureau identifies patterns in productivity or business entry and exit that are predictive of innovative activity.

Chapter 13, the final chapter of the volume, is a synthetic contribution from Ben Jones, who undertook the task of explicitly linking these industry-level studies to the broader question of the potential sources and barriers to economic growth in the medium term. Jones leverages the industry studies to highlight the striking variation across sectors in their recorded levels of innovation and entrepreneurship, and he proposes a framework to explain this variation based on the interplay among demand, supply, and institutional factors. One important question is whether the differences across sectors are preordained or whether policymakers can influence outcomes. Demand and supply factors may in large part be determined by basic human preferences or the laws of nature, but to a large extent, they also appear to be sensitive to policy. For instance, in sectors for which it is possible to define intellectual property, patent laws and other forms of intellectual property can be used to alter the supply of innovators, and funding of basic research can also increase the supply of innovations in different sectors. Policies such as direct buyer mechanisms can be used to increase the demand for innovations. Jones also notes that policy can be used either to increase or impede the scalability of innovations. For instance, privacy rules reduce the ability of innovations in health services to diffuse widely, whereas ride-sharing services like Uber were able to expand rapidly while they remained outside existing regulations of the taxi industry. Overall, Jones appears optimistic that policy can be used to promote innovation in sectors in which it is currently lagging, although the relationship between demand, supply, and institutional features is nuanced, and determining the best policy is not likely to be easy.

Practitioner Perspectives

This conference was also unique in featuring participation from 11 practitioners from the innovation and entrepreneurship space to give their insights into the role of innovation and entrepreneurship in driving the future of economic growth. The following individuals contributed their perspectives to the conference, listed in the order in which they spoke:

- *Katie Finnegan* has long and broad experience at the intersection of technology and retail. In 2012, she founded the e-commerce firm Hukkster, which was later acquired by Jet.com, where she served in a leadership role. In 2016, she became Vice President of Incubation at Walmart.com and cofounded Walmart's incubator, Store No. 8. Most recently, she is the founder and principal of Katie Finnegan Consulting.

- *Alexsis de Raadt St. James* is an investor and venture capitalist with substantial experience working with technology firms. She has founded numerous companies and nonprofits, including the Althea Foundation, which seeks to support ideas that demonstrate social impact; and Youth Business America, Inc., which provides financial mentoring and loan capital to entrepreneurs who lacked funding from traditional sources. Alexsis is currently the managing partner of Merian Ventures, an early-stage venture firm focused on investing in women-founded firms. Alexsis is the US-UK Fulbright Commissioner and sits on several boards.
- *Jose Mejia* grew up in rural Venezuela and moved to the US when he was 16. Since then, Jose has been a senior vice present at Juniper Networks, chair and CEO of Medis Technologies, and president of Lucent Technologies' Worldwide Operations and Customer Support/Installation organization. Jose currently sits on the board of numerous software service firms, including RapidSOS. Jose has received the Ellis Island Medal of Honor, awarded by the US Congress to distinguished immigrants, and been named the Engineer of the Year by the Hispanic Engineer National Achievement Awards Corporation.
- *James Cham* is a principal at Bloomberg Beta, which invests in firms that attempt to shape the future of work. Prior to Bloomberg Beta, James has served as a principal at Trinity Ventures and a vice president at Bessemer Venture Partners. He serves on the boards of numerous firms and has spent time working as a consultant and software developer.
- *Barb Stuckey* is a longtime innovator in the food and restaurant industry. Barb has been involved in the food industry in some form or another since spending time in her best friend's parents' Chinese restaurant in suburban Baltimore while growing up. Since then, she has worked for Kraft Foodservice, Brinker International (which operates Chili's, among other restaurants), and Whole Foods. Barb is currently the president and chief innovation officer at Mattson, one of the largest developers of new foods and beverages. Barb is widely recognized as an expert in foods trends and product development, is the authors of a book on food science for the general public (Stuckey 2012), and is featured in the *New Yorker* article "The Bakeoff" (Gladwell 2005).
- *Dr. Arati Prabhakar* is the former head of the US Defense Advanced Research Projects Agency (DARPA) from 2012 to 2017 and is currently the founder and CEO of Actuate, a nonprofit organization funding R&D to solve societal problems. In 1984, she became the first woman to receive a PhD in applied physics from CalTech. She was the head of the National Institute of Standards and Technology (NIST) from 1993

to 1997 and has held numerous positions in government, nonprofit, and private research organizations.

- *Dr. Chris Kirchhoff* is currently a senior fellow at the Schmidt Futures Foundation. He began his career on staff of the Space Shuttle Columbia Accident Investigation and went on to serve numerous advisory positions to the Department of Defense in Iraq, writing the US government's history of the conflict (Special Inspector General for Iraq Reconstruction 2009), which the *New York Times* called "the Iraq Pentagon Papers." He founded and led the Pentagon's Silicon Valley Office, Defense Innovation Unit X, which harnesses emerging commercial technology for national security innovation.
- *Dr. Bob Kocher* is currently a partner at Venrock focusing on health-care IT and services instruments. A trained physician and Howard Hughes Medical Institute fellow, He was a partner at McKinsey & Company, where he led the McKinsey Global Institute's healthcare economic program. After that, he joined the Obama Administration as Special Assistant to the President for Healthcare and Economic Policy on the National Economic Council, where, among other things, he helped shape the Affordable Care Act, the "Let's Move" childhood obesity initiative, and the Health Data Initiative.
- *Dr. Jean Rogers* is the chief resilience officer at the Long-Term Stock Exchange. She founded and served as the CEO for the Sustainability Accounting Standards Board. Prior to that, she worked with Deloitte and at Arup, a global engineering consultancy.
- *Dr. Ilan Gur* is the founder of the Lawrence Berkeley National Laboratory's Cyclotron Road and the CEO of Activate.org, both of which manage fellowship programs that support entrepreneurial scientists. Prior to that, Gur founded multiple science-based startups and served as a program director at the Department of Energy's Advanced Research Projects Agency, ARPA-E.
- *Sal Khan* is the founder and CEO of Khan Academy, a free online education platform. He also founded the Khan School Labs, a brick-and-mortar school designed to experiment with educational approaches, and he sits on the board of the Aspen Institute. In 2012, *Time Magazine* named him one of the 100 most influential people in the world (Gates 2012).

While we do not attribute specific views to specific practitioners (some of whom elected to speak off the record), several common themes emerged.

First, most practitioners expressed optimism about the abilities of our current innovation and entrepreneurial system to effectively drive growth in certain domains. For instance, US science and high-tech R&D is second to none in the world, and this manifests itself in, for instance, US dominance in biopharmaceuticals and ICTs. But outside these domains, most concluded that the US faces severe challenges. One challenge is translating high-quality science to practice, especially when there is no well-defined career path for individuals with a technical background. This can lead to different parts of the US innovation system working well in isolation but ultimately measuring up to less than the sum of their parts.

Second, many expressed their frustration with the difficulties in making innovation and entrepreneurship democratic. Some sectors, of course, are more democratic than others. But especially in highly technical fields, most innovators and entrepreneurs come from similar backgrounds, and most are white and male. While some were concerned about issues of representation for their own sake, most worried that the homogeneity of backgrounds likely deprives the economy of diverse and radical new ideas—the leaky pipeline problem discussed in chapter 12 by Biasi, Deming, and Moser.

Finally, several of the practitioners expressed concern that the good economic times of the previous several years meant that many younger entrepreneurs never developed the skills to succeed during adversity. During good economic times, funding for projects is more readily available, which also makes it challenging for funders to distinguish great ideas from the merely good ones. These practitioners expressed concern that, were economic conditions to change, the innovation and entrepreneurship system had not developed the requisite resilience. Unfortunately, within 2 months of the conference, these concerns were realized, as we discuss in the final section of this introduction.

Broad Lessons

While the individual chapters contribute on their own to our understanding of the prospect for innovation and entrepreneurship across various sectors of the US economy, the ability to compare and contrast the findings that arise from this collection of sectoral studies also allows us to draw some broader, if still tentative, lessons.

Heterogeneity and the "Vannevar Bush Sectors"

The most striking takeaway from this volume is that there are several sectors in which innovation and entrepreneurship are proceeding at a rapid pace, in line with the proclamations of the technological optimists (although even in those sectors, the authors in this volume point out several potential headwinds), while in other sectors, the amount of innovation and entrepreneurship is very low. We can see this clearly in table I.1 (displayed earlier in this introduction): the manufacturing sector produces 5.6 patents for every 1,000 employees, while the education sector produces 1.6 patents for every *100,000* employees. The detailed industry studies are necessary to move beyond these headline numbers to examine within-industry heterogeneity.

For example, while health care performs poorly on the patenting metrics presented in table I.1, our data for the health-care sector are for health-care *services*; as Chandra, Foroughi, and Mostrom show in chapter 11, biotech, pharmaceuticals, and medical devices see the vast majority of health-care venture funding.

The detailed industry studies are also valuable for helping us understand potential reasons that some sectors see so much more innovation and entrepreneurship than others. One possible explanation for the observed heterogeneity is that sectors experiencing little innovation are already quite advanced (Baumol 1967; Baumol and Bowen 1966), or are "fully grown," to use Vollrath's (2020) phrase. While this may be part of the explanation and deserves further study, we do not believe it can completely explain the patterns that we observe. Instead, we note that the sectors that have seen successful innovation and entrepreneurship have been science-based (the productivity drivers: IT, energy, and agriculture) or have been able to incorporate technologies from those fields (manufacturing and the on-demand sectors). In the sectors for which progress has been more mixed, such as health care, the parts of the sector that rely on science have typically seen large advances (i.e., biotech, pharmaceuticals, and medical devices), whereas those that do not have largely stagnated (health-care delivery, financing, non-pharmaceutical health interventions).

While the sector-specific studies in this volume do not allow us to make causal claims about why some sectors have been more innovative than others—after all, technological opportunities are not evenly distributed across sectors—we find it telling that the innovative sectors are those for which an innovation system is well established. By "innovation system," we mean not only well-funded public institutions to conduct R&D, although such an institution is certainly in place for the innovative sectors (i.e., the NSF, NIH, and numerous large R&D projects funded by the Department of Defense and Department of Energy), but also well-defined research jobs, career ladders, rewards for innovative success (such as intellectual property), and an ecosystem in place to develop and support high-growth entrepreneurs.

We term these sectors for which an established innovation system is in place the "Vannevar Bush sectors." US innovation policy today hews remarkably closely to the proposals laid out by Bush in his famous report, *Science: The Endless Frontier* (Bush 1945b), as exemplified by the major US research institutions identified above. The modern IT industry likewise reflects Bush's vision for recording, storing, accessing, and sharing the world's knowledge (Bush 1945a).

While we again stress that causation is difficult to establish, the evidence leads us to suspect that constructing innovation systems for the non–Vannevar Bush sectors will lead, after a long delay, to technological and entrepreneurial opportunities in these areas. Jones reaches a similar conclusion in his synthetic chapter (chapter 13) when he notes that the institutional environment—and hence the innovation system embedded in it—is often malleable, and that in many cases, innovation outcomes appear quite elastic to the institutional environment. Many of the non–Vannevar Bush sectors are focused in the social sciences, and more specifically, on determining how to innovate complicated systems with many stakeholders. It is up to future researchers and policymakers to determine what the equivalent of the NIH for education or housing might look like. But at present it appears that, to a first order, we aren't even trying to build such a system for these sectors.

Measurement Challenges

One challenge with determining the role of innovation and entrepreneurship in economic growth relates to measurement. Indeed, there are challenges both with quantifying innovation-related activities as well as with quantifying productivity and growth. As Foster describes in her panel remarks, US statistical agencies are both hardworking and creative at tackling the measurement challenge, but there remain fundamental challenges associated with creating definitive ways to measure new things. We are certainly not the only people to note the difficulties with measuring these types of activities; see for instance the recent Brookings Institution initiative (Hutchins Center on Fiscal and Monetary Policy 2019).

When it comes to quantifying innovation, several chapters in this volume make extensive use of patent data. This is especially true in chapter 2 by Forman and Goldfarb on the IT sector and, to a lesser degree, in chapter 10 by Chandra, Foroughi, and Mostrom on the health-care sector. Notably, these are two sectors in which the ability to protect innovations via patents (on molecular compounds in the health sector and software in the IT sector) was questionable until fairly recently and is still on uncertain ground. Of course, patents are at best an incomplete and imperfect measure of the universe of innovations. But this is likely to be a much larger problem in some sectors than others. For instance, in both the education and government sectors, many improvements take the form of organizational changes, which are not generally patentable.

Productivity and growth are likewise harder to measure in some sectors than others. While statistical agencies have more than a century and a half of experience quantifying output improvements in manufacturing and agriculture, there is less agreement on how to measure successful government or good education. For instance, in the education sector, a large debate surrounds the use of teacher value added measures to assess input quality (Bitler et al. 2019; Chetty, Friedman, and Rockoff 2014a,b, 2017; Jackson, Rockoff, and Staiger 2014; Rothstein 2017) and of testing data to assess educational outcomes (Ballou and Springer 2015; Carrell and West 2010; Shavelson et al. 2010). It is clear that no consensus exists on which measures to use comparable to that related to measuring productivity in, say, manufacturing (Syverson 2011). Relating to the previous lesson, it is probably not a coincidence that we see so little innovation-driven growth exactly in the sectors for which identifying and quantifying improvements—and rewarding the people who make those improvements—is most difficult.

While it is often difficult to measure how innovations in some sectors contribute to productivity growth, innovations in many sectors are, by construction, not reflected in standard measures of growth like GDP. This is particularly apparent with Internet-related technologies. The Internet undoubtedly makes firms more productive, but it also provides valuable free services to consumers, which are not captured in GDP data (Brynjolfsson and Oh 2012; Byrne, Fernald, and Reinsdorf 2016; Goolsbee and Klenow 2006). Other approaches are therefore needed to quantify the value of innovations in IT, as well as in sectors as diverse as education (the value of better-educated citizens is not counted in GDP), energy (a cleaner environment is not included in standard GDP calculations), or health care (health-care innovations improve quality of life far above and beyond their contributions to output). Chapter 8 by Waldfogel in this volume is therefore a valuable contribution, as he moves beyond traditional productivity accounting to discuss how technological changes in the creative sectors have led to an increase in consumer surplus.

Classification Challenges

Closely related to measurement challenges are challenges of classifying where in the economy innovation and entrepreneurship are occurring. The in-depth sectoral studies approach taken in this volume allows the authors of each chapter to move beyond crude industry classifications, documenting how each sector is both affected by innovations in upstream sectors and affects performance in downstream sectors. For instance, in chapter 12, Biasi, Deming, and Moser make clear that innovations in the education sector affect every other sector by supplying future innovators and entrepreneurs. And as we note above, IT now pervades nearly every industry. Chapter 11 by Kung and chapter 5 by Choe, Oettl, and Seamans document that the emergence of on-demand housing and rides are among the most important recent innovations in housing and transportation, respectively. Whether these innovations are classified as occurring in the IT sector or in the housing or transportation sector is in some sense irrelevant; they will shape the way we consume housing and transportation services regardless of their official classification.

But how innovations are classified matters a great deal for statistical agencies and, consequently, for policy. Table I.1 shows how naively relying on NAICS codes, which are the standard industry classification used by the US government, may lead to distorted conclusions about where innovative activity is occurring. For example, the NAICS code for health includes only health-care services; as Chandra, Foroughi, and Mostrom (chapter 10) show, health-care services have seen little innovation compared to biotech, pharmaceuticals, or medical devices. As another example, the NAICS codes for manufacturing include such activities as automobile and aviation manufacturing; automobiles and aircraft experience regular innovation, while there has been little measured innovation in transportation infrastructure, making the transportation sector appear middling in table I.1.

This issue is no less challenging at the firm level: should Netflix be classified as a media and entertainment firm, or as an IT firm? E-commerce firms similarly fall between the transportation, retail, and IT sectors. As Fuchs et al. show in chapter 1, official classifications of the manufacturing sector include firms from a wide array of seemingly disparate sub-industries, from animal slaughtering to oil refining, and Lafontaine and Sivadasan (chapter 6) show that, for a long time, official classifications of the retail sector included restaurants. Nor do firms remain in one sector over their entire lifetimes; in chapter 7, Delgado, Kim, and Mills highlight several firms that began as manufacturing firms but are now primarily in the supply chain traded services sector.

To the extent that our data are collected by industry-specific censuses or surveys, that official statistics are organized by industry, or that policy is targeting specific sectors, taxonomical issues threaten both our ability to study innovation and entrepreneurship-driven growth as well as to design policies to improve it.

Challenges of Place

We have mentioned that, while the health-care sector is innovative in producing new drugs and medical devices, it has struggled to improve delivery of health-care services to those who need it. The problem of delivering products to potential users is likewise a major challenge in the delivery of government services. Even in the IT sector, arguably the largest bottleneck to growth is providing the infrastructure to allow consumers to take advantage of new innovations. Indeed, this issue seems so ubiquitous that it is worth considering the extent to which failures of innovation and entrepreneurship to generate economic growth are really problems about urban economics and economic geography, that is, challenges related to place.

As we noted, even in the best of cases it can be difficult to draw a line between different sectors. But this is especially the case when the delivery of goods and services is involved. The problems in transportation, retail, and housing all relate to the fact that agents on different sides of a transaction are in different places. As Kung reviews in chapter 11 on housing, frictions related to relocating resources through space (for instance, due to strict zoning laws) can have large economic costs. And we expect these kinds of frictions to be especially damaging to innovation and entrepreneurship in sectors that involve many stakeholders; the more parties there are to coordinate, the more costly relocation frictions will be. In this sense, we see issues in the housing and transportation sectors as affecting innovation throughout all other sectors, in the same way that the performance of the education and IT sectors affect all other sectors.

Issues of place may also matter for innovation and entrepreneurship if the type and quality of ideas generated depend on where people are located. Two chapters in this volume, chapter 2 on IT by Forman and Goldfarb and chapter 10 by Chandra, Foroughi, and Mostrom on the health sector, make the point that patenting in these sectors has become increasingly geographically concentrated in recent decades, and this is likely to be problematic if individuals from outside the major sectoral innovation hubs are excluded from the innovation process. At a time when the concentration of overall patenting is the highest it has been in a century and a half (Andrews and Whalley 2021), this is likely to be an issue for the other sectors as well. And innovation and entrepreneurship may be even more spatially concentrated than these statistics suggest: Guzman and Stern (2015) show that even in highly innovative regions, entrepreneurship is clustered in a few zip codes.

Some important open questions relate to quantifying the costs of spatial concentration of innovation and entrepreneurship. Others relate to understanding whether non-innovative regions can better reap the rewards of innovation and entrepreneurship-driven growth through policies to promote such growth in those regions or by better diffusion of innovations created in other places, for instance, through better transportation and communication technologies (Glaeser and Hausman 2020).

The Future Is Already Here

Several times during the conference, we were reminded of science fiction writer William Gibson's famous quip: "The future is already here—it's just not very evenly distributed" (Gibson 1999). While making concrete predictions about the future path of innovation and entrepreneurship is typically a good way to appear foolish in the eyes of future readers, it seems safe to conclude that the innovations that will most profoundly shape the next decade already exist, at least in a nascent form.

For many of the most impactful technologies of the past, there was a long lag between the first introduction of the technology and when its use became widespread. This is most clearly seen in this volume in chapter 3 by Alston and Pardey on agriculture. While hybrid and genetically engineered crops diffused fairly quickly, reaching more than 80 percent adoption within a decade or two of their introductions, other technologies like the tractor took almost half a century to see similar levels of adoption. One reason for this, as David (1990) famously points out, is that for the most important innovations, widespread adoption is more complicated than simply switching from one technology to another; changes in organization, in the use of complementary technologies, and in the behavior of customers, suppliers, or rivals also must take place. In addition to examples from agriculture, clean energy (discussed by Popp et al. in chapter 4) and autonomous vehicles (discussed by Choe, Oettl, and Seamans in chapter 5) are other technologies with long gestation periods that have seen slow but steady improvements in performance and appear poised to make meaningful impacts on future economic growth in the coming decades.

While we are thus living in the future, it is also the case that we are living in the past, with the current distribution of economic activity across sectors determined at least in part by historical innovations. We see this most clearly once again in agriculture, which used to employ almost a third of the entire US population in 1916; today only about 1.5 percent of the population is in agriculture. This dramatic change is largely driven by productivity improvements in the agricultural sector, most notably mechanization and biological innovations. A similar story is playing out today in manufacturing. While the manufacturing sector is clearly highly innovative, many of those innovations decrease manufacturing's share of employment and GDP. Moreover, as the manufacturing sector continues to shrink as a share of GDP, productivity improvements in manufacturing will have a limited ability to increase aggregate productivity growth. Such observations help forecast where the future of economic growth is likely to occur. As we noted above when discussing heterogeneity across sectors, we do not see this as a reason to celebrate low rates of innovation, nor do we believe that the rate and direction of economic growth are entirely determined by past innovations. Instead, we believe there are opportunities to increase the rate of innovation in sectors that account for a growing share of the economy but have historically received little investment in innovation and entrepreneurship, namely, sectors like services, housing, education, and the government.

Innovation and Entrepreneurship during the 2020 COVID-19 Pandemic

Shortly after the conference took place, the novel coronavirus SARS-Cov-2 caused a pandemic, leading to shelter-in-place orders throughout the US and the cancellation of most in-person activities. While it is far too early to assess the long-term effects of the pandemic on innovation and entrepreneurship across different sectors, here we offer some initial observations based on events that occurred throughout the remainder of 2020.

Those sectors that had already embraced general-purpose technologies to achieve past productivity growth—namely, our productivity driver and especially on-demand sectors—were able to respond reasonably well to the pandemic, highlighting that innovation can drive not only growth but also resilience. For instance, online retailers like Amazon saw large gains in share prices as consumers minimized shopping in-person, by necessity rapidly accelerating the trend toward online shopping; in chapter 6, Lafontaine and Sivadasan provide a brief overview of the large adverse effect of COVID-19 on brick-and-mortar retail establishments and restaurants. Many supply chain service sector jobs were also able to switch to online work with minimal disruption. The online delivery of media and entertainment content allowed media platforms to weather the storm as well.

Our impression is that the transition to a pandemic economy appears to have been more difficult for the cost disease sectors, which have historically struggled to incorporate innovations from other sectors. School closures forced the education sector to embrace online education technologies at a rate and scale that would have been unthinkable prior to the pandemic. It is far too early to know how the adoption of these technologies has affected educational outcomes, much less the extent to which they will continue to be used when the pandemic subsides. Finally, in the health-care sector, the pandemic brought into sharp relief the gap between health-care innovation and delivery, echoing themes from chapter 10 by Chandra, Foroughi, and Molstrom: the SARS-Cov-2 genome was sequenced in record time, and trials for vaccines and antiviral therapies were launched rapidly, but sourcing, manufacturing, and distribution of "low tech" health-care materials like masks and other personal protective equipment proved difficult in the early stages of the pandemic.

Of course, we do not yet know whether the choices of participants in different sectors to adopt new technologies in the face of the pandemic will prove to be permanent or transitory, nor whether the events of the past year will induce the development of new technologies in sectors that had previously struggled to innovate. Obtaining answers to these questions will shed light on the future role of innovation and entrepreneurship in driving economic growth across sectors.

References

Abramovitz, Moses. 1956. "Resources and Output Trends in the United States since 1870." *American Economic Review* 46(2): 5–23.

Acemoglu, Daron, and Pascual Restrepo. 2020. "Robots and Jobs: Evidence from US labor markets." *Journal of Political Economy* 128(6): 2188–2244.

Aguiar, Luis, and Joel Waldfogel. 2018. "Quality Predictability and the Welfare Benefits from New Products: Evidence from the Digitization of Recorded Music." *Journal of Political Economy* 126(2): 492–524.

Andreessen, Marc. 2011. "Why Software Is Eating the World." *Wall Street Journal*, August 20. Accessed May 29, 2020. https://www.wsj.com/articles/SB10001424053 111903480904576512250915629460.

Andrews, Michael J., and Alexander Whalley. 2021. "150 Years of the Geography of Innovation." Forthcoming in *Regional Science and Urban Economics*.

Ballou, Dale, and Matthew G. Springer. 2015. "Using Student Test Scores to Measure Teacher Performance: Some Problems in the Design and Implementation of Evaluation Systems." *Educational Researcher* 44(2): 77–86.

Baumol, William J. 1967. "Macroeconomics of Unbalanced Growth: The Anatomy of Urban Crisis." *American Economic Review* 57(3): 415–26.

Baumol, William J., and William G. Bowen. 1966. *Performing Arts: The Economic Dilemma.* Cambridge, MA: MIT Press.

Bitler, Marianne, Sean Corcoran, Thurston Domina, and Emily Penner. 2019. "Teacher Effects on Student Achievement and Height: A Cautionary Tale." NBER Working Paper No. 26480. Cambridge, MA: National Bureau of Economic Research.

Bloom, Nicholas, Charles I. Jones, John Van Reenen, and Michael Webb. 2020. "Are Ideas Getting Harder to Find?" *American Economic Review* 110(4): 1104–44.

Bresnahan, Timothy. 2010. "General Purpose Technologies." In *Handbook of the Economics of Innovation*, Vol. 2, edited by Bronwyn H. Hall and Nathan Rosenberg. Amsterdam: Elsevier.

Brynjolfsson, Erik, and JooHee Oh. 2012. "The Attention Economy: Measuring the Value of Free Digital Services on the Internet." *Proceedings of the International Conference on Information Systems.*

Buera, Francisco J., and Joseph P. Kaboski. 2012. "The Rise of the Service Economy." *American Economic Review* 102(6): 2540–69.

Bush, Vannevar. 1945a. "As We May Think." *The Atlantic*, July. Accessed March 30, 2021. https://www.theatlantic.com/magazine/archive/1945/07/as-we-may-think /303881/.

———. 1945b. *Science: The Endless Frontier.* Washington, DC: US Government Printing Office.

Byrne, David M., John G. Fernald, and Marshall B. Reinsdorf. 2016. "Does the United States Have a Productivity Slowdown or a Measurement Problem?" *Brookings Papers on Economic Activity.*

Carrell, Scott E., and James E. West. 2010. "Does Professor Quality Matter? Evidence from Random Assignment of Students to Professors." *Journal of Political Economy* 118(3): 409–32.

Chatterji, Aaron K. 2018. "Innovation and American K–12 Education." *Innovation Policy and the Economy* 18: 27–51.

Chetty, Raj, John N. Friedman, and Jonah E. Rockoff. 2014a. "Measuring the Impact of Teachers I: Evaluating Bias in Teacher Value-Added Estimates." *American Economic Review* 104(9): 2593–2632.

———. 2014b. "Measuring the Impact of Teachers II: Teacher Value-Added and Student Outcomes in Adulthood." *American Economic Review* 2014(9): 2633–79.

———. 2017. "Measuring the Impact of Teachers: Reply to Rothstein." *American Economic Review* 107(6): 1685–1717.

Congressional Research Service. 2019. *Federal Research and Development (R&D) Funding: FY2020.* CRS Report R45715, November 26.

Cowen, Tyler. 2011. *The Great Stagnation.* New York: Dutton.

David, Paul. 1990. "The Dynamo and the Computer: An Historical Perspective on the Modern Productivity Paradox." *American Economic Review: Papers and Proceedings* 80(2): 355–61.

Davis, Clint. 2019. "Music Stars Who Were Discovered on YouTube." *The Delite*, December 16. Accessed August 19, 2020. https://www.thedelite.com/music-stars -who-were-discovered-on-youtube.

Decker, Ryan, John Haltiwanger, Ron Jarmin, and Javier Miranda. 2014. "The Role of Entrepreneurship in US Job Creation and Economic Dynamism." *Journal of Economic Perspectives* 28(3): 3–24.

Delgado, Mercedes, and Karen G. Mills. 2020. "The Supply Chain Economy: A New Framework for Understanding Innovation and Services." *Research Policy* 49(8).

Eckert, Fabian, Sharat Ganapati, and Conor Walsh. 2019. "Skilled Tradable Services: The Transformation of U.S. High-Skill Labor Markets." Federal Reserve Bank of Minneapolis Institute Working Paper 25.

Fuchs, Victor. 1980. "Economic Growth and the Rise of Service Employment." NBER Working Paper No. 486. Cambridge, MA: National Bureau of Economic Research.

Gates, Bill. 2012. "Salman Khan." *Time*, April 18. Accessed May 28, 2020. http://content.time.com/time/specials/packages/article/0,28804,2111975_2111976_2111942,00.html.

Gibson, William. 1999. "The Science in Science Fiction." Interview on *NPR Talk of the Nation*, November 30.

Gladwell, Malcolm. 2005. "The Bakeoff." *The New Yorker*, August 28. Accessed May 27, 2020. https://www.newyorker.com/magazine/2005/09/05/the-bakeoff.

Glaeser, Edward L., and Naomi Hausman. 2020. "The Spatial Mismatch between Innovation and Joblessness." *Innovation Policy and the Economy* 20: 233–99.

Goldschlag, Nathan, Travis J. Lybbert, and Nikolas J. Zolas. 2020. "Tracking the Technological Composition of Industries with Algorithmic Patent Concordances." *Economics of Innovation and New Technology* 29(6): 582–602.

Goolsbee, Austan, and Peter J. Klenow. 2006. "Valuing Consumer Products by the Time Spent Using Them: An Application to the Internet." *American Economic Review: Papers and Proceedings* 96(2): 108–13.

Gordon, Robert J. 2000. "Does the 'New Economy' Measure Up to the Great Inventions of the Past?" *Journal of Economic Perspectives* 14(4): 49–74.

———. 2012. "Is US Economic Growth Over? Faltering Innovation Confronts the Six Headwinds." NBER Working Paper No. 18315. Cambridge, MA: National Bureau of Economic Research.

———. 2016. *The Rise and Fall of American Growth: The U.S. Standard of Living since the Civil War*. Princeton, NJ: Princeton University Press.

———. 2018. "Declining American Economic Growth Despite Ongoing Innovation." *Explorations in Economic History* 69: 1–12.

Griliches, Zvi. 1957. "Hybrid Corn: An Exploration in the Economics of Technological Change." *Econometrica* 24(4): 501–22.

Guzman, Jorge, and Scott Stern. 2015. "Where Is Silicon Valley?" *Science* 347(6222): 606–9.

———. 2020. "The State of American Entrepreneurship: New Estimates of the Quantity and Quality of Entrepreneurship for 32 U.S. States, 1988–2014." *American Economic Journal: Economic Policy* 12(4): 212–43.

Hsieh, Chang-Tai, and Enrico Moretti. 2019. "Housing Constraints and Spatial Misallocation." *American Economic Journal: Macroeconomics* 11(2): 1–39.

Hutchins Center on Fiscal and Monetary Policy. 2019. "Productivity Measurement Initiative." Washington, DC: Brookings Institution. Accessed August 20, 2020. https://www.brookings.edu/productivity-measurement-initiative/.

Jackson, C. Kirabo, Jonah E. Rockoff, and Douglas O. Staiger. 2014. "Teacher Effects and Teacher-Related Policies." *Annual Review of Economics* 6: 801–25.

James, E. L. 2011. *Fifty Shades of Gray*. Fifty Shades Ltd.

Manso, Gustavo. 2016. "Experimentation and the Returns to Entrepreneurship." *Review of Financial Studies* 29(9): 2319–40.

Mokyr, Joel. 2018. "The Past and the Future of Innovation: Some Lessons from Economic History." *Explorations in Economic History* 69: 13–26.

Mokyr, Joel, Chris Vickers, and Nicolas L. Ziebarth. 2015. "The History of Technological Anxiety and the Future of Economic Growth: Is This Time Different?" *Journal of Economic Perspectives* 29(3): 31–50.

Rothstein, Jesse. 2017. "Measuring the Impacts of Teachers: Comment." *American Economic Review* 107(6): 1656–84.

Schumpeter, Joseph A. 1942. *Capitalism, Socialism and Democracy.* New York: Harper & Brothers.

Shavelson, Richard J., Robert L. Linn, Eva L. Baker, Helen F. Ladd, Lind Darling-Hammon, Lorrie A. Shepard, Paul E. Barton, Edward Haertel, Diane Ravitch, and Richard Rothstein. 2010. "Problems with the Use of Student Test Scores to Evaluate Teachers." Economic Policy Institute Briefing Paper 278.

Solow, Robert M. 1956. "A Contribution to the Theory of Economic Growth." *Quarterly Journal of Economics* 70(1): 65–94.

———. 1957. "Technical Change and the Aggregate Production Function." *Review of Economics and Statistics* 39(3): 312–20.

Special Inspector General for Iraq Reconstruction. 2009. *Hard Lessons: The Iraq Reconstruction Experience.* Washington, DC: US Government Printing Office.

Stuckey, Barb. 2012. *Taste What You're Missing.* New York: Simon & Schuster.

Syverson, Chad. 2011. "What Determines Productivity?" *Journal of Economic Literature* 49(2): 326–65.

Thiel, Peter. 2011. "What Happened to the Future?" *Founders Fund.*

Vollrath, Dietrich. 2020. *Fully Grown: Why a Stagnant Economy Is a Sign of Success.* Chicago: University of Chicago Press.

I

Productivity Drivers

1

The "Weighty" Manufacturing Sector
Transforming Raw Materials into Physical Goods

Erica R. H. Fuchs, Christophe Combemale,
Kate S. Whitefoot, and Britta Glennon

1.1 Introduction

Manufacturing has historically played a significant role in productivity and R&D. Jorgenson (2001) suggests that advances in microprocessors alone were associated with 50 percent of total factor productivity growth in the US and worldwide in the 1990s. This outsized role in R&D and productivity appears to continue today, even with significant changes across the sector in technology and globalization. US manufacturing is a disproportionate source of private R&D spending relative to its share of employment and global value added (GVA)[1,2] and has higher than average labor productivity relative to other sectors.[3]

Erica R. H. Fuchs is a professor in the Department of Engineering and Public Policy at Carnegie Mellon University and a research associate of the National Bureau of Economic Research.

Christophe Combemale is a PhD student in engineering and public policy at Carnegie Mellon University.

Kate S. Whitefoot is an assistant professor of mechanical engineering and of engineering and public policy at Carnegie Mellon University.

Britta Glennon is an assistant professor at the Wharton School of Business at the University of Pennsylvania and a faculty research fellow of the National Bureau of Economic Research.

For acknowledgments, sources of research support, and disclosure of the authors' material financial relationships, if any, please see https://www.nber.org/books-and-chapters /role-innovation-and-entrepreneurship-economic-growth/weighty-manufacturing-sector -transforming-raw-materials-physical-goods.

1. The ratio of R&D spending in manufacturing relative to its share to GVA share went from 4.52 in 1997 to 5.45 in 2015 (i.e., a 21 percent relative increase). The share of research funding proportional to employment in manufacturing grew from 1982 to 2015 and was "overrepresented" on a per-capita basis by a factor of 5 relative to other sectors. The manufacturing share of GDP parallels the trajectory of its share of GVA.

2. The manufacturing share of GDP parallels the trajectory of its share of GVA.

3. Manufacturing productivity per capita employed (measured as its share of the US GVA versus its share of employment) is higher than that of the overall US economy by a factor of

For the manufacturing sector as a whole, the past few decades have been marked by increases in R&D and productivity and a declining share of the US economy as other sectors grew faster. US manufacturing value added (MVA)[4] has grown in real terms from the 1980s to the present (as far back as public data allow us to observe) in addition to real growth in US private R&D spending by manufacturing industries. However, both absolute employment and share of total US employment in the sector have declined over the same period.[5] Despite MVA growth, manufacturing today accounts for a smaller share of total US value added than it did in the 1980s and 1990s.[6] While a majority of US industrial R&D spending still occurs in manufacturing, this too is a declining share of the US total. Manufacturing is a sector whose apparent role in the economy on these important dimensions would seem to be in decline, but it remains unusually productive per employee and highly research intensive.

Despite these average trends and commonalities, drawing implications from sector-wide manufacturing trends can be misleading because of the variation in these indicators across manufacturing subsectors. By definition, the manufacturing sector includes all establishments engaged in mechanical, physical, or chemical transformation of materials, substances, or components into new products (US Census Bureau 2017). The industries in the sector vary widely with respect to value added, workforce size and composition, and level of R&D effort. At the five-digit NAICS code level, the top sources of employment are animal processing, aerospace products, and printing (on various materials, including textiles, metals, and plastics); the top sources of revenue are petroleum refineries and automotive; and the top source of R&D spending is pharmaceuticals followed by semiconductors and other electronic components.

The rate and direction of technology change also varies greatly across subsectors. Indeed, industrial R&D spending is not only disproportionately driven by manufacturing, it is also disproportionately driven by the top five subsectors: pharmaceuticals, semiconductors and other electronic components, automobiles and light duty vehicles, communications, and aerospace. Unpacking the relationship among globalization, innovation, and labor outcomes requires not only understanding how the manufacturing sector can be different than other sectors, but also addressing the sector's diversity. Here, deep subsector-level knowledge and empirical detail may prove particularly

---

1.39. Manufacturing's share of GVA relative to its share of employment has grown since 1997 (the first available US MVA data) from a ratio of shares at 1.18 to a ratio of 1.40 in 2016.

4. Manufacturing value added is calculated (as in the US Census Bureau 2018) by the difference between input costs and output values from a firm or other entity.

5. US manufacturing employment also went from 19 percent of total employment in 1982 to 8.7 percent in 2015 (and is still falling slightly as of 2019, beyond our R&D funding dataset, at 8.5 percent).

6. MVA share of US GVA shifted from 16.7 percent in 1997 to 12.1 percent in 2015 (i.e., a 27.9 percent relative decline).

valuable for unpacking the puzzling (and sometimes conflicting) results in today's state-of-the-art analyses.

This chapter is structured as follows. We begin with a brief history of manufacturing technologies and systems. Second, we provide a birds-eye view of the trends in manufacturing based on available data on manufacturing value added, R&D spending, and human capital and demographic composition of the labor force. Third, we explore why manufacturing contributes to a majority (66 percent) of US industrial R&D spending but a much smaller (12 percent) proportion of US domestic value added. Fourth, we highlight subsectoral level differences in our birds-eye view measures, and potential subsectoral differences in the dichotomy between US industrial R&D spending and US value added (and potential explanations for that dichotomy). Finally, we engage with the existing literature and discuss implications of the chapter's findings for the relationship among globalization, innovation, and labor outcomes.

1.2 A Brief History of Manufacturing Technologies and Systems

US manufacturing began in the seventeenth and eighteenth centuries as a craftwork system imported from Europe to the American colonies. Craftwork was performed by skilled artisans, often working with tools that they owned themselves. Labor was organized into master craftsmen with apprentices or in small firms. In this period, most craftwork was for domestic consumption, and exports were dominated by raw materials (Shepherd and Williamson 1972).

In the mid-eighteenth century, what later came to be known as the first industrial revolution emerged in Great Britain. This revolution would eventually reach its maturity in the United States during the first quarter of the nineteenth century (Crafts 1996). The first industrial revolution shifted the sources of production power from human and animal toward chemical sources such as coal and wood, and water sources such as riverside mills (Crafts 1996). Faced with abundant materials but scarce, relatively skilled labor, US manufacturers in this period strongly favored innovations in mechanization (even compared with Great Britain; Rosenberg 1972). This mechanization reduced the demand for labor on the production line but increased material waste and produced new demands for skilled machinists to construct the machines. At the same time as the demand for skilled machinists grew, the shift in production organization from artisanal work to factory production saw a decline in the demand for skilled artisanal labor while shifting demand toward less skilled production labor in the factory (Goldin and Katz 1998).

After the first and into the second industrial revolution, US manufacturing saw the emergence, national prominence, and international export of the "American system," a mechanized approach to producing separate, interchangeable parts that made up final goods (Hounshell 1984). Eli Whitney originally popularized the concept of interchangeable parts in response to the needs of American small arms manufacture for high performance and easier repair, maintenance, and logistics (Hounshell 1984). Progress toward interchangeability was further developed by such entities as the Springfield Armory (Ford 2005). In addition to facilitating higher production volumes, interchangeability also expanded opportunities for the division of labor (Tyson 1990). Novel modes of organizing production activity at larger scales were driven in large part by the demand of US armories that emerged in the late eighteenth century and proliferated in the first quarter of the nineteenth century. Production volumes grew around US conflicts, such as the Mexican-American War and the American Civil War as well as arms production for national and international use in the later nineteenth and early twentieth centuries (Malone 1988; Smith 1980, 1985).

By the 1870s and the coming of the second industrial revolution, major productivity gains had been achieved through specialized labor and tools (Atack, Margo, and Rhode 2019) and innovations in power sources (e.g., from coal to oil; Mokyr 1992). As infrastructure, transportation, and communication technologies expanded and improved, production was able to further increase in scale, scope, and complexity. Along with increases in these dimensions came an enlarged role for salaried managers who did not own the industrial enterprises but rather were organized according to functions in the overall system of the firm, such as sales, purchasing, or research (Chandler 1990).

The organizational implications of the increasing scale economies of production gave rise in the early twentieth century to what became known as the American system of mass production (Hounshell 1984). Under mass production, further division of labor and specialization were made possible by the realization of interchangeable parts combined with a high degree of product and process standardization under organizational structures, such as the assembly line and scientific management approaches pioneered by Frederick Winslow Taylor (Chandler 1990; Hounshell 1984; Taylor 1914). These innovations also drove a further complementarity between capital and low skilled labor (Lafortune, Lewis, and Tessada 2019). Standardization of tools, processes, and products would remain a driving feature of production into the post-war era (Mowery and Rosenberg 1999).

After a slowdown in productivity growth in manufacturing from the 1960s to the 1970s (Hulten and Schwab 1984), US manufacturing in the mid-1970s and 1980s experienced what some have referred to as the third industrial revolution (Greenwood 1997; Mowery 2009). Manufacturing tasks shifted from humans and active machine control toward industrial robots and computer numerical control (CNC) systems (Bollinger and Duffie 1988; Moore 1997; Nichols 1976). Flexible manufacturing exploited CNC and other systems to allow medium-sized batch production. This batch production enabled product variety over the low-variety scale economies of mass production (Browne et al. 1984; Buzacott and Yao 1986). Human resource management approaches, such as employee training programs and flexible job assignments, also expanded (Bartel 1994; Ichniowski, Shaw, and Prennushi 1995).

In contrast to the American system of mass production, shifts associated with the third industrial revolution coincided with higher demand for skilled labor (Autor and Dorn 2013; Autor, Levy, and Murnane 2003; Katz and Murphy 1992). In some contexts, changes in the methods of production coincided with changes in the organization of production: from mass production, product standardization, and strict task specialization for equipment and personnel toward flexible manufacturing and lean production approaches (Mansfield 1993; Ohno 1988). Lean manufacturing, pioneered at Toyota through the Toyota Production System (TPS), differed from the material-rich roots of early US manufacturing by focusing on minimizing material as well as other resource wastage (Shah and Ward 2003; Womack, Jones, and Roos 1990). The system established just-in-time manufacturing strategies, which encouraged firms to entwine production and supply chains with the goal of narrowing the lead time between production and suppliers and time in production (Cheng and Podolsky 1996; Sakakibara et al. 1997). Among US manufacturers, lean manufacturing methods were adopted, among other places, in metal fabrication and computer, electrical machinery, and automotive production (Swamidass 2007). US firms did not adopt all dimensions of TPS, due to concerns about possible limitations on creativity and innovation (Mehri 2006), keeping many traditional compensation and labor relations arrangements (Doeringer, Lorenz, and Terkla 2003).[7]

Throughout the third industrial revolution, multiple manufacturing contexts actively pursued increasing the modularity of designs, led by computer hardware and other electronics. Modular computer systems composed of smaller, simpler subsystems (including such elements as hard disk drives and microprocessors) paralleled rapid innovations in component-specific performance that did not require costly (from the perspective of both time and money) total-system overhauls. In some cases, this modularity in design was mirrored in the design of organizations and supply chain composition of modern industries (Baldwin and Clark 2000, 2003; Colfer and Baldwin 2016). Suppliers also often took an active role in the innovative process (Helper and Sako 1995). Increasing modularity, including in the organization of suppliers, coincided with an increasing globalization of manufacturing supply chains (Gereffi, Humphrey, and Sturgeon 2005). At the same time, system-level innovations were often associated with (often temporary) reintegration of modular elements to facilitate technologies

---

7. While strong performers adopting TPS realized inventory-to-sales reductions, weaker performers saw an increase in their ratio of inventory to sales (Swamidass 2007).

that affected characteristics across modular boundaries. The integrated circuit, a key innovation in microprocessors that enabled technology across the US economy (Bresnahan and Trajtenberg 1995), was itself an integration of components (Moore 1965); other components, such as lasers, saw continuing integration during the twentieth and twenty-first centuries (Liu et al. 2007). Drawing on industries such as computer hardware and other electronics, academics hypothesized a dynamic of modularity, and integration in contrast, increasing and decreasing apace with technological shifts (Chesbrough 2003).

Organizational innovations and production technologies continue to evolve in the twenty-first century. Though lean and flexible approaches have become prominent trends in manufacturing, the American system of mass production continues in new permutations, as does the development of new automation and information technologies that hold potential to transform the nature of work (Bartel, Ichniowski, and Shaw 2007; Mindell 2015). Automation has begun to include collaborative dimensions, bringing workers into direct production roles supported by robots (Cherubini et al. 2016; Kaber and Endsley 2004). However, collaborative robots are in their infancy and are unlikely to be appropriate in all settings (Hayes and Scassellati 2013). Additive manufacturing approaches present new possibilities for small batch, high variety production with the promise of mass customization in such industries as food, metals, and plastics (Atzeni and Salmi 2012; Fralix 2001; Herrigel 2010; Mellor, Hao, and Zhang 2014) and material savings complementary to lean manufacturing approaches. That said, additive manufacturing is likely to be limited, at least in the near term, in the complexity of components that it can build and the degree of economically feasible customization that it enables, limiting its appropriateness in a wide range of contexts (Bonnín-Roca et al. 2017a). Through all these changes, large scale, mechanized systems with intellectual roots in nineteenth- and even eighteenth-century US manufacturing continue to play a major role informed by subsequent innovations (Achillas et al. 2015; Hu 2013; Kumar and Ando 2010).

1.3 Manufacturing Value Added and R&D

Global measurements of manufacturing value added and R&D offer an important birds-eye perspective on the US and world economies.

1.3.1 US and Global Value Added

Value added is the amount (in our data, dollars) contributed by an entity to the value of a good or service (US Census Bureau 2018). Value added thus comes from the changes made to an intermediate good or service (the price minus all inputs). While value added is a useful economic indicator, in that it isolates an individual firm or nation's contribution in the global supply chain, it has several limitations. First, market power can affect prices of goods, which can then affect the measurement of value added. Second, our global manufacturing value added statistics are from the World Bank Database. The World Bank measures of value added come from its national accounts data. As not all national accounts are handled in the same way, cross-country comparisons are imprecise. The World Bank lacks gross (and thus nonmanufacturing sector) value added data for many countries, including China. We therefore limit our international comparisons of gross value added across all sectors to Appendix A (this section includes international comparisons of manufacturing value added only).[8] The World Bank data on MVA includes more countries, although notably the World Bank only starts including China as of 2004. Our US domestic value added data by sector thus comes from the Bureau of Economic Analysis (BEA). The BEA's data collection on value added by industry follows the North American Industry Classification System (NAICS) codes, whereas the World Bank's data collection across countries follows the International Standard Industrial Classification (ISIC) codes.[9] These sector classification differences in part explain the numerical differences between figure 1.1 (World Bank) and figure 1.2 (BEA).

The US has seen a decline in its global share of MVA since 2000. While US MVA grew in real terms (indeed, at a higher rate than the growth of key manufacturing countries, such as Germany or Japan), it did not outpace the overall growth of the rest of the world. In particular, the US decline in global share of MVA is due in large part to the significant rise in China's MVA, leaving the US with a reduced share.

US manufacturing has seen a decline in its share of US value added (Bureau of Economic Analysis 2019). While manufacturing value added stagnated in real terms in 1997–2015, other sectors, such as services, grew. Thus, the relative role of manufacturing in the overall value added of the economy decreased (see figure 1.2). Outside of services, manufacturing, and information (reported in figure 1.2), the largest nongovernmental sectors by

8. The United States has seen growth in its GVA over the past 25 years, and modest growth in its share of world GVA from 2011 to 2016 after a year-on-year decline since 2001 (World Bank 2019). The US share of GVA is likely less than reported by the World Bank and perhaps is declining more sharply due to growth in unmeasured nations.

9. Moreover, the World Bank has changed which versions of the ISIC codes it uses, with data up to 2008 reflecting Revision 2 and a shift toward ISIC Revision 3 thereafter. After 2008, however, some international comparative data continue to follow ISIC Revision 2, and the World Bank notes that it attempts to reconcile these with its Revision 3 standard. The ISIC Revision 2 system did not break out manufacturing by industry or subsector, and this rougher classification likely resulted in the discrepancies between World Bank and BEA values for US MVA that are observable in figures 1.1 and 1.2. Even the ISIC Revision 3 codes differ slightly from the NAICS categorization and could result in further discrepancies. For example, ISIC Revision 3 includes recycling (absent from NAICs) but no category for "miscellaneous manufacturing" (NAICS 339). We thus reserve World Bank data for rough international comparisons of manufacturing and do not attempt a subsectoral international comparison.

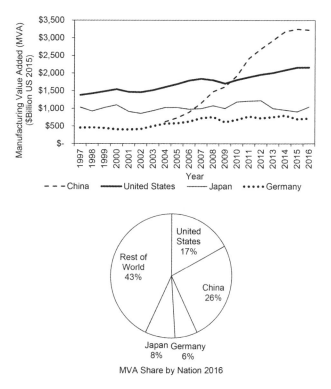

Fig. 1.1 Global manufacturing value added of top four manufacturing nations, 1997–2016

value added are finance (21 percent) and retail and wholesale trade (10 percent). Though the greatest proportional growth in 1997–2015 was in mining (89 percent increase in value added 1997–2015), the largest real growth was in services and finance, with manufacturing among the slowest growing sectors proportionately and in real terms (Bureau of Economic Analysis 2019).

In short, the manufacturing industry in the US offers an undersized—and shrinking—contribution to domestic value added.

1.3.2   US and Global R&D Spending

Our data on global industrial R&D spending is based on the OECD Science, Technology and Patents Database.[10] The OECD database consists of the OECD nations and 28 nonmember countries (including all countries

10. International R&D spending statistics are collected by the European Union and the OECD. The European Union's World Input Output Database (WIOD) covers the 28 EU countries and 15 other major countries, including the US and China. However, the WIOD database lacks detailed breakouts of the sources of R&D spending, such as industry and government.

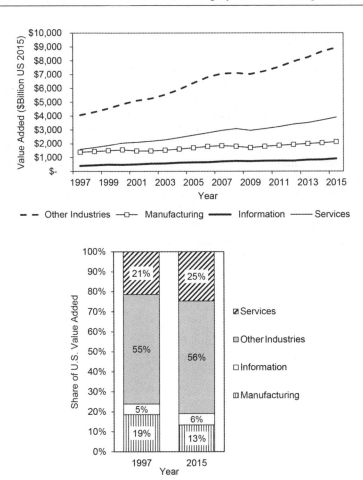

Fig. 1.2   US domestic value added, by sector
Source: Bureau of Economic Analysis (2019).

in the G20), with data covering the US, China, and some other nations beginning in 2008 only. While the OECD data does not include sectoral-level data, it captures industrial R&D activity in each nation distinctly from government spending for each sector (including manufacturing).[11] Similar to value added, the OECD database on R&D spending has limitations for cross-country comparisons: While the National Science Foundation (NSF), on which OECD bases its US R&D calculations, excludes historical and other nonscientific research, the definition of R&D used by OECD in tabu-

11. Internationally, federal R&D spending is a greater share of expenditure relative to industrial spending than it is in the United States.

lating the R&D spending of EU nations and possibly others in the database includes a broader set of cultural and historical research.[12]

For sectoral level comparisons of industrial R&D spending in the US, we use the NSF Science and Technology Indicator data.[13] The OECD data are submitted by nations following the Frascati Manual (OECD 2015): for each nation, these data report all spending on R&D by establishments in a focus country's borders (regardless of the country in which those establishments have their headquarters), combined with the R&D spending of foreign subsidiaries not within the focus country's borders, but whose parent company is headquartered in the focus country.[14] While the NSF also reports these values (referred to by NSF as "US world-wide R&D spending," and which match OECD's numbers), as our focus in later sections is on R&D spending by business establishments located in the US, we use NSF's (smaller) US domestic industrial R&D values rather than the worldwide spending. As can be seen in comparing figures 1.3 and 1.4, the difference between the NSF's US world-wide R&D spending (as used in the OECD global industrial R&D spending data) and the NSF US domestic industrial R&D spending in 2015 was about $50 billion or 21 percent.

Under OECD's measurement, Chinese establishments and Chinese-owned subsidiaries account for the most R&D spending internationally. While US manufacturing R&D has increased since 1980s, growth has stagnated since 2008. The same trends are true in Japan and Germany (the nations with the third and fourth greatest R&D spending by manufacturing business establishments located within them). In contrast, R&D expenditures by manufacturing business establishments located in China have more than doubled in the same period, exceeding spending in the US in 2013 (OECD 2019).[15] Figure 1.3 captures these trends in R&D spending by

12. The OECD (2015) definition of R&D is: "Research and development (**R&D**) comprise creative work undertaken on a systematic basis in order to increase the stock of knowledge (including knowledge of man, culture and society) and the use of this knowledge to devise new applications."

13. Historic NSF R&D indicators classify firms into industries and sectors based on the industry that receives the plurality of R&D funding for the firm. Although more recent NSF work (NSF 2019) has sought to classify R&D indicators based on the revenue sources of firms, we focus in this chapter on the historic data.

14. It is thus possible for international aggregate statistics to double-count R&D spending when the country in which a multinational enterprise in headquartered counts the R&D spending of that enterprise's foreign affiliates, and the country where those affiliates are located also counts the R&D spending of those affiliates.

15. While offering the most complete international data on R&D spending by nation and industry, the OECD Science, Technology and Patents Database is based on a different definition of R&D spending from that used by the US government (and OECD notes that US R&D inputs to its database are based on a different definition). OECD's R&D "comprise creative work undertaken on a systematic basis in order to increase the stock of knowledge (including knowledge of man, culture and society) and the use of this knowledge to devise new applications." The inclusion of social sciences expands the scope of relevant R&D activity outside that used in the US and thus may understate the level of non-social science R&D spending in the US relative to other countries.

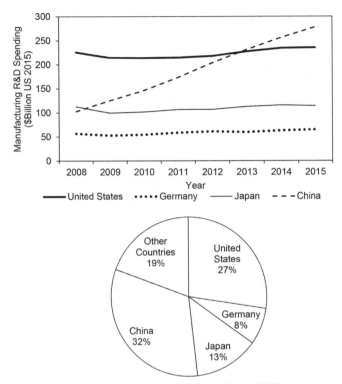

Fig. 1.3 **Expenditures on manufacturing R&D by business establishments located in a country, top four nations**
Source: OECD (2019).
Note: Other countries are OECD nations + Taiwan + Argentina + Romania.

manufacturing business enterprises in key nations. The named countries' shares of global R&D activity by manufacturing business enterprises are overstated in the figure, because the dataset for 2015 (the latest available year with broad, reliable international data) includes data from China, the US, Japan, Germany, the OECD nations, Taiwan, Argentina, and Romania, but not the rest of the world.

Among the nations captured by the OECD data (OECD Nations and China, Taiwan, Argentina, and Romania), 72 percent of industrial R&D expenditures recorded by OECD were in manufacturing. In China, that share was 88 percent, while in OECD's figures, the share of US industrial R&D expenditure in manufacturing was only 66 percent. That is, the US spends proportionally less on manufacturing R&D than do OECD members and other nations.

Between 1982 and 2015, the US rate of federal R&D funding declined as a relative share of total R&D funding (National Science Foundation n.d., American Association for the Advancement of Science 2019), with industrial R&D funding growing relative to federal funding over the same period (see appendix J). Industrial and federal R&D show significant differences in the funding of basic versus applied research: while 30–36 percent of overall federal funding was allocated to basic research during 2006–2015, in 2015 only 5.5 percent of industry R&D spending was directed toward basic research, the rest going to applied research and development.[16] Arora, Belenzon, and Patacconi (2015) show declining R&D spending and capability-building by US companies in basic research. Fleming et al. (2019) suggest that companies are increasingly relying on federally supported research.

In the US, manufacturing remains the dominant source of industrial R&D. Industrial R&D spending originating from manufacturing grew significantly in real terms during 1982–2015 (National Science Foundation n.d.). However, after 1997, this growth in manufacturing R&D was accompanied by growth in R&D spending from other sectors, including services and information, such that the overall share of industrial R&D spending from manufacturing has actually declined (see figure 1.4).

In short, R&D spending by manufacturing sector business establishments located in the US continues to dominate US-based industrial R&D spending, far outstripping that spent by other sectors. This dominance is in stark contrast to manufacturing's comparatively small role in contributing to US value added.

1.4   The US Manufacturing Labor Force

The IPUMS Current Population Survey Annual Social and Economic Complement microdata from 1968 to 2018 reveal differences between the US manufacturing and nonmanufacturing labor force along several demographic dimensions, including educational attainment, age, gender, and wage and salary income groups.[17] Figure 1.5 shows the magnitude of the labor force each year in manufacturing and nonmanufacturing; during this period, growth in the US labor force has come entirely from the nonmanufacturing sector, with a reduced manufacturing labor force post-1981.

1.4.1   Human Capital and Demographics of the Labor Force

Educational attainment, as measured by years of formal education, has risen for the overall labor force, manufacturing sector, and manufacturing subsectors. Across the economy, the proportion of workers with a high school (HS) education or less has declined across the past five decades. Ber-

16. Federal funds to industry were also disproportionately allocated to applied R&D, with 8 percent of funds going to basic research.
17. Each individual observation in the data is weighted by the Annual Social and Economic Complement population weight.

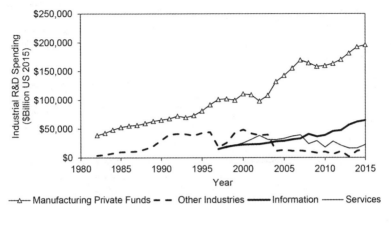

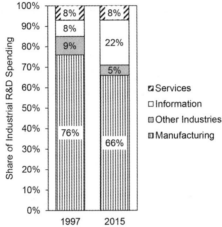

Fig. 1.4   US industrial R&D spending, by sector

Source: National Science Foundation (n.d.).

Note: While manufacturing and overall R&D data extend to 1982, we use 1997 as a basis of comparison, because it is the first year for which information and service data are available.

man, Bound, and Griliches (1994) argue that labor-saving technological change is the leading cause of this trend. Berman, Bound, and Machin (1998) find further international evidence of manufacturers increasing demand for skilled workers and increasing skill premiums, in line with the skill-biased technological change hypothesis.

However, the manufacturing sector still provides many jobs for workers with less education, especially in contrast with other sectors. As can be seen in figure 1.6, the manufacturing sector (solid line) consistently has a higher proportion of workers with a HS education or less relative to nonmanufacturing sectors (dashed line); each year, the manufacturing labor force has

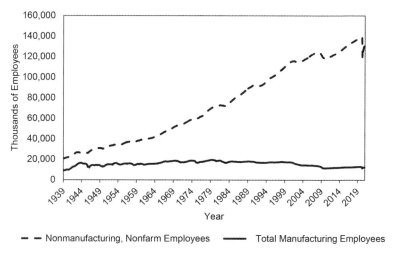

Fig. 1.5   Absolute magnitude of the US nonmanufacturing and manufacturing labor force

Source: St. Louis Fed.

Note: In this figure, 2014 is omitted to allow for use of consistent weighting by the ASEC population weight, as the CPS underwent an experimental redesign.

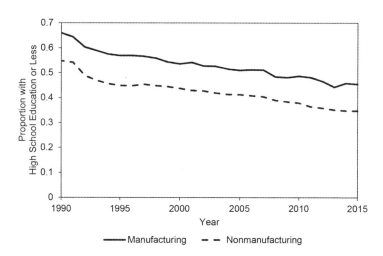

Fig. 1.6   Manufacturing and nonmanufacturing labor force educational attainment exhibiting a consistent difference

Source: IPUMS-CPS ASEC microdata (1990–2015).

8–12 percentage points more workers with HS education or less relative to the nonmanufacturing sector.

The manufacturing industry's labor force has remained nearly completely private wage or salary workers: 98 percent in 1975 and 95 percent in 2015. The proportion of the manufacturing labor force earning less than $10,000

(2017 dollars) remains less than the proportion of the nonmanufacturing labor force (8 percent manufacturing, 19 percent nonmanufacturing). The proportion of the manufacturing labor force whose earnings fall between $10,000 and $250,000 is also higher than the nonmanufacturing labor force (91 percent manufacturing, 81 percent nonmanufacturing).

1.5   Manufacturing Share of Value Added and Share of R&D Funding

1.5.1   Disproportionate R&D Funding from Manufacturing Relative to MVA

As described in sections 1.1 and 1.3, manufacturing historically and currently makes up a disproportionate source of industrial R&D funding in the US: about 96 percent in 1982 and about 66 percent in 2015. Though shrinking proportionally, R&D funds from manufacturing grew in real terms by 197 percent in the same period. Manufacturing represents a much smaller proportion of US nongovernmental value added (14 percent), and manufacturing's proportion of value added has been declining since 1997 (the earliest available BEA data), when MVA share of total value added stood at 19 percent. At that time, the manufacturing share of industrial R&D spending was 76 percent. With a proportional decline in R&D share of 13 percent and a proportional decline of MVA share of 26 percent since 1997, the proportional difference between manufacturing subsector's contribution to US R&D spending and to value added has been growing. As can be seen in figure 1.7, this difference between a sector's contribution to US industrial R&D spending versus a sector's contribution to US value added, while most pronounced in manufacturing, is not unique to the sector. For example, the information sector comprises 22 percent of US industrial R&D spending but 6 percent of US value added. In contrast, professional, scientific, and technical services comprise 7 percent of US industrial R&D spending but a much larger percentage of US value added. Uncovering the sources of these differences in other sectors is outside the scope of this chapter but is an important broader phenomena to unpack in the US economy.[18]

1.5.2   Hypotheses, Evaluation, and a Partial Explanation

We propose and evaluate three hypotheses for what might in part account for the disproportionate share of US industrial R&D spending from manufacturing: (1) Other sectors of the economy underreport their R&D spend-

---

18. More recent work by NSF (2019) has sought to reclassify R&D spending based on the dominant revenue source of a firm, rather than on the dominant industry focus of its R&D. This approach suggests that about 40 percent of industrial R&D performance occurs in firms whose primary revenue source is manufacturing. This figure is less than the 66 percent of industrial R&D spending with a manufacturing focus but remains much greater than the share of manufacturing in US value added. We choose to focus on industrial R&D spending by sector of spending rather than by revenue stream, as our interest is in manufacturing as a destination of R&D activity.

A. US Value Added (Nongovernment)

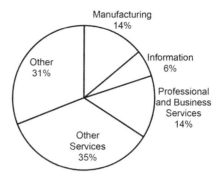

B. US Industrial R&D Spending

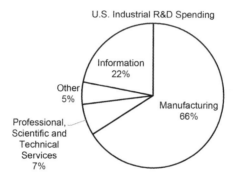

Fig. 1.7   Share of value added and industrial R&D spending by sector, 2015
Source: A: BEA: *The Use of Commodities by Industries.* B: NSF.
Note: Professional and Business Services includes Professional, Scientific and Technical Services.

ing, possibly due to incentives in the R&D tax credits available under the US tax code or because research activities that are not performed through traditional R&D channels are not counted by NSF. (2) The returns from manufacturing R&D accrue to nonmanufacturing sectors, for instance, through R&D embodied in manufactured capital or through the development of general-purpose technologies (GPTs) using manufacturing R&D funds. (3) The returns to domestic manufacturing R&D are realized abroad, for instance, by multinational firms, and thus are not reflected in value added statistics from US manufacturing. Our ingoing hypothesis was that all three hypotheses could be acting simultaneously.

We do not find strong evidence to support our first two hypotheses. We briefly discuss our conclusions regarding hypotheses 1 and 2 here, and provide the details of our explorations of the first two hypotheses in appendix K. We present our findings regarding hypothesis 3 in greater depth in the next section.

For hypothesis 1, we were not able to find clear incentives for other sectors of the economy to underreport their R&D spending under the US Research and Development Tax Credit. We find that personnel expenditures and, in small firms, payroll taxes, can be offset by R&D tax credits, suggesting that there are strong incentives for software and other technology firms to report their R&D activities. Firms may in fact have less incentive to report the capital-intensive R&D activities more common to manufacturing, because the credit excludes spending on fixed capital. We also find that one possible form of R&D spending not counted by the NSF, venture capital (VC) funding, is disproportionately directed toward sectors other than manufacturing. That said, even counting all VC funding as a form of R&D spending still leaves manufacturing the majority source of industrial R&D spending (although at this extreme only by a very small margin). It is important to note that the definition of R&D used both in NSF's data collection and for the R&D Tax Credit does not include the development of internal capabilities or of incremental product improvements. For example, there is significant patenting in finance (Lerner et al. 2020) and software (Branstetter et al. 2019), but some of those patents are, for example, for new algorithms consumed internally by the firm. Manufacturing also has cases where firms develop, for example, their own equipment for internal use. These activities would not count as R&D according to NSF's definition. Future work is needed to unpack whether such internal R&D expenditures are more significant in some sectors than in others.

Hypothesis 2 proposes that the disproportionate share of US industrial R&D from manufacturing is in part due to the returns from manufacturing R&D accruing to nonmanufacturing sectors, for instance, through R&D embodied in manufactured capital or through the development of general-purpose technologies (GPTs) using manufacturing R&D funds. We do not find evidence to support an outsized role for manufacturing in producing capital that embodies R&D. Leveraging the World Input-Output Database (WIOD), we conduct a rudimentary regression analysis of output and value added of other sectors on intensity-adjusted R&D stock from manufacturing subsectors (described in detail in appendix K.2). Preliminary evidence based on the rudimentary regression instead suggest that the magnitude of embodiment may be greater for nonmanufacturing sectors, such as information. We also do not find any preliminary evidence to support GPT as a primary explanation for the outsized role of manufacturing overall. A GPT is defined as having (1) general applicability (i.e., it performs some generic function vital to the functioning of a large number of products or processes that use it); (2) technology dynamism (i.e., continuous innovation over time improves the efficiency with which the general function is performed, benefiting existing users and prompting further sectors to adopt the GPT);

and (3) innovation complementarities (i.e., technology advances in the GPT make it more profitable for users to innovate in their own technologies) (Rosenberg and Trajtenberg 2004). We do not find any association between value added in nonmanufacturing sectors and their manufacturing inputs. We do not do a sufficient test to track whether innovation in one sector leads to innovation in another sector. GPT dynamics have clearly been a significant part of the story historically in some sectors, such as microprocessors (Jorgenson 2001).[19]

1.5.2.1   MVA Returns Abroad: A Partial Solution to the Puzzle

In this section, we examine the hypothesis that returns to domestic manufacturing R&D are realized abroad and therefore are not reflected in value added statistics that are bounded by country borders (hypothesis 3). We do so by looking at the activities of US multinational companies (MNCs) in the US and at their foreign affiliates, using publicly available BEA data from the US Direct Investment Abroad surveys (Bureau of Economic Analysis 2019). Statistics on value added and R&D performed in the US exclude the foreign affiliate activities of multinational firms and may hide some significant activity undertaken by these firms. The focus on multinational firms is especially significant given their disproportionate role in performing R&D; the National Center for Science and Engineering Statistics[20] reports that US multinational companies performed 79 percent of all R&D conducted by US-located businesses.

Figure 1.8 illustrates that concentrating attention on US MNCs—and including all their global activity—significantly shrinks the gap between value added and R&D performed for manufacturing firms vs. nonmanufacturing firms. Panel A is a bar graph representation of the pie chart from figure 1.7 and shows the original motivating puzzle: manufacturing firms contribute disproportionately to R&D, and yet very little value added results from this. Panel B focuses attention on US multinational firms and—importantly—includes both the parent activities and the foreign affiliate activities. By concentrating attention on MNCs—and their global activity—the gap between value added and R&D for manufacturing firms compared to nonmanufacturing firms shrinks significantly.

Figure 1.9 provides some insight into why the gap shrinks so much when looking at MNC global activity rather than domestic activity alone: a larger share of value added is abroad compared to R&D, which is highly concentrated in the US.

The picture becomes even more clear when we take this one step further

---

19. Jorgenson's (2001) approach is a technology-specific analysis of quality improvements in information technology relative to pricing, which then informs a model of the production possibility frontier of the US economy and its shifts relative to the quality of IT equipment. We were unable to replicate this detailed analysis for goods and services throughout manufacturing.
    20. Moris (2016).

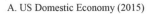

A. US Domestic Economy (2015)

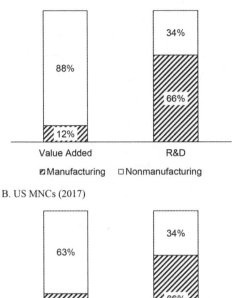

Fig. 1.8   Share of value added and R&D contributed to by manufacturing vs. non-manufacturing firms
Source: BEA.

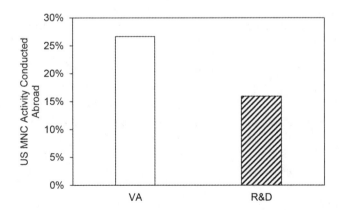

Fig. 1.9   Percentage of US MNC activity conducted abroad in 2017
Source: BEA.

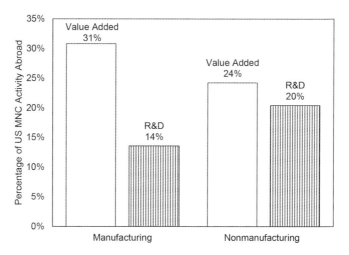

Fig. 1.10   Percentage of US MNC activity conducted abroad in 2017, by sector
Source: BEA.

and consider how US MNCs in the manufacturing sector geographically distribute their value added and R&D activities relative to those in the non-manufacturing sector. Figure 1.10 illustrates this point: US MNCs in the manufacturing sector do only 14 percent of their R&D activities abroad, while those in the nonmanufacturing sector do 20 percent of their R&D activities abroad, as of 2017. In contrast, they are much likely to have value added abroad; 31 percent of manufacturing value added is at their foreign affiliates, while only 24 percent of nonmanufacturing value added is at their foreign affiliates.

The above data support our hypothesis and suggest that a significant part of the gap between manufacturing's share of R&D spending and their realization in value added can be explained by recognizing that production is no longer constrained by national borders, while manufacturing R&D—in general terms—is more constrained.

1.5.2.2   R&D Increasingly Moving Abroad, but Less So in Manufacturing

R&D is increasingly moving abroad, especially in services and some manufacturing sectors. Although we document in section 6.2.3 that R&D is more concentrated at home than production is, when explaining the differences in manufacturing's contribution to R&D vs. value added in US domestic borders, it is important to recognize that (1) R&D is increasingly moving abroad, and (2) the concentration of R&D at home is only true for some sectors.

As shown in figure 1.11, there has been tremendous growth—in real terms—of foreign R&D. Since the late 1990s, the amount of R&D conducted overseas by US MNCs has grown nearly fourfold.

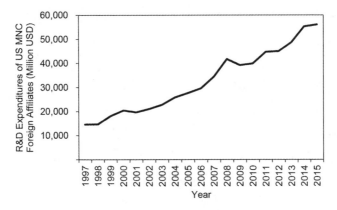

Fig. 1.11   R&D expenditures of US MNC foreign affiliates (millions USD)
Source: BEA.

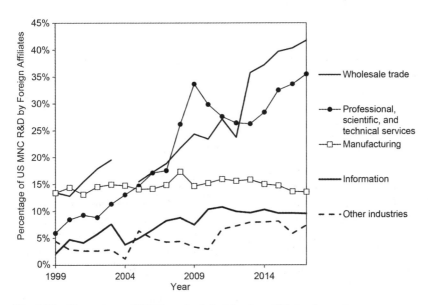

Fig. 1.12   Percentage of R&D conducted at foreign affiliates, by sector
Source: BEA.

Figure 1.12 and figure 1.13 illustrate that the expansion abroad has largely been driven by nonmanufacturing sectors. In particular, the services sector—and especially the professional, scientific, and technical services sector—has dramatically increased the amount of R&D conducted at foreign affiliates rather than at the US parent company location. In contrast, at the aggregate level, the manufacturing industry as a whole has continued to keep the vast majority of its R&D at home.

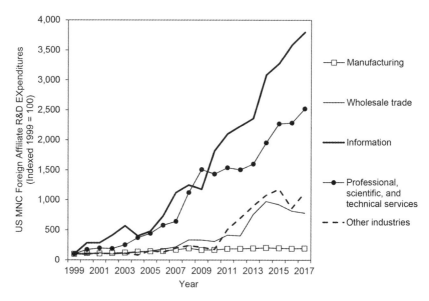

Fig. 1.13   R&D expenditures by US MNC foreign affiliates, by industry of foreign affiliate, indexed (1999 = 100)
Source: BEA.

1.6   Manufacturing Subsectoral Variations in the Concentration of Value Added, R&D Funding, Employment, and Revenue

Today, the US manufacturing sector is composed of industries that vary in the level of spending that they dedicate to R&D, with key industries representing dominant sources of current investment. The disproportionate role of manufacturing in R&D activity becomes starker when considering the top five manufacturing subsectors by R&D spending. These subsectors contributed 42 percent of US industrial R&D Spending in 2015 (National Science Foundation n.d.), despite representing only 18 percent of manufacturing value added and thus 2.1 percent of total value added in the economy (Bureau of Economic Analysis 2019; US Census Bureau 2018). The role of these key subsectors offers further insight into the puzzle of outsized manufacturing R&D spending versus value added.

In contrast to manufacturing industrial R&D spending, MVA is not dominated by any core sector or sectors, nor are the top subsectors necessarily the largest by R&D spending. Appendix L shows the share of total MVA by the top five subsectors by MVA and by industrial R&D spending.

Figure 1.14 illustrates the concentration of R&D spending, employment, and value added in the manufacturing sector by four-digit NAICS subsector. As the figure illustrates, the industries that provide the most funding for industrial R&D are not necessarily the largest employers or sources of value

A. Industry R&D Spending ($Billion), NSF, Top 5 Industries

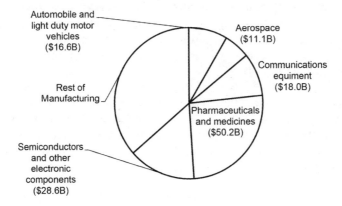

B. Industry Employment (thousands), ASM, Top 5 Industries

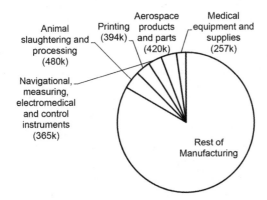

C. Industry Receipt ($Billion), ASM, Top 5 Industries

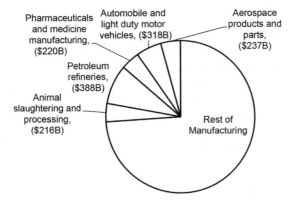

Fig. 1.14   Concentration of R&D spending, employment, and value added in manufacturing, 2015

added. Pharmaceuticals rank as the top R&D spending industry and the top source of value added, while animal slaughtering is the top employer. Only aerospace overlaps the top five ranking for all three indicators. The largest industries by value added include only two of the five largest by R&D funding (pharmaceuticals and aerospace) and only one of the largest by employment (aerospace).

The pharmaceutical industry leads manufacturing R&D spending with 26 percent of the total, followed by semiconductors and electronic components with 15 percent of the total and communications, automobile and aerospace manufacturing contributing a cumulative 23 percent, for a total of 64 percent of Industry R&D funded by the top five industries. The gap between pharmaceuticals and medicines and the next largest subsector by R&D spending, semiconductors and other electronic components, is just over twice the gap between the second and third largest industries. Thus, not only are the largest five sectors by R&D spending disproportionately dominant, but the concentration continues to scale within the top five.

Employment and value added show a wider dispersion across manufacturing industries. The five largest manufacturing industries by revenue make up 24 percent of total manufacturing revenue, while the five industries with the highest employment represent 15 percent of total employment. While the pharmaceutical industry is a major source of R&D funding, it does not solely drive the disproportionate concentration of R&D funding among type funds: even without pharmaceuticals, the next four industries account for 38 percent of R&D spending by manufacturing, more than half again the concentration of employment or revenue among top five sectors and more than twice the concentration among the second through fifth place sectors.

The top five manufacturing industries by R&D funding are consistent from 1994[21] to the latest NSF data by sector in 2015. Figure 1.15 illustrates that while the overall composition was consistent, the relative positions of top industries by R&D funding evolved over this period. The automotive industry, which ranked fourth for R&D funding in 2015, was the largest manufacturing funder of R&D from 1994 to 2003, with pharmaceuticals and medicines dominating from 2004 to 2015. While pharmaceuticals and semiconductors grew in R&D funding after 2004, aerospace, automotive, and communications equipment manufacturing appeared to largely stagnate or decline throughout the period, except for modest growth in communications R&D funding after 2011. The relative composition of R&D funding in manufacturing has shifted over the 2004–2015 period, with the bottom three industries remaining fairly close to one another in level of funding

---

21. The NSF annual reports on "Research and Development in Industry" include annual data extending back to 1982, but classification shifts from the 1993 to 1994 reports limit comparisons before 1994: the composition of the top five sectors may have changed prior to 1994, but comparison is infeasible before and after the reclassifications.

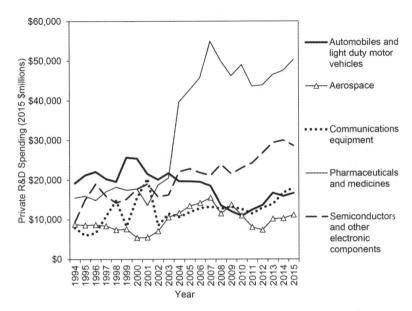

Fig. 1.15   Industrial R&D funding by top five R&D funders in manufacturing, 1994–2015 (NSF)

and a growing gap between both the top and bottom three and between pharmaceuticals and semiconductors.

1.7   Subsectoral Nuances in the Offshore Realization of Manufacturing R&D Returns

1.7.1   Globalization of MVA and R&D Subsector Story

To better understand the dichotomy between MVA and industrial R&D spending, we looked at the changes in share of intermediates imported for the subsectors in the ISIC classification that most closely correspond to the manufacturing subsectors under NAICS with the top industrial R&D spending.[22] While US manufacturing overall saw a 10 percent increase in the share of intermediates imported from 2005 to 2014 (the latest available data from WIOD), the manufacturing subsectors with the highest industrial R&D spending experienced far greater shifts in their share of intermediate inputs imported than did manufacturing overall (see figure 1.16). Motor vehicles and machinery had nearly double an increase in their share of inter-

22. While some research (e.g., Los, Timmer, and de Vries 2015) has imputed value added from the input-output data of the WIOD, sectoral and gross national value added data are not collected for all countries in the WIOD, and available measures of input and output by national industry or sectors may overstate value added by omitting inputs from countries in the database.

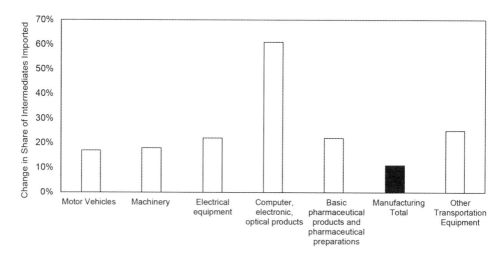

Fig. 1.16   Manufacturing subsector differences in shifting inputs offshore, 2005–2014

Source: World Input Output Database.

Note: Classification system used is ISIC, not NAICS as in NSF R&D and ASM data.

mediates imported, at 17 percent and 18 percent, respectively, compared to manufacturing on average. The largest industrial R&D spending subsector in manufacturing, pharmaceuticals, saw a 22 percent in its share of intermediate inputs imported between 2005 and 2014. Meanwhile, computer, electronic, and optical products saw a 61 percent increase in the share of intermediates imported. While these R&D-intensive subsectors showed strong increases in importing, further research would be necessary to understand what in these sectors was and was not shifted abroad and why.

Although in aggregate, US MNCs in the manufacturing industry concentrate their R&D activity in the US, figure 1.17 demonstrates the degree to which this varies. Industries like petroleum conduct almost no R&D abroad, while textiles and printing conduct almost a third of their R&D at their foreign affiliates.

In short, while US MNCs continue to concentrate their R&D activity predominately in the US, even as they have expanded production overseas, R&D is increasingly a global activity—particularly in the services sector and some manufacturing sectors.

1.7.2   Globalization of MVA: Labor Subsector Story

The realization of MVA returns abroad in key manufacturing subsectors by R&D spending also aligns with differences in the educational demand of those subsectors relative to the rest of manufacturing. While the overall manufacturing distribution of employment and wages is characterized by higher employment and wages for non-college educated workers (see section 1.4), we show in figure 1.18 that the largest manufacturing subsectors

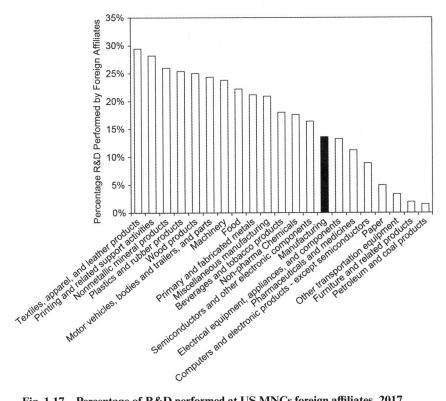

Fig. 1.17   Percentage of R&D performed at US MNCs foreign affiliates, 2017
Source: BEA.

by R&D spending (panel A) tend to skew less toward HS-level employees than the largest subsectors by employment (panel B).[23]

Our findings suggest that the role of manufacturing in R&D spending may be relatively decoupled from the sector's overall labor profile, so that value added gains from R&D may not translate directly into value added or employment growth for HS-intensive subsectors. Of the five largest subsectors by R&D spending, all but motor vehicle manufacturing have proportionally fewer employees with HS education or less than do nonmanufacturing industries. The contrast is especially apparent between high-employment, low-R&D subsectors, such as animal slaughtering and processing, and the high-R&D subsectors. Aerospace, the only subsector in the top five by R&D spending and employment, highlights the potential decoupling of high-R&D spending from HS employment, with a lower proportion of HS employees than manufacturing overall and nonmanufacturing industries.

23. The figure reports on some subsectors at higher levels of aggregation than the NSF data due to imperfections in data cross-walking between the IPUMS database and NAICS classification, but the aggregation occurs across sectors with similar R&D spending and offshoring profiles (e.g., motor vehicles and aerospace).

A. Top 5 R&D Spending Subsectors

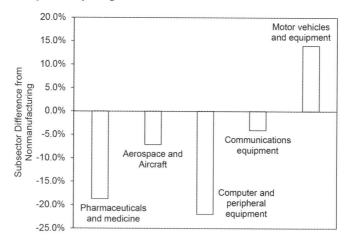

B. Top 5 Employment Subsectors

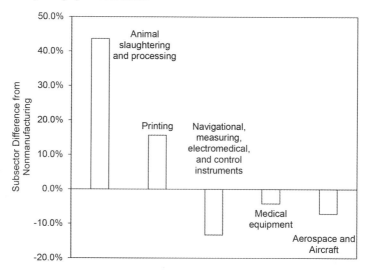

Fig. 1.18   Manufacturing industry differences from share of high-school level employees in nonmanufacturing, 2015
Source: IPUMS-CPS ASEC microdata, 2015.

It is also important to note that significant employment in other sectors (e.g., retail and warehousing services) is connected to the output of manufacturing industries and that innovative effort in manufacturing can have effects along the supply chain. Sectoral and subsectoral boundaries do not fully capture the characteristics (e.g., educational) of workforces, which may be affected by innovations coming out of manufacturing.

1.8   Discussion: Potential Relationships between Manufacturing Location, Innovation, and Labor Outcomes—A Need for Technology Differentiation

1.8.1   The Potential Relationship between Manufacturing and Innovation

Economic theory suggests that shifts in manufacturing away from a nation may hurt wages there, but global innovation and productivity gains will not suffer (Samuelson 2004). However, empirical research suggests that, at least in certain contexts, moving the location of manufacturing can alter whether and which next-generation products are profitable (Fuchs and Kirchain 2010, Fuchs et al. 2011). Production characteristics (wages, yields, downtimes, organization of production) can differ greatly across nations (especially developed and developing ones). In two cases—automobile bodies and high-end optoelectronic components for communications—when US firms shifted production to developing East Asia, differences in these production characteristics meant that products developed in the US based on the most advanced technologies were no longer immediately profitable. The overseas firms stopped producing these products and, in optoelectronics, also stopped innovation (measured as patenting) in the most advanced products in all their locations overseas and in the US (Fuchs and Kirchain 2010; Yang, Nugent, and Fuchs 2016).

Recent work has further underscored the potential negative relationship between overseas activities and innovation. Dorn et al. (2020) find that foreign competition (in the form of import substitution) reduces US innovation. One potential mechanism behind this finding could be cost reductions giving a longer life to older-generation products by raising the barrier for next-generation products to be profitable. We find that while US multinationals in the manufacturing sector have increased their industrial R&D spending proportionally in the US and at foreign locations, as of 2013, the most industrial R&D spending on manufacturing globally is occurring in China. Notably, Branstetter et al. (2018) find—in contrast to software, where a growing number of patents are in developing countries or "new knowledge hubs" (like China)—a disproportionate number of manufacturing patents remain in "old knowledge hubs" (like Germany).[24] It is unclear whether it will just be a matter of time for levels of manufacturing pat-

---

24. Branstetter et al. (2021) find that the largest fraction of patents in emerging economies is in services, while developed countries continue to do a disproportionate amount of manufacturing patenting. Such results could be suggestive of less manufacturing innovation in developing countries or could reflect the fact that process innovations are dominant in developing countries, and process innovations are less likely to be patented. Patenting by developing countries with high manufacturing value added (in particular, China), is slowly growing in some manufacturing subsectors but not equally across all.

ents in China to catch up to levels of manufacturing value added (China's manufacturing value added superseded that of the US in 2010) and R&D spending (OECD's measure of R&D spending by establishments located in China and Chinese foreign subsidiaries exceeded that of US-based establishments and US foreign subsidiaries), and how that will differ by subsector and technology.

Indeed, more research is needed on the relationship between manufacturing location and innovation, and how that may differ by technological and industrial context. Increased distance, electronic dependence, time zone changes, and national differences all can reduce knowledge flows (Gibson and Gibbs 2006). In certain contexts—particularly, unfamiliar, unstructured problems—problem solving can require physically present experts to recognize embedded clues, exploit specialized tools, and find and interpret relevant information (Tyre and von Hippel 1997). Yang, Nugent, and Fuchs (2016) find that offshoring by US firms to developing East Asia (including producers in Taiwan, Singapore, Malaysia, and Shenzhen) is associated with fewer patents in the most advanced products by the firms, but more patents in other technological areas likely to be related to general production. Branstetter et al. (2021), exploiting a policy shock in Taiwan that allowed Taiwan's electronic and IT firms to legally offshore their manufacturing to China, find that offshoring has a negative impact on firm innovation as measured by patents. In addition to negatively affecting the level of innovation, they find that the offshoring shock shifted the direction of innovation in offshored products toward process innovation. That said, they argue that firms did not experience an across-the-board decline in innovation, but rather a reallocation of innovation away from offshored parts of their R&D portfolio and toward the non-offshored parts. The findings of Yang et al. (2016) suggest that in some cases, firms are not necessarily offshoring production activities in which it is no longer desirable to innovate. Indeed, the high share of US manufacturing R&D spending performed by MNCs and the realization of value added overseas raise the possibility that offshored activities may still be desirable and productive foci for domestic R&D funding.

Fuchs (2014) suggests that three conditions shape the impact of manufacturing location on global technology development: (i) the number of manufacturing facilities that a firm can sustain (potentially influenced by the ratio of their minimum efficient plant size to the size of the market and their share thereof); (ii) the location of product and process design expertise and whether the designers need to be physically present at the production line; and (iii) the importance, security, and enforcement of intellectual property rights. These conditions particularly affect early-stage high technology start-ups involving early-stage advanced materials and processes (Fuchs 2014). Challenges separating design from manufacturing are common for early-stage products in industries, such as semiconductors (Lécuyer 2006), pharmaceuticals (Pisano 2000), and additive manufacturing (Bonnín-Roca et al. 2017b), in which product innovations are fundamentally linked to advances in process. In these contexts, a lack of codified knowledge about the relationships between inputs and outputs, and the underlying science supporting outcomes, leads to low yields and can make production more of an "art" than a science in the early stages of new products (Bohn 2005, Bonnín-Roca et al. 2017b; Fuchs and Kirchain 2010). A small market compared with the production output required to take advantage of economies of scale is also common for early-stage high technology start-ups, forcing them to choose just one manufacturing location. In contrast, firms that can sustain multiple manufacturing facilities and don't struggle with separating design from production could potentially leverage location-based differences in production characteristics to diversify their product development portfolio and potentially increase their innovation.

Furthermore, national differences in consumer preferences may also have a role in incentives for innovation. Today approximately one-third of conventional vehicles are produced in China, but more than half of electric vehicles are produced in China. While the conventional vehicles are produced predominantly by joint ventures with multinational firms, the electric vehicles are produced predominantly by independent domestic Chinese firms. Helveston et al. (2015) find that, all else being equal, consumers in China are more willing to pay for electric vehicles than are consumers in the US. Local and national policy can then further shift the playing field. Helveston et al. (2019) finds a combination of local and national policies in China associated with significant regional experimentation in electric vehicle technologies by independent domestic manufacturers. Specifically, joint venture requirements may be creating disincentives for multinationals or their Chinese joint venture counterparts to undertake electric vehicle production or innovation in China, leaving open—with a combination of supportive resources and protectionism from regional governments—for independent domestic Chinese firms to move into the Chinese electric vehicle market (Helveston et al. 2019).

1.8.2 Technology Change in Manufacturing and Labor Outcomes

Recent research has investigated how employment and labor skill demands in manufacturing, and industry more broadly, are associated with globalization, technology change, changes in what is being manufacturing, and other factors. The adoption of new technologies in manufacturing has the potential to alter the demand for labor, including biases toward certain types of skill (Card and Dinardo 2002). There is a documented polarization of skill demand (measured as education or wage percentile) in the US economy, which Autor and Dorn (2013) attribute to a combination of sectoral shifts in demand toward low-skill service work and increases in automation (capital intensity). Research suggests that automation (measured as increases in capital to labor share) shifts manufacturing labor demand away from middle income jobs, as capital substitutes for labor in routine tasks and (Autor, Levy, and Murnane 2003; Autor and Dorn 2013). In particular, industrial robots may reduce employment and wages overall (Acemoglu and Restrepo 2017). Contributing at the high end of the observed polarization, technological shifts in production toward continuous processing may also drive an increase in the demand for worker skill (Goldin and Katz 1998), shifting from line operators toward labor involved in equipment support. Some technology changes may shift the skill requirements of an occupation (e.g., more operators pressing buttons and monitoring equipment than hand-assembling parts) while keeping the demand for labor in that occupation constant; other technology changes may shift skill requirements, such as a shift in the demand for occupations (e.g., fewer operators and more engineers). In the context of optoelectronic semiconductors, Bartel et al. (2004, 2007) suggest that information technology adoption in production facilities, coincides with increased skill requirements for machine operators, particularly in technical and problem-solving dimensions. In contrast, Combemale et al. (2021) find that automation polarizes the demand for skill in manufacturing operator occupations, eliminating demand for middle-skilled tasks while shifting demand toward low- and high-skilled tasks. Relatedly, Combemale et al. (2021) find that parts consolidation drives a convergence in skill demand toward middle skills (again in the context of optoelectronic semiconductors). Of potential policy interest, Combemale et al.'s work finds that competing technologies with seemingly comparable production cost outcomes can be associated with different outcomes for labor and skill demand.

1.9   Conclusions, Potential Policy Implications, and Future Work

The manufacturing sector dominates industrial R&D spending in the US as measured; however, manufacturing's share of US value added and share of US domestic employment have been in decline. This disproportionate contribution of manufacturing firms to US-based industrial R&D compared to total US employment or US gross value added is in part driven by the offshoring of manufacturing facilities from the US to other nations, and in particular China, without equivalent offshoring of US-based manufacturing R&D. The US manufacturing sector's dominant role in private funding of R&D is driven by five industries: aerospace, automobile, pharmaceuticals, semiconductors and telecommunications. Further research is necessary to understand the relationship between offshoring of manufacturing facilities and research in each of these industries and in specific technologies in these industries and technology directions. The changes, however, have not been small: according to the WIOD, between 2005 and 2014 US-based firms in motor vehicles increased intermediate inputs imported by

18 percent, pharmaceuticals increased intermediated imported by 22 percent (classification ISIC, not NAICS).

The manufacturing sector is not alone in disproportionately contributing to US-based R&D compared to value added: the information sector's fraction of US-based R&D spending is also greater than its fraction of US-based value added, although the difference is not quite as large as for manufacturing. While globalization still plays a dominant role, the information sector's greater contribution to US-based R&D than value added is in part driven by different underlying factors. Multinationals in the information sector conduct a greater proportion of their R&D at foreign affiliates than do multinationals in the manufacturing sector (the latter whose R&D spending has risen equally in the US and at foreign affiliates). Furthermore, the information sector receives a significant amount of funding from private equity and venture capital, which don't count toward R&D spending even though some of those funds likely contribute to R&D activities. In contrast, the proportion of deals by count (2 percent) and monetary volume (3 percent) aimed at manufacturing industries is comparatively quite small. This lower investment in manufacturing is perhaps surprising, given that Lerner (2000) finds that VC in manufacturing is more productive (measured by patents per dollar) than corporate R&D. However, the capital intensity of manufacturing (Levinson 2017; Pierce and Schott 2016) might contribute to this pattern: large manufacturing firms are likely better positioned to capture the returns of their basic research efforts (Cohen and Klepper 1996).

While inputs to the innovation process (e.g., industrial R&D expenditures) are clearly high in manufacturing, it is more difficult to measure outputs. Patents are often not the dominant mechanism used by manufacturing firms to appropriate innovation (Arora, Cohen, and Walsh 2015; Cohen, Nelson, and Walsh 2000; Levin et al. 1987). The research insights available into manufacturing innovation outputs, however, primarily use patents as measures of innovation. Trade theory suggests that shifts in manufacturing away from a nation may hurt wages there, but global innovation and productivity gains will not suffer (Samuelson 2004). However, empirical research has found that at least in certain contexts, moving the location of manufacturing can alter whether and which next generation products are profitable (Fuchs and Kirchain 2010, 2011). Likewise, Dorn et al. (2020) find that foreign competition (in the form of import substitution) reduces US innovation (measured in patents). Branstetter et al. (2021) find that the largest fraction of patents in emerging economies is in services, while developed countries continue to do a disproportionate amount of manufacturing patenting. However, manufacturing patenting in China has been rising, and it is unclear how long it will be until—like manufacturing value added and manufacturing industrial R&D expenditures—manufacturing patenting (and innovation) in China will also supersede that in the US, and in which industrial and technological contexts. Indeed, in some industrial and technological contexts, China's patenting and innovation activities likely already do supersede those in the US. More research is imperative on the global innovation landscape in manufacturing using measures other than patents, how the relationship between manufacturing and innovation differs by technological and industrial context, and how to think about the role of manufacturing in the US economy.

While the size of the US manufacturing labor force has remained relatively constant in the past half century, growth in US jobs outside manufacturing has led to manufacturing being a small fraction of today's overall US labor force. That said, in those US jobs that remain, manufacturing is an outsized employer of non-college educated workers, and generally has better-paying jobs than nonmanufacturing. It is important to separate the employment profile of manufacturing from its role in industrial R&D spending: the industries that drive manufacturing R&D spending tend to employ a more educated workforce than the rest of manufacturing. Industries such as food manufacturing, which help drive the sector's greater-than-average employment of less-educated workers, are relatively small contributors to the sector's R&D spending. It is also important to note that many manufacturing companies employ workers in establishments classified as part of retail, wholesale, and services that complement the production of manufactured goods (Whitefoot, Valdivia, and Adam 2018). Along with globalization, the adoption of new technologies in manufacturing over time is contributing to changes in the nature and demand for labor, including biases toward certain types of skill (Card and Dinardo 2002). Further research will be necessary to determine the relative contribution of offshoring, import competition, and technology change to observed economy-wide polarization in wages and education (Autor and Dorn 2013), and how different technologies may lead to different labor outcomes (Combemale et al. 2021).

Appendix A

The Share of Manufacturing in US GVA and the Share of the US in Global Manufacturing and GVA

Figure 1.A.1 illustrates the continually declining share of US GVA from manufacturing over the 20 years from 1997 to 2017. While US MVA rose in real terms over the same period, its relative contribution to the economy shrank. The US share of global MVA and GVA both declined from 1997 to 2017: the decline of manufacturing as a share of the US economy is mirrored in the steeper decline of the US share of global MVA, relative to world GVA (figure 1.A.2).

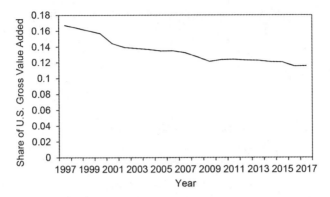

Fig. 1.A.1   Manufacturing share of US GVA, 1997–2017

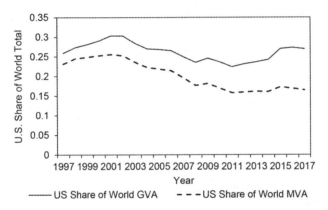

Fig. 1.A.2   US share of world MVA and GVA, 1997–2017

Appendix B

Additional Visualizations of the Manufacturing Labor Force

Subsector analysis reveals heterogeneity among leading R&D and employment subsectors. Figure 1.B.1 displays the difference in educational attainment of a few selected subsectors relative to the nonmanufacturing sector. These subsectors include the top five subsectors by private R&D spending and the top two subsectors by employment in 2015. As can be seen, the manufacturing subsector that contributes the most to employment—the food manufacturing subsector—has on average a 10 percent higher proportion of employees with HS education or less than nonmanufacturing sectors have. It also had an approximately 12 percentage higher proportion of employees

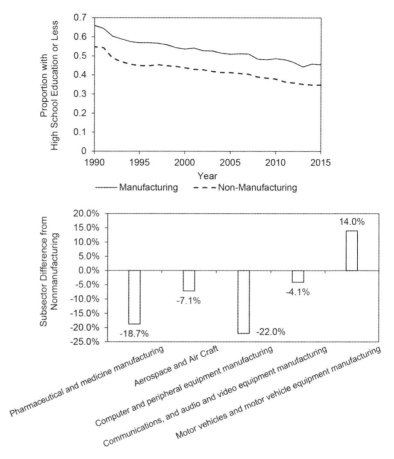

Fig. 1.B.1   Select manufacturing subsectors difference from nonmanufacturing's educational attainment, 2015

Source: Flood et al. (2020) (IPUMS-CPS ASEC microdata 2015).

Note: the NAICS imperfectly crosswalks to the Industry Codes in the IPUMS-CPS data, given the level of aggregation for our analysis aerospace and automotive subsectors were combined as were navigating instruments and medical equipment.

with HS education or less than the overall workforce proportion in the 1970s, with that gap widening in the recent decade to around 22 percentage points (IPUMS). Other subsectors with a relatively large proportion of workers with HS education or less include apparel, textile, furniture, leather, and lumber manufacturing. In contrast, the top R&D spending manufacturing subsectors have larger proportions of their labor force who are higher educated: consider the chemical/drug subsector and the communications subsector, which both contain a larger proportion of higher educated workers than do nonmanufacturing sectors.

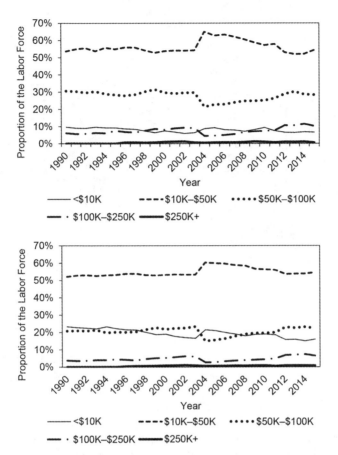

Fig. 1.B.2   Individual wage and salary income categories
Source: CPS microdata, 1990–2015.
Note: Data interval set for consistent industry classifications starting from 1990 industry re-classification by IPUMs.

Worker class falls into one of four categories: private wage or salary worker, federal or state government employee, self-employed (incorporated or unincorporated), or unpaid family worker. The manufacturing industry's labor force has remained nearly completely private wage or salary workers: 98 percent in 1975 and 95 percent in 2015. In the nonmanufacturing sector, private wage and salary workers have increased over time: 67 percent in 1975 and 74 percent in 2015. Figure 1.B.2 shows annual individual wage and salary income, CPI adjusted to 2017 dollars, between 1988 and 2018 (as shown in figure 1.B.2). While the proportion of nonmanufacturing workers with earnings less than $10,000 declines over time, the proportion of the manufacturing labor force earning less than $10,000 (2017 dollars)

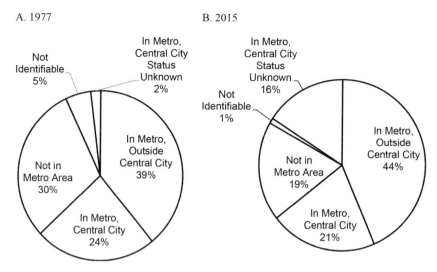

A. 1977   B. 2015

Fig. 1.B.3   Geographic location of the manufacturing labor force
Source: IPUMS-CPS ASEC microdata.

remains less than the proportion of the nonmanufacturing labor force. The total proportion of the manufacturing labor force whose earnings fall in the categories between $10,000 and $250,000 is also higher than that for the nonmanufacturing labor force.

It is well known that given manufacturing's floor space requirements and the higher cost of building space per square foot in metro areas and their central cities, manufacturing firms are often located outside of central cities/ metropolitan statistical areas. Figure 1.B.3 exhibits the manufacturing labor force's geographic location in 1977 and 2015.

The age distribution of the manufacturing labor force is quite similar to the nonmanufacturing workforce for prime aged workers (ages 25 to 64). Across time, the manufacturing labor force consistently has a lower proportion of participants aged 16–19 and 20–24 and consistently has a larger proportion of participants aged 25–64 relative to the nonmanufacturing labor force. As can be seen in figure 1.B.4, in manufacturing, the proportion of labor force participants aged 16–19 and 20–24 has fallen across time. Meanwhile, the largest mass of the labor force has been increasing in age across time: the largest proportions of workers were aged 35–44 in the 1990s, and aged 45–54 in the mid-2000s. Finally, the proportion of participants aged 65 and older in manufacturing is consistently lower relative to the nonmanufacturing labor force, although it has increased slightly.

Figure 1.B.5 shows the gender composition of the manufacturing and

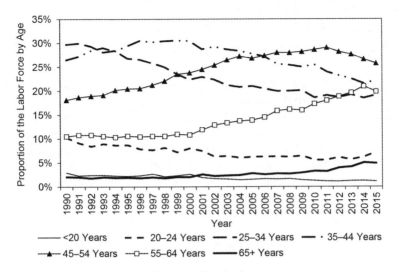

Fig. 1.B.4   Manufacturing labor force age distributions
Source: Flood et al. (2020) (IPUMS-CPS ASEC microdata, 1990–2015).

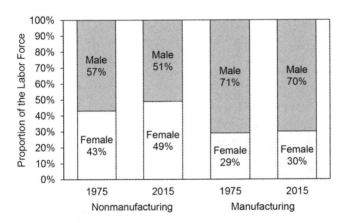

Fig. 1.B.5   Gender composition of the nonmanufacturing and manufacturing labor force
Source: Flood et al. (2020) (snapshots of 1975 and 2015).

nonmanufacturing labor force in 1975 and 2015. Across both nonmanufacturing and manufacturing sectors, the majority of the labor force is composed of male workers; however, manufacturing sectors have proportionately fewer female workers and thus more male workers. Across time, the gap in the labor force composition of manufacturing is quite stagnant, whereas nonmanufacturing subsectors have made progress toward parity.

Appendix C

Private Equity/Venture Capital Measures

Figure 1.C.1 shows the trends in median deal size and annual number of deals for nonmanufacturing and for manufacturing industries. As seen in figure 1.C.2, the US's percentage of global PE/VC deals in manufacturing dominate that of China, Germany, and Japan; however, PE/VC to manufacturing industries in China and Germany feature a higher median and mean deal size. Figure 1.C.3 features a similar visualization of the global distribution of nonmanufacturing deals. Note that the global geographic dispersion of PE/VC deals is quite similar for both manufacturing and non-manufacturing industries.

A. Nonmanufacturing Industries, US

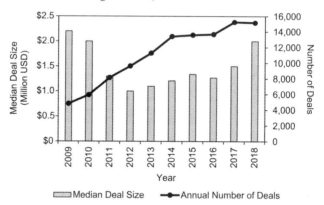

B. Manufacturing Industries, US

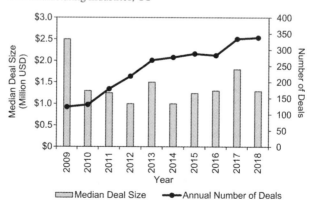

Fig. 1.C.1   PE/VC in nonmanufacturing industries and PE/VC in manufacturing industries, each with median deal size

Source: Data retrieved from CB Insights (2019).

A. Share of Global Manufacturing Industries PE/ VC Deals by Country. 2009–2019

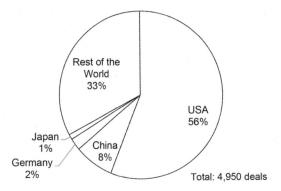

B. Median and Mean deal Size by Geography

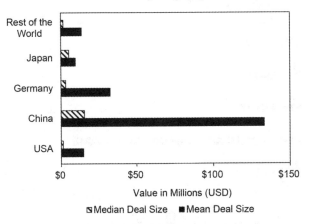

Fig. 1.C.2   Comparison of global manufacturing industries PE/VC, inclusive of top four countries by MVA

Source: Data retrieved from CB Insights (2019).

A. Share of Global Nonmanufacturing Industries PE/ VC Deals by Country, 2009–2019

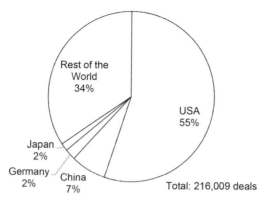

B. Median and Mean Deal Size by Geography

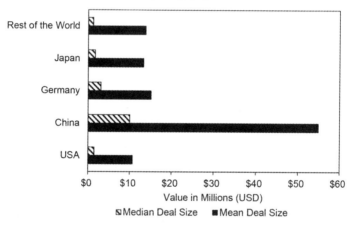

Fig. 1.C.3   Comparison of global nonmanufacturing industries PE/VC, inclusive of top four countries by MVA

Source: Data retrieved from CB Insights (2019).

Appendix D

"Public VC": Data Visualization of SBIR and STTR Awards

The distribution of Small Business Innovation Research (SBIR) and Small Business Technology Transfer (STTR) awards by funding agency are exhibited in figure 1.D.1 (data from SBIR.gov).[25] Notably, most of the awards have been given by two agencies: the Departments of Defense and of Health and Human Services.

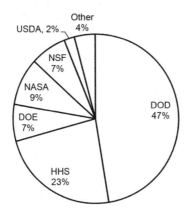

Fig. 1.D.1   Distribution of SBIR and STTR awards by federal funding agency
Source: SBIR.Gov, July 2019.

Appendix E

Firm Counts and Firm Size Distribution

The total number of firms (irrespective of industry) in the US has ranged from over 6.05 million firms in 2007 to 5.96 million firms in 2016, featuring a trough closely coincident with the business cycle: declining to 5.68 million firms in 2011, before increasing again (US Census Bureau, "Statistics of US Businesses, 2007–2016"). The proportion of manufacturing firms relative to the total number of firms' averages ~4.5 percent between 2007 and 2016 and has featured a slight decline in recent years, attributable to the lack of a sustained expansion in manufacturing firm counts relative to nonmanufacturing firm counts following the Great Recession. The proportion of information sector firms to all firms has been relatively stable at ~1.2 percent over the same period.

There are several differences between the firm size distribution of US firms in nonmanufacturing versus those in manufacturing (see figure 1.E.1). The

25. "Other" agencies include DHS, ED, EPA, DOT, DOI, and NRC.

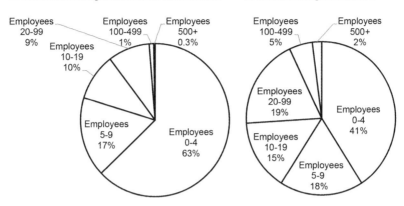

Fig. 1.E.1   **Firm size distributions, 2015**

Source: Data retrieved from Census Statistics of US Businesses.

Note: Nonmanufacturing Industries calculated by subtracting manufacturing firm counts (NAICS codes 31–33) from the total firm counts using the 2015 Census Statistics of US Businesses.

firm size distribution across nonmanufacturing firms is monotonic, that is, the density of firms in each category declines as the firm size grows. In contrast, manufacturing proceeds from 41 percent of firms with 0–4 employees, to 18 percent with 5–9 employees, to 15 percent with 10–19 employees, then a larger proportion 19 percent with 20–99 employees and 5 percent with 10–499 employees. These results may suggest that given manufacturing's capital intensity in many sectors, fewer firms find having 10–19 employees to be an efficient scale. In contrast, the 0–4 employees may reflect machining shops and similar undertakings.

Buera, Kaboski, and Shin (2011) argue that manufacturing, with larger scales of operation, is relatively more exposed to financial frictions than are other sectors. The differences between small and large manufacturing firms across the business cycle is explored in Gertler and Gilchrist (1994), who find that in a high interest rate environment, small firms shed inventories and contract relatively more than large firms. Davis and Haltiwanger (1992) document the countercyclical nature of the job reallocation rate,[26] which they argue is driven by larger, older, multi-establishment manufacturers. Comparatively, manufacturing has a lower proportion of firms with 0–4 employees and a higher proportion of each of the other categories. Overall, large firms (500 or more employees) comprise .3 percent of all nonmanufacturing firms; however, in manufacturing, large firms comprise 1.5 percent of all manufacturing firms. That is, the manufacturing firm size distribution

---

26. Davis and Haltiwanger (1992) define the job reallocation rate to be the sum of the gross job destruction and gross job creation rates. Their study employs data from 1972 to 1986 and finds these rates to be 11.3 percent and 9.2 percent, respectively.

has proportionally 5 times as many large firms as the overall distribution. In other words, large (500+ employees) manufacturing firms made up 20 percent of all large (500+ employees) firms in the US in 2015. The relatively larger proportion of large manufacturing firms is consistent with Neumark, Wall, and Zhang (2011), who document the importance of large firms in manufacturing to job creation. Dunne, Roberts, and Samuelson (1989) provide one explanation for the presence of more large firms. These authors argue that manufacturing firms' plant failure rates fall with plant size and age, however there is a tradeoff between a manufacturer's rate of growth and probability of failure. Klepper and Simons (2000) also address the effects of firm size (among other factors) on the US tire industry, arguing that larger and older firms influence technological evolution in the industry, increasing their survivability. Still, the disproportionate presence of large firms is quite interesting, given that the literature has documented a wage premium paid to workers of large US manufacturing employers which can only be partially explained by observable characteristics of the workers and establishments (Troske 1999). It has also been documented that larger firms proportionally face higher relative prices of labor than their smaller competitors (Söderbom and Teal [2003] in the case of African manufacturing firms).

Appendix F
Science and Technical Employees by Sector

Manufacturing represents 20 percent of employment for engineers, mathematical and computer science and scientific occupations, compared with 8 percent employment share for information and 5 percent share for R&D service companies.

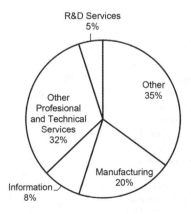

Fig. 1.F.1   Share of industrial STEM employees by sector
Source: Data from Bureau of Labor Statistics, 2019.

Appendix G

Example of Data Format

Table 1.G.1   BEA input-output subsector data format example

Industry Code	Commodities/Industries Name	111CA Farms	113FF Forestry, fishing, and related activities
111CA	Farms	71893	901
113FF	Forestry, fishing, and related activities	23901	9627
211	Oil and gas extraction	. . .	. . .
212	Mining, except oil and gas	2771	2
213	Support activities for mining	. . .	. . .
22	Utilities	4500	139

Appendix H

Linear Regression of Inputs and Intensity-Adjusted R&D by Sector

In addition to our production function estimation approach, we also attempt a very simple linear regression of output and value added over intensity-adjusted R&D stock from key R&D spending subsectors. For example, we use the change in the ratio of value added by a subsector to the output of

Table 1.H.1   Regression outputs for change in value added over output (annual)

	Coefficient	Standard error	p-value
Change in subsector value added/output ($R^2 = .274$)			
Intercept	1.70E−03	1.23E−03	0.17
Change in gross value added (US economywide)	1.29E−16	6.90E−17	0.06
Change in inputs (sector)	−6.71E−07	3.81E−08	0.00
Machinery intensity adjusted 3-year R&D	2.81E−11	1.02E−10	0.78
Computer and electronic intensity adjusted 3-year R&D	3.06E−12	2.69E−12	0.26
Motor vehicles, bodies and trailers, and parts intensity adjusted 3-year R&D	−5.39E−12	5.66E−12	0.34
Publishing industries, except internet (includes software) intensity adjusted 3-year R&D	1.18E−10	7.10E−11	0.10
Computer systems design and related services intensity adjusted 3-year R&D	−3.34E−10	6.40E−10	0.60
Miscellaneous professional, scientific, and technical services intensity adjusted 3-year R&D	9.84E−12	8.46E−12	0.24

Sources: Bureau of Economic Analysis (2019), NSF (2019).

that subsector as a measure of the productivity of inputs to a sector, and then regress this value on intensity-adjusted R&D stock from key subsectors.

We are unable to find evidence in these preliminary regressions to suggest that the returns to manufacturing R&D are captured by consumers of manufactured goods in a manner accounting for the underrepresentation of manufacturing in overall value added.

Appendix I

Regression Outputs for Estimation of Subsector Output with Time Fixed Effects

To account for possible exogenous factors in each year of our time series (curtailed at either end by the limitations of our NSF time series R&D data and the construction of our intensity-adjusted measure of R&D stock), we conduct and report on an estimation of the regression model in table 1.I.1 extended to include time fixed effects for each year. We do not find that this revised model affects our evaluation that there is little initial evidence to support the R&D embodiment hypothesis for the dominance of manufacturing R&D spending.

Table 1.I.1   **Regression outputs for estimation of subsector output with time fixed effects**

Dependent variable: ln(Output) (R^2 = .86)			
Independent variable	Coefficient	Standard error	p-value
Intercept	0.394	0.186	0.034
ln(Intensity-adjusted top manufacturing R&D stock)	0.022	0.007	0.002
ln(Intensity-adjusted service and information R&D stock)	0.122	0.011	4.84E−24
ln(Inputs from other sectors)	0.952	0.013	1E-25
Time-fixed effects (year)			
2002	−0.066	0.065	0.305
2003	−0.086	0.065	0.185
2004	−0.087	0.065	0.178
2005	−0.104	0.065	0.108
2006	−0.097	0.065	0.134
2007	−0.117	0.065	0.072
2008	−0.114	0.065	0.079
2009	−0.051	0.065	0.435
2010	−0.057	0.065	0.381
2011	−0.046	0.064	0.471
2012	−0.051	0.064	0.432
2013	−0.036	0.064	0.578
2014	−0.048	0.064	0.456

Sources: Bureau of Economic Analysis (2019), NSF (2019).

Appendix J
US R&D Funding by Federal Government and Industry

Figure 1.J.1 illustrates industrial R&D spending overtaking federal R&D spending, growing most acute after the 1980s.

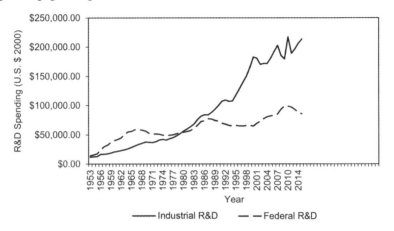

Fig. 1.J.1   Industrial and federal R&D, 1953–2015 (NSF, AAAS)

Appendix K
Exploration of Alternative Hypotheses

K.1   Mismeasurement and Reporting Incentives

We examine three possible sources of mismeasurement of R&D spending and conclude that they cannot account for the dominance of manufacturing R&D spending.

The first possible source is measurement error through sampling bias in the NSF's data collection process for industrial R&D spending. The NSF used the "Business R&D and Innovation Survey" (BRDIS) from 2008 until the 2016 survey cycle. The BRDIS defines R&D as "planned, creative work aimed at discovering new knowledge or developing new or significantly improved goods and services."[27] R&D returns manifest outside of manu-

27. This definition includes (a) activities aimed at acquiring new knowledge or understanding without specific immediate commercial application or use (basic research); (b) activities aimed at solving a specific problem or meeting a specific commercial objective (applied research); and (c) systematic use of research and practical experience to produce new or significantly improved goods, services, or processes (development). The term "research and development" does not include expenditures for: routine product testing, quality control, and technical services unless

facturing, or manufacturing does not appropriate all returns. The survey covers a population consisting of all firms in the Business Register, with or without known R&D activities. As part of the survey, firms are asked to report whether they engage in R&D activity and how many employees are engaged. NSF notes the risk of bias from different definitions of R&D but identifies government contractors and R&D service companies as the major risk items, possibly overstating their level of R&D spending activity. Industrial R&D funding as reported by NSF does not include funds from the federal government for performance, so that federal funding activity is not included in the dominance of manufacturing industrial R&D spending (NSational Science Foundation n.d.), and R&D service providers are already measured in the NSF data to account for a share of industrial R&D spending less than one-sixth that of manufacturing. These potential sources of measurement error in the NSF's survey methodology appear unlikely to account for the dominance of manufacturing in R&D spending.

The second possible source of mismeasurement is that some spending activities that further R&D objectives are not included in traditional R&D spending channels. For example, venture capital investment is not factored into industry R&D spending as measured by NSF, but nevertheless may support innovation effort from firms that engage in research-like activity (Kortum and Lerner 2001). The Venture Capital and Private Equity (VC/PE) market's nominal value of $0.53 trillion during 2009–2015 (CB Insights 2019) compares with nominal private industrial R&D spending of $1.76 trillion from 2009 to 2015. Assuming that every dollar spent in the VC and PE market was a form of R&D investment and given that about 3 percent of VC/PE spending went to manufacturing, manufacturing would still represent at least 52 percent of nominal combined industrial and VC R&D spending. Even under the most expansive assumptions about the share of VC spending dedicated to research activities, manufacturing would remain the majority source of combined VC and traditional R&D spending (at least 52 percent; see figure 1.K.1).

The third possible source of error that we examine is differences by sector in the incentives to report R&D spending. US firms have a financial incentive to report their R&D activities under the terms of the Federal R&D Tax Credit, in place since 1981 and established in perpetuity since the 2015 PATH Act. The terms of the credit have been consistent since before the PATH Act, however (Holtzman 2017). The terms for accessing the tax credit for R&D activity could produce different incentives to report R&D. The credit is available to businesses developing "new, improved, or technologically advanced products or trade processes" (IRS 2020). Qualified applications

---

they are an integral part of an R&D project; market research; efficiency surveys or management studies; literary, artistic, or historical projects, such as films, music, or books and other publications; or prospecting or exploration for natural resources.

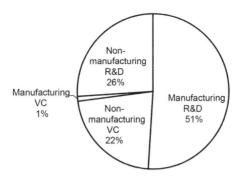

Fig. 1.K.1   Manufacturing and nonmanufacturing shares of R&D and venture capital spending, 2009–2015

include wages for qualified services, supplies used and consumed in R&D, contract research expenses on behalf of government, and basic research payments to qualified institutions. The credit also places constraints on qualified activities, which must be intended to resolve technological uncertainty; consist of a process of experimentation to resolve that uncertainty; and rely on engineering, computer science, biological science, or physical science.

Under the conditions for the credit, manufacturing firms may have less incentive to report R&D than other sectors have, not more. The credit notably excludes fixed capital, while wages, contracts and supplies are creditable (IRS 2020). Given the capital intensity of manufacturing R&D (Nadiri and Mamuneas 1991), there may be less incentive for manufacturing firms to report their R&D spending than for other, less capital-intensive sectors (such as information). The credit is also not available for incremental product development (such as post-launch software fixes). One major change brought by the PATH act is that startup businesses with no federal tax liability and gross receipts of less than $5 million may take the R&D tax credit against their payroll taxes. While NSF does not report data on firm R&D spending by revenue, US firms with fewer than 100 employees accounted for 6.3 percent of US industrial R&D in 2016 (after the PATH act took effect) (NSF 2019), insufficient to displace the dominance in prior years of manufacturing, even if other sectors had proportionately more firms with revenues less than $5 million.

Finally, we note in figure 1.K.2 that among the largest publicly traded US firms by R&D spending (PricewaterhouseCoopers 2019), manufacturing remains a dominant sector that key firms outside manufacturing (such as Google, Amazon, and Microsoft) help drive the spending of top firms. That is, these firms claim heavy R&D spending but do not displace the dominance of manufacturing, even under the whole population measure of the top 340 publicly traded US firms used by PricewaterhouseCoopers.

A. U.S. R&D Spending by Top 340 Public Firms: Share by Sector (2018), PwC 2019

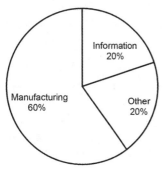

Fig. 1.K.2   R&D spending, by sector

Table 1.K.1   Top 10 US firms by R&D spending, 2018

2018 Spending rank	Company name	Sector
1	Amazon.com, Inc.	Retail
2	Alphabet, Inc.	Information
3	Intel Corporation	Manufacturing
4	Microsoft Corporation	Information
5	Apple, Inc.	Manufacturing
6	Johnson & Johnson	Manufacturing
7	Merck & Co., Inc.	Manufacturing
8	Ford Motor Company	Manufacturing
9	Facebook, Inc.	Information
10	Pfizer, Inc.	Manufacturing

K.2   Returns across Sectors and General-Purpose Technologies

Our second hypothesis, that the returns to manufacturing R&D may accrue in other sectors of the US economy, is motivated by the literature on General Purpose Technologies (Aghion and Howitt 2000; Helpman and Tratjenberg 1996). Under this framework, manufacturing could generate R&D returns that are not accounted for until they are sold in other sectors, for example. Manufacturing R&D could also generate technical knowledge that is adapted and appropriated by other sectors.

Our first subcase is motivated by descriptions of GPT embodied in capital (cf. Aghion and Howitt 2000). We evaluate this subcase of the GPT hypothesis using input-output accounts data by subsector from the Bureau of Economic Analysis (2019). This dataset, collected at the annual level, relates the inputs from individual subsectors of the US economy to other US subsectors and reports the output and value added of each subsector, with subsectors reported at four- and five-digit NAICS code levels. In total, the dataset covers 71 subsectors of the economy, each described in terms of the dollar value of its inputs from and outputs to the other 70. We select the 66 of these 71 subsectors that are nongovernmental and construct a time series dataset from 1997 to 2017 relating the inputs from each subsector to every other subsector and subsector outputs and value added by year. For intertemporal comparison, all annual input, value added, and output data were adjusted to 2015 dollars in our analysis.

We undertake a simple first-order statistical evaluation of the embodiment hypothesis to suggest whether an outsized productivity effect from manufacturing R&D might supply an explanation for its dominant role in R&D spending.

To reconstruct the possible embodiment of R&D in the outputs of manufacturing subsectors, we create a composite variable intensity-adjusted embodied R&D stock going into each nongovernmental subsector from each top R&D spending nongovernmental subsector (including manufacturing industries but also subsectors under information and technical services). This embodied stock is calculated for each year and subsector in the time series and has the form:

$$S_{j,i,t} = \frac{I_{j,i,t}}{\sum_{k=1}^{66} I_{j,k,t}} R_{i,t}$$

where $S_{j,i,t}$ is the intensity-adjusted embodied R&D stock in subsector j from sector i at time t; $I_{j,i,t}$ is the input to subsector to j from i in time t; $\sum_{k=1}^{66} I_{j,k,t}$ is the sum of nongovernmental inputs to subsector j; and $R_{i,t}$ is a research spending term for subsector i in time t. We test several different constructions of $R_{i,t}$ to account for lags between R&D spending and the realization of returns. We find that the "best" fit formulation is a 3-year running average from subsector spending in $t - 2$ to spending in t, as measured by NSF (thus limiting the upper bound of our time series to 2015).[28]

As a preliminary estimate of a relationship between this embodied R&D stock and subsectoral output, we use a Cobb-Douglas production function of the form:

$$O_{j,t} = a \left(\sum_{k=1}^{66} I_{j,k,t} \right)^{\alpha} \left(\sum_{i \in M} S_{j,i,t} \right)^{\beta} \left(\sum_{i \in V} S_{j,i,t} \right)^{\gamma}$$

where $O_{j,t}$ is the output of subsector j in time t; a, α, β, γ are constant terms; $\sum_{k=1}^{66} I_{j,k,t}$ is the value of intermediate inputs to $O_{j,t}$; $\sum_{i \in M} S_{j,i,t}$ is the sum of intensity-adjusted embodied R&D stock from subsectors $i \in M$, where M is the set of high R&D spending subsectors in manufacturing; and $\sum_{i \in V} S_{j,i,t}$

---

28. We also test alternate formulations for our intensity measure $I_{j,i,t} / (\sum_{k=1}^{66} I_{j,k,t})$, including 3- and 5-year averages to reflect accumulation of R&D-embodying stock, with no improvement of fit.

is the same for V the set of information and service subsectors with high R&D spending. The analysis reported below excludes high R&D spending subsectors that produce end consumer goods (e.g., pharmaceuticals) and focuses instead on machinery, electronics, and various transportation goods.

We perform a simple regression analysis estimating $\ln(O_{j,t})$, giving an equation of the form:

$$\ln(O_{j,t}) = \ln(a) + \alpha \ln\left(\sum_{k=1}^{66} I_{j,k,t}\right) + \beta \ln\left(\sum_{i \in M} S_{j,i,t}\right) + \gamma \ln\left(\sum_{i \in V} S_{j,i,t}\right)$$

In table 1.K.2, we report the results of our regression estimating subsectoral output from inputs and intensity-adjusted R&D stock from manufacturing and from service and information (see appendix I for estimation output with annual time fixed effects—these effects do not affect our evaluation). Though a basic first evaluation, this simple analysis does not give any preliminary suggestion that manufacturing R&D stock in other sectors is disproportionately contributing to output relative to information and technical services, which it far outweighs in spending. We note that the coefficient for top manufacturing subsector R&D stock is in fact less than one-fifth the coefficient for service and information R&D stock—if manufacturing R&D spending is embodied in inputs to other subsectors, service and information inputs may outweigh it. Thus, embodiment of R&D spending does not appear to account for the dominance of manufacturing.

We also perform several simple linear regressions relating variation in value added, output and year-on-year change in these measures to R&D stock from specific subsectors, without any further evidence of a dominant role for manufacturing (see appendix I).

In this rudimentary analysis, we do not find evidence to support GPT as the sole explanation for the outsized role of manufacturing in R&D across all manufacturing subsectors. GPT not being an explanation for all manufacturing subsectors, however, does not rule out it being an explanatory

Table 1.K.2   **Regression outputs for estimation of subsectoral output**

Dependent variable: ln(Output) ($R^2 = .86$)			
Independent variable	Coefficient	Standard error	p-value
Intercept	0.394	0.186	0.034
ln(Intensity-adjusted top manufacturing R&D stock)	0.022	0.007	0.002
ln(Intensity-adjusted service and Information R&D stock)	0.122	0.0118	4.84E−24
ln(Inputs from other sectors)	0.952	0.0128	1.E−25

Sources: Bureau of Economic Analysis (2019), NSF (2019).

Note: Assuming an intercept $a = 1$, $\ln(a) = 0$ does not alter the finding that manufacturing R&D stock contributes a smaller effect than services and information or other sectors.

factor for some subsectors, such as innovation in microprocessors enabling innovation in other sectors throughout the economy (Jorgenson 2001).

The second subcase is that manufacturing is a source of GPTs that are adopted and adapted by other sectors. A GPT is a technology of generic function and general applicability, whose efficiency improves over time by continuous innovation, and it enables innovation and improvement by users in their own technologies (Rosenberg and Tratjenberg 2004). The third element of this definition suggests sector- or firm-specific R&D investment supported by the GPT (Helpman and Tratjenberg 1996; Jovanovic and Rousseau 2005), while many of the sectors and subsectors whose growth outperformed that of manufacturing were not engaged intensively in R&D (BEA 2019). Jorgenson (2001) finds that up to half of US economic growth in the 1990s was associated with advances in information technology and hardware (a form of GPT), including microprocessors (a manufactured good). While we were unable to unable to construct technology-specific factor productivity analysis (cf. Jorgenson 2001), we also note that top manufacturing R&D spenders include pharmaceuticals and other consumable end-use products, which do not fit the profile of GPT. That is, top sources of manufacturing R&D spending generate products that are not generalist in their function (e.g., pharmaceuticals) or that would directly facilitate further innovation in other sectors in the same manner as information technology or microprocessors. While manufacturing and the semiconductor subsector in particular have historically been a source of GPT, it does not appear that manufacturing R&D spending across all sectors engaged in producing GPTs nor that the emergence of GPTs from manufacturing is a plausible explanation for its disproportionate share of R&D activity.

Appendix L

Figure 1.L.1 displays the share of overall manufacturing value added from both the top five manufacturing subsectors by value added and the top five manufacturing subsectors by R&D spending. We see that the top five manufacturing subsectors by R&D have a total value added about a third lower than the top five subsectors by value added. Two subsectors, aerospace and pharmaceuticals, are both among the top five largest subsectors by MVA and R&D spending, but the remaining top subsectors by R&D spending are outweighed in value added by less R&D-intensive subsectors.

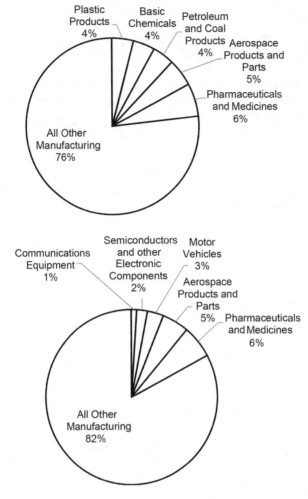

Fig. 1.L.1   Share of total manufacturing value added by subsector, 2015 (ASM)

Appendix M

US Share of R&D Spending by Top 1,000 Firms by R&D Spending Worldwide

A. U.S. Share of Manufacturing R&D Spending from Top 1000 World Firms by R&D Spending

B. U.S. Share of Nonmanufacturing R&D Spending from Top 1000 World Firms by R&D Spending

Fig. 1.M.1   US share of manufacturing and nonmanufacturing R&D spending by top 1,000 world firms by R&D spending

References

Acemoglu, Daron, and Pascual Restrepo. 2017. "Robots and Jobs: Evidence from US Labor Markets." NBER Working Paper No. 23285. Cambridge, MA: National Bureau of Economic Research.

Achillas, C., D. Aidonis, E. Iakovou, M. Thymianidis, and D. Tzetzis. 2015. "A Methodological Framework for the Inclusion of Modern Additive Manufacturing into the Production Portfolio of a Focused Factory." *Journal of Manufacturing Systems* 37: 328–39.

Acs, Zoltan, and David B. Audretsch. 1989. "Patents as a Measure of Innovative Activity." *Kyklos* 42(2): 171–80. https://onlinelibrary-wiley-com.proxy.library.cmu.edu/doi/epdf/10.1111/j.1467–6435.1989.tb00186.x.

Aghion, Philippe, Antoine Dechezleprêtre, David Hémous, Ralf Martin, and John Van Reenen. 2016. "Carbon Taxes, Path Dependency, and Directed Technical Change: Evidence from the Auto Industry." *Journal of Political Economy* 124(1): 1–51. doi:10.1086/684581 https://dash.harvard.edu/bitstream/handle/1/27759048/SSRN-id2186325.pdf.

Aghion, Philippe, Peter Howitt, and Giovanni L. Violante. 2002. "General Purpose Technology and Wage Inequality." *Journal of Economic Growth* 7(4): 315–45.

Aghion, Philippe, and Peter Howitt. 2000. "On the Macroeconomic Effects of Major Technological Change." In *The Economics and Econometrics of Innovation*, edited by D. Encaoua, B. H. Hall, F. Laisney, and J. Mairesse, 31–53. Springer, Boston: Springer.

American Association for the Advancement of Science. 2019. Historical Trends in Federal R&D. AAAS.

Amirapu, A., and M. Gechter. 2017. "Labor Regulations and the Cost of Corruption: Evidence from the Indian Firm Size Distribution." Working Paper, February.

Arora, Ashish, Sharon Belenzon, and Andrea Patacconi. 2015. "Killing the Golden Goose? The Decline of Science in Corporate R&D." NBER Working Paper No. 20902. Cambridge, MA: National Bureau of Economic Research.

Arora, Ashish, Marco Ceccagnoli, and Wesley Cohen. 2003. "R&D and the Patent Premium." NBER Working Paper No. 9431. Cambridge, MA: National Bureau of Economic Research. https://papers.ssrn.com/sol3/papers.cfm?abstract_id=368187.

Arora, Ashish, Wesley Cohen, and John Walsh. 2015. "The Acquisition and Commercialization of Invention in American Manufacturing: Incidence and Impact." NBER Working Paper No. 20264. Cambridge, MA: National Bureau of Economic Research. https://www.nber.org/papers/w20264.

Atack, Jeremy, Robert A. Margo, and Paul W. Rhode. 2019. "'Automation' of Manufacturing in the Late Nineteenth Century: The Hand and Machine Labor Study." *Journal of Economic Perspectives* 33(2): 51–70.

Atzeni, Eleonora, and Alessandro Salmi. 2012. "Economics of Additive Manufacturing for End-Usable Metal Parts." *International Journal of Advanced Manufacturing Technology* 62(9–12): 1147–55.

Autor, David, and David Dorn. 2013. "The Growth of Low-Skill Service Jobs and the Polarization of the US Labor Market." *American Economic Review* 103(5): 1553–97.

Autor, David H., David Dorn, Gordon H. Hanson, Gary Pisano, and Pian Shu. Forthcoming. "Foreign Competition and Domestic Innovation: Evidence from U.S. Patents." *American Economic Review: Insights.*

Autor, David H., David Dorn, Gordon H. Hanson, and Jae Song. 2014. "Trade Adjustment: Worker-Level Evidence." *Quarterly Journal of Economics* 129(4): 1799–1860.

Autor, David H., Frank Levy, and Richard J. Murnane. 2003. "The Skill Content of Recent Technological Change: An Empirical Exploration." *Quarterly Journal of Economics* 118(4): 1279–1333.

Baldwin, Carliss Y., and Kim B. Clark. 2000. *Design Rules: The Power of Modularity*, vol. 1. Cambridge, MA: MIT Press.

Baldwin, Carliss Y., and Kim B. Clark. 2003. "Managing in an Age of Modularity." *Managing in the Modular Age* 149: 84–93.

Bartel, Ann P. 1994. "Productivity Gains from the Implementation of Employee Training Programs." *Industrial Relations* 33(4): 411–25.

Bartel, Ann, Casey Ichniowski, and Kathryn Shaw. 2004. "Using 'Insider Econometrics' to Study Productivity." *American Economic Review*, 94(2): 217–23.

———. 2007. "How Does Information Technology Affect Productivity? Plant-Level Comparisons of Product Innovation, Process Improvement, and Worker Skills." *Quarterly Journal of Economics* 122(4): 1721–58.

Berman, Eli, John Bound, and Zvi Griliches. 1994. "Changes in the Demand for Skilled Labor within US Manufacturing: Evidence from the Annual Survey of Manufactures." *Quarterly Journal of Economics* 109(2): 367–97.

Berman, Eli, John Bound, and Stephen Machin. 1998. "Implications of Skill-Biased Technological Change: International Evidence." *Quarterly Journal of Economics* 113(4): 1245–79.

Bernard, Andrew B., Jonathan Eaton, J. Bradford Jensen, and Samuel Kortum. 2003. "Plants and Productivity in International Trade." *American Economic Review* 93(4): 1268–90.

Bernard, Andrew B., and Charles I. Jones. 1996. "Comparing Apples to Oranges: Productivity Convergence and Measurement across Industries and Countries." *American Economic Review* 86(5): 1216–38.

Bohn, R. 2005. "From Art to Science in Manufacturing: The Evolution of Technical Knowledge." *Foundations and Trends in Technology, Information, and Operations Management* 1(2): 1–82.

Bollinger, John G., and Neil A. Duffie. 1988. *Computer Control of Machines and Processes*. New York: Addison-Wesley.

Bonnín-Roca, Jaime, P. Vaishnav, M. G. Morgan, J. Mendonça, and E. Fuchs. 2017. "When Risks Cannot Be Seen: Regulating Uncertainty in Emerging Technologies." *Research Policy* 46(7): 1215–33.

Bonnín-Roca, Jaime, Parth Vaishnav, Joana Mendonça, and Millett Granger Morgan. 2017. "Getting Past the Hype about 3-D Printing." *MIT Sloan Management Review* 58(3): 57.

Branstetter, Lee, Matej Drev, and Namho Kwon. 2015. "Get with the Program: Software- Driven Innovation in Traditional Manufacturing" NBER Working Paper No. 21752. Cambridge, MA: National Bureau of Economic Research.

Branstetter, Lee, Britta Glennon, and J. Bradford Jensen. 2018. "The IT Revolution and the Globalization of R&D." NBER Working Paper No. 24707. Cambridge, MA: National Bureau of Economic Research.

———. 2019. "The IT Revolution and the Globalization of R&D." *Innovation Policy and the Economy* 19: 1–37.

Branstetter, Lee, Guangwei Li, and Francisco Veloso. 2014a. "The Rise of International Coinvention." In *The Changing Frontier: Rethinking Science and Innovation Policy*, edited by Adam Jaffe and Benjamin Jones, 135–68. Chicago: University of Chicago Press.

Branstetter, Lee, Jong-Rong Chen, Britta Glennon, and Nikolas Zolas. 2021. "Does Offshoring Manufacturing Reduce Innovation? Firm-Level Evidence from Taiwan." NBER Working Paper No. 29117. Cambridge, MA: National Bureau of Economic Research.

Bresnahan, Timothy F., and Manuel Trajtenberg. 1995. "General Purpose Technologies: 'Engines of Growth'?" *Journal of Econometrics* 65(1): 83–108.

Browne, Jim, Didier Dubois, Keith Rathmill, Suresh P. Sethi, and Kathryn E. Stecke. 1984. "Classification of Flexible Manufacturing Systems." *FMS Magazine* 2(2): 114–17.

Buera, Francisco J., Joseph P. Kaboski, and Yongseok Shin. 2011. "Finance and Development: A Tale of Two Sectors." *American Economic Review* 101(5): 1964–2002.

Bureau of Economic Analysis. "U.S. Direct Investment Abroad (USDIA)." Retrieved November 2019. https://www.bea.gov/international/di1usdop.

———. 2019. "The Use of Commodities by Industries." https://apps.bea.gov/iTable /iTable.cfm?reqid=52&step=102&isuri=1&table_list=4&aggregation=sec.

Bureau of Labor Statistics. 2019. "Manufacturing: NAICS 31–33." Industries at a Glance. Updated April 11, 2019. https://www.bls.gov/iag/tgs/iag31–33.htm.

Buzacott, John A., and David D. Yao. 1986. "Flexible Manufacturing Systems: A Review of Analytical Models." *Management Science* 32(7): 890–905.

Card, David, and John E. Dinardo. 2002. "Skill-Biased Technological Change and Rising Wage Inequality: Some Problems and Puzzles." *Journal of Labor Economics* 20(4): 733–83.

Caro, Felipe, and Jérémie Gallien. 2010. "Inventory Management of a Fast-Fashion Retail Network." *Operations Research* 58(2): 257–73.

CB Insights, Private Equity and Venture Capital Data. Retrieved June 2019. https://www.cbinsights.com/industries.

Chandler, Alfred Dupont. 1990. *Scale and Scope: The Dynamics of Industrial Capitalism.* Cambridge, MA: Harvard University Press.

Charles, Kerwin Kofi, Erik Hurst, and Mariel Schwartz. 2018. "The Transformation of Manufacturing and the Decline in U.S. Employment." NBER Working Paper No. 24468. Cambridge, MA: National Bureau of Economic Research.

Cheng, T. C., and Susan Podolsky. 1996. *Just-in-Time Manufacturing: An Introduction.* New York: Springer Science & Business Media.

Cherubini, Andrea, Robin Passama, André Crosnier, Antoine Lasnier, and Philippe Fraisse. 2016. "Collaborative Manufacturing with Physical Human–Robot Interaction." *Robotics and Computer-Integrated Manufacturing* 40: 1–13.

Chesbrough, Henry. 2003. "Towards a Dynamics of Modularity: A Cyclical Model of Technical Advance." In *The Business of Systems Integration*, edited by Andrea Prencipe, Andrew Davies, and Michael Hobday, 181. Oxford: Oxford University Press.

Cohen, L., and R. Noll. 1991. "The Technology Pork Barrel." Washington, DC: Brookings Institution.

Cohen, Wesley, Richard Nelson, and John Walsh. 2000. "Protecting Their Intellectual Assets: Appropriability Conditions and Why U.S. Manufacturing Firms Patent (or Not)." NBER Working Paper No. 7552. Cambridge, MA: National Bureau of Economic Research.

Cohen, Wesley M., and Steven Klepper. 1996. "Firm Size and the Nature of Innovation within Industries: The Case of Process and Product R&D." *Review of Economics and Statistics* 78(2): 232–43.

Colfer, Lyra J., and Carliss Y. Baldwin. 2016. "The Mirroring Hypothesis: Theory, Evidence, and Exceptions." *Industrial and Corporate Change* 25(5): 709–38.

Combemale, Christophe, Kate S. Whitefoot, Laurence Ales, and Erica R. H. Fuchs. 2021. "Not All Technological Change Is Equal: Disentangling Labor Demand Effects of Automation and Parts Consolidation." Available at SSRN 3291686.

Crafts, Nicholas F. R. 1996. "The First Industrial Revolution: A Guided Tour for Growth Economists." *American Economic Review* 86(2): 197–201.

David, H., and David Dorn. 2013. "The Growth of Low-Skill Service Jobs and the Polarization of the US Labor Market." *American Economic Review* 103(5): 1553–97.

David, H., David Dorn, and Gordon H. Hanson. 2013. "The China Syndrome: Local Labor Market Effects of Import Competition in the United States." *American Economic Review* 103(6): 2121–68.

Davis, Steven J., and John Haltiwanger. 1992. "Gross Job Creation, Gross Job Destruction, and Employment Reallocation." *Quarterly Journal of Economics* 107(3): 819–63.

Doeringer, Peter B., Edward Lorenz, and David G. Terkla. 2003. "The Adoption and Diffusion of High-Performance Management: Lessons from Japanese Multinationals in the West." *Cambridge Journal of Economics* 27(2): 265–86.

Dorn, David, Gordon H. Hanson, Gary Pisano, and Pian Shu. 2020. "Foreign Competition and Domestic Innovation: Evidence from US Patents." *American Economic Review* 2(3): 357–74.

Dunne, Timothy, Mark J. Roberts, and Larry Samuelson. 1989. "The Growth and Failure of US Manufacturing Plants." *Quarterly Journal of Economics* 104(4): 671–98.

Fleming, L., H. Greene, G. Li, M. Marx, and D. Yao. 2019. "Government-Funded Research Increasingly Fuels Innovation." *Science* 364(6446): 1139–41.

Flood, Sarah, Miriam King, Renae Rodgers, Steven Ruggles, and J. Robert Warren. 2018. Integrated Public Use Microdata Series, Current Population Survey: Version 6.0 [dataset]. Minneapolis, MN: IPUMS.

————. 2020. Integrated Public Use Microdata Series, Current Population Survey: Version 8.0 [dataset]. Minneapolis, MN: IPUMS. https://doi.org/10.18128/D030 .V8.0.

Ford, Robert C. 2005. "The Springfield Armory's Role in Developing Interchangeable Parts." *Management Decision* 43(2): 265–77.

Fralix, Michael T. 2001. "From Mass Production to Mass Customization." *Journal of Textile and Apparel, Technology and Management* 1(2): 1–7.

Fuchs, Erica R. H. 2014. "Global Manufacturing and the Future of Technology." *Science* 345(6196): 519–20.

Fuchs, Erica, and Randolph Kirchain. 2010. "Design for Location? The Impact of Manufacturing Offshore on Technology Competitiveness in the Optoelectronics Industry." *Management Science* 56(12): 2323–49.

Fuchs, Erica R. H., Frank R. Field, Richard Roth, and Randolph E. Kirchain. 2011. "Plastic Cars in China? The Significance of Production Location over Markets for Technology Competitiveness in the United States versus the People's Republic of China." *International Journal of Production Economics* 132(1): 79–92.

Gallien, Jérémie, Yann Le Tallec, and Tor Schoenmeyr. 2004. "A Model for Make-to-Order Revenue Management." Cambridge, MA: Sloan School of Management, Massachusetts Institute of Technology.

Gereffi, Gary, John Humphrey, and Timothy Sturgeon. 2005. "The Governance of Global Value Chains." *Review of International Political Economy* 12(1): 78–104.

Gertler, Mark, and Simon Gilchrist. 1994. "Monetary Policy, Business Cycles, and the Behavior of Small Manufacturing Firms." *Quarterly Journal of Economics* 109(2): 309–40.

Gibson, Cristina B., and Jennifer L. Gibbs. 2006. "Unpacking the Concept of Virtuality: The Effects of Geographic Dispersion, Electronic Dependence, Dynamic Structure, and National Diversity on Team Innovation." *Administrative Science Quarterly* 51(3): 451–95.

Goldin, Claudia, and Lawrence F. Katz. 1998. "The Origins of Technology-Skill Complementarity." *Quarterly Journal of Economics* 113(3): 693–732.

Gordon, Bart. 2007. "US Competitiveness: The Education Imperative." *Issues in Science and Technology* 23(3): 31–36.

Greenwood, Jeremy. 1997. *The Third Industrial Revolution: Technology, Productivity, and Income Inequality*. Washington, DC: American Enterprise Institute.

Hall, B., A. Jaffe, and M. Trajtenberg. 2001. "The NBER Patent Citations Data File: Lessons, Insights and Methodological Tools." NBER Working Paper No. 8498. Cambridge, MA: National Bureau of Economic Research. http://www.nber.org /papers/w8498.

Hall, B. H., and R. H. Ziedonis. 2001. "The Patent Paradox Revisited: An Empirical Study of Patenting in the US Semiconductor Industry, 1979–1995." *Rand Journal of Economics* 32(1): 101–28.

Hayes, Bradley, and Brian Scassellati. 2013. "Challenges in Shared-Environment Human-Robot Collaboration." *Learning* 8(9).

Helper, Susan R., and Mari Sako. 1995. "Supplier Relations in Japan and the United States: Are They Converging?" *MIT Sloan Management Review* 36(3): 77.

Helpman, Elhanan, and Manuel Trajtenberg. 1996. "Diffusion of General Purpose

Technologies." NBER Working Paper No. w5773. Cambridge, MA: National Bureau of Economic Research.

Helveston, John P., Yanmin Wang, Valerie J. Karplus, and Erica R. H. Fuchs. 2019. "Institutional Complementarities: The Origins of Experimentation in China's Plug-In Electric Vehicle Industry." *Research Policy* 48(1): 206–22.

Helveston, John Paul, Yimin Liu, Elea McDonnell Feit, Erica Fuchs, Erica Klampfl, and Jeremy J. Michalek. 2015. "Will Subsidies Drive Electric Vehicle Adoption? Measuring Consumer Preferences in the US and China." *Transportation Research Part A: Policy and Practice* 73: 96–112.

Herrigel, Gary. 2010. *Manufacturing Possibilities. Creative Action and Industrial Recomposition in the United States, Germany, and Japan.* New York: Oxford University Press.

Holtzman, Yair. 2017. "US Research and Development Tax Credit: A First Look at the Effect of the PATH Act." *CPA Journal* 87(10): 34–37.

Hounshell, David. 1984. *From the American System to Mass Production, 1800–1932: The Development of Manufacturing Technology in the United States.* Baltimore: Johns Hopkins University Press.

Hu, Albert Guangzhou, and Gary H. Jefferson. 2009. "A Great Wall of Patents: What Is Behind China's Recent Patent Explosion?" *Journal of Development Economics* 90(1): 57–68.

Hu, S. Jack. 2013. "Evolving Paradigms of Manufacturing: From Mass Production to Mass Customization and Personalization." *Procedia CIRP* 7: 3–8.

Hulten, Charles R., and Robert M. Schwab. 1984. "Regional Productivity Growth in US Manufacturing: 1951–78." *American Economic Review* 74(1): 152–62.

Ichniowski, Casey, Kathryn Shaw, and Giovanna Prennushi. 1995. "The Effects of Human Resource Management Practices on Productivity." NBER Working Paper No. 5333. Cambridge, MA: National Bureau of Economic Research.

Internal Revenue Service (IRS). 2020. "Instructions for Form 6765: Credit for Increasing Research Activities." https://www.irs.gov/pub/irs-pdf/i6765.pdf.

Jovanovic, Boyan, and Peter L. Rousseau. 2005. "General Purpose Technologies." In *Handbook of Economic Growth, Vol. 1*, edited by Philippe Aghion and Steven N. Durlauf, 1181–1224. Amsterdam: Elsevier.

Jorgenson, Dale W. 2001. "Information Technology and the US Economy." *American Economic Review* 91(1): 1–32.

Jorgenson, Dale W., Frank M. Gollop, and Barbara Fraumeni. 2016. *Productivity and US Economic Growth.* Vol. 169. Philadelphia: Elsevier.

Kaber, David B., and Mica R. Endsley. 2004. "The Effects of Level of Automation and Adaptive Automation on Human Performance, Situation Awareness and Workload in a Dynamic Control Task." *Theoretical Issues in Ergonomics Science* 5(2): 113–53.

Katz, Lawrence F., and Kevin M. Murphy. 1992. "Changes in Relative Wages, 1963–1987: Supply and Demand Factors." *Quarterly Journal of Economics* 107(1): 35–78.

Klepper, Steven, and Kenneth L. Simons. 2000. "The Making of an Oligopoly: Firm Survival and Technological Change in the Evolution of the US Tire Industry." *Journal of Political Economy* 108(4): 728–60.

Kortum, Samuel, and Josh Lerner. 2001. "Does Venture Capital Spur Innovation?" In *Entrepreneurial Inputs and Outcomes: New Studies of Entrepreneurship in the United States*, edited by Gary D. Libecap, 1–44. Bingley: Emerald Group Publishing.

Kumar, Mukul, and Yoshinori Ando. 2010. "Chemical Vapor Deposition of Carbon Nanotubes: A Review on Growth Mechanism and Mass Production." *Journal of Nanoscience and Nanotechnology* 10(6): 3739–58.

Lafortune, Jeanne, Ethan Lewis, and José Tessada. 2019. "People and Machines: A Look at the Evolving Relationship between Capital and Skill in Manufacturing, 1860–1930, Using Immigration Shocks." *Review of Economics and Statistics* 101(1): 30–43.

Lécuyer, Christophe. 2006. *Making Silicon Valley: Innovation and the Growth of High Tech: 1930–1970.* Cambridge, MA: MIT Press.

Lerner, Josh. 1999. "The Government as Venture Capitalist: The Long-Run Effects of the SBIR Program." *Journal of Business* 72: 285–318.

———. 2000. "Assessing the Impact of Venture Capital on Innovation." *RAND Journal of Economics* 31(4): 674–92.

Lerner, Josh, and Paul Gompers. 1999. Introduction. *The Venture Capital Cycle.* Cambridge, MA: MIT Press.

Lerner, Josh, and Kristle Romero-Cortes. 2013. "Bridging the Gap? Government Subsidized Lending and Access to Capital." *Review of Corporate Finance Studies* 2(1): 98–128.

Lerner, Josh, Amit Seru, Nicholas Short, and Yuan Sun. 2020. "21st Century: Evidence from U.S. Patenting." Working Paper.

Levin, Richard, Alvin Klevorick, Richard Nelson, and Sidney Winter. 1987. "Appropriating the Returns from Industrial Research and Development." *Brookings Papers on Economic Activity* 3 (1987): 783–831.

Levinson, Marc. 2017. "US Manufacturing in International Perspective." Washington, D.C.: Congressional Research Service.

Liu, Jifeng, Xiaochen Sun, Dong Pan, Xiaoxin Wang, Lionel C. Kimerling, Thomas L. Koch, and Jurgen Michel. 2007. "Tensile-Strained, n-Type Ge as a Gain Medium for Monolithic Laser Integration on Si." *Optics Express* 15(18): 11272–77.

Locke, Richard M., and Rachel L. Wellhausen, eds. 2014. *Production in the Innovation Economy.* Cambridge, MA: MIT Press.

Los, Bart, Marcel P. Timmer, and Gaaitzen J. de Vries. 2015. "How Global Are Global Value Chains? A New Approach to Measure International Fragmentation." *Journal of Regional Science* 55(1): 66–92.

Malone, Patrick M. 1988. "Little Kinks and Devices at Springfield Armory, 1892–1918." *IA. The Journal of the Society for Industrial Archeology* 14(1): 59–76.

Mansfield, Edwin. 1993. "The Diffusion of Flexible Manufacturing Systems in Japan, Europe and the United States." *Management Science* 39(2): 149–59.

Mehri, Darius. 2006. "The Darker Side of Lean: An Insider's Perspective on the Realities of the Toyota Production System." *Academy of Management Perspectives* 20(2): 21–42.

Mellor, Stephen, Liang Hao, and David Zhang. 2014. "Additive Manufacturing: A Framework for Implementation." *International Journal of Production Economics* 149: 194–201.

Mindell, David A. 2015. *Our Robots, Ourselves: Robotics and the Myths of Autonomy.* New York: Viking Adult.

Mokyr, Joel. 1992. *The Lever of Riches: Technological Creativity and Economic Progress.* Oxford: Oxford University Press,

Moore, Gordon E. 1965. "Cramming More Components onto Integrated Circuits." *Electronics* 38(8) (April 19): 114–17.

———. 1997. "The Microprocessor: Engine of the Technology Revolution." *Communications of the ACM* 40(2): 112–15.

Moris, Francisco. 2016. "R&D Performance of US-Located Multinational Companies: Results from Multiagency Survey Linking Project." February 2016. National Center for Science and Engineering Statistics. NSF 16–305. https://www.nsf.gov/statistics/2016/nsf16305/nsf16305.pdf.

Mowery, David C. 2009. "Plus ça change: Industrial R&D in the 'Third Industrial Revolution.'" *Industrial and Corporate Change* 18(1): 1–50.

Mowery, David C., and Nathan Rosenberg. 1999. *Paths of Innovation: Technological Change in 20th-Century America*. Cambridge: Cambridge University Press.

Nadiri, M. Ishaq, and Theofanis P. Mamuneas. 1991. "The Effects of Public Infrastructure and R&D Capital on the Cost Structure and Performance of US Manufacturing Industries." NBER Working Paper No. 3887. Cambridge, MA: National Bureau of Economic Research.

National Academy of Engineering. 2015. Committee on Foundational Best Practices for Making Value for America. *Making Value for America: Embracing the Future of Manufacturing, Technology, and Work*. Washington, DC: National Academies Press.

National Science Foundation. n.d. "Business Research and Development and Innovation: 1991–2015." Retrieved May 2019. https://www.nsf.gov/statistics/surveys.cfm.

———. 2019. "Examining Different Industry Classification Methods for Business R&D." NSF 19–324. https://www.nsf.gov/statistics/2019/nsf19324/.

Neumark, David, Brandon Wall, and Junfu Zhang. 2011. "Do Small Businesses Create More Jobs? New Evidence for the United States from the National Establishment Time Series." *Review of Economics and Statistics* 93(1): 16–29.

Nichols, A. J. 1976. "An Overview of Microprocessor Applications." *Proceedings of the IEEE* 64(6): 951–53.

OECD. 2015. *Frascati Manual 2015: Guidelines for Collecting and Reporting Data on Research and Experimental Development*.

———. 2019. *STAT: Gross Domestic Spending on R&D*.

Ohno, Taiichi. 1988. *Toyota Production System: Beyond Large-Scale Production*. Boca Raton, FL: CRC Press.

Pierce, Justin R., and Peter K. Schott. 2016. "The Surprisingly Swift Decline of US Manufacturing Employment." *American Economic Review* 106(7): 1632–62.

Pisano, Gary P. 2000. "In Search of Dynamic Capabilities: The Origins of R&D Competence in Biopharmaceuticals." In *The Nature and Dynamics of Organizational Capabilities*, edited by Giovanni Dosi, Richard Nelson, and Sidney Winter, 129–154. New York: Oxford University Press.

PricewaterhouseCoopers. 2019. "What the Top Innovators Get Right." *Global Innovation 1000*. https://www.strategyand.pwc.com/gx/en/insights/innovation1000.html.

Relihan, Tom. 2019. "Setting the Record Straight on Lean." *MIT Sloan Management Review*. https://mitsloan.mit.edu/ideas-made-to-matter/setting-record-straight-lean.

Revenga, Ana L. 1992. "Exporting Jobs? The Impact of Import Competition on Employment and Wages in US Manufacturing." *Quarterly Journal of Economics* 107(1): 255–84.

Rodrik, Dani. 2012. "Unconditional Convergence in Manufacturing." *Quarterly Journal of Economics* 128(1): 165–204.

Rosenberg, Nathan, and Manuel Trajtenberg. 2004. "A General-Purpose Technology at Work: The Corliss Steam Engine in the Late-Nineteenth-Century United States." *Journal of Economic History* 64(1): 61–99.

Sakakibara, Sadao, Barbara B. Flynn, Roger G. Schroeder, and William T. Morrism. 1997. "The Impact of Just-in-Time Manufacturing and Its Infrastructure on Manufacturing Performance." *Management Science* 43(9): 1246–57.

Samuelson, Paul A. 2004. "Where Ricardo and Mill Rebut and Confirm Arguments of Mainstream Economists Supporting Globalization." *Journal of Economic Perspectives* 18(3): 135–46.

SBIR.gov. July 2019. "Award Information" SBIR*STTR America's Seed Fund Powered by SBA. Data retrieved July 2019. https://www.sbir.gov/analytics-dashboard.

————. 2019. "About SBIR" SBIR*STTR America's Seed Fund Powered by SBA. https://www.sbir.gov/about/about-sbir.

Shah, Rachna, and Peter T. Ward. 2003. "Lean Manufacturing: Context, Practice Bundles, and Performance." *Journal of Operations Management* 21(2): 129–49.

Shepherd, James F., and Samuel H. Williamson. 1972. "The Coastal Trade of the British North American Colonies, 1768–1772." *Journal of Economic History* 32(4): 783–810.

Shu, Pian, and Claudia Steinwender. 2019. "The Impact of Trade Liberalization on Firm Productivity and Innovation." *Innovation Policy and the Economy* 19: 39–68.

Smith, Merritt Roe. 1980. *Harpers Ferry Armory and the New Technology: The Challenge of Change.* Ithaca, NY: Cornell University Press.

————, ed. 1985. *Military Enterprise and Technological Change: Perspectives on the American Experience.* Cambridge, MA: MIT Press.

Söderbom, M., and F. Teal. 2003. "Size and Efficiency in African Manufacturing Firms: Evidence from Firm-Level Panel Data." *Journal of Development Economics* 73: 369–94.

Swamidass, Paul M. 2007. "The Effect of TPS on US Manufacturing during 1981–1998: Inventory Increased or Decreased as a Function of Plant Performance." *International Journal of Production Research* 45(16): 3763–78.

Taylor, Frederick W. 1914. "Scientific Management: Reply from Mr. FW Taylor." *Sociological Review* 7(3): 266–69.

Troske, Kenneth R. 1999. "Evidence on the Employer Size–Wage Premium from Worker-Establishment Matched Data." *Review of Economics and Statistics* 81(1): 15–26.

Tyre, Marcie J., and Eric Von Hippel. 1997. "The Situated Nature of Adaptive Learning in Organizations." *Organization Science* 8(1): 71–83.

Tyson, Thomas. 1990. "Accounting for Labor in the Early 19th Century: The US Arms Making Experience." *Accounting Historians Journal* 17(1): 47–59.

US Census Bureau. "Statistics of U.S. Businesses, 2007–2016." Retrieved November 2019. https://www.census.gov/programs-surveys/susb.html.

————. 2017. *2017 North American Industry Classification System Manual.* Washington, DC.

————. 2018. *Annual Survey of Manufactures.* Washington, DC.

US Internal Revenue Service. 2019. *About Form 6765m Credit for Increasing Research Activities.*

USPTO. PatentsView, Data Query. Retrieved May 2019. http://www.patentsview.org/query/#step/selectCriteria.

Whitefoot, Kate, Walter Valdivia, and Gina Adam. 2018. *Innovation and Manufacturing Labor: A Value-Chain Perspective.* Washington, D.C.: Brooking Insitution.

Williams, Heidi. 2017. "How Do Patents Affect Research Investments?" NBER Working Paper No. 23088. Cambridge, MA: National Bureau of Economic Research. https://www.nber.org/papers/w23088.

Womack, James P., Daniel T. Jones, and Daniel Roos. 1990. *The Machine That Changed the World.* New York: Simon & Schuster.

World Bank. 2019. *World Bank National Accounts Data, and OECD National Accounts Data Files.*

Yang, Chia-Hsuan, Rebecca Nugent, and Erica R. H. Fuchs. 2016. "Gains from Others' Losses: Technology Trajectories and the Global Division of Firms." *Research Policy* 45(3): 724–45.

2

Concentration and Agglomeration of IT Innovation and Entrepreneurship
Evidence from Patenting

Chris Forman and Avi Goldfarb

"We wanted flying cars, instead we got 140 characters."
—Peter Thiel

2.1 Introduction

This volume is partly motivated by Peter Thiel's criticism of recent innovation. Thiel's business success came in the field of information technology. The product he criticized as not sufficiently exciting—Twitter's 140 characters—is information technology. The product he emphasizes as something to aspire to—flying cars—will depend on information technology if it is to appear.

Information technology (IT) is at the center of much innovation over the past 50 years. As Brynjolfsson and McAfee (2014) have emphasized, IT matters to prosperity. Many of the most prominent companies and emerging industries either produce IT, use IT as a critical input, and/or produce digital goods and services. For example, of the top 10 companies in market capitalization in May 2019, seven are primarily IT companies (Statista 2019). The most valued startups (for example, as measured by billion-dollar valuations) are overwhelmingly IT (Evans and Gawer 2016). Recently there have been significant technological advances in IT, most prominently related to artificial intelligence and cloud computing.

Chris Forman is the Peter and Stephanie Nolan Professor of Strategy, Innovation, and Technology at the Charles H. Dyson School of Applied Economics and Management, Cornell University.

Avi Goldfarb is the Rotman Chair in Artificial Intelligence and Healthcare and Professor of Marketing at the Rotman School of Management, University of Toronto, and a research associate of the National Bureau of Economic Research.

We thank Mike Andrews, Erik Brynjolfsson, Ronnie Chatterji, Scott Stern, and participants at the conference for helpful comments and suggestions. We thank David Balter and Xiaomeng Chen for outstanding research assistance. All opinions and errors are ours alone. For acknowledgments, sources of research support, and disclosure of the authors' material financial relationships, if any, please see https://www.nber.org/books-and-chapters/role-innovation-and -entrepreneurship-economic-growth/concentration-and-agglomeration-it-innovation-and -entrepreneurship-evidence-patenting.

IT is central to innovation, and this centrality has been increasing over time. Much of this innovation is focused on software (Arora, Branstetter, and Drev 2013). Manufacturing firms that are more software-intensive have been shown to have more patents per dollar spent on research and development (R&D), and their investments in R&D are more highly valued in equity markets (Branstetter, Drev, and Kwon 2019). More recently, Cockburn, Henderson, and Stern (2019) argue that advances in machine learning are primarily valuable because they make innovation more efficient. To the extent that recent advances in machine learning represent advances toward artificial intelligence, innovation would accelerate more. Demis Hassabis of Google DeepMind asserted, "Our goal is to solve intelligence, and then use that to solve the other problems in the world." In that way, Erik Brynjolfsson, in his discussion of this chapter at the conference, argued that artificial intelligence—a field of IT—is "The most G of all GPTs [general purpose technologies]."

Furthermore, IT is an input to other industries. Jorgenson, Ho, and Stiroh (2005) examine how IT impacted productivity in the 1990s. They examine differences between IT-producing and IT-using industries. They document a large increase in the productivity of IT-producing industries. This increased productivity then led to a substantial reduction in the (quality-adjusted) cost of IT. In turn, the reduced cost led to a productivity increase downstream. IT-using industries produced more efficiently with the same inputs, because the inputs became much less expensive. This role of IT as a key input into other industries continues today, though effective adoption of IT depends on complementary innovation by the using firm (Bresnahan and Greenstein 1996; Bresnahan and Yin 2017).

Table 2.1 shows the top 10 patenters in US patent data by half decade since 1976. It is suggestive of the increasing importance of innovation in IT to the broader economy. Between 1976 and 1980, just four of the top 10 patenters were also top patenters in IT, as defined by the "Computers and Communications" patent category. Those include RCA and the US Navy,

Table 2.1   **Top 10 patenters by 5-year period**

1976–80	1981–85	1986–90	1991–95	1996–2000	2001–05	2006–10
GE	GE	**GE**	**IBM**	**IBM**	**IBM**	**IBM**
AT&T	IBM	GM	Motorola	**Micron**	HP	**Microsoft**
IBM	AT&T	Kodak	GE	Lucent	**Microsoft**	**Qualcomm**
Westinghouse	Westinghouse	**IBM**	Kodak	**Intel**	**Intel**	GE
RCA	Dow Chemical	Dow Chemical	GM	HP	Micron	**AT&T**
USA/Sec. Navy	DuPont	DuPont	**AT&T**	Motorola	GE	**Intel**
DuPont	**GM**	AT&T	Xerox	GE	Texas I	HP
GM	Mobil	**Motorola**	**Texas I**	Kodak	**Cisco**	Honeywell
Dow Chemical	**RCA**	Westinghouse	3M	**AMD**	Honeywell	**Apple**
Phillips Petro.	Allied Chemical	Allied Signal	DuPont	Xerox	**Broadcom**	Micron

neither of which was an IT-focused company. By 2006–2010, seven of the 10 were top patenters in that category, and one of the remaining three, Micron, makes computer memory products.

Despite this evidence of continuing innovation in IT and its implications for innovation and productivity in IT-using industries, there is simultaneously evidence of a productivity slowdown in the US and in other OECD countries (e.g., Brynjolfsson, Rock, and Syverson 2021; Syverson 2017). Various reasons have been given for this recent productivity slowdown, including mismeasurement, lags in benefits due to need for costly implementation and complementary adjustments, as well as market concentration that may dissipate the benefits of productivity improvements (Brynjolfsson, Rock, and Syverson 2021). Moreover, there is evidence that the benefits of increasing innovation in, and pervasiveness of, IT has not been shared equally across firms, individuals, and regions (Autor et al. 2020; Brynjolfsson and McAfee 2014; Forman, Goldfarb, and Greenstein 2012).

Given the centrality of IT to innovation and recent concerns that the benefits of IT innovation are being captured by a subset of the economy, we study the concentration of innovation in IT over time. By studying trends in US patenting, we provide evidence that is suggestive of an increase in concentration in inventive activity in IT innovation. We measure concentration in two ways: firm level and location level. Specifically, we document trends in patenting concentration over time and across patent categories. We calculate Gini coefficients by firm and by location, annually from 1976 to 2010. We document trends in the fraction and geographic concentration of patents by first-time inventing firms and by individual inventors. Some trends are general, but the focus of our argument is on those specific to IT.

Our empirical results depend on our definition of IT and the data we have available. The dictionary definition of IT is: "The technology involving the development, maintenance, and use of computer systems, software, and networks for the processing and distribution of data" (Merriam-Webster 2020). *The Handbook of the Economics of Information Systems* (Hendershott and Zhang 2006) defines it as "the hardware and software used in the processing and communication of information." Our focus on innovation and inventive activity in IT focuses but also narrows our analysis in several ways. In particular, we measure inventive output using patents. Identifying IT inventions in the patent data is difficult, as highlighted by Graham and Mowery (2003), Bessen and Hunt (2007), Hall and MacGarvie (2010), and others. We define innovations in IT using the classification systems initially developed and described in Hall, Jaffe, and Trajtenberg (2001). We think are our results are suggestive of a broad and important phenomenon that requires further exploration. We discuss the limitations of this definition in detail below.

Firm concentration in patenting could arise for several reasons. One is due to concentration in output markets. A large and still-growing literature has documented an increase in market concentration over the past few decades and its implications, in some cases highlighting trends in IT-intensive industries. De Loecker, Eeckhout, and Unger (2020) document a rise in markups and an increase in market share across a wide range of US industries. Eggertsson, Robbins, and Wold (2018) take a macroeconomic perspective and argue that increased market power and high profits have caused a decline in labor share. Autor et al. (2017, 2020) demonstrate a connection between a rise in superstar firms and a decline in the labor share. Superstar firms are able to take advantage of globalization and technological change facilitated by IT, and such firms increasingly dominate their industries. The documented increase in market concentration has therefore been blamed for the recent rise of inequality in the US and elsewhere (Furman and Orszag 2015) and for a decline in investment in real and intangible assets (Gutiérrez and Philippon 2017). Andrews, Criscuolo, and Gal (2019) identify a divergence in productivity between the most productive firms and the rest of the distribution, and note that this trend is strongest within ICT services. Both Gutiérrez and Philippon (2017) and Andres, Criscuolo, and Gal (2019) review a broad literature that documents this increase in concentration.

While the line of work cited above has documented increased concentration across the economy, there may be features that are specific to IT that lead to increases in concentration. Shapiro and Varian (1998) highlighted a different set of forces leading to concentration in the IT industry. Emphasizing software, they note that "information is costly to produce but cheap to reproduce" (p. 21). High fixed costs and low marginal costs lead to concentration. Furthermore, they highlight the role of positive feedback loops or network externalities. They note that "positive feedback makes the strong grow stronger" (p. 174). This positive feedback loop is particularly prevalent in many IT contexts, particularly for digital marketplaces. A rich literature (e.g., Einav, Farronato, and Levin 2016; Jullien and Pavan 2019) has emphasized a potential connection between market power and the rise of online marketplaces in advertising (Google, Facebook), goods (Amazon, Ebay), and services (Uber, Airbnb, Upwork). The Stigler Committee on Digital Platforms produced a report that summarized many of these issues (Stigler Center for the Study of the Economy and the State 2019). This documentation of an increase in concentration in IT contexts has led to regulatory attention to the largest IT firms, including Google, Facebook, and Amazon; however, it is important to recognize that antitrust attention to IT has existed for decades, for example, in the 1970s IBM case and the 1990s Microsoft case.

The use of IT as an input to production in other industries can also lead to concentration. Investments in IT are often accompanied by complementary innovation and organizational change (e.g., Aral, Brynjolfsson, and Wu 2012; Bresnahan, Brynjolfsson, and Hitt 2002; Bresnahan and Greenstein 1996). Historically these investments have required substantial fixed costs and have been shown to have the highest payoff in large organizations (Tambe and Hitt 2012; however, for a recent counterexample, see Jin and McElheran 2018). These investments lead to a stock of intangible capital (Tambe et al. 2019). Industries that are characterized by large investments in IT have seen growth in market concentration (Brynjolfsson et al. 2008; McAfee and Brynjolfsson 2008).

Sutton (1998) highlighted how technology can lead to concentrated market structure through endogenous sunk costs. Specifically, as firms compete by investing in R&D, it becomes harder and harder for new firms to enter. The investment required to achieve the same quality as the leading firms is too high. As a consequence, a relatively small number of firms can dominate the market. IT is an R&D-intensive industry. This is especially true in hardware, but also for some aspects of software. Therefore, we expect the forces Sutton highlighted to lead to concentration in IT-producing industries.

Characteristics specifically related to IT may either facilitate or inhibit concentration. For instance, IT products are often composed of subsystems of components that interact with one another through interfaces that are defined by standards. In this environment, industry firms will compete to define standards through which products and technologies work together and also compete in product markets. This can lead to a circumstance of divided technical leadership, in which multiple firms compete to provide key technologies and products (Bresnahan and Greenstein 1999).

However, the changing nature of innovation in IT can also lead to increases in concentration. Innovation in IT has become increasingly software intensive (Andreesen 2011; Arora, Branstetter, and Drev 2013; Branstetter, Drev, and Kwon 2019). However, the strength of formal measures of intellectual property protection, such as patents, are weaker in software than in other fields of IT innovation, such as IT hardware (Cohen, Nelson, and Walsh 2000; Graham et al. 2009). Changes in the strength of patents can create uncertainty for market participants and inhibit well-functioning markets for technology. For example, increases in the strength of software patents and software patenting can give rise to packet thickets that could lead to declines in de novo entry (Cockburn and MacGarvie 2011).

For geographic concentration, there are many reasons we expect invention to agglomerate. Carlino and Kerr (2015) summarize many of these, emphasizing the role of input sharing, labor market matching, and knowledge spillovers, among others.[1] There is recent evidence that the productivity of inventors is higher in technology clusters (Moretti 2019). In prior work (Forman, Goldfarb, and Greenstein 2016), we documented a sharp rise in the share of US patenting in a small number of cities, and particularly in the

---

1. A large literature examines the competing effects of convergence and agglomeration. We will not attempt to survey it here. For some examples of how agglomeration can impact regional economic performance, see Glaeser et al. (1992); Henderson, Kuncoro, and Turner (1995); and Fernández-Delgado et al. (2014).

San Francisco Bay Area. A similar phenomenon has been documented in medical devices (Foroughi and Stern 2018). These types of agglomeration economies can give rise to superstar cities (Gyourko, Mayer, and Sinai 2013). A few cities have comprised an increasing share of US (and global) output.

Before we proceed with the chapter, we emphasize that this exercise is entirely descriptive. We will not identify why this is happening, whether the trends are robust to other definitions of innovation, or whether the trends in IT explain the overall changes in market concentration, location concentration, labor share, or productivity.

2.2   Data

We use patents granted by the US Patent and Trademark Office (USPTO) as our measure of invention. Because of the delay between patent application and grant date, we date patents using the year of application. Our starting point is the data provided by the UPSTO through the PatentsView program (www.patentsview.org). We have data on patents granted between 1976 and 2018, and our analysis dataset includes patents with application dates between 1976 and 2010.

To assess trends on IT patents compared to other patents, we use the six patent categories defined in Hall, Jaffe, and Trajtenberg (2001): Chemical; Computers & Communication; Drugs & Medical; Electrical & Electronic; Mechanical; and Other. We consider the Computers & Communication category to represent IT. For some analysis, we look at subcategories related to IT, specifically Communications; Computer hardware & software; Computer peripherals; Information storage; Electronic business methods & software; and Semiconductor devices.

The Hall, Jaffe, and Trajtenberg (HJT) approach is a widely used means to categorize patents based on technology. However, because of recent changes to the patent data, it imposes some limitations on our ability to observe recent trends in our data. The HJT categorization is based on the US Patent Classification (USPC) system. Beginning in 2010, the European Patent Office and USPTO initiated the Cooperative Patent Classification System (CPC), and patents granted after 2015 may no longer have a USPC class and so similarly have no HJT category. Given the lag between the patent application and patent grant dates, we end our sample with patents applied for in 2010 to mitigate truncation bias arising from patents that were applied for and granted after 2010 but were not assigned a USPC class. Even with this sample end date, a small fraction of patents in our sample did not receive a USPC class because of a lengthy application-grant delay.

We focus on patents because they are available in a consistent form over time and across categories. Patents have been shown to provide a useful measure of a firm's intangible stock of knowledge (Hall, Jaffe, and Trajtenberg 2005). Their limitations are well known. Not all patents meet the USPTO criteria for patentability (Jaffe and Trajtenberg 2002). Not all inventors seek to patent, and many use alternative means to appropriate value from their inventions. In particular, for our purposes, the propensity to patent innovations related to IT is thought to be different from other technology sectors. Cohen, Nelson, and Walsh (2000) note that IT hardware firms (such as semiconductor and communications equipment) report that patenting was effective at protecting about one-quarter of their product innovations in comparison to secrecy, which was effective at protecting one-half of product innovations. There is evidence this may have changed over time, however. In a more recent survey focused on entrepreneurial firms, Graham et al. (2010) note that venture-backed IT hardware firms report that patenting is at least as important as secrecy. However, the same survey notes that among software startups, patenting was the least important among all appropriability strategies (Graham et al. 2010).

Furthermore, the propensity to patent has changed over time during our sample (e.g., Hall and Ziedonis 2001). This was particularly the case for patents related to software, which grew rapidly toward the end of our sample period due to legal changes that strengthened the legal rights of patents in this area (e.g., Graham and Mowery 2003; Hall and MacGarvie 2010). It was only after our sample ends that the *Bilski* and *Alice* cases led to a decrease in the propensity to patent software and business processes. Our approach will lead to bias in our results if large firms are more likely to patent relative to others over time in IT relative to other industries.

We map patents to firms based on several sources. First, we map patents to the CRSP (Center for Research in Security Prices) "permco" list of publicly traded firms using a mapping generously provided to us by the authors of Kogan et al. (2017) and Stoffman, Woeppel, and Yavuz (2019). Further details on the construction of that data are provided in these papers. The method provides a consistent measure of patenting in publicly traded firms over time. For the remaining patents, we grouped patents into organizations based on names provided in the PatentsView data. Our starting point is the disambiguated Assignee names in those data. Then, following procedures detailed in Kogan et al. (2017), we compared assignee names by calculating the Levenshtein edit distance between them. If one assignee name is close to another that is associated with many more patents, then the more common assignee name is substituted for the less common one. This procedure will lead to biased estimates of the number of patents assigned to firms when, for example, patents are assigned to subdivisions of firms with different names and when firms change their names over time. The procedure will influence our results if these events are disproportionately likely to happen in firms that produce IT patents relative to those that patent in other technological areas.

Our primary means of mapping patents to counties is based on the mapping provided in the PatentsView.org data. In cases where this mapping is unavailable, we used the longitude and latitude provided by the USPTO and the Stata program GEOINPOLY (Picard 2015) to map the locations to counties.

For most of the analysis that follows, we do not weight by citations. For multi-author patents, we divide by the number of authors. For example, if a patent has one author in the Bay Area and two authors in Boston, it would count as 1/3 of a patent in the Bay Area and 2/3 of a patent in Boston. Our results are generally robust, and often stronger, using 3-year and 5-year citation-weighted measures. In the few instances where the citation-weighted results differ qualitatively from the counts, we show both. Otherwise, we focus on the counts.

Our data contain a total of 2,448,280 patents. In 1976, 41,122 new patents were issued by the USPTO. At the peak of our data in 2007, there were 107,744 patents.

We present our results at the year level, as aggregated values over the 35 years from 1976 to 2010 inclusive. This is therefore a descriptive exercise that tests whether the results are consistent with increasing concentration of patents in larger firms over time, for patents related to IT compared to other technological areas. We have not determined the primary cause(s) of the observed patterns.

We measure concentration using Gini coefficients. The Gini coefficient is a measure of statistical dispersion. While typically used to measure economic inequality, it is also a useful measure of concentration (Giorgi 2019). Unlike the Hirschman-Herfindahl index, the Gini coefficient captures whether there are many observations that have very little share. A value of 0 means perfect dispersion, and a value of 1 means perfectly concentrated. In general, a higher Gini coefficient means higher concentration.

One weakness of the Gini coefficient as we use it in the context of patenting is that it will not capture firms with zero patents. In other words, our measures condition on patenting. This will bias our results if the increase in the number of firms patenting over time systematically decreases the Gini coefficient. This is not the case in our data, as the top handful of firms and counties represent an increasing share of patenting, even as the number of firms and counties with at least one patent increases over time.

Overall, these data give us a sense of the general patterns in the concentration of patenting by firm and location over time.

2.3   Results

We present five key results. We compare patenting in Computers and Communications to other HJT categories. In some cases, for brevity, we will refer to patenting in Computers and Communications as "IT patenting." We first show that firm concentration in IT patenting is increasing over time and then show that geographic concentration in IT patenting has similarly grown. We

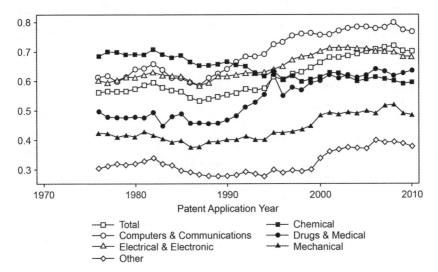

Fig. 2.1   Firm-level concentration in IT patenting, Gini for firm concentration

then turn to an analysis of first-time patenters, showing that the percentage of patents coming from new firms has declined over time, and we show that there has been an increase in the geographic concentration of IT patenters. Last, we further probe our earlier results by showing the increases in firm and location concentration are robust across subcategories of IT patents.

Firm concentration in IT patenting is increasing over time. Figure 2.1 shows that the Gini coefficient for patents in the Computers & Communications patent category fell from 0.66 to 0.59 from 1983 to 1987, an 11 percent fall. This coincided with the diffusion of decentralized computing devices like personal computers. The Gini has been almost continually rising since then, though the rate of growth has slowed in recent years: the Gini rose to 0.77 in 2010. The Electrical & Electronic category has followed a similar pattern, though the decline in the 1980s was not as pronounced and the subsequent rise not as great. Other categories of invention have increased over the same time period. In particular, Drugs & Medical rose from 0.45 to 0.63 between 1988 and 2010. However, what is unique about Computers & Communications was the pronounced fall followed by significant rise observed over our sample period. This rise was largest in the 1990s.

Figures 2.2a and 2.3a show that the total number of patents and patenters (patenting firms) in Computers & Communications is growing, even as concentration also increases. Based on total patents, Computers & Communications became the largest patent category in the 1990s, and it is now by far the largest category. Some of this rise is driven by an increasing propensity to patent, as highlighted by Hall and Ziedonis (2001). Figures 2.2b and 2.3b show these values weighted by citations over the 3 years following

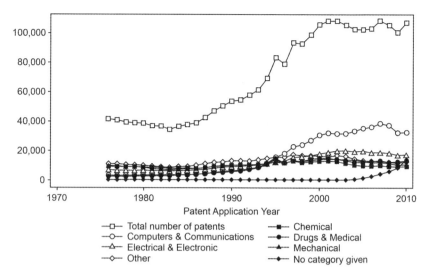

Fig. 2.2a   Total patents

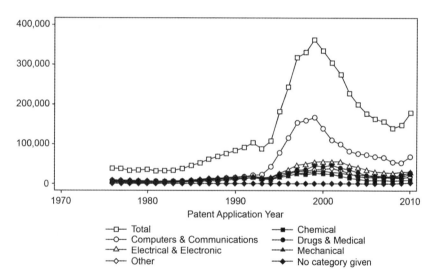

Fig. 2.2b   Total patents, weighted by 3-year forward citations

the application. These citation weights are a proxy for quality (Hall, Jaffe, and Trajtenberg 2005). Comparing figures 2.2a and 2.2b, until 2000, the patterns for the citation-weighted data in Computers & Communications look similar to non-citation-weighted data, with the number of patents in both categories increasing over time. After 2000 they diverge, however. While the total number of citation-weighted patents declines after 2000, the number

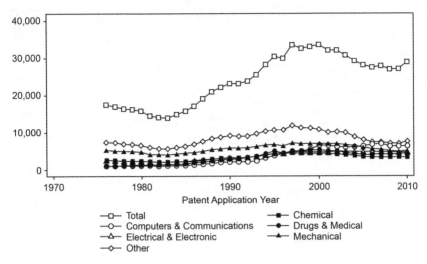

Fig. 2.3a   Number of patenters (firms and individuals)

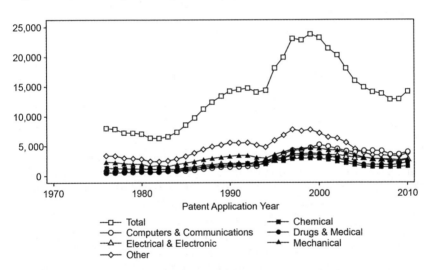

Fig. 2.3b   Number of patenters (firms and individuals), weighted by 3-year forward citations

of citation-weighted patents in Computers & Communications experiences the sharpest absolute and relative declines over time. Nevertheless, the difference between IT patents and other patents remains. IT patents continued to represent the largest share of patenting, whether citation weighted or not.[2]

---

2. The other figures in this chapter show similar trends for counts and for citation-weighted measures. Therefore, to keep the paper streamlined, we show only the counts.

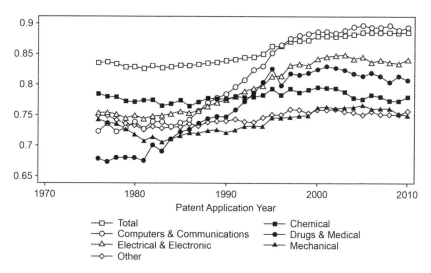

Fig. 2.4   Location-level concentration in IT patenting over time, Gini for location concentration

We further note that in figures 2.2a and 2.2b, some patents have no technology category. This is because of the transition from USPC to CPC codes mentioned in section 2.2. We provide these results to demonstrate how this transition influences our data. Because our analysis requires comparing patents across technology categories, in other figures, we drop these patents from our sample.

Geographic concentration of IT patenting has grown. Figure 2.4 shows the increasing Gini by location over time. Location is defined by county, and so there has been a large increase in location concentration in Computers & Communication since 1985. This increase is particularly pronounced in the 1990s. This result is similar to Forman, Goldfarb, and Greenstein (2016) who found a large increase in IT patenting in the San Francisco Bay Area in particular. As was the case with firm concentration, we see similar but more muted patterns in Electrical & Electronic and a similarly strong trend of increases in concentration among Drugs & Medical. Of course, if invention is increasingly concentrated in fewer firms then firm concentration could contribute to geographic concentration if firms have a limited number of geographic centers of invention (Ellison and Glaeser 1997). We explore this possibility in further detail below.

Decline in new patenters 2000–2010. We now explore changes in the number of new (first time) patenters. Figures 2.5a–c show a steady decline in new patenters over time. These figures compare the share of new patents that are coming from new firms for each year. Since our data begin in 1976, all patenters in 1976 are new, and the subsequent decline across all catego-

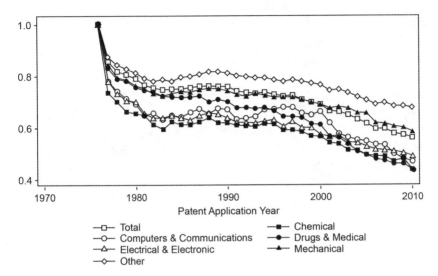

Fig. 2.5a   Percentage of new patenters over time

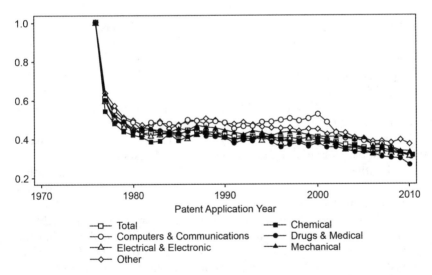

Fig. 2.5b   Percentage of new patenting firms, not including individuals, over time

ries of invention subsequently is in part mechanical. Figure 2.5a shows all patenters, and figure 2.5b excludes individual patenters and focuses on firms only. Figure 2.5c shows the individual patenters only. All three figures reveal similar patterns.

The share of patenters from new firms in Computers & Communications remained fairly stable between 1980 and 2000. After that, it declined

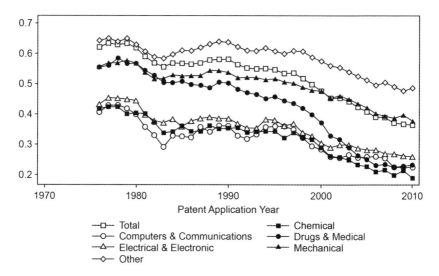

Fig. 2.5c   Percentage of individual patenters over time

sharply. Beginning in the late 1990s, a series of court decisions and action by the USPTO changed perceptions about the patentability of software.[3] As a result, the sharp decline post-2000 could be shaped by changes in the composition of patenting in Computers & Communications during this period. However, the percentage of new patenters continued to fall until the end of our sample period. Put differently, the surprise here is that IT didn't fall in 1980–2000, rather that it did fall thereafter.

Increased geographic concentration of new IT patenters. Figures 2.6a–b show that the geographic concentration of new IT patenters has grown over time. In other words, the increasing geographic concentration of patenting shown in figure 2.4 is not mechanically a result of the increased firm-level concentration of patenting. New firms are also geographically concentrated. Figure 2.6a shows all first-time patenters. Figure 2.6b shows firms only.

Similar results across IT subcategories. Figures 2.7a–b shows that the general trends in concentration by firm and concentration by location are robust across the different categories of Computers & Communications: Communications, Computer hardware & software, Computer peripherals, Information storage, Semiconductor devices, and Electronic business methods & software.

Figure 2.7a shows firm-level concentration. For Electronic business methods & software, results prior to the late 1990s are difficult to interpret because of the uncertainty of the patentability of software. However, between 2000 and 2010, this category shows the fastest rate of growth in concentration, from 0.53 in 2000 to 0.60 in 2010. Semiconductor devices has the highest

---

3. See Hall and MacGarvie (2010) and Cockburn and MacGarvie (2009) for further details.

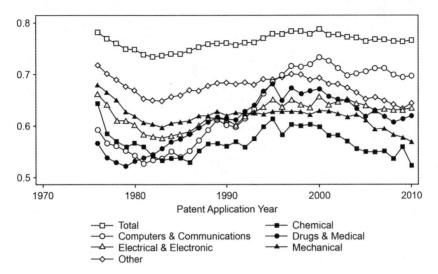

Fig. 2.6a   Geographic concentration (Gini by location) of first time patenters over time, firms and individuals

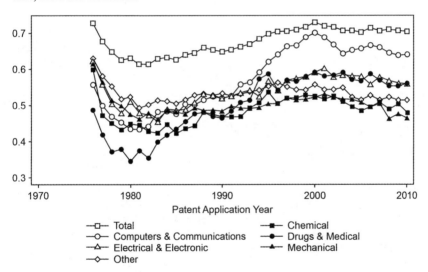

Fig. 2.6b   Geographic concentration (Gini by location) of first time firm patenters over time

Gini coefficient throughout most of the sample, but it declines between 2000 and 2010. Figure 2.7b shows that the increases in the Gini coefficient by location hold across all subcategories of IT.

Figure 2.8 provides context, showing the trend in total patents over time for each subclass. It suggests that the category of Electronic business methods & software grows from effectively zero in mid-1990s to comprise a meaningful share of all IT patents.

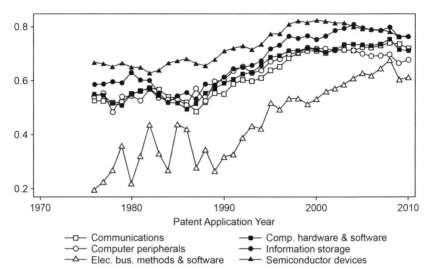

Fig. 2.7a   Firm-level concentration (Gini by firm) over time by IT subclass

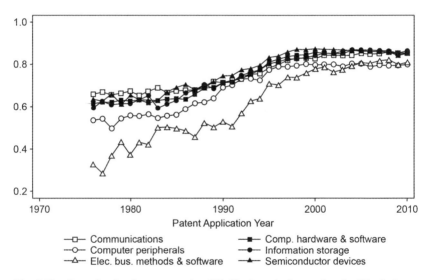

Fig. 2.7b   Location-level concentration (Gini by location) over time by IT subclass

2.4   Hypotheses on the Rise of Concentration

The above analysis presents a puzzle. We have documented that the firm-level and location-level concentrations of IT patenting have risen over time, particularly since 1990. Here we present several hypotheses that could explain this rise. In this chapter, we will not test these hypotheses, leaving that for future work.

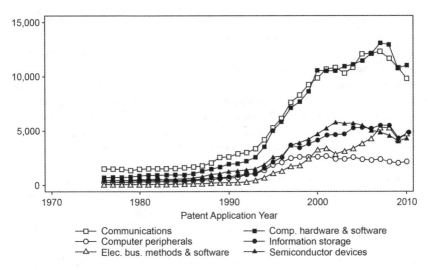

Fig. 2.8   **Total patents over time by IT subclass**

2.4.1   Why Is Firm-Level Concentration Rising?

We identify 10 possible (sometimes overlapping) reasons that we measure an increase in firm-level concentration in IT patenting over time:

1. *Network externalities in IT*: Network externalities are important for a variety of IT applications (Shapiro and Varian 1998). If the value of a technology rises with the number of users, either directly as for a communication technology or indirectly as for online platforms, then this can lead to an increase in industry concentration (e.g., Armstrong 2006; Katz and Shapiro 1985). If these network externalities have been increasingly important to IT over time (or if interoperability and common standards have become less important), then this could lead to a concentration of the industry overall and a concentration in firm-level IT patenting.

2. *Superstar effects in demand for IT*: IT has lowered the cost of searching for information (Goldfarb and Tucker 2019; Shapiro and Varian 1998), which has made comparison across products easier. Combined with low marginal costs, this can lead to a superstar effect, in which a small number of firms that offer superior quality dominate (Bar Isaac, Caruana, and Cuñat 2012; Rosen 1981).

3. *High fixed costs*: In addition to superstar effects, industries with high fixed costs and low marginal costs have barriers to entry and a minimum efficient scale. As Shapiro and Varian (1998) emphasize, information goods have high fixed costs and low marginal costs. Many IT products are information goods. Furthermore, high fixed cost and low marginal cost are also characteristics of IT hardware. Generally, this will lead to a barrier to entry

and a relatively small number of firms. To the extent that fixed costs have risen over time, this could explain the increased concentration.

4. *Endogenous sunk costs*: Sutton (1998) emphasized that the cost structure of an industry is endogenous. As leading firms compete with one another in R&D, an increasing amount of resources is required for a new entrant to compete. These endogenous sunk costs increase concentration of an industry over time. As the leading IT firms invest in R&D, it may have become harder for new entrants to join the industry. In this way, competitive pressure among the leading firms can lead to the concentration of an industry over time.

5. *Intangible capital*: There has been a sustained increase in the importance of intangible capital over time. This increase in the role of management practices, business processes, and firm-specific employee skills is not captured in standard measures of investment (Corrado, Hulten, and Sichel 2009). This growth is particularly pronounced among firms using IT (Brynjolfsson et al. 2008; Tambe et al. 2019). Intangible capital represents a fixed cost (and perhaps an endogenous sunk cost). It is also difficult to imitate; there is no easy strategy for a new entrant to invest in generating the intangible capital needed to compete. Intangibles can therefore lead to firm-level concentration among firms using IT. These firms may also create patents that use IT as a critical input (Branstetter, Drev, and Kwon 2019).

6. *The burden of knowledge*: Jones (2009) demonstrated that innovation has been getting harder over time. Similarly, Bloom et al. (2020) demonstrated that the productivity of innovation is falling. New ideas are getting harder to find. While these ideas have not been shown to be specific to the IT industry, they would increase the costs associated with patenting and might therefore benefit large firms over small.

7. *Anticompetitive behavior*: The Stigler Report (Stigler Center for the Study of the Economy and State 2019) emphasizes the increasing concentration of many aspects of the IT industry. More generally, the IT industry has been the subject of antitrust scrutiny for decades, with cases against IBM, AT&T, and Microsoft. If antitrust scrutiny and merger control have become more lenient over time in the IT industry (e.g., Gutiérrez and Philippon 2017; Valletti and Zenger 2019), then this would lead to increased concentration of the industry generally and therefore increased firm-level concentration of patenting behavior.

8. *Maturity of the industry*: Our data begin in 1976. At that time, the IT industry was relatively new. In the early stages of an industry, it is not unusual for many competitors to enter and then for a few firms to dominate over time (Klepper 2002; Klepper and Graddy 1990). While there is evidence that recent IT innovations have reduced barriers to entry for small firms (Jin and McElhcran 2018), these forces may be dominated by the increasing maturity of the industry.

9. *Uncertainty and changes in intellectual property protection*: The strength

of patents historically has been weaker for some inventions based on IT, particularly those based on business methods and software. As we noted above, strengthening of intellectual property protection in software was coincident with an increase in patenting in these categories. This increase in patenting may have made it more difficult for de novo startups to receive financing and enter markets (Cockburn and MacGarvie 2009, 2011). Conversely, uncertainty about the strength of patents can lead to concerns about expropriation of intellectual property assets when startups contract with established firms, making it more difficult for markets for specialized suppliers to develop (Gans and Stern 2003; Gans, Hsu, and Stern 2002).

10. *Bias in our analysis*: The result may be driven by our use of patent data. If the largest firms have become increasingly likely to patent their innovations (however marginal) over time, then this will lead to an increase in measured concentration of patenting without a meaningful increase in the underlying concentration of innovation. This is related to the prior point in that both are based on changes in the patent system. However, the earlier point is about changes in equilibrium outcomes brought about by these changes, rather than mismeasurement of invention caused by our use of patents. Many of our other empirical choices may lead to results that are not robust to other measures of innovation and other measures of patenting. While we have examined robustness to some of these choices, such as citation weighting, our goal has not been to emphasize robustness. Instead, we have focused on identifying a puzzle that warrants further examination.

The above hypotheses are not mutually exclusive. Furthermore, many of them build on the same idea of fixed costs leading to concentration. Overall, the relationship between concentration and welfare depends on the relative importance of these hypotheses. For example, given fixed costs to innovation, increased concentration of innovation may be efficient. Other hypotheses, such as the burden of knowledge, imply that increased concentration and a reduced growth rate for welfare are consequences of other forces. Clearly, if increased concentration is driven by an increase in anticompetitive behavior, then it is welfare reducing.

2.4.2   Why Is Location-Level Concentration Rising?

While there is a significant body of work on location-level concentration in invention,[4] there is less literature that might explain why we see differences in trends in location-level concentration in IT relative to other types of technologies. Therefore, our hypotheses mostly draw on work that has highlighted the reasons for location-level concentration more generally and leave for future work an explanation for why the benefits of concentration might be different in IT. We identify four possible reasons:

---

4. See, for example, Carlino and Kerr (2015), Audretsch and Feldman (2004), and Feldman and Kogler (2010).

1. *Productivity of inventors in high-tech clusters*: Forman, Goldfarb, and Greenstein (2016) find a general increase in innovation in the San Francisco Bay Area over time and across all patent classes. They suggest that this increase might be due to agglomeration economies in invention. Moretti (2019) provides direct evidence of this, demonstrating that inventors are increasingly productive in high-tech clusters. This could explain the increased location-level concentration of patenting in IT. As a high-tech industry, invention has increased in those clusters, either because investors move to those clusters to be more productive or because the inventors in the clusters become more productive over time (or both).

2. *Agglomeration economies*: More generally, there may be increased agglomeration economies in the IT industry, independent of the productivity of inventors. Forman, Goldfarb, and Greenstein (2012) and Dranove, Garthwaite, and Ody (2014) show that IT adoption is more effective in cities. Outside IT, the increased importance of agglomeration economies between 1980 and 2010 is well documented in the urban economics literature (Duranton and Puga 2004; Glaeser 2012; Helsley and Strange 2014). If industrial activity is increasingly concentrated in a few locations and effective application of IT in using industries is increasingly concentrated in those locations, then IT innovation will be increasingly concentrated.

3. *Firm-level concentration*: For the most part, the hypotheses on the increase in firm-level concentration are unrelated to those on location-level concentration. This hypothesis is an important exception. An increase in firm-level concentration could mechanically increase location-level concentration. If a small number of firms increasingly dominate patenting, and if each firm focuses its patenting in a small number of locations, then the increase in firm-level concentration directly leads to an increase in location-level concentration. If this is the primary reason for increased location-level concentration, the location-level concentration is relatively uninteresting in itself.

4. *Bias in our analysis*: The result may be driven by our use of patent data. As with our analysis of firm-level concentration, to the extent that our measures of increased concentration in patenting are attempts to measure concentration in innovation, then we are limited by what can be learned from patent data. If there is an increased propensity to patent in certain locations over time (particularly in IT), then this increase could drive our result, and it might have little to do with innovation generally.

2.5   Conclusions

We document a change in concentration in patenting at both the firm level and the location level. We also document a decline in the fraction of new patenters from 2000 to 2010, especially in IT. We further find that patenting has become increasingly concentrated in a smaller number of locations. These patterns are found across different categories of IT, though some evidence suggests that the patterns may be stronger in Electronic business methods & software. These findings complement other recent evidence, found elsewhere, that the effects and incidence of technological change in IT are not shared equally across industries, firms, locations, and people.

These findings are important, because many prominent companies and emerging industries use IT as a critical input or are inherently digital. Furthermore, IT is an input to other inventions. There is rising concentration across firms both in and outside IT. There are reasons to expect IT to lead to concentration. Therefore, maybe IT is to blame. As noted in the introduction, this possibility has recently been more prominently raised in industries that are most easily digitized and that have been affected by digital platforms (Stigler Center for the Study of the Economy and the State 2019). However, there is a long-run trend of increasing use of IT and software in other industries, like manufacturing (Branstetter, Drev, and Kwon 2019), which may accelerate with the increasing diffusion of artificial intelligence (e.g., Cockburn, Henderson, and Stern 2019).

The increasing concentration of software innovation in a smaller number of locations is also important. The tendency for innovation to agglomerate in and across industries, the increasing concentration of innovation in IT, and IT's increasing use as an input in innovation may encourage the development of superstar cities, as documented elsewhere (Gyourko, Mayer, and Sinai 2013).

Increases in firm and geographic concentration will have important implications for the issues surrounding innovation, entrepreneurship, and growth that are the focus of this volume. A rich literature has explored the relationship between competition and innovation (for a review, see Gilbert 2006). Further, as noted at the beginning of this chapter, recent work has highlighted how increases in firm concentration can have important implications for the labor share and corporate investments, both of which have important growth implications. Likewise, increases in firm and geographic concentration could contribute to a rise in income inequality in the US. For economic growth more generally, increased productivity and innovation in this sector are likely to impact growth substantially in the short term. Over time, however, as in other sectors, as productivity improves, we can expect the industry to be a smaller part of overall economic output (Baumol 1967), and the impact of this industry on overall geographic and industrial concentration of economic activity should decline over time.

Our research is subject to several limitations. For one, we use patents as our measure of invention. Patents are a useful way to study concentration in innovation, particularly because they provide a consistent measure that is available over a long time. However, they are less frequently used as a measure of intellectual property protection than in other technologies and settings discussed in this book, and their strength has varied over time, both inside and outside our sample period. As a result, it is well known that the propensity to patent has varied over time, particularly in software; thus our results must be viewed with some care. Furthermore, our results end with patents applied for in 2010. Thus, our results miss recent developments that may arise because of changes in digitization, artificial intelligence, and cloud computing, among others. It is an open question whether the results are stronger or persist to the present day. Finally, our results are preliminary in the sense that we do not seek to explain why they are happening and what their implications are, if any. In particular, we do not show whether technological trends in IT explain the overall changes in market concentration, location concentration, labor share, or productivity.

Our approach also highlights important limitations to measuring concentration of IT innovation and entrepreneurship going forward. As famously highlighted in Marc Andreessen's statement that "Software Is Eating the World" (Andreessen 2011) and documented across chapters in this volume, innovation that is enabled by IT hardware and software is pervasive across industries. In our study, this pervasiveness made it difficult to identify IT-related patents in the patent system, but the same phenomenon also makes it difficult to identify new firm formation and growth in employment and production that is IT enabled. This occurs not only through the transformation of traditional industries like housing and real estate by de novo software start-up companies, such as Zillow and Redfin (Edward Kung, chapter 11, this volume), but also by attempts by large existing firms like General Electric to become digital businesses.

Despite these limitations, our contribution is to document a new pattern in the time trends in IT patenting. Both firm-level concentration and location-level concentration have increased over time.

References

Andreessen, Marc. 2011. "Why Software Is Eating the World." *Wall Street Journal*, August 20.

Andrews, Dan, Chiara Criscuolo, and Peter N. Gal. 2019. "The Best versus the Rest: Divergence across Firms during the Global Productivity Slowdown." CEP Discussion Paper No. 1645, August. London: Centre for Economic Performance.

Aral, Sinan, Erik Brynjolfsson, and Lynn Wu. 2012. "Three-Way Complementarities: Performance Pay, Human Resource Analytics, and Information Technology." *Management Science* 58(5): 913–31.

Armstrong, Mark. 2006. "Competition in Two-Sided Markets." *RAND Journal of Economics* 37(3): 668–91.

Arora, Ashish, Lee G. Branstetter, and Matej Drev. 2013. "Going Soft: How the Rise of Software-Based Innovation Led to the Decline of Japan's IT Industry and the Resurgence of Silicon Valley." *Review of Economics and Statistics* 95(3): 757–75.

Arora, Ashish, Andrea Fosfuri, and Alfonso Gambardella. 2004. *Markets for Technology: The Economics of Innovation and Corporate Strategy.* Cambridge, MA: MIT Press.

Audretsch, David, and Maryann Feldman. 2004. "Knowledge Spillovers and the Geography of Innovation." In *Handbook of Regional and Urban Economics*, vol. 4, edited by J. Vernon Henderson and Jacques-François Thisse, 2713–39. Amsterdam: Elsevier.

Autor, David, David Dorn, Lawrence F. Katz, Christina Patterson, and John Van Reenen. 2017. "Concentrating on the Fall of the Labor Share." *American Economic Review* 107(5): 180–85.

———. 2020. "The Fall of the Labor Share and the Rise of Superstar Firms." *Quarterly Journal of Economics* 135(2): 645–709.

Bar-Isaac, Heski, Guillermo Caruana, and Vicente Cuñat. 2012. "Search, Design, and Market Structure." *American Economic Review* 102(2): 1140–60.

Baumol, William J. 1967. "Macroeconomics of Unbalanced Growth: The Anatomy of Urban Crisis." *American Economic Review* 57(3): 415–26.

Berry, Steven, Martin Gaynor, and Fiona Scott Morton. 2019. "Do Increasing Markups Matter? Lessons from Empirical Industrial Organization." *Journal of Economic Perspectives* 33(3): 44–68.

Bessen, James, and Robert M. Hunt. 2007. "An Empirical Look at Software Patents." *Journal of Economics and Management Strategy* 16(1): 157–89.

Bloom, Nicholas, Charles I. Jones, John Van Reenen, and Michael Webb. 2020. "Are Ideas Getting Harder to Find?" *American Economic Review* 110(4): 1104–44.

Branstetter, Lee G., Matej Drev, and Namho Kwon. 2019. "Get with the Program: Software-Driven Innovation in Traditional Manufacturing." *Management Science* 65(2): 459–954.

Bresnahan, Timothy, Eric Brynjolfsson, and Lorin M. Hitt. 2002. "Information Technology, Workplace Organization, and the Demand for Skilled Labor: Firm-Level Evidence." *Quarterly Journal of Economics* 117(1): 339–76.

Bresnahan, Timothy, and Shane Greenstein. 1996. "Technical Progress and Co-Invention in Computing and in the Uses of Computers." *Brookings Papers on Economic Activity: Microeconomics* 27: 1–83.

———. 1999. "Technological Competition and the Structure of the Computer Industry." *Journal of Industrial Economics* 47(1): 1–40.

Bresnahan, Timothy, and Pai-Ling Yin. 2017. "Adoption of New Information and Communications Technologies in the Workplace Today." *Innovation Policy and the Economy* 17: 95–124.

Brynjolfsson, Erik, and Andrew McAfee. 2014. *The Second Machine Age: Work, Progress, and Prosperity in a Time of Brilliant Technologies.* New York: W. W. Norton & Company.

Brynjolfsson, Erik, Andrew McAfee, Michael Sorell, and Feng Zhu. 2008. "Scale without Mass: Business Process Replication and Industry Dynamics." Unit Research Paper No. 07-016, Harvard University.

Brynjolfsson, Erik, Daniel Rock, and Chad Syverson. 2021. "The Productivity J-Curve: How Intangibles Complement General Purpose Technologies." *American Economic Journal: Macroeconomics* 13(1): 333–72.

Carlino, Gerald A., and William Kerr. 2015. "Agglomeration and Innovation." In *Handbook of Regional and Urban Economics*, vol. 5A, edited by Gilles Duranton, J. V. Henderson, and William Strange, 349–404. Amsterdam: Elsevier.

Cockburn, Iain, and Megan MacGarvie. 2009. "Patents, Thickets and the Financing of Early-Stage Firms: Evidence from the Software Industry." *Journal of Economics and Management Strategy* 18(3): 729–73.

————. 2011. "Entry and Patenting in the Software Industry." *Management Science* 57(5): 915–33.

Cockburn, Iain M., Rebecca Henderson, and Scott Stern. 2019. "The Impact of Artificial Intelligence on Innovation: An Exploratory Analysis." In *The Economics of Artificial Intelligence*, edited by Ajay K. Agrawal, Joshua Gans, and Avi Goldfarb, chapter 4. Chicago: University of Chicago Press.

Cohen, Wesley M., Richard R. Nelson, and John P. Walsh. 2000. "Protecting Their Intellectual Assets: Appropriability Conditions and Why U.S. Manufacturing Firms Patent (or Not)." NBER Working Paper No. 7552. Cambridge, MA: National Bureau of Economic Research.

Corrado, Carol, Charles Hulten, and Daniel Sichel. 2009. "Intangible Capital and U.S. Economic Growth." *Review of Income and Wealth* 55(3): 661–85.

De Loecker, Jan, Jan Eeckhout, and Gabriel Unger. 2020. "The Rise of Market Power and the Macroeconomic Implications." *Quarterly Journal of Economics* 135(2): 561–644.

Dranove, David, Craig Garthwaite, and Christopher Ody. 2014. "Health Spending Slowdown Is Mostly Due to Economic Factors, Not Structural Change in the Health Care Sector." *Health Affairs* 33(8): 1399–1406.

Duranton, Giles, and Diego Puga. 2004. "Micro-Foundations of Urban Agglomeration Economies." *Handbook of Regional and Urban Economics* 4: 2063–2117.

The Economist. 2018. "How to Tame the Tech Titans." Available at https://www.economist.com/leaders/2018/01/18/how-to-tame-the-tech-titans.

Eggertsson, Gauti B., Jacob A. Robbins, and Ella Getz Wold. 2018. "Kaldor and Piketty's Facts: The Rise of Monopoly Power in the United States." NBER Working Paper No. 24287. Cambridge, MA: National Bureau of Economic Research.

Einav, Liran, Chiara Farronato, and Jonathan Levin. 2016. "Peer-to-Peer Markets." *Annual Review of Economics* 8(1): 615–35.

Ellison, Glenn, and Edward Glaeser. 1997. "Geographic Concentration in U.S. Manufacturing Industries: A Dartboard Approach." *Journal of Political Economy* 105(5): 889–927.

Evans, Peter C., and Annabelle Gawer. 2016. The Rise of the Platform Enterprise: A Global Survey. The Center for Global Enterprise. Available at https://www.thecge.net/app/uploads/2016/01/PDF-WEB-Platform-Survey_01_12.pdf.

Feldman, Maryann P., and Dieter Kogler. 2010. "Stylized Facts in the Geography of Innovation." In *Handbook of the Economics of Innovation*, edited by Bronwyn Hall and Nathan Rosenberg, 381–410. Amsterdam: Elsevier.

Fernández-Delgado, Manuel, Eva Cernadas, Senén Barro, and Dinani Amorim. 2014. "Do We Need Hundreds of Classifiers to Solve Real World Classification Problems?" *Journal of Machine Learning Research* 15(90): 3133–81.

Forman, Chris, Avi Goldfarb, and Shane Greenstein. 2012. "The Internet and Local Wages: A Puzzle." *American Economic Review* 102(1): 556–75.

————. 2016. "Agglomeration of Invention in the Bay Area: Not Just ICT." *American Economic Review Papers & Proceedings* 106(5): 146–51.

Foroughi, Cirrus, and Ariel Dora Stern. 2018. "Digital Innovation with High Costs of Entry: Evidence from Software-Driven Medical Devices." Working Paper, Harvard Business School, Cambridge, MA.

Furman, Jason, and Peter Orszag. 2015. "A Firm-Level Perspective on the Role of Rents in the Rise in Inequality." Presentation at "A Just Society" Centennial Event in Honor of Joseph Stiglitz, Columbia University, New York.

Gans, Joshua S., David H. Hsu, and Scott Stern. 2002. "When Does Start-Up Innovation Spur the Gale of Creative Destruction?" *RAND Journal of Economics* 33(4): 771–86.

Gans, Joshua S., and Scott Stern. 2003. "The Product Market and the Market for 'Ideas': Commercialization Strategies for Technology Entrepreneurs." *Research Policy* 32: 333–50.

Gilbert, R. 2006. "Looking for Mr. Schumpeter: Where Are We in the Competition-Innovation Debate?" In *Innovation Policy and the Economy*, vol. 6, edited by Adam B. Jaffe, Josh Lerner, and Scott Stern, 159–215.

Giorgi, Giovanni M. 2019. "Gini Coefficient." In *SAGE Research Methods Foundations*, edited by Paul Atkinson, Sara Delamont, Alexandru Cernat, Joseph W. Sakshaug, and Richard A. Williams. Thousand Oaks, CA: Sage Publications.

Glaeser, Edward. 2012. *Triumph of the City: How Our Greatest Invention Makes Us Richer, Smarter, Greener, Healthier, and Happier*. London: Penguin Books.

Glaeser, Edward L., Hedi D. Kallal, José A. Scheinkman, and Andrei Shleifer. 1992. "Growth in Cities." *Journal of Political Economy* 100(6): 1126–52.

Goldfarb, Avi, and Catherine Tucker. 2019. "Digital Economics." *Journal of Economic Literature* 57(1): 3–43.

Graham, Stuart J. H., Marco Ceccagnoli, Matthew J. Higgins, and Jeongsik Lee. 2010. "Productivity and the Role of Complementary Assets in Firms' Demand for Technology Innovations." *Industrial and Corporate Change* 19(3): 839–69.

Graham, Stuart J. H., Robert P. Merges, Pam Samuelson, and Ted M. Sichelman. 2009. "High Technology Entrepreneurs and the Patent System: Results of the 2008 Berkley Patent Survey." *Berkley Technology Law Journal* 24(4): 1275–1328.

Graham, Stuart J. H., and David C. Mowrey. 2003. "Submarines in Software? Continuations in US Software Patenting in the 1980s and 1990s." *Economics of Innovation and New Technology* 13(5): 443–56.

Gutiérrez, Germán, and Thomas Philippon. 2017. "Declining Competition and Investment in the U.S." NBER Working Paper No. 23583. Cambridge, MA: National Bureau of Economic Research.

Gyourko, Joseph, Christopher Mayer, and Todd Sinai. 2013. "Superstar Cities." *American Economic Journal: Economic Policy* 5(4): 167–99.

Hall, Bronwyn H., and Megan MacGarvie. 2010. "The Private Value of Software Patents." *Research Policy* 39(7): 994–1009.

Hall, Bronwyn H., and Rosemarie Ham Ziedonis. 2001. "The Patent Paradox Revisited: An Empirical Study of Patenting in the U.S. Semiconductor Industry, 1979–1995." *RAND Journal of Economics* 32(1): 101–28.

Hall, Bronwyn H., Adam B. Jaffe, and Manuel Trajtenberg. 2001. "The NBER Patent Citations Data File: Lessons, Insights and Methodological Tools." NBER Working Paper No. 8498. Cambridge, MA: National Bureau of Economic Research.

Hall, Bronwyn H., Adam Jaffe, and Manuel Trajtenberg. 2005. "Market Value and Patent Citations." *RAND Journal of Economics* 36(1): 16–38.

Helsley, Robert W., and William C. Strange. 2014. "Coagglomeration, Clusters, and the Scale and Composition of Cities." *Journal of Political Economy* 122(5): 1064–93.

Hendershott, Terrence, and Jie Zhang. 2006. "A Model of Direct and Intermediated Sales." *Journal of Economics and Management Strategy* 15(2): 279–316.

Henderson, J. Vernon, Ari Kuncoro, and Matthew Turner. 1995. "Industrial Development in Cities." *Journal of Political Economy* 103(5): 1067–90.

Huang, Peng, Marco Ceccagnoli, Chris Forman, and D. J. Wu. 2013. "Appropriability Mechanisms and the Platform Partnership Decision: Evidence from Enterprise Software." *Management Science* 59(1): 102–21.

Jaffe, A., and M. Trajtenberg. 2002. *Patents, Citations, and Innovations: A Window on the Knowledge Economy*. Cambridge, MA: MIT Press.

Jin, Wang, and Kristina McElheran. 2018. "Economies before Scale: Survival and

Performance of Young Plants in the Age of Cloud Computing." Working paper, Rotman School of Management, Toronto.

Jones, Benjamin F. 2009. "The Burden of Knowledge and the 'Death of the Renaissance Man': Is Innovation Getting Harder?" *Review of Economic Studies* 76(1): 283–317.

Jorgenson, Dale W., Mun S. Ho, and Kevin Stiroh. 2005. *Productivity: Information Technology and the American Growth Resurgence*, vol. 3. Cambridge, MA: MIT Press.

Jullien, Bruno, and Alessandro Pavan. 2019. "Information Management and Pricing in Platform Markets." *Review of Economic Studies* 86(4): 1666–1703.

Katz, Michael L., and Carl Shapiro. 1985. "Network Externalities, Competition, and Compatibility." *American Economic Review* 75(3): 424–40.

Klepper, Steven. 2002. "Firm Survival and the Evolution of Oligopoly." *RAND Journal of Economics* 33(1): 37–61.

Klepper, Steven, and Elizabeth Graddy. 1990. "The Evolution of New Industries and the Determinants of Market Structure." *RAND Journal of Economics* 21(1): 27–44.

Kogan, Leonid, Dimitris Papanikolaou, Amit Seru, and Noah Stoffman. 2017. "Technological Innovation, Resource Allocation, and Growth." *Quarterly Journal of Economics* 132(2): 665–712.

McAfee, Andrew, and Erik Brynjolfsson. 2008. "Investing in the IT That Makes a Competitive Difference." *Harvard Business Review*, July–August 2008.

Merriam-Webster. 2020. https://www.merriam-webster.com/.

Moretti, Enrico. 2019. "The Effect of High-Tech Clusters on the Productivity of Top Inventors." NBER Working Paper No. 26270. Cambridge, MA: National Bureau of Economic Research.

Picard, Robert. 2015. "GEOINPOLY: Stata Module to Match Geographic Locations to Shapefile Polygons." Statistical Software Components, Boston College Department of Economics, Boston.

Rosen, Sherwin. 1981. "The Economics of Superstars." *American Economic Review* 71(5): 845–58.

Rosenthal, Stuart, and William Strange. 2004. "Evidence on the Nature and Sources of Agglomeration Economies." In *Handbook of Regional and Urban Economics*, vol. 4, edited by J. Vernon Henderson and Jacques-François Thisse, 2119–71. Amsterdam: Elsevier.

Shapiro, Carl, and Hal R. Varian. 1998. *Information Rules: A Strategic Guide to the Network Economy*. Cambridge, MA: Harvard Business Press.

Statista. 2019. The 100 Largest Companies in the World by Market Value in 2019. Available at https://www.statista.com/statistics/263264/top-companies-in-the-world-by-market-value/.

Stigler Center for the Study of the Economy and the State. 2019. "Stigler Committee on Digital Platforms: Report." Chicago: Chicago Booth.

Stoffman, Noah, Michael Woeppel, and M. Deniz Yavuz. 2019. "Small Innovators: No Risk, No Return." Kelley School of Business Research Paper No. 19-5, Bloomington, IN.

Sutton, Stephen. 1998. "Predicting and Explaining Intentions and Behavior: How Well Are We Doing?" *Journal of Applied Social Psychology* 28(15): 1317–38.

Syverson, Chad. 2017. "Challenges to Mismeasurement Explanations for the US Productivity Slowdown." *Journal of Economic Perspectives* 31(2): 165–86.

Tambe, Prasanna, and Lorin M. Hitt. 2012. "Now IT's Personal: Offshoring and the Shifting Skill Composition of the U.S. Information Technology Workforce." *Management Science* 58(4): 678–95.

Tambe, Prasanna, Lorin M. Hitt, Daniel Rock, and Erik Brynjolfsson. 2019. "IT, AI and the Growth of Intangible Capital." Working paper, Wharton Business School, Philadelphia.

Valletti, Tommaso M., and Hans Zenger. 2019. "Increasing Market Power and Merger Control." *Competition Law & Policy Debate* 5(1): 26–35.

Innovation, Growth, and Structural Change in American Agriculture

Julian M. Alston and Philip G. Pardey

3.1 Introduction

During the twentieth century, American agriculture was dramatically transformed, and its role in the economy changed markedly. The progressive introduction and adoption of a host of technological innovations and other farming improvements enabled much more to be produced with less land and a lot less labor; farms became many fewer, much larger, and more specialized. However, while agriculture continued to grow, it shrank in relative importance. The US farm population peaked at 32.5 million, 31.9 percent of the total US population in 1916; since then it declined to an estimated 4.5 million in 2019, just 1.4 percent of the total. And while agriculture's share of GDP increased (somewhat erratically) from 12 percent in 1889 to

Julian M. Alston is a Distinguished Professor in the Department of Agricultural and Resource Economics and Director of the Robert Mondavi Institute Center for Wine Economics at the University of California, Davis, and a member of the Giannini Foundation of Agricultural Economics. He is also a research fellow at InSTePP at the University of Minnesota.

Philip G. Pardey is a professor in the Department of Applied Economics, Director of Global Research Strategy for CFANS, and Director of the International Science and Technology Practice and Policy (InSTePP) center, all at the University of Minnesota.

The authors are grateful for the excellent research assistance provided by Connie Chan-Kang, Xudong Rao, and Shanchao Wang; for helpful advice provided by James (Jess) Lowenberg-DeBoer, Abigail Okrent, J. B. Penn, and David Schimmelpfennig; and for helpful comments provided by Brian Wright, other participants in the symposium, and the organizers. The work for this project was partly supported by the California Agricultural Experiment Station; the Minnesota Agricultural Experiment Station (MIN-14–161); the USDA National Research Initiative; and the Giannini Foundation of Agricultural Economics. For acknowledgments, sources of research support, and disclosure of the authors' material financial relationships, if any, please see https://www.nber.org/books-and-chapters/role-innovation-and -entrepreneurship-economic-growth/innovation-growth-and-structural-change-american -agriculture.

17 percent in 1917, it declined steadily thereafter to just 0.81 percent in 2018. Innovation on and off farms played a central role.

This chapter provides detailed documentation, evidence, and analysis of the past and ongoing sources of innovation and structural change in American agriculture. To begin, we describe the profound structural transformation of American agriculture over the course of the past century and the implications for changing patterns of inputs, outputs, and productivity. Then we turn to a consideration of the sources of change. We pay particular attention to the impact of innovation as a driver of productivity and employment in the agricultural sector; to the role of private entrepreneurship in the process; and to the distinctive features of the agricultural sector—still largely atomistic and heavily dependent on a host of natural, often location-specific, inputs, in which changes can undercut past productivity gains—and its evolution (shrinking as a share of the economy). Digging deeper, we present evidence on inputs to and outputs from innovation, on the resulting gains in productivity, what those gains are worth, prospects for the coming decades, hurdles to be overcome, and roles played by government policies.

Before getting into the meat of this chapter, we briefly broach some conceptual, measurement, and other data issues that are integral to the structural changes we are studying. One hundred years ago, farmers would themselves produce energy and traction for farm operations and fertilizer for crops (using horses and mules), seed and other inputs, as well most if not all of their own food. This aspect of farm life has changed considerably. Over time, farms became increasingly specialized in a narrower range of market goods. Many productive activities progressively shifted off farms to be undertaken by specialized (pre-farm) agribusiness firms that nowadays produce farm machinery, seed, chemicals, energy, and other inputs that were once largely (and in some instances entirely) produced on-farm. Likewise, farm households once made many food and fiber products that are now produced entirely off-farm by agribusiness firms in other (post-farm) sectors of the economy. These shifts have implications for where the lines are drawn in distinguishing between farms and other firms and thus between agriculture and the rest of the economy.

In industrial organization parlance, farms and farmers are now less vertically integrated and more specialized, and the nature of the farm firm has changed (Coase 1937). So, too has the statistical definition of a farm—whether specified in terms of acres farmed, the value of sales, or some combination of the two.[1] The large changes over the decades in the actual and

---

1. As discussed by Sumner (2014), concepts of farm firm size based on land area, which might work well for cropping farms in the US Midwest, are less useful for intensive livestock producers or for horticulture, where gross value of sales, total employment of labor, or total value of the capital stock   as sometimes used to measure size of nonfarm firms—might be more useful. Issues surrounding the statistical definition of what is a farm are linked with issues about how to measure farm size since many of the USDA definitions, which themselves have changed from time to time, are based on a farm size criterion involving land area or value-of-sales attributes.

recorded nature of farms and farming pose challenges for economists who measure inputs and outputs and seek to make intertemporal comparisons. Moreover, the data are not always collected and presented in the preferred ways that make it possible to develop consistent measures that match the conceptual constructs. Nonetheless, the available measures are informative.

The data issues associated with the changing structure of agriculture and the distinction between agriculture and other sectors of the economy extend to the corresponding concepts and measures of public and private investments in agricultural and food R&D. In our discussion of these issues we take pains to place agricultural R&D spending in the context of broader measures of public and private R&D, maintaining a consistent set of definitions of agricultural versus non-agricultural, and private versus public as used by other publications dealing with these concepts applied to R&D. A perennial challenge in this context is how to treat more fundamental scientific inquiries, the ultimate application of which, by definition, remains to be seen. Likewise, the treatment of spillovers and attribution in empirical work often entails assumptions that are hard to validate. Where possible, we address these aspects.

3.2 Special Features of Agriculture

Innovation in agriculture has many features in common with innovation more generally, but agriculture differs in terms of its industrial structure and the nature of market failures in innovation; the spatial dimensions of production and the site-specific nature of the technology; the biological nature of the production process; and the nature of food and farming as perceived by the broader public and groups that define technological regulations and requirements.[2] It is helpful to have those differences in mind as we review the past and prospective changes in agriculture and the roles of entrepreneurship and innovation in shaping them.

Like other parts of the economy, agriculture is characterized by market failures associated with incomplete property rights over inventions. The small-scale, competitive, atomistic industrial structure of farming means that the attenuation of incentives to innovate is more pronounced than in other industries that are more concentrated in their industrial structure. Agriculture is further distinguished by the biological and spatial nature of its production technology (Joglekar, Pardey, and Wood-Sichra 2016). Agricultural production takes up a lot of space—indeed, about 40 percent of the world's land area is occupied by agriculture (including 12 percent used for crops), and 44 percent of US land is in agriculture. And the nature of the space varies in ways that are relevant for the choice of technology: since agricultural production involves biological systems, appropriate technologies

2. Parts of this section draw from Pardey, Alston, and Ruttan (2010).

can vary with changes in climate, soil types, topography, latitude, altitude, and distance from markets. Hence, unlike most innovations in manufacturing, food processing, or transportation, agricultural technology has a degree of site specificity, which circumscribes the potential for knowledge spillovers and the associated market failures.

The biological nature of agricultural production also means that production processes take time, during which outcomes are susceptible to the influence of such factors as weather and pests that are difficult or costly to control. Moreover, the agricultural production consequences of pests and weather vary in ways that are often uncontrolled and difficult to predict with present knowledge and technology, not only within a season but also systematically over time and space. Climate change and the co-evolution and adaptation of pests and diseases mean that maintenance research is required to prevent yields from declining—the "Red Queen" effect, as discussed by Olmstead and Rhode (2002), for instance.[3] These features of agriculture give rise to a demand for innovations that reduce the susceptibility of production to uncontrolled biotic and abiotic stresses and allow technology to adapt to changes in the farming environment or changes in technological regulations.

Agriculture is also subject to different kinds of public and policy scrutiny, because, compared with most other industrial outputs, people care differently about food and the way it is produced, and increasingly so as they become richer. US consumers are increasingly demanding foods that have "credence" attributes associated with the products and the processes used to produce them—such as organic, locally produced, and raised using humane livestock and poultry practices (see, e.g., Rausser, Zilberman, and Kahn 2015; Rausser, Zilberman, and Sexton 2019). Alston (2021) discusses this demand and the related demand for technological regulation coming from what he terms the "woke farm and food policy reform movement," which blames the agricultural and food industry for various societal ills (see, e.g., Willett et al. 2019). Some food processors, manufacturers, and retailers are requiring foods to be produced in ways that accommodate these demands (see, e.g., Saitone, Sexton, and Sumner 2015). All these forces have implications for the types of innovations that will be relevant for American farms in the coming decades—as they or forces like them were in the past.

3.3   Structure of American Agriculture

Land-saving and especially labor-saving innovations were central to the structural transformation of American agriculture in the twentieth century.

---

3. For example, a 1986 survey of 744 US agricultural scientists suggested that "maintenance research" accounted for around one-third of production-oriented agricultural research at that time (Adusei and Norton 1990).

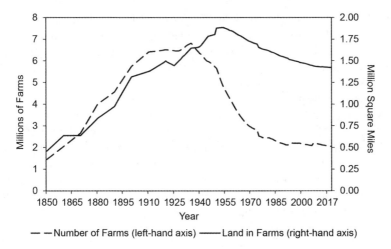

Fig. 3.1   US farm area and farm numbers, 1850–2017
Source: Pardey and Alston (2021, figure 3).
Note: For number of farms, missing intercensal values were estimated by linear interpolation.

The number of US farms grew from 1.4 million in 1850 to a peak of 6.8 million in 1936 before falling to 2.9 million in 1970 and 2.1 million in 2017; land in farms peaked in 1954 (figure 3.1; Pardey and Alston 2021). Farms became much larger and more specialized in terms of their output mix, and the input mix shifted to use much less labor and a little less land, combined with more capital and purchased material inputs.[4]

3.3.1   Farm Labor

These changes in the structure of agriculture entailed changes in the structure of the farm labor force, reflecting both the pull from growth in nonfarm demand for labor (driving up the opportunity cost of farmers' time as well as the cost of hired farm labor) and the push from technological changes on farms that permitted more to be produced with much less labor and more land per farm. Farmers responded to these incentives and opportunities by consolidating farms and substituting other inputs for labor, in part by developing and adopting labor-saving innovations that favored higher

---

4. These aggregate figures encompass highly diverse farm sizes and types. In 1920, the US had 735 million acres on 6.4 million farms, at an average of 8.7 acres per farm. None of those farms had more than 1,000 acres. By 2012, the total number of farms had fallen by more than two-thirds compared with 1920. Now 9.2 percent of a total of 2.1 million farms had more than 1,000 acres. Notably, more than 10 percent of today's "farms" have less than 10 acres, but many of today's small farms are "hobby farms," and many are part-time occupations for people for whom living on a farm is a lifestyle choice more than a way of making a living. See MacDonald (2020) for further details.

land-labor ratios and larger optimal farm sizes.[5] Figure 3.2 captures the main elements of the post–World War II changes in farm labor use. In figure 3.2, panel A, total labor use in agriculture—measured in hours per year and taking account of the major shift to part-time farming—fell by two-thirds from 1949 to 2007. Within this total, operator labor fell by more than three-quarters, and the hired labor share increased from 20 percent to 32 percent.[6]

As farmers substituted other inputs for more-expensive labor, the cost share of labor fell from more than 42 percent in 1949 to less than 30 percent in 2007. Mainly, farmers increased their use of materials inputs purchased off farm (such as seed, fuel, electricity, fertilizer and other agricultural chemicals, and hired machines); the total use of land and capital (measured with appropriate indexes) remained relatively constant—albeit with considerable variation in these details over time and among states.[7] The mix of agricultural output has also changed over time, reflecting the effects of changes in US and foreign demand for US farm products, as well as the effects of changing production possibilities enabled by new technologies.[8] The category of nursery and greenhouse marketing in particular has grown rapidly, and it constituted the fastest growing category of output for all but five of the 48 contiguous US states during the second half of the twentieth century (Alston et al. 2010, p. 69).[9]

5. MacDonald, Hoppe, and Newton (2018) report: "By 2015, 51 percent of the value of US farm production came from farms with at least $1 million in sales, compared to 31 percent in 1991 (adjusted for price changes). . . . [Now] few farms specialize in a single crop, field crop operations increasingly grow just 2 or 3 crops, versus 4–6 crops previously. Livestock production continues to shift toward farms that produce no crops, and instead rely on purchased feed. . . . Despite increased consolidation, most production continues to be carried out on family farms, which are owned and operated by people related to one another by blood or marriage. Family farms accounted for 90 percent of farms with at least $1 million in sales in 2015."

6. Growth of the rural nonfarm economy has facilitated growth in off-farm employment for farm household members. Between 1930 and 2012, the share of full-time farm operators fell from 70 percent to 40 percent, and their average number of days per year worked off-farm increased from 86.5 to 143.2.

7. Alston et al. (2010) provide detailed state-level and national data on inputs, outputs, and productivity in US agriculture during 1949–2002 in a book-length treatment. State- and national-level data for 1949–2007 are available on the InSTePP website (see Pardey et al. 2006 for data documentation) and are discussed by Pardey and Alston (2021).

8. Among other changes, improved communications, electrification, transportation, and logistical infrastructure meant that perishables and pre-prepared foods could be moved efficiently over much longer distances. This contributed to the changing spatial patterns of production.

9. "Nursery and greenhouse marketing" produces ornamental and diverse other plants and has grown in comparative importance as Americans have become more affluent. Much of it is highly intensive horticulture, often located in the urban fringe, and it probably lies outside common and traditional perceptions of "agriculture." But it counts as part of agriculture in official agricultural statistics and other manifestations of agricultural policy—whereas golf courses and forestry, for example, do not—and in many instances, this is as good a basis as any we may have for drawing the distinction between what we reasonably should or should not count as part of the sector. The essential idea is "agriculture" is economic activity that happens on farms. As the balance of that activity has changed, implicitly the concept and measures of agriculture have evolved in ways that make consistent intertemporal comparisons harder.

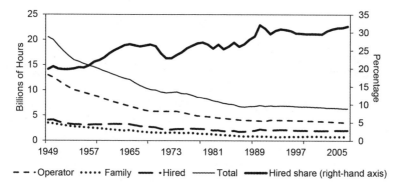

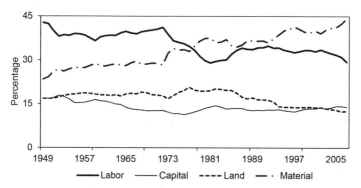

Fig. 3.2   Labor use in US agriculture, 1949–2012

Source: Pardey and Alston (2021, figure 5).

Note: In all census years up to 1997, the reported number of operators was set equal to the total number of farms. From 2002 on, the census reported information on the total number of operators. If a farm had more than one operator, it was counted accordingly. In all census years up to 1997, data are reported in terms of operators by days worked off-farm cohorts (e.g., 0 days, 1–49 days, 50–99 days). For 2002, 2007, and 2012, data are reported in terms of cohorts of days worked off-farm by the principal operator. In 1974, data were collected only for individual or family operations (sole proprietorships) and partnerships. Thus, corporations and other types of organizations (e.g., cooperative, prison farms, grazing associations, and Indian reservations) were excluded (for more details, see US Bureau of Census, 1977, Appendix A, p. A4). In all other years, data on days worked off-farm were collected for all types of farms.

To calculate the average number of days worked off-farm per operator, we proceeded as follows. First, the total number of days worked off-farm in each cohort was estimated by multiplying the mid-point number of days worked off farm in each cohort (e.g., 25 days for 1–49 days, 75 days for 50–99 days etc. and 200 days for 200 and more) by the corresponding total number of operators. The total number of days worked off farms was obtained by summing the estimated number of days worked off-farm across cohorts. The number of days worked off-farm per operator is given by the total number of days worked off-farm divided by the total number of operators.

Data for intercensal years were estimated by linear interpolation.

The total number of operators working full time was estimated by subtracting the number of operators working off-farms from the total number of operators.

Panel C. Part time farm operators

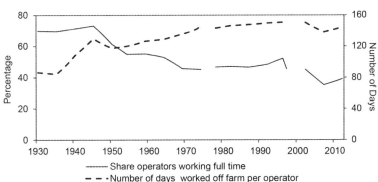

------- Share operators working full time
— — ·Number of days worked off farm per operator

Fig. 3.2   (cont.)

Table 3.1   Growth rates in US agricultural input, output, and productivity, 1910–2007

| Period | Input | Output | Productivity indexes | | |
			MFP	Labor	Land
			Percent per year		
1910–1950	0.46	1.29	0.83	2.16	0.62
1950–1990	−0.21	1.91	2.12	4.07	1.92
1990–2007	0.31	1.48	1.16	1.90	1.88
1910–2007	0.16	1.58	1.42	2.90	1.38

Source: Growth rates of productivity indexes were calculated by the authors using the In-STePP Production Accounts, version 5, augmented with data from USDA-ERS (1983). See Pardey and Alston (2021).

Note: All figures are annual average growth rates, computed as logarithmic trends.

3.3.2   Agricultural Productivity

Reflecting these and other changes, over the past 100 years and more, US agricultural productivity grew rapidly—albeit unevenly over time and across states. During 1910–2007, multifactor productivity (MFP) in US agriculture grew at an average annual rate of 1.42 percent, reflecting average annual growth of 1.58 percent in the index of aggregate output and 0.16 percent in the index of inputs (table 3.1). These averages reflect shrinking total inputs (and even total output) in some states as they shifted out of agriculture, in contrast to comparatively rapid expansion in inputs and output in some other states. And they also reflect changes in the composition of inputs and outputs, as already discussed. Since World War II, MFP has grown generally rapidly in US agriculture, but this reflects a surge (during the 1950s–1980s) followed by a slowdown such that MFP has been growing at about 1 percent

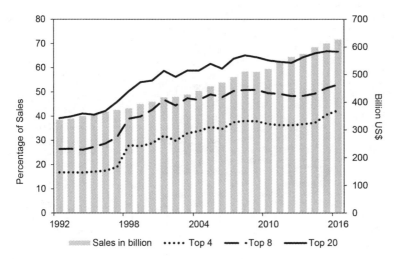

Fig. 3.3   Top 4, 8, and 20 firms' shares of US grocery store sales, 1992–2016
Source: USDA, Economic Research Service, using data from US Census Bureau, Monthly Retail Trade Survey, company annual reports, and industry sources. Sales based on North American Industry Classification System (NAICS).

per year since 1990, compared with about 2 percent per year during 1950–1990 (see Andersen et al. 2018; Pardey and Alston 2021).[10]

3.3.3   Off-Farm Changes

The pre- and post-farm elements of the farm-based food and fiber supply chain have also been transformed, especially during the past half-century. The pre-farm agribusiness industries that supply inputs used by farmers, many of which embody technological innovations—whether genetic, chemical, mechanical, or digital—have become more concentrated, more global, and more vertically integrated, while accounting for an increasing share of total value added by the sector. Likewise, the post-farm sector has become more concentrated and more economically important, such that the farming sector represents an ever-shrinking share of the total food value chain (figure 3.3). In 2017, the average farm share was down to 14.6 cents per dollar of food expenditure by consumers (USDA-ERS 2019a).

The income elasticity of demand for food per se is quite low for most Americans (see, e.g., Okrent and Alston 2011), but the demand for ser-

---

10. This raises questions about the relative productivity performance of agriculture compared with other sectors of the US economy. Following Jorgenson and Gollop (1992), it has become a stylized fact among agricultural and other economists to say productivity has grown comparatively quickly in agriculture. In a more nuanced comparison, Pardey and Alston (2021) document and discuss a surge and slowdown in nonfarm productivity during 1910–1960, two decades prior to the surge and slowdown in farm productivity.

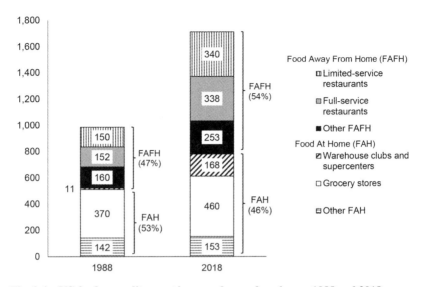

Fig. 3.4   US food expenditures at home and away from home, 1988 and 2018

Source: Calculated by USDA, Economic Research Service, from various sources. See details in Okrent et al. (2018).

Note: Nominal 1988 values inflated to 2018 values using CPI data from the US Bureau of Labor Statistics: https://www.bls.gov/data/inflation_calculator.htm. Units are billions of 2018 dollars.

vices associated with food and other "quality" attributes of food is much more income elastic. With rises in per capita incomes and the opportunity cost of time—especially for women as they have progressively entered the workforce—Americans have increasingly demanded more food away from home (accounting for more than half of food expenditure and more than one-third of calories since 2010) and more prepared foods and ready-to-eat foods for consumption at home (Okrent et al. 2018; Saksena et al. 2018) (figure 3.4). In addition, they are demanding food differentiated in various ways according to both product attributes (related to nutrients, food safety, and so on) and process attributes (related to technologies used on farms, such as genetically engineered varieties, organic practices, pesticide use, animal husbandry practices, and so on).

The choices of technologies available to farmers and the types of food products available to consumers are increasingly being mediated by the food processing, manufacturing, and retailing sector (e.g., Saitone, Sexton, and Sumner 2015), cognizant of the evolving consumer marketplace and the influence of activist organizations (Alston 2021; Rausser, Zilberman, and Kahn 2015; Rausser, Zilberman, and Sexton 2019). Indeed, private regulation of farm technologies imposed by food manufacturers and retailers might come to supplant government regulation in this domain. In turn, these shifts have implications for the demand for technologies expressed by farmers and the derived demand for investment in R&D and innovation. And ultimately, these processes will shape the future path of demand for farm inputs, supply of farm outputs, productivity, and prices.

3.4   Investments in Innovation

Farmers are tinkerers. The 10,000-year history of agriculture and agricultural innovation includes only a century or two of organized science and other institutions that foster innovation (Pardey, Roseboom, and Anderson 1991; Ruttan 1982). In the US, since 1862—which marked both the establishment of the US Department of Agriculture (USDA) and the passage of the Morrill Land Grant College Act—state and federal governments have become progressively more involved through both public investments in and the public performance of food and agricultural R&D. So too has the private sector, especially in more recent decades, as the incentives for investing in food and agricultural innovation have strengthened. In particular, changes in intellectual property (IP) protection enhanced the appropriability of the returns to biological innovations as more fundamental discoveries in the basic biological sciences opened up new (applied) R&D possibilities. Food and agricultural innovation investments also evolved in conjunction with, benefited from, and contributed to R&D spending directed to other sectors of the economy. During the past half-century, the patterns of R&D spending overall (or gross domestic expenditures on R&D, GERD) and R&D spending directed to the food and agricultural sector (or agGERD) have continued to change in ways that we quantify and discuss in this section.

3.4.1   GERD vs. agGERD

While clear statistical guidelines for collecting and compiling R&D statistics (see, e.g., OECD 2015) are widely accepted, the practical application of those guidelines is tricky and involves choices that have implications for the resulting measures and their interpretation. Pardey et al. (2016a) provide a detailed description of the conceptual and practical methods they used to identify agGERD as the "gross domestic expenditures on food and agricultural R&D" series reported here, as distinct from R&D (or other related activities) performed for other purposes; the sector (e.g., business enterprise, government, higher education, and private nonprofit) associated with the performance of the research; and the geographical jurisdiction of the research.

Thus, for example, the private agGERD series reported here represents R&D purposely targeting food and agriculture, where the research is performed by business enterprises in the US, whether by domestic or foreign-owned firms. (An alternative measure could include all private food and agricultural R&D performed by firms headquartered or operating in the US, irrespective of where in the world the research occurred.) Creating this series often requires parsing research spending totals into US vs. rest-of-world components. This distinction is increasingly difficult to make, as many large multinational companies (US-based and foreign) continue to diversify their R&D activities globally but only report total company-wide spending. Moreover, business activities of some firms are only partially associated with the agricultural and food sectors, or they span multiple subsectors in the general scope of food and agricultural research. For example, a single firm may undertake chemical research (only some of which is related to food and agriculture) and may also undertake biological or varietal development research related to agriculture, and the mix of that research may change over time. For this subset of firms, absent any other information, the US private-sector series reported here was developed from firm-specific data, where, if required, each firm's total R&D spending was parsed in line with the share of that firm's sales associated with its agricultural or food-related business segments.

In 1953, the US economy invested $34.4 billion (2011 prices here and below unless otherwise stated) in GERD—that is, total public and private gross domestic expenditures on R&D. Over the subsequent six decades, GERD in deflated terms grew 13.5-fold (or 4.2 percent per year on average) to total $465 billion in 2015 (figure 3.5, panel A). Over the same period, agGERD carried out in the United States also grew markedly—albeit at a slightly slower average annual rate of 3.7 percent per year, again in constant prices—from $1.27 billion in 1953 to $12.6 billion in 2015 (figure 3.5, panel B).

As a consequence of these differential rates of R&D spending growth, the share of agGERD in total GERD gradually trended down from 3.7 percent in 1953 to 2.7 percent in 2015, in tandem with the secular decline in the agricultural share of overall economic activity. However, while the agGDP/GDP ratio shrank in a reasonably steady fashion, the reduction in the agricultural share of total R&D was less regular. Overall US spending on R&D grew faster than spending on agricultural R&D during the 1950s. During the agricultural productivity surge of the 1960s and 1970s, spending on agGERD grew substantially faster than spending on GERD, such that the food and agricultural share of total R&D spending peaked in 1977 at 4.2 percent (vs. 2.5 percent in 1961). Thereafter, GERD grew faster than agGERD, such that by 2015, the food and agricultural share of GERD had reverted to the low point of the early 1960s.

Although the food and agricultural share of GERD has gradually declined over recent decades, the food and agricultural sector continues to invest more intensively in R&D than does the US economy as a whole. Investments in food and agricultural R&D when expressed relative to agGDP grew steadily from just 0.7 percent in 1950 to a peak of 9.2 percent in 2002, shrinking thereafter to 7.7 percent in 2015 (figure 3.6). At 2.75 percent in 2015, the economywide intensity of R&D investments in the US was one-third of

Panel A. GERD

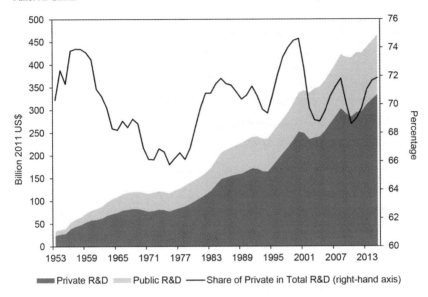

Panel B. AgGERD

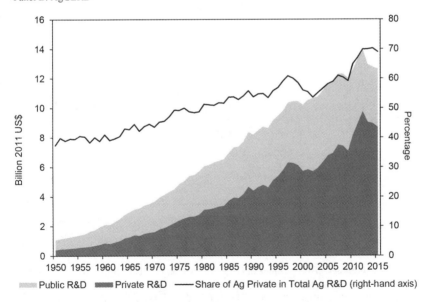

Fig. 3.5   GERD vs. agGERD spending trends, 1950–2015

Source: GERD data are from NSF (2019); AgGERD data are from InSTePP International Innovation Accounts: Research and Development Spending (2019).

Note: Public GERD include R&D expenditures from federal, nonfederal, higher education and other nonprofit organization.

Panel A. GERD, BERD, and PERD as a share of GDP

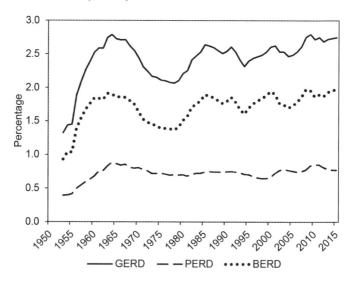

Panel B. AgGERD, AgBERD, and AgPERD as a share of AgGDP

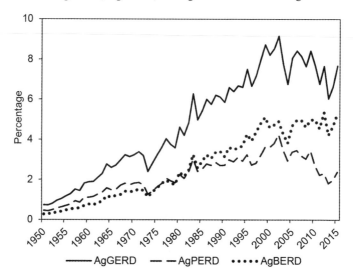

Fig. 3.6   Intensity of investment in GERD versus agGERD, 1950–2015

Source: GERD (total), BERD (business) and PERD (public) R&D spending data are from National Science Board (2018); AgGERD, AgBERD and AgPERD data are from InSTePP International Innovation Accounts: Research and Development Spending (2019); GDP data are authors' compilation based on data from United Nations Statistics Division (2017), World Bank (2017), and Johnston and Williamson (2017); AgGDP data are authors' compilation based on data from United Nations Statistics Division (2017), and Bureau of Economic Analysis (2017).

the corresponding food and agricultural research intensity, and it was roughly equivalent to the intensity of GERD investment that prevailed half a century earlier (i.e., 2.79 percent in 1964).

3.4.2 Private vs. Public Research

The private sector has long accounted for a significant share of US GERD, averaging 70.2 percent of the total since 1953, albeit with a period during the 1960s and 1970s when the share of private R&D investments fell to a low of 65.7 percent in 1975 (figure 3.5, panel A). While the private share of US agGERD (70.0 percent in 2015) is now roughly in line with the private share of research overall, this is a relatively recent development, with the private sector accounting for just over one-third of US agGERD in the early 1950s (figure 3.5, panel B).

Changes in the scope of US IP protection were associated with a rise in agricultural innovations coming from the corporate sector. Mechanical, chemical, storage, transport, and processing inventions pertinent to food and agriculture have long been subject to patent protection (as well as copyright, trademark, trade secrecy, and eventually other legal means) enabled by Article 1, Section 8 of the US Constitution that became operational on March 4, 1789. However, little protection was afforded biological inventions, such as new crop varieties (likewise for genetics-related innovations in the health sector). Trademarks and trade secrecy laws were applicable, but these did not protect against reverse engineering or self-replication, and so the common practice of saving seeds for own reuse—or for sharing with other farmers or selling to them—did not constitute legal infringement of new seed varieties.

In 1930, legal forms of plant varietal rights were first introduced in the US, and the corporate share of such rights issued rose from 55 percent in the 1930s and 1940s to 82 percent by 2008 (Pardey et al. 2013). The 1930 Plant Patent Act covers asexually reproduced plants, a category that largely encompasses ornamental plants and fruits. Sexually reproduced crops, a category that includes grains, oilseed crops, and grasses, gained IP protection in 1970 by way of the Plant Variety Protection Act (PVPA). A third form of protection became possible in 1980 with Diamond v. Chakrabarty, in which the US Supreme Court narrowly found that "anything under the sun that is made by man" is patentable subject matter (Wright et al. 2007). In practice, this case and subsequent legal rulings clarified that plant varieties, parts of plants, genetically engineered organisms, and gene products themselves were eligible for the same US utility patents that cover most other inventions.

This IP landscape evolved hand-in-hand with important changes in the genetics and genomics sciences that support crop varietal development— notably, mechanical (Taylor and Fauquet 2002) and bacterial (Gelvin 2003) means of manipulating genes to produce genetically engineered crops, as well as more recent, more precise, and more cost-effective means to edit genes, such as TALEN and Crisper-Cas9 technologies (Baltes, Gil-Humanes, and Voytas 2017). Legislative and legal changes that gathered momentum in the 1970s and 1980s (Pardey et al. 2013) preceded a substantial rise in the amount of private research oriented toward biological innovations during the subsequent decades by such firms as Monsanto (acquired by Bayer in June 2018) and Pioneer-Dupont (now Corteva Agrisciences).

In addition, over the past 50 years, food, beverage, and tobacco processing and manufacturing R&D has continued to be a big part of total US private spending on agGERD (averaging 42.2 percent over the past two decades) as industry has sought to respond to changing consumer demands, including an increase in the share of food and beverages consumed away from home and the desire for prepared foods and those packaged in more convenient forms (see figure 3.4).

Notably, the more expansive IP protection afforded the food and agricultural sector in the past few decades was associated with a continuing increase (albeit at a slower rate) in the intensity of private food and agricultural R&D, while the intensity of public agGERD has trended down over the past 15 years (see figure 3.6, panel B). In contrast, the intensity of public GERD has changed little since the mid-1960s, such that most of the increase in overall GERD intensity since the late 1970s is attributable to an upward trend in the intensity of private investments in R&D (see figure 3.6, panel A).

These overall intensities mask considerable differences among sectors in the intensity of R&D investment by private firms. Table 3.2 reports aggregate firm sales and R&D spending data grouped into sectors, along with their corresponding intensity of investments (here measured relative to their net domestic sales). Pharmaceutical and medical firms, on average, spent $12.9 on R&D for every $100 of sales in 2015, while chemical companies averaged $6.7 and information-related companies $5.9, making them the three most R&D-intensive sectors in the National Science Foundation compilation. The InSTePP compilation of data on 132 firms undertaking research related to food and agriculture has an R&D intensity that averages 1.2 percent in 2014 (Lee et al. 2021).[11] But the intensity of research varied markedly among categories of firms in that sector. Although total sales for food companies were more than double those of agricultural companies in 2014, food companies invested less in R&D such that their intensity ratios averaged just 0.7 percent, versus 2.6 percent for agriculture-related companies. Nonetheless, these data place food companies on par with "other nonmanufacturing companies" in terms of their R&D intensities, while the intensity of research investments by agricultural companies exceeds those of the automobile, other manufacturing, other chemical, and finance sectors.

While the increasing investments in innovation by private (food and agri-

---

11. InSTePP is the International Science and Technology Practice and Policy center at the University of Minnesota, details of which are at www.instepp.umn.edu.

Table 3.2   **Company sales and R&D intensity, 2015**

	Sales ($ millions)	R&D expenditures ($ millions)	R&D intensity (percentage)
Manufacturing industries	**5,358,542**	**235,776**	**4.4**
Chemicals	1,023,512	68,575	6.7
Pharmaceuticals and medicines	456,424	58,879	12.9
Others	567,088	9,640	1.7
Machinery	360,719	13,347	3.7
Automobiles, trailers and parts	795,662	19,096	2.4
Others	1,901,685	28,525	1.5
Nonmanufacturing industries	**3,691,358**	**118,123**	**3.2**
Information	1,105,520	65,226	5.9
Finance and insurance	709,990	5,680	0.8
Others	1,453,882	10,177	0.7
All industries	**9,049,901**	**352,946**	**3.9**
Food and agriculture	**767,857**	**9,447**	**1.2**
Food	554,237	3,821	0.7
Agriculture (machinery, chemicals and biology)	213,620	5,626	2.6

Sources: Manufacturing, non-manufacturing and all industries data are from National Science Board (2018, Table 4.10); Food and Agriculture data are from Lee et al. (2021) taken from InSTePP International Innovation Accounts: Research and Development Spending (2019).

Notes: Sales from manufacturing and non-manufacturing industries includes domestic net sales of companies that perform or fund R&D, transfers to foreign subsidiaries, and export sales to foreign companies; excludes intracompany transfers and sales by foreign subsidiaries. R&D intensity from manufacturing and non-manufacturing industries represents domestic R&D paid for by the company and others, and performed by the company, divided by domestic net sales.

cultural) firms have obviated the need for some public research, much of the private research stands firmly on the shoulders of publicly performed research.[12] The different roles played by public and private research are revealed to some extent by the large differences in the composition of the research performed by the two sectors. Around 41 percent of the agGERD performed by the public sector during 2016–2018 was considered "basic" research (USDA-CRIS 2020), where the notional objective is the pursuit of new knowledge or ideas without specific applications in mind (OECD 2015, p. 29). This squares with the "basic" research share (44 percent in 2015) of public GERD (National Science Board 2018, table 4-3). Another 48 percent of public GERD in 2015 was classified as "applied," or research done to meet a specific need, the same as the applied share of public agGERD in 2016–2018. Only 12 percent of GERD was deemed "developmental" (versus 11 percent of agGERD) and directed toward the production of specific products and processes with nearer-term commercial potential. In con-

12. See Fuglie and Schimmelpfennig (2000) and Pardey and Beddow (2013) for examples of public-private research complementarities in the food and agricultural sector.

trast, 78 percent of private GERD was developmental in nature, intended to develop prototypes, new processes, or products for commercialization, with only 16 percent of private research considered applied and 6 percent basic.

3.4.3   International Dimensions of US Research

In 1960, the US accounted for 18.6 percent of the entire world's expenditures on publicly performed food and agricultural R&D. But by 2015, that share had shrunk to 9.4 percent, and the US was eclipsed by China, which by 2013 had begun outspending the US on both public and private food and agricultural research (Chai et al. 2019). Part of this shifting research geography reflects policy choices in the US vs. those in China and other countries—especially other large agricultural economies, such as Brazil and India—regarding public spending and other forms of legislative support for agricultural R&D. These changing international R&D relativities also reflect more fundamental economic forces shaped by major changes in the economic geography of agriculture itself (Pardey et al. 2016b).

In 1961, the US accounted for 14.8 percent by value of the world's agricultural output, compared with China's 8.5 percent. Less than six decades later, the tables had turned. The US share of global agricultural production had declined to 10.0 percent in 2016, while China now accounted for almost one-quarter (23.7 percent) of the total, propelled by historically unprecedented and sustained rates of growth in Chinese agricultural production and productivity. These Chinese agricultural developments were enabled by several radical institutional reforms beginning in the late 1970s; notably, the introduction of the household responsibility system for farming that incentivized farmers to increase output and spurred the off-farm migration of labor (J. Lin 1992), and the doubling down on investments in agricultural R&D (Chai et al. 2019). Meanwhile, the US government first slowed growth in agricultural R&D and then of late has scaled back public support for it.

These shifts in the global landscape for food and agricultural R&D also paralleled broader changes in the world's economic geography and the country composition of global GERD. In 1980, the US accounted for 19.8 percent of the world's $6.4 trillion (2009 PPP prices) GDP, compared with 2.1 percent for China. By 2014, the global GDP had grown to $99.3 trillion, but the US share had shrunk to 16.2 percent and China's had grown to 16.9 percent. Dehmer et al. (2019) estimated that over the period, global GERD grew from $0.48 trillion in 1980 to $1.67 trillion in 2014 (2009 PPP prices), and of this total, the US share declined a little from 31.2 to 27.0 percent, while China's share increased dramatically from 1.2 to 20.0 percent.

Where in the rest-of-the-world agricultural R&D takes place matters as much as the amount and type of research conducted in the US for the innovative future of US agriculture. Just as genetic innovations conceived in the health sector have benefited agriculture (and vice versa), rest-of-world agricultural knowledge stocks have spatial spillover consequences for US agriculture (see, e.g., Clancy et al. 2020). However, location matters more for agriculture, and many agricultural innovations are site specific. Consequently, taking wheat as an example, research targeted for agroecologies (or production systems) that are agroecologically distant from current or prospective wheat areas in the US are likely to be less consequential for wheat innovation in the US than if they were targeted to US agroecologies.[13] Thus, with an increasing share of the world's agricultural research taking place outside the US, the global stock of scientific knowledge can be expected to have less relevance for innovations within US production agriculture in the decades ahead relative to decades past.[14]

3.5 Payoffs to Investments in Agricultural Innovation

In the economic evidence on the payoffs to investment in R&D, various summary statistics have been used to summarize the streams of costs and benefits associated with R&D activities that typically take (sometimes considerable) time for the research to be conducted, and years if not decades for the resulting innovations to be diffused and realize their full economic consequences. For the most part, however, the internal rate of return (IRR) has been used as the statistic of choice. This is true, for example, for researchers summarizing the economic consequences of manufacturing R&D (see the tabulation in Hall, Mairesse, and Mohnen 2010, table 2) and health-related research (e.g., Deloitte Centre for Health Solutions 2014; Glover et al. 2014; HERG, OHE, and Rand Europe 2008). Notwithstanding Griliches' (1958) objection to the use of IRRs in this context, it is also the preferred summary statistic for the now extensive literature on the returns to agricultural R&D, which he initiated.[15]

The InSTePP agricultural returns-to-research database (version 3)

---

13. At any given time, hundreds of different wheat varieties are being grown or bred that are adapted to specific agroecologies, and the productive potential of any particular variety of wheat varies greatly, depending on where in the world, precisely, that variety is to be grown.

14. As discussed by Alston (2002) and emphasized by Alston et al. (2010), agricultural technology spillovers are significant, and they run in both directions, though not always symmetrically or spontaneously. Cognizant of this fact, private foundations based in the US together with the US government led the funding (as well as the founding) of the system of international agricultural research centers now known as the CGIAR. This institutional innovation was conceived for essentially humanitarian purposes to address the global food crisis of the 1960s and was a primary source of the so-called "Green Revolution" technologies (see, e.g., Alston et al. 2006 and Wright 2012). It reduced but did not eliminate a global market failure in agricultural R&D that persists today. The donor countries also benefited by adopting the resulting technologies, as quantified, for example, by Pardey et al. (1996) in relation to the spill-ins of CGIAR crop varietal technologies into the US. See also Alston, Pardey, and Rao (2020).

15. With reference to using the IRR as a summary returns-to-research measure, Griliches (1958, p. 425) wrote "My objection to this procedure is that it values a dollar spent in 1910 at $2,300 in 1933. This does not seem very sensible to me. I prefer to value a 1910 dollar at a reasonable rate of return on some alternative social investment."

includes 3,426 rate-of-return estimates gleaned from 492 studies worldwide, of which 1,298 (37.9 percent) of the estimates evaluate research conducted in the US (Rao, Hurley, and Pardey 2019a). Among the US estimates, 76 percent (986 estimates) report IRRs, while 24 percent (312) report benefit-cost ratios (BCRs) (table 3.3). Given the wide dispersion and positive skewness in the distribution of the reported rates of return, the median is a more informative measure of the central tendency than the mean. The median of the reported IRRs for US agricultural R&D is 31.9 percent per year, and the median of the reported BCRs is 12.0, roughly in line with the corresponding medians for the reported rest-of-world evidence.[16]

Although the IRR is merely a breakeven interest rate, equating the present values of costs and benefits, many policymakers (and even some economists!) treat IRRs as compounding rates of interest, analogous and comparable to the returns reported for financial products (e.g., mortgages, mutual funds, and certificates of deposit). However, Hurley, Rao, and Pardey (2014) showed that such an interpretation is generally incorrect and often leads to incredible implications.[17] They also pointed out how the modified internal rate of return, MIRR (A. Lin 1976), offers an alternative to the IRR that can be reasonably interpreted as an annual percentage rate of return.

Hurley, Rao, and Pardey (2014, 2017) provide a detailed account of the properties of MIRRs and the implicit (often undesirable) assumptions made in the calculation of IRRs, especially in the returns-to-research context. One of the desirable properties of an MIRR is its one-to-one correspondence with a BCR if a common discount rate and research timeline are used to calculate the rates of return for different projects. Using the BCR-IRR relationship elucidated by Hurley, Rao, and Pardey (2014), Rao, Hurley, and Pardey (2019b) recalibrated the reported IRRs into a standardized set of imputed BCRs and MIRRs, where the discount rates and research timelines are held constant, thus improving comparability among the estimates. Table 3.3 presents these imputed BCRs and MIRRs for the United States and the rest-of-world using a common discount rate of 5 percent and a research evaluation timeline (from the initiation of costs to the cessation of benefits) of 30 years, roughly the average timeline of the reported evidence. These results indicate a median BCR of 7.5 for investments in US agricultural R&D, corresponding to a MIRR of 12.3 percent per year. The comparable median rest-of-world estimates are a BCR of 9.0 and a MIRR of 13.0 per-

16. However, such direct comparisons of broad aggregates are of limited value, given differences in the nature of the evidence across countries and over time in terms of what commodities and types of research are being evaluated, and the details of the evaluation methods (Rao, Hurley, and Pardey 2019a).

17. As Alston et al. (2011, pp. 1271–72) showed, "if the roughly $4 billion invested in public agricultural R&D in 2005 earned a return of 50% per annum compounding over 35 years, by 2040 the accumulated benefits would be worth $5,824,000 billion (2000 prices)—more than 100 times the projected US GDP in 2040 and more than 10 times the projected global GDP in 2040."

Table 3.3   Returns to agricultural R&D

		Number of		Values			
	Units	Studies	Estimates	10th percentile	Mean	Median	90th percentile
Reported data							
United States							
Internal rate of return	Percent per year	80	986	12.5	63.0	31.9	101.2
Benefit-cost ratio	Ratio	21	312	0.5	19.3	12.0	45.0
Rest of world							
Internal rate of return	Percent per year	381	1,641	16.0	57.6	41.2	101.0
Benefit-cost ratio	Ratio	147	487	1.7	31.4	12.1	69.6
Imputed data							
United States							
Benefit-cost ratio	Ratio	66	796	2.1	34.4	7.5	44.6
Modified internal rate of return	Percent per year	66	796	7.7	11.4	12.3	19.2
Rest of world							
Benefit-cost ratio	Ratio	345	1,330	2.6	25.7	9.0	57.3
Modified internal rate of return	Percent per year	345	1,330	8.4	13.6	13.0	20.2

Sources: Derived from InSTePP compilation used by Rao, Hurley, and Parday (2019a,b).

cent per year. These estimates are indicative of a sustained and substantial underinvestment in agricultural science both in the US and globally. In spite of this government failure on top of market failure, innovation in US agriculture has accomplished a great deal and has contributed positively to global agricultural growth and change.

3.6   Clusters of Innovation in US Agriculture

Pardey and Alston (2021) discuss and document a century of transformative change in US agriculture (1910–2007), in which they pay particular attention to the potential sources of a mid-century (1950s–1980s) surge and subsequent slowdown in farm productivity growth. They liken this farm productivity pattern to the earlier surge and slowdown in the broader economy identified by Gordon (2000, 2016), which he associated with great "clusters of inventions."[18] Borrowing those ideas and in a similar spirit, Pardey and Alston (2021) suggest that much of the past time path of US agricultural input use, production, productivity, and prices can be understood in terms of clusters of agricultural inventions and the structural changes in the farm economy they enabled, including (1) "mechanical" (mostly labor-saving) technologies; (2) improved animal breeds and crop varieties and other "biological" innovations; (3) synthetic fertilizers, pesticides, and other "chemical" technologies; and more recently, (4) "information" technologies. All of these were employed in conjunction with ever-evolving knowledge and improved understanding of and changes in agricultural production and practices. This section builds on the discussion of innovation clusters by Pardey and Alston (2021), paying greater attention to the more recent period while placing the newer innovations in a longer-run historical context.

Mechanization played a large early role in the twentieth century transformation of US agriculture. As well as much human labor, machines saved considerable amounts of land from having to be used to produce feed for horses and mules, and they facilitated the consolidation of farms into many fewer and larger units. The tractor in particular saved millions of acres of land and the work of many men and women. In 1910, the US had a total of 6.4 million farmers, farming 881 million acres using a total of 24 million horses and mules and just 1,000 tractors. After its peak in 1917 at 27 million animals, the stock of work horses and mules on US farms dropped eventu-

---

18. Rasmussen (1962) had a similar notion of technological clusters or sequential technological revolutions driving the arc of history regarding US agriculture, noting that up to the time of his writing: "Two revolutions in American agriculture reflect the impact of technological change on farming during the past century. The first revolution saw the change from manpower to animal power, and centered about the Civil War. The second revolution saw the change from animal power to mechanical power and the adaptation of chemistry to agricultural production. It centered around the post-World War II period. The transition from animal power to mechanical power is virtually complete" (Rasmussen, 1962, p. 578).

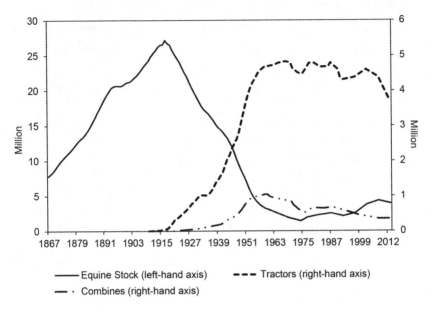

Fig. 3.7   **American agricultural mechanization, 1867–2012**
Source: Pardey and Alston (2021, figure 4).
Note: See Alston et al. (2010, p. 29) for notes on equine stock.

ally to a low of 1.4 million in 1974 (figure 3.7). Meanwhile, from just 50,000 tractors in 1917, the total grew to 4.5 million tractors in 1957.

Along with tractors, farmers also adopted automobiles and motor trucks that were not developed specifically or exclusively for agriculture, as well as other machines that were useful only in agriculture, such as reapers, mowers, binders, and combines (figure 3.8, panel A). To a great extent, this was a private-sector process, in which many of the innovations were patented technologies embodied in tractors and related machines produced privately and sold to farmers. Public agricultural (and other) R&D was complementary but played a minor role here compared with its role in other types of innovations, such as new crop varieties and farming systems.

As can be seen in panel A of figure 3.8, biological innovations, in particular improved crop varieties that were responsive to chemical fertilizers, took center stage a little later—although they were clearly part of the story all along (Olmstead and Rhode 2008). For example, hybrid corn varieties were adopted rapidly in Iowa in the early 1930s, but it took until the 1960s for vastly improved hybrids to achieve 100 percent adoption throughout the US (Dixon 1980; Griliches 1957; Hallauer and Miranda 1981). Varietal improvement has continued for corn and other crops, including food crops, such as wheat and rice, for which public investments have been more

Panel A. Mechanical, chemical and conventional genetic improvement technologies

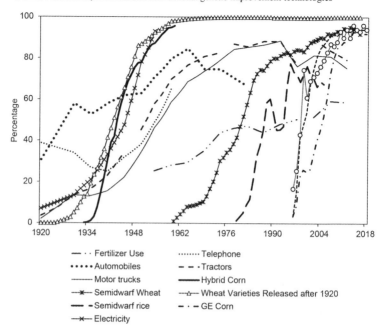

Fig. 3.8   Waves of technological adoption in US agriculture

Source: Mechanical, infrastructure and fertilizer data were developed by authors based on estimates from the US Census of Agriculture (US Bureau of Census and USDA-NASS, various years). Data for intercensus years were linearly interpolated. Data on hybrid corn are from Alston et al. (2010); GE soybeans, GE corn, and GE cotton data are from Alston et al. (2010) and USDA-NASS "June Agricultural Survey" (available at www.ers.usda.gov/data-products /adoption-of-genetically-engineered-crops-in-the-us/). Semidwarf wheat and rice areas and area of wheat varieties released after 1920 are unpublished data from InSTePP. Estimated precision agriculture technologies cropland area shares are from Erickson et al. (2017).

Note: For automobiles, motor trucks, tractors, electricity, and telephone, the data represent the shares of farms using the designated technology. For hybrid corn, semidwarf rice, semidwarf wheat, GE soybeans and GE corn, the data represent the shares of area planted to the designated technology. For fertilizer, the data represent the share of cropland with fertilizer application. For precision agriculture technologies (autosteer, yield monitor with GPS, grid/zone soil sampling, satellite or areal imagery, VRT nutrient application, and VRT seeding prescription) data represent the share of the market area of various precision ag technologies used by farmers.

Tractors: From 1920 to 1945, tractors include wheel, crawler, and garden; from 1950 to 1969, tractors include wheel and crawler; from 1978 to 1997, tractors include wheel tractor only; from 2002 to 2012, tractors include wheel and crawler.

Automobiles: Details concerning the sudden and sustained drop in the number of automobiles in 1969 are reported in US Bureau of Census (1973, p. 11).

Fertilizer: From 1954 to 1997 fertilizer do not include lime whereas from 2002 to 2012 lime is included. Manure is excluded in all years. From 1978 to 2012, acres on which fertilizers were applied are reported for cropland only, pastureland, and total (i.e., cropland and pastureland). In 1959, 1964, 1969 and 1974 however, data were reported for pastureland and total acres fertilized. Thus, acres of cropland fertilized were estimated for those years by subtracting acres of pastureland fertilized from total acres fertilized. In 1954, only data on total acres fertilized was available. Thus, we estimated the area of cropland fertilized in 1954 by applying the share of cropland fertilized in 1959 to the 1954 cropland area.

Panel B. Modern genetic transformation technologies and precision agriculture technologies

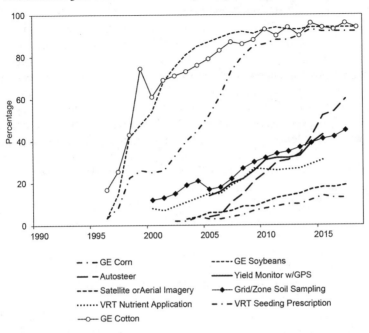

Fig. 3.8   (cont.)

important. These innovations, with others, laid the foundation for genetically engineered (GE) hybrid corn varieties to be developed and adopted, beginning in 1996 (Fernandez-Cornejo et al. 2014). Similar, though typically less dramatic genetic innovations were common to many agricultural crop and livestock species, and they contributed to the rapid rise of yields and aggregate productivity during the second half of the twentieth century (Olmstead and Rhode 2008).

Chemical technologies for agriculture became more important beginning in the 1960s. In particular, the early twentieth-century invention of the Haber-Bosch process for the economical manufacturing of synthetic nitrogen fertilizer was profoundly important for enhanced crop yields, especially when combined with complementary genetics and crop management practices. The US on-farm adoption process for these fertilizers and associated varieties was notable in the 1960s and 1970s. Partly as a post-war dividend, synthetic pesticide technologies took off around the same time, soon to become subject to environmental regulation following the publication of Rachel Carson's *Silent Spring* (1962). A great many forms of agricultural chemical technologies have been developed, registered, and approved for commercial use, and they have been adopted by farmers (and in many cases, subsequently deregistered or heavily regulated and disadopted)—including fertilizers, growth promotants, herbicides, fungicides, insecticides, and antibiotics and other veterinary medicines.

More recently, GE crop varieties have been developed that could serve as better complements to or substitutes for these chemical technologies. Predominant among these are herbicide tolerant (HT) varieties of cotton, corn, soybeans, and canola, which permit herbicides to replace mechanical tillage for weed control, and pesticide inherent (PI) varieties (e.g., Bt cotton and corn) that reduce (or eliminate) requirements for chemical pesticides for controlling specific pests. These technologies tend to predominate where they are available for adoption and confer significant benefits to farmers, consumers, and technology firms (see, e.g., Fernandez-Cornejo et al. 2014; Qaim 2016). Furthermore, HT technologies are complementary to conservation tillage practices (Perry, Moschini, and Hennessy 2016), such that minimum-till and no-till systems are now used on a majority of acres of US wheat (67 percent in 2017), corn (65 percent in 2016), and soybeans (70 percent in 2012) (Claassen et al. 2018). Conservation tillage practices reap their own rewards in terms of reduced soil compaction, improved water infiltration (and reduced runoff), promotion of soil fauna and biological processes, and increased soil organic matter, most of which have beneficial agricultural production and environmental outcomes.[19]

To date, however, GE varieties have been developed and adopted widely for only a few crops (in particular, soybeans, cotton, corn, canola, and papaya) and only in a few countries (Qaim 2016). This reflects a combination of regulatory and market resistance, which has discouraged the development of technologies for these and other applications in the countries that are open to GE technologies; more so in those that are opposed. The US is predominant both as a developer and adopter, but even there, the regulatory barriers are substantial, adding years of delay and hundreds of millions of dollars in costs (see, e.g., Kalaitzandonakes, Alston, and Bradford 2006).[20] Panel B of figure 3.8 displays the US adoption paths for GE varieties of corn and soybeans on a truncated time scale, where they can be juxtaposed with adoption paths for digital (and related information) technologies used in US crop production in the modern era. This panel captures key elements of the

19. Changes in the emphasis of agricultural innovation might have changed the requirements for maintenance research as a share of total research, since the Red Queen effect applies particularly to genetic and chemical pest- and disease-management technologies, and less so to mechanical or digital innovations. This might help account for the mid-twentieth-century surge (associated with adoption of mechanical innovations) in US farm productivity and the subsequent slowdown (during the decades emphasizing chemical and biological innovation). In this respect, digital technologies may be more like mechanical technologies, although rapid (planned) obsolescence is a predominant feature in much of digital technology.

20. Compared with the earlier path for hybrid corn, these paths are shorter, reflecting the advantages of modern science and communications technologies, but once we allow for an additional decade of regulatory lags, the overall post-research development and adoption process is still on the order of 20 years for these technologies—like hybrid corn in Iowa, six decades previously.

current innovative landscape for agriculture, emphasizing genetic innovation and other data-intensive technologies.

Digital farming technologies (including "precision agriculture" or "variable rate" technologies), which help farmers gather information and adjust production practices according to changes in field conditions over space and time, are beginning to gain ground in US farm production. Major examples include global positioning system (GPS)-based remote-sensing and guidance systems, soil and yield mapping based on GPS (perhaps in conjunction with satellite and aerial photography), and variable-rate technology (VRT) (Jia et al. 2019; Lowenberg-DeBoer and Erickson 2019).

Field operators can use GPS guidance systems to auto-steer tractors, combines, and other machines, which helps pinpoint precise field locations and reduce operator fatigue (Schimmelpfennig 2016). Precision technologies can also help farm operators map their fields better. Yield monitors mounted on harvesters can be used to record data on yields with GPS coordinates that the operator can use to monitor changes in crop yield across the field and from year to year. These data can be combined with data from soil maps using related technology—based on core samples or soil sensors that use electrical conductivity to test soil—to better understand the sources of yield variation and act on the information. And VRT allows farmers to customize the application of irrigation water, fertilizer, chemicals, and pesticides spatially and over time using data from remote sensors or GPS data—often from yield and soil maps or guidance systems. Farmers can even use VRT to plant different types of seeds or to apply different agricultural chemicals at different rates at different locations with a single pass of the tractor. And, looking forward, these technologies will be used to allow precise mechanical or chemical weeding and cultivation around individual plants, among other things.

Panel B of figure 3.8 includes adoption curves for six types of technology in this context, as well as three types of GE crops (corn, cotton, and soybeans). The plots for the GE crops start earlier and rise more rapidly. By 2006, GE varieties had already been adopted on 61 percent of corn, 83 percent of cotton, and 89 percent of soybean acres. In contrast, the adoption curves for most of the digital and related precision farming technologies are much flatter. Autosteer technology, which was first introduced around the same time as the GE crop varieties, was used on 60 percent of acres in 2015, while the other digital technologies were less widely adopted.

As discussed by Schimmelpfennig (2016), some of these technologies are simple to adopt and easy to use, while others may come at a relatively high cost in terms of requiring specialized equipment or specific skills. These factors, along with functionality, have contributed to the differences observed in the rate of development and adoption of these technologies. Many of these tools are knowledge and skill intensive, and their profitable use requires location-, application-, and site-specific adaptation, all of which takes time to work out. Primarily, their limited use to date reflects the fact that it is still early days for many of these technologies in terms of matching data to models and real-time processing of very large data sets, engineering the machinery to go with the data and knowledge, and software development. The technologies themselves have been changing rapidly, and the prospects are very bright.

In some cases, we can understand the differences in adoption rates in terms of the nature of the technology as it relates to the factors mentioned by Schimmelpfennig (2016). For example, adoption of GE seeds did not require any significant investment in new knowledge (instead, in some ways, the technology replaced a requirement for knowledge about pest management with pest-management-inherent seeds). Nor did it require any new equipment or new business relationships; it was a routine transition in an environment where farmers were used to adopting new hybrids reasonably often. The benefits were reasonably clear, the costs of change were small, and the benefit-cost calculus was straightforward—facilitated by much opportunity to begin small and observe neighbors and learn from their experience. However, the subsequent (implied) transition from conventional cropping to lo-till and no-till enabled by GE varieties took considerably longer, because it required sometimes considerable own-farm-specific learning-by-doing about what works and what does not, which can be a time-intensive process.

Likewise, autosteer is a relatively simple technology and easy to learn to use (like GE seed, it replaces a more difficult technology with a simpler one), and the benefit-cost calculus is reasonably straightforward. However, the same is not true for many other digital technologies. Some may require very significant up-front investment in physical capital and acquisition of technical know-how (and thus implying large economies of size) to make use of a technology for which the benefits might be quite uncertain or where the technology landscape is changing rapidly, so that even better options may become available soon. It is also pertinent to note that in 2017, the average age of farmers was 57.5 years (USDA-NASS 2019). Other things being equal, older farmers are less likely to adopt innovations generally (Feder and Umali 1993) and perhaps more so for digital versus more traditional technologies with which they may be more comfortable.

Schimmelpfennig and Ebel (2016, p. 97) propose an additional possible explanation for sluggish adoption, if potentially complementary technologies are adopted and worked into production practices sequentially: "The one-technology-at-a-time approach to adoption may seem inefficient and time-consuming compared to adoption of complete, possibly complementary, packages of technologies, but this scheme has been shown to occur in other settings." If one part of the package is seen as costly or risky to adopt, this might have implications for the rates of adoption of other elements that are less useful alone.

In addition to these types of technologies, which are most apparent in the context of major field crops, other types of digital technologies are being developed and used in the context of specialty crops or livestock production, as well as field crops. For example, in crop production, automated irrigation systems based on sensors that measure precipitation, evapotranspiration, and soil moisture in the root zone are used to improve the efficiency of water use and save labor; these are in their early stages of adoption. USDA-ERS (2019b) report that "fewer than 10 percent of irrigators make use of soil- or plant-moisture sensing devices or commercial irrigation scheduling services [and less than] 2 percent make use of computer-based simulation models to determine irrigation requirements based on consumptive-use needs by crop-growth stage under local weather conditions."

Autonomous or articulated weeding machines are under development, and some are already being used in farmers' fields (see, e.g., BlueRiver Technology 2020). These include machines that can selectively spray or physically cut out weeds based on GPS references or computer vision (or image identification) technologies, thereby saving labor and reducing the environmental burden of herbicide (see, e.g., Fennimore and Cutulle 2019; Filmer 2019). Drones and other self-driving machines fitted with cameras, sniffers, and other types of sensors are being developed and deployed to monitor the crop for drought and other stresses and check for pests and diseases. Analogous sensing technologies are being developed for monitoring soil nutrient (see, e.g., Teralytic 2020) and health status, including soil microbiome activity. Robotic and other devices fitted with sensors are also being developed and deployed to selectively harvest crops (e.g., apples, strawberries) with variable maturation dates.

In livestock production, digital technologies are already widely used, and their use is progressing. For example, companies such as Lely (2020) have already commercialized robotic milking machines and digital cow tag systems that can be used to monitor and help manage animal health and feeding status for dairy cows.[21] As with crop production, "smart" livestock production technologies involve precision technologies and variable rate technologies, where the unit of observation now becomes the individual animal. Using modern information technology, farmers now can monitor and record details of numerous attributes of each animal, including its health status, its consumption of feed and other inputs, and its productivity and reproductive performance. These data can be collected and interpreted using machine learning and other processes in ways that make the information economically useful and permit better livestock management and more profitable decisions, with respect to both individual animals and the entire herd or

21. For example, an active smart ear tag can get data from individual animals, such as temperature and activity patterns, which can be used to identify illness, heat stress, estrous, and so on, and to enable livestock producers to identify sick animals sooner and more accurately. This early detection leads to reduction in costs by lowering retreatment rate and death loss and by getting animals back to peak performance faster.

flock. Decisions regarding optimal culling age and feeding regimes can now be individualized based on individualized performance measures, such as fertility, yield of meat (or milk), quality of meat (or milk), feed-conversion efficiency, and their implications for profitability. Other precision livestock technologies serve to save labor and perform tasks more precisely, such as robotic milkers and automated feeders, and climate control technologies for housed livestock.

Growing from "just" $2.6 billion in 2012, new agrifood startup companies attracted $16.6 billion of investments worldwide in 2018 (AgFunder 2018, p. 15).[22] The US accounted for $7.9 billion (48 percent) of the total, China $3.5 billion (21 percent), and India $2.4 billion (14 percent). Startups based in California accounted for almost one-third of global investment and two-thirds of all US investment; the number rises to 92 percent of the US total if funding to firms located in Massachusetts, New York, North Carolina, Colorado, and Minnesota are also included. Some $6.9 billion (41.5 percent of the global total) went to investments in startups closer to the farmer—spanning such areas as soil testing, pest detection, precision agriculture, digital agricultural management, agronomic data, and predictive analytics. The remaining $9.7 billion went to firms focused on the off- (or vertical-) farm segments—including food processing and production companies (such as Impossible Foods, Zymergen, and Bowery Farming Inc.) and, especially, food delivery companies (such as Instacart and DoorDash).

3.7   The Next Wave of Agricultural Innovation: Ripple or Tsunami?

Looking forward, we can see great potential for new product and process innovations—in particular, digital and other data- and knowledge-intensive technologies, including genetic innovations—that will enable more and better food, fiber, and industrial raw materials to be produced on farms at much lower cost and with a smaller environmental footprint, worldwide. Realizing this potential will matter for the future trajectory of global public goods, including climate change, other natural resource stocks, the world food equation, poverty, and related civil or military strife. The extent to which these opportunities will be captured, and when, will be determined to a great extent by forces outside agriculture and outside the R&D and technology sector. These forces will determine the availability and direction of resources available for public-sector agricultural R&D; the regulations and rules governing the development, deployment, and adoption of new

---

22. Other studies, such as Graff, de Figueiredo Silva, and Zilberman (2021), provide alternative quantification and discussion of venture capital investments in (R&D intensive) agriculture startups, developed for different purposes. Not all the venture capital being invested in these (technology-oriented) companies is necessarily directed to activities that are consistent with R&D measures reported in this chapter. Some of the funds are also invested in market development, promotion, and related business activities, so that only some (and often an unknown) fraction of the venture capital total is spent on R&D per se.

farm and food technologies; and the demand for products depending on the technologies used to produce them.

3.7.1   Induced Innovation

As noted above, agriculture is unusual in that it faces knowledge deprecia-tion arising from climate change and, in particular, the coevolution of pests and diseases. This gives rise to a demand for maintenance R&D—simply to preserve past productivity gains. Much of the past work on crop varietal innovations can be seen in this light. The demand for innovation on farms is also driven by (1) changing factor supply conditions; (2) evolving demand for farm products (now including feedstock for biofuels and other indus-trial raw materials as well as traditional feed, food, and fiber); and (3) the peculiar regulatory environment for agriculture related to issues including varietal technologies, animal welfare in livestock production, and landscape amenities (and dis-amenities) from agricultural production. Farmers also face a changing market environment with demands for food products and food production processes mediated through private standards and mass media messages.

Over the long history, a major element of change was labor-saving inno-vation induced by farm labor scarcity. Past labor savings notwithstanding, reliable and timely availability of suitably skilled labor is a major concern of farmers today—especially in California's labor-intensive specialty crops— and they are actively seeking technological alternatives for harvesting, weed-ing, irrigating, and a host of other farm operations as well as post-farm packing and handling.[23] Farmers are also increasingly concerned about the reliability of natural rainfall and irrigation water, with variability and uncertainty in these dimensions exacerbated by climate change. Drought- and heat-tolerant varieties are being developed to mitigate these conse-quences (see, e.g., Cooper et al. 2014 and McFadden et al. 2019 in the case of drought-tolerant corn). Information technologies combined with more precise and selective water delivery systems can reduce total water usage and vulnerability to drought.

Changing technological regulations generate a demand for replacement technologies. In recent years, significant agricultural pesticides have been banned in some jurisdictions and are threatened in others owing to concern about their risks to the environment or human health.[24] These include soil

---

23. Today's farm labor environment with its implications for the demand for labor-saving innovations is reminiscent of the period when the Bracero Program was terminated in 1964, stimulating the rapid deployment and adoption of the mechanical tomato harvester. Olmstead and Martin (1985) analyze the resulting controversy.

24. Donley (2019, p. 1) reports: "There are 72, 17, and 11 pesticides approved for outdoor agricultural applications in the USA that are banned or in the process of complete phase out in the EU, Brazil, and China, respectively. Of the pesticides used in USA agriculture in 2016, 322 million pounds were of pesticides banned in the EU, 26 million pounds were of pesticides banned in Brazil and 40 million pounds were of pesticides banned in China. Pesticides banned in the EU account for more than a quarter of all agricultural pesticide use in the USA."

fumigants (e.g., methyl bromide), insecticides (e.g., neonicotinoids) and herbicides (e.g., glyphosate, aka Roundup®). When significant pesticides are deregistered, farmers demand new solutions. In some cases, the alternative to a banned chemical is another chemical or new genetics, but sometimes it simply means technological regression. For example, Roundup-resistant® varieties of corn, soybeans, and canola, combined with the herbicide glyphosate, permitted the widespread adoption of lo-till or no-till production systems that resulted in significant improvements in soil structure and reduced greenhouse gas emissions. If glyphosate were to be banned in the US and Canada—as it has been (either totally or for selected uses) in some other countries recently—we could expect to see a reversion to older production systems using mechanical tillage for weed control and environmentally less benign herbicides. The pressure will be on to come up with an alternative to glyphosate that will be as effective for farmers and more acceptable to the regulators. This is a serious challenge.

Agriculture has generated various other environmental concerns related to air pollution (including greenhouse gases, particulate matter, and odors from livestock production) and water pollution (including nitrates in groundwater and surface water that give rise to human health and environmental issues). With increasing awareness of these issues, and the likelihood of government intervention in one form or another, demand is growing for alternative technologies that will enable more precise use of inputs and better control of unwanted outputs. Likewise, whether motivated by animal welfare concerns or other issues, new regulations on livestock production practices—such as castration; dehorning; the size and structure of pens for calves, sows, and egg-laying hens; and use of antibiotics and other veterinary medicines—give rise to demand for new technologies.

In many instances, genetic innovations offer promising solutions to the problems created by the changing regulatory environment. However, genetic technologies also are subject to considerable regulatory weight. The science of genetic innovation has improved by leaps and bounds over recent decades, but society has placed arbitrary strictures (unsupported by scientific evidence) on some of the most powerful tools in the toolkit available to the modern-day geneticist. In the US, genetically engineered crop varieties are subject to much greater regulatory control than their conventionally bred counterparts, even though they pose no greater risk to human health or the environment (see, e.g., Qaim 2016). In many other countries, GE crops are effectively banned. More recent innovations, such as gene-editing techniques, promise much greater possibilities for targeted genetic changes in commercial species, but they also might face serious regulatory barriers that could stifle that potential.[25] Some countries have already opted to treat

25. Van Eenennaam (2019) provides a review of the gene-editing targets for cattle, while Baltes, Gil-Humanes, and Voytas (2017) provide an overview of the gene editing opportunities and technical challenges for plant transformations. Qaim (2020) discusses the risk of overregu-

gene-edited varieties as GMOs, subject to severe restrictions (see, e.g., Wight 2018, regarding the European Court of Justice ruling regarding the use of gene editing in the EU).

It is not easy to get a good handle on the innovations in the pipeline or on the drawing board, especially since so much of what is going on is being undertaken privately, and in private—in particular when we talk about digital agriculture but also for some aspects of genetic innovations.[26] As we have discussed, genetic innovation in plants and animals includes the results from conventional breeding (albeit supported by the tools of modern biotechnology, such as marker-assisted breeding), genetic engineering, and gene editing. Much of the emphasis of this work tends to be focused on the main agricultural species and the main production systems, for sound economic reasons. Apart from yield potential, tolerance of abiotic stresses (drought, frost, and heat), and resistance to pests and diseases, crop geneticists are looking for various other agronomic advantages and product quality attributes. In the case of apples and table grapes, for example, fruit quality attributes are an important focus of private and public breeding efforts, and the varieties in use are changing rapidly.[27]

As noted, digital farming innovations (including precision technologies and variable rate technologies) have the potential to save (and also reduce dependence on uncertain supplies of) labor and irrigation water; they also have the potential to save on materials and reduce environmental spillovers associated with fertilizers and pesticides (see, e.g., Schimmelpfennig 2018). Some of these technologies also have the potential to reduce the requirement for farm labor to perform dangerous and arduous tasks that can be done better by machines. Some of these prospects will be enhanced by government policies and the political action of various interest groups, including the woke food policy movement, and others will be hampered. Issues have begun to arise over the IP rights to the data generated by farmers about their business, using machines embodying technology owned by others (AFBF 2018; Janzen 2019). A related issue is the changing scope for farmers as "tinkerers" to economically modify increasingly complex and sophisticated technologies. There can be no doubt that farmers will continue to be busy tinkering, modifying machines and using them in ways that were not imagined by the engineers that built them in the first instance. But it seems likely that an increasing share of the total innovation in American agriculture will

---

lation of new plant breeding technologies (NPBTs). He suggests: "While the science is exciting and some clear benefits are already observable, overregulation and public misperceptions may obstruct efficient development and use of NPBTs. Overregulation is particularly observed in Europe, but also affects developing countries in Africa and Asia, which could benefit the most from NPBTs" (Qaim 2020, p. 1).

26. The public sector also is active in these areas, and public-sector science is less secretive.

27. Alston and Sambucci (2019) discuss and document the rapid rate of innovation in table grape varieties in California, reflecting both public and increasingly private innovative activity. A total of 85 varieties are currently in production, and the mixture in vineyards is changing.

be based on patented technologies developed in the for-profit sector, continuing recent trends—whether we are talking about mechanical, genetic, chemical, or digital technologies.

3.7.2 Policy Perspectives

Government policy has been a central theme in our discussion of agricultural innovation, because the government plays a central role both in contributing directly to the innovation process, as a major provider of agricultural R&D, and in setting the rules of the game that determine the supply of and demand for agricultural innovations. In the current environment for agriculture, demands for private innovation investments are being influenced by government through the prospect of new regulations (or taxes) applied to agricultural production, including technological regulations and environmental regulations to reduce greenhouse gas emissions and other spillovers from agriculture; and through the influence of policy on the supply of inputs (especially labor and water) to agriculture, and on the markets for farm products. A more subtle influence of government is through changing support for public sector R&D (in terms of both the total investment and the balance of investments) influenced by the changing role of scientific evidence in policy and shifting public preferences.[28] These shifts create some opportunities for the private sector and foreclose other opportunities.

The National Academies of Science, Engineering and Medicine (2019) recently published a new agricultural research agenda for the US titled *Science Breakthroughs to Advance Food and Agricultural Research by 2030*. This report identifies innovative, emerging scientific advances for making the US agricultural and food system more efficient, resilient, and sustainable. The report presents five priorities:

1. Increasing understanding of the animal, soil, and plant microbiomes and their broader applications across the food system.

2. Harnessing the potential of genomics and precision breeding to improve plant and animal traits.

3. Capitalizing on agri-food informatics to enable advanced analytics using data sciences, information technology, and artificial intelligence.

4. Employing existing sensors and developing new sensing technologies to enable rapid detection and monitoring.

5. Prioritizing transdisciplinary science and systems approaches.

A fundamental motivation for this effort was concern about the shrinking total support for public agricultural R&D in the US and the loss of direction in terms of the focus of the shrinking public funds. Among these

---

28. For example, Pardey et al. (2013) show that the share of research by state agricultural experiment stations focused on farm productivity fell steadily from 69 percent in 1985 to 56 percent in 2009.

five priorities, most of the topics entail significant opportunities for private entrepreneurial activity to generate proprietary research products. Notably, three of the five are predominantly digital, data-intensive systems.

3.8 Conclusion

US agriculture was transformed during the twentieth century by waves of innovation involving mechanical, biological, chemical, and information technologies. Compared with a few decades ago, today's agriculture is much less labor intensive, and farms are much larger and more specialized, supplying a much-evolved market for farm products. Over recent decades, the global landscape for agricultural R&D has shifted away from farms, away from the public sector and toward the private sector, and away from the US and toward agriculturally important middle-income countries (especially China, India, and Brazil). Investments are stalling, even though meta-evidence shows that past US investments in R&D have yielded very favorable returns: median reported benefit-cost ratios in the range of 12:1. Sustained US investment and innovation will be required simply to preserve past productivity gains in the face of climate change, coevolving pests and diseases, and changing technological regulations—let alone to increase productivity. Great potential exists for innovation in crop and livestock genetics and digital farming technologies to generate new products and production processes, but innovators must overcome increasingly strong headwinds from social and political forces that seek to dictate technology choices.

Appendix

Table 3.A.1   US food expenditures at home and away from home, 1988 and 2018 (billion $US)

		1988 (Nominal)	1988 (Inflated)*	2018
FAH	Grocery stores	177.9	385.9	460.0
	Warehouse clubs and supercenters	5.1	11.1	168.0
	Other	68.4	148.4	153.0
	Total	251.3	545.4	780.9
FAFH	Full-service restaurants	73.1	158.7	337.8
	Limited-service restaurants	72.2	156.7	340.2
	Other	76.7	166.5	252.6
	Total	222.1	481.9	930.6

*Calculated using CPI data from the US Bureau of Labor Statistics: https://www.bls.gov/data/inflation_calculator.htm.

Source: Calculated by USDA, Economic Research Service, from various sources. See Okrent et al. (2018) for details.

Table 3.A.2 **Regional growth in US agricultural inputs, outputs, and productivity (percent per year)**

	United States	Pacific	Mountain	N. Plains	S. Plains	Central	Southeast	Northeast
All inputs	−0.11	0.82	0.45	0.16	−0.12	−0.27	−0.41	−0.84
Land	−0.10	0.59	0.41	−0.13	0.21	−0.51	0.29	−0.67
Labor	−1.74	−0.47	−0.90	−1.64	−1.80	−1.92	−2.15	−2.26
Capital	−0.07	0.08	0.02	0.25	0.13	−0.06	−0.74	−1.16
Materials	1.88	2.58	2.35	2.09	2.05	1.57	2.29	0.65
All outputs	1.68	2.50	1.97	2.12	1.66	1.44	1.63	0.84
Livestock	1.39	2.32	2.03	1.44	2.16	0.44	2.34	0.78
Field crops	1.65	0.76	1.00	2.60	0.95	2.29	0.27	0.60
Specialty crops	2.21	2.82	2.60	1.20	1.55	1.62	2.36	0.60
Multifactor productivity								
1949–2002	1.78	1.82	1.59	1.89	1.88	1.61	2.09	1.64
1949–1990	2.02	2.02	1.89	2.31	2.01	1.70	2.49	2.16
1990–2002	0.97	1.15	0.57	0.43	1.47	1.30	0.72	−0.14

Sources: InSTePP production accounts version 5 (revised) available at https://www.instepp.umn.edu/united-states.

Note: Average annual growth rates for inputs and multi-factor productivity span the period 1949–2002; for outputs they span the period 1949–2006.

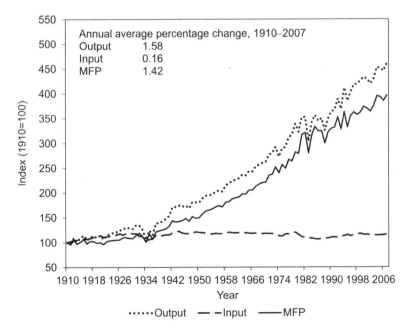

Fig. 3.A.1 **Quantity indexes of output, input, and MFP, US agriculture, 1910–2007**
Source: Pardey and Alston (2021, figure 1).

References

Adusei, E. O., and G. W. Norton. 1990. "The Magnitude of Agricultural Maintenance Research in the USA." *Journal of Production Agriculture* 3: 1–6.

AFBF (American Farm Bureau Federation). 2016. "Privacy and Security Principles for Farm Data." www.fb.org/issues/technology/data-privacy/privacy-and-security-principles-for-farm-data.

AgFunder. 2018. *AgriFood Tech Investing Report 18-Year in Review*. https://agfunder.com/research/agrifood-tech-investing-report-2018/.

Alston, J. M. 2002. "Spillovers." *Australian Journal of Agricultural and Resource Economics* 46 (3): 315–46.

———. 2018. "Reflections on Agricultural R&D, Productivity, and the Data Constraint: Unfinished Business, Unsettled Issues." *American Journal of Agricultural Economics* 100 (2): 392–413. doi:10.1093/ajae/aax094

———. 2021. "Woke Farm and Food Policies in the Post-Truth Era: Calamitous Consequences for People and the Planet." In *Modern Agricultural and Resource Economics and Policy: Essays in Honor of Gordon C. Rausser*, edited by Harry de Gorter, Jill McCluskey, Johan Swinnen and David Zilberman, chapter 6. New York: Springer.

Alston, J. M., and P. G. Pardey. 2014. "Agriculture in the Global Economy." *Journal of Economic Perspectives* 28(1): 121–46.

———. 2019. "Transforming Traditional Agriculture Redux." In *The Oxford Handbook of Structural Transformation*, edited by C. Monga and J. Lin. Oxford: Oxford University Press.

Alston, J. M., and O. Sambucci. 2019. "Grapes in the World Economy." Chapter 1 of Dario Cantu and Andrew M. Walker, eds., *The Grape Genome*, for the Springer Publishers *Compendium of Plant Genomes*.

Alston, J. M., S. Dehmer, and P. G. Pardey. 2006. "International Initiatives in Agricultural R&D: The Changing Fortunes of the CGIAR." In *Agricultural R&D in the Developing World: Too Little, Too Late?*, edited by P. G. Pardey, J. M. Alston, and R. R. Piggott, chapter 12. Washington, DC: International Food Policy Research Institute.

Alston, J. M., P. G. Pardey, and X. Rao. 2020. *The Payoff to Investing in CGIAR Research*. Research Report. Washington, DC: SoAR Foundation (forthcoming).

Alston, J. M., M. A. Andersen, J. S. James, and P. G. Pardey. 2010. *Persistence Pays: U.S. Agricultural Productivity Growth and the Benefits from Public R&D Spending*. New York: Springer.

Alston, J. M., M. A. Andersen, J. S. James, and P. G. Pardey. 2011. "The Economic Returns to U.S. Public Agricultural Research." *American Journal of Agricultural Economics* 93(5): 1257–1277.

Andersen, M. A., J. M. Alston, P. G. Pardey, and A. Smith. 2018. "A Century of U.S. Farm Productivity Growth: A Surge Then a Slowdown." *American Journal of Agricultural Economics* 100(4): 1072–90. doi.org/10.1093/ajae/aay023.

Baltes, N. J., J. Gil-Humanes, and D. F. Voytas. 2017. "Genome Engineering and Agriculture: Opportunities and Challenges." In *Gene Editing in Plants*, edited by D. P Weeks and B. Yang, 1–26. Progress in Molecular Biology and Translational Science, Vol. 149. Amsterdam: Elsevier. https://www.sciencedirect.com/bookseries/progress-in-molecular-biology-and-translational-science.

BlueRiver Technology. 2020. "Our See and Spray Machines." http://smartmachines.bluerivertechnology.com/.

Bureau of Economic Analysis (BEA). 2017. *National Income and Product Accounts Tables*. Table 1.3.5. Gross Value Added by Sector. Downloaded February 14, 2017.

https://www.bea.gov/iTable/iTable.cfm?ReqID=9&step=1#reqid=9&step=3& isuri=1&904=1929&903=24&906=a&905=1000&910=x&911=0.

Carson, R.1962. *Silent Spring*. Boston: Houghton Mifflin.

Chai, Y., P. G. Pardey, C. Chan-Kang, J. Huang, K. Lee, and W. Dong. 2019. "Passing the Food and Agricultural R&D Buck? The United States and China." *Food Policy* 86. doi.org/10.1016/j.foodpol.2019.101729.

Claassen, R., M. Bowman, J. McFadden, D. Smith, and S. Wallande. 2018. *Tillage Intensity and Conservation Cropping in the United States*, EIB-197, US Department of Agriculture, Economic Research Service.

Clancy, M., P. Heisey, Y. Ji, and G. Moschini. 2020. "The Roots of Agricultural Innovation: Patent Evidence of Knowledge Spillovers." In *Economics of Research and Innovation in Agriculture*, edited by P. Moser. Chicago: University of Chicago Press. Forthcoming.

Coase, R. H. 1937. "The Nature of the Firm." *Economica* 4(16): 386–405.

Cooper, M., C. Gho, R. Leafgren, T. Tang, and C. Messina. 2014. "Breeding Drought-Tolerant Maize Hybrids for the U.S. Corn Belt: Discovery to Product." *Journal of Experimental Botany* 65(21): 6191–6204.

Dehmer, S. P., P. G. Pardey, J. M. Beddow, and Y. Chai. 2019. "Reshuffling the Global R&D Deck, 1980–2050." *PLOS ONE* (March). https://doi.org/10.1371/journal.pone.0213801

Deloitte Centre for Health Solutions. 2014. "Measuring the Return on Pharmaceutical Innovation 2014: Turning a Corner?" Deloitte LLP (United Kingdom).

Dixon, R. 1980. "Hybrid Corn Revisited." *Econometrica* 48(6): 1451–61.

Donley, N. 2019. "The USA Lags Behind other Agricultural Nations in Banning Harmful Pesticides." *Environmental Health* 18 (Article 44). https://doi.org/10.1186/s12940-019-0488-0.

Erickson, B., J. Lowenberg-DeBoer, and J. Bradford. 2017. *2017 Precision Agriculture Dealership Survey*. Lafayette, IN: Departments of Agricultural Economics and Agronomy, Purdue University. December.

Feder, G., and D. L. Umali.1993. "The Adoption of Agricultural Innovations: A Review." *Technological Forecasting and Social Change* 43: 215–39.

Fennimore, S., and M. Cutulle. 2019. "Robotic Weeders Can Improve Weed Control Options for Specialty Crops." *Pest Management Science* 75(7): 1767–74. https://doi.org/10.1002/ps.5337

Fernandez-Cornejo, J., S. Wechsler, M. Livingston, and L. Mitchell. 2014. *Genetically Engineered Crops in the United States*. USDA Economic Research Report No. 162. Washington, DC: United States Department of Agriculture.

Filmer, A. 2019. "Automated Weeders Are Attracting More Interest: Steve Fennimore Explains." *Farms.Com News*, September 26. www.farms.com/news/automated-weeders-are-attracting-more-interest-steve-fennimore-explains-149734.aspx

Fuglie, K. O., and D. Schimmelpfennig, eds. 2000. *Public-Private Collaboration in Agricultural Research: New Institutions and Economic Implications*. Ames: Iowa State University Press.

Gelvin, S. B. 2003. "Agrobacterium-Mediated Plant Transformation: The Biology behind the 'Gene-Jockeying' Tool." *Microbiology and Molecular Biology Reviews* 67(1): 16–37. doi: 10.1128/MMBR.67.1.16–37.2003.

Glover, M., M. Buxton, S. Guthrie, S. Hanney, A. Pollitt, and J. Grant. 2014. "Estimating the Returns to UK Publicly Funded Cancer-related Research in Terms of the Net Value of Improved Health Outcomes." *BMC Medicine* 12: 99. doi.org/10.1186/1741-015-12-99.

Gordon, R. J. 2000. "Interpreting the 'One Big Wave' in U.S. Long-Term Productivity Growth." NBER Working Paper 7752. Cambridge, MA: National Bureau of Economic Research, June.

———. 2016. *The Rise and Fall of American Growth*. Princeton, NJ: Princeton University Press.

Graff, G. D., F. de Figueiredo Silva, and D. Zilberman. 2021."Venture Capital and the Transformation of Private R&D for Agriculture." In *Economics of Research and Innovation in Agriculture*, edited by P. Moser. Chicago: University of Chicago Press. Forthcoming.

Griliches, Z. 1957. "Hybrid Corn: An Exploration in the Economics of Technological Change." *Econometrica* 25(4): 501–22.

———. 1958. "Research Costs and Social Returns: Hybrid Corn and Related Innovations." *Journal of Political Economy* 66(5): 419–31.

———. 1963. "The Sources of Measured Productivity Growth: United States Agriculture, 1940–60." *Journal of Political Economy* 71(4): 331–46.

Hall, B. H., J. Mairesse, and P. Mohnen. 2010."Measuring the Returns to R&D." In *Handbook of the Economics of Innovation, Volume 2*, edited by B. Hall and N. Rosenberg, chapter 24. Amsterdam: Elsevier.

Hallauer, A. R., and J. B. Miranda.1981. *Quantitative Genetics in Maize Breeding*. Ames: Iowa State University Press.

HERG (Health Economics Research Group), OHE (Office of Health Economics), and RAND Europe. 2008. *Medical Research: What's It Worth? Estimating the Economic Benefits from Medical Research in the UK*. London: UK Evaluation Forum. www.mrc.ac.uk/publications/browse/medical-research-whats-it -worth/.

Hurley, T. M., X. Rao, and P. G. Pardey. 2014. "Re-examining the Reported Rates of Return to Food and Agricultural Research and Development." *American Journal of Agricultural Economics* 96(5): 1492–1504.

———. 2017. "Re-examining the Reported Rates of Return to Food and Agricultural Research and Development—Reply." *American Journal of Agricultural Economics* 99(3): 827–36.

Janzen, T. 2019. "Do Farmers Still Care About Ag Data Privacy?" Janzen Ag Law. www.aglaw.us/janzenaglaw/2019/1/3/farmers-care-about-data.

Jia, X., A. Khandelwall, D. J. Mulla, P. G. Pardey, and V. Kumar. 2019. "Bringing Automated, Remote-Sensed, Machine Learning Methods to Monitoring Crop Landscapes at Scale." *Agricultural Economics* 50(S1): 41–50.

Joglekar, A. B., P. G. Pardey, and U. Wood-Sichra. 2016. *Where in the World Are Crops Grown?* HarvestChoice Brief. St. Paul, Minnesota and Washington, DC: University of Minnesota and International Food Policy Research Institute.

Johnston, L., and S. H. Williamson. *What Was the U.S. GDP Then?* MeasuringWorth .com. Downloaded January 2017 from https://www.measuringworth.com/data sets/usgdp/.

Jorgenson, D. W., and F. M. Gollop. 1992. "Productivity Growth in U.S. Agriculture: A Postwar Perspective." *American Journal of Agricultural Economics* 74(3): 745–50.

Kalaitzandonakes, N., J. M. Alston, and K. J. Bradford. 2006. "Compliance Costs for Regulatory Approval of New Biotech Crops." In *Regulating Agricultural Biotechnology: Economics and Policy*, edited by R. E. Just, J. M. Alston, and D. Zilberman, chapter 3. New York: Springer-Verlag.

Lee, K., P. G. Pardey, S. Miller, and S. Dehmer. 2021. "An Examination of Private (Sectoral and Firm-Level) Investments in U.S. Food and Agricultural R&D, 1950–2014." InSTePP Working Paper. St. Paul: University of Minnesota, Department of Applied Economics (in process).

Lely. 2020. "Milking: More Milk in the Tank with Less Effort." https://www.lely
.com/us/solutions/milking/.

Lin, A. Y. S. 1976. "The Modified Internal Rate of Return and Investment Criterion." *Engineering Economist* 21(4): 237–47.

Lin, J. Y. 1992. "Rural Reforms and Agricultural Growth in China." *American Economic Review* 82(1): 34–51

Lowenberg-DeBoer, J., and B. Erickson. 2019. "Setting the Record Straight on
Precision Agriculture Adoption." *Agronomy Journal* 111: 1–18. doi:10.2134/
agronj2018.12.0779.

MacDonald, J. M. 2020. "Tracking the Consolidation of U.S. Agriculture." *Applied
Economic Perspectives and Policy*. Accessed August 25, 2020. doi.org/10.1002/aepp
.13056.

MacDonald, J. M., R. A. Hoppe, and D. Newton. 2018. *Three Decades of Consolidation in U.S. Agriculture*, EIB-189. Washington, DC: US Department of Agriculture, Economic Research Service, March.

McFadden, J., D. Smith, S. Wechsler, and S. Wallander. 2019. *Development, Adoption, and Management of Drought-Tolerant Corn in the United States*, EIB-204.
Washington, DC: US Department of Agriculture, Economic Research Service.

National Academies of Science, Engineering and Medicine. 2019. *Science Breakthroughs to Advance Food and Agricultural Research by 2030*. Washington, DC:
National Academies Press.

National Science Board. 2018. *Science and Engineering Indicators 2018*. NSB-
2018–1. Alexandria, VA: National Science Foundation. https://www.nsf.gov
/statistics/indicators/

National Science Foundation (NSF), National Center for Science and Engineering
Statistics. 2019. *National Patterns of R&D Resources (annual series)*. Accessed
December 27, 2019. https://www.nsf.gov/statistics/2018/nsb20181/data/appendix.

OECD (Organisation for Economic Co-operation and Development). 2015. *Frascati
Manual 2015: Guidelines for Collecting and Reporting Data on Research and Exper-
imental Development, The Measurement of Scientific, Technological and Innovation
Activities*. Paris: OECD Publishing.

Okrent, A. M., and J. M. Alston. 2011. *Demand for Food in the United States:
A Review of Literature, Evaluation of Previous Estimates and Presentation of New
Estimates of Demand*. Giannini Foundation Monograph Series No. 48. Berkeley,
CA: Giannini Foundation of Agricultural Economics.

———. 2012. *The Demand for Disaggregated Food-Away-from-Home and Food-at-
Home Products in the United States*. Economic Research Report No. 139. Washington, DC: US Department of Agriculture, Economic Research Service.

Okrent, A. M., H. Elitzak, T. Park, and S. Rehkamp. 2018. *Measuring the Value of
the U.S. Food System: Revisions to the Food Expenditure Series*. TB-1948. Washington, DC: US Department of Agriculture, Economic Research Service.

Olmstead, A. L., and P. L. Martin. 1985. "The Agricultural Mechanization Controversy." *Science* 227(4687): 601–6. doi: 10.1126/science.227.4687.601.

Olmstead, A. L., and P. W. Rhode. 2002. "The Red Queen and the Hard Reds: Productivity Growth in American Wheat, 1800–1940." *Journal of Economic History*
62(4): 929–66.

———. 2008. *Creating Abundance: Biological Innovation and American Agricultural
Development*. Cambridge: Cambridge University Press.

Pardey, P. G., and J. M. Alston. 2021. "Unpacking the Agricultural Black Box: The
Rise and Fall of American Farm Productivity Growth." *Journal of Economic
History* 81(1): 114–55.

Pardey, P. G., and J. M. Beddow. 2013. *Agricultural Innovation: The United States in a Changing Global Reality*. CCGA Report. Chicago: Chicago Council on Global Affairs.

Pardey, P. G., J. M. Alston, and C. Chan-Kang. 2013. *Public Food and Agricultural Research in the United States: The Rise and Decline of Public Investments, and Policies for Renewal*. AGree Report. Washington, DC: AGree.

Pardey, P. G., J. M. Alston, and V. W. Ruttan. 2010. "The Economics of Innovation and Technical Change in Agriculture." In *Handbook of the Economics of Innovation*, edited by B. H. Hall and N. Rosenberg, chapter 22. Amsterdam: Elsevier.

Pardey, P. G., J. Roseboom, and J. R. Anderson. 1991. "Regional Perspectives on National Agricultural Research." In *Agricultural Research Policy: International Quantitative Perspectives*, edited by P. G. Pardey, J. Roseboom, and J. R. Anderson, chapter 7. Cambridge: Cambridge University Press.

Pardey, P. G., J. M. Alston, J. E. Christian, and S. Fan. 1996. *Hidden Harvest: U.S. Benefits from International Research Aid*. Food Policy Report. Washington, DC: International Food Policy Research Institute.

Pardey, P. G., M. A. Andersen, B. J. Craig, and A. K. A. Acquaye. 2006. "Primary Data Documentation: U.S. Agricultural Input, Output, and Productivity Series, 1949–2002, Version 4." St. Paul: International Science and Technology Practice and Policy (InSTePP), University of Minnesota. https://www.instepp.umn.edu /products/instepp-primary-data-documentation-us-agricultural-input-output -and-productivity-series.

Pardey, P., B. Koo, J. Drew, J. Horwich, and C. Nottenburg. 2013. "The Evolving Landscape of Plant Varietal Rights in the United States, 1930–2008." *Nature Biotechnology* 31(1): 25–29.

Pardey, P. G., C. Chan-Kang, J. M. Beddow, and S. M. Dehmer. 2016a. "InSTePP International Innovation Accounts: Research and Development Spending, Version 3.5 (Food and Agricultural R&D Series)-Documentation." St. Paul, MN: International Science and Technology Practice and Policy (InSTePP). https:// www.instepp.umn.edu/sites/instepp.umn.edu/files/product/downloadable/In STePP%20International%20Innovation%20Accounts-R%26D%20ver3.5%282 SEPT2016%29.pdf.

Pardey, P. G., C. Chan-Kang, S. P. Dehmer, and J. M. Beddow. 2016b. "Agricultural R&D Is on the Move." *Nature* 15(537): 301–3.

Pardey, P. G., J. M. Alston, C. Chan-Kang, T. M. Hurley, R. S. Andrade, S. P. Dehmer, K. Lee, and X. Rao. 2018. "The Shifting Structure of Agricultural R&D: Worldwide Investment Patterns and Payoffs." In *From Agriscience to Agribusiness: Theories, Policies and Practices in Technology Transfer and Commercialization*, edited by N. Kalaitzandonakes, E. G. Carayannis, E. Grigoroudis, and S. Rozakis, chapter 1. Cham, Switzerland: Springer.

Perry, E. D., G. Moschini, and D. A. Hennessy. 2016. "Testing for Complementarity: Glyphosate Tolerant Soybeans and Conservation Tillage." *American Journal of Agricultural Economics* 98(3): 765–84. doi: 10.1093/ajae/aaw001.

Pollan, M. 2007. *The Omnivore's Dilemma: A Natural History of Four Meals*. New York: Penguin.

Qaim, M. 2016. *Genetically Modified Crops and Agricultural Development*. New York: Palgrave-Macmillan.

———. 2020. "Role of New Plant Breeding Technologies for Food Security and Sustainable Agricultural Development." *Applied Economic Perspectives and Policy*. https://doi.org/10.1002/aepp.13044.

Rao, X., T. M. Hurley, and P. G. Pardey. 2019a. "Are Agricultural R&D Returns Declining and Development Dependent?" *World Development* 122: 27–37.

———. 2019b. "Recalibrating the Reported Returns to Agricultural R&D: What If

We All Heeded Griliches?" InSTePP Working Paper P19–07. St. Paul: University of Minnesota, Department of Applied Economics.

Rasmussen, W. D. 1962. "The Impact of Technological Change on American Agriculture, 1862–1962." *Journal of Economic History* 22(4): 578–91.

Rausser, G., D. Zilberman, and G. Kahn. 2015. "An Alternative Paradigm for Food Production, Distribution, and Consumption: A Noneconomist's Perspective." *Annual Review of Resource Economics* 7: 309–31. doi.org/10.1146/annurev-resource-100913-012549.

Rausser, G., D. Zilberman, and S. Sexton. 2019. "The Economics of the Naturalist Food Paradigm." *Annual Review of Resource Economics* 11: 217–36. doi.org/10.1146/annurev-resource-100516-053623.

Ruttan, V. W. 1982. *Agricultural Research Policy*. Minneapolis: University of Minnesota Press.

Saitone, T., R. Sexton, and D. Sumner. 2015. "What Happens When Food Marketers Require Restrictive Farming Practices?" *American Journal of Agricultural Economics* 97(4): 1021–43.

Saksena, M. J., A. M. Okrent, T. D. Anekwe, C. Cho, C. Dicken, A. Effland, H. Elitzak, J. Guthrie, K. S. Hamrick, J. Hyman, and J. Young. 2018. *America's Eating Habits: Food Away from Home*. Washington, DC: US Department of Agriculture, Economic Research Service.

Schimmelpfennig, D. 2016. *Farm Profits and Adoption of Precision Agriculture*. Economic Research Report No. 217. Washington, DC: US Department of Agriculture.

———. 2018. "Crop Production Costs, Profits, and Ecosystem Stewardship with Precision Agriculture." *Journal of Agricultural and Applied Economics* 50(1): 81–103.

Schimmelpfennig, D., and R. Ebel. 2016. "Sequential Adoption and Cost Savings from Precision Agriculture." *Journal of Agricultural and Resource Economics* 41(1): 97–115.

Sexton, R. J., and T. Xia. 2018. "Increasing Concentration in the Agricultural Supply Chain: Implications for Market Power and Sector Performance." *Annual Review of Resource Economics* 10: 229–51.

Sumner, D. A. 2014. "American Farms Keep Growing: Size, Productivity, and Policy." *Journal of Economic Perspectives* 28(1): 147–66.

Taylor, N. J., and C. M. Fauquet. 2002. "Microparticle Bombardment as a Tool in Plant Science and Agricultural Biotechnology." *DNA and Cell Biology* 21(12): 963–77.

Teralytic. 2020. "Soil Probes to Soil Insight." https://teralytic.com/how-it-works.html.

United Nations Statistics Division. 2017. *UN National Accounts Main Aggregates Database*. New York: United Nations. http://unstats.un.org/unsd/snaama/dnlList.asp.

USDA-CRIS (Current Research Information System). 2020. Unpublished CRIS data files for various years, authors' extraction. Washington, DC: United States Department of Agriculture, Current Research Information System.

USDA-ERS (US Department of Agriculture, Economic Research Service). 1983. "Economic Indicators of the Farm Sector: Production and Efficiency Statistics, 1981." ECIFS 1–3. Washington, DC: USDA, Economic Research Service.

———. 2019a. *Food Dollar Series*. Washington, DC: USDA, Economic Research Service. www.ers.usda.gov/data-products/food-dollar-series/.

———. 2019b. "Trends in Water Use and Onfarm Irrigation Efficiency." https://www.ers.usda.gov/topics/farm-practices-management/irrigation-water-use/#trends.

USDA-NASS. 2019. *Farm Producers. 2017 Census of Agriculture Highlights.* Washington, DC: United States Department of Agriculture. https://www.nass.usda.gov/Publications/Highlights/2019/2017Census_Farm_Producers.pdf.

———. Various years. *Census of Agriculture. United States, Summary and State Data.* Washington, DC: United States Department of Agriculture. http://agcensus.mannlib.cornell.edu/AgCensus/.

US Bureau of the Census. 1973. *1969 Census of Agriculture—Volume II General Report, Chapter 1 General Information, Procedures for Collection, Processing, Classification.* US Department of Commerce. Washington, DC: Government Printing Office.

———. 1977. *1974 Census of Agriculture—United States Summary and State Data, Volume I Part 51.* US Department of Commerce. Washington, DC: Government Printing Office.

———. Various years. *Census of Agriculture. United States, Summary and State Data.* Washington, DC: Government Printing Office. http://agcensus.mannlib.cornell.edu/AgCensus/.

Van Eenennaam, A. L. 2019. "Application of Genome Editing in Farm Animals: Cattle." *Transgenic Research* 28: 93–100.

Wight, A. J. 2018. "EU Gene-Editing Rule Squeezes Science." *Nature* 563: 15.

Willett, W., J. Rockström, B. Loken, M. Springmann, T. Lang, S. Vermeulen, T. Garnett, D. Tilman, F. DeClerck, A. Wood, M. Jonell, M. Clark, L. J. Gordon, J. Fanzo, C. Hawkes, R. Zurayk, J. A. Rivera, W. De Vries, L. M. Sibanda, and A. Afshin. 2019. "Food in the Anthropocene: The EAT–Lancet Commission on Healthy Diets from Sustainable Food Systems." *The Lancet* 393.10170: 447–92.

World Bank. 2017. *World Development Indicators Online.* Washington, DC: World Bank. Downloaded January 25, 2017, from http://data.worldbank.org/data-catalog/world-development-indicators (last updated January 3, 2017).

Wright, B. D. 2012. "Grand Missions of Agricultural Innovation." *Research Policy* 41: 1716–28. http://dx.doi.org/10.1016/j.respol.2012.04.021.

Wright, B. D., and P. G. Pardey. 2006. "The Evolving Rights to Intellectual Property Protection in the Agricultural Biosciences." *International Journal for Technology and Globalization* 2(1/2): 12–29.

Wright, B. D., P. G. Pardey, C. Nottenburg, and B. Koo. 2007. "Agricultural Innovation: Economic Incentives and Institutions." In *Handbook of Agricultural Economics*, Vol 3, edited by R. E. Evenson and P. Pingali, 2533–2603. Amsterdam: Elsevier.

Comment   Brian Davern Wright

I have removed discussions of some issues included in my conference remarks that have been addressed in a subsequent revision by Alston and Pardey. For acknowledgments, sources of research support, and disclosure of the author's material financial relationships, if any, please see https://www.nber.org/books-and-chapters/role-innovation-and-entrepreneurship

Brian Davern Wright is a professor of agricultural and resource economics at the University of California, Berkeley.

-economic-growth/comment-innovation-growth-and-structural-change
-american-agriculture-wright.

The US agricultural sector offers a fascinating and possibly unique case for study of sectoral innovation. The production technologies, factor proportions, and the productivity of the sector have been radically transformed by waves of innovation. However, the principal food and fiber products supplied at the farm gate, and the competitive organization of farms as the managerial units that produce them, have changed relatively little over the past century, so that comparable data on production, prices, and input use are available spanning an unusually extended period. Hence we have the opportunity to observe waves of research, innovation, and diffusion in a highly dynamic sector in the short and long views. A shelf containing all of Alston's and Pardey's highly cited books on the topic would need to be wide and sturdy. They are eminently qualified to meet the challenge of covering this multidimensional topic in a single chapter, for an audience not necessarily familiar with key elements of the story.

Figure 3.1 in Alston and Pardey (chapter 3, this volume) offers a dramatic illustration of one aspect of the story. For almost a century, beginning in 1850, farmland and farm families increased apace. This ended around 1936, when the number of farm families began a steep and persistent descent.[1] Then, as argued by Alston and Pardey, a 40-year productivity surge started in the 1950s and lasted for four decades.

Subsequently, they argue, a decline in public research intensity (relative to farm GDP) reduced farm productivity growth. Private agricultural research spending has risen to pass public funding, but it is focused on applied research and especially development expenditures off-farm, which does not generally compensate for the effect of reduced public support for research related to farm productivity.

Many observers of the trends in farm area and farm numbers embrace a very different narrative. Family farms, the backbone of US productivity, increased at a relatively constant size behind an expanding frontier through the mid-1930s. Subsequently, larger corporate oligopolies have been driving families off most off their land, relegating them to a low-income, impoverished rural fringe or to urban slums. Productivity growth has become less sustainable as corporate substitution of chemicals and machines for family management and labor has taken its toll, and urban sprawl has taken some of the best land out of production. This narrative might seem all the more convincing to those who know that the published data vastly overstate the current number of minimally productive family farms.[2] In 2012, less than 4 percent of farms generated two-thirds of farm sales, while the bottom half

---

1. Although land area shown in the figure continued to increase through 1955, total cropped area was about the same in 1936 and 1955. https://www.ers.usda.gov/data-products/major -land-uses.aspx (last accessed May 15, 2020).
2. US Department of Agriculture (2015, p. 1).

shared less than 1 percent. This might seem consistent with the notion that large farm corporations are getting the lion's share, leaving family farmers to struggle for the scraps. If so, no wonder public support for agricultural research has declined!

At a time when we all have good reason for concern about many heart-rending social phenomena, let me assure you that the process as character-ized in the above narrative should not be numbered among them. It is true that, for the majority of "farm families," farm income is trivial at best. Does this mean they are impoverished? Not at all. Beginning in the 1960s, aver-age nonfarm income of most farm families has risen fast.[3] In 2014, only 2 percent of farm households were in the bottom half of all households in terms of *both* income and wealth. Most farm households are families of wealthy retirees (many of them former farmers), or families with large off-farm income who choose to live in a rural residence.

Furthermore, even the top 4 percent constitute 80,000 farms, the vast majority of which are family operations with negligible market power, even if incorporated for tax or other reasons. It is interesting that talk of farm size increasing always focus on land or output. Measured by the aggre-gate of management and other labor, farm size in the US has very different dynamics. Indeed, it has changed remarkably little on average in more than a century—and remains quite similar to farm size in other countries in which farm income is dramatically lower, including India and China.[4]

As the number of farm families has fallen and acres and output per farm have risen, the share of measured farm output in GDP had plummeted to about 1 percent.[5] As the authors note, this is largely an accounting phe-nomenon. Many products once included as farm output are now located elsewhere.

Nevertheless, the secular decline in labor used in production on farms is striking. Is this driven by innovation? The answer is yes, but the question is where. A third narrative takes a macro perspective. Wages in the US since the end of the Great Depression been set in the nonfarm economy. The increasing opportunity cost of farm managers and labor meant that other factors—land and capital—must be substituted for labor to raise its mar-ginal productivity to approximate off-farm opportunities generated by off-farm innovation, with some adjustment lag. This would have happened, and the number of farm managers and agricultural laborers could have declined, even if total factor productivity in farming had not risen nearly as rapidly.

3. US Department of Agriculture (2014), table 10.
4. The persistence of the family organization of farming is a problem for those who see Adam Smith's extreme functional specialization as a key to increased productivity. Its advantage lies in the necessity for self-motivated labor and management in a dispersed and highly stochastic local environment. The extent to which this might change as information technology evolves is a very interesting question.
5. https://www.erata-producs.usda.gov/dts/ag-and-food-statistics-charting-the-essentials/ag-and-food-sectors-and-the-economy/ (last accessed May 15, 2020).

Advances in hydroponics and vertical farming notwithstanding, the business of growing plants for food, animal feed, or fiber remains located on farms. Alston and Pardey focus principally on innovations that raise the productivity of land, management, labor, water, and fertilizers in producing crops or animal products, or sustains existing productivity of plants and animals as pests and diseases evolve. Many of these innovations are relevant to farms in other countries with very different labor intensities. The US history of innovation in this line of business begins with the important work of selecting plant varieties, often taken by immigrants and prospectors from other lands, and choosing those appropriate for new local environments. The federal government helped, for example, by distributing seed samples via the Post Office. Evenson demonstrated that, in the nineteenth century, the key mechanical inventions for farming the newly settled lands originated with farmers or local blacksmiths, often members of farm families, subsequently to be perfected by engineering firms.[6]

Given this history, agricultural economists have become accustomed to the fact that major inputs used by farmers (land services, seed, draft animals, breeding animals, forage, and management) are sourced from within agriculture. They tend to expect that research and innovative activities likewise will be located in the sector.

The establishment of US agricultural education at the Land Grant Colleges by the Morrill Act of 1862, and later of federal support for State Agricultural Research Stations by the Hatch Act of 1887, signaled a commitment of public support specifically targeted at productivity-increasing agricultural education and research of direct use to farmers, insufficiently fostered by the atomistic competitive private farm sector. The result was a string of innovations that facilitated the transformation of agriculture in the twentieth century.

In a volume on the role of innovation and entrepreneurship in economic growth, the contributions of private entrepreneurship, government policies, and the patent system in the innovation called the "agricultural research station," and indeed, the necessity and feasibility of public support, are questions worthy of a little further discussion. US agricultural experiment stations as public initiatives deserve the attention that the authors give to them. However, the initial motivations for the development of the idea of the agricultural research stations are complex.[7]

Consider two key figures. The first is Justus von Liebig, the son of merchant who compounded and sold paints and dyes, who has been called the founder of the modern chemistry laboratory. He experienced the "year without summer" in 1816 as a 13-year-old boy and became a chemist interested

---

6. Evenson, personal communication with author, 1993.
7. For a wide-ranging international perspective on this, and more detail on the influence of von Liebig, see Pardey, Roseboom, and Anderson (1991).

in agriculture. His education included study in the private laboratory of Gay-Lussac under a grant from the Hessian government. As professor at the state University of Geissen, in 1840, he authored the pioneering publication, *Organic Chemistry in its Relation to Agriculture and Physiology*. He founded his research laboratory as an initially private initiative, with the approval of his university. His experiments identified the role of nitrogen as a plant nutrient, and he influenced the competitive development of agricultural research stations in other states that would later become part of a unified Germany; by 1873, there were 25 such stations. He proclaimed the famous "law of the minimum" regarding the constraints imposed by available nutrients on plant growth. Besides his innovation of the modern chemistry laboratory and methods of teaching chemistry, von Liebig also developed key instruments for chemical analysis. His later applied research included the use of silver to replace the toxic mercury used in the making of mirrors. Although he was essentially an academic, some of his work was more entrepreneurially oriented. For example, his research on meat enabled the private sector development of what became Oxo beef cubes.

Consider, in contrast, John Bennet Lawes, a land-owning entrepreneur interested in chemistry applied to agriculture. Having learned some chemistry as an undergraduate at Oxford, he prematurely returned to Rothamsted Estate, which he had inherited as a boy, on the bankruptcy of its tenant. Around 1837, he began small experiments on ammonium salts as nitrogen fertilizers, and he identified ammonium phosphate as producing the greatest yield increase in cabbages. Further experiments resulted in the production of a highly effective phosphate fertilizer, succeeding in competition with von Liebig (founder of the chemistry laboratory), by treating phosphatic minerals with sulphuric acid. He patented his invention of superphosphate (Patent 93530) in November 1842. In 1843, he hired Dr. J. Henry Gilbert, who had studied under von Liebig in 1840, to manage his laboratory, and constructed what has been called the world's first fertilizer factory (Warington 1900). A few years later, he purchased another related patent from a competitor. His factory marked the highly successful commercial beginnings of a fertilizer industry that became established as the major customer for sulphuric acid.

Lawes' Rothamsted Experimental Research Station was no doubt a useful complement that encouraged growth of his highly successful fertilizer business. His subsequent endowment of Rothamsted furnished the base for its continued operation today as the oldest agricultural research station in the world.

The establishment of Rothamsted affected the development of the US Land Grant Universities. For example, Evan Pugh, who had worked at Rothamsted in 1857–59 on the sources of nitrogen for plants, became the first president of the new Pennsylvania State University. In the 1920s, R. A. Fisher, as head of the statistics department at Rothamsted, transformed experimental agricultural research with his work on analysis of variance

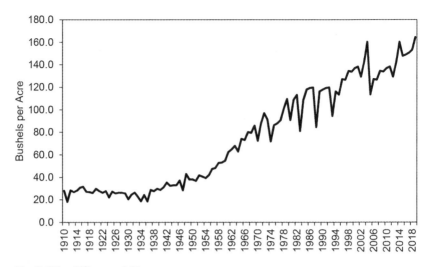

Fig. 3.C.1   US corn yield
Source: USDA, ERS, 2019.

and experimental design. However, the German experiment stations in the tradition founded by von Liebig around 1840 had greater influence on the design of the US public agricultural research effort (Finlay 1988). The first director of a US agricultural experiment station, Samuel W. Johnston, was trained by a founder of the German system.

What was the effect of this US research effort on the productivity of US crops? Yield per acre is one relatively straightforward indicator, even though the contributions of complementary inputs, such as fertilizer and irrigation, should properly be considered. Let us focus on yields of corn and domestic wheat. Both are grasses, but one is an open-pollinating diploid, the other a self-pollinating hexaploid. Nothing outstanding happened to their average national yields for nearly a century. Then, as shown in figures 3.C.1 and 3.C.2, during the mid-1930s, yields of both began an increasing trend that in the past six decades has displayed an approximately constant arithmetic rate, consistent with Malthus' assumption about the nature of technical progress.

How can we explain the beginnings of such persistently higher trends in yields in the 1930s? There is no obvious common biological or entrepreneurial element. For corn, the increasing yield coincided with introduction of hybrid varieties. Seeds produced from hybrid parents have a yield disadvantage that discourages farmers from replanting their output. Under this protection commercial firms, notably Pioneer Hi-Bred, came to dominate breeding, production and sales of hybrid seed, but not more basic research. In wheat there was no such abrupt change in the breeding strategy and no sustained shift to commercial breeding.

A third crop, soybeans, became a major complement to corn as its yield

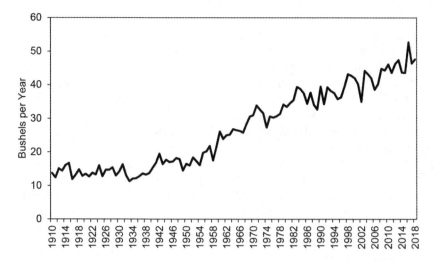

Fig. 3.C.2   US wheat yield
Source: USDA, ERS 2019.

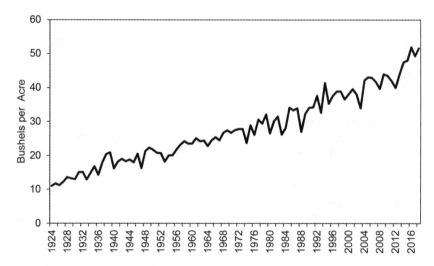

Fig. 3.C.3   US soybean yield
Source: USDA, ERS, 2019.

increased, also at a relatively constant arithmetic rate, starting a little earlier (figure 3.C.3). This was a very different crop, a legume supplied with atmospherically derived nitrogen via symbiotic bacteria, and hence lacking the potential response to nitrogen fertilizer inherent in corn or wheat, which generated research opportunities in both crops.

With these yield histories in mind, look again at figure 3.1 of Alston and

Pardey. They identify the productivity surge as starting in 1950. But the number of farm families began to fall fast in the mid-1930s. Some of this fall is related to the ending of the Great Depression and the re-emergence of urban employment opportunities. Even so, it is remarkable that in the mid-1930s, the yields of both crops began to increase persistently (figures 3.C.1 and 3.C.2). Could this be the true date of the beginnings of the productivity surge discussed by Alston and Pardey? Could Fisher's work on design and analysis of crop experiments have a role in the sharp discontinuity in yield gains for wheat and maize?

The postwar public agricultural research expenditures also increased monotonically (Alston and Pardey's figure 3.5b) until the downturn in expenditure intensity in the new millennium. Figure 3.6b shows that research intensity per unit agricultural GDP also increased remarkably. In reading the chapter, it is easy to miss the fact that public inputs into agricultural research were not only high relative to other sectors but were also increasing fast through the millennium.

Crop yields have continued to increase as agricultural research intensity waxed and waned.[8] This might well partly reflect the long lag of the returns to agricultural research. Alternatively, crop research intensity might not be well aligned with agricultural research intensity. This could be true; the authors are uniquely equipped to tell us. An alternate conjecture might be that the correlation of yield changes with research intensity might be spurious: public research might not be a proximate determinant of yield increase.

Private research intensity had surpassed public by the new millennium, mainly focused on innovations in fields that the authors classify as in the agricultural sector but are currently outside the farm sector. Measures of private research intensity must depend heavily on the components counted in the numerator and in the denominator. This is a daunting task. There seems to be no consensus as to the definition of private agricultural research, and the authors have no doubt spent a lot of time and effort on getting it right. Clancy et al. (2020) include animal health, biocides, fertilizers, agricultural machinery, agricultural plants, and agricultural research inputs. Graff et al. (2020) define the fields of agricultural venture capital as online businesses, software, commodity processing, and agricultural research inputs. They find that only 2 percent of all the firms included in at least one of three sources of venture capital startups in agriculture, PitchBook, VentureSource, and Crunchbase, appear in all three databases.

I wonder whether the effort to locate relevant research in and outside the agricultural sector might seem a little puzzling to economists who spend most of their time on other sectors of the economy. A century ago, most agricultural research was public, much of it actually located on (experimen-

---

8. In particular, wheat figures might be complicated by changes in area planted and average land quality, perhaps affecting average yield in recent years.

tal) farms and directed at familiar and clearly agricultural processes. "Spillovers" from other sectors were exceptional. Now most off-farm research is less obviously restricted to agricultural users and more difficult to relate to specifically agricultural off-farm activity. In this sense, is the agricultural sector becoming more like most of the rest of the economy?

Finally, let us turn to the key question of the returns to public agricultural research. Historically, calculation of returns to agricultural research was particularly important, because there was thought to be a need to justify public expenditures to taxpayers as well as to farmers. Farmers have recently become less interested in public expenditure on research as a source of increased wealth. They understand more clearly that most of the benefits accrue in the long run to consumers at home and abroad. Further, they have learned that returns to lobbying for favorable market distortions have a much larger payoff. US grain farmers gained greatly from biofuels mandates enacted in 2005 and 2007 that resulted in the speedy diversion of around 30 percent of the feed value of the US corn crop to biofuels, effectively eliminating the effects of a decade or more of progress in corn yields (Wright 2014). The gains in income and land values were far beyond the most optimistic predictions of the financial benefits farmers might get from keeping agricultural research intensity on track.

There is no doubt that overall, the social returns have been very good for the nation as a whole, with spillovers worldwide. But problems arise in measuring those returns. The authors allude to problems with the internal rate of return, a topic that they have pursued in greater depth elsewhere, and prefer benefit-cost ratios. However, benefit-cost ratios are also problematic. High benefit-cost ratios may well be useful in the quest for political support for public agricultural research. Unfortunately, these ratios can be manipulated. As long as the ratio is above unity, reclassification of costs as negative benefits, or vice versa, can get you a number close to unity, or as high as you like.

For allocation of research dollars across and within sectors, high average returns as indicated by benefit-cost ratios are not sufficiently informative. We would like to use measures more relevant to identification of marginal and submarginal projects, or better yet (if feasible), the marginal productivity of resource allocation in each project. Perhaps the relatively constant yield increases for three major crops over a long period reflects the fact that long-run programs in this area (including private sector research on corn in particular) are thought to be about the right size and have been protected as the attractiveness of other public opportunities for allocating marginal research dollars has recently declined, justifying some reduction in funding of such opportunities, and a reduction in overall research intensity? After decades of careful data collection and illuminating research, the authors are well qualified to address this question.

For any measure of returns to research investment, a widely acknowledged problem is posed by the long and variable lags. Even 150 years of data are not sufficient to identify the correct lag structures, and controlled experiments to answer the question are not feasible. Another obvious but unavoidable difficulty is that empirical studies are of necessity retrospective, and so of limited utility for high-level decisions on research plans for a changing world. Nevertheless, careful construction, maintenance, and analysis of data sets (exemplified by the work at InStePP) are crucially important tasks. Building on this knowledge base, decisions on resource allocations to agricultural research must rely on informed reviews of perceived needs and potential technical and economic opportunities based on the state of the art, as exemplified in this chapter.

References

Alston, J. M., and P. G. Pardey. 2020. "Innovation, Growth, and Structural Change in American Agriculture." In *The Role of Innovation and Entrepreneurship in Economic Growth*, edited by Aaron Chatterji, Josh Lerner, Scott Stern, and Michael J. Andrews. Chicago: University of Chicago Press. This volume.

Clancy, M., P. Heisey, Y. Ji, and G. Moschini. 2020. "The Roots of Agricultural Innovation: Patent Evidence of Knowledge Spillovers." In *Economics of Research and Innovation in Agriculture*, edited by P. Moser. Chicago: University of Chicago Press. Forthcoming.

Finlay, M. R. 1988. "The German Agricultural Experiment Stations and the Beginnings of American Agricultural Research." *Agricultural History* 62(2): 41–50.

Graff, D., F. de Figueiredo Silva, and D. Zilberman. 2020. "Venture Capital and the Transformation of Private R&D for Agriculture." In *Economics of Research and Innovation in Agriculture*. Chicago: University of Chicago Press. Forthcoming.

Pardey, P. G., J. Roseboom, and J. R. Anderson. 1991. "Regional Perspectives on National Agricultural Research Policy." In *Agricultural Research Policy: International Quantitative Perspectives*, edited by P. G. Pardey, J. Roseboom, and J. R. Anderson, 265–308. Cambridge: Cambridge University Press.

US Department of Agriculture, Economic Research Service. 2014. *Structure and Finances of U.S. Farms: Family Farm Report, 2014 Edition*. Economic Information Bulletin No. EIB-132.

US Department of Agriculture, National Agricultural Statistics Service. 2012. *Census of Agriculture*, Farm Typology, Vol. 2, Part 10, January 2015, p. 1.

———. 2019. *Crop Production: Historical Track Records*, April.

Warington, R. 1900. "Sir John Bennett Lawes, Bart, F.R.S." *Nature* (1900): 467–68.

Wright, Brian D. 2014. "Global Biofuels: Key to the Puzzle of Grain Market Behavior." *Journal of Economic Perspectives* 28(1) (Winter): 73–98.

Innovation and Entrepreneurship in the Energy Sector

David Popp, Jacquelyn Pless, Ivan Haščič,
and Nick Johnstone

4.1 Introduction

Energy markets are going through a period of profound structural change. With significant cost declines and performance improvements in renewable energy technologies over the past decade, electricity grids must manage higher levels of generation from intermittent renewable energy resources. These resources lower greenhouse gas (GHG) emissions associated with the power sector but also create new challenges for grid operators, who must balance supply and demand in real time. Furthermore, the rise of "unconventional" gas and oil in the past decade puts downward pressure on fossil

David Popp is a professor in the Department of Public Administration and International Affairs at Syracuse University, and a research associate of the National Bureau of Economic Research.

Jacquelyn Pless is the Fred Kayne (1960) Career Development Professor of Entrepreneurship and an assistant professor at the MIT Sloan School of Management.

Ivan Haščič is senior economist in the Environment Directorate at the Organisation for Economic Co-operation and Development (OECD).

Nick Johnstone is chief statistician in the Energy Data Centre of the International Energy Agency (IEA).

We thank Julie Lassébie for helpful discussions on obtaining and working with Crunchbase data, Miguel Cárdenas Rodríguez for precious help with patent searches, and Myriam Gregoire-Zawilski for helpful research assistance. Hunt Allcott and participants at the NBER Conference on The Role of Innovation and Entrepreneurship in Economic Growth provided helpful comments on an earlier draft. A special thank you to Aaron Chatterji, Josh Lerner, Scott Stern, and Mike Andrews for their efforts organizing this project and for helpful comments throughout. Funding from the National Bureau of Economic Research project on The Role of Innovation and Entrepreneurship in Economic Growth was used to purchase data for this research. The views expressed in this chapter are the authors' own and do not necessarily reflect those of the OECD, the IEA, nor their member countries. For acknowledgments, sources of research support, and disclosure of the authors' material financial relationships, if any, please see https://www.nber.org/books-and-chapters/role-innovation-and-entrepreneurship -economic-growth/innovation-and-entrepreneurship-energy-sector.

fuel prices, resulting in natural gas replacing coal as the primary fuel for electricity generation in the US.

Despite these advances, improving the environmental performance of the energy sector requires continued innovation. Limiting global warming to no more than 1.5° Celsius, which would reduce (but not eliminate) projected climate change impacts, is only possible by achieving zero net carbon emissions by mid-century (IPCC 2018). Replacing vast amounts of fossil fuels with alternative, carbon-free energy sources, such as solar and wind energy, will require long-term energy storage solutions and smart grid technologies to integrate these intermittent energy sources into the grid (International Energy Agency 2019a; International Renewable Energy Agency 2017). These challenges must be overcome while also ensuring energy security in the face of rapidly changing market conditions.

Yet innovation in the energy sector has historically proceeded slowly. Energy firms invest less in R&D than almost all other sectors of the economy. There are also several unique features of the energy sector that make innovation in the energy context particularly challenging. Energy production is capital intensive, and especially long-time horizons between initial idea and commercialization create a "Valley of Death" for energy innovation (e.g., Mowrey, Nelson, and Martin 2010; Weyant 2011). Such long time horizons also make energy firms less attractive to venture capitalists, who typically expect to see returns within 5–7 years. In addition, because the social benefits of clean energy associated with pollution reductions are not reflected in market prices without government intervention, the potential demand for clean energy technologies is dependent on effective environmental policy. As a result, while small, nimble startups are frequently the vehicle through which innovation reaches the market in many sectors, they have historically played a smaller role in the energy sector (Gaddy et al. 2017; Nanda, Younge, and Fleming 2015).

Could this be changing, given the evolving nature of energy markets? Many of the latest energy technologies are smaller and more modular (e.g., solar panels, smart meters for homes) relative to conventional technologies. They also increasingly rely on advancements in other sectors in which fast-moving startups are more prominent players. For instance, new smart grid technologies depend on software and information technology (IT)—a sector where entrepreneurial firms play important roles (e.g., Gaddy et al. 2017). How is the nature of innovation in energy changing? Are entrepreneurial firms now playing a larger role? Do more energy innovations contain a software or IT component? Do energy startups with a high-tech component perform better than other energy startups?

We explore these questions in three parts. We begin by providing an overview of the energy industry and energy innovation literature, exploring how both unconventional natural gas and oil and increasingly affordable renewable energy technologies are changing the industry. We focus on the electricity sector, considering the generation of electricity and the supply of fuel (e.g., coal and natural gas) to power plants. While we do not directly address energy in the transportation sector, there are technological needs that overlap both sectors, such as innovation in batteries for energy storage on the power grid and for powering electric vehicles.

We then provide two new descriptive data analyses on the changing nature of innovation in energy, with a particular focus on the increasing role of digitalization. First, we examine patenting activity and document that, despite rapid growth in the late 2000s, energy patenting activity overall has fallen since about 2010 or 2011. We consider possible explanations for this decline, such as the rise of hydraulic fracturing, changing regulations, diminishing returns to research, and the existence of a cleantech bubble. The share of power sector patents that can also be considered "high-tech," though, began to increase in the past couple of years of our sample (2013–2014). This increase suggests that digitalization may be an increasingly important aspect of energy innovation moving forward.

Second, we present data on startup activity in the energy sector, with a similar focus on entrepreneurial energy firms that operate in high-tech fields. The findings are consistent with what we observe in the patenting data. We document a similar decline in energy startups since about 2010, but again, an increasing share of these energy startups are also "high-tech" firms. We also show that high-tech energy startups are more likely to attract venture capital (VC) investments, but they do not necessarily perform better than non-high-tech energy startups. Furthermore, conditional on receiving funding, energy startups generally do not perform better than the average funded firm, although there is some evidence of overinvestment in clean energy, corresponding with growth and a subsequent fall in both patenting and VC funding during the 2006–2012 period.

The rest of this chapter proceeds as follows. In section 4.2, we provide industry background and a review of the energy innovation literature so far. Sections 4.3 and 4.4 present our patenting and startup analyses, respectively. We conclude with a discussion of emerging trends in the energy sector and suggestions for future research in section 4.5.

4.2   Industry Background

Fossil fuel combustion generated nearly 5 billion metric tons of greenhouse gases in 2016, accounting for 76 percent of all US emissions (US Environmental Protection Agency 2019). While electricity generation historically was the largest source of US greenhouse gas emissions, increased generation from natural gas and clean renewable energy resulted in emissions from the power sector falling below those of the transportation sector for the first time in 2016 (US Environmental Protection Agency 2019). Nonetheless, significant innovation and progress is still needed to mitigate the potential impacts of climate change and to meet future energy policy goals in a cost-effective manner, and innovation in the energy sector has historically moved relatively slowly.

Examining historical R&D investment trends can begin to shed light on this phenomenon. Consider the data provided in table 4.1, for instance, which shows domestic R&D paid for and performed by US companies in select industries, as a percentage of net sales. Over the past 10 years, the industrial sector as a whole spent between 2.5 to 3.5 percent of sales on R&D. For manufacturing industries, the share ranges from 3.1 to 3.9 percent, with shares approaching 10 percent in R&D-intensive industries, such as pharmaceuticals and computers. In contrast, mining and extraction industries, which include the oil and gas sector, were spending less than 1 percent of sales on R&D until 2015. Utilities spend just 0.1 percent of sales on R&D. Only the engine and turbine manufacturing component of the energy industry has R&D spending levels comparable to the rest of the manufacturing sector.

Fostering and accelerating innovation, though, is not simply a matter of increasing R&D expenditures. Such spending must effectively translate into the commercialization and diffusion of new technologies, processes, business models, and management practices that improve performance, such as the financial and environmental performance of the power sector. Beyond the lessons from innovation economics, strategy, and management that apply broadly to many sectors, there are several unique features of the energy industry that make the process of technological change different in this sector:

1. Energy is a commodity. Consumers want the lights to go on when they flip a switch. While environmental considerations are becoming more important to consumers in many countries, most do not care about the source of that energy and are unwilling to pay a premium for clean energy. As a result, successful entrepreneurs cannot fully capture the rents associated with differentiating their product. Instead, reducing costs is the measure of successful innovation.

2. Regulation plays an important role in the industry. Electrical and gas service is usually distributed by regulated natural monopolies, and regulation of energy production varies across jurisdictions. Because consumers focus on cost rather than quality, until recently, cleaner energy sources (such as solar or wind) were viewed as too expensive in the absence of interventions to address externalities. Unlike sectors where the government is a primary consumer (such as the military or space exploration), energy is somewhat unique in that government regulation shapes demand, but final consumption decisions are made in the private sector. As a result, uncertainty over future policy can dampen incentives for R&D.

3. Energy generation is capital intensive. Economies of scale are pervasive

Table 4.1 Domestic R&D as a percentage of net sales, selected industries

	2006	2007	2008	2009	2010	2011	2012	2013	2014	2015	2016
Energy industry											
NAICS 21: Mining, extraction and support activities	0.7	0.9	0.4	0.7	0.5	0.4	0.9	0.8	0.8	1.2	1.4
NAICS 22: Utilities	0.1	0.1	0.1	0.1	N/A	0.1	0.1	0.1	0.1	0.1	0.1
NAICS 3336: Engines, turbines, & power trans. equip.	N/A	N/A	4.1	3.3	5.1	3.0	3.3	2.7	N/A	5.1	6.0
Comparison industries											
NAICS 21–23, 31–33, 42–81: All industries	3.4	3.5	3.0	3.0	2.5	2.6	2.7	2.7	2.9	3.3	3.5
NAICS 31–33: All manufacturing industries	3.6	3.7	3.5	3.7	3.3	3.2	3.1	3.1	3.3	3.7	3.9
NAICS 3361–63: Automobiles, bodies, trailers, & parts	2.4	2.4	2.5	2.4	1.8	2.1	2.2	2.0	2.2	2.1	2.2
NAICS 3254: Pharmaceuticals and medicines	13.5	12.7	12.2	12.3	11.7	10.6	11.2	9.0	11.3	11.0	9.7
NAICS 334: Computer and electronic products	9.2	8.4	10.1	9.2	8.2	8.5	8.6	9.0	8.9	8.7	8.7

Source: National Science Foundation *Business Research and Development and Innovation*, various years.

Notes: Table shows domestic R&D paid for and performed by the company as a percentage of domestic net sales (percent of domestic sales of R&D performers or funders). Data for 2006 and 2007 are not comparable to other years due to changes in data availability. Data in those years represent company and other nonfederal funds for industrial R&D as a percent of net sales of companies performing industrial R&D in the US.

in large power plants. For example, new natural gas-fired combined cycle plants are three times as large as similar plants built in the 1980s, leading to lower costs per kilowatt (EIA Today in Energy 2019a). Demonstrating commercial viability of a new energy production technology requires hundreds of millions of dollars, making entry into the industry difficult for small startup firms (Nanda, Younge, and Fleming 2015).

4. Long time horizons between initial idea and commercialization in the energy sector also make it more difficult for small startup firms to raise capital (e.g., Howell 2017; Popp 2016). Venture capital investors expect returns within 3 to 5 years of their investments. But the development and testing of new energy technologies takes longer (Gaddy et al. 2017).

Measuring the returns to R&D in the energy sector is also challenging. Since energy is a commodity, reducing costs and environmental impacts matter more than increasing productivity. On these measures, the energy industry has seen remarkable changes in the twenty-first century. The rise of unconventional gas and oil sources obtained using hydraulic fracturing increased supplies and lowered prices of oil and gas. At the same time, costs of renewable energy sources fell to levels that make them competitive with fossil fuels. Below we describe the impact of each of these technological advances on the energy industry.

4.2.1   The Rise of Shale Gas and Oil

Access to natural gas and oil reserves in shale deposits on competitive terms has changed global energy markets. Shale deposits were too expensive to access until technological advances, such as horizontal drilling and hydraulic fracturing (colloquially known as "fracking"), reduced drilling costs (Jacoby, O'Sullivan, and Palstev 2012). These unconventional wells use a mixture of water, sand, and other chemicals to cause cracks and fissures in the rock formation that allow crude oil to escape (Fetter et al. 2018). Horizontal drilling is often used to widen access to shale plays. Improved access to shale gas and oil caused US crude oil reserves to grow (figure 4.1), allowing the US to play a larger role in global oil markets. In September 2019, the US exported more petroleum than it imported for the first time since monthly recordkeeping began in 1973 (EIA Today in Energy 2019b). Domestically, increased access to natural gas lowered natural gas prices (figure 4.2), leading to increased use of natural gas by electric utilities. Natural gas surpassed coal as the primary fuel source for US electric utilities in 2016 (figure 4.3). Since 2010, US power plant emissions of sulfur dioxide (SO_2) fell by 75 percent, and carbon dioxide emissions fell by over 25 percent. As a result, annual damages from emissions fell from $245 billion to $133 billion. Roughly $60 billion of this reduction is due to changing shares of fuels in power generation (Holland et al. 2018).

The rise in hydraulic fracturing began in the early 2000s, stimulated by

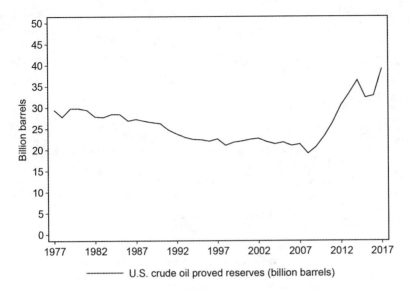

U.S. crude oil proved reserves (billion barrels)

Fig. 4.1   US crude oil proved reserves
Source: US Energy Information Administration (2018).
Note: US crude oil proved reserves, in billions of barrels.

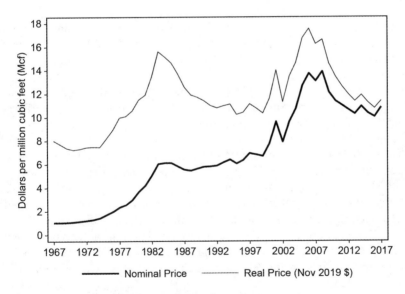

Nominal Price ———— Real Price (Nov 2019 $)

Fig. 4.2   Annual residential natural gas price
Source: US EIA Short-Term Energy Outlook, November 2019.
Note: Average annual price of residential natural gas in the United States, in 2019 US dollars.

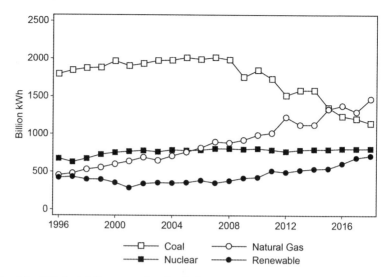

Fig. 4.3   US electricity generation, by fuel source
Source: US Energy Information Administration (2019).
Note: "Renewable" includes conventional hydropower, wind, wood biomass, waste biomass, geothermal, and solar.

the high price of conventional crude oil at the time. These higher prices made shale oil viable, and the initial activity in shale oil led to efficiency improvements that further reduced the costs (Killian 2016). Both private and public sector investments in the US aided the development of shale gas technologies. The US invested in government R&D to develop unconventional natural gas, but oil industry innovations, such as horizontal drilling and three-dimensional seismic imaging, were also important (Krupnick and Wang 2017). In particular, Mitchell Energy, an independent natural gas firm, made large investments in shale gas development before it was proven profitable (Krupnick and Wang 2017). Mitchell Energy had experimented with shale development for several years without finding a way to make it profitable. Their technological advance came in 1997, when they used new "slickwater" fracking treatments (Cahoy, Gehman, and Lei 2013). In 2001, Devon Energy, with expertise in horizontal drilling, acquired Mitchell Energy. Combining horizontal drilling and hydraulic fracturing led to the boom in shale gas production that would soon follow (Cahoy, Gehman, and Lei 2013).

Hydraulic fracturing has affected both energy markets and the environment in several ways:

- Increased drilling has led to local economic booms. Employment in oil and gas extraction grew from nearly 74,000 workers in 2000 to over 113,400 workers in 2016 (table 4.2). Communities in the top quartile of

Table 4.2   Total employment (thousands): Select industries

	2000	2005	2010	2011	2012	2013	2014	2015	2016
21111: Crude petroleum and natural gas extraction	73.7	72.4	99.5	109.0	114.5	120.1	126.7	124.8	113.4
2121: Coal mining	70.7	74.3	81.4	86.2	89.4	84.0	76.6	69.9	55.0
23712: Pipeline construction		86.3	126.9	127.9	143.4	163.1	167.7	178.3	163.7
22111: Electric power generation	143.9	120.8	132.8	135.7	134.5	135.4	137.5	134.9	135.2
22114: Solar					0.8	0.9	1.2	1.4	1.6
22115: Wind					2.4	2.9	2.8	3.1	3.2
335911: Battery manufacturing	22.8	17.1	17.8	18.9	19.3	18.9	19.2	19.7	20.8
3361–3: Automobiles	1198.1	1033.2	627.6	667.3	727.1	769.7	811.1	865.6	901.9
31–33: All manufacturing	16474.0	13667.3	10862.8	10984.4	11192.0	11276.4	11424.3	11605.5	11590.4

Source: US Census Bureau: Statistics of US Businesses, various years.

Note: Table shows total employment, in thousands, for select industries.

potential hydraulic fracturing productivity experienced a 4.8 percent growth in employment and a 5.8 percent increase in household income (Bartik et al. 2019). Taking into account indirect impacts, Maniloff and Mastromonaco (2017) estimate that the shale boom created about 550,000 local jobs. Feyrer, Mansur, and Sacerdote (2017) find that every million dollars of new oil and gas extracted creates 0.85 jobs in the county, and 2.13 jobs within 100 miles of the drilling site. To put this in perspective, $393 billion of new oil and gas production occurred between 2005 and 2014.

- At the same time, expansion of natural gas has hurt the coal industry. Employment in coal mining fell from a peak of 89,367 in 2012 to just 55,008 in 2016 (table 4.2).
- Shale gas and oil reduce market volatility. While shale wells take longer to drill and reach production, they produce more per well and have less variation in production. Thus, shale gas is more responsive to market prices (Newell and Prest 2017).
- While the development of shale gas helped reduce air pollution from US power plants, it also raised new environmental concerns. Hydraulic fracturing requires several times more water than does conventional drilling. Moreover, there are concerns that leaks and spills from hydraulic fracturing activity may contaminate groundwater. As a result, several countries and some US states have banned hydraulic fracturing while further study is conducted (Krupnick and Wang 2017).

4.2.2 Increased Penetration of Renewable Energy Sources

Increasing electricity generation from wind and solar energy provides a second opportunity for the energy sector, but it also comes with its own set of challenges. The costs of electricity generated from solar photovoltaic (PV) and onshore wind turbines has fallen dramatically since 2010, making both competitive with electricity generated from fossil fuels (figure 4.4). While renewable energy sources are still a small share of electricity generation in the US (17 percent), their use is growing rapidly (figure 4.3). Solar and energy generation typically occurs at a smaller scale than for fossil fuels. Figure 4.5 shows trends in the percentage of employment in small and medium-sized establishments for various industries. While the average for all manufacturing industries is just over 40 percent, power generation, turbine manufacturing, and battery manufacturing all have percentages around 20 percent or less. In contrast, most solar and wind energy generation occurs in small and medium-sized establishments. Because solar and wind establishments are smaller and these enterprises still make up a small share of the overall power generation industry, the growth in renewable energy during the past decade did not lead to growth in employment in the power generation sector (table 4.2).

Wind and solar energy are examples of *intermittent* sources of power, as

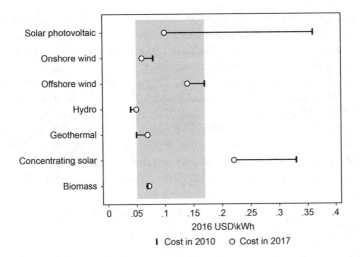

Fig. 4.4   Costs of electricity from selected sources

Note: Figure shows the levelized cost of energy (LCOE) for various renewable energy sources. Data taken from figure 2.1 in International Renewable Energy Agency (2018), which uses costs of individual projects in the IRENA Renewable Cost Database. Costs are the global weighted average of LCOE for newly commissioned projects in a given year, where the weights are based on capacity deployed by country/year. The shaded region shows the equivalent cost range for fossil fuels. Note that, by 2017, all renewable sources except concentrating solar power were competitive with fossil fuels.

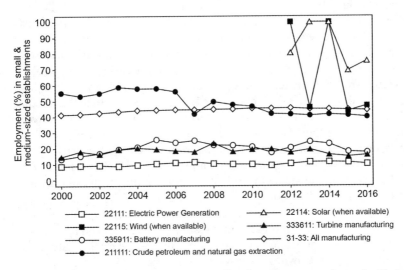

Fig. 4.5   Percentage of employment in small and medium enterprises, select industries

Source: US Census Bureau: Statistics of US Businesses, various years.

Note: Figure shows the percentage of employees working in small and medium enterprises, which include establishments of 500 workers or fewer. Separate breakdowns for solar and wind are unavailable until 2011.

the electricity generated depends on factors beyond the operator's control, such as wind speeds. Intermittent sources create challenges for managing the electricity grid (Borenstein 2012). Because electricity is very expensive to store, what goes on the grid must match what comes off, requiring *balancing authorities* to equate power supply and demand in real time (EIA Today in Energy 2016; International Energy Agency 2019a). To illustrate, consider the structure of the US electricity grid. The continental US electricity grid is divided into three mains sections: the Eastern Interconnection, the Western Interconnection, and the Electricity Reliability Council of Texas (ERCOT). Except for ERCOT, these interconnections are divided into smaller balancing authorities managing smaller regions. Some balancing authorities are independent utilities, such as the Tennessee Valley Authority (TVA). Others are regional transmission organizations—independent nonprofit organizations, such as the Midwest Independent System Operator or the New York Independent System Operator (EIA Today in Energy 2011).

The increased penetration of intermittent renewable sources poses two additional challenges. First, because the marginal cost of renewables is close to 0, it is offered to wholesale markets at very low costs. At times when renewable energy generation is high, wholesale prices fall. In some cases, oversupply of electricity from mid-day solar energy has created *negative* electricity prices—power producers were willing to pay grid managers to use the electricity they generate (Bajwa and Cavicchi 2017). Low wholesale prices have particularly hurt nuclear plants (International Energy Agency 2019b). While these plants also have low marginal costs, they have high fixed costs that are difficult to recover when wholesale prices are low. Nuclear plants are also costly to shut down and restart. As a result, competition from natural gas and wind is forcing some nuclear plants to retire early (Roth and Jaramillo 2017) rather than accept low wholesale prices and operating at a loss. Second, modular sources, such as solar PV panels, exacerbate the fluctuations in electricity demand that occur during a typical day. As homeowners generate more of their own power during the day using solar photovoltaic panels, demand for electricity purchased from the grid falls but then picks up again in early evening as the sun sets and people return home for the day.

Addressing the challenges of grid integration requires both technological and management innovations. Cross-border power markets increase flexibility and make balancing supply and demand easier (Martinot 2016). Developing affordable energy storage options would reduce the need to instantaneously balance supply and demand. Currently, most electricity stored on the grid uses pumped hydro reserves: water is pushed to a higher elevation using excess electricity, where it can be released to generate electricity using hydropower when needed. The use of pumped hydropower storage is limited geographically. Technological advances, such as better batteries, could greatly expand the potential of energy storage (Greenblatt et al. 2017). Similarly, smart grid technologies allowing for automated demand-load management can better match supply and demand (Greenblatt et al. 2017). Smart grid technologies allow for two-way communication between customers and utilities, facilitating management strategies, such as peak-load pricing, where electricity prices to consumers rise and fall based on market conditions. Consumers can, for example, then choose to run appliances at times when prices are lowest (US Department of Energy n.d.).

4.2.3 Innovation in the Energy Sector

The increased use of both hydraulic fracturing and renewable energy creates new technological challenges, but it also creates new opportunities for innovation. New energy technologies are often smaller and modular (e.g., solar panels, smart meters for homes), reducing the need for large capital costs. While energy remains a commodity, the popularity of products such as Nest thermostats suggests that product differentiation is possible for end-use technologies that improve energy efficiency and potentially improve grid management. The rise of hydraulic fracturing depended in part on improved seismic imaging to help locate new shale resources (Krupnick and Wang 2017). Today, energy companies are turning to data analytics and artificial intelligence to further improve their search for new energy (Anonymous 2019).

Before turning to our analysis of the changing nature of energy innovation, we provide a brief review of evidence so far in the literature examining the effects of policies and regulations on energy innovation. See Popp (2019) for a more comprehensive review. Several distinct features of energy innovation make it particularly important to study today. First and foremost, addressing climate change and mitigating its harm in the time required will require significant innovation at speed and scale. Furthermore, in addition to the four challenges outlined at the beginning of this section, innovation in clean energy faces a "double-externality" challenge. As there are for any innovation, knowledge spillovers associated with clean energy innovation reduce private incentives for investing. However, the social benefits of clean energy associated with pollution reductions are also not reflected in market prices without government intervention. Thus, the potential demand for clean energy technologies is dependent on effective environmental policy. Policies addressing these *environmental externalities* increase the potential market size for clean energy innovation and are often referred to as *demand-pull* policies in the literature. Policies supporting technology development directly are often referred to as *technology-push* policies.

These two market failures could, in principle, be addressed separately. Since knowledge market failures apply generally across technologies, economy-wide policies affecting all types of innovation could address knowledge market failures, leaving it to environmental policy to "get the prices right" to encourage green innovation. A carbon tax exemplifies the economist's goal of "getting prices right" by putting a price on emissions related to climate change. Evidence on the impact of market forces, such as higher energy prices or price corrections from broad-based policies (e.g., carbon taxes), show that prices matter for innovation. Over the long term, a 10 percent increase in energy prices leads to a 3.5 percent rise in the number of US patents in 11 different alternative energy and energy efficiency technologies (Popp 2002). Most of the response occurs quickly after a change in energy prices, with an average lag between an energy price change and patenting activity of 3.71 years. Verdolini and Galeotti (2011) find similar results using a multi-country sample from 1975 to 2000. Similarly, when facing higher fuel prices, firms in the automotive industry produce more innovations on clean technologies, such as electric and hybrid cars, and less in fossil-fuel technologies that improve internal combustion engines (Aghion et al. 2016). A 10 percent higher fuel price is associated with about 10 percent more low-emission energy patents and 7 percent fewer fossil-fuel patents. In contrast, energy prices are less effective for promoting innovation for home energy efficiency, particularly for less-visible technologies, such as insulation, that are installed by builders and are not easily modified. Instead, building code changes induce innovation for home energy efficiency (Noailly 2012).

However, in addition to broad-based policies, such as carbon taxes or cap-and-trade that target all greenhouse gas emissions, governments use a variety of targeted policies to promote clean energy and reduce emissions. Examples include energy efficiency standards, renewable energy mandates, tax incentives for purchasing rooftop solar photovoltaic equipment, and investment credits and subsidies for specific clean energy technologies. The type of policy support chosen also affects both the pace and direction of innovation. Policies to promote clean energy can either be *technology-neutral* or *technology-specific*. Technology-neutral policies provide broad mandates, such as reducing emissions to a certain level but leave it to consumers and firms to decide how to comply. Examples include a carbon tax, which targets all emissions equally, as well as more targeted policies, such as renewable energy mandates. Such mandates can require that utilities generate a set portion of electricity from renewable energy, but they do not dictate what types of renewable sources be used. In contrast, technology-specific policies stipulate the use of individual technologies. For example, tax credits for electric vehicles or rooftop solar energy are only available to consumers who purchase these products.

Technology-neutral policies promote technologies closest to being competitive in the market without policy support. The Johnstone, Haščič, and Popp (2010) study of renewable energy innovation is an example. Because wind energy was the closest to being competitive with traditional energy sources at the time of that study, innovation in countries with mandates to provide alternative energy focused on wind. In contrast, direct investment incentives such as feed-in tariffs supported innovation in solar and waste-to-energy technologies. These technologies were less competitive with traditional energy technologies and required the guaranteed revenue from a feed-in tariff to compete. Thus, although technology-specific policies may raise short-term costs, judicious use of them helps promote the development of low-emission technologies further from the market, such as offshore wind or carbon capture and sequestration.

Recent theoretical work provides support for the use of such targeted policies—particularly those technologies furthest from market. Other market failures (such as learning-by-doing, path dependency, and capital market failures) limit incentives to invest in these emerging technologies (Acemoglu et al. 2016; Fischer, Preonas, and Newell 2017; Lehmann and Söderholm 2018). Both learning-by-doing and path dependency justify technology-specific deployment policies, such as feed-in tariffs or tax credits—most notably when the resulting cost reductions benefit not only early adopters but also those who wait to adopt until costs fall (e.g., Lehmann and Söderholm 2018). However, the existing literature on learning-by-doing generally suggests that the benefits of learning-by-doing are not sufficient to justify current levels of deployment subsidies (e.g., Fischer, Preonas, and Newell 2017; Nemet 2012; Tang 2018). Empirical evidence on path dependency is slim. Path dependency creates a market failure if switching costs make it difficult for firms previously investing in one type of technology to switch to profitable opportunities in another. While some recent studies find evidence of path dependency in energy innovation (e.g., Aghion et al. 2016; Stucki and Woerter 2017), none of these studies tests whether the observed path dependency results from high switching costs or is simply a reaction to better research opportunities. More research on the relationship between switching costs and path dependency is needed.

In contrast, the evidence on capital market failures for energy is limited but suggestive of such market failures. In a study using financial microdata, Cárdenas Rodríguez et al. (2015) find that price-based policy instruments, such as feed-in tariffs and tax credits, have a positive effect on private investment for renewable energy. It is hypothesized that such instruments provide a more predictable revenue stream, potentially making them more suitable for alleviating the particular risk-return profile of renewable energy investments. In contrast, quota-based policy instruments, whose support levels are more difficult to ascertain ex ante, have no significant effect on private finance investment. Moreover, if credit markets are functioning well, price schemes will induce private finance for less mature technologies (e.g., solar PV), while a quota schemes will induce private finance for more mature technologies (e.g., onshore wind). However, if credit markets are not functioning well, only price schemes will have an effect on private finance flows, and only for the case of onshore wind power.

In an evaluation of the US Department of Energy Small Business Innovation Research (SBIR) program, Howell (2017) provides evidence that early financing helps overcome capital market failures in clean energy. SBIR grants improve the performance of new clean energy firms, but they are ineffective for older technologies, such as coal, natural gas, and biofuels. Similarly, Popp (2017) provides evidence that bringing new energy technologies to market takes longer in clean energy than in other fields (e.g., Branstetter and Ogura 2005; Finardi 2011), suggesting that the length of time necessary for commercialization of energy R&D creates a barrier to raising private sector financial support.

Given the importance of financing constraints, a recently emerging literature considers the role of venture capital for renewable energy. Nanda, Younge, and Fleming (2015) provide descriptive data comparing clean energy innovations supported by venture capital to other clean energy innovations, showing that patents from firms receiving venture capital are cited more frequently. However, they argue that the nature of energy markets may reduce the potential of venture capital in clean energy. These concerns include the capital intensity of energy production, the long time frame, and the difficulty for successful ventures to find an "exit" strategy, in which they are purchased by a larger company. Similarly, comparing venture capital investments in clean energy, software, and medicine, Gaddy et al. (2017) find that clean energy ventures do not perform as well as software, but they do not perform worse than medicine. They also argue that their study suggests venture capital is poorly suited for clean technology. Cumming, Leboeuf, and Schwienbacher (2017) consider crowdfunding as an alternative to venture capital. They collect data on crowdfunded projects from Indiegogo, with 7.4 percent of projects pertaining to clean technology. While potential entrepreneurs are able to use the crowdfunding platform to reduce information asymmetries with investors, clean technology offerings are no more successful than other crowdfunded projects, and they appear to be perceived as more risky.

Finally, climate change is a global problem. Innovators partake in global markets and are influenced by regulation not only at home but also in other countries where they do business. As such, policies in both local and foreign markets matter. Dechezleprêtre and Glachant (2014) compare wind energy patents across OECD countries, using data from 1991–2008. Their observations consist of country pairs, as they look at both the source (e.g., where the invention is developed) and destination (e.g., where patents are granted) of invention. Although the marginal effect of policies implemented at home is 12 times higher, the larger size of foreign markets makes the overall impact of foreign policies twice as large on average as the overall impact of domestic policies on innovation. In a study of 15 OECD countries using patent data from 1978 to 2005, Peters et al. (2012) also find both domestic and foreign demand-pull policies (such as renewable portfolio standards or feed-in tariffs) are important for the development of solar PV technology. However, technology-push policies (such as R&D subsidies) only increase domestic innovation, as firms must be in the local market to take advantage of them.

Fabrizio, Poczter, and Zelner (2017) find similar results for energy storage. In addition, as their sample includes patents from countries not directly regulating energy storage, they also show that demand-pull policies encourage innovation and increase technology transfer coming into the country, measured as domestic patent applications filed for technologies that originally filed for patent protection elsewhere.

4.3   Patenting in the Energy Sector

In this section, we present patenting trends for a range of energy technologies, focusing on technologies related to the changing nature of energy: clean energy technologies and hydraulic fracturing. A large literature on energy innovation has shown that clean energy patenting is responsive to both higher energy prices (e.g., Aghion et al. 2016; Newell, Jaffe, and Stavins 1999; Popp 2002; Verdolini and Gaelotti 2011) and policy (e.g., Dechezleprêtre and Glachant 2014; Fabrizio, Poczter, and Zelner 2017; Johnstone, Haščič, and Popp 2010; Nesta, Vona, and Nicolli 2014; Peters et al. 2012). However, with a few exceptions, patent levels have fallen since a peak in the early 2010s. We explore possible explanations for this decline below.

Our patent data are taken from the European Patent Office (EPO) World Patent Statistical Database (PATSTAT), which includes over 100 million patent applications from 90 patent authorities. To control for patent quality, we only include patent applications having two or more family members in different jurisdictions. Inventors must file a patent at each patent office for which they desire protection. Filing in multiple offices is a signal that the patented invention is of higher quality (e.g., Harhoff, Scherer, and Vopel 2003; Lanjouw, Pakes, and Putnam 1998). We use the EPO's "Y scheme," which provides separate classifications for technologies pertaining to climate change mitigation and adaptation, to identify relevant patents. These classifications complement standard patent classification schemes, such as the Cooperative Patent Classification (CPC) scheme, grouping together relevant technologies that may appear in a wide range of traditional patent classes (Angelucci, Hurtado-Albir, and Volpe 2018; Veefkind et al. 2012).

We first present data for 11 clean energy technologies, categorized in two main groups. Clean energy technologies include new or improved energy sources. Enabling technologies include those technologies that will help integrate a rapidly diversifying set of energy sources, such as energy storage, smart grids, and systems integration. Appendix table 4.A1 lists the patent classes used to identify each technology below. In the following three figures, the trend for all technologies is included for comparison.

Figures 4.6 through 4.8 present our patent data. Panels A and B of figure 4.6 show global trends for clean energy and enabling energy technologies, respectively. Our data include patents applied for between 1997 and 2015, so that our focus is on innovation since the Kyoto Protocol. Because the

A. Clean Energy Technologies

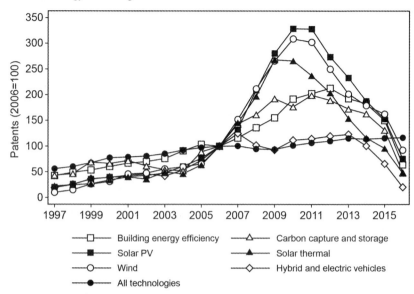

B. Enabling Energy Technologies

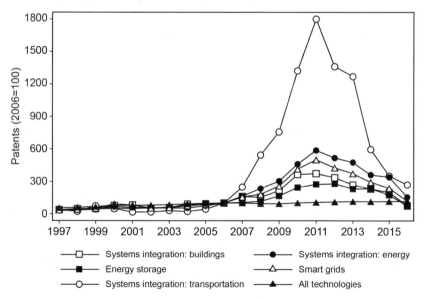

Fig. 4.6 Global energy patents

Note: Figures show global counts of energy patents for patents filed in two or more countries. Patents are sorted by priority year. All counts normalized so that 2006 = 100. Patent extractions from the EPO World Patent Statistical Database (PATSTAT).

number of patents in each group varies, we normalize each patent series so that 2006 equals 100.[1] Two notable trends stand out. First, each energy technology experiences dramatic growth in the early 2010s. For most technologies, global patent counts increased by a factor of 3 or more from 2006 to 2011. Growth is larger for several of the enabling technologies, which are less mature. The only exception to this pattern is hybrid and electric vehicles, whose patent counts peak in 2007. For the remaining technologies, this sudden increase in clean energy patenting followed already significant growth in the early twenty-first century, as patent counts for most technologies doubled from 1997 to 2006. Second, this sudden increase in patenting was followed by a rapid decline. By 2015, patent levels were around half of what they had been at the 2010–2011 peak. This stands in contrast to the small, steady increases in patenting for all technologies.

Figures 4.7 and 4.8 show that these trends are truly global. Based on the home country of each inventor, we present clean energy patents and enabling technology patents from inventors from the US, the European Union (EU), Japan, and China. While the downturn is not as noticeable for China (or perhaps begins a year or two later), overall patenting is also increasing more rapidly in China, so that much of the growth in energy patenting in China simply corresponds to an overall increase in patenting activity. With few exceptions, such as building energy efficiency patents in the US and EU, similar peaks and declines are observed for clean energy technologies in the US, EU, and Japan.

4.3.1   Why Has Clean Energy Patenting Fallen?

While it is beyond the scope of this chapter to provide definitive evidence on any one possible explanation for the recent decline in clean energy patenting, we suggest several possible explanations below. When relevant, we cite evidence from recent working papers that have begun exploring this decline. In other cases, we provide our own descriptive data to look for correlations between potential mechanisms that might explain the decline.

4.3.1.1   Innovation Follows Energy Prices

As previously noted, energy prices are an important driver of energy innovation (e.g., Aghion et al. 2016; Popp 2002; Verdolini and Galeotti 2011). Both the recent increase and decrease in patenting coincide with trends in energy prices, particularly in the fuel sector (figure 4.9). Similar spikes in patenting also occurred during the period of high energy prices in the late 1970s and early 1980s. Figure 4.10 provides a longer-term look at patenting for selected technologies.[2] To control for overall growth in patenting, we

1. We normalize in the middle of the sample, rather than in 1997, because some technologies have very few patents in the early years of the sample.
2. Because our search terms use the EPO's Y-scheme, which uses internal EPO classifications, we cannot extend the data prior to 1978. The EPO was founded in late 1977.

A. United States

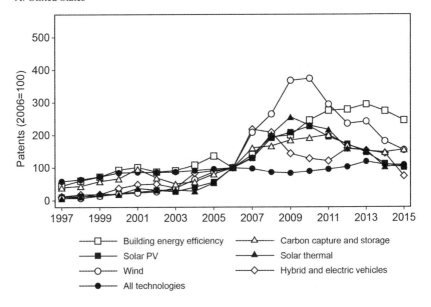

B. European Union

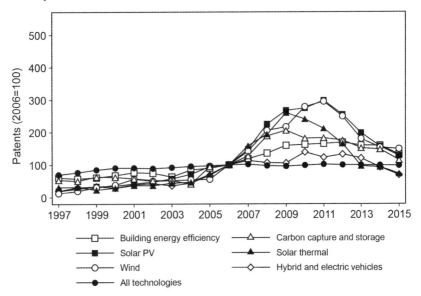

Fig. 4.7   Clean energy patents by country

Note: Figures show global counts of clean energy patents for patents filed in two or more countries. Patents are sorted by priority year. Fractional counts used for patents with inventors from multiple countries. All counts normalized so that 2006 = 100. Patent extractions from the EPO World Patent Statistical Database (PATSTAT).

C. Japan

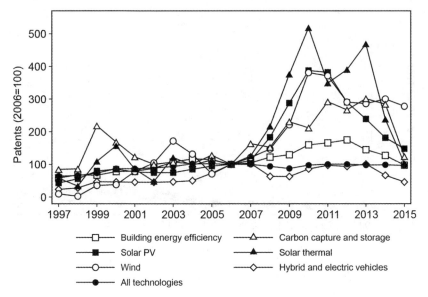

D. China

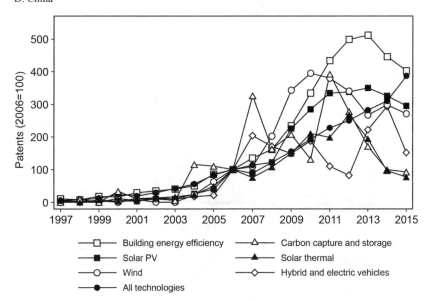

Fig. 4.7   (cont.)

A. United States

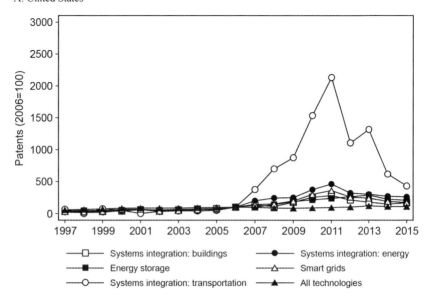

B. European Union

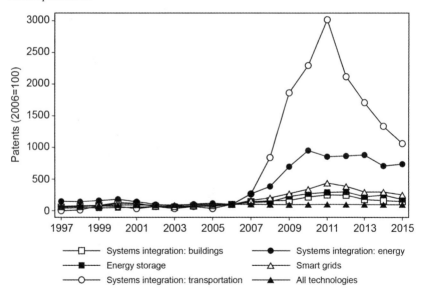

Fig. 4.8 Enabling energy technology patents, by country

Note: Figure shows global counts of enabling energy technologies for patents filed in two or more countries. Patents are sorted by priority year. Fractional counts used for patents with inventors from multiple countries. All counts normalized so that 2006 = 100. Patent extractions from the EPO World Patent Statistical Database (PATSTAT).

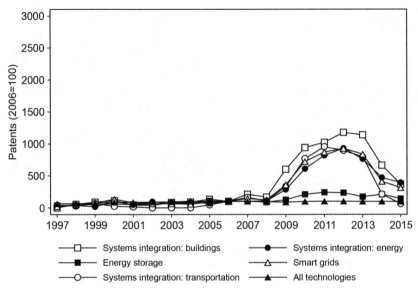

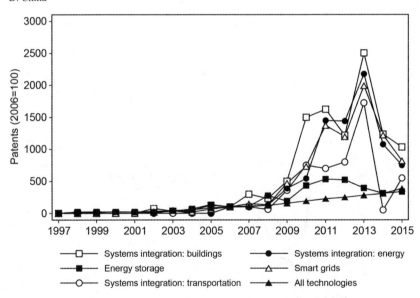

Fig. 4.8   (cont.)

A. United States

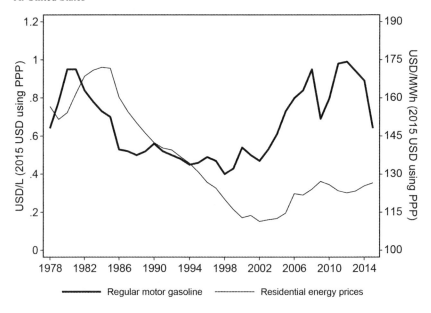

B. European Union

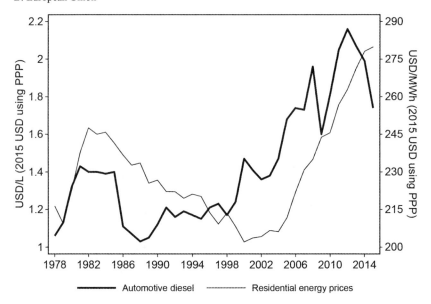

Fig. 4.9   Energy prices, selected countries

Source: IEA (2019c).

Note: Figures show gasoline and residential electricity prices for select countries, in 2015 US dollars.

C. Japan

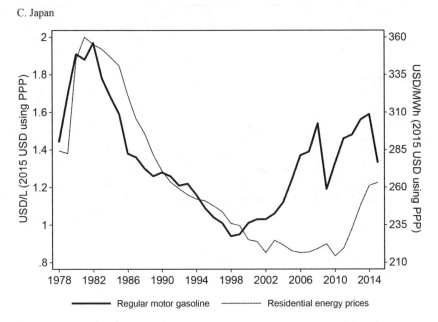

Fig. 4.9   (cont.)

present these data as the share of all global patents pertaining to a given technology. The trends clearly suggest that clean energy patenting fell as energy prices declined in the mid-1980s.

While it is tempting to conclude that history is simply repeating itself, the most striking take-away from figure 4.10 is the unprecedented growth in patenting through the late 2000s. The share of patents devoted to such technologies as wind, energy efficiency, and energy storage is three to five times higher in the late 2000s and very early 2010s than during the first energy crisis. Only solar thermal technology experienced a peak in the late 1970s comparable to its peak just after 2010. Presumably this is a result of changing emphasis in solar energy, where modular solar photovoltaic panels, rather than large-scale solar thermal installations, have become the cost-effective technology. Recall from figure 4.4 that concentrated solar power was cheaper than solar PV in 2010, but by 2017, solar PV was three times less expensive than concentrated solar power. As figure 4.10 shows, these cost reductions followed a remarkable growth in solar PV innovation.

The observation that "peak" patenting is so much higher at the turn of the last decade emphasizes how other energy policies complemented the incentives provided by energy prices. During the energy crisis of the 1970s, government R&D investments for clean energy were the main targeted clean energy policy. By the 2000s, direct subsidies (such as feed-in tariffs guaranteeing a minimum price for clean energy or government mandates for renew-

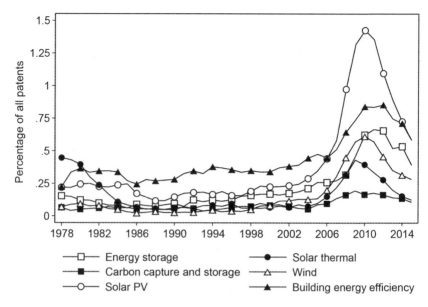

Fig. 4.10   Historical patent counts, selected technologies

Note: Figure shows the share of all patents in selected technologies, for patents filed in two or more countries. Patents are sorted by priority year. Fractional counts used for patents with inventors from multiple countries. Patent extractions from the EPO World Patent Statistical Database (PATSTAT).

able energy sources) became more prevalent, as did broad-based carbon pricing following the introduction of the EU Emissions Trading Scheme in 2005 (e.g., Ang, Röttgers, and Pralhad 2017; EIA 2004). The importance of both targeted and broad-based energy policy for promoting innovation is further supported by recent evidence that consumers are more responsive to energy price changes driven by carbon taxes than to other market dynamics, as tax changes may be more salient and are perceived as being more persistent (Davis and Kilian 2011; Li, Linn, and Muehlegger 2014; Rivers and Schaufele 2015). Furthermore, targeted subsidies are particularly important for fostering innovation in technologies that had not yet become cost-effective, such as solar PV in the early 2000s (Johnstone, Haščič, and Popp 2010). While increases in the price of fossil fuels, either due to market forces or carbon-pricing policies, may affect which energy technology is cheapest at the margin, price increases tend to not spur producers or consumers to choose technologies that remain relatively costlier, even with higher fossil fuel prices. Given the important supporting role of policy, the drop in energy prices alone is not sufficient to explain the recent decline in patenting.

4.3.1.2   *The Rise of Hydrofracturing*

The decline in clean energy patenting comes soon after the expansion of US natural gas production due to hydrofracturing. Recall that natural gas

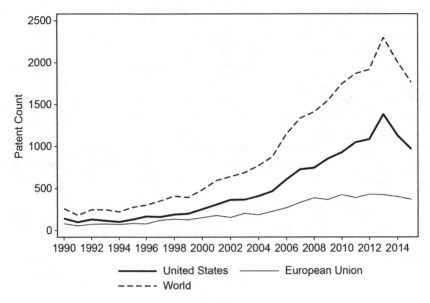

Fig. 4.11   Hydrofracturing patents, 1990–2015

Note: Figure shows hydrofracturing patents with applications in two or more countries, sorted by priority year and inventor country. Fractional counts used for patents with inventors from multiple countries. Patent extractions from the EPO World Patent Statistical Database (PATSTAT).

prices in the US began to decline after 2007. Similarly, increased oil supply and decreased demand after the global recession led to decreased oil and gasoline prices (e.g., figure 4.9). Acemoglu et al. (2019) posit that the shale boom caused energy innovation to shift from clean energy to fossil fuels.

Data on hydraulic fracturing patents provide some support for this argument. Figure 4.11 shows patent counts related to hydrofracturing for the world, the US, and the EU.[3] Together the US and EU account for 79 percent of these patents. Two trends emerge. First, after a period of relatively flat innovation, hydrofracturing innovation took off during the first decade of the twenty-first century. Between 1990 and 1999, fracking patents grew by just over 50 percent. From 2000 to 2009, they grew by more than a factor

---

3. As in other figures, data include patents with applications in two or more countries, sorted by priority year and inventor country. As the patent classes used to identify these innovations are limited in scope, we also perform a robustness check using a broader set of classes, which may however include unrelated technologies. For this reason, they are combined with a keyword search on patent titles and abstracts using the terms "hydraulic fracturing," "horizontal drilling," and "well completion" (following Cahoy, Gehman, and Lei 2013). These counts are not directly comparable to our other patent trends, as the keyword searches are only possible for patents applications registered at the US and European Patent Offices. Although the resulting patent counts are much lower, the trends for those patents are similar, with a three-fold increase during the 2000s and dominance by US inventors. Search terms for both search strategies are listed in Appendix A.

of 3. While they do not grow as fast as most clean energy patents, hydraulic fracturing patents do not peak until 2013.

Second, recent innovations in hydrofracturing are dominated by the US, as nearly all growth during the 2000s comes from US inventors. Fracking faces strong public opposition in Europe due to concerns over surface water diversion, groundwater quality, and consistency with climate policy goals (Krupnick and Wang 2017). While the US is responsible for about 20 to 30 percent of most energy inventions (table 4.3), it is responsible for over 50 percent of fracking patents. Nonetheless, the fall in clean energy patenting has occurred globally. Moreover, while hydrofracturing contributed to the fall in oil and gas prices during this time, electricity prices are a more important driver of innovation for renewable technologies, such as solar and wind energy. Trends in electricity prices vary across countries (see figure 4.9). Electricity prices were relatively stable in the US, thanks in part to lower natural gas prices, but they were steadily increasing in the EU and began to rise in Japan after bottoming out in 2010. Thus the rise of hydrofracking offers at best a partial explanation for the decline in clean energy patents.

4.3.1.3   Weakened Regulations

Because market prices do not internalize environmental externalities for clean energy versus other energy sources, regulatory support is an important driver of innovation in the energy sector. Both weakened regulation and uncertain regulation dampen incentives to innovate. Some regulatory changes that occurred as renewable energy reached its peak include:

- The election of President Barack Obama in the US increased expectations that the US would enact nationwide climate legislation. While several proposals were considered—most prominently the American Clean Energy and Security Act (more commonly known as the Waxman-Markey bill), which would have instituted a cap-and-trade system for US carbon emissions—health care was the first priority of the new administration, and prospects for nationwide climate policy fell once Republicans took control of the Senate in 2010.
- The initial run-up of clean energy innovation coincides with the beginning of the EU's Emissions Trading Scheme (EU-ETS), an EU-wide cap-and-trade program for carbon emissions. Phase I of EU-ETS began in 2005. This pilot phase lasted until 2007. Phase II, which began in 2008, lowered the supply of allowances available. While allowance prices initially rose to 30 euros as a result, they fell to below 10 euros after the financial crisis in late 2008 (Ellerman, Marcantonini, and Zaklan 2016). Allowance prices would not reach pre-crisis levels again until phase IV began in 2018.[4]
- As the cost of renewable energy technology fell, government support

4. https://sandbag.org.uk/carbon-price-viewer/, accessed November 14, 2019.

Table 4.3   **Percentage of patents with inventors from selected countries and regions**

	2000	2005	2010	2015
United States				
Fracking	52.0	53.4	53.3	54.8
Solar PV	17.2	22.7	21.5	20.6
Wind	10.5	21.9	19.9	15.6
Hybrid and electric vehicles	15.7	20.7	19.0	18.7
Carbon capture and storage	35.3	31.9	38.3	41.8
Energy storage	17.8	9.9	14.4	19.4
Smart grids	33.8	41.7	33.4	33.3
All technologies	27.0	24.6	21.9	23.4
European Union				
Fracking	31.2	25.8	24.4	20.8
Solar PV	18.8	26.2	17.8	17.8
Wind	69.0	47.8	50.7	51.5
Hybrid and electric vehicles	18.7	23.2	30.9	26.1
Carbon capture and storage	27.4	30.9	30.1	25.6
Energy storage	16.8	13.8	19.1	17.9
Smart grids	34.2	22.6	20.3	26.2
All technologies	31.1	26.7	25.9	22.7
China				
Fracking	0.7	1.6	2.7	3.8
Solar PV	0.4	2.1	3.4	7.6
Wind	0.0	3.8	5.0	6.5
Hybrid and electric vehicles	0.5	0.5	2.9	3.9
Carbon capture and storage	0.8	2.0	1.2	1.1
Energy storage	1.0	3.4	4.4	4.8
Smart grids	0.0	1.1	2.7	5.3
All technologies	1.0	2.8	6.1	10.7
Japan				
Fracking	1.7	2.3	0.9	1.5
Solar PV	57.2	33.0	31.4	25.8
Wind	8.5	7.6	8.7	12.0
Hybrid and electric vehicles	60.2	51.5	39.3	35.6
Carbon capture and storage	27.7	15.7	13.1	10.3
Energy storage	52.6	49.4	38.2	36.0
Smart grids	18.2	13.1	21.9	16.6
All technologies	28.4	26.7	24.5	21.2

Source: Authors' calculations using data from the EPO World Patent Statistical Database (PATSTAT).

Notes: Table shows the percentage of inventors coming from each country for selected technologies. Fractional counts used for patents with inventors from multiple countries.

also began to decline. Germany, Spain, and Italy—three major supporters of solar PV—all cut subsidies to PV after the financial crisis. While Spain cut subsidies to PV in September 2008, Germany announced cuts in late 2010—right at the peak of patenting activity. Italy announced cuts to subsidies beginning in 2012. Moreover, Spain's subsidy cut was retroactive, increasing uncertainty among investors. A working paper by Ko and Simons (2020) argues that these subsidy cuts affected innovation not only domestically but abroad as well. They link the subsidy cuts to a decline in R&D by South Korean manufacturers, who exported 70 percent of PV production.

Weakened regulations are a plausible explanation for the worldwide decline in clean energy innovation. Both energy supply technologies and the enabling technologies needed to complement these technologies peak after 2010, corresponding with when the US election reduced the likelihood of climate policy in the US and Germany reduced solar subsidies. In contrast, technologies less directly linked to these policies, such as building energy efficiency and hybrid vehicles, peak at different times. That global innovation fell as a result is consistent with such studies Dechezleprêtre and Glachant (2014) and Peters et al. (2012), who demonstrated the importance of global markets for wind and solar innovation, respectively.

4.3.1.4   Was There a Clean Technology Bubble?

While most discussions of the recent decline in clean energy patents attempt to explain the decline, perhaps instead it is the rapid growth in clean energy patenting around 2010–2011 that requires an explanation. Clean energy patenting has fallen from its peak, but it still witnessed impressive growth compared to overall technological progress since 2006. Except for hybrid/electric vehicles and solar thermal, growth in patenting 2006–2015 is still greater for energy patents than for all patents in general. For instance, by 2015, overall patent counts are 16 percent higher than they were in 2006. In contrast, solar PV patent counts are 53 percent higher, wind energy patents 62 percent higher, energy storage patents 74 percent higher, and smart grid patents 138 percent higher. Perhaps investors were overly optimistic about the future potential of clean energy, leading to a cleantech bubble. Our venture capital data allow us to explore this possibility further, by looking for evidence of a clean technology bubble in venture capital around the same time.

4.3.1.5   Diminishing Returns to Research

Both demand-side and supply-side pressures affect energy innovation (Popp 2002). As research in a field progresses, promising opportunities may be used up, making it harder for further progress. Given how quickly clean energy patenting increased in the early 2010s, might promising avenues of research have simply dried up?

Popp (2002) uses forward citations made to patents in a given year to assess the quality of innovation from a given year. However, that requires several years of patent data to assess, which is not possible for the recent decline in patents. Instead, we present data on two measures of patent quality that make use of data on *backward* citations (that is, citations made by a given patent to the prior art):

- *Radicalness*, first proposed by Shane (2001), measures the extent to which patents are building on ideas outside the patented technological domain. For a given patent p, it is the count of the number of International Patent Classification (IPC) classes included in patents cited by patent p that are not included in the classifications of patent i itself. It is calculated as:

$$Radicalness_p = \sum_{j}^{n_p} \frac{CT_j}{n_p} \text{ for } IPC_{pj} \neq IPC_p,$$

  where CT_j is the count of IPC 4-digit classifications IPC_{pj} cited by patent p that are not assigned to patent p, and n_p represents the total number of IPC classes in the prior art cited by patent p (Squicciarini, Dernis, and Criscuolo 2013).

- *Originality*, first proposed by Trajtenberg, Jaffe, and Henderson (1997), measures the breadth of technology fields on which a patent relies. It also relies on backward citations, but is based on the percentage of citations made by patent p to each possible IPC 4-digit patent class. Patents building on a more diverse set of knowledge are more original. We calculate originality as:

$$Originality_p = 1 - \sum_{j}^{n_p} s_{pj}^2,$$

where s_{pj} is the percentage of citations made by patent p to patent class j out of the n_p IPC 4-digit classifications in all patents cited by patent p (Squicciarini, Dernis, and Criscuolo 2013).

Figures 4.12 and 4.13 present radicalness and originality for a select set of our energy patent technologies, as well as for all patents (bold lines) for comparison. Because the annual averages for small technological fields are noisy, we present the data as 3-year moving averages. In each figure, panel A includes "traditional" clean energy technologies, such as renewables and electric and hybrid vehicles. A few things stand out here. Among these technologies, there are some noticeable peaks for radicalness, although except for vehicles and wind in the mid-1990s, these peaks appear to coincide with a similar peak for all technologies. Pertaining to the recent drop in clean energy pat-

A. Clean Energy Technologies

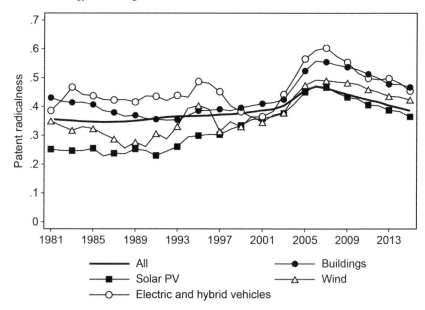

B. Enabling Energy Technologies

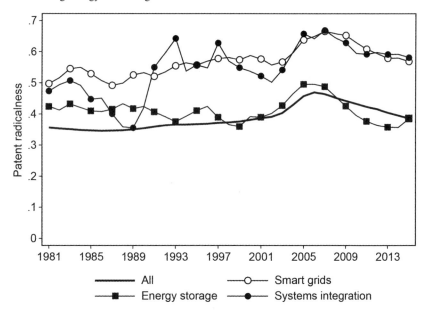

Fig. 4.12   Radicalness
Source: Authors' calculations using data from the EPO World Patent Statistical Database (PATSTAT).
Note: Figure shows the 3-year moving average of radicalness for selected energy technologies.

A. Clean Energy Technologies

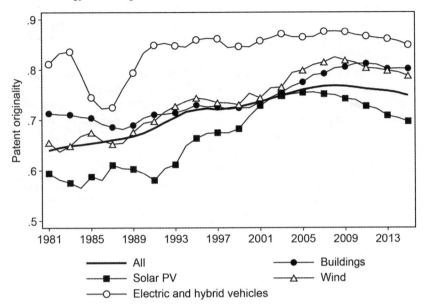

B. Enabling Energy Technologies

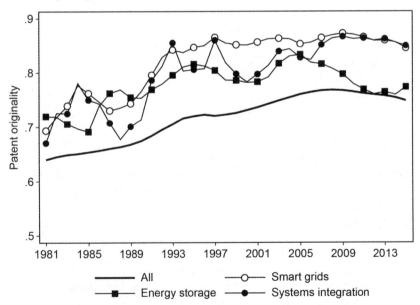

Fig. 4.13   Originality
Source: Authors' calculations using data from the EPO World Patent Statistical Database (PATSTAT).
Note: Figure shows the 3-year moving average of originality for selected energy technologies.

enting, radicalness for patents for solar, wind, and energy efficiency buildings all peak right before the spike in patenting. That radicalness begins to fall along with patenting provides some suggestive evidence of diminishing returns. However, the radicalness of these technologies remains higher than the radicalness of technology as a whole. The originality of both wind and solar patents appear to peak slightly before the spike in patenting, although the drop-offs in recent years are not large. Electric and hybrid vehicles are both more radical and more original than other clean energy technologies or all technologies in general (in bold). Nonetheless, while their originality has been fairly constant since the early 1990s, the radicalness of electric and hybrid vehicles peaks in 2007, which is when patenting peaks for these vehicles. In contrast, the radicalness of building energy efficiency technology peaks in 2006, although patenting doesn't peak until 2012. Solar PV is nearly always less radical and less original than the average technology. This result also suggests that the era of "peak patenting" for solar PV may be ending.

The bottom panel of each figure presents radicalness and originality for three enabling energy technologies: systems integration, energy storage, and smart grids. While originality has fallen for energy storage, all three are more original than the average technology, suggesting that advances in these types of technologies may be increasingly important for driving the energy transition and integration of new resources. Interestingly while both systems integration and smart grids technology are more radical than the average technology, the radicalness of energy storage almost perfectly follows the trends for the average technology. Energy storage appears to build off a diverse range of technologies (i.e., it is more original), but not necessarily off technological classes outside its own domain (i.e., it is not more radical).

The measures for enabling technologies are inconsistent with diminishing returns as an explanation for decreasing patenting in these technologies. Particularly for systems integration and smart grid technology, the patent applications being filed are still radical and original. It may be that the fall in patenting for these technologies has occurred because they are complements to intermittent renewable energy sources, such as wind and solar. Decreased patenting in those technologies may have been seen as a sign of reduced opportunities for smart grids and systems integration. However, diminishing returns appear to be only a partial explanation at best for decreased clean energy patenting.

4.3.1.6 Innovation Has Worked

Concerns about diminishing returns pertain to the supply-side of innovation. Related to the possibility that research has hit diminishing returns is the possibility that clean energy research in existing technologies has been a success. In such a case, there will be less demand for continued research and relatively more resources devoted to incremental innovations that cannot be patented. Recall from section 4.2 that the costs of wind and solar PV have fallen to levels that make them competitive with traditional sources of electricity. In fact, by 2017, solar PV costs had fallen below what experts had earlier predicted for the year 2030 (Nemet 2019)! Clean energy innovation peaking at the point where costs become competitive is consistent with innovation on other clean technologies. For instance, Popp (2006) shows both how innovation on sulfur dioxide and nitrogen oxide pollution control quickly increased after the passage of regulations in the US, Japan, and Germany, and returned to pre-peak levels once the goals of the regulation were met.

But unlike these examples, more innovation is still needed—urgently—to enable the clean energy transition in the time required. Wind and solar energy still make up just a small fraction of electric generation. Complementary technologies to integrate rising shares of wind and solar into the grid are needed. Electric vehicles must improve to be widely accepted by consumers. Innovation in new technologies altogether—such as long-term storage solutions for seasonal balancing—are needed in some regions. The decrease in innovation, at least as measured by patent counts, may suggest a challenge for business and policymakers moving forward. At the same time, it may be that these trends do not fully capture some innovation that is crucial for the clean energy transition. Cost-effective integration of clean energy resources increasingly relies on innovation in other high-tech sectors, like IT, and it may be that traditional measures of energy patenting and innovation do not reflect the benefits that these advances bring to the energy sector. Further development of measures and methods for capturing these innovations is needed.

4.3.2 The Challenges of New Energy Technologies

For many reasons, relative to past trends, the remaining technological needs for a clean energy transition are more challenging and are likely to grow more so in the future. Overcoming these challenges will require additional government support. First, the next wave of energy innovation will emphasize public infrastructure, such as smart-grid technologies, the integration of intermittent renewable energy technologies into the grid, the adoption of connected vehicle infrastructure, and charging infrastructure for electric vehicles. How will private sector innovation respond when the demand for new equipment comes from the government itself in the form of infrastructure investment, rather than from the private sector?

Second, if successful, these emerging technologies will generate large spillovers. Much of their social value comes from making it easier to use complementary technologies, such as intermittent renewables. For example, as the share of electricity generated by intermittent renewable power grows, advances in energy storage would greatly improve grid management. Energy storage breakthroughs leading to better batteries would also make electric vehicles more attractive to consumers, both by reducing costs and increasing vehicle range. Because of its novel nature, Dechezleprêtre, Martin, and Mohnen (2017) find evidence of large spillovers in many areas of clean energy research.

Third, the value of energy storage also depends on the cost of solar and wind generation. Complementarities among technologies make future benefits from innovation uncertain. The potential private sector rewards from energy storage innovation are connected to progress in intermittent renewables. As the cost of solar and wind falls, so must the cost of storage to continue to add value (Braff, Mueller, and Trancik 2016). This interdependency raises uncertainty about the future profits from innovation.

Finally, grid integration and energy storage innovations also provide examples of how the building blocks of energy innovation are changing. The high degree of radicalness and originality of both smart grids and system integration technologies suggests that technologies will require more innovation across different businesses and different lines of technology. As an example of the changing nature of energy technology, we look at the extent to which information and communication technology (ICT) has permeated both energy and other sectors.

Figure 4.14 illustrates the penetration of digital technology in different technological domains, measured as the 3-year moving average of the percentage of patents in different fields that also have an ICT patent classification. Appendix table 4.A.1 lists the patent classes used to identify each technology discussed here. Overall, the share of patents also having an ICT class rose through the end of the twentieth century, plateauing at around 40 percent by 2006. Trends in ICT penetration among climate mitigation technologies is similar (figure 4.14, panel A), although a bit lower. For climate mitigating energy and building technologies, ICT penetration is just a few percentage points below all technologies, and it follows similar trends. ICT penetration is a bit lower for climate mitigation technologies in the manufacturing sector, and much lower in the transportation sector. For comparison, we also include the health sector, which has a lower ICT penetration of just 10 percent.

Panel B of figure 4.14 provides evidence from other energy and engineering technologies. Compared to these technologies, ICT penetration appears more important for climate mitigation. ICT penetration for power technologies plateaus at around 25 percent. Patents related to general engineering, engines, or combustion have ICT penetration rates below 10 percent.

As energy innovation moves forward, bringing in new knowledge from disparate sectors such as ICT could change the nature of energy R&D. Traditionally, energy R&D has been dominated by large firms that move slowly. While redesigning a turbine requires the physical transformation of equipment, improvements in software and information technology can be made more quickly (Branstetter, Drev, and Kwon 2019). ICT improvements are also modular. Software components can be developed remotely and inte-

A. Climate change mitigation technologies

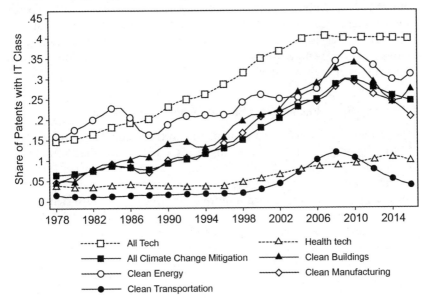

B. Broad energy technologies

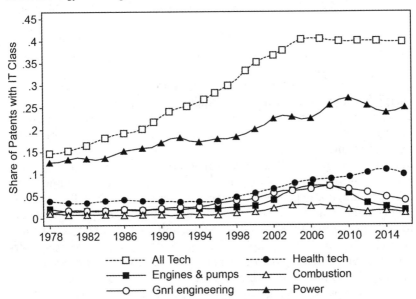

Fig. 4.14 Penetration of digital technologies in various technologies

Note: Three-year moving average of percentage of "claimed priorities" (i.e., patent family size > 1) in the different fields which also have an ICT co-class. Patent extractions from EPO World Patent Statistical Database (PATSTAT) by OECD/ENV and IEA/EDC (2019).

grated into larger systems, allowing R&D to be done in more locations, both domestically and abroad (Branstetter, Glennon, and Jensen 2019). These changes suggest that innovation in other sectors, especially those that are high-tech, is likely to become more important during the next wave of energy innovation. To examine this possibility, we turn next to data on venture capital in the energy industry.

4.4   Early-Stage Financing for Startups in the Energy Sector

Startups historically played a minor role in the energy sector (Gaddy et al. 2017; Nanda, Younge, and Fleming 2015). Existing distribution systems and regulatory frameworks were designed for a centralized system, and combined with high capital costs, there were significant barriers to entry. However, the transition toward a more decentralized energy system characterized by increasing levels of renewable energy and storage technologies may change the role of energy startups. Furthermore, the successful integration of these resources relies on progress and innovation in other sectors as well, where entrepreneurial firms do play a larger role. For example, IT and blockchain technology are further helping to facilitate this transition to a more decentralized energy system and are becoming increasingly abundant. Blockchain energy startups are multiplying, raising more than 265 million euros for applications in the energy sector in 2017 (European Commission 2018).

At the same time, startups need to raise capital to survive or successfully exit, but venture capital (VC) investments for clean energy firms have fallen in recent years after large investments through the 2000s. There are multiple potential explanations for this perceived failure of the VC model for clean energy. Some observers point to inadequate risk-return profiles (Gaddy et al. 2017). Long time horizons between technology idea, development, and commercialization in the energy sector offer an alternative explanation: firms may have achieved the desired returns but on a time scale that is typically not attractive to VCs. This suggests that a different form of more patient capital may be needed. If high-tech is becoming more important in the energy sector, it also could be that it is just increasingly difficult to evaluate energy startups as they become increasingly complex and perhaps difficult to evaluate ex ante. While Nanda, Younge, and Fleming (2015) and Gaddy et al. (2017) provide initial explorations of venture capital in the energy sector, the changing nature of energy markets in recent years suggests further investigation is warranted to better understand the historical and potential role of startups in enabling and driving the clean energy transition.

In this section, we explore trends in the types of companies founded since the year 2000 as well as the funding raised by different startups. We also examine the performance of different types of energy firms, such as whether they raised funding, whether they had a successful exit (i.e., as measured by an acquisition or initial public offering (IPO)), and the time to exit conditional on a successful exit. While the analysis remains purely descriptive and does not attempt to estimate any causal relationships, our exploration of heterogeneous correlations reveals a few key insights that warrant more rigorous evaluation in future research.

4.4.1   Data Overview

We gather firm-level data on startup companies and VC activity from Crunchbase, a commercial database of innovative companies.[5] Crunchbase provides detailed information on organizations—such as their founding date, headquarter country, funding raised (with detailed funding round information), and exits—generating real-time updates from a community of partners and machine learning algorithms. It has become a leading provider of data on startups and investment activity, especially for the US, and it has been embraced by the investor community as a leading platform for discovering and connecting with innovative companies.

That said, the data come with limitations. There are certainly selection concerns, for instance, as more innovative companies are more likely to appear in the data. There is also increasing coverage over time but with less comprehensive coverage in the final year or two, given time lags. Furthermore, some firms may misleadingly indicate that they operate in a certain sector for self-promotion purposes in an effort to attract more funding, as sector categories are not cross-checked against traditional sectoral classifications. Finally, the coverage for firms in some countries, such as China, is very low, which may be particularly important in the energy context.

We do not attempt to address these selection biases from a statistical perspective. However, we do try to engage with some of the concerns descriptively when we graphically explore trends and outcomes of firms across sectors by using shares of total firms founded and total funding allocated each year per sector in addition to the totals. We also focus mainly on comparisons across sectors and across energy types (rather than changes over time) in our correlation analysis and discussion. Insofar as the selection biases impacting performance metrics are not systematically different across sectors or firms of different energy types in the energy sector, our analyses still provide some meaningful insight about energy startups that is new to the literature.

We link several Crunchbase datasets to compile our dataset for analysis. First, we start with the full cross-section of 733,133 organizations.[6] We keep only those that were founded in 2000 or later and those that indicated their

5. The database can be accessed at www.crunchbase.com. Crunchbase was created in 2007; however, the data cover firms that were founded in preceding years as well. See Dalle, den Besten, and Menon (2017) for a discussion of the use of Crunchbase data in economic and managerial research.
6. We accessed the data in summer 2019.

primary business as operating as a company (as opposed to an investor, for instance). We match this organization-level data to funding round-level data, and we convert all funding amounts (in US dollars) to real 2010 dollars using the consumer price index from the World Bank. The funding deal dataset includes 268,774 observations with about 71,000 missing actual funding amount information, so the totals used throughout the analysis are lower bounds for this sample of firms.[7] We find each firm's total funding raised and the number of successful funding rounds (where each observation in the funding deal dataset is defined as a funding round) and match these data to the organization-level cross-sectional data. We also match this to Crunchbase's data on firm exits (i.e., acquisitions and IPOs). After dropping duplicate observations, the datasets include information on about 87,000 acquisitions and 17,000 IPOs.

Perhaps most interestingly for our analysis, Crunchbase sector classifications allow us to identify startups that operate in multiple (and possibly complementary) fields, such as IT. We classify firms based on whether they indicate that they are in the energy sector, and separately firms also indicating that they operate in a high-tech sector. Table 4.4 provides a summary of how we classify different types of firms and the number of observations we have for each category. Our final sample consists of 604,884 firms founded from 2000 through 2018, including 13,515 energy firms. Panel A provides the breakdown of firms based on high-level sectors. We classify different types of energy firms in Panel B, and in Panel C, we further break down the energy firms based on whether they also operate in a high-tech sector. Of the 13,515 energy firms, 10,129 are energy only (e.g., not also high-tech) versus 3,386 being energy as well as high-tech. Panel C also shows the number of firms that are also high-tech by energy type.

4.4.2   Trends in Companies Founded and Funding Raised

We begin by graphically exploring trends in companies founded each year and funding raised for energy firms relative to those in manufacturing, science, health and biotech, transportation, and financial services.[8] Figure 4.15 illustrates these trends from 2000 through 2018 in four panels. In panels A and B, we plot the total number of companies founded each year and the share of companies founded each year by sector, respectively. The number of energy firms founded appears to peak in 2012, which is a little later than when it peaks when measured as a share of founded firms. This suggests

---

7. These also are lower bounds from the perspective of firms not appearing in Crunchbase at all. When examining the impact of this funding on various outcomes, these correlations will embed selection bias, such as endogeneity associated with these firms perhaps being more visible (and thus perhaps more successful) than those that do not appear in the data or do not have fully populated funding data.

8. Note that because some firms may participate in multiple sectors, some firms and their associated funding are double counted.

Table 4.4   **Firm classifications and descriptions**

Firm type (1)	Crunchbase categories (2)	Number of firms (3)
	A. High-level sectoral groupings	
All firms	Total sample of firms across sectors	604,884
Energy	All energy types	13,515
Financial services	Financial services, lending, and payments	48,923
Science	Science and engineering	40,464
Health/biotech	Health care and biotechnology	62,414
Manufacturing	Manufacturing	32,116
Transport	Transportation	22,300
High-tech	Apps, AI, data, hardware, IT, internet services, telecommunications, mobile, platforms, and software	300,251
	B. Energy types	
Clean	Clean energy, renewable energy, storage, solar, wind	6,276
Fossil fuel	Fossil fuels, fuel cells, and oil and gas	2,265
Grid management	Electricity distribution, energy management, and power grid	887
Energy efficiency	Energy efficiency	466
Other energy	All other energy types, including biomass and biofuel	3,621
	C. Energy and high-tech firms	
Energy only	Energy firms not in high-tech	10,129
High-tech only	High-tech firms not in energy	296,865
Energy and high-tech	Energy firms that are also high-tech	3,386
Clean and high-tech	Clean energy firms that are also high-tech	1,414
Fossil fuel and high-tech	Fossil fuel energy firms that are also high-tech	341
Grid and high-tech	Grid management and high-tech	386
Energy efficiency and high-tech	Energy efficiency firms that are also high-tech	238
Other energy and high-tech	Other energy firms that are also high-tech	1,007

that founding energy firms was still on the rise throughout the Great Recession, but not as quickly relative to firms in other sectors. Furthermore, the number and share of startups in financial services, science, and engineering all increase more quickly than energy startups following the recession, with the share of firms founded that are energy-related falling from about 2007 onward.

Panels C and D illustrate similar patterns for the share of total funding each year allocated to each sector (panel C) and the share of total funding deals by sector (panel D).[9] These figures also clearly illustrate the "bubble" of investments flowing to energy at different times. There are two spikes in the share of energy funding levels—in 2008 and 2012—and also a spike in the share of funding deals for energy firms in 2008. This aligns with energy

9. A "share of funding deals" refers to the share of the total number of VC funding rounds completed each year that go to each sector.

A. Number of Companies Founded Each Year

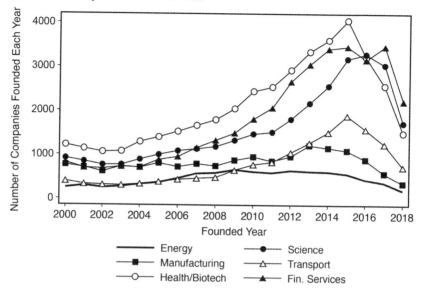

B. Share of Companies Founded Each Year

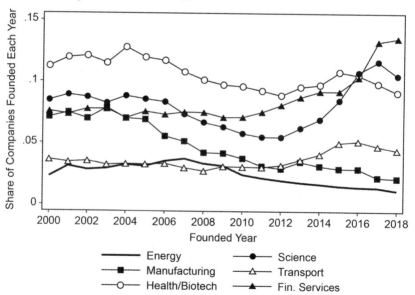

Fig. 4.15   Comparison of energy firms to other sectors

Note: Panel A compares the number of firms founded each year. Panel B compares the share of firms founded each year as a proportion of all firms. Panel C is the share of total VC funding going to each sector, and Panel C is the share of total number of completed VC rounds going to each sector.

C. Share of Total Funding by VCs Each Year

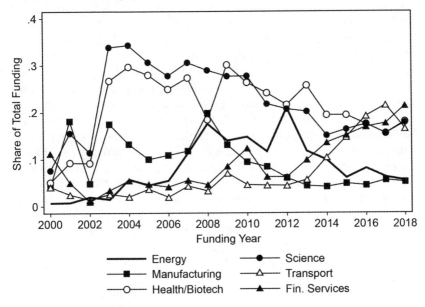

D. Share of Total Funding Deals by VCs

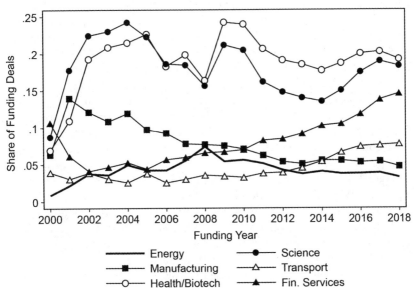

Fig. 4.15 (cont.)

firm founding year peaks, descriptively suggesting that such funding may be correlated with the successful startup of energy firms. The decrease in funding for energy firms corresponds with decreases in science and health/ biotech as well, whereas funding to financial services and transportation are on the rise following the Great Recession. We will explore the relationship between funding and startup performance in section 4.4.3.

The rise and fall of the share of VC funding going to energy firms also closely mirrors the trends in patenting presented in section 4.3. In both cases, rapid growth begins in the mid-2000s. While the peak in venture capital funding comes slightly later than the peak in many clean energy patents, both drop significantly after 2012, and both remain above the levels achieved prior to the initial increase in 2006. These data are only suggestive, but it does appear that the rise and fall in patenting seen during the 2006–2012 period may be indicative of broader trends in energy investment.

Next, given the increasing penetration of high-technology innovations broadly over the past decade—combined with the need for high-tech innovations in the energy sector for the integration of variable renewable energy resources—we explore trends in high-tech companies as well as energy firms that are either energy-only or high-tech energy. We first compare high-tech companies to all companies in figure 4.16. Panel A plots the number of companies (total and high-tech) over time, and panel B plots the share of companies founded each year that are high-tech. These figures illustrate how the share of companies that are high-tech has risen starkly from about 2006 onward. Panels C and D explore VC funding allocated, revealing that most funds do go to firms that are high-tech. The share of funds going to high-tech firms fell in the years leading up the recession and through 2010, but then rose again quickly from 2010 onward, suggesting that VCs may be particularly drawn to firms reporting to operate in high-tech sectors.

We explore this further to see whether a similar relationship holds in the energy sector specifically (figure 4.17). Panel A of figure 4.17 plots the share of all companies founded that are energy firms also categorized as high-tech vs. those that are energy only (i.e., not also operating in the high-tech space), and panel B plots the share of energy firms founded each year that are also high-tech. While the overall number of energy-only startups has been falling since about 2006, the number of energy firms that are also high-tech rose sharply after 2006 and plateaued throughout the Great Recession, falling again from 2009 onward (but then leveling off from about 2012 onward). The proportion of energy startups that are also high-tech have therefore been rising quickly. Comparing these findings with funding for these types of firms in panels C and D, we can see that the spike in the number of high-tech energy startups around the year 2008 also aligns with a spike in funding (both in totals and in shares) at the same time.

We explore this distinction between energy-only and high-tech energy firms by energy type as well (see figure 4.18). Panel A plots the number of

A. Number of Companies Founded Each Year

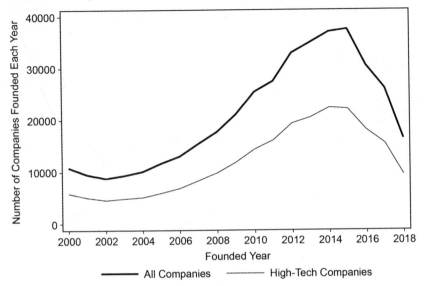

B. Share of Companies that are High-Tech

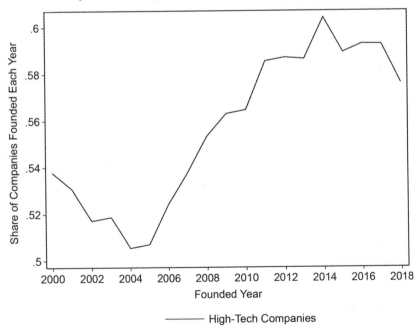

Fig. 4.16   Growing share of companies founded are high-tech, 2005–2014

C. Total Funding for All Companies vs. High-Tech

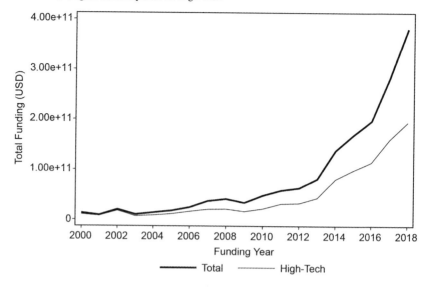

D. Proportion of Funding to High-Tech

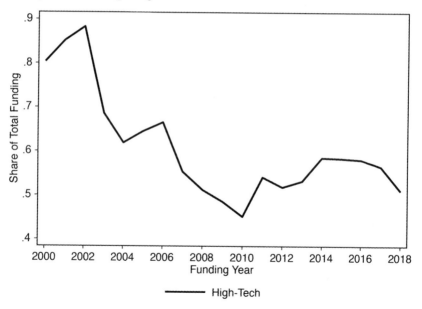

Fig. 4.16 (cont.)

A. Share energy-only vs. energy and high-tech

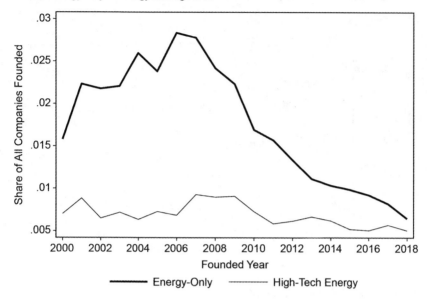

B. Increasing share of high-tech energy cos.

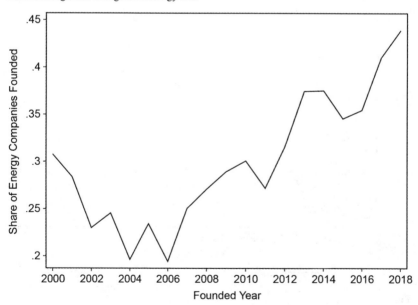

Fig. 4.17   Energy-only and high-tech energy companies

C. Total Funding: Energy & Energy High-Tech

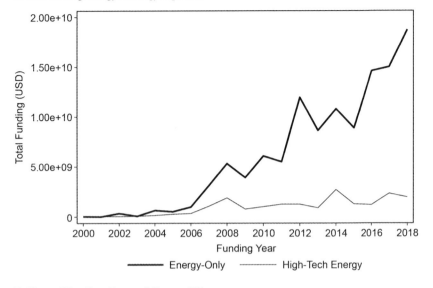

D. Share of Funding: Energy & Energy HT

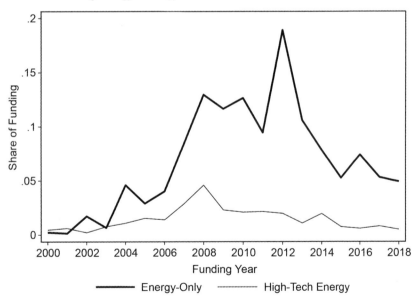

Fig. 4.17   (cont.)

A. Number of Companies by Energy Type

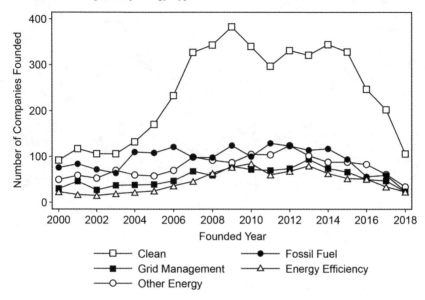

B. Share of All Companies by Energy Type

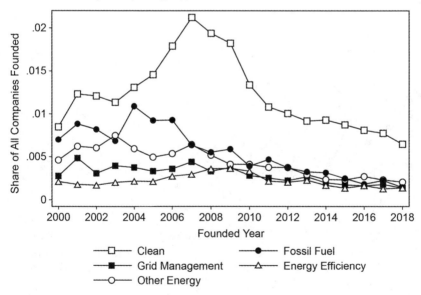

Fig. 4.18   Energy companies founded each year, by energy type

Note: Shares (panels B and D) are proportions of all companies founded in a given year.

C. Number of Companies by Energy Type

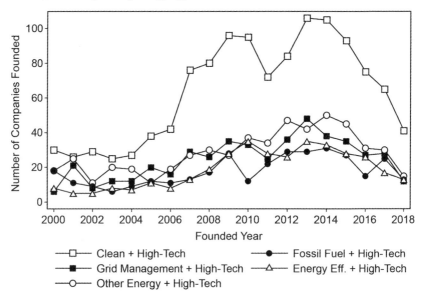

D. Share of All Companies by Energy Type

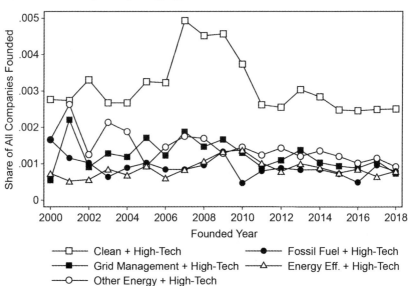

Fig. 4.18   (cont.)

companies by energy type (clean, fossil fuel, grid management, energy efficiency, and other), and panel B plots the share of all firms that fall into each category. These figures very clearly show the "bubble" of clean energy firms that emerged through the Great Recession: while the number of firms in fossil fuel, grid management, and so forth remained relatively flat (or increased slightly), there was a major spike in clean energy from about 2004 to 2008, with the proportion of firms in clean energy then falling sharply from about 2009 onward. When examining firms that specifically are also high-tech in these energy subcategories in panels C and D, we can see that these trends may have been at least partially driven by high-tech energy firms. The proportion of firms that are high-tech clean energy firms jumped sharply from 2005 to 2007, and then began to fall in 2008 before leveling off in 2011.

As one final exploration of whether energy startups are increasingly also high-tech, we examine the share of *energy* firms (rather than of total firms) that are also high-tech by energy type. Panel A of figure 4.19 plots energy firms that are also high-tech by energy subgroup as shares of all energy companies founded each year, and panel B of figure 4.19 plots firms that are also high-tech as shares of their own subgroup. In other words, in panel A, high-tech clean firms are plotted as a proportion of all energy firms; in panel B, high-tech clean firms are plotted as a proportion of all clean energy firms. The story is clear: across all energy subgroups, startups are increasingly either claiming to be high-tech or actually are high-tech. This growth is similar to that observed in the share of energy patents also classified as high-tech, as well as supporting the anecdotal evidence presented in section 4.2 that IT is also of growing importance in the search for new energy resources.

Last, we examine whether these trends are correlated with VC funds flowing to energy firms that are also high-tech, as this could provide some insight into one potential explanation of why VC funding has not performed as well in the energy sector relative to others. That is, it could be that being labeled or marketed as "high-tech" helps these firms attract VC, but they may not actually end up performing any better than energy-only firms. This could be for several reasons. High-tech energy firms may be particularly complex and difficult to assess, or such firms could take longer to commercialize their products or exit if they are working on a more complex technology. It also could be that some firms simply claim to be high-tech when they are not as a means of attracting VC—a hypothesis that's been posed in light of Crunchbase being used as a platform by VCs. This could mean that VCs overvalue them, or alternatively, that they just don't perform as well as energy-only firms. We explore firm performance in the next section, but first we present graphical evidence of funding trends for these types of firms.

Figure 4.20 plots the share of total funding (panels A and C) and the share of successful funding deals each year (panels B and D) by energy subcategory (panels A and B) and then by energy subcategory for firms that are also high-tech. Panels A and B illustrate the clean energy funding

A. Share of All Energy Companies Founded

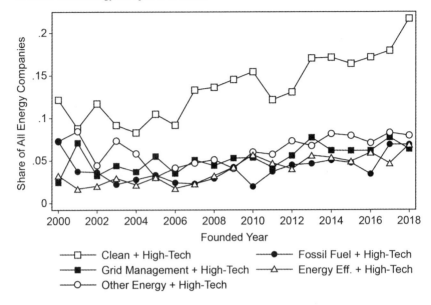

B. Share of Each Energy Sub-Group Also HT

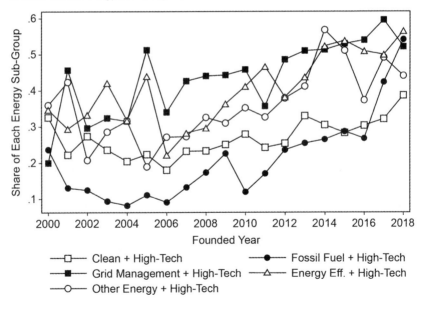

Fig. 4.19   Increasing trends in energy firms that are also high-tech

Note: All shares are of totals corresponding to all energy firms.

A. Share of Total Funding by Energy Type

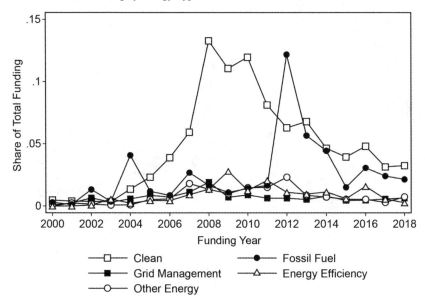

B. Share of Funding Deals by Energy Type

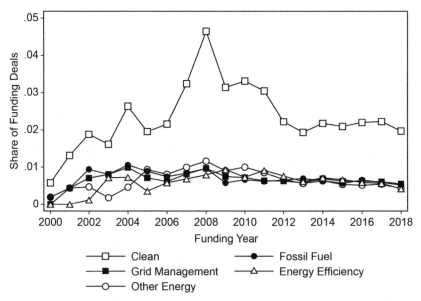

Fig. 4.20   Share of funding going to energy firms

Note: Energy funding as shares of total funding (panels A and C) and shares of funding deals (panels B and D). Panels C and D show shares by energy type for energy firms that are also high-tech.

C. Share of Total Funding by Energy Type

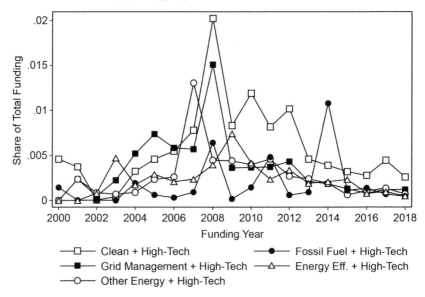

D. Share of Funding Deals by Energy Type

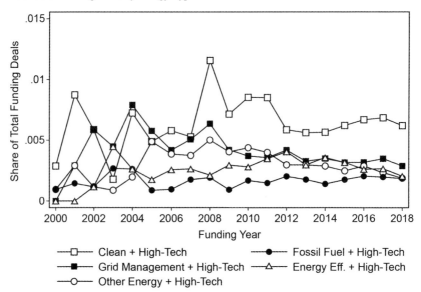

Fig. 4.20   (cont.)

"bubble" that occurred around the year 2008, where a large spike occurs in the share of funding that goes to clean energy relative to other types of energy in terms of both levels of funding and the number of funding deals. Interestingly, there is also a spike in funding allocated to fossil fuel energy around 2012–2013, which is likely driven by the fracking revolution. Panels C and D specifically look at high-tech energy firms by subcategory. Despite there only being a spike in funding for clean energy firms in general around 2008, it appears as though a spike occurs in funding for *all* energy types that are also at least labeled as "high-tech," and this is particularly pronounced for clean energy and grid management firms.

Taken together, these findings suggest that at least part of the explanation for changes in clean energy VC funding is that energy firms are increasingly high-tech. The energy transition requires complementary high-tech endeavors, such as innovation in smart technologies, platforms, and the artificial intelligence required for managing a more complex and distributed system. However, this may present new challenges for VCs. It may be that "high-tech" firms are more attractive to VCs, but they may not necessarily perform better (which we explore in the next section). It also could be that the firms in our data are actually not necessarily in high-tech industries but rather just claiming to be in an effort to attract funding. Any of these stories could at least partially explain the unexpectedly low returns to investments in the clean energy sector so far.

This also presents a new challenge for researchers studying energy innovation: studying firms or patents that are only identified as being in the energy sector will vastly underestimate innovation and startup activity that is relevant for advancing the clean energy transition. Accounting for innovation in high-tech sectors that are also applicable for the exploration, integration, and management of new energy systems and resources is more important than ever for fully understanding the energy innovation landscape.

4.4.3 The Performance of Energy Firms

Insufficient returns to investments are often pointed to as the key explanation for why VC funding has not been as successful in the clean energy sector relative to other sectors. This could be due to low returns—or lower returns than expected—or it could be that the time horizons for achieving returns are just longer than average and thus the returns have not yet been realized. A third hypothesis is that it is difficult to identify promising energy VCs that are increasingly complex and operating not just in the energy sector but also often in other high-tech sectors, or that VCs overvalue such firms. To explore these potential explanations, we examine the success of energy firms relative to average firms and other high-tech firms, as well as performance metrics across energy types as measured by whether they had a successful exit (i.e., acquisition or IPO), whether they ever raised funds, the amount raised conditional on raising funds, and the time to exit as measured by the difference

Table 4.5   Energy firms relative to the average firm

Dependent variable	Acquired (1)	IPO (2)	Raised funds (3)	Amount raised (4)	Time to exit (5)
Energy	0.042***	0.063***	0.145***	23.609***	−0.845***
	(0.006)	(0.009)	(0.009)	(4.300)	(0.132)
Sample mean for dependent variable	0.086	0.011	0.283	13.81	7.141
No. of observations	398,473	398,473	398,473	112,618	36,414

Notes: Regression results for various dependent variables to assess energy firms relative to the average firm. The dependent variable is a dummy equal to 1 if the firm is acquired or has an IPO in columns 1 and 2, respectively. In column 3, the dependent variable is a dummy indicating whether the firm raised VC funding. In column 4, the dependent variable is the amount of funding raised conditional on raising funds. In column 5, the dependent variable is the time to exit conditional on having a successful exit. Controls include founded year fixed effects and a dummy for being located in the US. Standard errors are clustered by founded year. Asterisks denote * $p < 0.10$, ** $p < 0.05$, *** $p < 0.01$.

between the founding and exit years. In each case, we regress these outcomes on indicator variables that capture firm type (energy only, high-tech only, high-tech energy, etc.), along with founding-year fixed effects and a dummy variable indicating whether the firm is located in the US. We cluster our standard errors by founding year. We focus on two broad sets of questions:

1. Are energy startups more or less likely to raise funds and/or successfully exit via acquisition or IPO? Does this vary by the type of energy firm (see tables 4.5–4.8)?

2. Conditional on having received funds, are energy startups more or less likely to successfully exit? While differences in the likelihood of receiving funding may occur if the expected potential returns differ across sectors, conditional on receiving funding, any differences across sectors observed are suggestive evidence that investors are not valuing expected returns across sectors correctly (see table 4.9).

Since the firms listed in Crunchbase are not a random sample of startups, our results should not be interpreted as causal. However, they reveal correlations in the data worthy of exploration in future research.

We begin by examining all firms and comparing the relative performance of energy firms (of any type) as a baseline. Table 4.5 presents the correlations between being an energy firm and the five measures of firm performance. Across all metrics, energy firms perform better than the average firm in our sample. They are 4.2 percent, 6.3 percent, and 14.5 percent more likely to be acquired, go public, or raise funds over their lifetimes, respectively. They also raise more money conditional on raising funds (column 4), and they take 0.85 fewer years on average to exit conditional on either being acquired or going public.

Given that VC has been considered a "failed" financing model for the

Table 4.6   **Energy + high-tech firms relative to the average firm**

Dependent variable	Acquired (1)	IPO (2)	Raised funds (3)	Amount raised (4)	Time to exit (5)
Energy + high-tech	0.005	0.003	0.292***	−3.251**	−0.382
	(0.006)	(0.004)	(0.011)	(1.298)	(0.261)
Energy only	0.043***	0.058***	0.182***	22.928***	−1.011***
	(0.006)	(0.008)	(0.010)	(4.368)	(0.150)
High-tech only	0.002	−0.009***	0.062***	−1.028	−0.305***
	(0.002)	(0.002)	(0.005)	(0.742)	(0.069)
Sample mean for dependent variable	0.086	0.011	0.283	13.81	7.141
No. of observations	398,473	398,473	398,473	112,618	36,414

Notes: Regression results for various dependent variables to assess energy firms relative to the average firm. The dependent variable is a dummy equal to 1 if the firm is acquired or has an IPO in columns 1 and 2, respectively. In column 3, the dependent variable is a dummy indicating whether the firm raised VC funding. In column 4, the dependent variable is the amount of funding raised conditional on raising funds. In column 5, the dependent variable is the time to exit conditional on having a successful exit. Controls include founded year fixed effects and a dummy for being located in the US. Standard errors are clustered by founded year. Asterisks denote * $p < 0.10$, ** $p < 0.05$, *** $p < 0.01$.

energy sector after some investments did not provide the expected returns, it is interesting that the energy startups listed in Crunchbase perform relatively *better* than the average startup. One potential explanation is that investors may place an unwarranted premium on energy firms that are also high-tech—or claim to be high-tech—relative to energy firms that are not high-tech. This might occur if there is a perception that high-tech firms are more likely to perform better, or perhaps generate returns in a shorter timeframe relative to energy-only firms. To test this hypothesis, we explore whether firms operating in both the energy and high-tech spaces raise more VC funding than their energy-only counterparts, and then also whether they perform better. We do this by regressing the performance outcomes on indicator variables for firm type (energy only, high-tech only, or both) and provide the correlations in table 4.6.[10] While firms that operate only in the energy space appear to do better than the average firm on every measure, high-tech energy firms are no more likely to be acquired or go public than the average firm, and they are far less likely to do so relative to energy-only firms (columns 1 and 2). They also do not take any less time to exit relative to the average firm, but they take longer to exit relative to energy-only firms (column 5). Yet high-tech energy firms are 11 percent *more* likely to

10. Note that these categories are mutually exclusive, so that the coefficients are, for example, the share of firms of each type that are acquired or have an IPO. The differences between the correlations for energy only and high-tech energy firms are statistically significant in all cases (at the 10 percent level in column 1, at the 5 percent level in columns 2 and 5, and at the 1 percent level in columns 3 and 4).

Table 4.7   Different types of energy firms relative to the average firm

Dependent variable	Acquired (1)	IPO (2)	Raised funds (3)	Amount raised (4)	Time to exit (5)
Clean energy	−0.016***	0.025***	0.164***	15.784***	−0.718***
	(0.005)	(0.007)	(0.010)	(4.602)	(0.239)
Fossil fuel energy	0.147***	0.133***	0.111***	29.873**	−0.923***
	(0.019)	(0.016)	(0.017)	(14.079)	(0.175)
Grid management	0.085***	0.014***	0.203***	−5.266**	0.245
	(0.016)	(0.005)	(0.014)	(2.076)	(0.316)
Energy efficiency	0.003	0.007	0.340***	−1.571	0.506
	(0.015)	(0.007)	(0.028)	(2.785)	(0.440)
Other energy firms	0.020***	0.040***	0.214***	12.236**	−0.906***
	(0.006)	(0.008)	(0.014)	(4.377)	(0.177)
Sample mean for dependent variable	0.086	0.011	0.283	13.81	7.141
No. of observations	398,473	398,473	398,473	112,618	36,414

Notes: Regression results for various dependent variables to assess energy firms relative to the average firm. The dependent variable is a dummy equal to 1 if the firm is acquired or has an IPO in columns 1 and 2, respectively. In column 3, the dependent variable is a dummy indicating whether the firm raised VC funding. In column 4, the dependent variable is the amount of funding raised conditional on raising funds. In column 5, the dependent variable is the time to exit conditional on having a successful exit. Controls include founded year fixed effects and a dummy for being located in the US. Standard errors are clustered by founded year. Asterisks denote * $p < 0.10$, ** $p < 0.05$, *** $p < 0.01$.

raise funds relative to energy-only firms (column 3).[11] This suggests that VC firms possibly were placing a premium on high-tech energy firms relative to energy-only firms but without reaping the expected rewards.

We also consider whether the performance of energy startups varies by the type of energy, as much of the discussion around the perceived failure of the VC model has centered around clean energy. For instance, do clean energy firms perform worse or take longer to exit (than the average firm or relative to other types of energy firms), thus making VC a poor vehicle for financing clean energy? The evidence presented in table 4.7 suggests that this is not the case.[12] Clean energy firms are less likely to be acquired relative to the average firm as well as to energy firms (column 1), but they are more likely to go public (column 2) and raise funds (on both the extensive (column 3) and intensive margins (column 4) relative to the average firm. They also take less time to exit (column 5). At the same time, relative to fossil fuel firms and

11. This is significant at the 1 percent level. Conditional on raising funds, energy plus high-tech firms raise fewer funds relative to energy-only funds (column 4), but this could be an artefact of the data. The graphical analysis demonstrated that the amount of funding per round decreased in later years, which is also when the number of energy plus high-tech firms is increasing.
12. Each of these categories is mutually exclusive.

Table 4.8   Impact of being high-tech for different types of energy firms

Dependent variable	Acquired (1)	IPO (2)	Raised funds (3)	Amount raised (4)	Time to exit (5)
Clean + high-tech	−0.007	−0.020***	0.050**	−24.806***	0.090
	(0.008)	(0.006)	(0.018)	(5.659)	(0.318)
Fossil fuel + high-tech	−0.135***	−0.140***	0.250***	−38.789***	1.498***
	(0.018)	(0.017)	(0.039)	(11.158)	(0.465)
Grid mgmnt. + high-tech	−0.119***	0.002	0.218***	6.456*	1.048*
	(0.028)	(0.017)	(0.039)	(3.571)	(0.593)
Energy efficiency + high-tech	0.084**	−0.001	0.045	0.987	1.800*
	(0.035)	(0.017)	(0.037)	(5.678)	(0.865)
General energy + high-tech	−0.018	−0.042***	0.093***	−28.626***	−0.336
	(0.013)	(0.010)	(0.023)	(6.414)	(0.526)
Clean energy	−0.041***	−0.021**	−0.029	0.792	0.047
	(0.012)	(0.008)	(0.019)	(9.992)	(0.332)
Fossil fuel energy	0.146***	0.100***	−0.111***	17.219	−0.196
	(0.020)	(0.020)	(0.022)	(19.833)	(0.306)
Grid management energy	0.120***	−0.043***	−0.088***	−34.000***	0.738
	(0.021)	(0.015)	(0.023)	(7.040)	(0.471)
Energy efficiency	−0.069***	−0.041**	0.144***	−25.193***	0.053
	(0.020)	(0.016)	(0.041)	(8.269)	(0.759)
Sample mean for dependent variable	0.137	0.059	0.456	30.16	6.826
No. of observations	8,689	8,689	8,689	3,965	1,512

Notes: Regression results for various dependent variables to assess energy firms relative to the average firm. The dependent variable is a dummy equal to 1 if the firm is acquired or has an IPO in columns 1 and 2, respectively. In column 3, the dependent variable is a dummy indicating whether the firm raised VC funding. In column 4, the dependent variable is the amount of funding raised conditional on raising funds. In column 5, the dependent variable is the time to exit conditional on having a successful exit. Controls include founded year fixed effects and a dummy for being located in the US. Standard errors are clustered by founded year. Asterisks denote * $p < 0.10$, ** $p < 0.05$, *** $p < 0.01$.

other "general" energy firms, they are less likely to go public and take slightly longer to exit. Taken together, these correlations may suggest that slightly longer time horizons relative to other energy firms may partially explain insufficient VC investment returns if expectations were incorrect. That is, if investors assumed that the exit time for clean energy firms is the same as fossil fuel energy firms, they would have (just slightly) underestimated the amount of time it would take for clean firms to exit. But nonetheless, clean firms do exit much faster than the average firm and perform better on most measures.

Finally, in table 4.8, we examine the same correlations for energy-only firms and high-tech energy firms conditional on energy type, with the omitted category being the average "general" energy firm. Once again, we find that venture capital investors appear to place a premium on energy firms that are also high-tech. With the exception of energy efficiency, high-tech energy firms raise more funds than their energy-only counterparts. The chances of raising funds are negative for fossil fuel energy-only and grid management-only relative to the average "general" energy firm (and there is zero correlation between being clean energy-only and raising funds), whereas they are positive for all three energy types when the firm is also high-tech. At the same time, the high-tech energy firms do not perform better (and actually perform worse on occasion) across the other performance metrics. Clean and fossil fuel high-tech energy firms are less likely to go public, and high-tech fossil fuel energy firms are also less likely to be acquired. Being high-tech also increases the time to exit for fossil fuel, grid management, and energy efficiency firms.

A core remaining question is whether differences in returns to energy investments relative to investments in other firms can at least partially explain the fall in energy funding (and founding of energy startups) over time. Our data do not allow us to directly examine returns to energy investments. However, we can compare the performance of energy firms that are funded relative to the average funded firm to better assess how well VC investments in energy fare. We test the likelihood of exit (either through acquisition or IPO) *conditional on receiving funding*. Correlation comparisons conditional on funding also at least partially account for selection bias associated with being more likely to receive funding. While energy firms in the Crunchbase dataset may do better than other firms on some measures of performance, selection into Crunchbase is not random.

We estimate these correlations across the full sample, as well as for subsamples based on the firm's founding year (2000–2005, 2006–2012, and 2013–2018) to test whether there may have been a "bubble" in clean energy finance. The years chosen correspond to the boom-and-bust period observed in clean energy patenting.[13] Lerner (2011) notes that venture capital funding is often cyclical, with investors overreacting to both good and bad news. Moreover, he finds that clean energy investment grew rapidly, albeit from a very low base, in the early 2000s. Overall returns on these investments were high, but primarily due to two very successful companies. He notes that the patterns observed in his data suggest overfunding may have occurred in the clean energy sector. If such a "bubble" exists, we expect firms funded during bubble years (i.e., roughly 2006–2012 in the clean energy investment context) to perform worse than those funded in other years, as clean energy investor expectations may have been unreasonably high.

Table 4.9 presents the results. Column 1 uses the full sample. We see that

13. We do not include separate categories for high-tech energy firms in table 4.9, as the small number of firms in each cell lead to imprecise estimates when splitting the sample. Overall, we find similar patterns for non-high-tech energy firms, but with nearly all coefficients insignificant when splitting the sample.

Table 4.9   **Exit of energy firms relative to the average funded firm**

	Any exit			
Dependent variable	Overall (1)	2000–2005 (1)	2006–2012 (2)	2013–2018 (3)
Clean energy	−0.026***	−0.025	−0.038**	−0.011
	(0.008)	(0.016)	(0.014)	(0.007)
Fossil fuel energy	0.018	0.069	0.023	−0.004
	(0.013)	(0.037)	(0.018)	(0.018)
Grid management	−0.012	−0.045	−0.011	0.007
	(0.017)	(0.047)	(0.027)	(0.022)
Energy efficiency	−0.009	0.098	−0.047*	−0.007
	(0.017)	(0.053)	(0.023)	(0.017)
Other energy firms	−0.025**	0.018	−0.040*	−0.023**
	(0.012)	(0.039)	(0.018)	(0.008)
Sample mean for dependent variable	0.116	0.328	0.152	0.04
No. of observations	112,618	13,605	41,836	57,177

Notes: Regressions include funded firms only. The dependent variable is a dummy equal to 1 if the firm is either acquired or has an IPO. Controls include founded year fixed effects and a dummy for being located in the US. Standard errors are clustered by founded year. Asterisks denote * $p < 0.10$, ** $p < 0.05$, *** $p < 0.01$.

clean energy and "other" energy firms are about 2.5 percentage points less likely to exit than the average firm. As the sample mean is just 11.6 percent, this difference is substantial. Unlike the estimates for the full sample in table 4.7 that do not condition on receiving funding, in no cases do we see that funded energy firms are more likely to exit. Recall that energy firms in Crunchbase are more likely to receive funding (see table 4.7), so that overall, they exit more frequently than do other firms. However, conditional on funding, energy firms do no better than other firms, and clean energy firms do worse. Understanding why energy firms are more likely to receive funding is left for future research. It may be that there are differences in the types of firms selecting into Crunchbase, or it may be that because entrepreneurs do not see venture capital as an appropriate model for energy, only relatively more promising energy companies choose to seek out venture capital. Since both factors may be different for the different subsets of energy startups, this may also help explain the differences we see in the sector.

Why do some funded energy firms fare worse than nonenergy funded firms? We provide suggestive evidence of a "bubble" in clean energy and energy efficiency investments that coincides with the peak patenting and VC period of 2006–2012. While energy firms funded in the early period perform just as well as the average firm across all energy types, clean energy, energy efficiency, and "other" energy firms perform worse during the boom-and-bust period of 2006–2012. These firms are 25 to 30 percent less likely to exit than funded nonenergy firms. Consistent with the "bubble" hypothesis, the share of total funding going to both clean energy and energy efficiency firms has a notable peak between 2006 and 2009 (see figure 4.19). Also consistent with a boom-and-bust story, energy efficiency firms are 30 percent more likely to exit during the prior 2000–2005 period, although this estimate is not statistically significant, with a p-value of 0.12. Fossil fuel energy funded firms are still just as likely to exit as nonenergy firms during this period, further suggesting that this boom-and-bust period was truly unique to investments in clean energy, energy efficiency, and "other" energy firms. In the 2013–2018 period, only "other" energy firms remain less likely to exit.

These results are consistent with the possibility of a clean-tech bubble, although we cannot rule out other potential explanations. If investors were overly exuberant about clean energy during the boom period and invested too much in clean energy relative to other sectors, we would expect to see poorer performance of funded energy firms founded during that time. Of course, this need not imply a bubble. Actual returns are uncertain. Investors may hold a portfolio of investments with negatively correlated risks to hedge against losses in any one sector. Investors may have acted rationally, only to see clean energy firms experience unexpectedly bad outcomes, for instance, because of changing regulations. Moreover, our analysis only looks at binary outcomes. We do not calculate a rate of return by comparing the valuation of these firms on exit to the amount raised. Exploration of competing explanations is left for future research.

4.4.4 Summary of Findings on Startups

To summarize our findings on venture capital in the energy sector, we find a growing interest in energy firms that also operate in the high-tech space. These firms are more likely to raise funds than are other types of energy firms, even though they are not more likely to exit than energy firms not also in high-tech. In general, all types of energy firms in the Crunchbase dataset perform better than the average firm on most performance metrics. However, once conditioning on having received funding, energy firms generally do not perform better than the average funded firm. There is some evidence of over-investment in clean energy during 2006–2012, but more research is needed.

One caveat worth noting is that we are unable to decipher whether these firms are actually working on high-tech technologies or whether they just claim to be doing so on the Crunchbase platform, perhaps in an effort to attract more funding. To truly measure the importance of high-tech activity, we would need a better measure of actual business activities. At a minimum, we provide evidence that energy firms claiming to be high-tech seem to attract more funding. This suggests that VCs may place a premium on these types of firms, which could be explained either by the fact that they are high-tech or by being high-quality if the savviness of claiming to be high-tech is correlated with other measures of firm quality.

4.5 Conclusions

Because energy is a commodity, measuring the returns to R&D in the energy sector requires different metrics than those used in other sectors. Reducing costs and environmental impacts matter more than increasing productivity. As our chapter has documented, the nature of innovation in the energy sector is changing in ways that both reduced costs and environmental impacts. In the past decade, the use of hydrofracturing technology in the US increased the prominence of natural gas. Increased usage of natural gas reduced carbon emissions as it replaced coal as the dominant fuel for electricity, but gas brought with it new environmental questions. The costs of wind and solar energy fell to levels making them competitive with fossil fuels. Innovative activity in the energy sector is also increasingly high-tech across all energy types.

The patent data presented in section 4.3 highlight the role of innovation promoting these trends. Patents for wind, solar, and hydrofracturing all peaked in the early 2010s. The data also illustrate the challenges faced by the industry moving forward. As electricity generation from wind and solar energy grows, integrating these intermittent energy sources into the electricity grid will become more challenging. To compound this challenge, not only has patenting in clean energy technologies (such as wind and solar energy) fallen from its early 2010s peak, but so has patenting in enabling technologies, such as grid integration, smart grids, and energy storage.

Our chapter posits several possible explanations for the fall of clean patenting over the past decade. While we leave it for future research to identify the relative contributions (if any) of the various explanations proposed in section 4.3, it is undoubtedly the case that innovation in the energy industry is changing in ways never seen before. Traditionally, energy R&D has been dominated by large firms that move relatively slowly compared to firms in other sectors. But increasingly, new energy innovation depends, at least in part, on high-tech innovations, such as IT. IT innovation moves much more quickly, is modular, and sees greater participation from smaller firms. Our venture capital data back this observation up. Energy startups attract funding at higher rates relative to the average firm, and energy firms with a high-tech component attract funding even more often. However, once conditioned on receiving funding, energy firms generally do not perform better than the average firm.

While our work is descriptive, not causal, it does raise several questions, both for research and for the industry moving forward. One set of research questions considers the relative importance of different policy instruments for promoting clean energy innovation. First, what role can marketwide increases in energy prices (such as through carbon taxation) play relative to targeted energy policies, such as renewable energy mandates for promoting clean energy innovation? While recent studies on the drivers of clean energy innovation consistently find that policies to increase clean energy demand promote innovation, those studies that also control for energy prices find mixed results. Some find that higher prices on their own have little effect on innovation once controlling for policy (e.g., Johnstone, Haščič, and Popp 2010; Nesta, Vona, and Nicolli 2014), while others find both policy and prices matter (e.g., Verdolini and Galeotti 2011; Peters et al. 2012). One important distinction is the difference between higher prices following the imposition of new taxes versus higher prices in response to market shocks. Studies of gasoline consumption suggest that consumers are more responsive to changes in taxes than market-generated fluctuations in price, as tax increases are perceived as more persistent (Davis and Kilian 2011; Li, Linn, and Muehlegger 2014; Rivers and Schaufele 2015). Similar studies comparing the effect of taxes versus market-generated price changes on innovation would help uncover the potential of broad-based policies, such as carbon taxes for promoting clean energy innovation.

Getting policies right is important. While energy prices remain a key driver of innovation in the sector, market prices do not capture the full social costs of energy use, absent a carbon tax. Public policy thus shapes both demand for green energy and the innovation necessary to meet this demand. Worldwide, policy goals are becoming more ambitions. The EU's Green Deal aims to reduce European greenhouse gas emissions to net zero by 2050. In the US, California plans to rely solely on zero-emission energy sources by 2045, and advocates of the Green New Deal propose using 100 percent zero emission power sources in just 10 years' time.

These ambitious goals raise new challenges for energy storage and smart grid technologies to integrate unprecedently large quantities of intermittent energy sources into the grid. Thus, a second set of questions considers how to promote innovative solutions to technical challenges, such as grid integration, that incorporate high-tech solutions. Do existing energy firms have the capability to incorporate high-tech solutions into their products, or will collaborative research become more important? As noted in International Energy Agency (2020), "low-carbon electricity systems are characterized by increasingly complex interactions of different technologies with different functions in order to ensure reliable supply at all times," placing a premium on collaborative research among different partners, stretching well beyond partners in the energy field. Distributed energy generation provides an example where such collaborative research is likely to yield significant benefits. With the costs of solar power generation now being extremely competitive and likely to become more so (International Energy Agency 2020), the potential for households to become significant producers of electricity presents technical challenges from the microscale to the grid infrastructure.

While there is scant evidence on the role of collaborative research in the energy sector, the work that does exist suggests government intervention can facilitate collaboration. However, this research primarily focuses on flows of knowledge across borders (e.g., Conti et al. 2018; Haščič, Johnstone, and Kahrobaie 2012) or across institutions. For alternative energy technologies, both scientific articles and patents with authors from multiple types of institutions (e.g., universities and corporations) are cited more frequently, suggesting that collaborations may have positive impacts on research quality (Popp 2017). In the EU, research networks enhance the effect of demand-side policies, particularly when high scientific profile network members, such as universities, are included in the network (Fabrizi, Guarini, and Meliciani 2018). Less research has been done on promoting collaborations across fields.

Do patents combining energy and high-tech come from incumbent firms or new entrants to the field? Are they more likely to be collaborative? While the growth in energy startups that are also high-tech observed in section 4.4 shows cross-fertilization of innovation across fields within the firm, are such firms more likely to have collaborative research strategies across firms and other institutions as they grow? The lines between sectors are blurring. Electricity is a general-purpose technology. As electricity costs fall and more stringent environmental regulation increases the costs of or even prohibits the use of fossil fuel energy, sectors such as transportation will increasingly depend on electricity. Efficient interaction between different technologies and firms from different sectors is essential for a smooth transition to an increasingly electric future.

Because of the potential growth in high-tech energy solutions, smaller firms, particularly those operating in the high-tech space, will play a larger role in driving energy innovation moving forward. Developing a better understanding of how policy interventions have heterogeneous effects on innovation outcomes depending on firm size—and whether firms focus on high-tech solutions as opposed to hardware—is therefore also important. For instance, Howell (2017) finds that Small Business Innovation Research (SBIR) funding from the Department of Energy has been effective, particularly for clean energy technologies. That support was most important for clean energy raises two points. First, it highlights that economies of scale may be less prominent for clean energy technology than for traditional energy technologies, so that smaller firms may play a more important role in clean energy innovation. Second, it raises the question of to what extent financial constraints hinder clean energy investment relative to a lack of demand, given how clean energy technologies historically have not been cost effective without government support. That is, is the Valley of Death for energy research really due to the special characteristics of energy innovation, or is it simply a result of historically underpriced environmental externalities reducing demand for cleaner technology? Both falling costs and increased policy support from governments may provide future researchers with the evidence needed to better identify the effects of financial constraints from other market failures holding back clean technology. Similarly, linking patent data with data on venture capital could provide new insights. For instance, how prominent were startup firms in the energy patenting boom of the early 2010s? Were their patents heavily cited? That is, did startups provide new insights to the evolving energy sector and even beyond?

Finally, it is important to note that much of the energy industry is still characterized by large firms with economies of scale. Even if fossil fuel plants are all replaced, large nuclear plants are likely to remain. Offshore wind technology, if successful, will also be capital intensive. The power grid itself is a natural monopoly. While startups may play a larger role for modular technologies, like solar PV or the emerging needs for innovation with a high-tech component, such as grid integration, they remain just part of an industry where high capital costs play an important role. Moving forward, both policymakers and industry leaders will need to identify when smaller, modular technologies are likely to be successful and when large-scale, capital-intensive technologies are needed (e.g., Nemet 2019, chapter 11) to devise policy solutions that recognize the different needs of each type of technology and the different implications of policy for small and larger firms. The climate problem is too expansive and complex for a one-size-fits-all solution, and so is the energy system on which solving the climate problem depends.

Appendix

Table 4.A.1   CPC classifications for energy technologies

Clean energy technologies

Building energy efficiency

Y02B 20/00–70/00	Aspects of energy efficiency related to lighting, appliances, etc.
Y02B 80/00	Aspects of energy efficiency related to building envelope

Carbon capture and storage

Y02C	Capture, storage, sequestration or disposal of greenhouse gases

Solar photovoltaic (PV)

Y02E 10/50	Photovoltaic (PV) energy

Solar thermal energy

Y02E 10/40	Solar thermal energy

Wind energy

Y02E 10/70	Wind energy

Hybrid and Electric Vehicles

Y02T 10/62	Hybrid vehicles
Y02T 10/64	Electric vehicles

Enabling technologies

Energy storage

Y02E 60/10	Energy storage

Smart grids

Y04S	Systems integrating technologies related to power network operation, communication or information technologies for improving the electrical power generation, transmission, distribution, management or usage, i.e. smart grids

Systems integration: building

Y02B 70/30–346	Systems integrating technologies related to power network operation and ICT for improving the carbon footprint of the management of residential or tertiary loads, i.e. smart grids as CCMT in the buildings sector or as enabling technology in buildings sector
Y02B 90/20–2692	Systems integrating technologies related to power network operation and communication or information technologies mediating in the improvement of the carbon footprint of the management of residential or tertiary loads, i.e. smart grids as enabling technology in buildings sector

(continued)

Table 4.A.1 (cont.)

Systems integration: energy	
Y02E 40/70–76	Systems integrating technologies related to power network operation and ICT for improving the carbon footprint of electrical power generation, transmission or distribution, i.e. smart grids as CCMT in the energy generation sector or as enabling technology in the energy generation sector
Y02E 60/70–7892	Systems integrating technologies related to power network operation and communication or information technologies mediating in the improvement of the carbon footprint of electrical power generation, transmission or distribution, i.e. smart grids as enabling technology in the energy generation sector
Systems integration: transportation	
Y02T 90/167–169	Systems integrating technologies related to power network operation and ICT for supporting the interoperability of electric or hybrid vehicles, i.e. smart grids as interface for battery charging of electric vehicles [EV] or hybrid vehicles [HEV]

Hydrofracturing
CPC codes included in Figure 10:

C10G 1	Production of liquid hydrocarbon mixtures from oil-shale, oil-sand, or non-melting solid carbonaceous or similar materials, e.g. wood, coal
E21B 43	Methods or apparatus for obtaining oil, gas, water, soluble or meltable materials or a slurry of minerals from wells

The robustness check in footnote 3 includes the above CPC codes and additional CPC codes in combination with keyword searches:[a]

E21B 36	Heating, cooling, insulating arrangements for boreholes or wells, e.g. for use in permafrost zones
C10G 2300	Aspects relating to hydrocarbon processing covered by groups C10G 1/00–C10G 99/00
Y10T 29	Metal working
C09K 8	Compositions for drilling of boreholes or wells; Compositions for treating boreholes or wells, e.g. for completion or for remedial operations
E21B 47	Survey of boreholes or wells
B32B 15	Layered products comprising a layer of metal
E21B 7	Special methods or apparatus for drilling
B32B 1	Layered products having a general shape other than plane

CPC and IPC codes used in Figure 14:

Climate change mitigation technologies

All Climate Change Mitigation

Y02	Technologies for mitigation or adaptation against climate change
Clean energy	
Y02E	Reduction of greenhouse gas emissions, related to energy generation, transmission, or distribution
Clean transportation	
Y02T	Climate change mitigation technologies related to transportation
Clean buildings	
Y02B	Climate change mitigation technologies related to buildings, and related end-user applications
Clean manufacturing	
Y02P	Climate change mitigation technologies in the production or processing of goods

Broad energy technologies

Engines and pumps	
F02	Combustion engines; hot-gas or combustion-product engine plants
General engineering	
F15	Fluid-pressure actuators; hydraulics or pneumatics in general
F16	Engineering elements and units; general measures for producing and maintaining effective functioning of machines or installations; thermal insulation in general
F17	Storing or distributing gases or liquids
Health technology	
A61	Medical or veterinary science; hygiene
Combustion	
F23	Combustion apparatus; combustion processes
Power	
H02	Generation; Conversion or distribution of electric power

ICT technologies

The patent search strategy follows the J-tags from Inaba and Squicciarini (2017)

[a] The patent search strategy follows Apenteng (2016). Keywords include "hydraulic fracturing," "horizontal drilling," and "well completion" following Cahoy, Gehman, and Lei (2013).

References

Acemoglu, D., U. Akcigit, D. Hanley, and W. Kerr. 2016. "Transition to Clean Technology." *Journal of Political Economy* 124(1): 52–104.

Acemoglu, D., P. Aghion, L. Barrage, and D. Hémous. 2019. "Climate Change, Directed Innovation, and Energy Transition: The Long-Run Consequences of the Shale Gas Revolution." Working paper. Accessed November 7, 2019. https:// scholar.harvard.edu/aghion/publications/climate-change-directed-innovation -and-energy-transition-long-run-consequences.

Aghion, P., A. Dechezleprêtre, D. Hemous, R. Martin, and J. Van Reenen. 2016. "Carbon Taxes, Path Dependency and Directed Technical Change: Evidence from the Auto Industry." *Journal of Political Economy* 124: 1–51.

Ang, G., D. Röttgers, and P. Pralhad. 2017. "The Empirics of Enabling Investment and Innovation in Renewable Energy." *OECD Environment Working Papers*, No. 123. Paris: OECD Publishing. https://dx.doi.org/10.1787/67d221b8-en.

Angelucci, S., F. J. Hurtado-Albir, and A. Volpe. 2018. "Supporting Global Initiatives on Climate Change: The EPO's 'Y02-Y04S' Tagging Scheme." *World Patent Information* 54: 585–92.

Anonymous. 2019. "Oil Rush." *The Economist*, March 16, 57.

Apenteng, Seth O. 2016. "Patent Analysis of Shale Gas Technology to Identify the U.S. Government's Role in Its Development." Thesis in Energy and Mineral Engineering, Pennsylvania State University, State College, PA.

Bajwa, Maheen, and Joseph Cavicchi. 2017. "Growing Evidence of Increased Frequency of Negative Electricity Prices in U.S. Wholesale Electricity Markets." *IAEE Energy Forum*, 37–41. https://www.iaee.org/newsletter/issue/47.

Bartik, Alexander W., Janet Currie, Michael Greenstone, and Christopher R. Knittel. 2019. "The Local Economic and Welfare Consequences of Hydraulic Fracturing." *American Economic Journal: Applied Economics* 11(4): 105–55.

Borenstein, Severin. 2012. "The Private and Public Economics of Renewable Electricity Generation." *Journal of Economic Perspectives* 26(1): 67–92.

Braff, William A., Joshua M. Mueller, and Jessika E. Trancik. 2016. "Value of Storage Technologies for Wind and Solar Energy." *Nature Climate Change* 6: 964–69.

Branstetter, L., and Y. Ogura. 2005. "Is Academic Science Driving a Surge in Industrial Innovation? Evidence from Patent Counts." NBER Working Paper No. 11561. Cambridge, MA: National Bureau of Economic Research.

Branstetter, Lee G., Matej Drev, and Namho Kwon. 2019. "Get with the Program: Software-Driven Innovation in Traditional Manufacturing." *Management Science* 65(2): 541–58.

Branstetter, Lee G., Britta Glennon, and J. Bradford Jensen. 2019. "The IT Revolution and the Globalization of R&D." In *Innovation Policy and the Economy*, vol. 19, edited by Josh Lerner and Scott Stern, 1–37. Chicago: University of Chicago Press.

Cahoy, Daniel R., Joel Gehman, and Zhen Lei. 2013. "Fracking Patents: The Emergence of Patents as Information-Containment Tools in Shale Drilling." *Michigan Telecommunications and Technology Law Review* 19: 279–330.

Cárdenas Rodríguez, M., I. Haščič, N. Johnstone, J. Silva, and A. Ferey. 2015. "Renewable Energy Policies and Private Sector Investment: Evidence from Financial Microdata." *Environmental & Resource Economics* 62(1): 163–88.

Conti, C., M. L. Mancusi, F. Sanna-Randaccio, R. Sestini, and E. Verdolini. 2018. "Transition towards a Green Economy in Europe: Innovation and Knowledge Integration in the Renewable Energy Sector." *Research Policy* 47: 1996–2009.

Cumming, D. J., G. Leboeuf, and A. Schwienbacher. 2017. "Crowdfunding Cleantech." *Energy Economics* 65: 292–303.

Dalle, J., M. den Besten, and C. Menon. 2017. "Using Crunchbase for Economic and Managerial Research." *OECD Science, Technology and Industry Working Papers*, No. 2017/08. Paris: OECD Publishing. https://doi.org/10.1787/6c418d60-en.

Davis, Lucas W., and Lutz Kilian. 2011. "Estimating the Effect of a Gasoline Tax on Carbon Emissions." *Journal of Applied Econometrics* 26(7): 1187–1214.

Dechezleprêtre, A., and M. Glachant. 2014. "Does Foreign Environmental Policy Influence Domestic Innovation? Evidence from the Wind Industry." *Environmental and Resource Economics* 58(3): 391–413.

Dechezleprêtre, A., R. Martin, and M. Mohnen. 2017. "Knowledge Spillovers from Clean and Dirty Technologies: A Patent Citation Analysis." Grantham Research Institute on Climate Change and the Environment Working Paper No. 135, London.

EIA Today in Energy. 2011. "About 60% of the U.S. Electric Power Supply Is Managed by RTOs." Accessed November 22, 2019. https://www.eia.gov/todayinenergy /detail.php?id=790.

———. 2016. "U.S. Electric System Is Made Up of Interconnections and Balancing Authorities." Accessed November 22, 2019. https://www.eia.gov/todayinenergy /detail.php?id=27152.

———. 2019a. "More New Natural Gas Combined-Cycle Power Plants Are Using Advanced Designs." Accessed October 17, 2019. https://www.eia.gov/todayin energy/detail.php?id=39912.

———. 2019b. "US Petroleum Exports Exceeded Imports in September." Accessed December 6, 2019. https://www.eia.gov/todayinenergy/detail.php?id=42176.

Ellerman, Denny, Claudio Marcantonini, and Aleksandar Zaklan. 2016. "The EU ETS: Eight Years and Counting." *Review of Environmental Economics and Policy* 10(1): 89–107.

European Commission. 2018. "10 Trends Reshaping Climate and Energy." European Political Strategy Centre. https://ec.europa.eu/epsc/sites/epsc/files/epsc_-_10 _trends_transforming_climate_and_energy.pdf.

Fabrizi, A., G. Guarini, and V. Meliciani. 2018. "Green Patents, Regulatory Policies and Research Network Policies." *Research Policy* 47: 1018–31.

Fabrizio, K. R., S. Poczter, and B. A. Zelner. 2017. "Does Innovation Policy Attract International Competition? Evidence from Energy Storage." *Research Policy* 46: 1106–117.

Fetter, T. R., A. L. Steck, C. Timmins, and D. Wrenn. 2018. "Learning by Viewing? Social Learning, Regulatory Disclosure, and Firm Productivity in Shale Gas." NBER Working Paper No. 25401. Cambridge, MA: National Bureau of Economic Research.

Feyrer, James, Erin T. Mansur, and Bruce Sacerdote. 2017. "Geographic Dispersion of Economic Shocks: Evidence from the Fracking Revolution." *American Economic Review* 107(4): 1313–34.

Finardi, U. 2011. "Time Relations between Scientific Production and Patenting of Knowledge: The Case of Nanotechnologies." *Scientometrics* 89(1): 37–50.

Fischer, C., L. Preonas, and R. Newell. 2017. "Environmental and Technology Policy Options in the Electricity Sector: Are We Deploying Too Many?" *Journal of the Association of Environmental and Resource Economists* 4(4): 959–84.

Gaddy, B. E., V. Sivaram, T. B. Jones, and L. Wayman. 2017. "Venture Capital and Cleantech: The Wrong Model for Energy Innovation." *Energy Policy* 102: 385–95.

Greenblatt, Jeffrey B., Nicholas R. Brown, Rachel Slaybaugh, Theresa Wilks, Emma

Stewart, and Sean T. McCoy. 2017. "The Future of Low-Carbon Energy." *Annual Review of Environment and Resources* 42: 289–316.

Harhoff, D., F. M. Scherer, and K. Vopel. 2003. "Citations, Family Size, Opposition and the Value of Patent Rights." *Research Policy* 32(8): 1343–63.

Haščič, I., N. Johnstone, and N. Kahrobaie. 2012. "International Technology Agreements for Climate Change: Analysis Based on Co-Invention Data." *OECD Environment Working Papers*, No. 42. Paris: OECD Publishing.

Holland, Stephen P., Erin T. Mansur, Nicholas Muller, and Andrew J. Yates. 2018. "Decompositions and Policy Consequences of an Extraordinary Decline in Air Pollution from Electricity Generation." NBER Working Paper No. 25339. Cambridge, MA: National Bureau of Economic Research.

Howell, S. T. 2017. "Financing Innovation: Evidence from R&D Grants." *American Economic Review* 107(4): 1136–64.

Inaba, T., and M. Squicciarini. 2017. "ICT: A New Taxonomy Based on the International Patent Classification." *OECD Science, Technology and Industry Working Papers*, No. 2017/01. Paris: OECD Publishing. https://doi.org/10.1787/ab16c396-en.

International Energy Agency. 2004. *Renewable Energy—Market and Policy Trends in IEA Countries*. Paris: International Energy Agency.

———. 2019a. "Status of Power System Transformation 2019." Paris: International Energy Agency. https://www.iea.org/reports/status-of-power-system-transformation-2019.

———. 2019b. "Nuclear Power in a Clean Energy System." Paris: International Energy Agency. https://www.iea.org/reports/nuclear-power-in-a-clean-energy-system.

———. 2019c. "World Energy Prices 2019." Paris: International Energy Agency. https://www.iea.org/reports/world-energy-prices-2019.

———. 2020. "Projected Costs of Generating Electricity 2020." Paris: International Energy Agency. https://www.iea.org/reports/projected-costs-of-generating-electricity-2020.

International Renewable Energy Agency. 2017. *Accelerating the Energy Transition through Innovation*. Abu Dhabi: International Renewable Energy Agency.

———. 2018. *Renewable Power Generation Costs in 2017*. Abu Dhabi: International Renewable Energy Agency.

IPCC. 2018. *Global Warming of 1.5°C. An IPCC Special Report on the Impacts of Global Warming of 1.5°C above Pre-industrial Levels and Related Global Greenhouse Gas Emission Pathways, in the Context of Strengthening the Global Response to the Threat of Climate Change, Sustainable Development, and Efforts to Eradicate Poverty*. Edited by V. Masson-Delmotte, P. Zhai, H.-O. Pörtner, D. Roberts, J. Skea, P. R. Shukla, A. Pirani, W. Moufouma-Okia, C. Péan, R. Pidcock, S. Connors, J. B. R. Matthews, Y. Chen, X. Zhou, M. I. Gomis, E. Lonnoy, T. Maycock, M. Tignor, and T. Waterfield. Geneva: IPCC.

Jacoby, Henry D., Francis M. O'Sullivan, and Sergey Palstev. 2012. "The Influence of Shale Gas on U.S. Energy and Environmental Policy." *Economics of Energy and Environmental Policy* 1(1): 37–51.

Johnstone, N., I. Haščič, and D. Popp. 2010. "Renewable Energy Policies and Technological Innovation: Evidence Based on Patent Counts." *Environmental and Resource Economics* 45(1): 133–55.

Killian, Lutz. 2016. "The Impact of the Shale Oil Revolution on U.S. Oil and Gasoline Prices." *Review of Environmental Economics and Policy* 10(2): 188–205.

Ko, Yu-li, and Kenneth L. Simons. 2020. "The Cross-Border Impact of Demand-Pull Policies on R&D: A Firm-Level Analysis." Working paper. Accessed April 3, 2020.

http://homepages.rpi.edu/~simonk/pdf/photovoltaicResearchAndSubsidies
.pdf.

Krupnick, Alan, and Zhongmin Wang. 2017. "Lessons from the U.S. Shale Gas Boom." In *Energy Tax and Regulatory Policy in Europe: Reform Priorities*, edited by Ian Parry, Karen Pittel, and Herman Vollebergh, 223–53. Cambridge, MA: MIT Press.

Lanjouw, J. O., A. Pakes, and J. Putnam. 1998. "How to Count Patents and Value Intellectual Property: The Uses of Patent Renewal and Application Data." *Journal of Industrial Economics* 46(4): 405–32.

Lehmann, P., and P. Söderholm. 2018. "Can Technology-Specific Deployment Policies Be Cost-Effective? The Case of Renewable Support Schemes." *Environmental and Resource Economics* 71: 475–505.

Lerner, J. 2011. "Venture Capital and Innovation in Energy." In *Accelerating Energy Innovation: Insights from Multiple Sectors*, edited by Rebecca M. Henderson and Richard G. Newell, 225–60. Chicago: University of Chicago Press.

Li, Shanjun, Joshua Linn, and Erich Muehlegger. 2014. "Gasoline Taxes and Consumer Behavior." *American Economic Journal: Economic Policy* 6(4): 302–42.

Maniloff, Peter, and Ralph Mastromonaco. 2017. "The Local Employment Impacts of Fracking: A National Study." *Resource and Energy Economics* 49: 62–85.

Martinot, Eric. 2016. "Grid Integration of Renewable Energy: Flexibility, Innovation, and Experience." *Annual Review of Environment and Resources* 41: 223–51.

Mowrey, D. C., R. R. Nelson, and B. R. Martin. 2010. "Technology Policy and Global Warming: Why New Policy Models Are Needed (or Why Putting New Wine in Old Bottles Won't Work)." *Research Policy* 39: 1011–23.

Nanda, R., K. Younge, and L. Fleming. 2015. "Innovation and Entrepreneurship in Renewable Energy." In *The Changing Frontier: Rethinking Science and Innovation Policy*, edited by A. B. Jaffe and B. F. Jones, 199–232. Chicago: University of Chicago Press.

Nemet, G. F. 2012. "Knowledge Spillovers from Learning by Doing in Wind Power." *Journal of Policy Analysis and Management* 31(3): 600–621.

———. 2019. *How Solar Energy Became Cheap: A Model for Low-Carbon Innovation*. New York: Routledge.

Nesta, L., F. Vona, and F. Nicolli. 2014. "Environmental Policies, Competition, and Innovation in Renewable Energy." *Journal of Environmental Economics and Management* 67: 396–411.

Newell, R., A. B. Jaffe, and R. Stavins. 1999. "The Induced Innovation Hypothesis and Energy-Saving Technological Change." *Quarterly Journal of Economics* 114(3): 941–75.

Newell, Richard G., and Brian C. Priest. 2017. "How the Shale Boom Has Transformed the US Oil and Gas Industry." Resources for the Future Issue Brief 17-11. Washington, DC: Resources for the Future.

Noailly, J. 2012. "Improving the Energy Efficiency of Buildings: The Impact of Environmental Policy on Technological Innovation." *Energy Economics* 34: 795–806.

Peters, M., M. Schneider, T. Griesshaber, and V. H. Hoffman. 2012. "The Impact of Technology-Push and Demand-Pull Policies on Technical Change—Does the Locus of Policies Matter?" *Research Policy* 41(8): 1296–1308.

Popp, D. 2002. "Induced Innovation and Energy Prices." *American Economic Review* 92(1): 160–80.

———. 2006. "International Innovation and Diffusion of Air Pollution Control Technologies: The Effects of NO_x and SO_2 Regulation in the U.S., Japan, and Germany." *Journal of Environmental Economics and Management* 51(1): 46–71.

———. 2016. "Economic Analysis of Scientific Publications and Implications for

Energy Research and Development." *Nature Energy* 1 (16020). https://doi.org/10.1038/nenergy.2016.20.

———. 2017. "From Science to Technology: The Value of Knowledge from Different Energy Research Institutions." *Research Policy* 46(9): 1580–94.

———. 2019. "Environmental Policy and Innovation: A Decade of Research." *International Review of Environmental and Resource Economics* 13(3–4): 265–337.

Rivers, N., and B. Schaufele. 2015. "Salience of Carbon Taxes in the Gasoline Market." *Journal of Environmental Economics and Management* 74: 23–36.

Roth, Michael Buchdahl, and Paulina Jaramillo. 2017. "Going Nuclear for Climate Mitigation: An Analysis of the Cost Effectiveness of Preserving Existing U.S. Nuclear Power Plants as a Carbon Avoidance Strategy." *Energy* 131: 67–77.

Shane, S. 2001. "Technological Opportunities and New Firm Creation." *Management Science* 47(2): 205–20.

Squicciarini, Mariagrazia, Hélène Dernis, and Chiara Criscuolo. 2013. "Measuring Patent Quality: Indicators of Technological and Economic Value." *OECD Science, Technology and Industry Working Papers*, No. 2013/03. Paris: OECD Publishing.

Stucki, T., and M. Woerter. 2017. "Green Inventions: Is Wait-and-See a Reasonable Option?" *Energy Journal* 38(4): 43–71.

Tang, T. 2018. "Explaining Technological Change in the US Wind Industry: Energy Policies, Technological Learning, and Collaboration." *Energy Policy* 120: 197–212.

Trajtenberg, M., A. Jaffe, and R. Henderson. 1997. "University versus Corporate Patents: A Window on the Basic-ness of Inventions." *Economics of Innovation and New Technology* 5(1): 19–50.

US Department of Energy. n.d. "What Is the Smart Grid?" Accessed November 22, 2019. https://www.smartgrid.gov/the_smart_grid/smart_grid.html.

US Energy Information Administration. 2018. *U.S. Crude Oil and Natural Gas Proved Reserves, Year End 2017*. Washington, DC: US Department of Energy.

———. 2019. "Monthly Energy Review: Table 7.2a: Electricity Net Generation (Total, All Sectors)." US Energy Information Administration, Washington, DC.

US Environmental Protection Agency. 2019. *Inventory of U.S. Greenhouse Gas Emissions and Sinks: 1990–2017*. EPA 430-R-19–001. Washington, DC.

Veefkind, V., F. J. Hurtado-Albir, S. Angelucci, K. Karachalios, and N. Thurman. 2012. "A New EPO Classification Scheme for Climate Change Mitigation." *World Patent Information* 34: 106–11.

Verdolini, E., and M. Galeotti. 2011. "At Home and Abroad: An Empirical Analysis of Innovation and Diffusion in Energy Technologies." *Journal of Environmental Economics and Management* 61: 119–34.

Weyant, J. 2011. "Accelerating the Development and Diffusion of New Energy Technologies: Beyond the 'Valley of Death.'" *Energy Economics* 33: 674–82.

II

The On-Demand Economy

5

What's Driving Entrepreneurship and Innovation in the Transportation Sector?

Derrick Choe, Alexander Oettl, and Rob Seamans

5.1 Introduction

The transportation sector—including the movement and storage of physical goods and the movement of people—is an important contributor to the US economy. It directly accounts for 3.2 percent of US gross domestic product (GDP) and indirectly affects many other sectors (figure 5.1). Personal transportation makes up a large portion of American consumption; according to the Bureau of Transportation Statistics, households spent an average of $9,737 on transportation in 2017, the second largest household expenditure category after housing.[1] Economists have highlighted the multiple ways in which transportation affects innovation and growth, including opening up geographically distant markets for entrepreneurs (Donaldson 2018), linking together people and thereby increasing the recombination of ideas (Agrawal, Galasso, and Oettl 2017), sparking new innovations by the arrival of a new product (Sohn, Seamans, and Sands 2019), and more.

Derrick Choe is a first-year doctoral student at NYU Stern School of Business.

Alexander Oettl is an associate professor of strategy and innovation at the Scheller College of Business, Georgia Institute of Technology, and a research associate of the National Bureau of Economic Research.

Rob Seamans is an associate professor of management and organizations at NYU Stern School of Business.

We thank Michael Andrews, Aaron Chatterji, Mercedes Delgado, Gilles Duranton, Jeff Furman, Adam Jaffe, Ben Jones, Shane Greenstein, David Popp, Scott Stern, Joel Waldfogel, and Kate Whitefoot for helpful comments and suggestions. Seamans acknowledges generous support from Google's Tides Foundation. For acknowledgments, sources of research support, and disclosure of the authors' material financial relationships, if any, please see https://www.nber.org/books-and-chapters/role-innovation-and-entrepreneurship-economic-growth/whats-driving-entrepreneurship-and-innovation-transport-sector.

1. https://www.bts.gov/browse-statistical-products-and-data/transportation-economic-trends/tet-2018-chapter-6-household.

Across the US economy, firms are increasingly adopting new technologies, including artificial intelligence (AI), robots, sensors, and others, and the transportation sector is no different. For example, Uber bought the autonomous trucking startup Otto for $680 million in 2016,[2] and Amazon bought warehouse robotics company Kiva for $775 million in 2012.[3] While fully autonomous vehicles (AVs) are still some ways off in the future—a topic we discuss later in this chapter—Kiva has led to dramatic changes in the way that Amazon organizes some of its fulfilment centers. Whereas in the past, a human picker would go up and down aisles of shelving units to pick the order, now the Kiva robots bring the shelving units to a central location, where the human picker is located (CEA 2016).

The costs associated with moving goods and individuals differ greatly. While the real cost of moving goods is 90 percent less than it was at the beginning of the twentieth century, transporting individuals remains costly (Glaeser and Kohlhase 2004). In this chapter, we review recent trends in the transportation sector and conduct deeper investigations into recent changes and innovations in the movement (and storage) of (1) goods and (2) people.

The key takeaways from this chapter include:

- Despite the rapid expansion of Internet-enabled services and the digital economy, the importance of transporting physical goods has not diminished.
- In aggregate, the transportation sector has grown (20 percent employment growth over 5 years), but this average increase masks large differences in the composition of the transportation sector (rail and sea transport are down, couriers and warehousing are up).
- Transportation's share of value added in the economy has also increased (an absolute increase of 0.3 percent over 5 years).
- As such, warehousing and the automation contained therein (robots, AVs, drones) will play a critical role in this increasingly important component of the transportation supply chain.

In the sections that follow, we first describe what we currently know about the sector from prior academic research and aggregate government statistics. We then highlight recent innovations in the transportation and storage of goods, with a deep dive into the warehouse sector—an area of increasing activity. We then review existing work in the personal mobility domain, focusing on the impact of ride sharing platforms and the potential for AVs to transform the economy. How these new innovations affect the sector and the economy more broadly will ultimately depend on a variety of factors, including government regulation, technological advancement, and customer

2. https://techcrunch.com/2016/08/18/uber-acquires-otto-to-lead-ubers-self-driving-car-effort-report-says/.
3. https://techcrunch.com/2012/03/19/amazon-acquires-online-fulfillment-company-kiva-systems-for-775-million-in-cash/.

demand. In our final section, we conclude and discuss opportunities for future work.

5.2 What Do We Know?

5.2.1 Prior Literature

Prior literature has highlighted the many ways in which transportation can affect innovation and economic growth. As the exchange of goods and services is contingent on the movement of materials and workers, transportation plays a key role in economic output. Investments in infrastructure and transportation technologies transform the urban landscape, and they spur productivity growth and innovative activity.

Innovations in transportation infrastructure directly impact the spatial distribution of workers. Baum-Snow (2007) finds that the development of interstate highways contributed to the post–World War II suburbanization of the US. Along with contributing to population shifts within cities, transportation influences the distribution of work across cities. Duranton and Turner (2012) estimate that a 10 percent increase in a city's initial stock of highways leads to a 1.5 percent increase in employment over a period of two decades. Taken together, these results indicate that transportation infrastructure has two distinct effects on input reorganization and growth: it can increase urban employment growth while also leading to population growth in surrounding areas (Redding and Turner 2015).

In addition to this work estimating the long-run effects of interstate highway development, other researchers have focused on the localized effects of within-city transportation infrastructure. In particular, studies have investigated the value of these transportation networks by estimating the proximal effects of subway line development on real estate prices. Billings (2011) finds that access to light rail transit increased single-family property values by 4 percent and condominium values by 11 percent. Gibbons and Machin (2005) study the London subway network and find that homes near newly developed stations experienced price increases of around 9 percent relative to those unaffected by transportation changes. The authors compare the price effects of proximity to subway stations to the price estimates of other local amenities, such as primary school performance, and find that households seem to value transportation higher relative to other local factors.

Changes to the flow of people are accompanied with innovative activity; transportation's positive impacts on economic performance through worker movement are also the product of resulting positive knowledge externalities. Agrawal, Galasso, and Oettl (2017) find that the stock of regional highways increases inventive productivity not only through its labor agglomeration effects but also through improvements to knowledge flows—increasing output beyond that explained by the influx of new innovators. Perlman (2016) provides historical evidence that the nineteenth-century "transportation revolution"—marked by the development of railroad networks—increased patenting activity through increased market access, among other covariates.

In addition to its impact on the geography of labor, transportation infrastructure serves as a catalyst to firm growth and productivity. Gains in accessibility to new roads lead to increases in the number of establishments, employment, and output per worker (Gibbons et al. 2019). Baum-Snow et al. (2017) further decompose the effects of highway growth on economic activity in China; they find that areas most proximal to dense highway networks show increased output, employment, and wages, and shift toward business services and manufacturing. Distal areas from these clusters demonstrate an opposite effect; they grow more slowly and specialize in agriculture.

These economic benefits to transportation may rely on improvements to the transfer of physical goods. The development of colonial India's railroad system transformed agricultural trade; by decreasing the cost of transporting origin-destination products and increasing trade flows, this expansive change in transportation infrastructure increased per capita agricultural incomes (Donaldson 2018). Additionally, economic gains to transportation may require sufficient ease of transporting capital along with goods. In examining the effects of railway access on economic growth, Banerjee, Duflo, and Qian (2012) find suggestive evidence that production factor immobility may limit the localized economic benefits to transportation infrastructure. These studies highlight the distinction between worker and capital flows; the regional benefits to government investment in transportation networks may be limited by the movement of physical production factors.

Historically, waterways have played a crucial role in determining market access, economic development, and innovation. Sokoloff (1988) finds evidence that navigable waterways explain early regional variation in patent activity across the US. The author suggests that during the Industrial Revolution, areas like southern New England and New York exhibited high growth in patenting due to increased access to low-cost river and canal transportation. The economic changes attributable to transportation infrastructure are persistent long after initial natural advantages afforded by geography become obsolete. Bleakley and Lin (2012) find that despite the decline in portage in the southeastern US, original portage cities remain denser than comparable regional counterparts, suggesting a degree of path dependence resulting from historical transportation activity.

More recent work has begun to focus on a more basic form of transportation infrastructure: the walkability of streets. In Roche (forthcoming), the author examines how the physical layouts of street networks facilitate idea exchange among knowledge workers. The paper demonstrates that neighborhoods that are easier to traverse by foot also produce more patents (even after controlling for population and other density related measures) and are more likely to build on geographically proximate knowledge inputs.

Table 5.1   Industry summary statistics

Industry title	NAICS code	2018 employment (in thousands)	2018 real average weekly wage (US$)	Five-year employment growth (percent) (2013–2018)	Five-year real wage growth (percent) (2013–2018)
All Transport/Warehousing	48/49	5419.1	940.0	20.3	1.7
Air Transport	481	501.4	1,107.1	12.8	1.2
Rail Transport	482	214.3		−7.4	
Water Transport	483	64.7		−0.9	
Truck Transport	484	1491.3	1,004.6	7.9	0.7
Transit/Ground Passenger Transport	485	487.4	663.0	8.7	8.7
Pipeline Transport	486	48.6		9.3	
Scenic/Sightseeing Transport	487	34.3		17.3	
Support Activities for Transport	488	711.8	955.5	18.9	0.6
Couriers and Messengers	492	725.5	784.6	33.4	14.9
Warehousing and Storage	493	1139.9	845.2	59.2	3.5

Note: These data come from BLS Current Employment Statistics. We omit the Postal Service, as well as wage data for rail, water, pipeline, and scenic/sightseeing transportation, as these aggregate data are not available from BLS CES.

5.2.2   Basic Statistics

In the US, the transportation sector (NAICS codes 48–49) contributes approximately 3 percent to US GDP and comprises multiple sub-industries, including air, rail, water, truck, pipeline, and passenger transport. It also includes couriers, messengering, warehousing, and storage businesses. Descriptive statistics of select sub-industries are presented in table 5.1. Between 2013 and 2018, sector-wide employment grew by over 20 percent, and real wages grew by 1.7 percent. However, this aggregate growth masks significant heterogeneity. Over the same period, rail and water transport saw 7 percent and 1 percent declines in employment, respectively. Conversely, the warehousing and storage (NAICS 493) and couriers and messengers (NAICS 492) sub-industries experienced the largest employment growth of all sub-industries with growth of 59 percent and 33 percent in employment, respectively. These two industries also saw real wage growth of 3 percent for warehousing and 15 percent for couriers and messengers. Providing a deeper understanding of the antecedents and consequences of this rapid growth in the warehousing sector will be an important point of focus for this chapter.

Figure 5.1 presents data on employment by transportation sub-industry over a longer period. Using data from the BLS Current Employment Statistics (BLS CES) survey to provide employment by transportation sub-industry, we see that the growth in warehousing started in 2010. Drawing from Bureau of Economic Analysis data, figure 5.2 plots value-added by

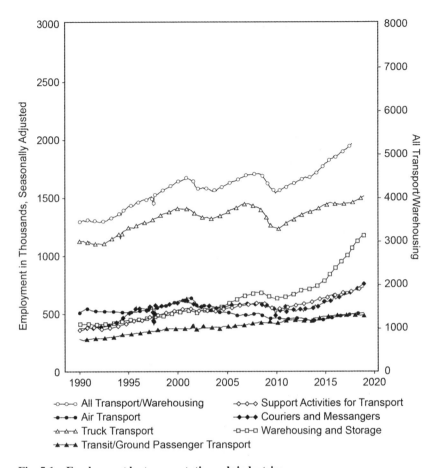

Fig. 5.1   Employment by transportation sub-industries
Source: Data are from the Bureau of Labor Statistics Current Employment Statistics survey (BLS CES).

transportation sub-industry, as a fraction of national GDP. We see that all transportation/warehousing industries make up an increasing share of aggregate economic activity, increasing from 2.8 percent in 2005 to 3.2 percent in 2018. Figure 5.3, using data from BLS CES, provides real average weekly earnings from 2006 onward,[4] by transportation sub-industry. On average, wages in the industry appear relatively flat over this entire period. However, there is some heterogeneity across sub-industries. These data suggest that as demand for transportation services increases, the industry is able to adjust relatively quickly at the margin by employing more individuals, such that wages do not rise much.

Figure 5.4 plots labor productivity by transportation sub-industry, mea-

4. The BLS CES only publishes wage estimates at the industry level from 2006 onward.

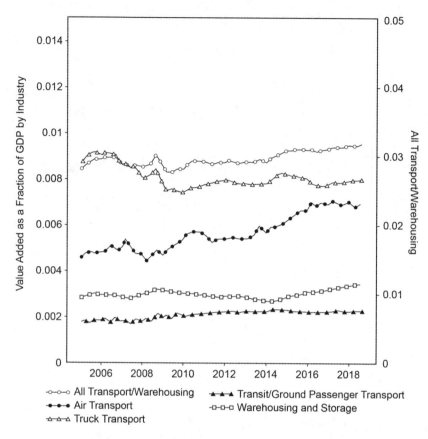

Fig. 5.2   Value added as a fraction of GDP
Source: Data are from the Bureau of Economic Analysis (BEA).

sured with BLS's Annual Index of Labor Productivity. The figure shows changes in output per hour relative to 2007 levels. Most sub-industries appear to have relatively flat productivity, although air transport has increased steadily over the almost 30-year times series between 1990 and 2018. As such, the employment growth in the sector appears not to be a result of changes in labor productivity and instead may stem from broader changes in market structure (Combes and Lafourcade 2005).

Figure 5.5 plots trends in the relative number of establishments by transportation sub-industry. The data come from the BLS Quarterly Census of Employment and Wages. The series is normalized to show establishment levels relative to 1990. While the number of establishments has increased in all sub-sectors, we find that growth in the Couriers and Messengers sub-industry outpaces that of all other sub-industries, followed by Warehousing and Storage.

Next we study two measures of innovative activity—patenting and ven-

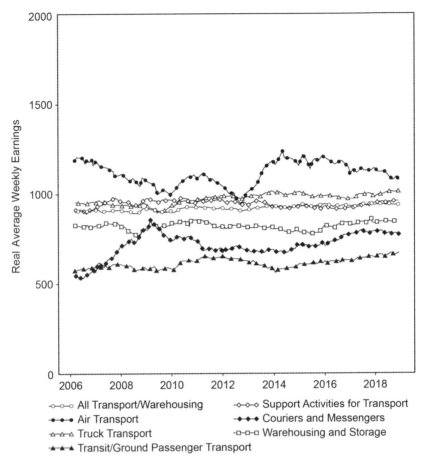

Fig. 5.3   Real average weekly earnings by transportation sub-industry
Source: Data are from BLS CES.
Note: Average weekly earnings are plotted by transportation sub-industry, adjusted for inflation using the CPI-U.

ture capital investment. Figures 5.6 and 5.7 compare patent activity by transportation sub-industry over time. The data come from PatentsView. We find that from 1980 onward, the number of vehicle-related patents outpaces the number of conveying, packing, storing, and other warehousing-related patents. Additionally, among less frequently patented codes, non-rail land vehicle and aircraft-related patents outpace other categories, including those for ships and railways.

Figure 5.8 plots transportation-related funding over time (in US dollars). The data come from CrunchBase. We find that relative to other activities, funding for warehousing companies shows dramatic growth later in our timeframe. Whereas funding for AVs, shipping, and general transportation-

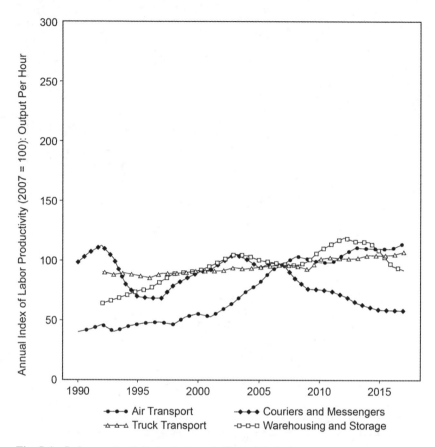

Fig. 5.4   Labor productivity by transportation sub-industry
Source: Data are from the BLS's Annual Index of Labor Productivity.
Note: These figures show changes in output per hour relative to 2007 levels.

related companies increases beginning in 2012, warehousing funding picks up in 2015 in our sample.

Finally, we consider adoption patterns from automotive technologies in the past. In figure 5.9, we plot technology adoption s-curves for various automobile transmission technologies. Our data come from the United States Environmental Protection Agency (EPA). We define advanced transmission as having six or more gears. These data show that advanced transmissions were adopted by the majority of manufacturers faster than automatic transmissions with lockup.

Figure 5.10 plots technology adoption s-curves for various engine technologies. These data come from the EPA. Variable valve timing (VVT) and gasoline direct injection (GDI) demonstrate considerable growth in production share. Multi-valve engines demonstrate a longer period of adoption, reaching around 90 percent of production share over 37 years. Stop/start and

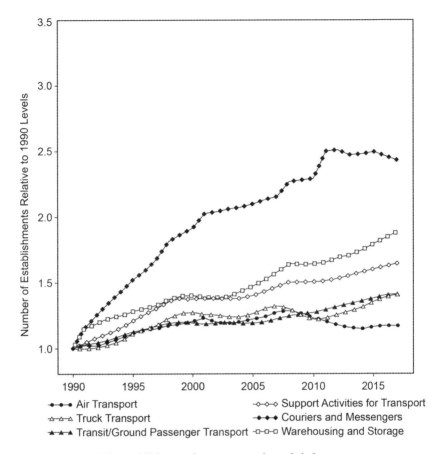

Fig. 5.5   Growth in establishments by transportation sub-industry

Note: These data come from the BLS Quarterly Census of Employment and Wages. The series are normalized to show establishment levels relative to 1990.

turbocharged engines do not yet make up a majority of engine production in our timeline. The broad takeaway from figures 5.9 and 5.10 is that new technologies can take many years before achieving widespread use, and there is heterogeneity across technologies. We keep these patterns in mind as we consider the potential effects of new technologies.

5.3   Moving and Storing Physical Goods

5.3.1   Literature

As noted, transportation's most aggregate industry classification (NAICS code 48–49) includes both transportation and warehousing-related activities. While transportation has received considerable interest from econo-

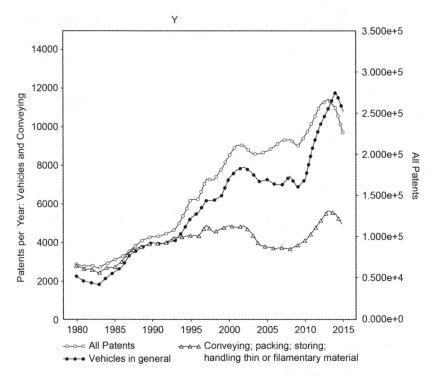

Fig. 5.6   Patenting activity: Vehicles in general and conveying

Source: Data are from PatentsView.

Note: We plot total patents per year for CPC codes B60 (vehicles in general) and B65 (conveying, packing, storing, etc.), as well as all patents.

mists, warehousing has received less attention. One reason for this may be the larger impact that air and truck transport have in contributing to GDP (see figure 5.1) relative to warehousing and storage. Yet over the past 5 years, growth in employment and in new establishments has been markedly higher in the warehousing sector than the overall transportation sector (see table 5.1). In this section, we examine this trend more deeply by exploring the changing role of warehousing, its interface with transportation, and its relationship with the economy at large.

The effects of transportation on economic growth have been extensively documented in the economics literature and well summarized in Redding and Turner (2015). Much less has been written on the role of warehousing in the transport supply chain. One exception is a recent paper by Chava et al. (2019); the authors find that when Amazon opens a fulfillment center in a county, employment levels at transportation and warehousing establishments in the same county grow by 2.1 percent, while worker wages at transportation and warehousing establishments in the same county grow by

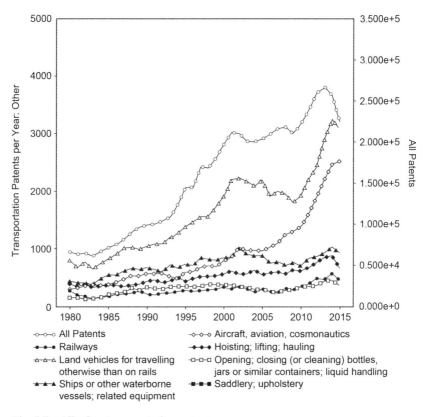

Fig. 5.7   All other transportation patents

Source: Data are from PatentsView.

Note: We plot patents per year for the remaining transportation CPC codes (B60–B68), excluding vehicles in general and conveying/packing.

1.7 percent. These numbers provide suggestive evidence of the complements that may exist between geographic co-location of warehousing/fulfillment centers of e-commerce players and local demand for additional transportation and warehousing services. It is unlikely, however, that the significant growth in warehousing employment is entirely attributable to the changing nature of retail. Figure 5.11 presents the warehousing employment plot first shown in figure 5.1 alongside retail employment growth.

More broadly, as others have noted, there may have been a shift in consumer purchase behavior. For example, Lafontaine and Sividasan (this volume, chapter 6) find marked growth in restaurant establishments and employment, which they attribute to an increase in consumer expenditure share for restaurant food. The authors also note that DoorDash and Instacart, two of the top delivery businesses, received substantial venture capital investments ($2.1 billion and $1.8 billion, respectively). As we indicate

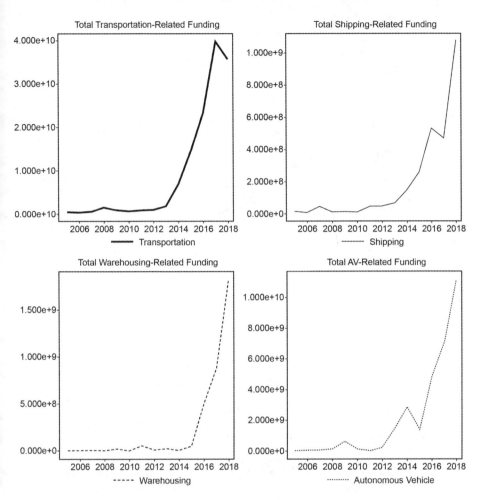

Fig. 5.8 Venture funding, by transportation sub-industry
Source: Data are from CrunchBase.
Note: Figures report annual funding by company type; amounts are reported in US dollars.

below, Instacart was the top hiring firm in the "transit and ground passenger" sector in 2017 and 2018 (see table 5.3 below). As another example, Relihan (2020) shows that consumers using online grocery delivery platforms change their consumption patterns by shifting time away from grocery shopping and toward visits to coffee shops. Relihan finds that early adopters of online grocery platforms reduce spending at grocery stores by 4.5 percent and increase spending at coffee shops by 7.6 percent.

Mandel (2020) points out that the shift from offline retail purchases to online purchases requires a substantial change in the architecture of supply chains. Notably, firms like Amazon and Walmart that want to engage with

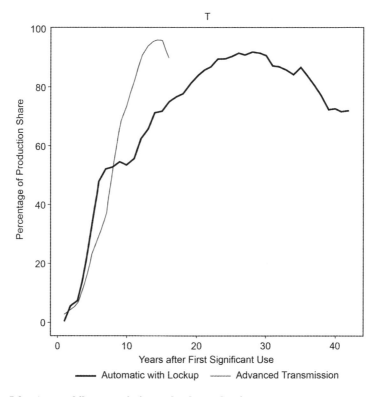

Fig. 5.9   Automobile transmission technology adoption

Note: Data are from the United States Environmental Protection Agency (EPA). We define advanced transmission as having six or more gears.

consumers on a large-scale basis need to invest in warehousing to hold merchandise, fulfilment systems to organize and pack orders, delivery infrastructure to ship packages to customers, and a complementary returns infrastructure to handle orders that are sent back or dropped off at physical locations. Some of these functions need to be available at local levels to serve customers quickly and efficiently, and others can be located far from customers.

5.3.2   Geography

The changes in employment documented in table 5.1 vary by geography. The majority of warehousing employment growth has come in rural counties, which have employment levels seven times higher than in 1990 (figure 5.12). However, growth in warehousing employment is not solely a rural phenomenon. Urban counties have not grown at the same pace as rural ones, but employment levels are 3.5 times higher than they were in 1990. Indeed, Chava et al. (2019) note that Amazon opens fulfillment centers in

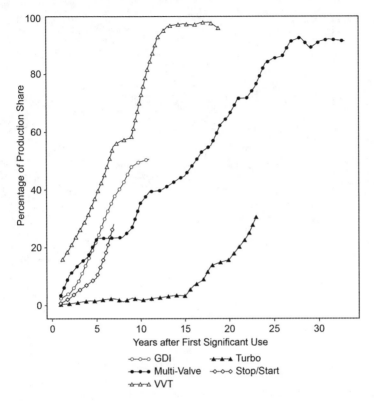

Fig. 5.10   Automobile engine technology adoption
Source: Data are from EPA.
Note: GDI, gasoline direct injection; VVT, variable valve timing.

counties with population densities 2.5 times higher than the average across all US counties. This trend is also in line with growth of transportation companies, in particular, truck transport. Figure 5.13 decomposes truck transport growth for establishments in urban and rural counties. As can be seen, truck transport employment growth follows similar patterns to those observed in figure 5.12 but at a much smaller scale. Rural truck transport has increased by 40 percent from 1990 levels, while urban truck transport has increased by 25 percent from 1990 levels. The extent to which this increase in warehousing activity is a complement or substitute for long- and short-haul trucking is difficult to fully assess, but time series data provide some suggestive relationships.

Figure 5.14 presents time series of warehousing and trucking employment relative to total US employment scaled to 1990 levels. As can be seen, general warehousing has increased the most—it has taken a 3.5 times larger share of US employment since 1990. Employment shares of used household and office goods moving as well as general freight trucking are unchanged since

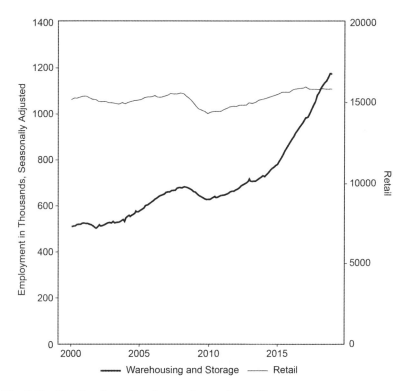

Fig. 5.11   Retail and warehousing employment over time
Note: Data are from the BLS Current Employment Statistics.

1990. In contrast, couriers and express delivery services, and local messengers and local delivery employment are both up, with local messengers up significantly since 2015—a possible reflection of the increasingly important role that e-commerce is playing in the retail industry. It may seem strange for us to observe such large increases in both urban-focused warehousing and transportation, given the higher real estate costs of urban areas compared to rural ones. Yet urban dwellers disproportionately make use of e-commerce retail, and this demand pull has strongly affected the way in which technology is deployed and the impact it has had on entrepreneurial activity.

Figure 5.15 plots the changes in rank of the top counties employing warehouse and storage workers. There have been some notable shifts between 2007 and 2017, with Cook County (IL), Franklin County (OH), and Harris County (TX) experiencing drops in their ranks, and San Bernardino County (CA), Riverside County (CA), San Joaquin County (CA), and Dallas County (TX) experiencing rises in their ranks. The results in figure 5.15 mirror, at a broad level, an observation made by Michael Mandel (2020) that California and Texas have been among the biggest gainers in the shift to what he

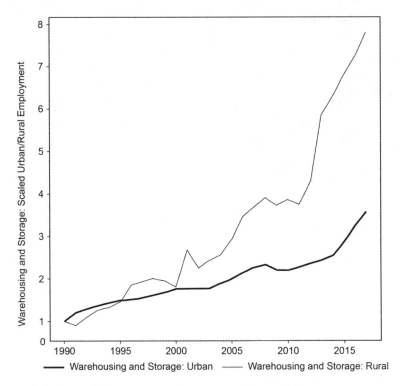

Fig. 5.12   Warehouse employment growth: Urban vs. rural
Source: Data are from BLS QCEW.
Note: Rural counties are defined as counties with more than half of their population living in rural areas as designated by the Census Bureau.

calls "consumer distribution" (e-commerce and brick and mortar retail).[5] Future research could investigate the causes and consequences of this shift.

5.3.3   Role of Incumbents and Entrants

Accompanying the change in economic activity for transportation and warehousing is an increase in startup activity. Much of this startup activity has been in logistics-focused firms attempting to reduce transport frictions and solving problems associated with delivering goods the "last-mile." One example is Fourkite, an e-commerce logistics company headquartered in Chicago that has received over $100 million in venture backed funding through a Series C round of funding. Fourkite has built a supply chain platform alongside a predictive shipment arrival time algorithm to lower shipping times and costs. Technologies like these are enabling new forms of warehousing to develop in urban areas, often referred to as "micro-fulfillment

5. https://www.progressivepolicy.org/blog/the-geography-of-ecommerce-industries/.

Fig. 5.13   Truck transport employment growth: Urban vs. rural
Source: Data are from BLS QCEW.
Note: Rural counties are defined as counties with more than half of their population living in rural areas as designated by the Census Bureau.

centers," that allow quicker delivery to urban customers. Another company that is working in the space of micro-fulfillment centers is Fabric. Founded in 2015, Fabric makes heavy use of robotics and small fulfillment centers in urban areas to fulfill order requests within an hour of purchase. They have raised $136 million through a Series B venture round and are growing rapidly.

As Fabric has demonstrated, technology—both in the form of AI predictive algorithms and robotics—is playing a critical role in the development of these new warehousing forms. The company Nuro is focused on developing AVs for the explicit purpose of delivering local goods and aiming to reduce the costs of the aforementioned last-mile delivery. They recently received $940 million in financing from Softbank. While Nuro is one of the most high-profile startups in this space, other startups also exist, including Startship Technologies, Marble, Boxbot, Robby Technologies, Kiwi Campus, Dispatch, and Unsupervised AI.[6] These technology trends may have

6. https://news.crunchbase.com/news/robot-couriers-scoop-up-early-stage-cash/.

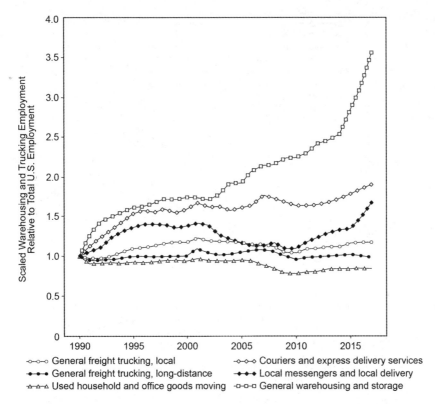

Fig. 5.14   Increasing importance of warehousing employment in the US
Source: Data are from BLS QCEW.
Note: Employment shares are plotted by transportation sub-industry (5-digit NAICS), normalized to 1990 levels.

divergent effects both for larger retailers continuing to vertically integrate into warehousing by operating ever-more efficient fulfillment centers and the arrival of technology-enabled specialized micro-warehouses lowering the cost of developing viable e-commerce business models for fledging direct-to-consumer startups.

Another technology that has the potential to impact last-mile delivery is that of unmanned aerial vehicles, also sometimes referred to as "drones." According to the CrunchBase database, there were at least 329 drone startups operating in late 2019.[7] While some of these startups will undoubtedly not focus on logistics and transportation (and focus more on leisure applications, military, etc.), this figure may also undercount numerous companies that are still in "dark mode." Apart from startups, many incumbents are also increasingly thinking about the impact of drones on their businesses, and growing numbers of transportation companies have received clearance

7. https://www.crunchbase.com/hub/drones-startups.

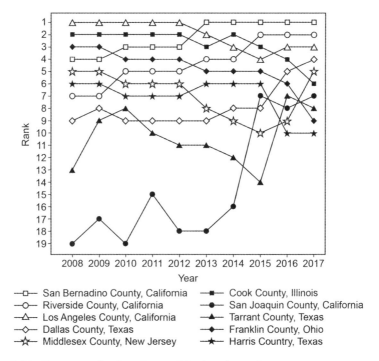

Fig. 5.15   Top county-level employers: Warehousing and storage

Source: Data are from BLS QCEW.

Note: Shown is a bump chart plotting the county ranks in terms of raw (not per capita) warehousing and storage employment. We include the top 10 counties in 2017 over a 10-year period (2008–2017).

from the Federal Aviation Administration (FAA) to run pilot programs. As an example, in October 2019, UPS's subsidiary UPS Flight Forward, Inc., was granted approval by the FAA to deliver medical packages by unmanned drone.[8] Not to be outdone, Amazon has launched a program named "Prime Air" with the express intent of delivering items in under 30 minutes from purchase. In both instances, the geographic location of warehouses will continue to be critical, as will advances in AV technologies. We next examine the implications of improvements in the viability of AVs on the transportation and warehousing sector.

Despite all the excitement about new firms and technologies, it appears that most of the employment activity by firms in this sector is by established, incumbent firms. Table 5.2 uses data from job postings, collected by Burning Glass, to list the top five "courier and messenger" firms by year. The top three in each year are UPS, FedEx, and DHL Express—which is no surprise,

8. https://pressroom.ups.com/pressroom/ContentDetailsViewer.page?ConceptType =PressReleases&id=15699339654.76–404.

as these are currently the dominant firms in the sector. Table 5.3, again using job posting data from Burning Glass, lists the top five "transit and ground passenger" firms by year. While most of the firms are engaged in transportation of people (covered in the next section), it is notable that in 2017 and 2018, the firm with the most listings was Instacart, a rapidly growing startup that specializes in same-day grocery store delivery.

Table 5.4 uses Burning Glass data to list the top five "warehouse and storage" firms by year. While the rank changes from year to year, it is interesting to note that most of the top firms are the same each year. For example, Exel is in the top five each year except 2018. Exel is a subsidiary of DHL, one of the world's largest courier and messenger firms. As another example, Americold, the owner and operator of a network of temperature-controlled warehouses used for storage of fruits, vegetables, meats, dairy, and other perishable products, is the top employer in 6 out of 9 years. Americold owned 160 such warehouses in the US in 2019.[9]

5.4   Entrepreneurship and Innovation in the Movement of People

5.4.1   Introduction

As section 5.3 demonstrates, the way in which physical goods are moved and stored has changed significantly over the past three decades. Yet media focus and public attention have centered disproportionately on the movement of people. Figure 5.16 presents Google Trends data of Internet search activity over the past two decades for the terms "Uber" and "Warehouse." As can be seen, warehousing has done little to change the attention (or Internet query interest) of Internet users, while interest in Uber and related ridesharing firms has grown significantly since the arrival of these services over the past 10 years. This section focuses on the movement of people with an emphasis on personal mobility and the implications for AVs, and it provides a brief discussion on the externalities that will arise as a result of the increased movement of people due to entrepreneurship and innovation in the transportation sector.

5.4.2   Personal Mobility

One of the biggest changes to personal mobility has been the rise of ride sharing firms such as Lyft and Uber, particularly in certain urban areas. These firms differ from standard taxi firms in at least two ways. First, unlike a traditional taxi company that manages a fleet of taxicabs which either search for passengers on city streets or wait for a dispatcher to tell them where to go, ride sharing firms rely on a digital application interface to manage the

Table 5.2   Top courier and messenger companies by job postings

	2010	2011	2012	2013	2014	2015	2016	2017	2018
1	UPS	UPS	UPS	UPS	UPS	UPS	UPS	UPS	UPS
2	FedEx	FedEx	FedEx	FedEx	FedEx	FedEx	FedEx	FedEx	FedEx
3	DHL Express	DHL Express	DHL Express	DHL Express	DHL Express	DHL Express	DHL Express	DHL Express	DHL Express
4	Republic Beverage	Republic Beverage	Midnite Express	Publisher's Circulation	Xpo Last Mile Inc	Spee Dee Delivery	Spee Dee Delivery	Spee Dee Delivery	Shipt
5	Courier	Courier	Republic Beverage	Ameriflight Incorporated	Spee Dee Delivery	Midnite Express	Midnite Express	Midnite Express	Ameriflight Incorporated

Note: These data come from Burning Glass. We report the top five companies by number of job postings (NAICS 492). Burning Glass does not report employer data for every single job posting.

Table 5.3 Top transit/ground passenger transport companies by job postings

	2010	2011	2012	2013	2014	2015	2016	2017	2018
1	MV Trans., Inc.	Firstgroup Plc	MV Trans., Inc.	MV Trans., Inc.	MV Trans., Inc.	Durham School Services	MV Trans., Inc.	Instacart	Instacart
2	Firstgroup Plc	MV Trans., Inc.	Firstgroup Plc	Veolia Trans.	Durham School Services	Uber	Amtrak	MV Trans., Inc.	MV Trans., Inc.
3	Veolia Trans.	Veolia Trans.	Westours Motor Coaches	First Student	Amtrak	Amtrak	Veolia Trans.	First Transit	Uber
4	Coach America	First Transit	Veolia Trans.	Firstgroup Plc	Veolia Trans.	MV Trans., Inc.	First Transit	Uber	First Transit
5	First Transit	Coach America	First Transit	Durham School Services	Firstgroup Plc	Veolia Trans.	Uber	Stock Trans.	Stock Trans.

Note: These data come from Burning Glass. We report the top five companies by number of job postings (NAICS 485). Burning Glass does not report employer data for every single job posting.

Table 5.4 Top warehousing and storage companies by job postings

	2010	2011	2012	2013	2014	2015	2016	2017	2018
1	Americold Logistics	Americold Logistics	Americold Logistics	Americold Logistics	Americold Logistics	Americold Logistics	Diversified Transfer Storage	Dematic	Dematic
2	Exel	Dematic	Dematic	Dematic	Exel	Exel	Americold Logistics	Americold Logistics	All My Sons Moving Storage
3	Dematic	Exel	After-market Tech. Corp,	Exel	Versacold Int. Corp.	Dematic	Dematic	Pure Storage, Inc	Life Storage, Inc
4	Document Storage Systems Inc.	After-market Tech. Corp.	Exel	After-market Tech. Corp.	Dematic	Diversified Transfer Storage	Exel	All My Sons Moving Storage	Pure Storage, Inc
5	Jk Moving Storage Inc.	Jk Moving Storage Inc.	Es3 Llc	Versacold Int. Corp.	Es3 Llc	Versacold Int. Corp,	Pure Storage, Inc	Exel	Americold Logistics

Note: These data come from Burning Glass. We report the top five companies by number of job postings (NAICS 493). Burning Glass does not report employer data for every single job posting.

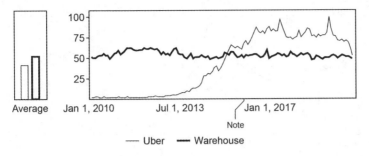

Fig. 5.16   **Google trends: Uber vs. Warehouse**

interaction between drivers and riders. Perhaps not surprisingly, ride sharing is more popular among younger generations. According to the Department of Transportation's National Household Travel Survey (2019), Millennials are almost twice as likely to use ride sharing services than Generation X or Baby Boomers.[10] In addition, ride sharing firms rely on complex, dynamic pricing models to "manage" the number of drivers and riders. As such, the interactions between drivers and riders are similar to those in other two-sided market settings (Parker and Van Allstyne 2005; Rochet and Tirole 2006). Second, ride sharing firms have argued that they should be regulated as technology firms instead of taxi firms, citing the prominent role that technology plays in providing their services. This regulatory arbitrage has led to the seeming proliferation of ride sharing services in various cities, arguably to the detriment of taxi companies. In some cases, cities have responded by banning ride sharing altogether (Paik, Kang, and Seamans 2019).

Recent research has sought to understand various economic and societal effects of these changes in personal mobility. To start, ride sharing apps provide efficiency benefits. Cramer and Krueger (2016) attribute Uber drivers' capacity utilization rate premiums of 30–50 percent to the company's matching rates, larger scale, freedom from inefficient regulation, and flexible labor and pricing models. These technologies also show social benefits. For example, Greenwood and Wattal (2017) find evidence that ride sharing has led to a decrease in vehicular fatalities associated with drunk driving. Burtch, Carnahan, and Greenwood (2018) provide evidence that driving for ride sharing firms may substitute for low-quality entrepreneurial activity. Gorback (2020) provides evidence that ridesharing's entry is associated with a doubling of net restaurant entry and an increase in housing prices. Some papers use incredibly rich and detailed data from ride sharing firms to study other economic issues. For example, Cook et al. (2018) use ride-level data from a ride sharing platform to study the determinants of gender earnings gap, and Liu, Brynjolfsson, and Dowlatabadi (2018) compare taxi and ride

10. https://nhts.ornl.gov/assets/FHWA_NHTS_Report_3E_Final_021119.pdf.

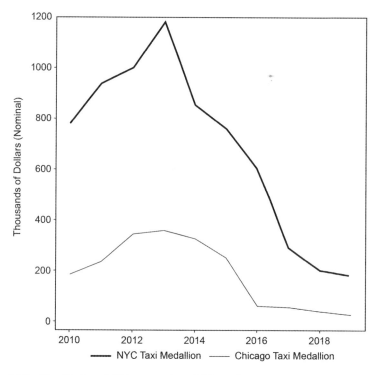

Fig. 5.17   New York and Chicago taxi medallion prices
Source: Data are from the NYC Taxi and Limousine Commission, as well as the Chicago Department of Business Affairs and Consumer Protection.

sharing ride-level data to study the extent to which digital monitoring via the ride sharing platform reduces moral hazard on the part of drivers.

To study competitive effects of ride sharing on traditional taxi businesses, we consider how ride sharing may affect taxi medallion sales. The 2016 *Economic Report of the President* (CEA 2016) shows that taxi medallion sales prices peaked in New York City in 2013 at over $1 million and in Chicago in 2013 at over $350,000. In figure 5.17, we extend this analysis with updated data through 2018 and find that medallion prices in both cities have continued a dramatic decline. In New York, medallions are now below $200,000 and in Chicago below $50,000. These dramatic changes provide suggestive evidence that ridesharing has substituted for traditional taxi service in many cities. Berger, Chen, and Frey (2018) decompose the resulting labor market effects; they find that Uber's entry coincides with a 10 percent decrease in relative taxi earnings. However, the authors note that the supply and composition of the taxi labor market has remained largely the same. Additionally, research suggests that ridesharing may have spurred adaptive changes in

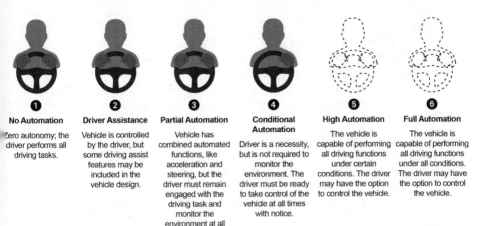

1	2	3	4	5	6
No Automation	**Driver Assistance**	**Partial Automation**	**Conditional Automation**	**High Automation**	**Full Automation**
Zero autonomy; the driver performs all driving tasks.	Vehicle is controlled by the driver, but some driving assist features may be included in the vehicle design.	Vehicle has combined automated functions, like acceleration and steering, but the driver must remain engaged with the driving task and monitor the environment at all times.	Driver is a necessity, but is not required to monitor the environment. The driver must be ready to take control of the vehicle at all times with notice.	The vehicle is capable of performing all driving functions under certain conditions. The driver may have the option to control the vehicle.	The vehicle is capable of performing all driving functions under all conditions. The driver may have the option to control the vehicle.

Fig. 5.18   Society of Automotive Engineers (SAE) automation levels

product quality among taxi drivers; Wallsten (2015) finds that increases in Uber's popularity are associated with decreases in taxi customer complaints in New York and Chicago.

5.4.3   Autonomous Vehicles

Automation of driving can take multiple forms. The current standards for autonomous driving were developed by the Society of Automotive Engineers (SAE International). According to the standards, autonomous driving ranges from Level 0, with no autonomy, to Level 6, which is full automation (see figure 5.18). Many vehicles sold today have features that would qualify as Level 1, including park assist, lane assist, and adaptive cruise control. A few vehicles claim to qualify as Level 2 or 3, including Tesla's vehicles, the Nissan Leaf, and Audi A8.[11] Google's Waymo would be considered Level 4 or 5. No Level 4 or 5 cars are certified for use on regular roads.[12]

Autonomous vehicles have generated a great deal of excitement. Some observers have referred to AVs as the "AI killer app."[13] However, a lot of disagreement exists around how long it will take for AVs to become widespread, and there is great uncertainty about the ultimate effect of AVs on the

11. https://www.pocket-lint.com/cars/news/143955-sae-autonomous-driving-levels -explained; https://techcrunch.com/2019/04/22/teslas-computer-is-now-in-all-new-cars-and -a-next-gen-chip-is-already-halfway-done/; https://www.forbes.com/sites/lanceeliot/2019/08 /01/eyes-on-hands-off-for-nissans-propilot-2-0-rouses-level-3-self-driving-tech-misgivings /#60e628627558; https://www.wired.com/story/audi-self-driving-traffic-jam-pilot-a8-2019 -availablility/.
12. https://crsreports.congress.gov/product/pdf/R/R45985.
13. https://www.forbes.com/sites/chunkamui/2013/08/23/google-car-uber-killer-app /#2620f33d600a.

economy. On one hand, in 2018 Elon Musk predicted that there would be a Tesla driverless taxi fleet by 2020.[14] On the other hand, Chris Urmson, who was a DARPA challenge winner, head of Google's Waymo AV unit, and is now CEO of a self-driving vehicle software company, argues it may take up to 30–50 years before widespread adoption of AVs.[15] To put these predictions into perspective, recall from figures 5.8 and 5.9 that historically, widespread adoption of new innovations in the auto sector can take several decades, as automobiles are long-lived, durable assets. Ultimately, several factors will affect the timing of adoption, including technological development, consumer preferences and tastes, and the regulatory landscape.

Researchers have begun to explore the economic and behavioral outcomes that may result from these technologies. Gelauff, Ossokina, and Teulings (2019) model two components of automation that lead to differing outcomes on population distribution: improved use of time during car trips, which lowers the cost of living at a distance from cities, and improved door-to-door public transit, which has the countervailing effect of lowering the costs of living in urban environments and may lead to increased population clustering in cities. Finding considerable welfare benefits resulting from these technologies, the authors suggest that these effects may lead to overall population shifts toward large, attractive cities at the expense of smaller urban as well as non-urban areas. Additionally, Kröger, Kuhnimhof, and Trommer (2019) project the adoption of AV technologies in the US and Germany. They estimate that the introduction of AVs will increase vehicle traffic by 2–9 percent, as a result of new automobile user groups, as well as lower generalized costs of car travel. However, others have argued that the conversion of all drivers into passengers may result in a substantial reduction in travel costs and thus substantially increase vehicle traffic (Duranton 2016).

5.4.4   Regulation

The speed of adoption of new technologies such as AVs will depend in large part on federal rules and regulations. We highlight two notable developments in this section. One notable development on the regulatory landscape is the US House and Senate nearing compromise language on legislation that would provide the National Highway Traffic Safety Administration (NHTSA) with the authority to regulate AVs. This is significant, as it would allow NHTSA to develop nationwide federal regulations for AVs, rather than allowing a patchwork of state-level AV regulations, which could slow down mass adoption. Federal regulation would provide clarity for various stakeholders, including car manufacturers and insurance companies, which

---

14. https://www.theverge.com/2019/4/22/18510828/tesla-elon-musk-autonomy-day-investor-comments-self-driving-cars-predictions.
15. https://www.theverge.com/2019/4/23/18512618/how-long-will-it-take-to-phase-in-driverless-cars.

should then lead to the development of AV vehicles and other technologies, and insurance products to complement these vehicles.

Another notable development is the Federal Communications Commission's (FCC) recent announcement of its plan to split the use of the 5.9 GHz spectrum between unlicensed Wi-Fi and vehicle-to-vehicle (V2V) communications standards.[16] This spectrum, a 75 Mhz band, had initially been set aside for use for vehicle-to-vehicle communications in 1999, and NHTSA, car manufacturers, and device manufacturers spent the ensuing two decades working on a standard for V2V communications. However, the standard that emerged, called "DSRC," faced lots of resistance, including from a competing standard called "C-V2V." Separately, Wi-Fi demands were growing, and the 5.9 GHz spectrum was increasingly used for unlicensed Wi-Fi. A recent study by Rand Corporation estimates the value of the consumer and producer surplus from using the entire band for Wi-Fi to be between $82.2 billion and $189.9 billion.[17] The FCC announced that 45 Mhz at the lower end of the band will be for Wi-Fi, the next 20 Mhz for C-V2V, and the top 10 Mhz potentially for C-V2V or DSRC. While it is too early to predict the ultimate outcome, the FCC's announcement seems to throw a lot of weight behind the C-V2V standard. The upshot is that this may hasten the resolution of what has been a battle over standards. Resolving this uncertainty over standards should then lead to the development of AV vehicles and other technologies.

In addition, the federal government will also play a role in addressing any externalities that may arise from these new technologies. We discuss some of these externalities, and the potential role for government to address them, in the next subsection.

5.4.5 Spillovers

Sections 5.4.2 and 5.4.3 highlight just two advances spurred by entrepreneurial entry and technological innovation, and while ride sharing and AVs certainly provide numerous benefits, they may, too, usher in costs and unintended consequences. These spillovers are discussed in more detail below, starting with the effect of AVs on jobs, followed by a broader discussion of ancillary spillovers that are unlikely to be properly priced.

5.4.5.1 *Jobs*

Scholars and pundits have speculated on a range of outcomes from AVs, including lower transport costs due to fewer drivers, better fuel efficiency, and better safety. The effect on driving jobs has garnered lots of attention. For example, the *Guardian* reports that autonomous driving puts 2 million

16. https://www.reuters.com/article/us-usa-spectrum/u-s-regulator-proposes-splitting -auto-safety-spectrum-to-boost-wi-fi-idUSKBN1XU2BJ.

17. https://www.rand.org/content/dam/rand/pubs/research_reports/RR2700/RR2720 /RAND_RR2720.pdf.

US truck drivers at risk of losing their jobs.[18] However, as Gittleman and Monaco (2017) point out, there are a variety of types of drivers, and autonomous driving will affect some more than others. The use of AVs is more likely for heavy and tractor trailer truck drivers (aka "long haul") rather than local delivery, given how difficult it would be to automate driving in a local or urban environment, and given all the other tasks associated with local delivery. According to analysis by Gittleman and Monaco, some of the other tasks performed by drivers include freight handling, paperwork, and customer service. Gittleman and Monaco estimate that Level 4 automation may ultimately displace 300,000 to 400,000 drivers. But the authors highlight that there are many practical limitations to automation. For example, they stress that one of the important functions of a truck driver is to serve as a security guard for the freight.[19]

Expected benefits stemming from autonomous trucking may need to be tempered in the event that the most likely application for autonomous trucking is in long haul and not local delivery. For example, most emissions and most accidents occur in urban environments (where local delivery is more common). Gately, Hutyra, and Wing (2015) report that urban vehicle emissions account for 60 percent of total emission and for 80 percent of growth in emissions since 1980. In other words, the most polluted areas are potentially the very areas where there will be little penetration of AVs. The Insurance Institute for Highway Safety reports that most accidents occur in urban and local roads, not rural interstates, and that 67 percent of fatalities occur outside the interstate system.[20] Again, the most dangerous areas are potentially the very areas where there will be little penetration of AVs.

Ultimately the costs and benefits of autonomous trucking will likely depend on the characteristics of government regulation. For example, one could imagine that consumer fear of AVs leads to regulations requiring humans to be in the cab of any AV, just in case the vehicle encounters unforeseen problems (in fact, in a 2018 survey, 71 percent of US drivers said they don't trust self-driving vehicles).[21] Such a regulation would attenuate any cost savings from replacing drivers. While the job displacement risk stemming from the arrival of AVs is but one of the many consequences of the changes in transportation arising from new products and services, numerous other spillovers also arise as result.[22]

---

18. https://www.theguardian.com/technology/2017/oct/10/american-trucker-automation-jobs.

19. The authors also cite an estimate of $175 million in losses to truck theft per year. https://www.trucks.com/2016/01/29/truck-thefts-result-in-large-losses/.

20. https://www.iihs.org/topics/fatality-statistics/detail/large-trucks.

21. https://www.theverge.com/2018/5/22/17380374/self-driving-car-crash-consumer-trust-poll-aaa.

22. We thank our discussant, Gilles Duranton, for articulating many of these.

5.4.5.2 Congestion and Vehicular Accidents

The effect of increased vehicle traffic on congestion, pollution, and the rate of accidents will depend on the source of increased vehicle usage. On one hand, ride sharing has been shown to lead to an increase in congestion[23] (and in turn pollution), in addition to an increase in accidents (Barrios, Hochberg, and Yi 2020). On the other hand, AVs may overcome these negative externalities as AVs with improved response times (compared to humans) can more safely drive close together.[24] These safety improvements should, in turn, reduce fatalities, and assuming the increase in capacity is greater than the reduction in transport costs, they should reduce congestion as well (Duranton and Turner 2011). Technologies that facilitate this vehicle-to-vehicle coordination, solutions that spread usage to off-peak hours, or improve passenger safety will all be important areas of both innovation and entrepreneurship. Policymakers will also need to strike the appropriate balance between usage patterns and how to allocate public space for various transportation modes.

5.4.6 Long-Run Effects

Ultimately, the successful proliferation of new transportation technologies will affect the geographic distribution of economic activity, but the impacts are likely to be heterogenous. As previously discussed, AVs will reduce the costs of transport, which in turn may reduce the need to live in proximity to one's place of work. This will have implications not only for the location of offices but also of domiciles, with commuters potentially moving to cheaper areas far from city centers. However, the wide adoption of electric vehicles may reduce the costs associated with living in urban areas (e.g., pollution) as well as heighten the value of face-to-face interactions and thus may lead to more densification/urbanization. Surely many other changes will emerge from the unanticipated interactions between individuals and new transportation technologies. These long-run effects are sure to be large, but at present, it is difficult to anticipate what equilibrium-level outcomes will look like, especially given the role that will be played by government regulators discussed in this chapter.

5.5 Conclusion

The transportation sector, which includes warehousing, plays a critical role in economic activity. In this chapter, we describe economic, entrepre-

---

23. As acknowledged by Chris Pangilinan, Uber's Head of Global Policy for Public Transportation, https://medium.com/uber-under-the-hood/learning-more-about-how-our-roads-are-used-today-bde9e352e92c.

24. https://www.economist.com/finance-and-economics/2018/01/20/why-driverless-cars-may-mean-jams-tomorrow.

neurial, and innovative activities in this area of the US economy. Recent trends suggest a shift emerging in this sector, with warehousing playing an increasingly important role. Prior economic research has focused primarily on innovations affecting the movement of goods (e.g., building new roads or railways), and there has been comparatively little research on innovations in storing goods. Thus, one takeaway from this chapter is for economists to conduct more research on the role of warehousing in the economy.

We also highlight several new transportation technologies, including ride sharing and AVs. There is much speculation about how these technologies will affect the sector, and eventually the economy as a whole. We note that prior innovations in this sector experienced heterogeneous rates of adoption. We believe this lesson from history suggests that we exercise much caution when speculating about the speed of adoption and impact of any new technology. Ultimately, the rate of adoption will depend on a range of factors, including technological development, consumer preferences and tastes, and regulatory landscape.

We believe there are areas for follow-on research, including addressing the following questions:

- Which firms are adopting new technologies in this sector, what are the barriers to adoption (if any), and what are the implications for the industrial organization of the sector?
- What accounts for the recent, rapid rise of employment in the warehousing sector? How much of this shift is attributable to online purchasing behavior or other shifts in consumer behavior?
- What is driving the rapid growth in warehousing employment in certain geographies of the US? What are the implications of this for the economic vitality of those regions that are gaining or losing employment in the sector?
- How much growth in the warehousing sector is coming from new firms vs. established incumbents? If, as appears to be the case, most growth is from established firms, what entry barriers are new firms facing?
- How will AVs affect employment and the economic geography of jobs?
- What are the implications of AVs for congestion, pollution, safety, and other by-products?
- How will transportation technologies interact with existing information technologies and the existing digital infrastructure?

On the first point, we note that the US statistical agencies can play a critical role in measuring the adoption and use of new technologies. The US Census Bureau has started to collect data on firm-level adoption of robots (Buffington, Miranda, and Seamans 2018) and other new technologies, such as machine learning, computer vision, and autonomous-guided vehicles. It appears that these technologies are primarily used by larger firms (Beede et al. 2020). This US data will soon be available for researchers to study the impact of these technologies on workers, firms, communities, and industries, including warehousing and transport. Consequently, the improved collection and increased availability of these data will play a critical role in answering many of the questions outlined in this chapter.

References

Agrawal, A., A. Galasso, and A. Oettl. 2017. "Roads and Innovation." *Review of Economics and Statistics* 99(3): 417–34. https://doi.org/10.1162/REST.

Banerjee, A., E. Duflo, and N. Qian. 2012. "On the Road: Access to Transportation Infrastructure and Economic." NBER Working Paper No. 17897. Cambridge, MA: National Bureau of Economic Research.

Barrios, J. M., Y. Hochberg, and H. Yi. 2020. "The Cost of Convenience: Ridehailing and Traffic Fatalities." NBER Working Paper No. 26783. Cambridge, MA: National Bureau of Economic Research.

Baum-Snow, N. 2007. "Did Highways Cause Suburbanization?" *Quarterly Journal of Economics* 122(2): 775–805.

Baum-Snow, N., J. V. Henderson, M. A. Turner, Q. Zhang, and L. Brandt. 2017. "Does Investment in National Highways Help or Hurt Hinterland City Growth?" *Journal of Urban Economics* 115 (September): 103124. https://doi.org/10.1016/j.jue.2018.05.001.

Beede, D., E. Brynjolfsson, C. Buffington, E. Dinlersoz, L. Foster, N. Goldschlag, K. McElheran, and N. Zolas. 2020. "Measuring Technology Adoption in Enterprise-Level Surveys: The Annual Business Survey." Washington, DC: US Census Bureau working paper.

Berger, T., C. Chen, and C. B. Frey. 2018. "Drivers of Disruption? Estimating the Uber Effect." *European Economic Review* 110: 197–210. https://doi.org/10.1016/j.euroecorev.2018.05.006.

Billings, S. B. 2011. "Estimating the Value of a New Transit Option." *Regional Science and Urban Economics* 41(6): 525–36. https://doi.org/10.1016/j.regsciurbeco.2011.03.013.

Bleakley, H., and J. Lin. 2012. "Portage and Path Dependence." *Quarterly Journal of Economics* 127(2): 587–644. https://doi.org/10.1093/qje/qjs011.

Buffington, C., J. Miranda, and R. Seamans. 2018. "Development of Survey Questions on Robotics Expenditures and Use in US Manufacturing Establishments." Working Paper No. 18-44. Washington, DC: US Census Bureau, Center for Economic Studies. https://ideas.repec.org/p/cen/wpaper/18-44.html.

Burtch, G., S. Carnahan, and B. N. Greenwood. 2018. "Can You Gig It? An Empirical Examination of the Gig Economy and Entrepreneurial Activity." *Management Science* 64(12): 5497–5520.

CEA (Council of Economic Advisers). 2016. "Economic Report of the President." https://obamawhitehouse.archives.gov/administration/eop/cea/economic-report-of-the-President/2016.

Chava, S., A. Oettl, M. Singh, and L. Zhang. 2019. "Creative Destruction? Assessing the Impact of E-Commerce on Employees at Brick-and-Mortar Retailers." Working paper, Georgia Tech Scheller College of Business.

Combes, P.-P., and M. Lafourcade. 2005. "Transport Costs: Measures, Determinants, and Regional Policy Implications for France." *Journal of Economic Geography* 5(3): 319–49.

Cook, C., R. Diamond, J. Hall, J. A. List, and P. Oyer. 2018. "The Gender Earnings Gap in the Gig Economy: Evidence from Over a Million Rideshare Drivers." NBER Working Paper No. 24732. Cambridge, MA: National Bureau of Economic Research.

Cramer, J., and A. B. Krueger. 2016. "Disruptive Change in the Taxi Business: The Case of Uber." *American Economic Review* 106(5): 177–82. https://doi.org/10.1257/aer.p20161002.

Donaldson, D. 2018. "Railroads of the Raj." *American Economic Review* 108(4–5): 899–934. https://doi.org/10.2307/1251838.

Duranton, G. 2016. "Transitioning to Driverless Cars." *Cityscape* 18(3): 193–96.

Duranton, G., and M. A. Turner. 2011. "The Fundamental Law of Road Congestion: Evidence from US Cities." *American Economic Review* 101(6): 2616–52.

———. 2012. "Urban Growth and Transportation." *Review of Economic Studies* 79(4): 1407–40. https://doi.org/10.1093/restud/rds010.

Gately, C. K., L. R. Hutyra, and I. S. Wing. 2015. "Cities, Traffic, and CO_2: A Multidecadal Assessment of Trends, Drivers, and Scaling Relationships." *Proceedings of the National Academy of Sciences* 112(16): 4999–5004.

Gelauff, G., I. Ossokina, and C. Teulings. 2019. "Spatial and Welfare Effects of Automated Driving: Will Cities Grow, Decline or Both?" *Transportation Research Part A: Policy and Practice* 121 (March): 277–94. https://doi.org/10.1016/j.tra.2019.01.013.

Gibbons, S., and S. Machin. 2005. "Valuing Rail Access Using Transport Innovations." *Journal of Urban Economics* 57(1): 148–69. https://doi.org/10.1016/j.jue.2004.10.002.

Gibbons, S., T. Lyytikäinen, H. G. Overman, and R. Sanchis-Guarner. 2019. "New Road Infrastructure: The Effects on Firms." *Journal of Urban Economics* 110 (January): 35–50. https://doi.org/10.1016/j.jue.2019.01.002.

Gittleman, M., and K. Monaco. 2017. "Truck-Driving Jobs: Are They Headed for Rapid Elimination?" *ILR Review*. https://doi.org/10.1177/0019793919858079.

Glaeser, E. L., and J. E. Kohlhase. 2004. "Cities, Regions and the Decline of Transport Costs." In *Fifty Years of Regional Science*, 197–228. Berlin and Heidelberg: Springer.

Gorback, C. 2020. "Your Uber Has Arrived: Ridesharing and the Redistribution of Economic Activity." Wharton working paper, Wharton School of the University of Pennsylvania, PA.

Greenwood, B. N., and S. Wattal. 2017. "Show Me the Way to Go Home: An Empirical Investigation of Ride-Sharing and Alcohol Related Motor Vehicle Fatalities." *MIS Quarterly* 41(1): 163–87.

Kröger, L., T. Kuhnimhof, and S. Trommer. 2019. "Does Context Matter? A Comparative Study Modelling Autonomous Vehicle Impact on Travel Behaviour for Germany and the USA." *Transportation Research Part A: Policy and Practice* 122 (April): 146–61. https://doi.org/10.1016/j.tra.2018.03.033.

Liu, M., E. Brynjolfsson, and J. Dowlatabadi. 2018. "Do Digital Platforms Reduce Moral Hazard? The Case of Uber and Taxis." NBER Working Paper No. 25015. Cambridge, MA: National Bureau of Economic Research.

Mandel, M. 2020. "Pre-Pandemic Retail and Warehouse Productivity and Hours Growth, and Post-Pandemic Implications." Washington, DC: Brookings Institution working paper.

Paik, Y., S. Kang, and R. Seamans. 2019. "Entrepreneurship, Innovation, and

Political Competition: How the Public Sector Helps the Sharing Economy Create Value." *Strategic Management Journal* 40(4): 503–32.

Parker, G. G., and M. W. Van Alstyne. 2005. "Two-Sided Network Effects: A Theory of Information Product Design." *Management Science* 51(10): 1494–1504.

Perlman, E. 2016. *Connecting the Periphery: Three Papers on the Developments Caused by Spreading Transportation and Information Networks in the Nineteenth Century United States.* PhD thesis, Boston University, Graduate School of Arts and Sciences.

Redding, S. J., and M. A. Turner. 2015. "Transportation Costs and the Spatial Organization of Economic Activity." In *Handbook of Regional and Urban Economics*, vol. 5, 1339–98. Amsterdam: Elsevier. https://doi.org/10.1016/B978-0-444-59531-7 .00020-X.

Relihan, L. 2020. "Is Online Retail Killing Coffee Shops? Estimating the Winners and Losers of Online Retail Using Customer Transaction Microdata." London: London School of Economics working paper.

Roche, M. P. Forthcoming. "Taking Innovation to the Streets: Microgeography, Physical Structure and Innovation." *Review of Economics and Statistics* 102(5): 912–28.

Rochet, J. C., and J. Tirole. 2006. "Two-Sided Markets: A Progress Report." *RAND Journal of Economics* 37(3): 645–67.

Sohn, E., R. Seamans, and D. Sands. 2019. "Technological Opportunity and the Locus of Innovation: Airmail, Aircraft, and Local Capabilities." New York: New York University Stern working paper.

Sokoloff, K. L. 1988. "Inventive Activity in Early Industrial America: Evidence from Patent Records, 1790–1846." NBER Working Paper No. 2707. Cambridge, MA: National Bureau of Economic Research.

Wallsten, S. 2015. *The Competitive Effects of the Sharing Economy: How Is Uber Changing Taxis?* Washington, DC: Technology Policy Institute.

Comment   Gilles Duranton

In their excellent chapter, Derrick Choe, Alexander Oettl, and Rob Seamans take a deep dive to examine two areas of the transportation sector, warehousing and personal travel with ridesharing services, and the future emergence of self-driving vehicles. Instead of trying to provide even more nuance to these thorough explorations, I would like to step back and draw some more general lessons, from these two case studies and from my own experience as someone who has been involved in transportation research for nearly 15 years. Doing this, I will highlight four key features of transporta-

Gilles Duranton is the Dean's Chair in Real Estate Professor at the Wharton School, University of Pennsylvania, and a research associate of the National Bureau of Economic Research.

For acknowledgments, sources of research support, and disclosure of the author's material financial relationships, if any, please see https://www.nber.org/books-and-chapters /role-innovation-and-entrepreneurship-economic-growth/comment-whats-driving -entrepreneurship-and-innovation-transport-sector-duranton.

tion and seek to understand what they imply for innovation in the sector and in the broader economy.

The first key feature of transportation is the presence of externalities. For many good reasons, transportation is often synonymous with congestion. While the true economic cost of congestion is still open to debate, Parry, Walls, and Harrington (2007) suggest a social cost of congestion of 5 to 7 cents per mile based on the best existing evidence. This seems small relative to some popular estimates, for two reasons. First, analysts often appraise congestion relative to a free-flow benchmark. This is not correct, since it would be deeply wrong to allow only a few vehicles (to allow them to travel at full speed) during peak hours when everyone wants to travel. Instead, we must assess congestion relative to some optimal level. Second, the bulk of travel takes place outside the most congested areas and not at peak hours. Commutes, according to the National Household Travel Survey, represent less than one in five trips and only account for about a quarter of total mileage. Despite these caveats, "fixing congestion" through a Pigovian tax seems like a no-brainer. Unfortunately, it is easier said than done. Only a tiny number of cities worldwide have managed to impose congestion pricing. Despite its advantages, taxing congestion is a deeply unpopular policy.

Unfortunately, the story does not end here. Most importantly, "innovations" in transportation often worsen congestion. While ride-hailing services offer many advantages, they also possibly lead to more vehicles on the road. Worse than that, these vehicles often block an entire lane for a short time to allow passengers to get in or out. This delay does not seem like much, but in a congested urban environment, traffic can only move as fast as the slowest vehicles. A similar assessment can be made for last-mile delivery or new forms of micro-mobility. Because they worsen congestion, these innovations do not generate as much social surplus as they should. Self-driving cars will have similar implications. To see this, note that human-driven and self-driving cars will have to share the road, at least during a long transition period when human-driven cars are phased out. Then, the lower cost of self-driven travel relative to human-driven travel will lead to more miles traveled. Unfortunately, the presence of human drivers will preclude the benefits from stacking cars close to one another or from keeping intersections fluid in urban environments.

Levying a congestion charge on these innovations could increase economic efficiency. The optimal congestion tax depends sensitively on the state of traffic in a given location at a given time. But even such fine-tuning, if it ever becomes possible, would not achieve the efficient outcome. Driver behavior also matters. A driver who tries to go through creates much less congestion than a driver who slows down while cruising for parking. To avoid this type of congestion-inducing behavior, we need "urban innovations" beyond charging for congestion. Such innovations include smart metering for parking and reinventing the curb for deliveries and for the pick-up and drop-offs of new mobility services. Because congestion is an externality, there is no direct way to provide the right market incentives. Much of the answer here will depend on the authorities in charge of the cities. Unfortunately, local governments face governance challenges of their own, weak incentives to innovate, and an increasing reluctance to tackle issues where their policies might create some losers.

The second major externality associated with motorized vehicles is accidents. According to the review by Parry, Walls, and Harrington (2007), we might face a cost of about 5 cents per mile, corresponding to the valuation of more than 35,000 deaths and 3 million injured on American roads every year. The situation is much worse in developing countries, with perhaps more than a quarter million deaths annually on the roads of India. Because accidents hurt others, the incentives for drivers to pay attention are too weak. This situation is compounded by a variety of behavioral traits, such as most drivers think they drive better than most others and get distracted by new communication technologies. Worse, innovations in this area are skewed toward improvements in one's own protection, regardless of the social cost imposed on others. For instance, American drivers keep driving heavier vehicles to protect themselves against the carelessness of other drivers. In equilibrium however, the resulting rat race makes the situation worse for everyone.

In practice, governments are in charge of road security nearly everywhere in the world. They impose a variety of security mandates on vehicle producers and decide on the appropriate driving behavior and how strictly (or leniently) to enforce it. This regulatory role is often conducted without much economic thinking and is constrained by both industry lobbying and potential political backlash from reluctant drivers.

The third main externality in transportation is pollution. CO_2 emissions leading to climate change are obviously important. However, and perhaps surprisingly, local emissions—small particulates especially—are even more important, as their effects are immediate and, all too often, lethal. Overall, the cost of pollution associated with motorized vehicles is estimated at around 3 cents per mile (Parry, Walls, and Harrington 2007). Relative to the previous two externalities, pollution is perhaps handled better in the US. The gas tax can be viewed as an antipollution instrument, albeit an imperfect one. That said, this outcome is largely incidental, since the primary objective of the gas tax is to fund the federal road system.

Electric vehicles and fuel cells look like a game changer for pollution, provided that the original source of energy is cleaner than the fuel burned by combustion engines. Here again, governments manage innovation in the absence of strong market incentives. They do so very unconventionally relative to what happens in innovative industries like high-tech or pharmaceuticals. The traditional tools of patents, prizes, and patronage play minor roles in reducing pollution. Instead, most of the impetus for innovation is coming from indirect instruments like fuel economy regulations or direct subsidies for cleaner vehicles. Because there is little entry into the automotive sector (with Tesla being a conspicuous exception), most existing innovations come from incumbent firms with little that could be called "entrepreneurship." While this innovation system is far from what the textbook would recommend, there is little evidence about its efficiency or lack thereof.

A second key feature of the transportation sector is the fundamental role of public goods. The Interstate Highway System is one of the most significant pieces of infrastructure in the US. The large public good component of transportation gives governments an important role, perhaps even more than because of the externalities discussed above. In the US, various levels of governments fund the bulk of the transportation infrastructure, own most transit vehicles, and extensively regulate the operation of transportation from parking to taxis.

This public good dimension opens up a range of issues related to innovation. First, in the US, as in many countries, the transportation infrastructure can be accessed freely or at very low cost. This acts as a subsidy. Historically, building and paving roads was instrumental to the diffusion of automobiles. Today, the challenges are about providing a charging infrastructure for electric vehicles or developing a system of communication between vehicles over a range of a couple of blocks to facilitate the operation of autonomous vehicles.

Second, we can ask whether infrastructure provision can be harnessed to promote innovation. This was certainly the case with digital infrastructure. We would like to see more evidence for the role of transportation in the innovation process. One of the authors of chapter 5 has provided some pioneering evidence (Agrawal, Galasso, and Oettl 2017), but more work is arguably needed. Third, another challenge arises from the management of existing infrastructure. How can we make infrastructure better and more efficient? For instance, how do we get governments to adopt state-of-the-art traffic management technologies or smart metering for parking? How can we make buses more attractive? Governments have a fundamental role to play in addressing these challenges, but a big part of the difficulty is that they do not act in a void. Extensive government intervention has favored the emergence of powerful vested interests, who have a large say in how the transportation infrastructure is used or regulated. Transit unions and taxi associations are two cases in point.

The third key feature of transportation is the durability of its assets. Motorized vehicles typically last for 10 years or more, while roads are extremely long lived. Duranton and Turner (2012) show that early exploration roads of North America are good predictors of contemporary roads in the US. This fundamental feature of transportation has several implications for innovation in the sector. First, innovations may generate large social losses through the traditional business stealing effect. For instance, new and better vehicles lead to the depreciation of the value of older vehicles. Hence, the benefits of a new vehicles must then be weighted against the depreciation losses they generate for the existing fleet. While the business stealing motive pushes toward more innovation than is socially desirable, other forces push in the opposite direction. First, since older and less efficient vehicles see their value depreciate instead of being retired, the adoption of new vehicles is slow. In turn, this slow pace of adoption possibly reduces the incentives to innovate, since the profits of new and better vehicles will only appear far in the future. Then, knowing that a lot of capital gets sunk into transportation assets, buyers facing some uncertainties about the pace of innovation will prefer to wait before investing in something new. In short, as often happens, asset durability implies strategic delays.

That said, not all transportation innovations are about improving durable and expensive assets. The recent past offers two conspicuous exceptions. First, ridesharing platforms like Uber or Lyft did not involve the development of new assets. Instead, these platforms redeployed existing assets. As a result, they could grow extremely fast, since minimal investments are needed to transform a regular car into an "Uber" or a "Lyft." Second, the ongoing micro-mobility revolution in many large cities relies on asset-light vehicles, like electric scooters. Despite desirable properties, these two innovations have some drawbacks. Taxi rents were capitalized into highly valued medallions. These values plummeted after the entry of Uber and Lyft, creating large losses for taxi drivers who had recently acquired one. Eliminating the medallions rents is a sign of the greater efficiency of ridesharing platforms, but it also created serious unease. New micro-mobility vehicles will eventually require a dedicated infrastructure. This will entail some costs for governments and, likely, reduced capacity for other road users. So even innovations that can seemingly be deployed in a short time, like ridesharing or micromobility, face resistance by losers (ridesharing) or require some complementary investments (micro-mobility) leading to long adjustment periods.

The last key feature of transportation is that it affects the entire economy well beyond the 3.2 percent share in US GDP of the transportation sector. For instance, Americans in 2018 devoted nearly 16 percent of their expenditure and more than an hour daily to transportation. Transportation and logistics are also at the heart of all economic activity and increasingly complex value chains. What happens to transportation has economy- and society-wide implications through powerful general equilibrium effects.

Most importantly, transportation links our choice of residence to our choice of workplace through commuting. Put differently, transportation dictates what happens to our cities. The mass adoption of the automobile combined with the development of highways led to a massive physical extension of cities in the US with initially the suburbanization of residents followed by the decentralization of jobs. At the same time, city centers suffered following the exodus of better-off residents who could afford a car. The new highways also scarred city centers by cutting through neighborhoods and generating noise and pollution. Closer to us, there is emerging evidence that ridesharing services have already affected our cities, boosting areas that were previously less accessible with transit (Gorback 2020). This gain may have come at the expense of more accessible locations.

Looking forward, self-driving cars will have a first-order effect on our cities. There is no consensus yet on the subject. A lower cost of travel will likely favor remote locations, as it did in the past. If true, this transportation innovation will lead to another major wave of urban expansion. At the same time, a strong case can be made that central locations also have a lot to win from self-driving cars. Time in traffic obviously represents an important fraction of trip time but far from all of it. Reaching one's vehicle, getting into traffic, finding parking, and reaching one's final destination all take time. Being able to ride door-to-door and avoid all these steps will save a lot of time in city centers. In turn, following their physical expansion and their densification, the most prosperous cities may be able to grow their population by a lot. If that growth exceeds nationwide demographic growth, something will have to give. Less prosperous cities and rural areas may be in for an extremely hard time.

To conclude, the four key features of transportation highlighted here affect how innovation works in transportation. The first two, transportation externalities and the public good nature of the transportation infrastructure, give governments overwhelming influence. As we saw, several elements point to a limited ability of governments to innovate, including a lack of incentives and a reluctance to adopt innovations for fear of alienating some voters or some powerful vested interests. The third key feature of transportation, the durability of its assets, also appears to slow down innovation through several channels. Despite this, changes are happening, as documented by the authors of chapter 5. These changes have wide-ranging implications through general equilibrium effects, the fourth key feature of transportation highlighted here. The research challenge is thus twofold. First, we need to understand the broader implications of changes in transportation. Second, how can we better incentivize innovation in transportation despite its complicated and unusual environment? While the first challenge has received a lot of attention by transportation scholars, the second has barely been touched. I very much hope innovation scholars will push this agenda forward.

References

Agrawal, Ajay, Alberto Galasso, and Alexander Oettl. 2017. "Roads and Innovation." *Review of Economics and Statistics* 99(3): 417–34.
Duranton, Gilles, and Matthew A. Turner. 2012. "Urban Growth and Transportation." *Review of Economic Studies* 79(4): 1407–40.
Gorback, Caitlin. 2020. "Your Uber Has Arrived: Ridesharing and the Redistribution of Economic Activity." Working paper, Wharton School of the University of Pennsylvania, PA.
Parry, Ian W. H., Margaret Walls, and Winston Harrington. 2007. "Automobile Externalities and Policies." *Journal of Economic Literature* 45(2): 1335–53.

6

The Recent Evolution of Physical Retail Markets
Online Retailing, Big Box Stores, and the Rise of Restaurants

Francine Lafontaine and Jagadeesh Sivadasan

6.1 Introduction

Much has been written in recent years, in both the trade press and the academic literature, about the decline of US retailing, or the "retail apocalypse."[1] This decline has typically been traced back to changes in technology, including the advent of UPC codes and scanner technology, and the creation of radiofrequency identification (RFID), whose adoption improved logistical and warehousing capabilities. Together, these innovations spurred the growth of large general merchandise retail chains, such as Walmart and

Francine Lafontaine is the Interim Dean and the William Davidson Professor of Business Economics and Public Policy at the Ross School of Business at the University of Michigan, and professor of Economics (courtesy) at the University of Michigan's Department of Economics.

Jagadeesh Sivadasan is the Buzz and Judy Newton Professor of Business Administration and a professor of Business Economics and Public Policy at the Ross School of Business, University of Michigan.

The bulk of this chapter focuses on the period 1999–2017 and was completed in January 2020, prior to the COVID-19 pandemic. Given the importance of this crisis for the retail sector, we have added a section 6.8 that undertakes a preliminary evaluation of the impact of the ongoing COVID-19 pandemic on the retail sector (including hotels and restaurants). We thank the organizers Michael Andrews, Aaron Chatterjee, and Scott Stern, and Shane Greenstein, Josh Lerner, Alexander Oettl, and other participants at the NBER pre-conference "Beyond 140 Characters: The Role of Innovation and Entrepreneurship in Economic Growth" (July 22–23, 2019) at Boston, and the participants at the final January 7–8, 2020, conference in Palo Alto for their support and comments. We especially thank our discussant Emek Basker for constructive and helpful comments at the Palo Alto conference; we have built on her suggestions in this final version of the chapter. We thank Jae Do Choi for research assistance. Any remaining errors are our own. For acknowledgments, sources of research support, and disclosure of the authors' material financial relationships, if any, please see https://www.nber.org/books-and-chapters /role-innovation-and-entrepreneurship-economic-growth/recent-evolution-physical-retail -markets-online-retailing-big-box-stores-and-rise-restaurants.

1. This notion of "retail apocalypse" has become so ingrained in the US that it has its own Wikipedia entry, which provides a long list of more than 50 references to related media stories.

Target, as well as the advent and growth of the Internet and resulting online retailing capabilities, themselves also supported by more efficient warehousing, logistics, and transportation operations (see Hortaçsu and Syverson 2015, various chapters in Basker 2016a, and papers cited therein).[2] To a large extent, then, the technologies that are associated with changing the face of the retail sector are not those developed by or necessarily for this sector, but rather the consequences of technological change occurring in other parts of the economy (e.g., Warehousing and Transportation, NAICS 48–49) that have had substantial implications for retailing.

In this chapter, we argue, using comprehensive data for the 1999–2017 period from the US Census, that the widely reported "retail apocalypse," illustrated by poignant stories of the exit of prominent chains (e.g., Borders, Circuit City, The Limited), presents an exaggerated picture of the decline of the brick-and-mortar retail sector in the aggregate. An important measurement issue (discussed in detail in section 6.2) plays a major role in explaining this discrepancy. Specifically, the definition of retail used by the Census does not fully account for the overall set of businesses that rely on the types of labor and real estate typically associated with the retail sector. This was not true in the (pre-1997) days of the old Standard Industrial Classification (SIC) system, which included restaurants in its definition. The newer NAICS (North American Industrial Classification System) classification scheme has separated restaurants from the retail sector, moving them to the sector Accommodations and Food Services (NAICS 72). Thus, the changing face of Main Street in many communities, where small retail stores are seemingly being replaced by a growing number of service-oriented businesses, especially restaurants, would imply a decrease in the official NAICS-based statistics about retailing. However, from the perspective of employment and usage of real estate, and we would argue from a "(wo)man on the street" perspective, it is not clear that "apocalypse" is an appropriate characterization of the transformation that we are witnessing.[3]

We document that the restaurant sector in particular showed remarkably strong growth, in terms of number of establishments, sales, and employ-

---

2. The chapters in the handbook (Basker 2016a) that complement our work include Basker (2016b), which examines the evolution of technology in the retail sector; Betancourt (2016), which examines distribution services; Carden and Courtemanche (2016), which focuses on general merchandise stores; Ellickson (2016), which examines the supermarket subsector; Foster et al (2016), which focuses on national retail chains; Ratchford (2016), which examines retail productivity; and Smith and Zentner (2016), which examines the effect of internet on retail markets. We use more recent data to extend analysis of related topics.

3. Other important measurement challenges are also associated with studying the retail sector, discussed in more detail in section 6.2. We further broaden the definition of retail to include services (e.g., auto repair and nail salons) and recreation (e.g., gyms, fitness centers, and yoga studios) in section 6.6.

ment, as well as payroll and value added, over the period in question.[4] Once restaurants are included, moreover, the broader physical retail sector had bounced back and, by 2017, exceeded its pre-Great Recession peak achieved in 2006 on a number of indicators. Despite this bounce back, we do find a significant drawn-out decline in the sector's share of aggregate value added, payroll, and number of establishments (employment share of physical retail, including restaurants, has held relatively steady) during 1999 to 2017. In other words, while the sector grew, it did so at a lower rate than the rest of the economy, and as such, there was a decline in the importance of the physical (inclusive of restaurants) retail sector in the overall economy during this time.

We begin our analyses by first investigating and confirming the negative impact that increased e-commerce has had on physical retail activity. Specifically, we find that sectors with the greatest increase in online sales during 1999–2017 (e.g., electronics, sporting goods, and furniture) also experienced the slowest growth in physical retail activity (in terms of number of establishments, employment, real sales, and real payroll). We then investigate the role of big box stores, emphasized by Hortaçsu and Syverson (2015). We find a stark flattening of the growth of big box stores' share of retail sales starting around 2009. Exploiting granular panel data from the US Census Bureau's county business patterns (CBP), we document that, contrary to expectations, the correlation between the growth of other physical activity and the growth of big box stores is actually positive across counties.

We next turn to a deeper investigation of the remarkable growth of restaurants. We first explore potential supply-side explanations. One possibility is that lower retail rental or property prices induced by the exit of other physical stores lowered fixed costs, which facilitated more entry by restaurants. However, aggregate data suggests a modest, if any, role for lower retail property prices; specifically, data from a National Association of Insurance Commissioners' report shows that the price indexes for retail commercial property bounced back to the pre-Great Recession levels by mid-2016, while retail vacancy rates have stayed stable at around 10 percent for several years (NAIC-CIPR 2017). Further, contrary to a pathway from exit of other physical stores to entry of restaurants, our analysis of county-level panel data

4. This strong growth in the restaurant sector was noted in an article in *The Atlantic* by Thompson (2017), which documented the strength of sales in food services relative to the rest of the retail sector (and termed this a "restaurant renaissance"). However, the strong performance in this sector has otherwise been underreported in the media. In a long and comprehensive report on Bloomberg.com, Townsend et al. (2017) present figures that portray a relatively gloomy picture of retail employment trends using Bureau of Labor Statistics (BLS) data, which relies on the NAICS classification, and thereby excludes restaurants (https://www.bls.gov/iag/tgs/iag44–45.htm). Following the NAICS definition, the BLS also classifies restaurants separately from retail, under the leisure and hospitality supersector (https://www.bls.gov/iag/tgs/iag70.htm).

on the growth of restaurants yields a positive correlation with the growth of other physical activity. That is, restaurant growth was slower in counties with relatively more decline in other physical retail activity. Thus, it appears that some locations have been successful in nurturing growth of all types of physical retail—big box stores, restaurants, and others—while other locations have seen a decline in all these physical retail activities.

The supply side explanation of lower fixed costs would, in most standard models, imply a reduction in the average scale of the restaurants.[5] We find that the data contradict this implication. In particular, we find that there was a significant increase in the real sales per restaurant, as well as employment per restaurant, during this period, suggesting an increase rather than a decrease in average scale. Further, if lower labor costs helped spur entry, we would expect lower growth of payroll per employee in the restaurant sector; in contrast, the data show significant growth in real payroll per employee for restaurants, notably faster than that for any other physical retail segments.

We next consider a demand-side explanation, albeit with limited aggregated data from the Bureau of Economic Data (BEA). We find evidence for a shift in expenditure from food at home (i.e., ingredients purchased from grocery stores and cooked at home) toward food away from home (i.e., at restaurants). Our back of the envelope calculations suggest that of the increase of roughly 150,000 restaurant establishments between 1999 and 2017, about 100,000 (or two-thirds of them) could be attributed to the increase in the share of restaurant expenditure.

We also investigate what types of restaurants grew and in what locations. We find evidence (from limited Yelp data) that the average quality as well as variety of restaurants has increased over recent years. Data from the CBP further show that both fast food and full-service restaurants grew, and that the growth of restaurants has been strongly positive in both rich and poor counties (though the number of bars has declined in poorer counties).

We address the question of whether the rise in restaurants was accompanied by a broader shift toward "servicification" of retail, by looking at the growth of three service and recreation sectors—repair services (NAICS 811), personal and laundry services (NAICS 812), and recreation (NAICS 713)—where a significant amount of the activity happens in establishments co-located with traditional physical retail establishments.[6] While we do find that some subsegments of services (specifically, personal service, including nail and hair salons) and recreation (specifically, fitness centers) experienced very strong growth, overall, these segments are small relative to traditional physi-

---

5. Technological change (e.g., facilitation of ordering over the Internet) could potentially be another pathway for a reduction of optimal scale, allowing for smaller restaurants to survive.

6. This analysis was prompted by comments from our discussant, Emek Basker, who showed that there has been strong growth in nail salons and fitness centers, albeit from a much smaller base level than restaurants, consistent with a shift toward more service/experience consumption in retail locations.

cal retail in terms of number of establishments, employment and payroll; and their shares in the aggregate (augmented to include these three sectors) physical retail remained largely flat during 1999–2017.

Finally, we examine emerging trends in retail by looking at data (from Crunchbase.com) on venture capital financing of retail-related startups. While most of the best-funded startups have a substantial online component, we find that a significant number of startups (e.g., delivery services) are in fact complementary to physical retail (and could facilitate entry by smaller physical retail firms). Of course, as discussed above, a dominant story in the retail sector over the past two decades has been the erosion of market share of physical retail stores due to competition from online merchants, such as Amazon. However, the recent purchase of Whole Foods has provided Amazon with a significant physical retail footprint, and the current trade press makes much of the complementarities between brick-and-mortar and online sales, and the importance of maintaining or developing physical locations for retail businesses (e.g., Kercheval 2014; Santa Cruz 2019).

As of this writing (mid-January 2021), the COVID-19 pandemic and associated adoption of social distancing norms and regulations have had a severe negative impact on the economy, with an overall decline in employment of over 8 million in December 2020 relative to December 2019 (per provisional Bureau of Labor Statistics [BLS] figures). Given the particularly large impact of the pandemic on the retail sector, we undertook a preliminary analysis of the evolving impact of the pandemic using data up to December 2020 from the US Census Advance Monthly Retail Trade Survey (MARTS) and monthly Current Employment (CE) statistics from the BLS, and using stock market data on retail stocks.[7] The data confirm a strong rebound overall for traditional retail by December 2020 from a severe initial negative impact of the pandemic in April, but with significant variation across subsectors. Specifically, and not surprisingly, we find a positive effect (in terms of aggregate sales and even employment) for grocery stores and online retailers, but sharp negative effects for restaurants and gas stations, and for nonessential retail goods sectors like clothing and electronics. The negative impact on restaurants, a sector that we highlighted above as a silver lining for an otherwise weak trend in brick-and-mortar retail, has been particularly striking and persistent throughout the crisis. Unlike other retail sectors (except gas stations), the percentage decline in cumulative year-to-date sales (compared to the prior year) was higher for restaurants in December 2020 than in April. While employment in the restaurant sector has rebounded somewhat from its largest year-on-year loss of 6.7 million jobs in April 2020, there has been a worrisome recent increase in year-on-year job loss from 2.6 million in November to 3 million in December 2020. The stock market data

---

7. Interestingly (and fortunately), the MARTS survey covers restaurants in addition to the NAICS retail subsectors. The BLS CE data is available for 3-digit NAICS subsectors.

are consistent with these aggregate trends, with online retailers and big box stores (clubs and supercenters) performing well, and restaurants and retail clothing firms being among the worst performers. The strong evidence that eating and speaking in groups in enclosed spaces is a significant risk for the spread of the disease has led to social distancing norms (adopted voluntarily or mandated by state governments) that have shifted consumption from restaurants toward eating at home and hence toward more grocery shopping. It seems clear that the prospects for the restaurant sector depend importantly on the control of the pandemic, which in turn appears to hinge on the rapid rollout of vaccines across the population. While we are circumspect about making long-term predictions given the unprecedented nature of this crisis, it is plausible that greater consumer familiarity with e-commerce platforms gained during the current lockdowns could help accelerate the growth of e-commerce and use of home delivery over the medium to long term, reinforcing some of the key trends already visible in the earlier data on venture capital investments (see section 6.7).[8] The duration of the crisis also may determine the extent to which restaurants, with their typically slim margins, will be able in the post-COVID era to reopen and regain the important role they have played in small towns and large cities alike.[9]

This chapter is organized as follows. In the next section, we discuss our data sources and some definitional and measurement challenges that arise in trying to capture the evolution of the retail sector using US Census and other data. In section 6.3, we document some of the trends we see in the retail sector in 1999–2017. We then turn, in section 6.4, to an analysis of potential drivers for the weak growth in physical retail stores during that time. Section 5.5 investigates potential supply and demand side explanations for the rise of restaurants and explores patterns in this rise across restaurant types and counties. Section 6.6 investigates broader servicification, by examining repair services, personal and laundry services, and recreation. Section 6.7 examines emerging trends in retail using venture capital data, and section

8. BLS data show a decline in employment relative to February 2020 of about 22.7 percent (about 2.31 million jobs) for restaurants (NAICS 722), and of 31.3 percent (about 0.30 million jobs) for clothing (NAICS 448), while general merchandise (+0.14 million, 4.6 percent) and building materials (+0.10 million, 7.1 percent) added the most jobs. The stock market data (as of January 8, 2020), show that all retail subsectors have recovered to pre-pandemic levels, but drugstores and clothing are notably weaker than the S&P500, while online retailers, home furnishing, and sporting goods stores outperformed the market. The strongest performing retail stocks include Etsy, Chewy, Wayfair, and Stamps.com, all major online retailers. The recovery of restaurant stocks suggests some potential good news, at least in terms of market expectations about the future of the sector. However, the weakest performing retail stocks include Groupon, Dave & Buster's, Arcos Dorados, and Denny's—all restaurant related stocks, and retail clothing firms. Note that some fast food stocks, including Chipotle and Domino's, have performed well, while the market appears less optimistic about the future of other prominent chains, including McDonald's and Yum! Brands, which have underperformed the market.

9. See e.g., https://www.nytimes.com/2020/05/07/us/coronavirus-restaurants-closings .html, and https://www.nytimes.com/interactive/2020/12/28/dining/restaurants-closings -usa.html.

6.8 presents preliminary analyses of the impact of the COVID-19 pandemic on the retail sector. Section 6.9 concludes.

6.2 Definitions, Data Sources, and Measurement Challenges

6.2.1 Defining the Retail Sector

The current industry classification scheme used by the US Census Bureau and other government statistical agencies, the North American Industry Classification System (NAICS), implemented for the Economic Census of 1997, defines retail to include 14 subcategories that encompass different goods retailing activities across two broad 2-digit codes (NAICS 44 and 45). This is the definition used in some recent research studies of the retail sector (e.g., Hortaçsu and Syverson 2015), as well as in many media stories on the widely reported "retail apocalypse" (e.g., Richter 2018; Townsend et al. 2017).

However, the earlier SIC, last revised in 1987, included what we term for brevity "restaurants" but is more precisely described as "Eating and Drinking Places" (SIC 58) in the broad retail sector (SIC codes 52–59). An important change made under the NAICS scheme was to move restaurants to a different major sector, NAICS 72, "Accommodation and Food Services," encompassing what we term for brevity as "hotels" (NAICS 721, Accommodation) and restaurants (NAICS 722, Food Services and Drinking Places).

We believe that including restaurants in the broader definition of retail can yield interesting insights, as consumers who see a shop replaced by a restaurant in their local town need not view this as a sign of crisis for what they view as retail. Relatedly, there is strong overlap in the inputs used by restaurants and the traditional NAICS retail sectors. In particular, some recent media articles contain anecdotal reports of restaurants taking over retail space from other traditional retail categories (e.g., Morris 2016; Takahashi 2018), and arguably there is significant overlap in labor markets as well.

Another important subsector worth examining separately, given the importance of e-commerce retailing, is that of nonstore retailers (NAICS 454), which includes online and catalog retailing, neither of which has traditionally included physical retail stores. Accordingly, in this chapter, we use the following breakdowns of retail industry aggregates and nomenclature:

- *Traditional Retail*, which includes retail per NAICS (NAICS 44–45), as well as restaurants (NAICS 722);
- *Traditional Physical Retail*, which is Traditional Retail as defined above, but excluding Nonstore retailers (NAICS 454);
- *Restaurants* (NAICS 722); and
- *Traditional Non-Restaurant Physical Retail*, which is traditional physi-

cal retail as defined above, but also excluding Restaurants (NAICS 722); in other words, this is NAICS 44–45 excluding 454.

6.2.2 Data Sources

For our work, we rely on several sources of data:

1. *Annual Retail Trade Survey (ARTS)*: This data source from the US Census Bureau provides annual sales data for retail subcategories. It also provides data on e-commerce activity levels. E-commerce activity data for the "Electronic Shopping and Mail-Order Houses" (NAICS 4541) or ESMOH, are provided separately and split by Merchandise line (see discussion in section 6.2.4). We accessed historical tables from the US Census Bureau websites; these tables help address some of the reclassification challenges discussed in section 6.2.4, as they provide consistent time series by classification codes (suitably adjusting historical data).

2. *County Business Patterns (CBP)*: These data, also provided by the US Census Bureau, include information on the number of establishments, employment, and payroll by NAICS in each county. One important limitation for employment data is that a significant proportion of these are suppressed (and reported as zero). We use a combination of interpolation and extrapolation in industry-county cells, along with the available employment range information (in the employment flag variable) to impute missing employment data. Note that in these data, employment is defined as all full- and part-time employees who were on the payroll during the pay period that includes March 12.[10] Because the extent of use of part-time employment could vary across sectors, caution must be exercised when comparing employment numbers. In part for this reason, in our analyses, we also pay attention to other outcome variables; in particular, value added (aggregated data available from BEA, discussed in point 3 below) and payroll (both aggregate and per employee) provide checks that are not affected by the variation in usage of part-time workers.

3. *BEA data*: We use two BEA tables, one with a breakdown of Personal Consumption expenditures (table 2.3.5) and one with a breakdown of value added by industry (table U), downloaded from the BEA websites. We also obtained county-level population and personal income per capita data from the BEA's regional economic accounts datasets available on the web.

4. *Yelp public-use microdata*: We use the Yelp dataset[11] to construct an aggregate annual measure of restaurant variety and quality (as discussed section 6.5.3). The Yelp dataset includes information about local businesses in 10 metropolitan areas across two countries. We undertake steps

---

10. See, e.g., definition of total employment provided online here: https://www.census.gov/quickfacts/fact/note/US/BZA110217.
11. We thank Alexander Oettl for pointing us to this data source. We accessed the data from: https://www.yelp.com/dataset/challenge.

to ensure validity of the data we use, including: (a) restricting attention to businesses with address information, review information, and time-series data; (b) restricting to restaurant businesses by matching a list of keywords in the "category" string; and (c) retaining only restaurants listed for states in the US.

5. *Crunchbase*: Crunchbase is an online platform that tracks data on companies and is an increasingly popular source for data on venture capital investments. We identify firms in retail-related activity during our study period (1999 to 2017) to provide some information on emerging technologies (in section 6.7). Related to the challenge of measuring innovation in the retail sector (discussed in section 6.2.4), we note a similar caveat about our measurement of startup retail activity using Crunchbase data that also arises from other large startups undertaking activity in retail-related activity. For example, Uber (a transportation/technology company) has a delivery service company (Uber Eats), and Alphabet (a technology company) is investing significantly in autonomous vehicles that have labor-saving implications for the retail sector. Many technology companies are also investing in warehouse, logistics, and e-commerce platforms that impact online retailing and hence affect the retail sector as well.

6.2.3 Heterogeneity in Retail—Auto Dealerships and Nonstore Retailers

While one might expect that retail activities are relatively similar for different types of goods, there are challenges when comparing activity levels across retail sectors, including the following:

Auto stores have significant sales but a small establishment/employment footprint. The automobile retailing (NAICS 441, Motor Vehicles and Parts Dealers) sector accounts for a large portion of retail sales that is not really representative of the level of economic activity in these dealerships because of the exceptionally high wholesale and unit prices in this sector compared to almost all other retail goods. In other words, this sector plays a less prominent role in terms of retail value added, employment, and number of establishments. Appendix figures 6.A.1 and 6.A.2 illustrate this point. They show that retail sales activity can be disproportionately affected by the fortunes of the automotive sector (e.g., the steep decline in the sector sales during the Great Recession had a significant impact of total retail sales), but the sector has a smaller role to play in explaining fluctuations in retail employment and number of establishments. Specifically, Figure 6.A.1 shows that the share of stores and employment of the auto sector relative to total retail are both low (less than 10 percent) and much more stable than their sales levels. In contrast, per figure 6.A.2, the sales share of restaurants understates the sector's contribution in terms of value added, employment and number of establishments.

Nonstore/online retailers have significant activities in other sectors. Another note of caution, for any analysis we undertake about nonstore retailers, is that a significant amount of labor input driving the sales levels achieved by the online retailers who form the main part of the nonstore sector would appear in the transportation and warehousing (48–49) industry classifications. Similarly, while technically categorized as "nonstore," these retailers now often do have retail establishments (and this physical presence has been growing over time). However, the count of establishments in this sector would not include the warehouses and storage facilities owned by nonstore retailers, such as Amazon; these would appear in transportation and warehousing again. To the extent that general merchandise and other stores that are in the Traditional Physical Retail Sector are also holding inventories in their stores, comparisons of their numbers of stores to the number of establishments associated with nonstore retailers in retail data are not comparing like to like.[12] Accordingly, sales or value added per employee or per establishment would need to be interpreted with caution, as we discuss again in section 6.5.

6.2.4   Other Measurement Challenges

In addition to the issues mentioned above that are specific to the measurement of economic activity in the retail sector and subsectors, there are additional measurement issues that are important to keep in mind as we proceed with our analyses. In particular:

Measuring innovation. As discussed above, transportation and warehousing, as well as the information technology sector and related technologies supporting these sectors provide vital inputs for the successful operations of online (and even physical) retail businesses. Thus, measuring innovation in the broad retail sector using traditional measures such as patenting is particularly challenging. For example, patents filed by online retailers like Amazon, or even technological innovations by traditional retailers like Walmart, are likely to be classified under patent classification codes related to the technology sector rather than to retail activity. Accordingly, a measure of patent counts in codes specifically linked to retail as a fraction of total patents filed in the US shows a miniscule level of patenting activity in this sector.[13] Appendix figure 6.A.3 shows that while patent counts have

12. We thank Ben Jones for raising this point at the pre-conference meeting. In particular, he noted that to the extent that the rise of online commerce is essentially shifting inventories from general merchandise and other physical retail stores to warehouses (and delivery using transportation workers rather than pickups by customers), the measured productivity benefits from the rise of online commerce would be lower than one may infer from the reduction of input use in the retail sector.

13. We thank Nathan Goldschlag for sharing USPTO patent count data by NAICS 4-digit sectors, which he and coauthors put together in connection with their work on patent concordances in Goldschlag, Lybbert, and Zolas (2019).

been going up in the retail sector, measured patenting in this sector constitutes less than 1.1 percent of total patents filed in the US. We believe that this measure significantly understates innovation in the sector, even in terms of patent counts. Moreover, because innovation affecting this sector comes from other sectors, and some of the innovation is related to changes in organizational structures as well, a patent-based measure for innovation in this sector simply does not capture much of the relevant innovative activity. For that reason, we do not pursue avenues to explain trends in this sector using such measures of technological change. Instead, in section 6.7, we frame our discussion of innovation around other sources of information.

Changes to industry classifications and related loss of data (apparently correlated with the extent of reduction in activity). Another challenge in studying the retail sector is that changes in the amount of economic activity in various sectors and subsectors have prompted several revisions to the NAICS, many of which have affected the retail sector in particular.[14] This classification, which was implemented with the Economic Census of 1997, was revised in 2002, 2007, 2012, and 2017. Our analyses were impacted by two major changes: (1) the codes for major subcategories of restaurant (full service and limited service restaurants) were changed in 2007, and (2) the code for Warehouse Clubs and Supercenters (which we term "big box" stores) was changed from NAICS 45291 (under the 2002 and 2007 NAICS versions) to NAICS 42311 (in the 2012 revision). While these changes call for extra care when collating the data, which we address below, some other changes are more difficult or infeasible to fully reverse. In particular, certain subcategories get folded into other more aggregate categories, likely because of a decline in economic activity in the subsector. For example, up to the 2007 version of the NAICS, music stores (NAICS 45211 Prerecorded Tape, Compact Disc, and Record Stores) were tracked in the broader subsector of NAICS 4512 (Book, Periodical, and Music Stores); this music stores subcategory was abandoned (i.e., was no longer tracked) from 2012 on, as the NAICS 2012 revision does not have a separate classification for these stores. Similarly, Camera and Photographic Supplies Stores (NAICS 44313) and Computer and Software Stores (44312) were tracked under Electronics and Appliance Stores (443), but in the NAICS 2012 revision, these subcategories were eliminated. These classification changes, and our desire to study trends over a relatively long time frame (1999 to 2017), require us in many cases to use data aggregated at the 3-digit NAICS code level, so that we can construct a comparable continuous data series for the period in question.

---

14. For a historical perspective on the development of the NAICS, and more information about changes implemented over time, see https://www.census.gov/eos/www/naics/history/history.html.

Imputing e-commerce data to retail sectors. A related classification challenge arises from the fact that e-commerce activity by online retailers is tracked in the ARTS based on product codes that do not directly relate to the NAICS classification scheme. We manually imputed NAICS 2012 codes to each of the merchandise lines, as documented in appendix table 6.A.1.[15]

6.3   Trends in Retail Sector Activity: A Decline in Brick-and-Mortar Goods Retailing and a Rise of Restaurants

In this section, we present data patterns for all Traditional Physical Retail (as defined in section 6.2.1) and break that down by Restaurants and Non-Restaurant Physical Retail, using data to 2017, the year of the last Economic Census as of this writing.

6.3.1   Trends in Number of Establishments

The most visible elements of retail are storefronts, with media stories on the retail apocalypse often focusing on closed storefronts and retail vacancies (e.g., Field 2018; Kestenbaum 2017; Kilgannon 2018). We examine whether those media stories of chain and other store closures reflect a broad decline in the number of brick-and-mortar establishments in the US, using data from the US Census Bureau's CBP.

Figure 6.1 panels a–c present trends in aggregate numbers of stores for Traditional Non-Restaurant Physical Retail, Restaurants, and Traditional Physical Retail, respectively. Consistent with the extensive media coverage of the "retail apocalypse," we show, in Figure 6.1a, that there was a sizable decline in the total number of establishments in the Traditional Non-Restaurant Physical Retail sector, from about 1.07 million establishments in 2007 down to 0.98 million in 2017, a nearly 10 percent reduction, with the bulk of the decline coincident with the time of the Great Recession (2008 and 2009). However, in figure 6.1b, we find that there has been a secular trend of strong growth in the number of restaurant establishments; despite a slowdown around the Great Recession, restaurant numbers have increased from about 475,000 establishments in 1999 to 650,000 establishments in 2017. This increase in restaurants more than offsets the decline in number of establishments in other physical retail, so that in figure 6.1c, the total number

---

15. One of the ARTS tables reports ESMOH data separated into NAICS categories. However, we did not use this categorization for two reasons. First, and as a practical limitation, we were unable to find this data series for the full 1999 to 2017 period; the two separate tables that we found covered data only from 2011 to 2017. Second, and importantly for our purposes, this table allocates most of the ESMOH sales into the NAICS 454 Nonstore retailer subsector (in 2017, the proportion allocated to nonstore retailers was 67.8 percent, or $269.4 billion of the total $397.5 billion). Because our goal is to find a good measure of the extent of penetration by online retailers in traditional categories, this very partial allocation of sales to traditional physical sales sectors means that these tables have very limited utility for us.

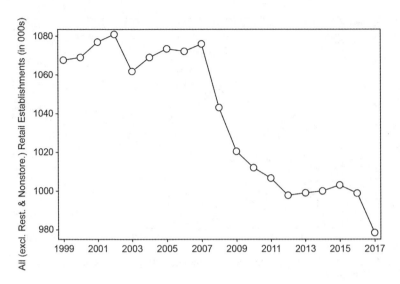

Fig. 6.1a   Decline in number of traditional non-restaurant physical retail establishments

Source: Data are from the US Census Bureau's County Business Patterns (CBP) dataset.

Note: This figure presents the trend in the aggregate number of establishments in Traditional non-Restaurant Physical Retail, which is all retail per the current classification code (i.e., NAICS 44–45) less all nonstore (NAICS 454 which includes ecommerce and catalog) retailer establishments.

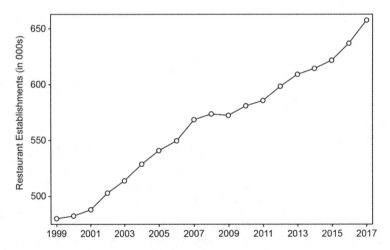

Fig. 6.1b   Strong growth in number of restaurants

Source: Data are from the US Census Bureau's County Business Patterns dataset.

Note: Restaurants is NAICS sector 722.

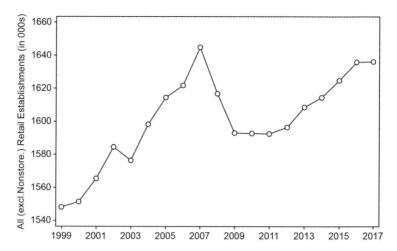

Fig. 6.1c   Traditional physical retail (including restaurants) bounces back after the Great Recession

Note: This figure presents trends for "Traditional Physical Retail," which refers to all retail establishments (NAICS 44–45) plus restaurants (NAICS 722) but excluding nonstore establishments (454). Data are from the US Census Bureau's County Business Patterns dataset.

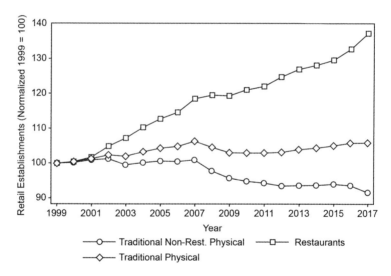

Fig. 6.1d   Numbers of establishments—normalized trends in retail categories

Note: "Traditional Physical" refers to traditional (per old SIC classification) retail stores excluding nonstore establishments (to exclude establishments of ecommerce and catalog companies)—this is NAICS 44, 45 and 722 excluding Nonstore Retailers (454). "Traditional Non-Rest. Physical" is the "Traditional Physical" excluding restaurants (722). Restaurants refers to NAICS 722. Data on number of establishments are from the US Census County Business Patterns (CBP).

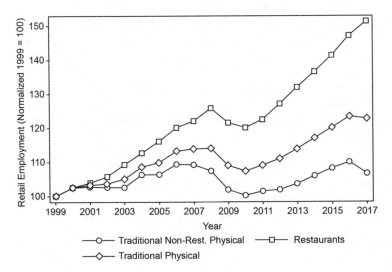

Fig. 6.2   Employment—normalized trends in retail categories

Source: Data on employment are from the US Census County Business Patterns (CBP).

Note: "Traditional Physical" refers to traditional (per old SIC classification) retail stores excluding nonstore establishments (to exclude establishments of ecommerce and catalog companies)—this is NAICS 44, 45 and 722 excluding Nonstore Retailers (454). "Traditional Non-Rest. Physical" is the "Traditional Physical" excluding restaurants (722). Restaurants refers to NAICS 722.

of traditional physical retail stores had bounced back almost all the way by 2017 (from a peak of about 1.64 million in 2007 to a trough of about 1.59 million in 2010, and back to about 1.63 million in 2017).

The interpretation of the decline in number of establishments in figure 6.1a, and of the trends in figures 6.1b and c, however, requires paying close attention to the vertical axes used. Figure 6.1d instead shows trends in terms of percentages by normalizing the 1999 level to 100 for each of the categories. This figure shows more clearly that the observed decline in figure 6.1a translates to somewhat less than a 10 percent decline in relative terms. Moreover, the stabilization from 2012 to 2016 is reassuring, though the further dip in 2017 may portend a further shakeout in the sector. Finally, the rise of the restaurant sector is evident in this figure as well, and we see that by 2017, the overall number of establishments in Traditional Physical Retail, as defined in this chapter, was about 5 percent above its 1999 equivalent (but still lower than its 2007 peak).

6.3.2   Trends in Employment

Figure 6.2 presents normalized trends in employment for retail subsectors, similar to figure 6.1d for establishments. We find a very similar pattern in employment as we did for establishments, except that even in the Traditional Physical Retail sector excluding restaurants, retail employment levels bounce back to the pre–Great Recession peak levels by 2016 (though there is again a notable dip in 2017). Restaurant employment shows a remarkably strong recovery from a decline coincident with the Great Recession, and this impetus from restaurants pushes employment in the overall Traditional Physical Retail sector to well above the pre–Great Recession levels.[16] Even after the dip in 2017, aggregate physical retail employment is about 21 percent above the 1999 levels.[17]

6.3.3   Trends in Sales, Value Added, and Total Payroll

Figure 6.3a shows the normalized trends for (real, in 1999 dollars) sales. Here, as for employment, we see that for the Non-Restaurant Traditional Physical Retail sector, there was a full recovery in sales to pre–Great Recession levels by 2017 (unlike the pattern for establishments in this sector). There is strong growth in restaurants, but the impact of this growth on total Traditional Physical Retail sales is more modest. This is in line with appendix figure 6.A.2 and the related discussion in section 6.2.3, which show that the sales share of restaurants in aggregate retail activity is considerably lower than their share in employment and establishments (implying lower sales per employee in the restaurant sector). We come back to this issue in section 6.5.

However, in terms of both aggregate real value added (figure 6.3b) and aggregate real payroll (figure 6.3c), we find that restaurants make a sizable contribution to the overall Traditional Physical retail sector. This is also in line with the larger value added and payroll share of total retail for Restaurants in figure 6.A.2. In particular, figure 6.3b shows that excluding restaurants, the traditional physical retail sector recovered to only a little below the 2007 peak in value added and total payroll, while including restaurants pushes the aggregate trend to above the 2007 indexed level. For both value added and payroll, the addition of restaurants leads to an increase of about 15 percent in the indexes for Traditional Physical Retail in 2017.

---

16. One caveat is that (as discussed in section 6.2.3), the employment variable in the CBP includes part-time employment. Because we are concerned, based on low average annual payroll per employee (see discussion in section 6.5.1.3), that the restaurant sector may have more than the typical—even relative to other retail—amount of part-time employment, we acknowledge that the total employment contribution from the restaurant sector to the retail sector corresponds to jobs with lower annual payroll per job than in other retail sectors. Nevertheless, as the analysis in section 6.3.3 shows, the restaurant sector experienced significant growth in value added and overall payroll, and this contribution helped both real value added and real payroll growth substantially (see figure 6.3).

17. We extend this figure to April 2020, using monthly data from BLS Current Employment statistics, in appendix figure 6.A.13, panel a. This shows that the trends seen in figure 6.2 largely continued up to March 2020, except for a small reversal in the growth of traditional non-restaurant physical retail. As we discuss in section 6.8.2, the ongoing COVID-19 crisis has triggered a historic plunge in employment levels, with only a partial recovery by December 2020.

A. Sales

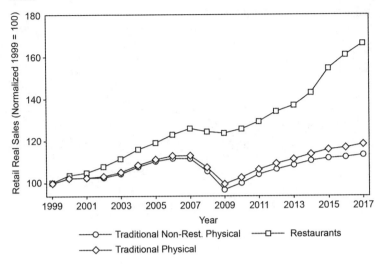

B. Value Added

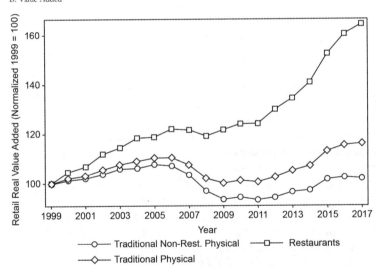

Fig. 6.3 Sales, value added, and payroll—normalized trends in retail categories

Source: Data on sales are from US Census Bureau's ARTS survey and antecedents, payroll are from the US Census Bureau's County Business Patterns (CBP) data, and value added are from the BEA.

Note: "Traditional Physical" refers to traditional (per old SIC classification) retail stores excluding nonstore establishments (to exclude establishments of ecommerce and catalog companies)—this is NAICS 44, 45, and 722 excluding Nonstore Retailers (454). "Traditional Non-Rest. Physical" is the "Traditional Physical" excluding restaurants (722). Restaurants refers to NAICS 722.

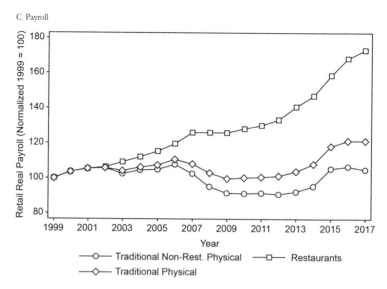

Fig. 6.3   (cont.)

6.3.4   Trends in Retail Share of the Overall Economy

The figures above suggest that, in general, the traditional physical retail sector inclusive of restaurants has bounced back to the pre-Great Recession peaks in level terms for establishments, and exceeded pre-recession peaks for employment, real sales, real value added and payroll.

However, because the rest of economy also experienced a strong (though drawn out) recovery from the Great Recession, these figures do not tell us how the different components of the retail sector fared *relative to the overall economy*. To understand this relative picture, in figure 6.4, we plot the trends for four indicators of the share of different components of retail in the overall economy, normalizing the share of each subcomponent in 1999 to 100.

Figure 6.4 shows that across all indicators, the share of restaurants in the overall economy has increased over 1999–2017, with shares of establishments and real value added increasing by about 20 percent, employment by about 30 percent, and real payroll by about 35 percent. Across all four indicators, traditional physical retail (excluding restaurants) shows significant decline in share of the overall economy: by about 20 percent for number of establishments and payroll, about 10 percent for employment, and about 28 percent for value added. The rise of restaurants is strong enough to more than offset the decline in the rest of traditional physical retail in terms of employment, so that employment in traditional physical retail including restaurants is higher in 2017 than in 1999. However, for the other three indicators, restaurant growth was insufficient to maintain retail's share in the overall economy. Thus, there is a small (about 7 percent) decline in the

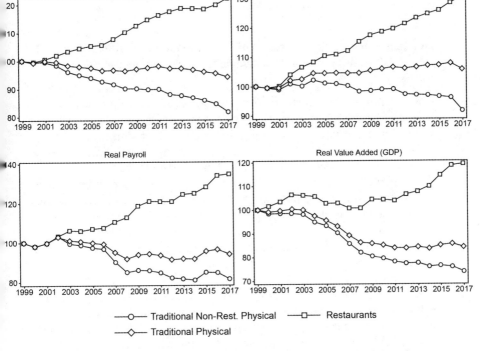

Fig. 6.4   Trends in retail share of the aggregate economy (normalized share in 1999 = 100)

Source: Data on establishments, employment and payroll are from the US Census Bureau's County Business Patterns (CBP) data and value added are from the BEA.

Note: "Traditional Physical" refers to traditional (per old SIC classification) retail stores excluding nonstore establishments (to exclude establishments of ecommerce and catalog companies)—this is NAICS 44, 45, and 722 excluding Nonstore Retailers (454). "Traditional Non-Rest. Physical" is the "Traditional Physical" excluding restaurants (722). Restaurants refers to NAICS 722.

share of establishments and payroll, and a steeper decline in the share of value added (about 16 percent), for traditional physical retail inclusive of restaurants.[18]

Overall, pre-COVID, we conclude that while restaurants have experienced an impressive rise relative to the rest of the economy, the traditional physi-

18. As discussed in section 6.8, we extend the figure for employment share of the aggregate economy, to April 2020 using BLS Current Employment statistics in appendix figure 6.A.13b. After 2017, the share of restaurants in the economy remained flat, while the share of traditional non-restaurant physical declined (similar to the sector's earlier decline in the other indicators). The plunge in employment triggered by the ongoing COVID-19 crisis initially (in April 2020) reduced the share of restaurants to even below the 1999 level; while there has been a rebound since, the recovery is only partial and restaurant share of private sector employment in December 2020 is well below the pre-pandemic peak.

cal retail (even inclusive of restaurants) has shrunk relative to the economy except in terms of employment.[19]

6.4   Innovation and the Slowdown of Non-Restaurant Traditional Physical Retail Activity: The Role of Online Retailing and Big Box Stores

Two main factors have been mentioned in the trade press and the academic literature (e.g., Hortaçsu and Syverson 2015) as main drivers of the decline in brick-and-mortar retail establishments or what we term Non-Restaurant Traditional Physical Retail: first, the development and growth of online retailing, and second, the growth of large general merchandise retail chains, in particular big box stores. By "big box," we mean chains of supercenters like Walmart and Target, as well as warehouse clubs, such as Costco and Sam's Club. Both online retailing and the success of big box stores arguably have been made possible by the development of new technologies permitting more efficient and better tracking of items as they move from manufacturers to consumers, including better inventory management, along with more efficient use of warehouse and transportation assets. In other words, exogenous technological innovation has allowed for growing scale economies that have benefitted national chains of very large general merchandise outlets and online retailers, which in turn have reduced demand for the products sold in Non-Restaurant Traditional Physical Retail stores (see Basker 2016a, which contains several chapters dedicated to technological and organizational changes in the goods retail sectors of the economy).

In this section, we examine in more detail the extent to which both sales by online retailers and big box stores have disrupted the retail sector. Figure 6.5 provides a summary by presenting how sales from these two sources have increased in terms of their share of the Traditional Retail sector (i.e., NAICS 44–45 plus NAICS 722).[20] This figure shows that in the first half of our study period, i.e., from 1999 to about 2010, the growth of big box stores was a more powerful trend, increasing share from about 4 percent of the market to nearly 9 percent, whereas in the same period online retailing grew from

---

19. We present a figure decomposing changes in the supersector share of GDP between 2017 and 1999 in appendix figure 6.A.4. Manufacturing and Retail sectors show the largest declines, while Finance, Professional services, and Education and health showed the largest gains over this period.

20. Figure 6.5 shows the aggregate share of ESMOH-Ecommerce, that is, e-commerce sales by firms in the NAICS 4541 (Electronic Shopping and Mail-order Houses) subsector, which includes online and catalog retailers, and hence, we believe that it includes Amazon and other big online retailers. We do not separate out e-commerce sales by retailers that operate mostly via brick-and-mortar stores, as this is small compared to ESMOH sales, and because such sales may not be competing but rather complementary activities for physical stores (e.g., for clothing stores that allow online customers to use stores for returns, and online orders from physical restaurants). Our analysis suggests that Restaurants (722), Clothing (448), Miscellaneous Stores (453), Motor Vehicles (441), and Sporting Goods (451) are the top subsectors in terms of direct e-commerce (i.e., e-commerce by physical retailers) share of subsector sales.

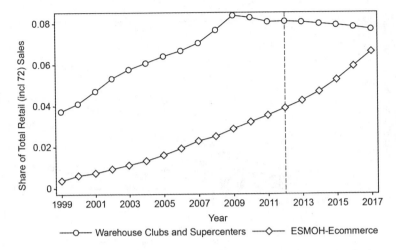

Fig. 6.5   Retail sales—trends for Big Box and non-store e-commerce

Source: Data are from US Census Bureau's Annual Retail Trade Survey (ARTS) and the Services Annual Survey (SAS) and their antecedents.

Note: Traditional Retail includes all subcategories of NAICS 44, 45 and 722. "Big Box" is the subsector 45291 (Warehouse Clubs and Supercenters) in the 2012 NAICS. ESMOH ecommerce refers to e-commerce by firms in the NAICS 4541 (Electronic Shopping and Mail-order Houses) subsector, which includes online and catalog retailers.

about 0.5 percent to 3.5 percent. However, in the latter half of our period, between 2009 and 2017, roles were reversed. In particular, there is a striking flattening of the share of big box stores starting in 2009, with their share actually declining slightly from about 8.5 percent in 2009 to 8 percent by 2017. In contrast, over that same time frame, online retailer e-commerce sales accelerated, increasing share from about 3.5 percent to 7 percent. Thus, it appears that the competition from big box stores has stabilized, while e-commerce competition shows no sign of slowing down.

In sections 6.4.1 and 6.4.2, we take a closer look at the trends for online retail and big box stores, and we undertake additional analyses to see whether competition from these sources explains variations in the decline of physical retail (excluding restaurants) over time and across US counties.

6.4.1   Nonstore Online Sales

The Census Bureau collects data on sales by nonstore retailers, under NAICS code 454. Within NAICS 454, retailers without physical (brick-and-mortar) stores are captured in the ESMOH (NAICS 4541) subsector. Specifically, the ESMOH subsector encompasses "establishments primarily engaged in retailing all types of merchandise using nonstore means, such as catalogs, toll free telephone numbers, or electronic media, such as interactive television or the Internet," per US Census Bureau documentation for

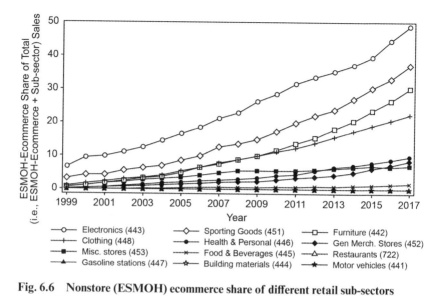

Fig. 6.6 Nonstore (ESMOH) ecommerce share of different retail sub-sectors

Source: This figure is based on imputing the breakdown of ESMOH ecommerce sales by merchandise lines in the US Census Bureau Annual Retail Trade Survey (ARTS) tables to individual retail NAICS codes (see Appendix Table 6.A.1 for the concordance used). Data on some merchandise lines for some years were suppressed in ARTS tables—these were interpolated on extrapolated based on data for adjacent years. *Note:* Categories sorted by 2017 share. Restaurants/Gasoline Stations/Building materials/Motor Vehicles are zero throughout.

the ARTS. It is a subsector in NAICS 44–45, which, as mentioned earlier, comprises all product retailing.

Because ESMOH includes non-ecommerce, primarily in the form of catalog sales, we can classify nonstore (NAICS454) retail sales into three subcategories: (1) ESMOH ecommerce (used in figure 5 discussed above), (2) ESMOH non-ecommerce, and (3) other nonstore retail sales. Appendix figure 6.A.5 shows how the level of retail sales achieved by retailers with no brick-and-mortar presence, as identified by the Census Bureau, has grown with the advent of the Internet. Panel B shows that, as a percentage of Traditional Retail (i.e., NAICS 44–45 plus restaurants; NAICS 722), nonstore retailing was a very minor component of retail in the late 1990s, at about 0.3 percent. This share increased (as seen earlier in figure 6.5) to about 7 percent of Traditional Retail sales, representing about $397.5 billion in sales in 2017.

This rise in e-commerce sales by online retailers has involved differential trends across retail subsectors, as illustrated in figure 6.6.[21] In particular, and in line with reports in the trade press (e.g., anecdotal explanations for the

---

21. See the last paragraph of section 6.2.3 for a discussion of how we imputed ESMOH data on e-commerce sales to retail subsectors.

bankruptcy of chains, such as Circuit City and Radio Shack), the data suggest that Electronic Stores (NAICS 443) faced the most intense competition from online sales, with the share of online retailers increasing from about 7 percent in 1999 to close to 50 percent in 2017. Sporting Goods (which also includes bookstores) was the subsector with the next highest penetration of online retailing, with shares increasing from below 5 percent in 1999 to about 37 percent in 2017. Somewhat surprisingly (given the likely high per item shipping costs), furniture stores are the next highest in terms of nonstore e-commerce share in 2017 (at 30 percent). Clothing stores are next, with about 22 percent in 2017, but then there is a sizable drop to the next subsector (Health and Personal Care Stores; NAICS 446) at just below 10 percent. The data yield no imputed e-commerce competition for Restaurants (722), Gasoline Stations (447), Building Materials (444) and Motor Vehicles (441).[22]

In figure 6.7 and corresponding table 6.1, we explore the correlation between the change in ESMOH e-commerce share between 1999 and 2016 for 11 traditional physical retail NAICS 3-digit sectors, and the decline in physical retail activity.[23] We find that, despite potentially significant measurement errors in the imputed e-commerce sales shares, there is a strong negative correlation between increases in e-commerce penetration and the level of retail activity by traditional retailers, as measured by the number of establishments, employment, sales, and payroll. Despite the small number of observations available, in table 6.1, we confirm the statistical significance of the negative correlation for two of our four measures of retail activity, namely, sales and total payroll (at the 5 percent level for sales and at the 10 percent level for total payroll).

Data limitations prevent a more granular investigation of the impact of online sales on physical retail activity. Nevertheless, the patterns in figure 6.7 provide solid support for several persuasive accounts from the trade press (e.g., Evangelista 2015) of the closure of physical stores (e.g., bookstores and electronic stores) that specifically refer to increased competition from online retailing as a trigger. Our results are also broadly in line with those of Chava et al. (2018), who use microdata from the National Establishment Time Series (NETS) to document a reduction in employment, sales, and entry,

---

22. Some of this result is likely due to one important source of measurement error, arising from a large unallocated "Other merchandise" category in the list of ESMOH merchandise lines, which had about $62.8 billion in e-commerce sales accounting for 16.13 percent of the total ESMOH e-commerce sales of $397.5 billion in 2017. The notes to the ARTS table describe this category as including "other merchandise such as collectibles, souvenirs, auto parts and accessories, hardware, and lawn and garden equipment and supplies"; hence it is likely that the imputed zero for the building materials subsector (NAICS 444, which includes lawn and garden equipment and supplies stores) and Motor Vehicles (NAICS 441, which includes 4413, Automotive Parts, Accessories, and Tire Stores) are underestimates, as they should include at least a portion of what is currently attributed to the "Other merchandise" category.

23. We chose 2016 as the end year of comparison, as the 2017 figures are the latest available and may be subject to revisions. In any case, there is only a modest difference in aggregate figures between 2016 and 2017 (see, e.g., figure 6.3).

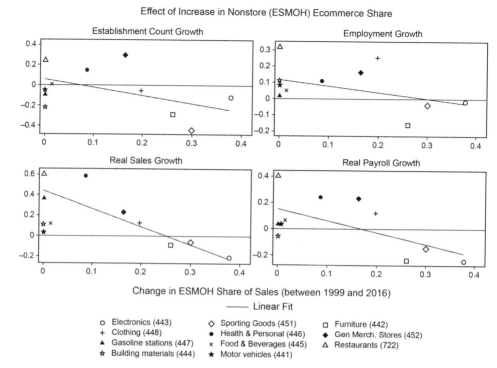

Fig. 6.7   **Cross-industry outcomes: Correlation with ESMOH ecommerce penetration**

Source: Establishment counts and employment from CBP, sales from ARTS and SAS (for restaurants); Excludes Nonstore retailers (454), and Misc. Stores (453).

Note: See table 6.1 for corresponding regression results. Y Growth = (Y2016 − Y1999)/Y1999.

and an increase in exit, of retail stores in counties nearest to e-commerce fulfillment centers. With the overall and sector-specific trends for online e-commerce (in figures 6.5 and 6.6) showing no signs of a slowdown, we expect pressure from online sales to continue to dampen physical retail activity in the most e-commerce-prone sectors of electronics, furniture, sporting goods, and clothing. Moreover, the current COVID-19 crisis is likely to only accelerate this effect as more customers, out of necessity, try out and become familiar with online shopping for such items.

6.4.2   The Role of General Merchandise Stores

In their overview paper on the evolution of US retail, Hortaçsu and Syverson (2015) use data up to 2012 to highlight the remarkable surge in the share of big box stores in retailing; in earlier work, Basker, Klimek, and Hoang Van (2012) documented this surge of general merchandise stores over the 1992–2007 period. The growth of this (NAICS 45291) subsector

Table 6.1   **Aggregate cross-industry exploration of the role of ESMOH e-commerce in the decline in physical stores**

	Establishment growth (1999 to 2016) (1)	Employment growth (1999 to 2016) (2)	Sales growth (1999 to 2016) (3)	Real payroll growth (1999 to 2016) (4)
Change in e-commerce share of sector	−0.655	−0.440	−1.754**	−0.881*
(1999 to 2016)	(0.481)	(0.285)	(0.695)	(0.391)
Constant	0.0338	0.139**	0.904***	0.154*
	(0.0888)	(0.0526)	(0.128)	(0.0722)
Observations	11	11	11	11
R-squared	0.171	0.209	0.414	0.360
Dependent variable mean	−0.0281	0.0768	0.797	0.0482
Dependent variable standard deviation	0.231	0.126	0.659	0.197
Mean of change in e-commerce share	0.112	0.112	0.112	0.112
Standard deviation of change in e-commerce share	0.129	0.129	0.129	0.129

Note: *, **, and *** denote statistical significance at 10%, 5%, and 1%, respectively.

was reflected also in figure 6.5, discussed above. Appendix figure 6.A.6 presents trends for big box and other general merchandise stores in dollar terms (panel A) and as a share of total traditional retail (i.e., NAICS 44–45 and Restaurants 722). The figures show that big box stores have grown from about a third of the general merchandise (NAICS 452) subsector to well above 50 percent of sales. While panel a of figure 6.A.6 shows that nominal sales continued to grow for big box stores through the entire 1999 to 2017 period, their growth slowed starting around 2008, as seen in a dramatic flattening of the trend in terms of share of retail sales (in appendix figure 6.A.6b just as in figure 6.5 above). Panel b also reveals that the non–big box stores in this subsector experienced considerable decline in their share of retail, so that the aggregate general merchandise subsector shrank from a peak of about 14.5 percent of retail sales (in 2009) to less than 12 percent in 2017. These trends suggest some challenges for stores in the general merchandise subsector, especially for non–big box general merchandise stores.[24]

These figures also confirm that while Hortaçsu and Syverson were correct to highlight the importance of the rise of big box stores up to the late 2000s as potentially more impactful than the rise of e-commerce in the same period, the rise of big box stores has stalled, so that since 2009, it seems likely that the continuing rise of e-commerce will be the prominent driver of changes in the physical retail sector. Having said that, with brick-and-mortar

24. In section 6.7, we discuss new approaches that physical retailers like Walmart are adopting, greater investments in online retailing, curbside pickups, and grocery home deliveries from stores, to defend and grow their market share.

retailers' increased involvement in online sales, and signs that e-commerce firms are finding their way into developing some brick-and-mortar presence, the lines between traditional and online retailing are blurring to an increasing degree as well, making it difficult to identify which is affecting which (see the discussion in section 6.7).

Despite the slowdown in big box share of retail starting in 2009, over the 1999 to 2016 time frame, this sector did see very significant growth. Did this growth reduce demand for other physical retail, especially since these supercenters and warehouse stores often carry a wide range of products that compete with almost every other retail store subsector? To investigate this in more granular detail, we use US Census Bureau CBP data and regress the 1999–2016 growth in measures of physical non-restaurant retail (i.e., NAICS 44–45 excluding nonstore retailers (454)) activity (specifically, the number of establishments and employment, with growth defined as ($Y2016 - Y1999)/Y1999$) on the growth in number of big box establishments in the county. Results are reported in table 6.2. We examine the effect of both a continuous measure of big box growth (in odd numbered columns) as well as a more flexible specification using dummy variables for different ranges of growth in the number of big box stores (in even numbered columns). In columns 5 to 7, we include variables to control for growth in county population and growth in county personal income. While we would not want to impute a causal interpretation to these regression results, these long-difference specifications are akin to using county fixed-effect regressions, and hence they control for omitted variable bias that would arise from omitted fixed county-specific characteristics (so long as they have static effects on the number of establishments and employment in the Non-Restaurant Traditional Physical Retail sector). Across all specifications, we find a strong *positive* correlation between growth of traditional retail activity and the growth of big box stores. As expected, population growth and income growth are also strongly positively correlated with growth in physical retail activity, but even in specifications controlling for these variables, we still find significant positive correlation between increases in big box presence and growth of the physical retail sector.

The results in table 6.2 contradict a narrative in which the growth of big box stores is associated with a decline in other retail physical activity over the full period of our data. Instead, these results suggest that places that saw increases in big box presence also saw a relative strengthening of other (non-restaurant) retail activity, even conditioning on income and population growth. We surmise that this occurs because big box stores expand in places that have a more than usual (over and above what is predicted from population and income growth) conducive environment for retail activity in general, rather than into less hospitable places where these stores try to replace other physical retail activity. Moreover, their presence in some

Table 6.2 Traditional nonrestaurant physical retail growth and big box growth—long difference estimates

Dependent variable: Growth (99 to 16) in Trad. (non-rest) Retail:	Estabs. (1)	Estabs. (2)	Emp. (3)	Emp. (4)	Estabs. (5)	Estabs. (6)	Emp. (7)	Emp. (8)
Growth in Big Box Estabs.	**0.0985***		**0.120***		**0.0512***		**0.0721***	
	(0.0087)		**(0.0074)**		**(0.0084)**		**(0.0065)**	
Big Box growth Cat 2 (growth=0)		−0.00634		0.0483		−0.00771		0.0445
		(0.0528)		(0.0452)		(0.0489)		(0.0380)
Big Box growth Cat 3 (growth>0 & <=1)		**0.0837***		**0.125***		**0.0477**		**0.0913***
		(0.0506)		**(0.0433)**		**(0.0469)**		**(0.0365)**
Big Box growth Cat 3 (growth>1)		**0.190***		**0.245***		**0.0840***		**0.139***
		(0.0506)		**(0.0433)**		**(0.0472)**		**(0.0367)**
Growth in county population					0.782***	0.781***	0.893***	0.903***
					(0.0336)	(0.0345)	(0.0259)	(0.0269)
Growth in county personal income (per capita)					0.276***	0.295***	0.701***	0.713***
					(0.0615)	(0.0621)	(0.0474)	(0.0484)
Constant	−0.108***	−0.132***	0.0238***	−0.0274	−0.333***	−0.350***	−0.443***	−0.487***
	(0.0103)	(0.0498)	(0.0087)	(0.0427)	(0.0353)	(0.0578)	(0.0272)	(0.0450)
Observations	3,088	3,088	3,088	3,088	3,088	3,088	3,088	3,088
R-squared	0.040	0.042	0.079	0.064	0.184	0.181	0.353	0.339

Note: Observations are weighted by county population. County population and income data are from the BEA regional economic accounts. (https://apps .bea.gov/regional/downloadzip.cfm). *, **, and *** denote statistical significance at 10%, 5%, and 1%, respectively.

Summary statistics for interpreting table 6.2

	Dependent variable: Growth in other (phys) retail establishments	Dependent variable: Growth in other (phys) retail employment	Growth in Big Box establishments	Growth in county population	Growth in county personal income (per capita)	Growth in Big Box establishments: breakdown by category bins			
						(Omitted) BB growth Cat 1 (gr < 0)	BB growth Cat 2 (gr = 0)	BB growth Cat 3 (gr > 0 & ≤ 1)	BB growth Cat 4 (gr > 1)
N	3,088	3,088	3,088	3,088	3,088	41	1,535	393	1,119
Mean	−0.013	0.140	0.968	0.159	0.531	−1.031	0.000	0.652	1.588
SD	0.335	0.290	0.677	0.169	0.090	0.787	0.000	0.225	0.349
P25	−0.139	−0.015	0.571	0.048	0.472	−2.000	0.000	0.500	1.294
P75	0.049	0.226	1.440	0.239	0.578	−0.400	0.000	0.857	2.000

Note: Observations are weighted by county population.

locations might drive other, potentially complementary, retailers to want to operate nearby.[25]

6.5 The Rise of Restaurants

In this section, we explore two broad (and potentially complementary) explanations for the rise in number of and economic activity in restaurants documented above: (i) a supply side explanation, where the increase in restaurants is induced by a reduction in retail real estate prices and retail wages,[26] and/or (ii) a demand side explanation, that the growth in the restaurant sector may have been propelled by a shift in expenditures/preferences away from other consumption, including home cooking, and toward restaurant food.

To explore explanation (i), in section 6.5.1, we examine data on real estate prices (section 6.5.1.1). And in section 6.5.1.2, we examine whether restaurant growth is directly negatively correlated with other physical retail growth, which would be the case if vacancies and displacement of workers from other physical retail activity played a role in the rise of restaurants. We explore trends in productivity and compensation in section 6.5.1.3. In section 6.5.2, we examine evidence for a shift in preferences toward restaurant food and explore a simple quantification of the impact of such a shift on restaurant activity. In section 6.5.3, we delve deeper into the expansion of restaurants to examine whether most of the growth was concentrated in a certain type of restaurant (in particular, limited service, or fast-food, versus full service restaurants) and the demographics of counties where the growth occurred.

6.5.1 Supply Side Factors and the Rise of Restaurants

6.5.1.1 *Trends in Retail Real Estate Vacancies and Prices*

The growth in online retailing and the growth of big box stores described above both would suggest a significant reduction in the demand for traditional retail space. Figure 6.8a shows the vacancy rate, at the national level, for retail (and other types) of commercial real estate. Figure 6.8b shows how the price of retail real estate has evolved over time. These figures, taken

25. For several years, Burger King was said to systematically locate its restaurants near McDonald's restaurants on the presumption that these were high-demand areas for fast food, and that the differentiation between the two chains in terms of products would allow them to capture some of that demand. Eaton and Lipsey (1982) argued that economies of scale and scope arising from multipurpose shopping trips lead to benefits from retail agglomeration that can be higher than the costs of locating close to competitors. See also Page (2007) for a theoretical paper that suggests that chains beget chains, based on a similar argument.

26. In simple, homogenous firm models, it is easy to show that a pure reduction in fixed costs, or pure reduction in variable costs, would lead to a higher equilibrium number of firms in the market.

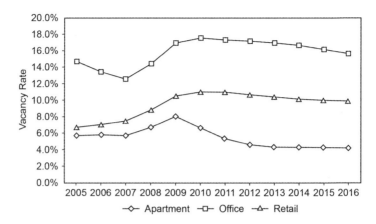

Fig. 6.8a Commercial real estate vacancies, by type

Source: From chart 3 in the "Capital Markets Special Report of the National Association of Insurance Commissioners and the Center for Insurance Policy and Research," https://www.naic.org/capital_markets_archive/170601.htm. Source data for the figure is cited as REIS Inc.

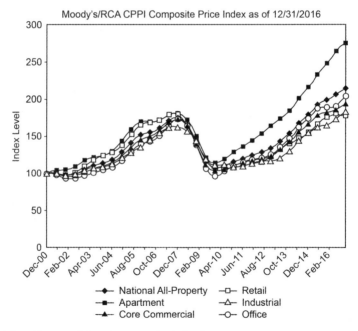

Fig. 6.8b Commercial real estate price index by property type

Source: From Chart 1 in the "Capital Markets Special Report of the National Association of Insurance Commissioners and the Center for Insurance Policy and Research," https://www.naic.org/capital_markets_archive/170601.htm.

Note: Core commercial includes retail, industrial and office. Core commercial includes retail, industrial, and office.

from NAIC-CIPR (2017), illustrate the large impact of the Great Recession in 2008–2009 on retail real estate. The effect on price is particularly pronounced, with the price index reaching about 175 right before the Great Recession (from 100 in 2000) and falling back down to almost 100 at the end of 2009. However, from that point on, the price recovers, reaching about 175 again in 2016.

Looking more closely at vacancies, figure 6.8a shows a sizable increase in the proportion of vacant retail space starting with the Great Recession, from a rate lower than 8 percent to a maximum of about 11 percent a few years later, in 2010–2011. The vacancy rate then decreases slowly, settling at 9.9 percent in 2016. This post-financial crisis rate is well above the rate of about 7 percent observed prior to the Great Recession, in 2005–2007.

While the data about vacancy rate and the price index for retail real estate clearly show the effect of the financial crisis of 2008–2009 on this market (an effect that was also very prominent in figures 6.1 and 6.3 for retail and restaurants), the evidence for a continued retail apocalypse way beyond the financial crisis is much less clear from these data. Instead, there is evidence of recovery from the Great Recession, with vacancy rates stabilizing, though at a higher level than before the recession, and the price index fully recovering by 2016.

We conclude that the growth in online retailing and general merchandise stores has been associated with reductions in the number of establishments and employment in the physical goods retail sector (NAICS 44–45), but that the effect on the retail real estate market has been less dramatic than might be expected: there is not the kind of secular reduction in the price of retail real estate, nor continued increases in the vacancy rate, that one might predict after the Great Recession based on the rate of growth in online retailing in particular. This, of course, is consistent with the idea that the demand for retail real estate at the aggregate level has not systematically declined over time or since the Great Recession. We would argue that this is likely due to the counterbalancing growth in the number of restaurants in the post-financial crisis, as shown in figure 6.2. In fact, the evolution of the price index in figure 6.8b is very similar to the evolution in the total number of establishments (the sum of establishments in NAICS 44–45 and restaurants) in figure 6.1d.

6.5.1.2   Correlation between Restaurant Growth and Traditional Non-Restaurant Physical Retail Growth at the County Level

As a further and more direct test of whether the rise in restaurants was induced by the decline in retail rents and wages, which themselves would be consequences of the collapse/apocalypse in the goods retail sector, we examined the correlation between restaurant growth and growth in the number of establishments or employment in such retail at the county level, using the US Census Bureau's CBP data.

In table 6.3, we show long difference regression results, where the depen-

Table 6.3   Restaurant growth and growth in traditional non-restaurant physical retail activity

Dependent variable: Growth (99 to 16) in Restaurant	Estabs. (1)	Emp. (2)	Estabs. (3)	Emp. (4)	Estabs. (5)	Emp. (6)	Estabs. (7)	Emp. (8)
Growth in other (Phys) retail establishments	**0.623*** (0.0108)	**0.595*** (0.0123)			**0.599*** (0.0110)	**0.572*** (0.0126)	**0.472*** (0.0105)	**0.443*** (0.0123)
Growth in non-restaurant phys. retail average payroll per worker			**−0.429*** (0.0391)	**−0.382*** (0.0411)	**−0.190*** (0.0277)	**−0.154*** (0.0315)	**−0.252*** (0.0244)	**−0.232*** (0.0285)
Growth in Big Box establishments					0.0303*** (0.0054)	0.0340*** (0.0061)	0.0049 (0.0048)	0.0129** (0.0056)
Growth in county population							0.639*** (0.0210)	0.634*** (0.0245)
Growth in county personal income (per capita)							0.274*** (0.0356)	0.529*** (0.0416)
Constant	0.321*** (0.0036)	0.411*** (0.0041)	0.454*** (0.0138)	0.529*** (0.0145)	0.354*** (0.0109)	0.429*** (0.0124)	0.150*** (0.0213)	0.0914*** (0.0249)
Observations	3,088	3,088	3,088	3,088	3,088	3,088	3,088	3,088
R-squared	0.519	0.433	0.038	0.027	0.531	0.443	0.640	0.552

Note: Observations are weighted by county population.

Summary statistics for interpreting table 6.3

	Dependent variable: Growth (99 to 16) in restaurant Estabs.	Dependent variable: Growth (99 to 16) in restaurant employment	Growth in other (physical) retail estabs.	Growth in other (physical) retail annual payroll per employee	Growth in Big Box estabs.	Growth in county population	Growth in county personal income (per capita)
N	3,088	3,088	3,088	3,088	3,088	3,088	3,088
Mean	0.313	0.404	−0.013	0.328	0.968	0.159	0.531
SD	0.289	0.303	0.335	0.131	0.677	0.169	0.090
P25	0.178	0.253	−0.139	0.287	0.571	0.048	0.472
P75	0.414	0.504	0.049	0.371	1.440	0.239	0.578

Note: Observations are weighted by county population.

dent variable is either the growth in number of restaurants in the county between 1999 and 2016 or the growth in the number of employees in that sector. The main explanatory variables are the growth in the number of establishments in Traditional Non-Restaurant Physical Retail and growth in average payroll per employee in that sector.[27] In our preferred specifications, we also control for growth in the number of big box stores, growth in county population, and growth in per capita income in the county.

In columns 1 and 2 of table 6.3, we find that there is a strong *positive* correlation between restaurant growth (both in terms of number of establishments and employment) and growth in the number of establishments in the brick-and-mortar goods retailing sector (NAICS 44–45 except nonstore retail). In columns 3 and 4, we find, as expected, that the average payroll per worker in the brick-and-mortar goods retailing sector is a deterrent to restaurant growth. In the remaining specifications, we show that the strong positive correlation between the growth in number of establishments in the brick-and-mortar goods retailing sector remains after we control for growth in the number of big box stores and demographics at the county level. Moreover, here again, as in table 6.2, we find that big box store growth is positively correlated with restaurant growth, and population and income growth are beneficial for restaurant growth as well.

Figure 6.9 presents a semi-parametric picture of the relationship between the growth in number of restaurants or restaurant employment on one hand and growth in the brick-and-mortar goods retailing sector on the other. Specifically, the figure reports the mean and the interquartile (p25 to p75) range for the growth rate for restaurants between 1999 and 2017, in 10 (population-weighted) deciles of county bins of growth in Traditional Non-Restaurant Physical Retail.[28] The graphs on the left confirm the results from the regression, that there indeed has been systematically higher growth of restaurants (both in terms of establishments in the top left panel, as well as employment

---

27. As mentioned in section 6.3, we do not have wage data in the CBP database. We use total payroll in the sector in the county and information about total numbers of employees in the sector to derive a measure of average yearly pay per worker. To the extent that some of the employment is part-time, this measure of average payroll indicates how much the average employee working the average number of hours brings home as compensation on a yearly basis. If all the employees were full-time, or if we knew hours worked, this measure could be further divided by the usual number of hours worked to yield a wage rate. However, we do not have data on hours worked, and we know many of the employees are in fact part-time, so we use "average payroll per employee" throughout.

28. The counties are divided into 10 groups with lowest to highest Traditional Physical Retail growth between 1999 and 2016. The *x*-axis shows the growth, so the top left panel of figure 6.9 has a mean Traditional Physical Retail physical establishments' growth rate of −38 percent. The population-weighting in the construction of the bins means (as indicated in the notes to the figure) that counties are divided into 10 groups with equal populations in each group; because the total US population in 2016 per the BEA data is about 320 million, each group refers to a collection of counties with population of about 32 million people. (The number of counties varies across bins as some bins may have a lot of low-population counties that together only have the population of a single large county in another bin.)

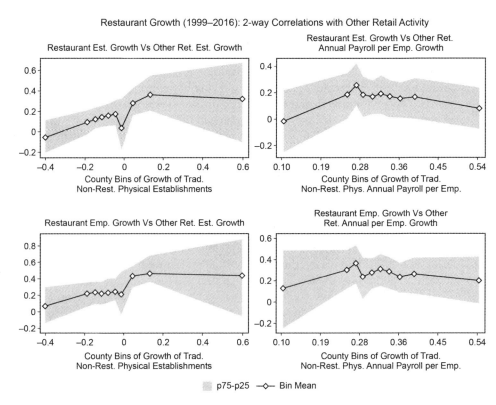

Fig. 6.9   Restaurant growth (between 1999 and 2016) vs. traditional non-restaurant physical retail activity

Note: Restaurants grew more where other physical retail grew, except in the counties with the highest growth in payroll per employee saw somewhat slower growth in restaurant establishments and employment. Growth = (Y2016—Y1999)/Y1999. County bins are 2016 population-weighted (i.e., each marker represents population of ~32 mn); *x*-axis represents (population-weighted means).

in the bottom left panel) in counties that experienced relatively lower decline or even positive growth in number of other physical retail establishments. The results in the panels on the right provide more nuance relative to the average negative effects we found in table 6.3 regarding compensation. Specifically, it appears that the growth in restaurants was lower in places with very low as well as very high growth in average payroll per worker in the physical goods retail sector. Thus, restaurant growth was focused on those counties with medium (.2 to .4) growth in the compensation of workers in the Traditional Non-Restaurant Physical Retail sector, not those with the highest but also not those with the lowest such growth.

In sum, these results indicate that restaurant growth is in fact stronger in places that experienced relatively less of a decline in other physical retail activity, suggesting that there is not a prominent role for a supply side explanation (i.e., the increase in restaurants is not correlated with a reduction in demand for real estate or labor due to reductions in other physical retail).[29]

6.5.1.3 Productivity and Compensation

While labor and real estate cost reductions do not seem to have spurred the growth in the restaurant sector, it is possible that costs in this industry might have been reduced, or productivity increased, through some other channel (e.g., some innovation or other cost-side shocks). Figures 6.10 and 6.11 present some interesting data in this regard.

In figure 6.10, we use data on sales from the US Census Bureau ARTS, and on employment and establishments from the US Census Bureau CBP, to calculate how both real sales per establishment (top left panel) and employment per establishment (bottom left panel) have grown at a very rapid rate in the restaurant sector since the Great Recession. In particular, sales per establishment (in 1999 dollars) increased from about 600,000 in 1999 to about 720,000 in 2017, with steep increases between 2013 and 2016.

Note that real sales per establishment in part grew as a result of sizable increases in the number of employees per establishment (top right panel) in this sector, so the story on real sales growth is not simply one of increased productivity per employee. Nonetheless, the increase in real sales per establishment implies, in the context of a simple model of homogenous competitive firms, that the observed increase in number of establishments was not triggered by a reduction in the optimal scale of restaurants (as could result from reduced fixed costs). Thus, the evidence suggests that the increase in number of restaurants is not a story of entry of small, previously inframarginal entrants induced by lower rents/labor costs triggered by the decline of other physical retail.[30] In fact, evidence shown in figure 6.10 suggests that the average scale of restaurants increased, in terms of real sales (top left), employment (top right) and real payroll (top middle), during this period.

The direct evidence on payroll per employee also argues against an explanation based on a decline in labor costs induced by exit of other physical retail stores. In particular, the bottom middle panel indicates a strong

29. One possible explanation for the lack of a positive correlation across regions between the rise of restaurants and the decline of other physical retail is that converting a non-restaurant location to a restaurant involves significant remodeling costs. Estimates based on a survey of independent restaurant owners by restaurantowner.com (presented at https://www.restaurant owner.com/public/CTOSurvey-SummaryReport.pdf) suggest that remodeling costs are indeed significant; a conversion from one restaurant to another is estimated to cost $275,000, while conversion of a non-restaurant to a restaurant is at the median about 54 percent more expensive, at $425,000. Though this is cheaper than new construction for a restaurant (median cost to open of $650,000), the significant additional up-front expenditure involved could be a sufficient deterrent, along with negative local demand factors that have weakened physical retail, to discourage restaurant entry even with potentially declining rents. A second source (Walters 2018) indicates a higher cost, suggesting a customized kitchen build out could cost an additional $250,000.

30. Even with a heterogeneous firm model, an increase in entry triggered by a reduction in fixed costs could be expected to result in a decline in equilibrium firm revenue per establishment as the cutoff productivity level drops (e.g., Hopenhayn 1992).

Fig. 6.10   Aggregate restaurant sector productivity
Note: These figures show trends in levels; see appendix figure 6.A.7 for normalized trends. Measures as based on national aggregates for the restaurant sector (722) in the numerator and denominator.

increase in real payroll per employee, suggesting compensation grew for restaurant workers over this period. The increases in real payroll per worker are large enough, in fact, to lead to overall decline in sales per dollar of payroll (bottom right panel).[31] Thus, while there has been labor productivity growth in this sector, the growth in real compensation has more than offset the benefits garnered by firms as a result of this productivity growth.

Figure 6.11 compares trends in labor productivity and compensation for workers in different retail sectors. In particular, it shows that real value added has been very stable throughout the period in all sectors except nonstore retailing. The latter's growth in value added should be interpreted with caution, because of the measurement issues discussed in sections 6.2.3 and 6.2.4, i.e., the idea that some of the labor that support sales in this sector likely appears under Warehousing and Transportation (NAICS 48–49) rather than under nonstore retail.

31. Both increased competition for workers and changing minimum wage laws in various jurisdictions are likely to be contributing to the growth in payroll per employee in the restaurant sector.

Trends in Aggregate Labor Productivity and Average Real Annual Payroll per Employee

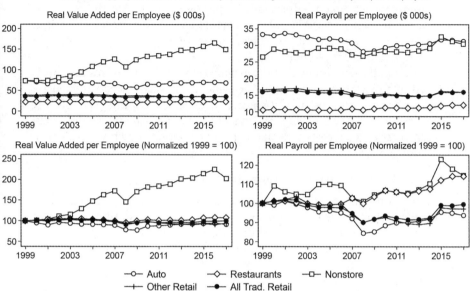

Fig. 6.11   **Real value added and payroll, per employee (labor productivity and average annual payroll per employee)**

Source: Data on sales are from US Census Bureau ARTS, employment and establishments are from the US Census Bureau County Business Patterns data, and value added are from BEA. Traditional retail is NAICS retail (NAICS 44–45)+ restaurants (NAICS 722). Data on value added are from BEA (https://apps.bea.gov/iTable/index_industry_gdpIndy.cfm), sales are from US Census Bureau ARTS, and other data are from US Census Bureau County Business Patterns.

Note: Auto refers to Motor Vehicles and Parts Dealers (NAICS 441), Nonstore refers to NAICS 454, and Restaurants refers to Food Services and Drinking Places (NAICS 722). Other Retail is total traditional retail (NAICS 44–45) less Auto and Nonstore.

Figure 6.11 (top panels) shows that real value added per worker, and real payroll per employee, are lower for restaurants than for other retail. This point provides a note of caution in interpreting some of the aggregate trends noted above. In particular, while the growth of restaurants has offset the decline in employment in the rest of the physical retail sector, figure 6.11 highlights the fact that the payroll per employee as well as contribution to GDP per employee (value added) in this sector are significantly lower than for other sectors. That is, we must be cautious when comparing employment numbers in restaurants to those in other physical retail sectors, because the range of payroll of around 10,000 to 12,000 per year per employee for restaurants is consistent with much of this work being part time, more so than what occurs in other retail sectors, even though some of them may also have part-time workers.

In terms of productivity and compensation, however, the main point with regard to restaurants is that while sales per establishment, and real sales per employee, have gone up dramatically (per figure 6.10) over the period of interest, in reality, real value added per employee has not. At the same time, real payroll per employee has inched up (figure 6.10, and figure 6.11, right top and especially right bottom panels).

Overall, the data imply that the explanation for the rise of restaurants is unlikely to be a supply side one. The evidence suggests instead an increase in average restaurant size, and relative wage growth appears to be steeper for restaurants (see bottom right panel of figure 6.11) than for other retail segments. This suggests a demand side explanation, which we explore in section 6.5.2.

6.5.2   The Demand for Food away from Home

As our results above suggest that no good supply side explanation exists for the growth in the number of restaurants, in this subsection, we turn to an examination of potential demand side explanations. A study projecting demand for restaurant food (Stewart et al. 2004) noted that increases in household income typically increase demand for restaurant food. In addition, increases in the proportion of single-person and no-children-multiple-adult households were also expected by the study authors to increase restaurant demand.

We use BEA data on personal expenditures to derive estimates of expenditures on food. Specifically, the BEA reports spending on Food and Accommodations (consistent with NAICS code 72) in a "Personal Consumption Expenditures by Major Type of Product" table. Comparing the dollar expenditure numbers in the BEA data to sales data for NAICS 72 according to the ARTS data, we find that the ratio of aggregate expenditure to sales in this sector remains within a tight range, between 92 percent and 98 percent, for 1999–2017. Assuming that the same personal expenditure (per the BEA) to sale (per ARTS) ratio holds for subcategories in Food and Accommodations, we use the available sales for restaurants to arrive at an estimated personal expenditure on restaurant food (by multiplying restaurant sales by the expenditure-to-sales ratio for the "Food and Accommodation" aggregate sector).[32] The BEA table also separately reports "Food and beverages purchased for off-premises consumption" as a subgroup within nondurable goods, which we take as a measure of expenditures on "food at home."

In figure 6.12a, we present the resulting trends in the share of expenditures on "food at home" vs. the share of (imputed) restaurant expenditures. We find that, consistent with a shift in consumer preferences toward restaurant food, there has been a decline in the share of total expenditures on nonres-

---

32. That is, we estimate personal expenditures on restaurant food $E_r \equiv S_R \times (E_{FA}/S_{FA})$, where S_R is total yearly sales in NAICS 722; S_{FA} is yearly data on sales for Food and Accommodations (NAICS 72), which are available from ARTS; and E_{FA} is yearly expenditure on Food and Accommodations (available in the BEA table).

Fig. 6.12a   Relative increase in restaurant expenditure share
Source: Data from BEA (https://www.bea.gov/data/consumers-spending/main), restaurant expenditure was imputed using the share of restaurant sales in Food & Accommodation per US Census Bureau's ARTS data.

taurant food from 8.2 percent to 7.2 percent (right axis), with an almost exactly offsetting increase in the share of restaurant food, from 4.2 percent to 5 percent (left axis).

We then undertake a simple quantification exercise to understand the role of this increase in share of expenditure on restaurant food in potentially explaining the observed increase in number of restaurants and employment in restaurants. To do this, we obtain a counterfactual number of restaurants in the absence of expenditure share growth by using the following simple relationship:

Projected number of restaurants in year t

  = *share of restaurants in total personal expenditure in 1999*

  × *observed total personal expenditure in year t*

  × *observed sales to expenditure ratio for restaurants in year t / observed*

    sales per restaurant in year t

We project the counterfactual employment using a similar formula. Figure 6.12b shows the actual and predicted (counterfactual) trends in number of establishments in the left panel, and in employment in the right panel. The left panel shows that without the expenditure shift, the aggregate number of restaurants would have reached only 550,000 instead of the observed 650,000 in 2017 (using the observed sales per establishment each year, which itself grew during this period). Thus, of the roughly 150,000 increase in

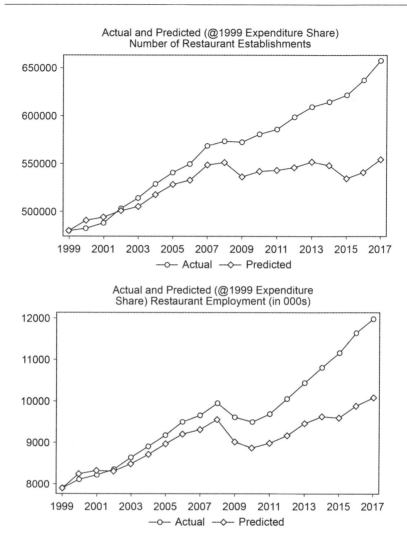

Fig. 6.12b   A simple estimate of the role of expenditure shift in the growth of restaurants

Note: Increase in expenditure share explains about 50 percent of the increase in employment and two-thirds of increase in number of restaurant establishments. Predicted number is based on holding the expenditure share of restaurants constant at the 1999 level, and adjusting by actual restaurant sales per establishment, or per employee.

establishments between 1999 and 2017, about 100,000 (or two-thirds) could be attributed to the increase in share of restaurant expenditures. Similar calculations for restaurant employment suggest that about 2 million of the observed 4 million increase in restaurant employment (from 8 million in 1999 to 12 million in 2017) can be attributed to this shift in expenditures.

Albeit highly simplistic, these estimates suggest an important role for a shift away from expenditures on food at home toward more food consumed away from home to explain the rise in the number of, and employment levels in, restaurants during the period of our study.

6.5.3   What Types of Restaurants Grew and Where?

In this section, we take a closer look at the growth in the number of restaurants. In particular, we address two questions: (i) Is the restaurant sector growing by adding high-quality restaurants, as suggested by our earlier analyses showing both increasing establishment size and employee productivity; and (ii) is the growth focused on particular types of customers (i.e., growth in full service vs. limited service restaurants, which might indicate a focus on high or low income customers, or in counties with high or low income levels).

Restaurant quality. Figure 6.10 presented trends for establishments and sales and payroll per worker. The fact that all these have grown over the period of our study suggests an overall increase in the quality of establishments and of jobs at these establishments. We explore this further in figure 6.13, where we use data from Yelp to calculate an inverse Herfindhal-Hirshman Index (HHI) measure of restaurant variety, as well as the fraction of restaurants with a rating at or above four stars. The Yelp public use data covering only a small number of US Metropolitan Statistical Areas (MSAs), which limits the generalizability of our results. Nonetheless, we combine the data from the different US MSAs into a single aggregate time series for both the inverse HHI and ratings data over time. The resulting time series data suggest that consumers today have access to a greater variety of types of restaurants, and a greater fraction of highly rated restaurants, even relative to 2010.[33]

Rich vs. poor counties, and limited vs. full service. In figure 6.14, analogous to figure 6.9, we present a semi-parametric analysis to show how the two different categories of restaurants identified in the Economic Census (namely, limited service restaurants and full service restaurants) have grown and how this might differ in rich vs. poor counties. Limited service restaurants are those where patrons normally order their food at a counter rather than

33. In addition to the limitation that the Yelp data reflect only the years 2010 to 2018, and only a few MSAs with significant coverage (more than 5,000 restaurant-year observations in the full panel) of just six states (Arizona, North Carolina, Nevada, Ohio, Pennsylvania, and Wisconsin), with some limited coverage of two others (Illinois [2,861 observations] and South Carolina [1,535 observations]), we also note that the definition of restaurant varieties is not systematic. We define varieties by looking for keywords in the "categories" description string variable for nationalities (e.g., Indian, Chinese, Afghan) or regions (e.g., Arabic, Asian, Mediterranean), as well as food types (e.g., deli, diner, halal, sandwich). The full list of restaurant types we use is provided in appendix table 6.A.2.

A. National index of variety: Inverse of HHI of restaurant types

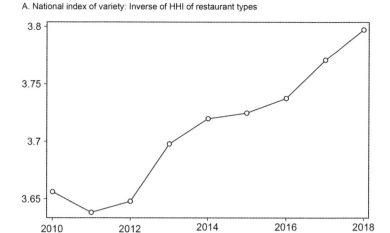

B. Fraction of restaurants rated 4 stars or above by reviewers

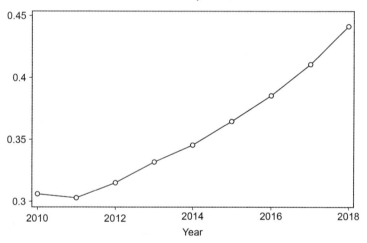

Fig. 6.13   Indicators of variety and quality of restaurants: Yelp restaurant data
Source: Yelp public dataset, https://www.yelp.com/dataset.

interacting with a server at their table; this category is often equated with fast food, although it also includes much more than the typical burger restaurant that this nomenclature conjures up. Full service restaurant refers to establishments where patrons are seated and order their food and are served while seated at their table. The figure shows strong positive growth across the full range of county income levels for both types of restaurants. In other words, both full service and limited service restaurants have grown in number across poor and rich counties. Bars (a small third category in the

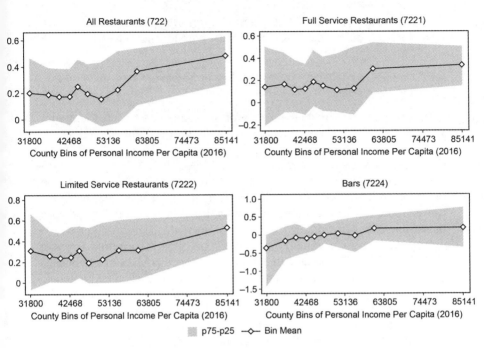

Fig. 6.14   Did restaurants grow in rich counties only? Restaurant categories employment growth (1999–2016): Correlations with county (2016) per capita income
Note: Growth = (Y2016−Y1999)/Y1999. County bins are 2016 population-weighted, that is, each marker represents population of ~32 million; *x*-axis represents (population-weighted means).

Food Services sector) have achieved slower growth generally (see appendix figure 6.A.8a), especially in poorer counties (appendix figure 6.A.8b).

Role of the largest chain restaurants. While many local restaurants are small businesses, there are also dominant firms, such as McDonalds, Starbucks, and Domino's, that have a very large presence in the sector and have grown considerably over the past couple of decades. Thus, an interesting question is whether the major restaurant chains have played an outsized role in the rise of restaurants overall. That is, could it be that the increase in establishments and sales is driven mostly by the expansion of the major chains? Comprehensive data on all restaurant chains are unavailable, but we have collated data on the number of establishments and sales for our time period for the top 200 (in terms of US sales) restaurant chains in the country. The data show (see appendix figure 6.A.9) that the shares of sales and establishments of the major restaurant chains held steady (or showed a slight increase) from 1999 to about 2009, but then have declined from that time on. We conclude that the rise of restaurants has not been primarily driven by the growth of the largest chains in the US nor accompanied by an increase in revenue or establishment share for these chains.[34]

6.6   Broader Servicification of Retail: Repair Services, Personal Services, and Recreation

In this section, we broaden the scope of our analyses to include some retail service categories that were not included under the definition of retail sector under the old SIC classification, and also are not included under the NAICS codes, but they are delivered to consumers in brick-and-mortar establishments that are often co-located with traditional physical retail stores. The inclusion of these additional service and recreation categories may help capture a broader shift of retail locations away from sales of goods toward sales of services or experiences.[35]

In particular, we examine three NAICS categories: (i) Repair Services (NAICS 811), (ii) Personal and Laundry Services (NAICS 812), and (iii) Amusement, Gambling, and Recreation Industries (NAICS 713). Repair services include auto repair and household goods (including cellphone) repair establishments that also provide retail services to consumers and are often co-located with traditional retail stores in malls and downtown locations. Personal and Laundry Services include some retail-located service providers, such as dry cleaners, beauty and nail salons, and barber shops. Finally, while amusement parks are typically not co-located with traditional retail, anecdotal evidence suggests that major retail malls increasingly are adding entertainment facilities, and historically, malls have included such options as carousels and videogame parlors, which fall under NAICS 713.[36] Further, gyms and fitness centers, which are common in retail locations, fall under this broader subsector as well.

We begin by defining a new aggregate (augmented) retail as traditional physical retail, per our earlier definition, plus these three sectors. In figure 6.15, we present the trends in shares of aggregate augmented retail

34. The data are from *Nation's Restaurant News*, "Top 200 Restaurants," various years. Note that the set of chains included in the top 200 ranking is not constant over time, as some chains shrink over time and thereby exit the ranking, while others grow to make the list.

35. We thank our discussant, Emek Basker, for raising this important point and presenting evidence that some subsegments, including nail salons and fitness centers, also have experienced considerable growth over our time period. We build on her comment by looking at broader industry definitions that include nail salons (Personal and Laundry Services, NAICS 812), and fitness centers (Amusement Parks, Gaming and Recreation, NAICS 713), and also examining repair services (NAICS 811).

36. For example, a story in the *New York Times* (Corkery and Maheshwari 2019) discussed the case of a megamall development called "American Dream," which planned to open in late October 2019 with an ice-skating rink and a Nickelodeon amusement park, with plans (at the time) to add 300 stores in March 2020. The development was delayed, and in the meantime, some original tenants (including Toys'R'Us and Barneys) went bankrupt. More examples of entertainment and recreation options at malls are discussed in a *Chicago Tribune* article by Zumbach (2016).

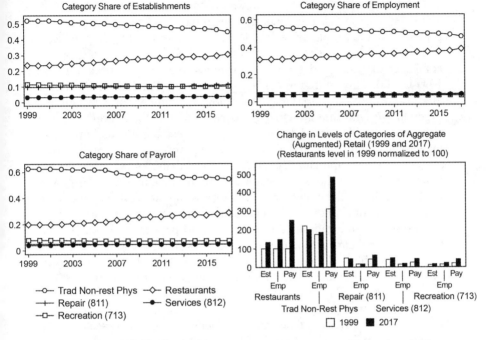

Fig. 6.15   Growth in Repair Services (811), Personal and Laundry Services (812) and Recreation (713)

Source: CBP, US Census Bureau.

Note: Aggregate (Augmented) Retail is Traditional Physical Retail + Repair (811) + Services (812) + Recreation (713).

for each of these three categories plus restaurants and traditional (non-restaurant) physical retail, separately for establishments (top left panel), employment (top right panel), and payroll (bottom left panel). All these figures confirm that, in terms of their contributions to the augmented retail sector, the shares of the three new sectors we include have not changed much at all during 1999–2017. In terms of establishments, the shares are roughly equal for repair (811) and services (812) and lower for recreation (713), but in terms of employment share, all three sectors are very similar. Moreover, their shares have remained relatively flat over time. In terms of payroll, the repair services sector has a persistently greater share relative to the other sectors, while recreation appears to have a very slight uptick in share relative to services. However, the figures confirm the narrative we discussed in the previous sections: whether one measures establishments, employment, or payroll, the dominant change in the past two decades, even when examining an "augmented" retail sector that includes these additional service and recreation categories, is that of a decline in the share of traditional non-restaurant physical retail sector, offset by a rise in the share of restaurants.

The patterns we see in shares, however, do not tell us about changes in levels. This is addressed in the bottom right panel in figure 6.15, where we present a summary picture of the levels of establishments, employment, and payroll in each of the subcategories, in 1999 and 2017. To allow for comparability and readability, we normalize the level for restaurants in 1999 to 100. This figure implies that between 1999 and 2017: (1) Across all three indicators (establishments, employment, and payroll), restaurants experienced significant growth; (2) the traditional non-restaurant physical sector experienced a small decline in number of establishments, but a small increase in employment and a large increase in total payroll; (3) the repair services, personal and laundry services, and recreation services sectors are much smaller than the restaurant sector on all three indicators; (4) given their small initial sizes, these three sectors saw only modest changes in the levels for our three indicators, much smaller than the changes we find for the restaurant and traditional (non-restaurant) physical retail sector; and (5) total payroll increased in the repair, services, and recreation sectors, but consistent with the share trends in the bottom left panel, this increase was not larger than the increase we see for restaurants or for the traditional (non-restaurant) physical retail sector.

Finally, for each of the three additional sectors, in appendix figure 6.A.10, we refine our analyses by focusing on the most important subsector in the sector. For repair services (panel of four sub-figures at top left), the auto repair segment is the dominant one. We find that this subsector has not grown in number of establishments or employment, but we see an upward trend in (nominal) total payroll. Overall, the auto repair's share of establishments and employment in total augmented retail has declined over our study period. For personal and laundry services, we examine personal services (NAICS 8121, which includes beauty and nail salons) vs. the rest (panel of four sub-figures at top right). We find that the personal services sector has grown considerably in terms of number of establishments and employment relative to the rest of the sector. Despite this strong growth, total payroll in this subsector has not grown that much more rapidly than in the rest of the sector, suggesting that the jobs in this subsector are not particularly well paid. The share of establishments providing personal services in the augmented retail sector increased by more than a percentage point (from about 4.7 to 6.1 percent), but the increase is much lower for employment and payroll. Finally, for the recreation sector, we examine fitness centers separately from the rest (panel of four sub-figures at bottom left); here also, we find that fitness centers have grown in number of establishments and employment at a more rapid pace than the rest of the sector. But again, the trend for overall payroll is flatter than the trend for establishments, suggesting that the work is not highly compensated in that subsector either. The share of fitness centers in the aggregate (augmented) retail went up on all three indicators, albeit less than a percentage point for number of establishments and payroll, and about 1 percentage point (from about 1.4 percent to 2.4 percent) for employment.

6.7 Pre-COVID-19 Trends in Venture Financing of Retail and Retail Firm Strategies

In this section, we draw on pre-COVID media news stories, company annual reports, and data from Crunchbase (as of December 30, 2019) to discuss some trends that already were emerging in the retail sector before the COVID-19 pandemic, and that, because they are technology enabled, might prove to be particularly important in the industry at this time and going forward. In particular, as noted earlier, new firms are offering services or technology that complement traditional physical retail. Our (admittedly rough) manual classification of the top 24 best-funded retail-related start-ups (in appendix table 6.A.3) shows that 55 percent of the funding went to companies that provide complementary services. Specifically, DoorDash with about $2.1 billion, and Instacart with about $1.8 billion in funding by end of December 2019, are delivery services companies that help physical retail firms provide home delivery for customers.

- *Omnichannel strategy—physical retailers offering online shopping, and the blurring of boundaries.* Physical retail firms are investing in their online presence and realigning their supply chain and distribution to serve customers through a blend of (a) online ordering, packaging at warehouses, and delivery to customer homes from warehouses; (b) online ordering, collation of order in physical store, and delivery to customer homes; and (c) online ordering and curbside pickup. Walmart has been an aggressive proponent of this "omnichannel" strategy, with plans "to have grocery pickup available at 3,100 stores and same-day delivery from 1,600 stores, covering about 80 percent and 50 percent of the US population, respectively" by the end of 2019 (Redman 2019). A prominent investment for Store 8, Walmart's incubation arm, is Walmart InHome Delivery, which aims to deliver groceries not just to the customer's door, but also to stock them in the home refrigerator. Arguably, Amazon's acquisition of Whole Foods (in 2017), and the Prime Now service (launched in June 2018), which offers same-day delivery in select locations from Whole Foods stores, is an example of the reverse trend (namely, online retailers embracing an omnichannel strategy as well). News reports (e.g., Weise 2019) suggest that Amazon is contemplating a new chain that "would be built for in-store shopping as well as pickup and delivery."
- *Independent on-demand delivery firms teaming up with physical retailers.* Related to the above, some new independent delivery firms are team-

ing up with physical retailers. For example, emerging grocery delivery firms, including Instacart, Shipt, and Burpy, offer on-demand delivery services from local stores, with online ordering and "personal shoppers" picking and putting together the order and delivering it to customer homes. These services could enable physical retailers to provide the comfort and convenience offered by online retailers. DoorDash (the top of our retail startup list in appendix table 6.A.3) and other startups (e.g., GrubHub) provide home delivery services for customers to buy from a range of local restaurants.[37]

- *Traditional retailers investing in curbside pickup and BOPIS (buy online pickup in store or "click and collect")*. Some media stories suggest investments by grocery stores, general merchandise stores, and other retailers in allowing shoppers to buy online and pick up curbside or in store (termed "BOPIS"). An infographic report on invesp.com cites studies showing that 67 percent of shoppers in the US have used BOPIS, and that 49 percent of shoppers using BOPIS report making additional purchases while picking up items in store. The report also mentions that 90 percent of retailers plan to implement BOPIS by 2021.[38] One of Walmart's investment, JetBlack, is a startup aimed at personalized shopping for time-constrained parents in Manhattan.

- *Autonomous vehicles/drone-based delivery*. Amazon, Domino's, and others have announced plans to experiment with delivery using drones. Amazon's Prime Air page highlights the fully autonomous (no human pilot) delivery made on December 7, 2016. UPS was recently awarded certification to use drones on medical campuses,[39] but UPS indicated that the possibility of use in urban areas was uncertain. News reports suggest delivery startups, such as Postmates, are experimenting with delivery robots as well.[40] Per our search of Crunchbase data, there are few startups focused specifically on drone or autonomous vehicles delivery for retail; with Nuro developing autonomous vehicles (total funding of $1 billion, and recent test-drive partnership with Walmart),[41] Starship Technologies developing drones (funding of $82.2 million),

37. One emerging measurement issue is the rise of "virtual restaurants," which are nonstore restaurants (including some operated from home kitchens, or operated under another name from a given physical restaurant) that serve as "online ordering and home delivery only" entities (Isaac and Yaffe-Bellany, 2019). These firms may be difficult to identify, in standard firm datasets such as the CBP. For instance, the *New York Times* news story reports a restaurateur with four operations, only one of which is physical, and the other "three are "virtual restaurants" with no physical storefronts, tables or chairs . . . [that] exist only inside a mobile app, Uber Eats" (https://www.nytimes.com/2019/08/14/technology/uber-eats-ghost-kitchens.html).

38. https://www.invespcro.com/blog/buy-online-pick-up-in-store-bopis/.

39. https://www.nytimes.com/2019/10/02/us/UPS-drone-deliveries.html.

40. https://www.forbes.com/sites/amyfeldman/2019/08/20/starship-technologies-raises -40m-to-expand-its-food-delivery-robots-on-college-campuses/#68b4487b1cec.

41. https://corporate.walmart.com/newsroom/2019/12/10/walmart-to-test-drive -autonomous-grocery-deliveries-with-nuro.

and Marble focused on land-based courier robots (funding $10 million) being the most prominent. However, autonomous vehicle (AV) development has seen significant investment by other large companies, including Alphabet, Uber, and Tesla, as well as mainstream car manufacturers (Ford, GM). If these vehicles reach so-called full automation "Level 5" capability, it would be an important labor-saving technology with major implications for the structure of retail markets. However, this capability seems many years away (see, e.g., Noonan 2019).

- *Artificial intelligence (AI) investments to improve stocking, inventory management, and customer services.* Some traditional retail companies report making investments in AI technologies to reduce costs throughout the supply chain, as well as to respond to and answer customer questions. Examples of such investments by physical retailers include the Intelligent Retail Lab by Walmart's Store 8, Domino's investments in AI-enabled automated phone ordering,[42] Macy's On Call app for in-store assistance, Uniqlo's in-store Kiosks to recommend products, the experimental Sam's Club Now store that allows customers to map the most efficient route through the store and leave without going through the traditional checkout line, the Kroger App (which makes in-store recommendations), and Starbucks' AI-enabled voice ordering.[43] AI technologies are also used by online retailers (e.g., Amazon for product recommendations), so it is unclear whether AI would systematically benefit physical retailers more than e-commerce retailers, but these investments may be needed to keep physical stores in a strong competitive position relative to e-commerce retailers.
- *Technological innovations in the restaurant sector.* Pre-COVID, restaurant operators also were looking for technological solutions to address some known pain points. Examples from the casual dining segment include the use of tablets in restaurants, which facilitate interactions with servers (i.e., flagging to get a drink refill or the bill), apps to allow diners to check table times and put their names on wait lists remotely, and General Motors' Marketplace, which allows for making reservations, food ordering, and payment while driving.

6.8 Preliminary Assessment of the COVID-19 Crisis: Retail Trade Survey, BLS Current Employment Statistics, and Stock Market Response

While the main focus of this chapter is on assessing changes in the retail sector for 1999–2017, for which key data sources were available, the ongoing COVID-19 crisis is clearly an extremely consequential event, with potential

---

42. https://www.mobilemarketer.com/news/dominos-lets-ai-assistant-dom-handle-incoming-phone-orders/522111/.
43. https://www.forbes.com/sites/blakemorgan/2019/03/04/the-20-best-examples-of-using-artificial-intelligence-for-retail-experiences/#6ea201574466.

profound implications for the economy in general and for several subsectors in retail in particular. The retail sector has been particularly heavily impacted as demand for all activities outside the home has constricted, with very severe effects for restaurants as well as nonessential shopping at brick-and-mortar stores. Anecdotal evidence from media reports suggests increased demand, and hence increased employment, for grocery stores and large general merchandise retailers (such as Walmart and Costco), as well as increased hiring by Amazon and other online retailers as consumers shift toward online shopping, and cooking and eating at home.

In this section, we attempt to provide a more systematic picture of the effect of COVID-19 on the retail sector by examining three sources of data that include some information on recent trends in retail: (i) recently released US Census data from the Monthly Advance Retail Trade Survey (MARTS), with sales data up to December 2020; (ii) BLS monthly Current Employment (CE) statistics, the latest of which (released January 8, 2020) includes data up to December 2020; and (iii) the stock market performance of retail firm stocks, which provides the market's view of the long-term prospects for the large public retail firms.

6.8.1   Retail Sales Response (From US Census MARTS Data)

We present data from MARTS in appendix figure 6.A.11. This figure shows the percentage change in cumulative year-to-date (YTD) sales compared to the same point a year earlier, for April (to capture short-run effects after the start of the pandemic) and for December 2020 (to capture longer-term changes), with sectors sorted from most negative to positive changes for December 2020.

The largest declines in YTD sales as of December 2020 are for the clothing and restaurants sectors, followed by gas stations; electronics stores; and to a much smaller extent; furniture stores. Subsectors that include grocery sellers (Food and Beverages (NAICS 445) as well as General Merchandise Stores (452)) saw some increase relative to the previous year, reflecting the shift in expenditure away from restaurants. But the biggest gains were for online retailers (included in NAICS 454), consistent with widespread media reports of expansion and hiring by Amazon. Building materials saw an increase as well, consistent with media reports of a boom in DIY and home improvement projects by homebound consumers, and increased online sales by major companies (like Home Depot and Lowe's).[44] Finally, the sporting goods category shows an exceptional pattern, in that sales swung from a steep decline relative to prior year in April to growth relative to the prior year by the end of the year, with anecdotes suggesting increased consumer

---

44. E.g., see https://www.cnbc.com/2020/11/20/home-depot-and-lowes-earnings-boosted -by-pandemic-induced-nesting.html.

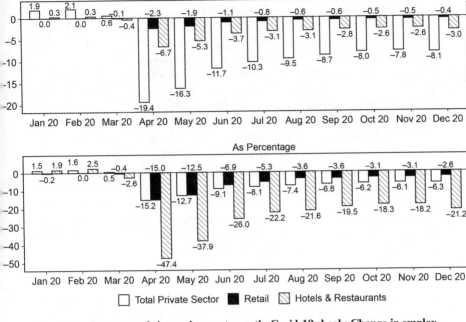

Fig. 6.16   Recent trends in employment growth. Covid-19 shock: Change in employment (relative to prior year-month)

Note: Data are from BLS Employment Statistics reports. Data for November and December 2020 are provisional.

expenditure on at-home fitness equipment and e-commerce sales by sporting goods retailers making up for reduced in-person shopping.[45]

6.8.2   Retail Employment Response in March and April 2020 (from BLS Data)

Figure 6.16 provides a summary of the effect of the pandemic on employment levels, using data from the BLS monthly Current Employment statistics. It illustrates the decline in employment (relative to the same month in 2019) for the private sector overall, for retail (per NAICS, i.e., excluding restaurants and hotels), and for hotels and restaurants (NAICS 722). The data show a significant rebound in the labor market from an overall employment loss of 19.4 million (in April 2020 compared to April 2019) to a much smaller, but still very substantial, deficit of 8.1 million jobs in December. The recovery was almost complete for the NAICS retail sector, as the deficit

45. E.g., see https://www.wsj.com/articles/dicks-sporting-goods-profit-and-e-commerce -sales-surge-11598441526.

is only 0.4 million (2.6 percent) by December. However, the restaurants and hotels sector experienced a much smaller recovery, going from a deficit of 6.7 million jobs in April to 3 million in December. The bottom panel of figure 6.16, which presents the decline in employment in percentage terms, shows that by December 2020, employment in the Hotels and Restaurant sector was still 21.2 percent below the December 2019 levels. Moreover, the figure shows that this sector experienced a further deterioration in employment in December relative to November 2020 (from 2.6 to 3.0 million), contributing to an increase in the job deficit for the private sector of the economy as a whole (which went up from 7.8 to 8.1 million in the same months).

Appendix figure 6.A.12 further illustrates the important reduction in employment in the Hotels and Restaurants sector compared to other segments of the economy, showing that it accounted for 36.7 percent of the overall decline in private sector employment between February and December of 2020, despite accounting for just 11.1 percent of private sector employment at the start of the pandemic, in February 2020. This figure also shows that the overall traditional retail sector, which includes online retail, was impacted to a much smaller degree by the pandemic relative to its share of employment.

To capture the severity of the recent decline, we present the long-run trends in retail employment in appendix figure 6.A.13 using monthly BLS data. Figure 6.A.13a illustrates well the historic nature of the COVID-19 shock, as the declines in March and April have led to employment levels for physical retail below the 1999 figures, though the subsequent rebound has lifted indexes back above the 1999 levels. Similar results are seen in figure 6.A.13b: for restaurants, the trend in terms of share of aggregate private sector employment plunged soon after the onset of the pandemic, reversing the gains accrued over a two-decade span. Again the rebound has lifted the share of employment in restaurants back above the levels from two decades ago. However, the recovery appears fragile over the last few months of data.

6.8.3   Stock Market Response

Finally, we present results from stock market data. Compared to data on past sales or employment trends, stock prices have the distinction of reflecting investor expectations about future prospects. However, there continues to be significant uncertainty about the pace of roll out of vaccines and other factors impacting the economy, reflected in higher market volatility (relative to prior years). Thus, the results here should be viewed with caution, representing an initial and noisy indicator of market expectations regarding the prospects of listed firms.

In appendix figure 6.A.14, we present trends in the stock index for different retail categories over the 1 year period from January 9, 2020, to January 8, 2021. The S&P 500 data is presented first as a benchmark, and the retail categories are shown in order of smallest to largest increase over this period. We find the smallest increases are for drugstores, clothing (consistent with decline in expenditure in figure 6.A.11), grocery, and general and department stores. It is somewhat surprising that grocery stores don't show a big increase, despite the much-reported shift to eating at home, possibly because additional expenditure may have gone to clubs and supercenters, which show a strong increase, and meal delivery from restaurants or online vendors. Restaurant chain stock prices have rebounded after a steep short-run decline in the early days of the pandemic, a rebound that has occurred despite evidence presented above of a steep decline in sales and employment in that sector over the past several months. This market swing for restaurants combined with the flattening of stock prices for grocery stores is consistent with market expectations for a shift back of consumer expenditure toward restaurants after the pandemic. Unsurprisingly, the online retail category (which has Amazon as a prominent member) has climbed after the onset of COVID—the maintenance of high stock price levels for the subsector is consistent with the market expecting that behavioral shifts to online retailing induced by the pandemic may be persistent. Interestingly, home furnishings, sporting goods stores (likely related to the rebound in expenditure seen in figure 6.A.11), and specialty retail have also outperformed the market.

Overall, all three data sources (MARTS sales, BLS employment, and stock market data) suggest a short and possibly longer run shift in retail purchasing behavior toward online, as well as a shift away from restaurants toward eating at home (at least during the pandemic). As noted earlier, the unprecedented nature of the pandemic, and uncertainty about the pace of vaccine rollout and recovery, make it difficult to assess the long-term effects of this crisis. Nevertheless, we offer a couple of speculative predictions.

First, as noted in the media, during this crisis, many more consumers have become familiar with online ordering and the convenience of using home delivery services. As the pandemic period stretches out, some of this behavior could become more ingrained, which could portend a longer-term shift that accelerates the growth of e-commerce as well as newer delivery services discussed in section 6.7.

For restaurants, depressed demand—and limited capacity to serve what were once full rooms of customers—will continue so long as social distancing guidelines remain in place, and/or customers continue to feel unsafe in crowded locales (full service restaurants) or in long lines in front of cash registers (limited service restaurants). Unfortunately, unlike for durable goods retailers, there is little prospect of a rebound in demand that would make up for lost sales in these types of businesses, so that many restaurants may be forced to exit (as suggested by initial survey studies).[46] As important as many

---

46. E.g., https://www.grubstreet.com/2020/09/restaurant-closing-national-restaurant
-association-survey.html.

of these businesses have been for their local communities, except for the traditional take-out or delivery model, it is not clear what other type of services might allow especially small local restaurant businesses to survive the likely protracted reduction in revenues that they are suffering through today and will continue to face in the near and perhaps even medium term. Because of the changing composition of economic activity toward more restaurants documented in this chapter, the economic consequences of the pandemic for retail, including restaurants, are perhaps of even greater concern today than they would have been otherwise. Restoring the vibrancy of the local retail landscape may require government assistance for new entrants, in addition to the ongoing Paycheck Protection Program that aims to sustain existing small and medium businesses.

6.9   Conclusion

In this chapter, we have discussed how the evidence about the so-called "retail apocalypse" is much less clear, and is in fact contradicted, if we examine sales or employment rather than the number of establishments or storefronts in retail. This is because sales and employment had bounced back to their pre–Great Recession levels by the end of 2017, while the number of establishments indeed is still lower today than it was before the Great Recession.[47] We noted that the changing face of retail in the US is mostly due to innovations that have arisen in other sectors of the economy, namely, in the logistics, warehousing, and transportation sectors, where cost-saving innovations and the capacity to track goods as they go from manufacturers to consumers have enabled the growth of large chains of general merchandise stores, such as Walmart and Target. And of course, the advent and growth of the Internet, along with these same innovations in warehousing and logistics, have had a large—and we expect will continue to have a large—effect on many segments of the physical goods retail sector. We also discussed briefly, in section 6.7, some innovations that brick-and-mortar stores are exploring, and even already exploiting, to address the needs of consumers.

Most important from our perspective, we documented throughout much of this chapter the remarkable growth in the restaurant sector during 1999–2017, and how, using what was the Standard Industrial Classification (SIC) version of the retail sector (which included restaurants), we found overall

47. Since our first presentation of these findings at the July 22–23, 2019, pre-conference for this volume, articles in the media have noted the strength of retail in government data. In particular, Woods (2019) notes the growing trends for the number of establishments in BLS data, and that the highly publicized closings of 40 chains (with Gymboree and Payless Shoes being the largest) accounted for only about 0.008 percent of all retail establishments. She also notes that the top 40 chain openings in the same period offset more than half of these closures, and she highlights the growth of restaurants, particularly relative to grocery stores.

growth in retail over the period of our study. We also showed that the number of restaurants grew in both lower and higher income counties and across types of restaurants (full vs. limited service, variety of food). The picture is less rosy for the retail sector in terms of its relative share of the economy. While the restaurant sector's share of the overall economy showed strong growth on all the indicators we examined (including establishment counts, employment, payroll, and value added), we found that, even inclusive of restaurants, the physical retail sector had shrunk between 1999 and 2017 relative to the overall economy (except in terms of employment), with about 16 percent decline in its share of aggregate GDP (value added), and about 7 percent decline in its shares of establishments and payroll.[48]

While the growth of restaurants has offset the decline in employment in the rest of the physical goods retail sector, figure 6.11 highlights that the payroll per employee as well as contribution to GDP per employee in the restaurant sector is significantly lower than for other sectors. The range of $10,000 to $12,000 per year for payroll per employee for restaurants also is consistent with much of this work being part time, more so than in other goods retailing sectors (which themselves tend to have part-time workers). However, there are signs that both worker productivity and pay had increased in the restaurant industry (figure 6.11).

We examined personal service categories that are often found in malls and other retail locations, and documented strong growth in those and in fitness clubs; but the broader service and entertainment/recreation categories are a small proportion of traditional retail, and this share has remained stable during 1999–2017. Thus, the shift toward more servicification and entertainment (per anecdotal evidence discussed in section 6.6) has not yet had a major impact on the aggregate retail landscape.

We find some evidence suggesting that the growth in the number and sales and employment in the restaurant sector was related to changing consumer tastes, from less food consumed at home to more food consumed away from home. Exploring the underlying factors that could explain this shift is beyond the scope of this chapter, but many articles in the trade press point to demographic changes along with increased desire for "experiences" outside the home along with less focus on purchasing durable goods among younger consumers as potential factors explaining the increased tendency to consume food outside the home. Moreover, we note that technology is increasingly being used in this sector as well, to relieve some of the pain points for consumers and increase efficiency as well. This, in turn, may lead to yet greater growth in this sector, as well as increases in productivity and

48. Over the 1999 to 2017 period, finance, professional services, and education and health care registered the biggest gains in share of GDP, while manufacturing and retail had the largest loss of share (appendix figure 6.A.4).

employee compensation. We leave further exploration of these issues and other potential explanations for the evolution of the retail sector broadly defined as avenues for future research.

As a postscript, the ongoing economic shock from the COVID-19 pandemic has severely negatively impacted the prospects of many brick-and-mortar retail firms. A full analysis of this shock as of this writing is limited by the uncertainty and volatility in the market and data about the pandemic and is beyond the scope of this chapter. A preliminary view based on an examination of the performance of retail stocks and of recently released US Census and BLS data suggests significant challenges for restaurants and nonessential goods merchants, while grocery store and online retailers, not surprisingly, appear to be relatively less affected, or have even benefited from the crisis. For restaurants in particular, voluntary or mandated social distancing, which may persist so long as the pandemic continues, will likely lead many customers to avoid even their favorite local eateries. It is our hope that, despite the small margins typical of these types of businesses, the dependence of local economies and communities on restaurants for both amenities and employment will encourage governments and local communities to find ways to support these businesses so they can bounce back on the other side of this crisis.

Appendix

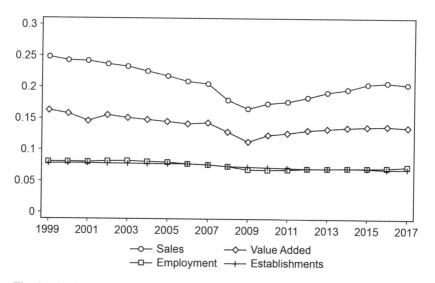

Fig. 6.A.1   Share of motor vehicle dealers in retail activity
Note: Traditional retail is NAICS retail (NAICS 44–45) + restaurants (NAICS 722)

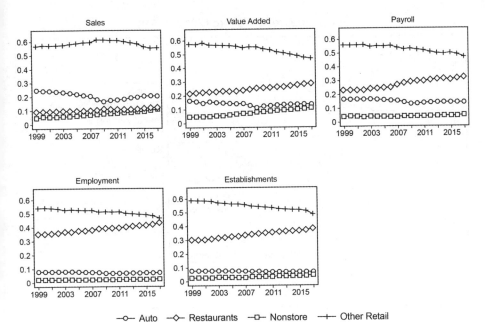

Fig. 6.A.2   Categorywise shares of sales, value added, establishments, and employment

Source: Data on value added are from BEA (https://apps.bea.gov/Table/index_industry _gdplndy.cfm), sales are from US Census Bureau ARTS, and other data are from US Census Bureau County Business Patterns.

Note: Traditional retail is NAICS retail (NAICS 44–45) + restaurants (NAICS 722).

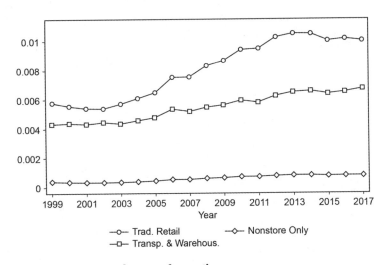

Fig. 6.A.3   Patent count share trends over time

Source: The data are from Goldschlag, Lybbert, and Zolas (2019), who concord UPSPTO patent classification codes to NAICS codes.

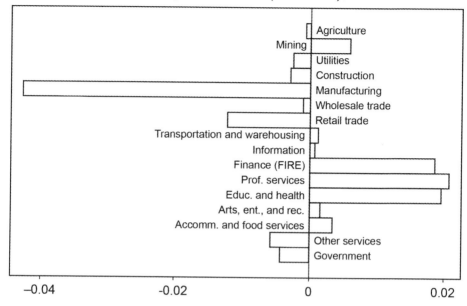

Fig. 6.A.4   **Change in sector share of GDP**

Source: Data are from BEA valued-added by industry statistics (release date October 29, 2019).

A. Components of Non-Store Retailer (454) Sales (in $ mn)

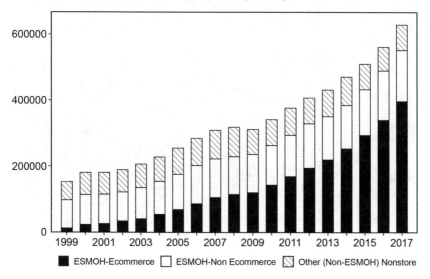

B. Components of Non-Store Retailer (454) as Share of Total Traditional Retail Sales

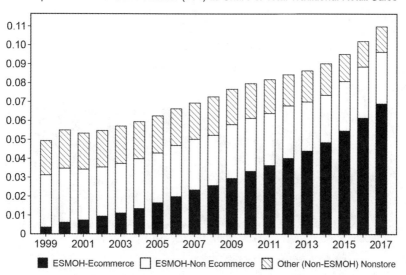

Fig. 6.A.5   Non-store sales—growth driven primarily by e-commerce

Source: ARTS & SAS, US Census Bureau.

Note: Traditional Retail includes all subcategories of NAICS 44, 45 and 722. ESMOH stands for NAICS 4541 (Electronic Shopping and Mail-order Houses). Other non-ESMOH Non-Store retailers (NAICS 454) includes Vending Machine Operators (NAICS 4542) and Direct Selling Establishments (4543). Data are from US Census Bureau's Annual Retail Trade Survey (ARTS) and the Services Annual Survey (SAS) and their antecedents.

A. Components of General Merchandise (452) Sales (in $ mn)

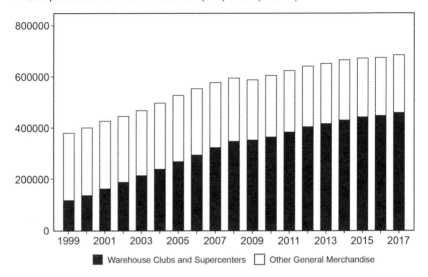

B. Components of General Merchandise (452) as Share of Total Traditional Retail Sales

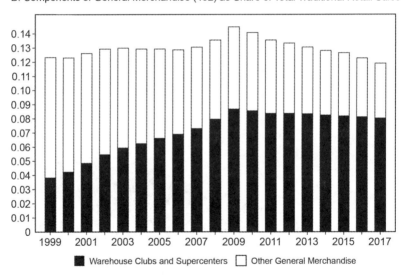

Fig. 6.A.6   Physical general merchandise sales—overall decline since 2009, Big Box share of total retail has flattened

Source: ARTS & SAS, US Census Bureau.

Note: Traditional Retail includes all subcategories of NAICS 44, 45 and 722. General Merchandise refers to NAICS 452, while "Big Box" is the sub-sector NAICS 45291 (Warehouse Clubs and Supercenters). Data are from US Census Bureau's Annual Retail Trade Survey (ARTS) and the Services Annual Survey (SAS) and their antecedents.

A. Restaurant Outcomes per Establishment (Normalized 1999 = 100)

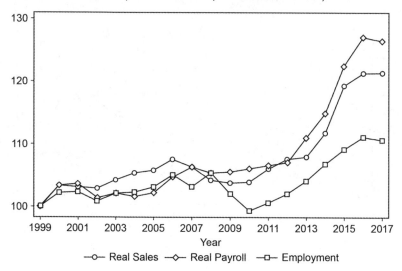

—o— Real Sales —◇— Real Payroll —□— Employment

B. Restaurant Outcomes per Employee & Sales to Payroll (Normalized 1999 = 100)

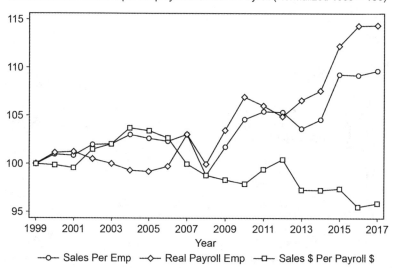

—o— Sales Per Emp —◇— Real Payroll Emp —□— Sales $ Per Payroll $

Fig. 6.A.7 Aggregate restaurant sector productivity—normalized trends
Note: These figures present normalized (1999 = 100) trends; see figure 6.A10 for level trends.

1. Aggregate Employment (Normalized 1999 = 100)

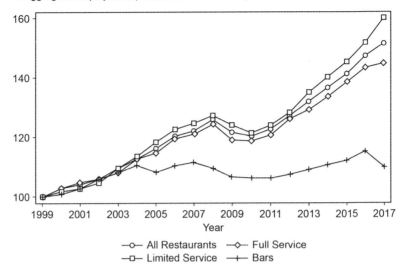

2. Aggregate Number of Establishments (Normalized 1999 = 100)

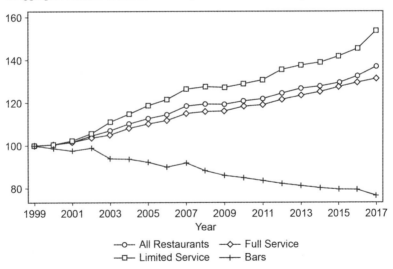

Fig. 6.A.8a   Restaurant category-wise growth

1. Employment Shares of Restaurant Categories
By year and county population-weighted income quintiles

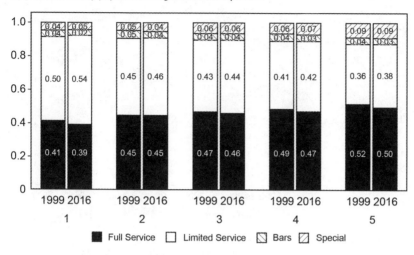

2. Establishment Shares of Restaurant Categories
By year and county population-weighted income quintiles

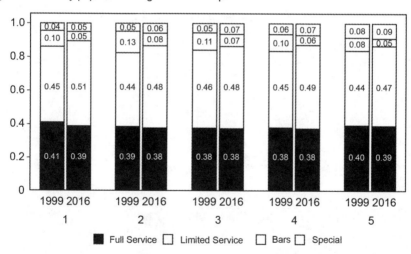

Fig. 6.A.8b   Restaurant category-wise shares by income quintile, 1999 vs 2016
Note: County income quintiles are defined within year

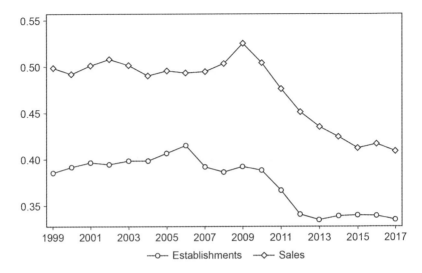

Fig. 6.A.9   Trends in share of the top 200 restaurant chains

Source: Data are from *Nation's Restaurant News*, "Top 200 Restaurants," various years.
Note: The set of chains included in the Top 200 ranking vary over time.

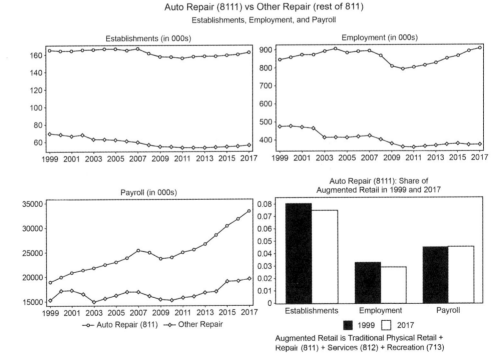

Fig. 6.A.10   Components of Repair (811), Services (812), and Recreation (713)
Source: CBP, US Census Bureau.

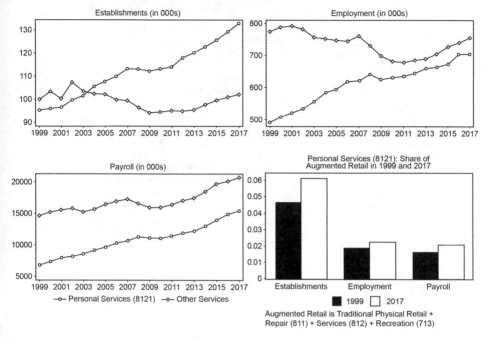

Fig. 6.A.10 (cont.)

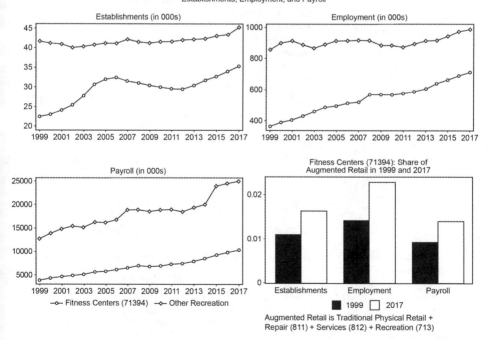

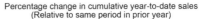

Percentage change in cumulative year-to-date sales
(Relative to same period in prior year)

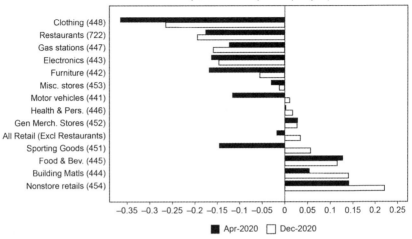

■ Apr-2020   ☐ Dec-2020

Fig. 6.A.11   Covid-19 shock: Change in cumulative year-to-date (YTD) retail sales in April and December 2020

Source: Data are from US Census MARTS dataset, accessed January 15, 2021, from https://www.census.gov/econ/currentdata/.

Note: Figures use unadjusted sales.

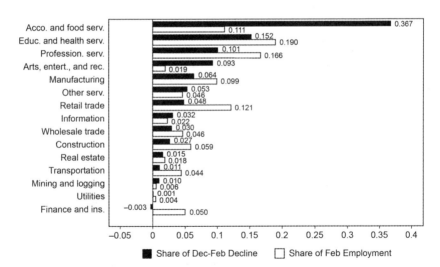

■ Share of Dec-Feb Decline   ☐ Share of Feb Employment

Fig. 6.A.12   Covid-19 Shock: Sector shares of Change in Aggregate Employment in December 2020, compared to February 2020

Source: Data are from BLS Current Employment statistics, https://download.bls.gov/pub/time.series/ce/ce.data.01a.CurrentSeasAE.

Note: Data for December are provisional. Data are the seasonally adjusted employment series for different sectors. Change in employment is (End-of-December Employment—End-of-February Employment). Share of "Level" in the title refers to the share of private sector employment level in February (red bars), i.e., End-of-February employment in sector divided by End-of-February total private sector employment.

A. Trends in Employment

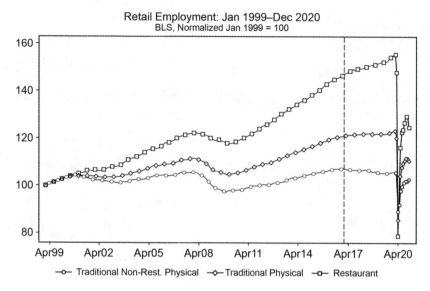

Retail Employment: Jan 1999–Dec 2020
BLS, Normalized Jan 1999 = 100

—o— Traditional Non-Rest. Physical —◇— Traditional Physical —□— Restaurant

B. Trends in Share of Total Private Sector Employment

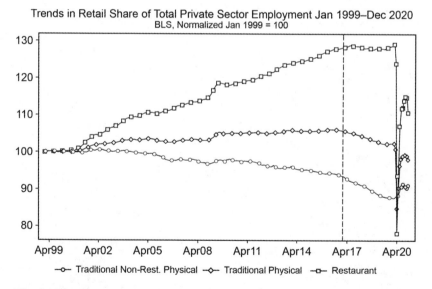

Trends in Retail Share of Total Private Sector Employment Jan 1999–Dec 2020
BLS, Normalized Jan 1999 = 100

—o— Traditional Non-Rest. Physical —◇— Traditional Physical —□— Restaurant

Fig. 6.A.13   Employment trends in retail: Monthly series January 1999 to December 2020, BLS CES data

Source: Data are from BLS Current Employment statistics, from https://download.bls.gov/pub/time.series/ce/ce.data.01a.CurrentSeasAE.

Note: Data for March and February are provisional. Data are the seasonally adjusted employment series for different sectors.

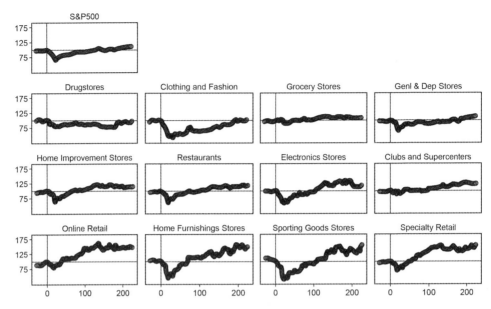

Fig. 6.A.14   Covid-19 shock: Trends in sector stock price indexes, January 9, 2020 to January 8, 2021

Note: Indexes are normalized to 100 on February 19, 2020; weights are market values at start of window. Day zero is set a February 19, 2020 pre-pandemic peak of S&P 500.

Table 6.A.1   **Concordance of merchandise lines to NAICS 2012 codes**

Merchandise lines (in ESMOH e-commerce data)	Imputed NAICS 2012 3-digit code	NAICS 2012 description
Books (includes audio books and e-books)	451	Sporting goods, hobby, musical instrument, and book stores
Clothing and clothing accessories (includes footwear)	448	Clothing and clothing access. stores
Computer and peripheral equipment, communications equipment, and related products (includes cellular phones)	443	Electronics and appliance stores
Computer software (includes video game software)	443	Electronics and appliance stores
Drugs, health aids, and beauty aids	446	Health and personal care stores
Electronics and appliances	443	Electronics and appliance stores
Food, beer, and wine	445	Food and beverage stores
Furniture and home furnishings	442	Furniture and home furnishings stores
Jewelry	448	Clothing and clothing access. stores
Audio and video recordings (includes purchased downloads)	443	Electronics and appliance stores
Office equipment and supplies	453	Miscellaneous store retailers
Sporting goods	451	Sporting goods, hobby, musical instrument, and book stores
Toys, hobby goods, and games	451	Sporting goods, hobby, musical instrument, and book stores
Other merchandise	452	General merchandise stores
Nonmerchandise receipts	499	Not classified

Table 6.A.2 Frequency distribution by keywords used to define restaurant "varieties" in Yelp data

Variety	Frequency	Percent	Variety	Frequency	Percent	Variety	Frequency	Percent
hot dog	79,530	50.15	chicken wings	337	0.21	gelato	33	0.02
american	13,046	8.23	buffet	324	0.2	mongolian	28	0.02
italian	10,164	6.41	street	243	0.15	portuguese	27	0.02
mexican	7,490	4.72	french	228	0.14	moroccan	25	0.02
burgers	5,396	3.4	bubble tea	227	0.14	british	24	0.02
chinese	5,210	3.29	southern	219	0.14	poke	23	0.01
sandwich	4,152	2.62	filipino	194	0.12	pub	22	0.01
tea	4,012	2.53	cafe	166	0.1	russian	22	0.01
ice cream	3,277	2.07	gluten-free	156	0.1	noodle	18	0.01
specialty	3,025	1.91	cajun/creole	155	0.1	indonesian	17	0.01
japanese	2,686	1.69	vegan	153	0.1	african	16	0.01
deli	1,976	1.25	asian	149	0.09	hungarian	16	0.01
bagel	1,135	0.72	pretzel	130	0.08	nepalese	16	0.01
donut	1,050	0.66	creperies	120	0.08	arabian	12	0.01
local	1,034	0.65	breweries	104	0.07	butcher	12	0.01
thai	961	0.61	middle eastern	98	0.06	polish	11	0.01
greek	923	0.58	spanish	98	0.06	belgian	10	0.01
fast food	866	0.55	fish & chips	87	0.05	argentine	9	0.01
soul food	808	0.51	shaved ice	80	0.05	soup	9	0.01
bakeries	758	0.48	kosher	79	0.05	comfort	7	0
wine	738	0.47	cupcake	77	0.05	european	7	0
indian	727	0.46	turkish	69	0.04	burmese	6	0
dessert	694	0.44	cuban	60	0.04	pakistani	5	0
barbeqe	504	0.32	ethiopian	54	0.03	halal	4	0
diners	498	0.31	cambodian	52	0.03	waffle	4	0
vietnamese	497	0.31	afghan	51	0.03	fondue	3	0
juice	493	0.31	taiwanese	51	0.03	poutineries	3	0
salad	492	0.31	brazilian	44	0.03	hot pot	2	0
hawaiian	466	0.29	irish	44	0.03	malaysian	2	0
mediterranean	442	0.28	german	42	0.03	diy	1	0
brunch	425	0.27	peruvian	37	0.02	honey	1	0
seafood	394	0.25	iranian	34	0.02	ukrainian	1	0
korean	352	0.22						
Total							**158,579**	**100**

Notes: See section 6.2.2 for description of Yelp public-use microdata.

Table 6.A.3   Top 24 funded retail-related startups founded after 1998 per Crunchbase data (as of December 2019)

Name	Description	Founding year	Total funding (to Dec 2019, USD million)	Complementary to physical retail?
DoorDash	DoorDash provides a delivery service that connects customers with local and national businesses.	2013	2,071.8	COMPLEMENT
Instacart	Instacart delivers groceries and home essentials from a variety of local stores.	2012	1,895.8	COMPLEMENT
Sears Holdings Corporation	Sears Holdings Corporation is a leading integrated retailer focused on seamlessly connecting the digital and physical shopping experiences	2005	1,710.0	NEUTRAL
Groupon	Groupon is a deal-of-the-day website that offers discounted gift certificates usable at local or national companies.	2007	1,387.0	COMPLEMENT
Affirm	Affirm is a financial technology services company that offers installment loans to consumers at the point of sale.	2012	1,020.0	COMPLEMENT
Postmates	Postmates powers local, on-demand logistics focused on fast deliveries from any type of merchant at scale.	2011	903.0	COMPLEMENT
Authentic Brands Group	Authentic Brands Group is a brand development and licensing company.	2010	875.0	NEUTRAL
Lineage Logistics	Lineage Logistics is a warehousing and logistics company built to deliver sophisticated, customized, and dependable cold chain solutions.	2012	700.0	COMPLEMENT
Jet	Jet operates an e-commerce platform that allows its member to shop online from various retailers.	2014	570.0	RIVAL
Rent the Runway	Rent the Runway is an online e-commerce website that allows women to rent designer apparel and accessories.	2009	541.2	RIVAL
Toast	Toast is an all-in-one point-of-sale and restaurant management platform for businesses in the food service and hospitality space.	2011	502.0	COMPLEMENT
Chewy	Chewy.com delivers pet happiness by conveniently shipping 500+ brands of pet food and goodies for free.	2011	451.0	RIVAL
Zume Pizza	Zume Pizza is a food delivery company that operates an automated pizza delivery platform.	2015	423.0	RIVAL
CloudKitchens	CloudKitchens is a real estate company that provides smart kitchens for delivery-only restaurants.	2016	400.0	COMPLEMENT
thredUP	thredUP is a fashion resale marketplace that enables individuals to buy and sell clothing for women and children.	2009	381.1	RIVAL

(continued)

Table 6.A.3 (cont.)

Name	Description	Founding year	Total funding (to Dec 2019, USD million)	Complementary to physical retail?
Wayfair	Wayfair is an online retailer of home products for bedroom, living room, kitchen and dining, home entertainment, bathroom, and more.	2002	358.0	RIVAL
MOD Super Fast Pizza	MOD Super Fast Pizza owns and operates a chain of pizza restaurants in the United States and the United Kingdom.	2008	352.0	NEUTRAL
Casper	Casper is a sleep startup that launches a comfortable mattress sold directly to consumers, eliminating commission-driven, inflated prices.	2013	339.7	RIVAL
TechStyle Fashion Group	TechStyle is a global membership fashion commerce company focused on reimagining the global fashion business.	2010	336.0	RIVAL
ezCater	ezCater is an online catering marketplace that allows individuals to order food from local caterers in the US	2007	319.8	COMPLEMENT
RetailMeNot	RetailMeNot is a marketplace for online coupons and deals that operates a portfolio of coupon and deal websites.	2007	299.5	NEUTRAL
Moda Operandi	The leading platform for fashion discovery. We connect consumers directly with established and emerging designers from around the world.	2010	293.7	RIVAL
Shift	Shift is an online marketplace for buying and selling used cars.	2013	293.0	RIVAL
Brandless	Brandless is a direct-to-consumer company providing household items.	2016	292.5	RIVAL
Total funding for top 24 companies			16,715	
Total complement funding			9,199	
Proportion complement			55.03 percent	

Notes: The data are from Crunchbase, as of December 30, 2019. We note a strong caveat that startups in other categories also operate and impact the retail market, e.g., Uber Eats is a competitor to DoorDash but is not listed here as Uber is not primarily a delivery startup. Similarly, Nuvo is primarily an autonomous vehicle startup, but it operates in the retail delivery space as well. Large online retailers (e.g., Amazon) are excluded if they were founded prior to 1999. Finally, funding data is missing for 55.6 percent (2,538 of 4,566) companies we identified as being involved in retail-related activity in the Crunchbase data.

References

Basker, Emek. 2012. "Raising the Barcode Scanner: Technology and Productivity in the Retail Sector." *American Economic Journal: Applied Economics* 4: 1–29.

———. 2016a. *Handbook on the Economics of Retailing and Distribution.* Cheltenham, UK: Edward Elgar Publishing.

———. 2016b. "The Evolution of Technology in the Retail Sector." In Basker, *Handbook on the Economics of Retailing and Distribution*, 38–53.

Basker, Emek, Shawn D. Klimek, and Van H. Pham. 2012. "Supersize It: The Growth of Retail Chains and the Rise of the 'Big Box' Store." *Journal of Economics and Management Strategy* 21: 541–82.

Betancourt, Roger R. 2016. "Distribution Services, Technological Change and the Evolution of Retailing and Distribution in the Twenty-First Century." In Basker, *Handbook on the Economics of Retailing and Distribution*, 73–96.

Carden, Art, and Charles Courtemanche. 2016. "The Evolution and Impact of the General Merchandise Sector." In Basker, *Handbook on the Economics of Retailing and Distribution*, 413–32.

Chava, Sudheer, Alexander Oettl, Manpreet Singh, and Linghang Zeng. 2018. "Impact of E-Commerce on Employees at Brick-and-Mortar Retailers." June 15. Georgia Tech Scheller College of Business Research Paper No. 18–23; 29th Annual Conference on Financial Economics & Accounting 2018. https://ssrn.com /abstract=3197326 or http://dx.doi.org/10.2139/ssrn.3197326.

Corkery, Michael, and Sapna Maheshwari. 2019. "After 15 Years, Dream Mall Finally Becomes a Reality." *New York Times*, October 24.

Eaton, B. C., and R. G. Lipsey. 1982. "An Economic Theory of Central Places." *Economic Journal* 92(365): 56–72.

Ellickson, Paul B. 2016. "The Evolution of the Supermarket Industry: From A&P to Walmart." In Basker, *Handbook on the Economics of Retailing and Distribution*, 368–91.

Evangelista, Benny. 2015. "How the 'Amazon Factor' Killed Retailers like Borders, Circuit City." SFGate.com, July 13. https://www.sfgate.com/business/article /How-Amazon-factor-killed-retailers-like-6378619.php.

Field, Hayden. 2018. "If Business Is Booming, Why Is Main Street America Still Full of Empty Storefronts?" *Entrepreneur*, November 29. https://www.entrepreneur .com/article/322979.

Foster, Lucia, John Haltiwanger, Shawn Klimek, C. J. Krizan, and Scott Ohlmacher. 2016. "The Evolution of National Retail Chains: How We Got Here." In Basker, *Handbook on the Economics of Retailing and Distribution*, 7–37.

Goldschlag, Nathan, Travis J. Lybbert, and Nikolas J. Zolas. 2019. "Tracking the Technological Composition of Industries with Algorithmic Patent Concordances." *Economics of Innovation and New Technology.* https://doi.org/10.1080/10 438599.2019.1648014.

Hopenhayn, Hugo A. 1992. "Exit, and Firm Dynamics in Long Run Equilibrium." *Econometrica* 60(5): 1127–50.

Hortaçsu, Ali, and Chad Syverson. 2015. "The Ongoing Evolution of US Retail: A Format Tug-of-War." *Journal of Economic Perspectives* 29: 89–112.

Isaac, Mike, and Yaffe-Bellany, David. 2019. "The Rise of the Virtual Restaurant." *New York Times*, August 14, 2019.

Kercheval, Michael. 2014. "Why Online Retailers Continue to Open Brick-and-Mortar Stores." TechCrunch, October 31. https://techcrunch.com/2014/10/31/why -online-retailers-continue-to-open-brick-and-mortar-stores/.

Kestenbaum, Richard. 2017. "This Is What Will Happen to All the Empty Stores You're Seeing." *Forbes*, May 30. https://www.forbes.com/sites/richardkestenbaum/2017/05/30/this-is-what-will-happen-to-all-the-empty-stores-youre-seeing/#2566157c4bb7.

Kilgannon, Corey. 2018. "This Space Available." *New York Times*, September 6. https://www.nytimes.com/interactive/2018/09/06/nyregion/nyc-storefront-vacancy.html.

NAIC-CIPR. 2017. "Capital Markets Special Report." National Association of Insurance Commissioners & the Center for Insurance Policy and Research. https://www.naic.org/capital_markets_archive/170601.htm.

Noonan, Keith. 2019. "What Does the Future Hold for Self-Driving Cars?" The Motley Fool, October 18. https://www.fool.com/investing/what-does-the-future-hold-for-self-driving-cars.aspx.

Page, Scott E. 2007. "Why Chains Beget Chains: An Ecological Model of Firm Entry and Exit and the Evolution of Market Similarity." *Journal of Economic Dynamics & Control* 31: 3427–59.

Ratchford, Brian. T. 2016. "Retail Productivity." In Basker, *Handbook on the Economics of Retailing and Distribution*, 54–72.

Redman, Russell. 2018. "More Whole Foods Locations Get Prime Now Pickup: Amazon to Offer Grocery Delivery Service on Thanksgiving." *Supermarket News*, November 8. https://www.supermarketnews.com/online-retail/more-whole-foods-locations-get-prime-now-pickup.

Richter, Felix. 2018. "Who's Surviving the 'Retail Apocalypse'?" statista.com, April 17. https://www.statista.com/chart/13550/change-in-retail-store-count-by-category/.

Santa Cruz, Justine. 2019. "Why E-Commerce and Brick-and-Mortar Are Stronger Together." TotalRetail. https://www.mytotalretail.com/article/why-e-commerce-and-brick-and-mortar-are-stronger-together/.

Smith, Michael D., and Alejandro Zentner. 2016. "Internet Effects on Retail Markets." In Basker, *Handbook on the Economics of Retailing and Distribution*, 433–54.

Stewart, H., N. Blisard, S. Bhuyan, and R. M. Nayga, Jr. 2004. *The Demand for Food Away from Home. Full Service or Fast Food?* Agriculture Economic Report No. 829. Washington, DC: US Department of Agriculture, Economic Research Service.

Takahashi, Paul. 2018. "Restaurants Eat Up More Space in Malls." *Houston Chronicle*, May 18. https://www.houstonchronicle.com/business/article/Restaurants-eat-up-more-space-in-malls-12925642.php.

Thompson, Derek. 2017. "The Paradox of American Restaurants." *The Atlantic*, June 20. https://www.theatlantic.com/business/archive/2017/06/its-the-golden-age-of-restaurants-in-america/530955/.

Townsend, Matt, Jenny Surane, Emma Orr, and Christopher Cannon. 2017. "America's 'Retail Apocalypse' Is Really Just Beginning." Bloomberg.com, November 8. https://www.bloomberg.com/graphics/2017-retail-debt/.

Walters, Nicole. 2018. "Restaurant Start-Up Costs (A Breakdown for New Restauranteurs)." Blogpost, shopkeep.com. https://www.shopkeep.com/blog/restaurant-startup-costs-breakdown.

Weise, Karen. 2019. "Amazon Wants to Rule the Grocery Aisles, and Not Just at Whole Foods." *New York Times*, July 28.

Woods, Sharon. 2019. "The 'Retail Apocalypse' Is a Myth, and That's Good News for the Shopping Industry and Downtowns." *Public Square*, September 23. https://

www.cnu.org/publicsquare/2019/09/23/%E2%80%98retail-apocalypse%E2%80
%99-myth-and-thats-good-news-shopping-industry-and-downtowns.
Zumbach, Lauren. 2016. "Shopping Centers Look to Entertainment, Recreation to
Fill Empty Anchors." *Chicago Tribune*, September 16. https://www.chicagotribune
.com/business/ct-retail-entertainment-0916-biz-20160916-story.html.

Comment   Emek Basker

Definitions

To understand the recent evolution of physical retail markets, it is useful to start by defining physical retail markets.

The retail sector, narrowly defined, consists of business establishments— stores—that primarily sell merchandise to consumers, generally without transformation. It is distinct from the wholesale sector, which sells merchandise to retailers (and sometimes transforms or packages the products).

In addition, the retail sector has long been considered distinct from other types of business that serve end customers and are often located in the same malls and streets as retailers but are primarily engaged in providing *services* rather than merchandise. For example, gyms are part of the arts, entertainment, and recreation sector; ceramics studios are classified under educational services; and hair salons, automotive repair shops, and dry cleaners are all classified under other services. Bank branches are classified in the finance and insurance sector, and rental locations (whether renting videos, formalwear, or furniture) are classified under real estate & rental & leasing.[1]

A major part of Lafontaine and Sivadasan's chapter (chapter 6, this volume) concerns restaurants, which provide both a good and a service. As noted by Lafontaine and Sivadasan, these were considered by the Census Bureau to be part of the retail sector under the Standard Industrial Classification (SIC) system used until 1997, but they are part of the accommodation and food services sector in the North American Industrial Classification System (NAICS), which has been used by the Census Bureau since 1997.

Emek Basker is an economist at the US Census Bureau.

Any opinions and conclusions expressed herein are those of the author and do not necessarily represent the views of the US Census Bureau. No confidential data are used in this comment. I thank Randy Becker, Cathy Buffington, and Shawn Klimek for helpful comments and conversations. For acknowledgments, sources of research support, and disclosure of the author's material financial relationships, if any, please see https://www.nber.org/books-and-chapters/ role-innovation-and-entrepreneurship-economic-growth/comment-recent-evolution-physi- cal-retail-markets-online-retailing-big-box-stores-and-rise.

1. Alternative classifications of businesses, based on type of customer or location, are feasible to create using the microdata collected by the Census Bureau.

In the retail sector (SIC 52–59, NAICS 44–45), stores' industrial classification codes have historically depended on their primary product. Thus, stores that primarily sell shoes are classified as shoe stores, and stores that primarily sell food for consumption off the premises are classified as grocery stores. There are only two exceptions to this rule. First, "general-merchandise" stores (SIC 53, NAICS 452) sell a variety of products—for example, a combination of shoes, groceries, home furnishings, and apparel. Second, "nonstore retailers" (SIC 596, NAICS 454) are classified not by what they sell but by how they sell it. These establishments have historically included catalog showrooms, vending-machine operators, mail-order retailers, and direct-selling retailers (such as door-to-door encyclopedia sales). Today, this industry also includes retailers primarily engaged in e-commerce.

The assignment of industry codes in Census Bureau business statistics is done at the establishment level, rather than at the firm level or at the worker level. An *establishment* is a location of business and employment; a *firm* is the owning entity. Some stores are so-called "mom-and-pop" businesses, which operate a single location. In those cases, there is no need to distinguish between the establishment's line of business and the firm's. Other stores belong to chains, and some chains own other types of establishments, such as warehouses, marketing arms, or manufacturing facilities. A retail chain may have one manufacturing facility, for example; workers in that facility are considered to be in manufacturing. Conversely, even if the primary business of the firm is manufacturing, the employees in its outlet store are considered retail workers in Census Bureau business statistics.

An establishment's industrial classification is determined by the line of business for which it either has the highest revenue or the largest employment or payroll. Thus, even if a hair salon sells some hair products, as long as it earns most of its revenue from the service of haircuts, styling, dyeing, and so on, it is classified as a hair salon. As a result, a worker whose job is to sell hair products could be classified as an employee of a hair salon (if the establishment at which she works is a hair salon) or as an employee of a retail establishment (if the establishment at which she works earns most of its revenue from the sale of merchandise to consumers). Likewise, a worker delivering restaurant food to consumers' homes could be classified as a worker of a restaurant (if he is employed by the restaurant) or as a worker in the delivery business (if he works for a delivery service).

Alternative classifications, based on the occupation of the workers, require information on workers rather than on businesses. The Current Population Survey and the American Community Survey collect such information on samples of workers; survey weights allow researchers to generate economy-wide statistics from these samples.

This background helps explain the big-picture trends presented by Lafontaine and Sivadasan. The rise in employment by restaurants, for example, excludes workers who support the restaurant business but work in warehouses or deliver food for delivery services. The increase in nonstore-retail employment excludes employees working at physical stores that have online channels (even if those workers are primarily engaged with website design and maintenance), as well as workers in the "customs computer programming services" industry (NAICS 541511) who may be contracted to design or maintain websites or apps.

Major Historical Developments in the Retail Sector

Next, it is useful to put the current surge in innovative activity in the retail sector into historical context. The modern retail sector arguably dates to the late 1800s, when many retail chains started their operations. In the grocery-retailing industry, chains were almost nonexistent in 1890. Of the 1,718 retail chains the Federal Trade Commission (FTC) identified in 1928, only 42 were created before 1900 (FTC 1932, table 29, p. 54). Interestingly, the growth of chains coincided with a technological innovation—the mechanical cash register—which was invented in 1878 and became standard equipment in all stores by the 1920s and which helped ameliorate retailers' principal-agent problem (Basker 2016, pp. 38–39).

If the first half of the twentieth century brought us chains, the second half brought us large general-merchandise stores, such as Walmart, Kmart, and Target, and large warehouse-style clubs, such as BJ's, Sam's, and Costco. Facilitating this development was the barcode scanner, which was first installed only in large grocery stores and subsequently became standard equipment across the retail sector by the 1990s (Basker and Simcoe 2021).

In the 2000s, the sector has seen another remarkable transformation with the growth of e-commerce. Now, instead of walking to the corner store (as in 1930) or driving to the strip mall on the edge of town (as in 1990), consumers purchase goods from the comfort of their homes and have the goods delivered to them. Like the previous transformations of retailing, this change has been attributed to a technological innovation—the rise of the Internet. This innovation has been transformative and stands apart from the prior changes. Whereas the cash register and the barcode scanner changed the way stores operated and affected the scale and scope of retailers, they remained recognizably *stores*; consumers continued to interact with them in much the same way. In contrast, as noted by Lafontaine and Sivadasan, the Internet has changed the very nature of retailing.

Measuring Retailing in the Internet Age

This major change has consequences for measuring economic activity, both in the retail sector and in other, related, sectors, particularly warehousing and transportation, services, and wholesale.

First, the classification system that distinguished "shoe stores" from "nonstore retailers" becomes meaningless when shoes are sold online. The Census Bureau has attempted to address this problem by including an e-commerce question in its Annual Retail Trade Survey (ARTS) and Monthly Retail Trade Survey (MRTS) since at least 1999.[2] However, the classification problem is likely to get more severe as more specialized businesses move entirely online.

Second, e-commerce has further blurred the lines between retail and service industries. For example, delivery services are an increasingly important line of business. While the Census Bureau's business statistics capture formal employment in delivery services (which has increased since 2012), measuring "gig" workers, who do not have formal employment contracts, has been a much more complex task (Abraham et al. forthcoming). At the same time, retailers are increasingly offering such services as delivery, shopping services, and curbside pickup, particularly in the grocery industry. The 2017 Census of Retail Trade asked supermarkets for the first time whether they offer "pre-ordering or delivery services by website, app, fax, phone, or other means." Responses to this question have not yet been tabulated, but I am hoping this question helps us quantify this type of industry blurring.[3]

In addition, as more businesses sell online, they often outsource website hosting, design, and maintenance, so the workers performing these functions are classified outside the retail sector. This type of measurement problem is not new—it has long been true that many firms outsource such tasks as marketing, accounting, and landscaping—but e-commerce represents a qualitative shift in this type of misclassification. For an online seller, the website *is* the business, so omitting the workers maintaining the web operations from the employment count is qualitatively different from omitting workers performing other support operations that are ancillary to the firm's primary business.[4]

---

2. The ARTS and MRTS are administered to taxpaying units (EINS) and firms rather than to establishments. For e-commerce questions, this is a better sampling unit than an establishment (store), because large retailers are likely to allocate e-commerce receipts to separate administrative units and not to individual stores. In 2019, the ARTS asked, "Did this [entity] have any e-commerce sales in 2019?" and, for those responding in the affirmative, followed up with: "What were the total e-commerce sales in 2019?" For the purposes of this survey, the Census Bureau defines e-commerce as "the sale of goods and services where the buyer places an order, or the price and terms of the sale are negotiated, over an Internet, mobile device (M-Commerce), extranet, EDI network, electronic mail, or other comparable online system. Payment may or may not be made online." (Source: 2019 ARTS form SA-44; https://www2 .census.gov/programs-surveys/arts/technical-documentation/questionnaires/2019/sa-44–19 .pdf. Accessed January 25, 2020.) Some, but not all, MRTS forms include similar questions.

3. See Basker et al. (2019) for details and background on this question. Another, tangentially related, issue is the rising importance of retailers' non-merchandise receipts, such as insurance and service contracts, particularly for consumer electronics stores. Census microdata on revenue breakdowns capture these revenues, albeit imperfectly, and could help determine when a retail establishment starts to become more of service provider.

4. This issue is akin to the measurement issues raised by "factoryless" manufacturing firms; see Bernard and Fort (2015).

Uneven Effects of E-Commerce on Retail and Consumer-Facing Service Industries

Finally, it is worth noting that the "retail apocalypse" discussed by Lafontaine and Sivadasan has not been uniform across retail industries. Lafontaine and Sivadasan focus on the growth of restaurant employment, but other, traditional, retail industries have also flourished. Published data from County Business Patterns show that employment in bookstores (NAICS 451211) has fallen from near 1 percent of all retail employment in the late 1990s to half as much by the late 2010s.[5] Employment in furniture stores (NAICS 442110) has also dropped dramatically, from about 1.9 percent of retail employment to only 1.4 percent. In contrast, employment in clothing stores (NAICS 448) increased over this period from 9 percent to over 11 percent of retail employment.

In addition, the patterns that Lafontaine and Sivadasan document in the restaurant industry have parallels in other "Main Street"-type businesses that fall outside the traditional retail sector. For example, there have been large increases in employment at fitness and recreational sports centers (NAICS 713940) and in nail salons (NAICS 812113).

These trends are consistent with Lafontaine and Sivadasan's conclusion that restaurants' gains are due to increased demand. Like restaurants, gyms and nail salons offer consumers something that cannot be easily replicated online: an experience beyond the purchase of a widget, and a chance for an in-person interaction. As even physical retail increasingly offers "self-service" options that remove personal interaction, consumers seem to find these alternative spending categories more fulfilling. The 2017 Census of Retail Trade asked stores for the first time whether they offer "self-service" checkout. This question was asked of home centers, supermarkets, convenience stores, health- and personal-care stores (including pharmacies and drug stores), department stores, and general-merchandise stores.[6] A question for further research is whether increased reliance on self-service in some retail outlets is correlated with an increase in demand for personal interaction in other outlets and industries.

References

Abraham, Katharine, John Haltiwanger, Kristin Sandusky, and James Spletzer. 2021. "Measuring the Gig Economy: Current Knowledge and Open Issues." In *Measuring and Accounting for Innovation in the 21st Century*, edited by Carol Cor-

5. County Business Patterns data since 1986 can be downloaded from https://www2.census.gov/programs-surveys/cbp/datasets/. (Accessed January 25, 2020.) Wu (2017) uses Census Bureau microdata to study the impact of e-commerce on traditional booksellers.
6. See Basker et al. (2019).

rado, Jonathan Haskel, Javier Miranda, and Daniel Sichel. Chicago: University of Chicago Press.

Basker, Emek. 2016. "The Evolution of Technology in the Retail Sector." In *Handbook on the Economics of Retailing and Distribution*, edited by Emek Basker, 38–53. Cheltenham, UK: Edward Elgar.

Basker, Emek, and Tim Simcoe. 2021. "Upstream, Downstream: Diffusion and Impacts of the Universal Product Code." *Journal of Political Economy* 129(4): 1252–86.

Basker, Emek, Randy Becker, Lucia Foster, Kirk White, and Alice Zawacki. 2019. "Addressing Data Gaps: Four New Lines of Inquiry in the 2017 Economic Census." CES Working Paper No. 19–28. Washington, DC: Center for Economic Studies.

Bernard, Andrew B., and Teresa C. Fort. 2015. "Factoryless Goods Producing Firms." *American Economic Review* 105(5): 518–23.

Federal Trade Commission. 1932. *Chain Stores: Growth and Development of Chain Stores*. Washington, DC: 73d Congress, 1st Session, Senate Document No. 100.

Wu, Sherry. 2017. "Adaptation or Death? Bookstore Chains Meet Online Competition." Unpublished paper, Duke University, Durham, NC.

The Servicification of the US Economy
The Role of Startups versus Incumbent Firms

Mercedes Delgado, J. Daniel Kim, and Karen G. Mills

7.1 Introduction

The past few decades have shown a fundamental shift in the US economy from manufacturing toward services (figure 7.1). This trend has raised concerns that the shrinking manufacturing sector may hamper the overall rate of innovation. However, unprecedented growth in one important subcategory of services—Supply Chain Traded Services—suggests a more optimistic view. SC Traded Services (i.e., service inputs sold to organizations) represents a set of industries that account for a disproportionately high share of science, technology, engineering and math (STEM) jobs in the US economy (Delgado and Mills 2020). The economic importance of these services is evidenced in the growth of such industries as computer programming, data processing and hosting, design, and logistics services (Bitner, Ostrom, and

Mercedes Delgado is an associate professor of strategy and innovation at Copenhagen Business School and a research scientist at the MIT Innovation Initiative.

J. Daniel Kim is an assistant professor of management at the Wharton School, University of Pennsylvania.

Karen Mills is a senior fellow at Harvard Business School and a member of the board of directors of the National Bureau of Economic Research.

Any opinions and conclusions expressed herein are those of the authors and do not necessarily represent the views of the US Census Bureau. All results have been reviewed to ensure that no confidential information is disclosed. We thank Annie Dang for wonderful research assistance. We are particularly grateful for comments from the editors (Mike Andrews, Aaron Chatterji, Josh Lerner, and Scott Stern), Lambert Chu, Ben Jones, Steven Eppinger, Sharat Ganapati, Mark Gillett, Shane Greenstein, and Manuel Trajtenberg, and from the participants at the NBER Conference on The Role of Innovation and Entrepreneurship in Economic Growth. For acknowledgments, sources of research support, and disclosure of the authors' material financial relationships, if any, please see https://www.nber.org/books-and-chapters /role-innovation-and-entrepreneurship-economic-growth/servicification-us-economy-role -startups-versus-incumbent-firms.

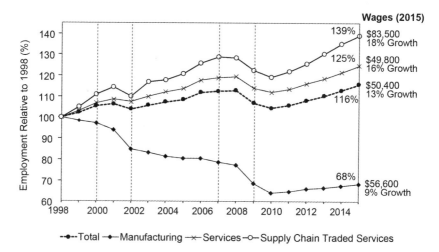

Fig. 7.1   Optimistic view of the economy: High growth of suppliers of service inputs

Source: Delgado and Mills (2020).

Note: Supply Chain (SC) industries are those that sell their goods and services primarily to businesses or the government.

Morgan 2008; Delgado and Mills 2020; Gawer and Cusumano 2002; Low 2013; Sheffi 2012).

While prior studies have documented the shift in the US economy from manufacturing to innovative services (see, e.g., Delgado and Mills 2020; Eckert, Ganapati, and Walsh 2019), understanding the causes and sources of this transition is in its infancy. In particular, little is known regarding the types of firms—startups or established firms—that are driving the transition to SC Traded Services. In this chapter, we explore the role of three types of firms as potential drivers of growth in these innovative services. First, we analyze the entry and growth of new and young firms enabled by new technology and data, like Okta and Rapid7. Second, we examine the transformation of incumbent manufacturing firms toward services over the past few decades, including Cisco, IBM, Intel, and Xerox (Baines et al. 2017; Lodefalk 2013; Vandermerwe and Rada 1988; Visnjic Kastalli and Van Looy 2013). Third, we explore the growth of incumbent SC Traded Services firms, such as Microsoft and Accenture.

To implement our analysis, we primarily use the Longitudinal Business Database (LBD) of the US Census Bureau, which is a panel dataset of all establishments in the US economy with at least one paid employee. The longitudinal nature of the LBD allows us to distinguish new and young startups from incumbent firms and to track important business characteristics, including employment and payroll. We then categorize each establishment's underlying industry using the categorization developed by Delgado and Mills (2020). Our sample covers all US establishments between 1998 and 2015, capturing the economic activity (employment and wages) in each sector by each firm type.

In this chapter, we focus on the types of firms and industries that are leading the transformation into high-wage, high-growth services. Our analysis provides a foundation for developing innovation and entrepreneurship policies specifically focused on building the skills and innovation ecosystems that better support innovative services, as this sector represents an important source of good jobs in the future.

7.2   Pessimistic View of the US Economy: Manufacturing vs. Services

Many US politicians and policymakers appear to believe that the best way to rebuild the economy is to bring manufacturing back. The innovation debate has remained largely centered on manufacturing because it accounts for the vast majority of patents, while services tend to be viewed as low-technology and lower-wage. The focus on manufacturing has resulted in a pessimistic view of the economy reflecting the decline in manufacturing jobs, which has been attributed in part to an increase in imports from China (Acemoglu et al. 2016). From 1998 to 2015, manufacturing employment declined by more than 32 percent, while services grew by 25 percent (figure 7.1). However, the pessimistic view about innovation is misleading: manufacturing currently comprises only about 9 percent of employment, and services are extremely heterogeneous—ranging from engineering and cloud computing to retail and restaurants. This chapter focuses on the hidden and growing role of suppliers of services in driving innovation and the jobs of the future.

7.2.1   A New Framework: The Supply Chain Economy

In recent work, Delgado and Mills (2020) develop a new innovation framework that focuses on the suppliers of goods and services to businesses and the government: the "supply chain economy." It includes businesses producing inputs (versus consumer products), such as semiconductors, cloud computing, design, and engineering services.

Suppliers are a source of innovation due to three important conceptual attributes. First, they create specialized inputs that can make the innovation process more efficient (Rosenberg 1963). Second, they tend to have numerous layers of buyer industries, so inventions developed by suppliers can diffuse broadly to multiple downstream industries. At the extreme, some innovative inputs (e.g., semiconductors) become general purpose technologies (GPTs) (Bresnahan and Trajtenberg 1995). Service industries, such as cloud computing and artificial intelligence, are becoming the next wave of GPTs (Brynjolfsson, Rock, and Syverson 2018; Cockburn, Henderson, and Stern 2018; Delgado and Mills 2020; Trajtenberg 2019). A third impor-

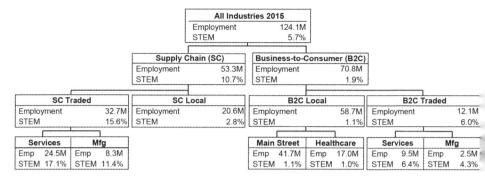

Fig. 7.2   Full supply chain categorization: Employment and STEM intensity, 2015

Source: Data from Delgado and Mills (2020); employment numbers from CBP 2015 data.

Note: Private-sector non-agricultural employment (excluding self-employed). Employment is in millions. STEM percent is the intensity of STEM jobs—the percentage of the subcategory jobs that are in STEM (e.g., 10.7 out of 100 SC jobs). Services includes non-manufactured goods.

tant attribute of suppliers is that they fuel geographical clusters, which spur innovation through the generation of agglomeration benefits (Chinitz 1961; Delgado, Porter, and Stern 2014).

To quantify the role of suppliers in innovation and jobs, Delgado and Mills (2020) provide a new industry categorization: Supply Chain vs. Business-to-Consumer industries. Using the 2002 Benchmark Input-Output Accounts of the Bureau of Economic Analysis (BEA), they separate supply chain (SC) industries (i.e., those that sell primarily to businesses or government) from business-to-consumer (B2C) industries (i.e., those that sell primarily to consumers).[1] They find that there is a distinct and large supply chain economy that accounts for 43 percent of US jobs (53 million) and for most STEM jobs and patents (87 percent) as of 2015 (figure 7.2).

In contrast to other industry categorizations that condition on industries that are STEM or knowledge-intensive (e.g., "knowledge-intensive business services" (Muller and Doloreux 2009); "advanced industries" (Muro et al. 2015); or "skilled traded services" (Eckert, Ganapati, and Walsh 2019), the supply chain industry categorization does not rely ex ante on innovation metrics. Industries that sell inputs to organizations are examined because of their conceptual importance for innovation, as described above. The empirical findings show that supply chain industries do, in fact, have a high concentration of innovative activity, as measured by STEM jobs and patents. Thus, the supply chain economy categorization reveals important insights on the sources of innovation in the US economy.[2]

1. SC industries are those with low sales to Personal Consumer Expenditures (≤ 35 percent); and B2C industries otherwise. Alternative SC industry definitions are tested in the appendix of Delgado and Mills (2020).

2. These alternative categorizations select industries based on particular innovation metrics, and therefore often include a mix of SC and B2C industries. For example, Eckert, Ganapati,

Delgado and Mills (2020) combine their categorization with two prior industry categorizations, Traded versus Local (Porter 2003) and Manufacturing versus Services, to analyze specific subcategories of the economy (see full SC versus B2C categorization in figure 7.2).[3] They find that SC Traded Services are a large and distinct segment that is a key driver of innovation. This subcategory encompasses more than 200 industries, including data processing and hosting, software, many professional services (like design, engineering, R&D, and advertising), financial, and logistics services. SC Traded Services constitute a significant part of the economy, with 20 percent of all jobs and 17 percent of firms. These services have the highest-wage jobs and are marked by the highest STEM intensity (17 out of 100 jobs are in STEM occupations), though interestingly, they account for relatively few patents (9 percent). Importantly, they have experienced fast growth in terms of jobs and wages during the 1998–2015 period (figure 7.1).

What could explain the high growth of these innovative service inputs? One answer is that these industries have many layers of buyer industries (based on the measure of industry upstreamness developed by Antràs et al. 2012).[4] This attribute, together with high STEM intensity, can increase their ability to produce specialized inputs for distinct industries and to cascade and diffuse innovation. In an increasingly knowledge- and data-driven economy, many of these services, like cloud computing, have become centrally important.

What firms are driving the growth in SC Traded Services? We examine three types of firms that may be contributing to the growth: new and young firms (e.g., Rapid7 and ShipHawk); manufacturing incumbents (e.g., IBM and Intel); and service incumbents (e.g., Microsoft and IDEO). Understanding the types of firms driving this change is important, as each may require distinct policy initiatives to access skilled labor, capital, buyers, and other growth-enhancing resources.

7.3   Data: Mapping Firms by Sector and Age

In this study, the Longitudinal Business Database (LBD) of the US Census Bureau serves as the primary dataset. The LBD is a panel dataset of all

---

and Walsh (2019) classifies as Skilled Tradable Services the NAICS codes 51 (*Information*), 52 (*Finance and Insurance*), 53 (*Real Estate and Rental and Leasing*), 54 (*Professional, Scientific, and Technical Services*) and 55 (*Management of Companies and Enterprises*). These services include 88 SC industries and 55 B2C industries (six-digit NAICS-2012 code). Among the 218 SC Traded Services industries in Delgado and Mills (2020) only a subset of 67 industries is also included in Eckert, Ganapati, and Walsh (2019)'s Skilled Tradable Services. Industry categorizations based on innovation metrics can be very useful, but they do not explore the conceptual reasons that an industry might be, or evolve to be, more STEM or innovation intensive.

3. Traded industries are those that sell their output across regions and countries, as opposed to industries that primarily serve the local market (e.g., retail). This categorization was initially developed by Porter (2003).

4. See Delgado and Mills (2020) for a detailed explanation of the upstreamness scores of SC vs. B2C industries.

employer establishments in the US economy. The LBD provides important establishment-level characteristics, including employment, payroll, industry, and location. Spanning 1976 to 2015, the LBD covers all industries in the private non-farm economy and every state in the US. While the underlying observations are at the level of the establishment, the LBD assigns a unique firm identifier to each establishment—a useful feature for tracking establishment-level activity for firms with multiple establishments.[5]

We also use the 2017 National Establishment Time-Series (NETS) database to examine and illustrate three incumbent firms that have been increasing their service activities: IBM, Intel, and Microsoft. The NETS database (by Walls & Associates, in collaboration with Dun & Bradstreet) is public and provides establishment-level employment data for many firms but with some limitations in its coverage and estimates.[6]

Our analysis is at the establishment level. Each LBD firm is decomposed into its portfolio of establishments. We then aggregate economic activity at the sector level by summing up across all establishments in a given sector (e.g., manufacturing vs. services). Therefore, a multi-unit firm with establishments spanning multiple sectors contributes to each sector based on its establishment-level activity. In measuring economic activity, we primarily use employment and payroll (adjusted to 2015 USD).

7.3.1   Firm-Level Attributes: Primary Industry and Age

As mentioned above, in measuring aggregate activity, we use establishment-level statistics to capture a multi-unit firm's contributions across multiple sectors. However, for analyses that examine firms in certain sectors (e.g., incumbent manufacturing firms in 1998; see figures 7.6–7.9 later in the chapter), we define each firm's primary industry using its firm-industry employment.[7] We then use the primary industry (six-digit NAICS) to classify whether an incumbent firm is in Manufacturing or SC Traded Services.

We also use the LBD to separate new firms (age 0), young firms (ages 1–10), and mature or incumbent firms (ages 11+). These cutoffs are based on the first year in which a firm's establishment appears in the LBD. It is important to note that a nontrivial share of establishments have a missing

---

5. See Jarmin and Miranda (2002) for more information regarding the LBD.

6. The NETS dataset follows over 60 million establishments during 1990–2017. Data are available for the whole country. Informed by Delgado and Mills (2020), we acquired data for a selected group of firms. While the NETS data are useful for examining firm dynamics, the dataset also has some limitations, including that data are often initially imputed for new establishments, there is considerable rounding of employment, and short-term employment changes are not measured very accurately (see Neumark, Zhang, and Wall 2005).

7. Specifically, for each multi-unit firm, we first identify the two-digit NAICS sector that accounts for the highest share of the firm's employment. Within this two-digit industry, we then identify the three-digit NAICS industry with the highest share of firm's employment. This process is repeated until the six-digit NAICS industry is determined—the firm's "primary" industry.

Table 7.1   SC Traded Services: Employment and wages by firm type (new, young, mature)

	Employment				Real wages (2015 USD)	
			1998–2015			1998–2015
	2015 (million) 1	Total (percent) 2	Growth (percent) 3	Net (million) 4	2015 ($000) 5	Growth (percent) 6
Total	**124.1**	**100**	**16**	**16.9**	**$50.4**	**13**
Services	112.5	91	25	22.3	$49.8	15
Supply Chain (SC) Traded						
Services	24.5	20	39	6.9	$83.5	18
New firms (age 0)	0.3	0	−50	−0.4	$53.1	−2
Young firms (ages 1–10)	3.5	3	−15	−0.6	$62.3	14
Mature firms (ages 11+)	14.1	11	60	5.3	$80.5	16
(unmatched)	6.5	5	66	2.6		

Note: The analysis of SC Traded Services by firm age uses the LBD. Firm age is a firm-level attribute based on the oldest establishment in the particular year. Total, Services, and SC Traded Services figures are sourced from Delgado and Mills (2020) and use the CBP data. Real wages in 2015 USD using CPI-U (All Urban Consumers; BLS).

(six-digit) industry in the LBD (e.g., see "unmatched" in table 7.1).[8] As a result, the overall levels in economic activity may be underestimated, but trends relative to 1998 should not be affected.

To quantify the economic activity in SC Traded Services in the US economy, we use the Supply Chain versus B2C Industry Categorization for six-digit NAICS (Delgado and Mills 2020).[9] For most of our analyses, we report aggregate economic activity in each sector (e.g., service) by each firm type (i.e., new, young, and mature).

7.4   SC Traded Services: Employment and Wage Trends by Firm Age

The US economy has witnessed a puzzling contraction in the rate of entrepreneurship. While research has demonstrated an overall decline in startup activity (Decker et al. 2014), there has simultaneously been a gradual rise in high-quality startups (Guzman and Stern 2019). One hypothesis is that the

8. The unmatched SC Traded Services employment primarily reflects LBD establishments with NAICS codes that are more aggregated (e.g., 4-digit) and therefore cannot be matched into the 6-digit NAICS industry categorization in Delgado and Mills (2020). In these cases, we can distinguish whether the establishment operates in Manufacturing versus Services, but cannot identify the type of service subcategory (e.g., SC Traded Services or SC Local Services). Some of these non-matches could be reduced in future work.

9. The full classification of the six-digit industries (NAICS-2012 definition) into these SC and B2C subcategories is available in Delgado and Mills (2020) in the supplemental online appendix B: Supply Chain and Business-to-Consumer Industry Categorization.

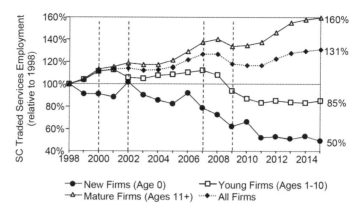

Fig. 7.3a   Supply chain traded services: Employment trends by firm type (new, young, mature)

Note: Age based on the oldest establishment of the firm in the particular year. Analysis based on the LBD.

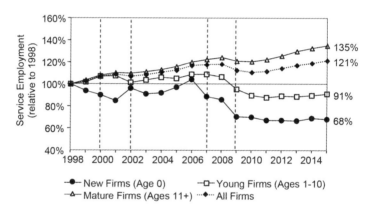

Fig. 7.3b   Total services: Employment trends by firm type (new, young, mature)

Note: Age based on the oldest establishment of the firm in the particular year. Analysis based on the LBD.

decline in new firm formation is concentrated in B2C Main Street services, but that high-growth startups are increasing in supply chain services that leverage STEM skills. Surprisingly, our preliminary findings suggest that this is not the case. We find a decline over time in the employment created by new and young firms in SC Traded Services as well as in total Services (figure 7.3).

Table 7.1 shows the level and growth in aggregate employment and payroll in the SC Traded Services sector for three firm types. Mature firms represent 11 percent of total US employment (with over 14 million jobs in 2015), followed by young firms (with 3.5 million jobs) and new firms (with barely 0.3

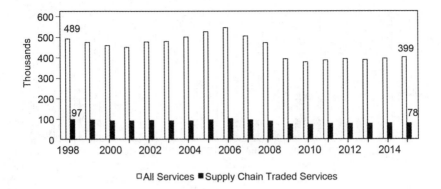

Fig. 7.4   Entry of new firms in services
Note: New firms are those with zero age. Analysis based on the LBD.

million). In terms of wages, all SC Traded Service firms have higher wages than the US average ($50,400), with the highest wages for mature firms ($80,500).

We find that the employment growth in SC Traded Services has been concentrated in mature firms (figure 7.3a), which created 5.3 million net jobs between 1998 and 2015 and also experienced significant growth in wages. In contrast, our analysis suggests a significant decline in the employment created by new firms and young firms (−50 percent and −15 percent growth rates, respectively), with a job loss of 1 million. For total services, we find similar trends but less variance across firm types (figure 7.3b).

7.5   The Declining Presence of New Firms in Services

As figure 7.4 illustrates, the decline in startup employment in SC Traded Services is largely due to a 20 percent decline in new firm entry (from 97,000 in 1998 to 78,000 firms in 2015). There was a similar reduction in the rate of startup entry in total Services (−18 percent).

While several studies have examined the decline of startup activity in the US economy (e.g., Decker et al. 2014; Guzman and Stern 2019), no conclusive answer has been found as to the underlying causes. Some high-quality startups have grown fast and, in some cases, have been acquired by established competitors (Kim 2020). Acquisitions of young firms could perhaps explain some of the decline in the employment created by young firms.[10]

Despite the decline in the overall startup entry, SC Traded Services startups continue to play an important role in innovation and employment, accounting for a steady 19 percent of US startups during 1998–2015 period

---

10. We should recognize that the inflow of new establishments may be recorded in the LBD data with some delay, with census years being most accurate in recording new establishments.

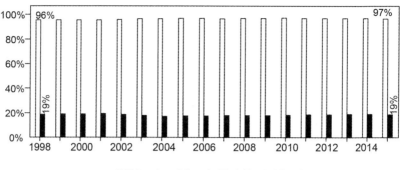

□ All Services ■ Supply Chain Traded Services

Fig. 7.5   Share of total new firms in services
Note: New firms are those with zero age. Analysis based on the LBD.

(figure 7.5). In contrast, in 2015, new manufacturing firms accounted for only 3 percent of US startups. Assuming startups are an important source of innovation (Romer 1990), a significant share of new ideas and new firms therefore reside in the SC Services industries. Removing barriers to startups in this sector could play a vital role in policies to promote and diffuse innovation across the economy.

7.5.1   Company Examples: Potential Challenges Faced by SC Traded Services Startups

There are many examples of new and young firms in SC Traded Services in the US economy (e.g., DirectDefense, Tulip, ShipHawk, Symbia Logistics, and WP Engine).[11] However, SC Traded Services firms, and startups in particular, face barriers that may limit their growth, particularly in access to skills and capital (Delgado and Mills 2021). To scale up, they must integrate their specialized service inputs in the value chain of business customers. For example, Tulip Interfaces produces an industrial app for the organization of work in manufacturing plants. To grow, they must create software that can be tailored to the needs of distinct customers, requiring access to capital, data, and nearby customers.

Another challenge is the protection of startup innovations from (big tech) competitors in the absence of intellectual property. Services are not patent intensive and can be easily copied or simultaneously developed by established firms with better access to complementary resources (e.g., data). For example, MIT startup Point API (previously called "EasyEmail") launched

---

11. These examples are based on public databases (including Crunchbase), an interview with Mark Gillett at Silver Lake Partners, and a startup panel (including the founders of Tulip Interfaces and Point API) organized by the authors.

in 2016 with software to predict and autofill e-mail replies. Soon after their launch, Google announced a similar tool during its annual conference for software developers, which discouraged some Point API investors.[12] The startup responded by positioning its software for customer support businesses, but it experienced difficulty in retaining users after Google released Smart Compose, and it closed operations by 2019.

7.6   Servicification of Manufacturing Incumbents

The employment growth in SC Traded Services has been concentrated in mature firms (figure 7.3). This raises the question of whether this growth is associated with manufacturing incumbents transforming into services, a phenomenon referred to as "servicification" in the economic literature (Low 2013) and "servitization" in the strategy literature (Vandermerwe and Rada 1988). Recent trade studies show an increasing servicification of manufacturing firms, which refers to the increased use of service inputs for the production of goods and increased sales of services (Lodefalk 2013, 2017; Low 2013; Timmer et al. 2014).[13] In the strategy literature, there has been a growing interest in understanding the servitization of mature manufacturing firms—a process of adding revenue streams from selling services (Baines et al. 2017; Vandermerwe and Rada 1988; Visnjic Kastalli and Van Looy 2013). Relatedly, new information and communication technologies and management practices can facilitate the modularity and separation of research, development, design, and manufacturing (Fort 2017; Tripathy and Eppinger 2013), making service inputs more tradable domestically and globally.

We are interested in quantifying the servicification of manufacturing firms and determining whether this trend has resulted in net job creation. To quantify the transformation of manufacturing firms into services, we use a sample of about 2,000 incumbent manufacturing firms that have survived between 1998 and 2015. We condition on firms that in 1998 (our initial year) are mature (11+ age), large (500+ jobs), and have their primary industry in manufacturing. In 1998, these firms accounted for 5.6 million jobs, 33 percent of total manufacturing employment.

We find that there is a large servicification of manufacturing incumbents that occurs gradually and continuously during the examined period (figures 7.6–7.9). The aggregated employment of the manufacturing incumbent sample is used to compute the share of employment in Manufacturing versus SC Traded Services versus Other Services over time (figure 7.6). The share of employment in total Services increased by 13 percentage points

12. "American Tech Giants Are Making Life Tough for Startups," *The Economist*, June 2, 2018.
13. In these studies, service inputs are often classified as "intangibles," and their contribution to the value added of final goods or services is poorly measured (Low 2013; Timmer et al. 2014).

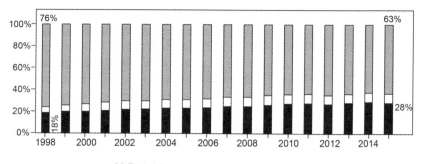

Fig. 7.6   Manufacturing incumbents: Share of employment in supply chain traded services

Note: LBD sample of large firms that are manufacturing incumbents in 1998 and survive 1998–2015. Their share of employment in SC Traded Services increased from 18 percent to 28 percent.

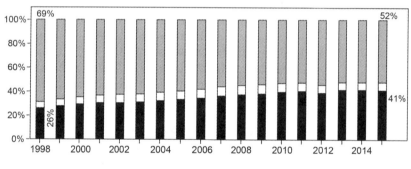

Fig. 7.7   Manufacturing incumbents: Share of payroll in supply chain traded services, 2015 dollars

Note: LBD sample of large firms that are manufacturing incumbents in 1998 and survive 1998–2015. Their share of payroll in SC Traded Services increased from 26 percent to 41 percent.

(24 percent to 37 percent). Most of the growth is in the share of employment in SC Traded Services, which increased by 10 percentage points (18 percent to 28 percent).

The servicification of manufacturing incumbents is even more pronounced when we examine payroll, indicating that the jobs in services exhibit higher average wages (figure 7.7). The share of payroll in Services has increased by 17 percentage points (31 percent to 48 percent) and in SC Traded Services by 15 percentage points (26 percent to 41 percent).

This servicification took place through the destruction of many manufacturing jobs and the creation of fewer yet very high-wage jobs (figures 7.8

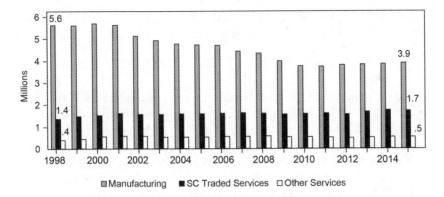

Fig. 7.8   Manufacturing incumbents: Employment trends, 1998–2015

Note: LBD sample of large firms that are manufacturing incumbents in 1998 and survive 1998–2015.

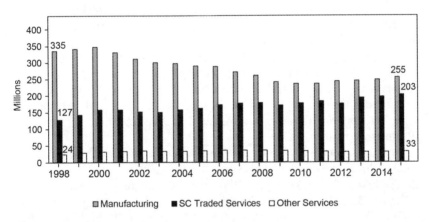

Fig. 7.9   Manufacturing incumbents: Payroll trends, 1998–2015, 2015 dollars

Note: LBD sample of large firms that are manufacturing incumbents in 1998 and survive 1998–2015.

and 7.9). From 1998 to 2015, these firms experienced a total job loss of 1.2 million but a payroll increase of $4.2 million. Manufacturing lost 1.7 million jobs and $80 million in payroll. In contrast, SC Traded Services gained 400,000 high-wage jobs, and payroll increased by $76 million (in 2015 USD).

Our results are not driven by a few "superstar" firms (Autor et al. 2020). The analysis suggests that many large manufacturing incumbents experienced servicification. We find that by the end of the period, about 20 percent of the firms have transformed into primarily SC Traded Service firms (i.e., the primary six-digit industry by employment is in SC Traded Services). Furthermore, we find similar servicification patterns for a large sample of small and medium manufacturing incumbents. To complement our empirical findings, we provide specific examples of manufacturing firms that have successfully evolved into SC Traded Services over the years.

7.6.1   Company Examples: The Continued Servicification of IBM and Intel

IBM: International Business Machines Corporation (IBM) was founded in 1896 as a punch-card data processing machine manufacturer. It found its footing as a hardware manufacturing company in the 1900s. Making all its components in-house, IBM became the leading computer company in the 1960s (Rothaermel et al. 2015). But with the emergence of Apple in 1976 and other competitors in the personal computer (PC) and related hardware space, IBM was forced to revise its strategy. Each change in top leadership has been associated with an increased focus on software and other services, particularly the bundling of these components together in an integrated sales offering.

When Louis Gerstner stood at the helm of IBM from 1993 to 2002, the company coined the term "e-business" in its marketing campaigns, highlighting the firm's strategy and new focus on the Internet and its capabilities for businesses. In 2002, Sam Palmisano stepped into the CEO role, reorganizing IBM around three complementary segments: hardware, software, and services. His focus on the services component was undeniable. During his tenure, IBM sold its PC business to Lenovo and over a 4-year period, spent $11.8 billion to acquire numerous software and computer service firms (Rothaermel et al. 2015).

Virginia Rometty continued the journey into services when she became CEO in 2012. She told the *Wall Street Journal* in 2015 that "Hardware was the original soul of this company," but "we can't hold on to our past" (Langley 2015). In a speech to shareholders in 2016, Rometty highlighted the company's transformation: "IBM . . . has reinvented itself through multiple technology eras and economic cycles . . . IBM is becoming much more than a 'hardware, software, services' company. We are emerging as a cognitive solutions and cloud platform company" (IBM 2016).

We used NETS data to quantify IBM's servicification. The analysis shows that while IBM's primary industry (6-digit NAICS) by employment in 1998 was *Electronic Computer Manufacturing*, it has transformed into a primarily SC Traded Service firm, with *Custom Computer Programming Services* as the primary industry in 2015. Specifically, the share of employment in SC Traded Services increased from 45 percent to 59 percent during 1998–2015. This transformation was accompanied by a large reduction of IBM's manufacturing and service jobs in the US (the compound annual growth rate [CAGR] was −5 percent).

Intel: Founded in 1968, Intel Corporation made a name for itself as a semiconductor chip manufacturer. It created a general-purpose technology (GPT) and a whole industry—semiconductors—with the Intel 4004 microprocessor (Bresnahan and Trajtenberg 1995). The success of the PC in the 1980s led to the prime positioning of the company as the go-to supplier of chips for PC manufacturers like IBM. Intel excelled at continuously developing improved versions of its popular microprocessor chips—faster and with increased capabilities—but ran into a significant hurdle when adoption of new models slowed. To combat this lag in sales, the company rolled out a brilliant marketing and branding campaign centered on the now ubiquitous "Intel Inside" tagline and logo (Moon 2005).

Since those early days, Intel has maintained its dominance in manufacturing PC components, but as the company faced declining PC sales, it has diversified into components for other devices, software, and cloud computing. Using NETS data, we find that while the company's primary industry remains in SC Manufacturing (*Semiconductor and Related Device Manufacturing*), it has continuously and rapidly increased its presence in SC Traded Services in the US economy (in particular in *Custom Computer Programming Services*). The percentage of firm employment in SC Traded Services increased from about 4 percent in 1998 to 26 percent by 2015, creating many service jobs (the CAGR was 8 percent). In 2016, Intel announced a significant restructuring effort, stating in a press release that the move was necessary to "accelerate its evolution from a PC company to one that powers the cloud and billions of smart, connected computing devices" (Intel 2016).

The servicification of this supply chain firm has been reflected in its branding and communication strategy. In January 2016, in a plan to expand beyond the extremely successful "Intel Inside" campaign, the company revamped its brand messaging: "Intel Inside makes amazing experiences outside." Penny Baldwin, VP and GM of global brand management and reputation explained: "By putting the focus on Intel Inside, we'd gone brand invisible. . . . We're trying to bring our brand from the inside to the outside. From being seen as a PC component to being an experiential exponent and an enabler of experience" (Schiff 2016).

7.7 The Growth of SC Traded Service Incumbents

Finally, we examine the role of large incumbent SC Traded Service firms (e.g., Microsoft) in the growth of this sector. Industries in SC Traded Services often have many layers of buyer industries, and therefore can themselves be important engines of innovation and growth. In fact, modern equivalents of GPTs like semiconductors reside increasingly in service or "digital" inputs, such as cloud computing and artificial intelligence (Brynjolfsson, Rock, and Syverson 2018; Cockburn, Henderson, and Stern 2018; Delgado and Mills 2020; Trajtenberg 2019).

For this analysis, we use a sample of about 1,000 incumbent SC Traded Service firms that survived from 1998 to 2015. These firms have the following attributes in our initial year (1998): they are mature (11+ age), large

(500+ jobs), and their primary industry is in SC Traded Services. Preliminary analysis shows that these firms experienced significantly high rates of net job creation during 1998–2015. Thus, while the job creation debate often focuses on manufacturing, the reality is that large service inputs firms have created many well-paying jobs. These firms play an important role in the servicification of the US economy.

7.7.1   Company Examples: Microsoft and Service Platforms

There is no shortage of incumbent service firms that have grown significantly during our time frame, capitalizing on the increasing use of data and the Internet, cloud computing, and AI technology. Examples range from high-growth enterprise software firms and consulting firms (e.g., Salesforce, Workday, SAP, and Red Ventures) to engineering and design service firms like Aecom and IDEO. Microsoft, a well-known incumbent services firm, illustrates the scalability of service inputs.

Microsoft: Founded in 1975, Microsoft was a software company from its outset, developing tools for the emerging PC industry. Microsoft Word was first released in 1983 and quickly took over the marketplace along with the Office suite of applications. Gawer and Cusumano (2002) demonstrated the importance of the Windows platform for the innovation capacity of many of Microsoft's customers. Focusing heavily on Windows and Office, Microsoft covered the enterprise software market through licensing agreements up through the 2000s.

By 2013, however, "the sale of prepackaged operating systems and software on PCs" was declining. Consumers were interacting with technology in varied ways with the increasing adoption of smartphones, tablets, and other mobile devices. Responding to these trends, Microsoft reorganized itself as a "devices and services company" and later, under Satya Nadella's leadership, as a company focused on a "mobile-first, cloud-first" strategy (Foley, Mayfield, and Boland 2017). The company developed its fast-growing cloud service, Microsoft Azure, and shifted to a constantly updating subscription model for Office 365. Related cloud-based products, such as Skype and SharePoint, have followed, as Microsoft continues to build out its software-as-a-service platform.

Our analysis (based on NETS data) illustrates the high scalability of this firm. During the entire period 1998–2015, over 90 percent of Microsoft's employment was in SC Traded Services, mainly in *Software Publishing*. These services experienced fast growth in employment (CAGR of 6 percent).

7.8   Conclusion: How to Support Innovative Service Firms

The servicification of the US economy is a significant source of anxiety due to the loss of well-paying jobs in manufacturing. However, strong growth in SC Traded Services businesses provides an important source of new, high-wage jobs (many of which require STEM skills). This raises important questions, particularly concerning policy initiatives that might support more of these businesses and create innovative service jobs.

One puzzling finding of our study is the decline in the number of entrepreneurial firms in SC Traded Services. While young firms in this sector continue to represent a large share of the overall entrepreneurial activity in the US economy, their decline raises questions regarding the missing start-ups in this increasingly important services sector. What are the barriers that stifle the entry and growth of entrepreneurial firms in high-tech services? Given the outsized role of startups in generating technological innovations and growth (e.g., Romer 1990), future research is needed to advance our understanding of the sources and solutions to these barriers. In particular, barriers related to access to STEM skills, capital, buyers, and data, as well as the ability to protect innovations, should be examined (Delgado and Mills 2021).

Another key finding in this study is that job creation in SC Traded Services is driven primarily by mature firms: the transformation of incumbent manufacturing firms into services and, especially, the growth of incumbent service firms. This pattern raises new questions about how incumbent firms are able to successfully transform from manufacturing into product-service or pure service firms. This transformation may be associated with firms moving manufacturing activities overseas (Fuchs et al., chapter 1 in this book) while choosing to produce innovative services in the US. The servicification of incumbent firms can generally occur by either organically developing their capabilities in-house (e.g., retraining their workers) or externally sourcing the necessary technology and skills. Organically, firms may train their workers with new skills that enable an effective response to the evolving competitive environment. Externally, firms may partner with—or acquire—other firms as a way to outsource new technology and talent. Relative to organic growth, how might an acquisition-based approach shape the incumbents' long-run innovation and growth? And what is the role of industry clusters and specialized STEM skills in the growth of these innovative services across regions (Delgado and Porter 2017; Eckert, Ganapati, and Walsh 2019)?

We conclude by discussing the prospects of SC Traded Services. We point to two directions. First, in terms of the overall size, we expect that this sector will continue to grow in both absolute and relative size. Especially with the global COVID-19 pandemic accelerating the economic trend toward digitization, the rising importance of data-driven services that rely on AI and Internet technologies (see e.g., Jones and Tonetti 2020; Mills 2019; Trajtenberg 2019) will likely catalyze further growth in many areas of SC Traded Services, such as cloud computing, financial technology, logistics, and health care. Second, in terms of the composition of firms, we expect that incumbents will continue to outpace the startups in this sector unless barriers to accessing data and other critical resources are addressed. Consistent with this view, a concurrent trend is the rise of superstar firms, which are industry giants with disproportionately high market shares (Autor et al. 2020). Another supporting trend is the growing prevalence of startup acquisitions in many industries (e.g., Kim 2020), which may further tilt the competitive landscape toward incumbent firms. A natural consequence of a startup acquisition is the transfer of market power from entrepreneurial firms to the acquiring incumbents before ventures can sufficiently mature and reach their innovation and size potential. As a result, young firms may play a declining role in driving jobs in SC Traded Services.

Overall, creating an appropriate business environment for new and young firms to overcome barriers to entry and growth, and for incumbent firms to adapt to changing trends, is essential to encourage growth in Supply Chain Services and innovation in the US economy.

References

Acemoglu, D., D. Autor, D. Dorn, G. H. Hanson, and B. Price. 2016. "Import Competition and the Great US Employment Sag of the 2000s." *Journal of Labor Economics* 34(1): 141–98.

Antràs, P., D. Chor, T. Fally, and R. Hillberry. 2012. "Measuring the Upstreamness of Production and Trade Flows." *American Economic Review* 102(3): 412–16.

Autor, D., D. Dorn, L. F. Katz, C. Patterson, and J. Van Reenen. 2020. "The Fall of the Labor Share and the Rise of Superstar Firms." *Quarterly Journal of Economics* 135(2): 645–709.

Baines, T. S., A. Z. Bigdeli, O. F. Bustinza, V. Guang Shi, J. S. Baldwin, and K. Ridgway. 2017. "Servitization: Revisiting the State-of-the-Art and Research Priorities." *International Journal of Operations & Production Management* 37(2): 256–78.

Bitner, M. J., A. L. Ostrom, and F. N. Morgan. 2008. "Service Blueprinting: A Practical Technique for Service Innovation." *California Management Review* 50(3): 66–94.

Bresnahan, T. F., and M. Trajtenberg. 1995. "General Purpose Technologies 'Engines of Growth'?" *Journal of Econometrics* 65(1): 83–108.

Brynjolfsson, E., D. Rock, and C. Syverson. 2018. "The Productivity J-Curve: How Intangibles Complement General Purpose Technologies." NBER Working Paper No. 25148. Cambridge, MA: National Bureau of Economic Research.

Chinitz, B. 1961. "Contrasts in Agglomeration: New York and Pittsburgh." *American Economic Review* 51(2): 279–89.

Cockburn, I. M., R. Henderson, and S. Stern. 2018. "The Impact of Artificial Intelligence on Innovation." NBER Working Paper No. 24449. Cambridge, MA: National Bureau of Economic Research.

Decker, R., J. Haltiwanger, R. Jarmin, and J. Miranda. 2014. "The Role of Entrepreneurship in US Job Creation and Economic Dynamism." *Journal of Economic Perspectives* 28(3): 3–24.

Delgado, M., and K. G. Mills. 2020. "The Supply Chain Economy: A New Industry Categorization for Understanding Innovation in Services." *Research Policy* 49(8): 104039.

———. 2021. "The Supply Chain Economy: New Policies to Drive Innovation and Jobs." *Economia Industrial* (forthcoming).

Delgado, M., and M. E. Porter. 2017. "Clusters and the Great Recession." DRUID Conference Paper. https://papers.ssrn.com/sol3/papers.cfm?abstract_id=3819293.

Delgado, M., M. E. Porter, and S. Stern. 2014. "Clusters, Convergence, and Economic Performance." *Research Policy* 43(10): 1785–99.

Eckert, F., S. Ganapati, and C. Walsh. 2019. "Skilled Tradable Services: The Transformation of U.S. High-Skill Labor Markets." Minneapolis: Federal Reserve Bank of Minneapolis Institute Working Paper 25.

Foley, F. C., S. E. Mayfield, and K. F. Boland. 2017. "The Transformation of Microsoft." HBS Case No. 218–048. Boston: Harvard Business School.

Fort, T. 2017. "Technology and Production Fragmentation: Domestic versus Foreign Sourcing." *Review of Economic Studies* 84(2): 650–87.

Gawer, A., and M. A. Cusumano. 2002. "Platform Leadership: How Intel, Microsoft, and Cisco Drive Industry Innovation." Boston: Harvard Business Review Press.

Guzman, J., and S. Stern. 2019. "The State of American Entrepreneurship: New Estimates of the Quality and Quantity of Entrepreneurship for 32 US States, 1988–2014." NBER Working Paper No. 22095. Cambridge, MA: National Bureau of Economic Research.

Hardy, Q. 2015. "Intel's Results Reflect Move to Cloud Computing." *New York Times*, October 14. https://www.nytimes.com/2015/10/14/technology/intels -results-reflect-move-to-cloud-computing.html.

Hecker, D. E. 2005. "High-Technology Employment: A NAICS-Based Update." *Monthly Labor Review* 128(7): 57–72.

IBM. 2016. Annual Meeting of Stockholders: Speech by Ginni Rometty. April 26. Accessed December 18, 2019. https://www.ibm.com/ibm/ginni/04_26_2016.html.

Intel. 2016. "Intel Announces Restructuring Initiative to Accelerate Transformation." Intel Newsroom, April 19. Accessed December 18, 2019. https://newsroom .intel.com/news-releases/news-release-intel-announces-restructuring/#gs.m7 go9o.

Jarmin, R. S., and J. Miranda. 2002. "The Longitudinal Business Database." https:// ssrn.com/abstract=2128793.

Jones, C. I., and C. Tonetti. 2020. "Nonrivalry and the Economics of Data." *American Economic Review* 110(9): 2819–58.

Kim, J. D. 2020. "Startup Acquisitions as a Hiring Strategy: Worker Choice and Turnover." https://ssrn.com/abstract=3252784.

Klara, R. 2016. "Intel Hopes This New Spot Will Shake Millennials from Their Malaise." *Adweek*, January 19. https://www.adweek.com/brand-marketing/intel -hopes-new-spot-will-shake-millennials-their-malaise-168998/.

Langley, M. 2015. "Behind Ginni Rometty's Plan to Reboot IBM." *Wall Street Journal*, April 20. https://www.wsj.com/articles/behind-ginni-romettys-plan-to -reboot-ibm-1429577076.

Lodefalk, M. 2013. "Servicification of Manufacturing—Evidence from Sweden." *International Journal of Economics and Business Research* 6(1): 87–113.

———. 2017. "Servicification of Firms and Trade Policy Implications." *World Trade Review* 16(1): 59–83.

Low, P. 2013. "The Role of Services in Global Value Chains." In *Global Value Chains in a Changing World*, edited by D. K. Elms and P. Low, 61–82. Geneva: WTO Publications.

Mills, K. G. 2019. *Fintech, Small Business & the American Dream: How Technology Is Transforming Lending and Shaping a New Era of Small Business Opportunity.* Cham, Switzerland: Palgrave Macmillan.

Moon, Y. 2005. "Inside Intel Inside." HBS Case No. 9–502–083. Boston: Harvard Business School.

390   Sharat Ganapati

Muller, E., and D. Doloreux. 2009. "What We Should Know about Knowledge-Intensive Business Services." *Technology in Society* 31(1): 64–72.
Muro, M., J. Rothwell, S. Andes, K. Fikri, and S. Kulkarni. 2015. *America's Advanced Industries: What They Are, Where They Are, and Why They Matter.* Brookings Advanced Industries Series. Washington, DC: Brookings Institution.
Neumark, D., J. Zhang, and B. Wall. 2005. "Employment Dynamics and Business Relocation: New Evidence from the National Establishment Time Series." NBER Working Paper No. 11647. Cambridge, MA: National Bureau of Economic Research.
Porter, M. E. 2003. "The Economic Performance of Regions." *Regional Studies* 37(6/7): 549–78.
Romer, P. M. 1990. "Endogenous Technological Change." *Journal of Political Economy* 98(5): Part 2, S71–S102.
Rosenberg, N. 1963. "Capital Goods, Technology, and Economic Growth." *Oxford Economic Papers* 15(3): 217–27.
Rothaermel, F. T., K. Grigoriou, G. Retana, and D. R. King. 2015. *IBM at the Crossroads.* New York: McGraw-Hill Education.
Schiff, A. 2016. "Inside Out: Intel Is Reinventing Itself with a Brand Overhaul." *AdExchanger*, February 18. https://adexchanger.com/advertiser/inside-intel-reinventing-brand-overhaul/.
Sheffi, Y. 2012. *Logistics Clusters: Delivering Value and Driving Growth.* Cambridge, MA: MIT Press.
Timmer, M. P., A. A. Erumban, B. Los, R. Stehrer, and G. J. D. Vries. 2014. "Slicing Up Global Value Chains." *Journal of Economic Perspectives* 28(2): 99–118.
Trajtenberg, M. 2019. "Artificial Intelligence as the Next GPT: A Political-Economy Perspective." In *The Economics of Artificial Intelligence: An Agenda*, edited by A. Agrawal, J. Gans, and A. Goldfarb, 175–86. Chicago: University of Chicago Press.
Tripathy, A., and S. D. Eppinger. 2013. "Structuring Work Distribution for Global Product Development Organizations." *Production and Operations Management* 22(6): 1557–75.
Vandermerwe, S., and J. Rada. 1988. "Servitization of Business: Adding Value by Adding Services." *European Management Journal* 6(4): 314–24.
Visnjic Kastalli, I., and B. Van Looy. 2013. "Servitization: Disentangling the Impact of Service Business Model Innovation on Manufacturing Firm Performance." *Journal of Operations Management* 31(4): 169–80.

Comment   Sharat Ganapati

Heterogeneity in the Great Sectoral Shift

The heart of US economic activity has broadly shifted away from manufacturing physical goods toward services over the past 70 years. While

Sharat Ganapati is an assistant professor of international economics at Georgetown University.
Thanks to the organizers Aaron Chatterji, Josh Lerner, Scott Stern, and Michael J. Andrews and to the chapter authors Mercedes Delgado, Daniel Kim, and Karen Mills. Thanks to Serena Sampler for research support. For acknowledgments, sources of research support, and disclosure of the author's material financial relationships, if any, please see https://www.nber.org/books-and-chapters/role-innovation-and-entrepreneurship-economic-growth/comment-servicification-us-economy-role-startups-versus-incumbent-firms-ganapati.

manufacturing accounted for nearly 40 percent of private US employment at the height of World War II, it accounts for just 8 percent today. In contrast, at the start of 2020, services account for 86 percent of total US employment (US Bureau of Labor Statistics 2020). While this broad trend has been widely studied, the broad "services" label masks massive heterogeneity in products, workers, and tasks.

Delgado, Kim, and Mills (chapter 7, this volume) study a particular set of service sub-industries, what they call "Supply Chain Traded Services." These services are not aimed at final consumption but are rather sold as intermediate inputs in the supply chain. Examples range from consulting firms to "Software as a Service" companies (Delgado and Mills 2018). This goal of this chapter is to study employment in this sector (wages and head counts), as well as study the types of establishments and firms operating in this sector. In doing so, Delgado, Kim, and Mills raise and address a series of important aggregate economy-wide consequences.

Splitting Up Services

Why should services be split up and considered separately? In particular, why does either "tradability" or location on a "supply chain" matter? Tradability is important, as it allows for production to be moved across space to places with greater comparative advantages. In the classic trade models, opening up sectors to trade will create a set of winners and losers; the winners being in locations with comparative advantage in that exported group. In today's world, winners include engineers in Silicon Valley, technicians in China, financiers in New York, and oil rig workers in North Dakota.

Service trade has recently opened up and taken off (Jensen et al. 2005). Traditionally, trade and spatial economics assumed a nontraded local service sector (See the Caliendo and Parro (2015) analysis of NAFTA), but newer work assumes that services are increasingly traded over space (Eckert 2019). The causes of the opening of services to trade and the mechanism underpinning it are still in their infancy (Juhász and Steinwender 2018). This chapter helps shed light on the black box of the wage and firm implications.

Supply chains are important for different reasons. Items "farther up" a value chain have an outsized influence on outcomes, ranging from environmental policy to market power (Baqaee and Farhi 2020; Shapiro 2021). In terms of policy, a tax on a consumer output (say, though a consumption tax) may have different effects from that on a primary input.

The intersection of these two divisions may be particularly informative. If a supply chain can be traded across space, forces (such as agglomeration economies) can amplify gains (Moretti 2012) and percolate throughout the economy to great effect. In particular, there should detectable wage and employment effects. As long as labor is imperfectly mobile, if a sector has a productivity jump from agglomeration, as well as increased demand from

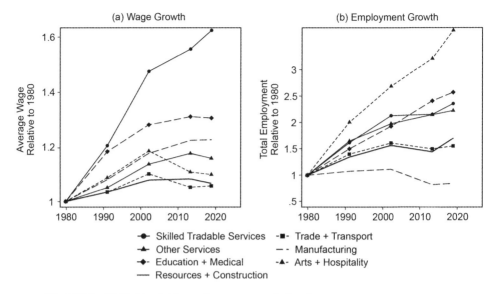

Fig. 7.C.1   Skilled tradable services—aggregate trends
Source: Eckert, Ganapati and Walsh (2019), adjusted by the Bureau of Labor Statistics Consumer Price Indices.

tradability, we should see large wage increases in those regions with productivity advantages.

Service Trend Robustness

Delgado, Kim, and Mills show the importance of these services, omitting the spatial aspect and focusing on the aggregate trends in employment and wages. The authors show that not only has "Supply Chain Trade Services" employment grown, but so have wages. However, it is worthwhile to revisit the spatial nature of these statistics. Eckert, Ganapati, and Walsh (2019) similarly approach this subject, but focusing on the scalable skill content of a task, looking at "Skilled Tradable Services." While conceptually different, this captures a similar set of industries to "Tradable Supply Chain Services" but drops remote call center workers and truck drivers, and adds software engineers and conglomerate executives.

As shown in figure 7.C.1, wages for these closely related "Skilled Tradable Services" have skyrocketed over the past 40 years. However, the employment figures are much more muted—while still growing, they have been outpaced by many other sectors. The question is: Why are these patterns so different? If wages are going up so much, why do we not see a rapid increase in employment? Is it due to the immobility of American workers today (Lee and Wolpin 2006)? Or is there something fundamental about the nature of the work (Garicano and Rossi-Hansberg 2006)?

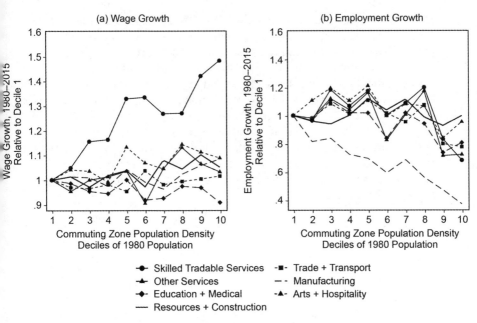

Fig. 7.C.2   Skilled tradable services—regional trends
Source: Eckert, Ganapti, and Walsh (2019).

In figure 7.C.2, Eckert et al. (2019) divide up all US commuting zones (a measure of labor markets) into 10 equally sized deciles. They show that the wage growth in "Skilled Tradable Services" is most significant in the largest and most dense labor markets, but employment growth is not unevenly distributed. Is there something different about these workers in large metropolitan areas? While the wages of engineers and bankers in New York and San Francisco have leapfrogged those of all other workers, their numbers have remained relatively modest. Is the work performed in both "Skilled Tradable Services" and "Supply Chain Services" different when comparing the most dynamic large markets to smaller and less dynamic areas (Hsieh et al. 2019; Rossi-Hansberg, Sarte, and Schwartzman 2019)?

The Role of Firms

The second part of this chapter delves into which firms are driving this trend. Dovetailing nicely with Ding et al. (2019), Delgado, Kim, and Mills find that this "Supply Chain Tradable Services" growth is entirely due to large incumbents growing in size, with the role of new entrants diminishing over time. However, many of these firms are not incumbents in supply chain services; instead, they are often former manufacturing behemoths that have transitioned to supply chain services. This trend echoes the trade literature, showing that China's ascension to the World Trade Organization caused US firms to shift employment away from manufacturing into services (Magyari 2017). This paper shows that this may be a broader part of American structural change—much broader than just from international trade.

The authors show that new firm creation in "Supply Chain Tradable Services" has slowed down, which has many potential economic implications. While it is not clear that the trends in this sector are any different from those in the rest of the economy (Haltiwanger, Jarmin, and Miranda 2013), implications in this sector may matter more due to the centrality of these services to economic growth. These trends tie to two literatures—the first focuses on the role of large firms in the economy and the second on the boundary of the firm.

Superstar Firms

Historically, large firms paid workers more than small firms (Troske 1999). However, this premium has recently fallen (Bloom et al. 2018). "Supply Chain Tradable Services" firms seem to keep up the historical trend in the large firm premium, as opposed to the larger economy. Why? In Autor et al. (2020), the trend in increasing national market concentration from large firms is linked to falling labor compensation. Are these "Supply Chain Tradable Services" different? In Ganapati (2018, 2021), these increases in concentration and market share are entirely due to new fixed-cost technologies, including the cost of communication infrastructure to trade services across space. In this case, the decline of new firms is not a negative thing; a few large firms are simply better than many little firms. Is it truly necessary to have millions of small shopkeepers?

Boundary of the Firm

Does it matter that "servicification" is happening mostly in incumbent firms? Too many sclerotic old firms may cause the economy to deteriorate. These old giants may not invest or innovate, facing the classic "Innovators Dilemma" (Christensen 2013). So why do we not see this? Delgado, Kim, and Mills have one answer. These firms have been forced to innovate due to structural change. As old manufacturing firms saw business dry up (perhaps due to foreign competition), they either died or adapted. The new survivors forged into new service markets, and they found new products and new customers. While observed firm entry seems "low," this is simply due to our ignorance. Many new service companies only look "old" due to their old names; they are effectively new companies that have nearly shed all their old business lines. The IBM of today bears little resemblance to your grandparent's IBM.

References

Autor, David, David Dorn, Lawrence F. Katz, Christina Patterson, and John Van Reenen. 2020. "The Fall of the Labor Share and the Rise of Superstar Firms." *Quarterly Journal of Economics* 135(2): 645–709.

Baqaee, David Rezza, and Emmanuel Farhi. 2020. "Productivity and Misallocation in General Equilibrium." *Quarterly Journal of Economics* 135(1): 105–63.

Bloom, Nicholas, Fatih Guvenen, Benjamin S. Smith, Jae Song, and Till von Wachter. 2018. "The Disappearing Large-Firm Wage Premium." *AEA Papers and Proceedings* 108: 317–22.

Caliendo, Lorenzo, and Fernando Parro. 2015. "Estimates of the Trade and Welfare Effects of NAFTA." *Review of Economic Studies* 82(1): 1–44.

Christensen, Clayton M. 2013. *The Innovator's Dilemma: When New Technologies Cause Great Firms to Fail.* Boston: Harvard Business Review Press.

Delgado, Mercedes, and Karen G. Mills. 2018. "The Supply Chain Economy: A New Industry Categorization for Understanding Innovation in Services." Technical Report, Working Paper 18–068. Boston: Harvard Business School.

Ding, Xiang, Teresa C. Fort, Stephen J. Redding, and Peter K. Schott. 2019. "Structural Change within versus across Firms: Evidence from the United States." Technical Report, Dartmouth Working Paper 2019. Hanover, NH: Dartmouth College.

Eckert, Fabian. 2019. "Growing Apart: Tradable Services and the Fragmentation of the US Economy." Mimeograph, Yale University, New Haven, CT.

Eckert, Fabian, Sharat Ganapati, and Conor Walsh. 2019. "Skilled Tradable Services: The Transformation of US High-Skill Labor Markets." SSRN 3439118.

Ganapati, Sharat. 2018. "The Modern Wholesaler: Global Sourcing, Domestic Distribution, and Scale Economies." US Census Bureau Center for Economic Studies Working Paper, CES-18-49. https://www.census.gov/library/working-papers/2018/adrm/ces-wp-18-49.html.

———. 2021. "Growing Oligopolies, Prices, Output, and Productivity." *American Economic Journal: Microeconomics* 13(3): 309–27.

Garicano, Luis, and Esteban Rossi-Hansberg. 2006. "Organization and Inequality in a Knowledge Economy." *Quarterly Journal of Economics* 121(4): 1383–1435.

Haltiwanger, John, Ron S. Jarmin, and Javier Miranda. 2013. "Who Creates Jobs? Small versus Large versus Young." *Review of Economics and Statistics* 95(2): 347–61.

Hsieh, Chang-Tai, Erik Hurst, Charles I. Jones, and Peter J. Klenow. 2019. "The Allocation of Talent and US Economic Growth." *Econometrica* 87(5): 1439–74.

Jensen, J. Bradford, Lori G. Kletzer, Jared Bernstein, and Robert C. Feenstra. 2005. "Tradable Services: Understanding the Scope and Impact of Services Offshoring [with Comments and Discussion]." In *Brookings Trade Forum 2005*, 75–133. Washington, DC: Brookings Institution Press.

Juhász, Réka, and Claudia Steinwender. 2018. "Spinning the Web: The Impact of ICT on Trade in Intermediates and Technology Diffusion." NBER Working Paper No. 24590. Cambridge, MA: National Bureau of Economic Research.

Lee, Donghoon, and Kenneth I. Wolpin. 2006. "Intersectoral Labor Mobility and the Growth of the Service Sector." *Econometrica* 74(1): 1–46.

Magyari, Ildikó. 2017. "Firm Reorganization, Chinese Imports, and US Manufacturing Employment." Columbia University Job Market Paper, January 16. http://www.columbia.edu/~im2348/JMP_Magyari.pdf.

Moretti, Enrico. 2012. *The New Geography of Jobs.* Boston: Houghton Mifflin Harcourt.

Rossi-Hansberg, Esteban, Pierre-Daniel Sarte, and Felipe Schwartzman. 2019.

"Cognitive Hubs and Spatial Redistribution." NBER Working Paper No. 26267. Cambridge, MA: National Bureau of Economic Research.

Shapiro, Joseph S. 2021. "The Environmental Bias of Trade Policy." *Quarterly Journal of Economics* 136(2): 831–86.

Troske, Kenneth R. 1999. "Evidence on the Employer Size-Wage Premium from Worker-Establishment Matched Data." *Review of Economics and Statistics* 81(1): 15–26.

US Bureau of Labor Statistics. 2020. "Current Employment Statistics." Washington, DC: US Bureau of Labor Statistics. https://download.bls.gov/pub/time.series/ce/.

8

Digitization and Its Consequences for Creative-Industry Product and Labor Markets

Joel Waldfogel

8.1 Introduction

Digitization has transformed many of the creative industries. Technological changes have sharply reduced the costs of creating, distributing, and promoting new products, with two broad consequences. First, there has been an explosion of new products—in movies, books, music, and television—with substantial welfare benefit for consumers. Second, because technological change has reduced the need for physical or financial capital for undertaking investment in new products, it has enabled individuals to bring new products to market largely by supplying their own labor to entrepreneurial creative projects. In this chapter, I explore the consequences of digitization for consumers via the product market as well as for entrepreneurial producers via their labor market activity.

A longstanding product market research tradition characterizes the effect of digitization on product markets generally, and markets for cultural goods in particular, through a "long tail" lens. The idea is that the Internet—and online retailing in particular—gives consumers access to a long tail of low-demand products not available at their local stores (Brynjolfsson, Hu, and Smith 2003). This is an important insight about a large welfare benefit made

Joel Waldfogel is associate dean of MBA Programs and holds the Frederick R. Kappel Chair in Applied Economics at the University of Minnesota, is a research associate of the ZEW and of the National Bureau of Economic Research.

I am grateful for comments from participants in the NBER pre-conference and conference on Innovation and Entrepreneurship. In particular, I thank Gustavo Manso for discussant comments and the editors for additional guidance. For acknowledgments, sources of research support, and disclosure of the author's material financial relationships, if any, please see https://www.nber.org/books-and-chapters/role-innovation-and-entrepreneurship-economic -growth/digitization-and-its-consequences-creative-industry-product-and-labor-markets.

possible by digitization that one might term a "long tail in consumption."
Having access to, say, a million books at Amazon rather than, say, 50,000
titles at a local store may deliver substantial welfare benefits to consumers.

The welfare benefits of digitization may be much larger, however. Digitization not only enables retailers to display products online without any
"shelf space" constraints; digitization also reduces the costs of creating new
varieties in the first place. For example, digitization has radically reduced
the costs of production, distribution, and even promotion for books, music,
movies, and television (Waldfogel 2018 and cites therein). The numbers of
new songs, books, television shows, and movies brought annually to market
have risen sharply. New song creation, for example, has more tripled.

Given the well-known unpredictability of product appeal at the time of
investment, an increase in the volume of new product entry—a "long tail
in production"—can have larger effects on welfare than the standard long
tail. In the conventional long tail narrative, online retailing gives consumers access to large numbers of new products with insufficient appeal to have
been stocked in local stores. All products whose availability is enabled by
digitization are therefore less appealing (on average) than the lowest-selling
product stocked offline. New products whose creation is made possible by
digitization-induced cost reductions are different. Although such products
had insufficient promise to justify their investment when costs were higher,
because of unpredictability, these products can end up throughout the sales
distribution and indeed, many turn out to be commercial successes. This
approach parallels a view of entrepreneurship as experimentation explored
in various studies.[1]

Aguiar and Waldfogel (2018) explore this mechanism explicitly using digitization of the recorded music industry as its context. Given the unpredictability of product success at the time of investment, they find that the change
in consumer surplus associated with the tripling of rate of new product
introduction after digitization gives rise to a welfare benefit 20 times the
size of the standard long tail. The music context is attractive because of
the quality of data on the availability and sales of new products; but as a
substantive matter, music sales are very highly concentrated in the top few
percent of products. For a fuller sense of the effect of the welfare benefits
of this mechanism, it is of interest to revisit these sorts of calculations for
books, movies, and television, three important cultural products whose sales
concentration among top products—and predictability of sales success at
release—may differ. That is the first goal of this chapter.

I also explore the implications of digitization for entrepreneurial creative

---

1. See, for example, Arrow (1969), Weitzmann (1979), Bergemann and Hege (2005), Manso
(2011), and Kerr, Nanda, and Rhoder-Kropf (2014), for studies viewing entrepreneurship as
experimentation. Ewens, Nanda, and Rhodes-Kropf (2018) study the effects of reduced costs
of entrepreneurial experimentation on innovation in cloud computing.

Table 8.1   **Media industries employment and receipts, 2002–2017**

Name	NAICS	Employment				Revenue ($ billion 2017)			
		2002	2007	2012	2017	2002	2007	2012	2017
Book publishers	51113	97,080	104,564	72,329	74,645	38.1	32.6	28.7	29.1
Motion picture and video industries	5121	271,225	308,740	280,679	316,612	85.8	93.7	86.7	88.6
Production	51211	111,112	142,620	120,803	130,640	63.7	70.3	64.7	65.9
Distribution	51212	3,760	5,083	2,843	3,196	1.6	2.4	1.8	1.4
Exhibition	51213	129,982	134,202	131,254	152,948	14.8	14.9	14.5	16.0
Sound recording industries	5122	31,923	27,067	23,818	24,369	20.9	17.8	12.0	13.5
Music publishers	51223	5,943	6,253	5,645	6,197	4.6	5.2	4.5	4.7
Sound recording studios	51224	6,150	6,566	6,311	5,421	0.9	1.0	1.0	0.9

Source: Economic Census, 2002, 2007, 2012, 2017. Based on api calls from, for example, api.census.gov/data /2017/.

labor markets. While digitization has lowered barriers to creating products available to broad audiences—and has therefore also enhanced entrepreneurial opportunities—the spread of digitization has also coincided with growing complaints from creators and intermediaries about earnings. This leads me to two broad questions. First, can I document evidence of new creative activity in various ongoing government databases confirming the growth in creative activity evident in product data? Second, what has happened to creators' earnings in the digital era?

I have four basic findings. First, available data on movies, television, and books confirm the findings of Aguiar and Waldfogel (2018) for music that the random long tail is large compared with the conventional long tail. Second and related, the welfare benefit of new creative products is substantial. Third, available evidence on creative labor markets confirms increased activity evidence in product market creation data (but in contrast with establishment-level data from the Economic Census). Fourth, while total earnings of creative workers are rising, average earnings per worker are falling, although it is not clear how much of the decline in average earnings is simply compositional.

8.2   Some Basic Facts about the Creative Industries

Table 8.1 provides a characterization of the major creative industries' sizes and growth, 2002–2017, from the Economic Census. The book publishing industry had receipts of $29.1 billion in 2017 and employment of about 75,000. The motion picture and video production industries had receipts of $88.6 billion and employment of 317,000. The sound recording industry had $13.5 billion in revenue, employing just under 25,000 people.

The Economic Census is an establishment-level survey; hence, its figures reflect activity that takes place inside firms.[2] While this would be an innocuous caveat for, say, automobiles, few of which are manufactured outside identifiable automobile firms, it is an important qualification for the creative industries, where digitization has allowed a great deal of creative production and distribution to take place outside established firms.

Based on table 8.1 alone, one would not expect or infer the "explosion of creative products" mentioned in the introduction to this chapter. Employment and revenue in book publishing and the sound recording industries have fallen by about a quarter. Motion picture revenue grew 3 percent in real terms between 2002 and 2017. This raises immediate questions about whether establishment-based statistics provide an accurate picture of what's happening to creative output or the experience of creators and consumers. We return to these questions below in our examination of labor-market data—including data on nonemployer establishments—covering creative industries.

8.3   Theory

New technology enables individuals, or smaller-scale groups, without much costly capital to engage in creative entrepreneurship. The specific circumstances vary across creative products, but the ability of individuals to create new products and bring them to market has increased across all creative industries.

Books provide an extreme example. Prior to digitization, an author needed to secure a contract with a major publisher to get a book created and brought to market. This was sufficiently difficult to prevent most would-be authors from attempting to create a book. With the advent of electronic self-publishing—in particular, with the appearance of Amazon's Kindle ecosystem—any author can create a text and make it available to millions of potential readers, without the permission or investment from the traditional gatekeepers (Waldfogel and Reimers 2015).

Music is similar in the extent to which digitization enables individual entrepreneurial product creation. Prior to digitization, artists sought investments from record labels. Without record deals, an artist might perform on a small scale, but there was no real chance of finding a large audience. Digitization changed this radically. Digitization allowed individuals to produce music using inexpensive hardware and software. Garageband software, for example, available on Apple computers and even iPhones, provides the functionality of a recording studio. Even more important, digital distribution—first via iTunes and more recently via streaming services—breaks the bottlenecks of both promotion and distribution. The resulting

2. See https://www.census.gov/data/developers/data-sets/economic-census.html.

increase in creativity is evidenced by the fact that Spotify added nearly a million songs to its system in 2017; essentially anyone can create music and make it available to a wide audience.

Digitization has had similar effects on movie and video production. First, digital photography has reduced the cost of literally producing content. Second, and more important, digital distribution has eliminated distribution bottlenecks. A few decades ago, broadcast television could accommodate about 10 new series per year; and even today, movie theaters in the US can accommodate about 250 films, given that many are released on substantial numbers of screens. But the possibility of watching films and serials directly over the Internet allows for the creation of a great deal more content. The past few years have seen the creation of thousands of new movies per year, as well as literally hundreds of new television series.

While digitization has reduced costs for video production and distribution, it is worth noting that these media remain more expensive than music or books. Music and books can be created by individuals or small groups. Video typically requires a larger number of participants, depending on the subject matter.

Another feature worthy of note is that, particularly in movies, there is a bifurcation between small-scale new products whose success is difficult to predict and larger-scale products, often derivative of prior works, that are both expensive and less risky. Even as the movie industry, broadly construed, has created a large and growing number of new works, most of them small-scale, the traditional major studio players in Hollywood have continued to invest substantial sums in large-scale movies, often sequels to previous movies (see Benner and Waldfogel 2020).

We would expect these technological changes to do two things. First, they would facilitate the participation of more potential creators. That is, they would allow greater participation in the entrepreneurial creative labor force. Second, they would make additional products available to consumers. These outcomes would provide greater competition in the product market as well as some possible benefit to consumers.

The workings of both mechanisms depend on the sorts of products facilitated by the easing of entry barriers. If the additional products are unappealing to consumers, then they would neither divert demand from existing products nor provide much benefit to consumers. However, if the additional products included some products that consumers found appealing, then the relaxation of entry constraints would both provide competition for existing creative products—and their producers—as well as delivering benefits to consumers.

One well-known feature of creative products is the unpredictability of their appeal to consumers. It is well known that most new creative products fail (Caves 2000; Vogel 2014). William Goldman summarized this succinctly with his description of Hollywood executives' ability to predict which movies would succeed, with the saying that "nobody knows anything." If this is correct, then a technological change that facilitates broad participation and many new products would be expected to deliver some products of value to consumers and therefore some consequential competition for other producers.

There is substantial evidence that this mechanism operates, the most corroborative of which is that large and growing shares of the successful products since digitization are products that entered the market with low ex ante promise. These include books originally released via self-publishing, music from independent record labels, and movies from independent producers. For example, over a tenth of the *USA Today* weekly top 150 bestselling books in 2012 began their commercial lives as self-published works. In the romance category, the share was over 40 percent (Waldfogel and Reimers 2015). Similar evidence exists for music, movies, and television (Waldfogel 2018).

Evidence that the random long tail mechanism operates does not directly indicate the size of the welfare benefit. The quantification of the welfare benefit is the task undertaken for music in Aguiar and Waldfogel (2018) and which we continue below for other creative products.

8.3.1   Products

An important research stream in digitization characterizes the benefit of the Internet through the lens of the long tail. The idea is that online retailing gives consumers access to a larger number of products than they could obtain from their local retailers. The idea is summarized simply in a diagram showing the cumulative share of sales on the vertical axis and the cumulative share of products on the horizontal.

If all products sold equally well, the cumulative sales would be a straight, 45 degree line. In reality, of course, some products sell more than others, so the top x percent of products tends to account for more than x percent of sales. As a result, realistic cumulative sales curves initially rise more steeply than the 45 degree line.

The cumulative sales diagram is useful for illustrating the traditional long tail idea. Suppose that traditional brick and mortar stores carry a share, say $1/3$, of the total extant products, as in figure 8.1. Then in the absence of online sales, consumers will have access to this share $1/3$, and sales will be at the quantity $q(1/3)$. Online retailing gives consumers access to the remaining share $(1 - 1/3)$ of products, and sales in the presence of online retailing are $q(1)$. Hence, the benefit from the additional sales relates to this difference, $\Delta = [q(1) - q(1/3)]$. This is the basis for standard estimates of the benefit of online retailing for consumers (Brynjolfsson, Hu, and Smith 2003).[3]

---

3. See also Quan and Williams (2018), who document that terrestrial retailers adapt their assortments to local tastes, so that analysis along the lines of figure 8.1 should be done separately by geography.

Fig. 8.1   Cumulative share of sales variance with the share of top products, with perfect prediction in contrast to a "nobody knows" environment.

The random long tail idea is different. The idea is not simply that digitization gives consumers access to more extant products. Rather, the idea is that digitization, by reducing the costs of bringing new products to market, allows the creation of more new products than would otherwise have been brought to market. The predictability of new product quality adds an important element to the story. If products' appeal to consumers were completely predictable at the time of investment, then while a reduction in cost would give rise to additional new products, all those products would be "worse" than the previous cost threshold. For ease of comparison with the previous example, consider a cost reduction that triples entry (from $1/3$ to 1). Under the old cost threshold, entry occurred out to $1/3$, with associated sales of $q(1/3)$. With lower costs—and perfect predictability—more entry occurs, but all products have lower realized sales than the products entering with higher costs. Hence, the additional entry—out to 1—raises total sales to $q(1)$. The benefit of additional entry with perfect predictability is formally equivalent to the traditional long tail benefit. Here, it is $\Delta = [q(1) - q(1/3)]$.

It is well known that new product success is very unpredictable in media industries (Caves 2000). Goldman (2012) colorfully declared that "nobody knows anything" about which potential Hollywood projects would find favor in the marketplace. Taken literally, the idea that nobody knows anything means that technological change giving rise to a growth in the number of products would bring forth products that are as good, on average, as existing products. In that extreme case—and putting aside substitutability across products—the growth in sales with a growth in products would lie along the 45 degree line, at least in expectation. A tripling in the number of products would then give rise to a tripling in sales and a tripling in the surplus associated with new production. It is useful to compare the welfare gain from new products under the "nobody knows" scenario with the standard long tail, in figure 8.1.

The term Δ_C represents the standard long tail benefits (of additional/online products, all of which are "worse" than existing/local products), while the term Δ_R represents the "random long tail" benefits of additional products that are as good, on average, as existing products.

While it is easy to conclude that product success is not perfectly predictable, the polar opposite—that "nobody knows anything"—is a strong assumption that is probably not correct. The crucial point to understand, however, is that the degree of predictability determines the extent to which the additional products made possible by digitization add to welfare. If predictability were perfect, then the additional products would have benefits similar to standard long tail benefits. The lower the degree of predictability is, the larger will be the benefit of new products. This analysis further points to the degree of predictability as a key determinant of the welfare benefits of new entry. Accordingly, the main empirical task of the product market part of this chapter is to use available (although imperfect) data on movies and books to assess the predictability of product success and the consequent size of the welfare benefit from new products, both absolutely and in comparison with traditional long tail approaches to measurement. That is, we will attempt to estimate Δ_C and Δ_R.

To be clear about the task, suppose we can observe the realized sales for a set of N products after an innovation that allows for additional entry. Order these products from the top-selling (q_1) to the bottom selling (q_N), and suppose that absent the innovation, only the share N_0/N of the eventual products would have been produced, where $N_0 < N$. Define $Q = \sum_{i=1}^{N} q_i$, and define $Q_o = \sum_{i=1}^{N_0} q_i$. Then the standard long tail benefit of the additional $(N - N_0)$ products is $Q - Q_0$.

To quantify the random long tail benefit, we need to determine which N_0 of the N entering products would have entered absent the innovation. We do this by developing a prediction of the realized sales of each product, based on information known at the time of investment decisions. Define the sequence of sales, ordered according to predicted sales, as $q_1', q_2', ..., q_N'$, where the predicted sales for q_k' exceeds the predicted sales for q_{k+1}', although the realized sales need not decline monotonically. That is, the ordering of products will differ from the ordering based on realized sales if there is imperfect predictability. Absent digitization, the N_0 products brought to market are the N_0 products with highest predicted sales. Output in the absence of digitization is given by $Q_0' = \sum_{i=1}^{N_0} q_i'$, and the welfare benefit of digitization is summarized by $Q - Q_0'$. The greater the predictability is, the smaller will be the benefit of new products.

In particular, I seek to quantify the relative size of the "long tail in production" relative to the "long tail in consumption" for books, television, movies, alongside the quantification for music. Doing this requires two things. First, I need to know the amount by which the entry of new products has increased. Second, I need to calculate the share of sales attributable to the new products.

8.3.2   Entrepreneurial Creative Labor Markets

Digitization facilitates entry into the creative product market. A substantial input into production—the predominant input for books and music—is creative labor. Hence, we expect digitization to have consequences for the entrepreneurial creative labor market. It is possible that new modes of consumption (for example, audio and video streaming) have expanded the market, raising demand for creative inputs enough for an increase in activity to be accompanied by higher earnings. It is also possible, however, that earnings would fall in the face of more competition. (It is worth noting here that average creative earnings, as opposed to earnings per hour, might also fall as more people are allowed to participate in create entrepreneurial labor markets on a part-time basis).

Since digitization, many artists have raised concerns about artist and intermediary earnings. Former Recording Industry Association of America head Cary Sherman raised concerns about the adequacy of streaming revenues, particularly for YouTube: "But it's harder and harder for more musicians to make a living. Because the revenue that they're getting from streaming isn't keeping pace with the revenue that they used to be able to earn. We're trying to get to a point where the streaming ecosystem works for everybody."[4] Entertainment executive Irving Azoff echoed Sherman's concerns in a tweet stating that "YouTube's below market rates are a threat to artists' livelihood."[5] Producer Kabir Seghal wrote: "Streaming services that we all use like Spotify and Apple Music offer great convenience to fans. But artists are getting a raw deal. The simple truth is musicians need to be paid more for their content."[6] Musician and business school professor David Lowery has written: "My song got played on Pandora 1 million times and all I got was $16.89, less than what I make from a single T-shirt sale."[7] Lowery continues, "streaming flattens and commoditizes the spin. So you just have one price for every spin of a song across the entire spectrum, whether it's some kind of avant-garde classical work or whether it's a Miley Cyrus song. So that will work if you have lots and lots of spins. But it won't work if you have just a few spins. So what that will do is push out—and you already

4. https://www.recode.net/2016/4/11/11586030/youtube-google-dmca-riaa-cary-sherman.
5. https://www.digitalmusicnews.com/2018/05/23/youtube-music-threat-artist-livelihood/.
6. https://www.cnbc.com/2018/01/26/how-spotify-apple-music-can-pay-musicians-more-commentary.html.
7. https://thetrichordist.com/2013/06/24/my-song-got-played-on-pandora-1-million-times-and-all-i-got-was-16-89-less-than-what-i-make-from-a-single-t-shirt-sale/.

see that happening—it will push out any sort of niche or, you know . . . Specialty genres."[8]

Rights holder concerns are not limited to the music industry. An Author's Guild Survey released in early 2019 describes a "crisis of epic proportions for American authors, particularly for literary writers."[9]

Below I seek to add to this discussion some information about official measures of labor market activity—numbers of people working in creative activities—as well as measures of earnings.

8.4   Data

We need two broad kinds of data for exploring the implications of digitization. First, we need data on the product markets. Second, we need data on creative labor markets. Both kinds of data are challenging to obtain; but some useful data are available. We describe them below.

8.4.1   Product Market Data

The ideal data for measuring the welfare consequences of new products consist of three elements. First, we need a measure of the sales of each product in the market. Second, we need relevant variables for predicting the success of products, and these variables need to be known to agents at the time that investment decisions are made. Finally, we need to know the effect of the innovation on the number of products brought to market (i.e., N_0 vs. N). These are all somewhat challenging to obtain, and I rely on different sources for different products.

8.4.1.1   Books

Rather than considering the entire distribution of sales, I observe the sales ranks for the top 150 best sellers, by week. These data are drawn from the *USA Today* best seller list, which I have available weekly from 1993 to 2016. For each entry on the list, I observe the author, title, genre, publisher, and original release date. I have 20,264 distinct titles from 8,239 distinct authors.

These data fall short of the ideal in two respects. First, I do not observe the full distribution of sales across all releases. Rather, I observe only those making the top 150 in at least one week of the year. Second, I do not observe sales quantities. Rather, I observe only sales ranks. I transform sales ranks into quantities using the rough approximation that sales are proportional to the reciprocal of the rank.[10] I then sum these (1/rank) terms across all

8. https://www.salon.com/2014/08/31/david_lowery_heres_how_pandora_is_destroying _musicians/.

9. https://www.authorsguild.org/industry-advocacy/six-takeaways-from-the-authors -guild-2018-authors-income-survey/.

10. This approach is common in the analysis of rank data. See, for example, Chevalier and Goolsbee (2003).

weeks for which a title enters the best seller list. This gives me an estimate of total sales. The estimate is deficient in two ways: the estimated sales are only approximations to the true values, and I attribute no sales to the titles in weeks when they don't appear in the top 150. Still, the resulting "sales" estimates allow me to calculate a scalar total sales quantity per title.

I have no direct way to deal with the problem that I observe only the head of the sales distribution, except to amend my empirical exercise. Rather than studying the predictability of product success among all released titles, I study the predictability of success among those achieving top-150 status in at least one week. Given the evidence, cited above, that many works with low ex ante promise become best sellers, I can be confident that the head of the sales distribution contains a diversity of works according to their ex ante promise. Because I have best seller lists back to 1993, I am able to construct author-specific past sales measures, which I can use to help predict the success of the current release. Other variables potentially relevant to predicting product success include genre and publisher.

8.4.1.2   Movies

I observe all US-released movies, 1980–2016. The movie data fall short of the ideal in one major respect. While I would like to observe the full distribution of revenue across movies, the only revenue data that are systematically available are box office revenues. These are important for movies in wide release, but this measure misses much of the revenue for movies made possible by digitization, which are generally distributed mainly—and sometimes exclusively—outside of theaters (see Benner and Waldfogel 2020).

What I use instead is a measure of interest that I can obtain for every movie, the number of IMDb users rating each movie. This measure is highly correlated with box office revenue for titles where box office revenue is available, providing some support for its use as a sales proxy. IMDb provides a great deal of information that is potentially relevant to the prediction of movie success (again, measured by the number IMDb ratings). These variables include the production budget, the genre, the identities and past success of the major actors, and the production company. My effective movie database contains 34,279 movies.

8.4.1.3   Television Data

My television data are also drawn from IMDb. I use have information on 16,159 television series produced between 1948 and 2016. I include those with a reported rating on IMDb, which therefore have at least five persons rating the show. As with movies, I use the number of persons rating the show as a measure of its success. I use the following variables for predicting success. I have the show's classification into one of 52 genres and its three most important cast members. I calculate each cast member's experience as the number of series they had appeared in prior to the current series.

Table 8.2   ACS creative occupations (2010 definition), plus taxi and limo

Occupation
Artists and related workers
Actors, producers, and directors
Musicians, singers, and related workers
Entertainers and performers, sports and related workers, all other
Editors, news analysts, reporters, and correspondents
Writers and authors
Media and communication workers
Broadcast and sound engineering technicians
Photographers
Television, video, and motion picture companies
Taxi drivers and chauffeurs

8.4.1.4   Labor Market Data

Ideally, I would have data on time spent on, and earnings derived from, new creative products. That way, I could measure both time spent making creative products, as well as both the overall earnings of those involved and the return to such activities (i.e., the earnings per hour of effort). What I actually have, while substantial, falls short of the ideal. I have household surveys as well as data from tax returns, indicating how many people filed a Schedule C as a nonemployer working in creative activities.

The household survey providing information on employment by occupation is the American Community Survey (ACS). The main purpose of the ACS is to provide "annual (or multi-year average) estimates of selected social, economic, and housing characteristics of the population for many geographic areas and subpopulations."[11] The ACS is based on surveys of 3 million addresses per year. The ACS asks respondents their occupations and their incomes, and it contains sampling weights that allow for the creation of population estimates. Table 8.2 lists the relevant creative occupations in the ACS.[12]

A second government data source of interest covers "nonemployer establishments." These data, from tax records, provide another possible glimpse into creators' labor force activity. Self-employed individuals with business income are required to complete a Schedule C. In filling out this form, the individual also indicates their industry. The Internal Revenue Service (IRS) maintains statistics on nonemployer establishments with Schedule C filings of $1,000 or more. Industries relevant to the creation of books, music, movies, and television include those listed in table 8.3.

11. https://www.census.gov/topics/income-poverty/poverty/guidance/data-sources/acs-vs-cps.html.
12. The Current Population Survey (CPS) has a similar approach but much smaller coverage. Efforts to detect evidence of an increase in creative activity among individuals in creative occupations were unsuccessful with the CPS.

Table 8.3   **Codes for schedule C and therefore for nonemployer statistics**

NAICS code	Name	2016 establishments
711510	Independent artists, writers, & performers	849,176
511000	Publishing industries (except Internet)	72,348
512100	Motion picture & video industries (except video rental)	83,331
512200	Sound recording industries	25,206

Notes: From 2018 Instructions for Schedule C, Principal Business or Professional Activity Codes, p C-17, at https://www.irs.gov/pub/irs-pdf/i1040sc.pdf. From page C-3: "Enter on line B the six-digit code from the Principal Business or Professional Activity Codes chart at the end of these instructions."

Nonemployer Statistics (NES) is an annual series that provides subnational economic data for businesses that have no paid employees and are subject to federal income tax. The data consist of the number of businesses and total receipts by industry. Most nonemployers are self-employed individuals operating unincorporated businesses (known as sole proprietorships), which may or may not be the owner's principal source of income. Statistics are available on businesses that have no paid employment or payroll, are subject to federal income taxes, and have receipts of $1,000 or more.[13]

While these data are technically available at the industry level, the nonemployer "establishments" are generally self-employed individuals.

8.5   Results: Welfare Benefit of New Products

A natural way to quantify the welfare benefit of new products is to estimate a utility-theory-consistent demand model that allows calculation of consumer surplus as a function of the products in the choice set. Aguiar and Waldfogel (2018) present such an approach, while also documenting that the size of the random long tail in relation to the conventional long tail is well summarized with a simple calculation. That simple calculation is the ratio of the share of sales accounted for by the ex ante long tail to the share of sales in the ex post long tail.

Accordingly, I estimate the welfare benefit of digitization by ascertaining which of recent products only exist because of digitization. To do this, I attempt to determine which, among a set of recent products, had modest ex ante probabilities of success. I assume that, say, x percent of products would not have come to market absent digitization. I then ask what share of current sales are accounted for by the products that would have been created without digitization. Finally, I compare this "random long tail" in production with something analogous to the standard long tail, the share of sales accounted for by the lowest-selling x percent of new products.

13. https://www.census.gov/programs-surveys/nonemployer-statistics/about.html.

Table 8.4   **Product success prediction**

	Television	Movies	Books
# possible variables	191	102	179
# chosen by LASSO	31	85	146
R2 out of sample	0.110	0.5721	0.2151

Note: For each product, a LASSO model is run relating log sales or its proxy to potential predictors, including past measures of author or actor success, genre, etc.

Doing this calculation requires two steps. First, I need to determine which among a crop of recent products would not have been produced but for digitization. For this purpose, I predict product success using information available at the time of entry. I assume that the products with low ex ante probabilities of success (the "ex ante losers") would have come to market without digitization. I then quantify the share of sales accounted for by the ex ante losers, which I view as a rough estimate of the welfare gain from digitization.

8.5.1   Predicting Ex Ante Product Success

I am interested in predictions of product success, as opposed to explanation. Hence, I use predictive tools suited to this purpose. In particular, I use cross-validated LASSO (Least Absolute Shrinkage and Selection Operator) regressions. For each of the three products—books, movies, and television series—I regress the log of my "sales" measure on interactions of the explanatory variables described above. I allow the cross-validation procedure to choose the penalty parameter that minimizes out-of-sample mean squared error.

To predict the success of individual books and movies, I regress measures of "sales" for an entering cohort of products on various explanatory variables and interactions. For books these include interactions of publisher, genre, publication year, and authors' prior sales, for a total of 179 possible explanatory variables. From these, the LASSO procedure selects 146 variables for inclusion. For movies, these include interactions of genre, budget, and year for a total of 102 explanatory variables. LASSO includes 85 of these variables. For television series, these include 191 possible variables, and LASSO selects only 31. The resulting models explain different shares of the variation across products. The R-squared for movies is 0.57, while it is 0.21 for books, and 0.11 for television shows. Table 8.4 summarizes the regressions. It is interesting that the movie industry, which inspired the phrase, "nobody knows anything," has the highest share of variance explained by the regression. The lower R-squared values for the other products suggest higher random long tail benefits for those products, relative to the conventional long tail.

8.5.2   Welfare Effects

The sales predictions ($\hat{q}_i$) allow us to order products according to ex ante promise. Then, given the number of products that would have been produced but for the innovation that reduced the cost threshold, we can calculate the realized sales that the chosen products would have delivered. The top panels of figures 8.2–8.4 report these results via comparisons between the cumulative sales distributions, ordered according to realized vs. predicted sales, for each of the three products for specific recent years (2016 for books and movies and 2015 for television). In these figures, the solid, upper line shows the cumulative sales in decreasing order according to realized sales. The lower, dashed line shows the cumulative realized sales but ordered according to expected sales. By construction, both lines begin at the origin and terminate in the sale cumulative sales. But they diverge between the extremes because of imperfect prediction.

The patterns differ fairly substantially among books, movies, and television series. First, realized sales are far more concentrated for movies and television shows than for books. We see this in the initial steepness of the realized sales for movies and television series. The Gini coefficients bear out the comparison: 0.935 for television and 0.938 for movies, compared with 0.806 for books. Thus, the conventional long tail is larger for books than for the other categories. Second, movie success is far more predictable than television or book success. We see this in the proximity of the dashed line— sales ordered by ex ante promise—to the solid one for movies.

What do these patterns mean for the welfare benefits of digitization? We have two measures of interest, both of which depend on the number of new products that would have been produced absent digitization. First, we can quantify the random long tail in relation to the conventional long tail (Δ_R / Δ_C). Second, we can measure the share of total sales attributable to products made possible by digitization.

Consider first the bottom panel of figure 8.2, for movies. The downward-sloping line shows the share of total sales accounted for by the new products made possible by digitization. The vertical line at 250 reflects the idea that the movie industry produced roughly 250 movies per year prior to digitization. At $N = 250$, the welfare gain—measured as additional revenue—is about 10 percent of revenue.[14] How large is this in absolute terms? As table 8.5 shows, US box office revenue in 2016 was $11.4 billion. As of the early 2000s, box office revenue accounted for 17.9 percent of overall Hollywood revenue. This suggests that total US movie industry domestic revenue is on the order

---

14. This 10 percent is the difference between the total revenue from all products and the value of the ex ante line at $N = 250$, divided by total revenue.

A. Cumulative sales of 2016 movies, ex post versus ex ante

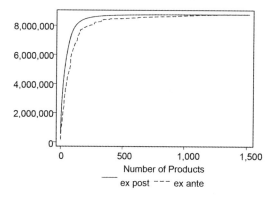

B. Welfare gain as a share of total 2016 sales, movies

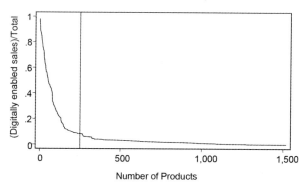

Fig. 8.2 **Cumulative sales of 2016 movies, ex post versus ex ante, and welfare gain as a share of total 2016 sales of movies**

Table 8.5   Revenue, products absent digitization, and Δ_R/Δ_C

	US Revenue	Products absent digitization	Δ_R/Δ_C
Books	$26.27 b (2016)	1500	8.62
Television	$37 billion (2013)	100	12.89
Movies	$63 billion = $11.4/0.179 (2016)	250	3.83

Notes: book revenue (https://www.statista.com/statistics/271931/revenue-of-the-us-book-publishing-industry/). Movie (https://www.latimes.com/business/hollywood/la-fi-ct-mpaa-annual-report-20180404-story.html)—US box office only. For box office as a share of total revenue, see http://www.edwardjayepstein.com/table2.htm. Box office = 17.9 percent. Television production revenue (https://www.statista.com/statistics/293450/revenue-of-television-production-in-the-us/).

A. Cumulative usage of 2015 TV shows, ex post versus ex ante

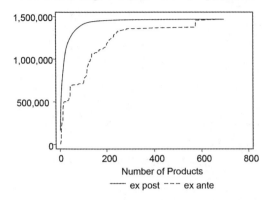

Number of Products

——— ex post − − − ex ante

B. Welfare gain as a share of total 2015 sales, TV

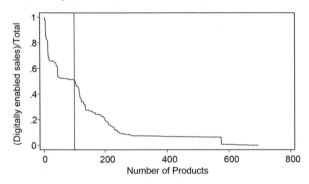

Number of Products

Fig. 8.3   Cumulative usage of 2015 TV shows, ex post versus ex ante, and welfare gain as a share of total 2015 sales, TV

of $63 billion. Hence, the share of revenue attributable to products that exist only because of digitization is 10 percent of $63 billion, or about $6.3 billion.

We can do a similar calculation for television. The bottom panel of figure 8.3 shows two things. First, prior to digitization, there were roughly 100 new shows per year. Second, the figure's downward-sloping line shows that roughly half of television industry "sales" are attributable to products beyond the first 100, those made possible by digitization. Television industry revenue is difficult to calculate, since some of television content is broadcast on ad-supported networks, while other television is distributed via subscriptions (e.g., HBO or Netflix). We can get a rough sense of the order of magnitude of the industry from annual production costs. These came to $37 billion in the US for 2013. On the logic that production occurs in the expectation of revenue in excess of production costs, the production

A. Cumulative sales of 2016 books, ex post versus ex ante

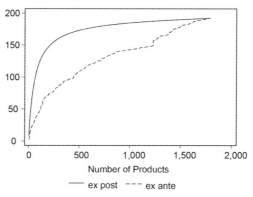

Number of Products

—— ex post   - - - ex ante

B. Welfare gain as a share of total 2016 sales of books

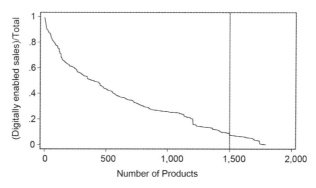

Number of Products

Fig. 8.4   Cumulative sales of 2016 books, ex post versus ex ante, and welfare gain as a share of total 2016 sales of books

expenditures would provide an underestimate of aggregate revenue. Half of the $37 billion would be $18.5 billion.

Books are slightly more complicated, in that we don't observe the entire population of new works. To perform the analogous calculation on books, we need to know the number of best sellers, rather than total works, that would have existed absent digitization. This is difficult to determine. Since the mid-2010s, about 10 percent of best sellers were works that came to market as self-published books. It is difficult beyond that to say what share of best sellers only came to market because of digitization. The bottom panel of figure 8.4 has a vertical line at 1,500, as if 1,500 of the best sellers would have existed absent digitization. Under that assumption, about 10 percent of the sales of best sellers would be for books made possible by digitization. US book sales were about $26 billion in 2016, so books made possible by digitization account for about $2.6 billion of this.

And how large is the random long tail relative to the conventional long tail? Evaluated at the vertical lines in the bottom panels of figures 8.2–8.4, the ratio Δ_R / Δ_C—which was roughly 20 for music in Aguiar and Waldfogel (2018)—is 3.83 for movies, 12.89 for television, and 8.62 for books. Here, too, the random long tail is much larger than its conventional counterpart.

8.6   Results: Labor Market Outcomes

We know that the numbers of new products have risen sharply in books, music, television, and movies. The creation of these products requires some activity by people, which might appear in labor market statistics, even if they do not appear readily in the Economic Census figures in table 8.1. That is, the product creation documented above reflects entrepreneurial labor market activity by creative individuals. The resulting products, as we have seen, have varying degrees of success. Moreover, the existence of many new products provides competition for other products, with possible consequences for the returns to creating new products. Below we explore each of these issues in turn. The questions here have clear parallels to research on whether entrepreneurship pays. Some important examples include Hamilton (2000) and Moskowitz and Vissing-Jørgensen (2002), who find that entrepreneurship does not pay, and Manso (2016), who finds that it does, when option value is properly measured.

8.6.1   Can We See Digitization-Enabled Creative Activity in the Government Data?

Our first question is a mundane but important one: Do the available data sources surveying individuals, the ACS and the IRS nonemployer statistics, reflect the activity underlying the increase in the number of creative products created? Before turning to this question, we can make an easier ask of these data sources: Do they indicate the growth in drivers apparently working for Uber and Lyft? Uber's revenue grew from $0.1 billion in 2013 to $6.5 billion in 2016 and reached $11.3 billion in 2018. The growth has been rapid and abrupt, and rides require drivers, so it should be possible to see evidence of this new digitization-enabled activity in the data.

Among the occupations in the ACS is the category of "taxi driver and chauffeurs." Figure 8.5 shows the number of people reporting that they work in this occupation in the ACS. The figure rises slowly from about 400,000 to 500,000 between 2000 and 2013. Between 2013 and 2017, the figure rises by another 300,000, topping 800,000 in 2017. This coincides well with the rapid growth in ridesharing apps, particularly Uber, documented in Hall and Krueger (2016).

The nonemployer statistics provide similar corroboration. Figure 8.6 shows the number of nonemployer establishments NAICS code 4853 ("taxi and limousine services") rising from about 100,000 in the late 1990s to about

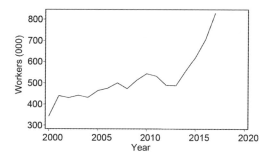

Fig. 8.5   Taxicab drivers and chauffeurs in the ACS

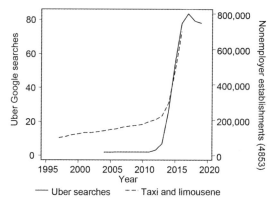

—— Uber searches   — — Taxi and limousene

Fig. 8.6   Uber and nonemployer establishment growth

200,000 in 2013. By 2016, the number was about 700,000. At least for occupations with abrupt growth, the ACS and IRS statistics corroborate what one expects for the underlying activity.

With figure 8.7, we turn to numbers of individuals working in creative occupations in the ACS. The four relevant occupations continuously available using the 2010 occupation classifications include actors, producers, and directors; musicians, singers, and related workers; writers and authors; and photographers. All show substantial growth during 2000–2016. The number of actors increase from 200,000 to nearly 300,000. Musician numbers increase from 200,000 to almost 280,000. The number of writers and authors increase from under 200,000 in 2000 to over 300,000 in 2016, and there is a jump in 2012, which coincides with the Kindle era at Amazon.[15] The number of photographers increases from 150,000 to nearly 250,000.

15. December 2011 saw the peak search volume on the term "Amazon Kindle" according to Google Trends. See https://trends.google.com/trends/explore?date=all&geo=US&q=%2Fm%2F03d068f.

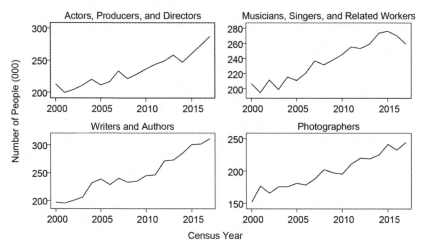

Fig. 8.7   Creative workers by occupation from ACS
Note: Graphs by occupation, 2010 basis.

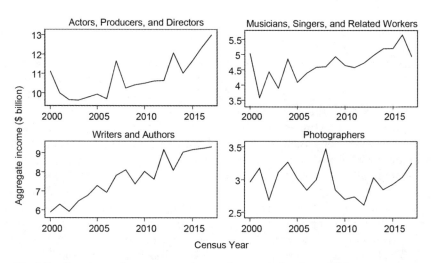

Fig. 8.8   Creative worker aggregate income by occupation from ACS
Note: Graphs by occupation, 2010 basis.

Figure 8.8 shows aggregate earnings in each category from the ACS. Despite fluctuations, aggregate earnings rise in all but the photography category. Figure 8.9 shows what happened to real average earnings in each of these categories. While all fluctuate year to year, there are clear downward trends. As the number of people working in these occupations has risen, the average earnings per worker have declined.

Figure 8.10 documents the evolution of creative occupation employment

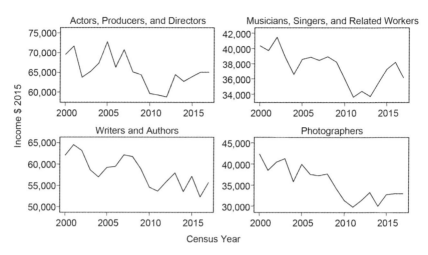

Fig. 8.9   Creative Worker Earnings from ACS
Note: Graphs by occupation, 2010 basis.

according to the IRS nonemployer statistics. Here the relevant categories are independent artists, writers, and performers (NAICS 7115), sound recordings (NAICS 5122), motion pictures (NAICS 5121), and publishing except Internet (NAICS 511). The first—and broad—category grows steadily and sharply over the digital era, from about 425,000 in 1997 to about 850,000 in 2016. Sound recording and motion picture nonemployer establishments also grow, but by much smaller absolute amounts. Publishing grows quickly from 1997 to about 2004, then holds steady. (See also Table 8.6, which compares employment growth according to IRS nonemployer statistics, with employment growth according to County Business Patterns.)

Digitization's enablement of creative work has no discrete date as clear as, say, the arrival of Uber. Hence, it is difficult to say whether the broad growth of individuals filing Schedule C forms for nonemployer establishments in creative industries is specifically caused by digitization.

The IRS data are nevertheless potentially useful for documenting the evolution of both total self-employment earnings in these occupations, as well as the average earnings per filer. Figure 8.11 aggregates the four NAICS codes. The top panel shows the substantial growth in individuals across these categories, from about a half million to a million. The second panel shows that the total earnings have risen from about $16 to $24 billion. The third panel shows that the average earnings have fallen from $30,000 in 1997 to about $24,000 in 2009 and have remained at that level in real terms to 2016.

The tax return–based figures appear to confirm much of what's evident in the ACS data. First, there is quite substantial growth in the number of

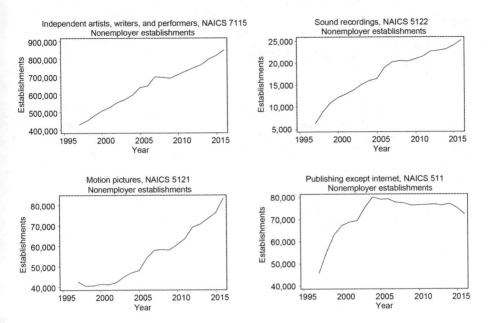

Fig. 8.10   Nonemployer establishments related to books, music, movies, and television

establishments (individuals) creating works for money. This provides evidence that the large outpouring of new works is generating income for the individuals creating it. The IRS data also show that the per capita business income of those individuals with this income is falling, by roughly 10 percent in the most general category and by much more in the more specific categories.

Even if the data are relatively clear, much remains unanswered. That is, while the government data do reflect the activity manifesting itself as a growth in new products, it is not clear that the reduction in average earnings reflects falling returns to creative entrepreneurship, as opposed to a changing mix of people involved in the activities.

Figure 8.12 provides suggestive evidence that composition—and the influx of new workers—explains the decline in average earnings over time. The figure presents the 90th, 50th, and 10th percentiles of the ACS log earnings distributions, by category. At the top and the middle of the distributions, earnings are stable over time. Earnings at the bottom of the distribution, by contrast, fall substantially.

One final comment is in order. The rather different pictures emerging from the establishment-level data cited in the introduction and the individual-level data analyzed here indicates that digitization—by enabling production to

Table 8.6   Disintermediating industries: Those in which nonestablishment growth exceeds employment growth, 1999–2016 (Creative industries in bold)

NAICS code	Industry name	Growth in nonemployer establishments, 1999–2016	Growth in CBP employment, 1999–2016	Nonemployer establishments, 2016	CBP employment, 2016
812	Personal and laundry services	1,208,604	179,902	2,720,918	1,441,285
531	Real estate	1,026,738	337,006	2,595,577	1,563,001
485	Transit and ground passenger Transportation	716,632	145,970	869,052	515,992
711	**Performing arts, spectator sports, and related industries**	**610,364**	**173,370**	**1,221,596**	**503,751**
7115	**Independent artists, writers, and performers**	**367,394**	**9,752**	**849,176**	**46,638**
484	Truck transportation	217,607	76,420	587,038	1,460,598
811	Repair and maintenance	128,181	−53,455	747,224	1,265,012
492	Couriers and messengers	70,242	33,578	197,355	611,946
115	Support activities for agriculture and forestry	26,013	−762	112,936	97,574
5122	**Sound recording industries**	**14,239**	**−265**	**25,206**	**22,940**
511	**Publishing industries (except Internet)**	**9,211**	**−88,098**	**72,348**	**916,599**
339	Miscellaneous manufacturing	8,972	−193,183	72,089	541,059
325	Chemical manufacturing	8,043	−119,583	14,302	766,771
336	Transportation equipment manufacturing	7,198	−401,944	10,769	1,504,272
221	Utilities	5,266	−28,145	19,613	638,917
332	Fabricated metal product manufacturing	5,020	−382,218	38,222	1,406,266
481	Air transportation	4,233	−116,398	20,585	466,440
442	Furniture and home furnishings stores	3,018	−72,091	40,015	453,251
315	Apparel manufacturing	2,176	−478,117	26,412	96,791
337	Furniture and related product manufacturing	2,046	−254,251	18,119	368,902
532	Rental and leasing services	1,445	−109,511	79,373	512,405
314	Textile product mills	1,355	−108,958	3,706	113,013
334	Computer and electronic product manufacturing	1,266	−828,790	9,461	786,387
316	Leather and allied product manufacturing	1,198	−48,288	5,246	25,678
313	Textile mills	1,056	−260,334	2,020	101,952
331	Primary metal manufacturing	622	−221,750	4,069	375,873
324	Petroleum and coal products manufacturing	441	−4,356	1,568	104,748
483	Water transportation	342	−6,712	6,645	65,132
333	Machinery manufacturing	95	−367,476	15,487	1,030,750

A. Creative nonemployer establishments, NAICS: 511, 5121, 5122, 7115

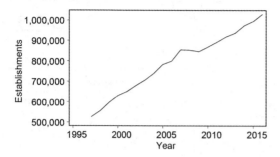

B. Aggregate earnings at nonemployer establishments, NAICS: 511, 5121, 5122, 7115

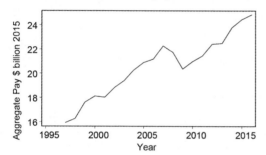

C. Earnings per nonemployer establishment, NAICS: 511, 5121, 5122, 7115

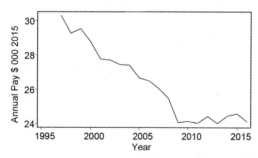

Fig. 8.11   Aggregate and per capita earnings at creative nonemployer establishments

take place outside traditional firms—has challenged the extent to which some statistical indexes reflect underling activity and the experiences of both creative workers and consumers.

8.7   Conclusion

Digitization has changed the conditions surrounding the production of creative products. Less capital is required, so not only has there been more

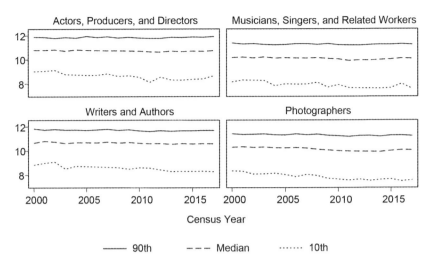

Fig. 8.12   Log earnings distribution over time
Note: Graphs by occupation, 2010 basis.

entry; there has also been a shift of new product creation outside traditional firms. To put this another way, digitization has enabled viable creative entrepreneurship that would have been difficult earlier. The results of these changes include substantial benefits to consumers, in the form of products accounting for substantial shares of sales that would not have existed without digitization. These products are made available because many more would-be creators are able to bring new products to market; and as with ridesharing drivers, we can see this activity in government data. Activity is increasing, as are total earnings of creative workers; but average earnings are falling, particularly at the bottom of the earnings distribution. It is difficult to draw more nuanced conclusions about returns with existing data; but it seems to be a topic that would be fruitful for additional research.

References

Aguiar, L., and J. Waldfogel. 2018. "Quality Predictability and the Welfare Benefits from New Products: Evidence from the Digitization of Recorded Music." *Journal of Political Economy* 126(2): 492–524.

Arrow, K. 1969. "Classificatory Notes on the Production and Diffusion of Knowledge." *American Economic Review* 59: 29–35.

Benner, M. J., and J. Waldfogel. 2020. "Changing the Channel: Digitization and the Rise of 'Middle Tail' Strategies." *Strategic Management Journal* 2020: 1–24. https://doi.org/10.1002/smj.3130.

Bergemann, D., and U. Hege. 2005. "The Financing of Innovation: Learning and Stopping." *RAND Journal of Economics* 36(4): 719–52.

Brynjolfsson, E., Y. Hu, and M. D. Smith. 2003. "Consumer Surplus in the Digital Economy: Estimating the Value of Increased Product Variety at Online Booksellers." *Management Science* 49(11): 1580–96.

Caves, R. E. 2000. *Creative Industries: Contracts between Art and Commerce*, No. 20. Cambridge, MA: Harvard University Press.

Chevalier, J., and A. Goolsbee. 2003. "Measuring Prices and Price Competition Online: Amazon.com and Barnes and Noble.com." *Quantitative Marketing and Economics* 1(2): 203–22.

Cuntz, A., and A. L. Miller. 2018. *Unpacking Predictors of Income and Income Satisfaction for Artists*, Vol. 50. Geneva: World Intellectual Property Organization.

Cuntz, A. 2018. *Creators' Income Situation in the Digital Age*, No. 755. Luxembourg: LIS Cross-National Data Center Luxembourg.

Ewens, M., R. Nanda, and M. Rhodes-Kropf. 2018. "Cost of Experimentation and the Evolution of Venture Capital." *Journal of Financial Economics* 128(3): 422–42.

Goldman, W. 2012. *Adventures in the Screen Trade*. London: Hachette UK.

Hall, Jonathan V., and Alan B. Krueger. 2016. "An Analysis of the Labor Market for Uber's Driver-Partners in the United States." NBER Working Paper No. 22843. Cambridge, MA: National Bureau of Economic Research.

Hamilton, B. H. 2000. "Does Entrepreneurship Pay? An Empirical Analysis of the Returns to Self-Employment." *Journal of Political Economy* 108(3): 604–31.

Jackson, Emilie, Adam Looney, and Shanthi Ramnath. 2017. "The Rise of Alternative Work Arrangements: Evidence and Implications for Tax Filing and Benefit Coverage." Office of Tax Analysis Working Paper 114, January. Washington, DC: US Department of the Treasury.

Katz, Lawrence F., and Alan B. Krueger. 2016. "The Rise and Nature of Alternative Work Arrangements in the United States, 1995–2015." NBER Working Paper No. 22667. Cambridge, MA: National Bureau of Economic Research.

———. 2019. "Understanding Trends in Alternative Work Arrangements in the United States." NBER Working Paper No. 25425. Cambridge, MA: National Bureau of Economic Research.

Kerr, W., R. Nanda, and M. Rhodes-Kropf. 2014. "Entrepreneurship as Experimentation." *Journal of Economic Perspectives* 28: 25–48.

Manso, G. 2011. "Motivating Innovation." *Journal of Finance* 66(5): 1823–60.

———. 2016. "Experimentation and the Returns to Entrepreneurship." *Review of Financial Studies* 29(9): 2319–40.

Moskowitz, Tobias J., and Annette Vissing-Jørgensen. 2002. "The Returns to Entrepreneurial Investment: A Private Equity Premium Puzzle?" *American Economic Review* 92(4): 745–78.

Quan, T. W., and K. R. Williams. 2018. "Product Variety, Across-Market Demand Heterogeneity, and the Value of Online Retail." *RAND Journal of Economics* 49(4): 877–913.

Ruggles, Steven, Sarah Flood, Ronald Goeken, Josiah Grover, Erin Meyer, Jose Pacas, and Matthew Sobek. 2018. IPUMS *USA: Version 8.0* [dataset]. Minneapolis, MN: IPUMS. https://doi.org/10.18128/D010.V8.0.

Vogel, H. L. 2014. *Entertainment Industry Economics: A Guide for Financial Analysis*. Cambridge: Cambridge University Press.

Waldfogel, J. 2016. "Cinematic Explosion: New Products, Unpredictabilty and Realized Quality in the Digital Era." *Journal of Industrial Economics* 64(4): 755–72.

———. 2017a. "The Random Long Tail and the Golden Age of Television." *Innovation Policy and the Economy* 17: 1–25.

————. 2017b. "How Digitization Has Created a Golden Age of Music, Movies, Books, and Television." *Journal of Economic Perspectives* 31(3): 195–214.

————. 2018. *Digital Renaissance: What Data and Economics Tell Us about the Future of Popular Culture.* Princeton, NJ: Princeton University Press.

Waldfogel, J., and I. Reimers. 2015. "Storming the Gatekeepers: Digital Disintermediation in the Market for Books." *Information Economics and Policy* 31: 47–58.

Weitzman, M. L. 1979. "Optimal Search for the Best Alternative." *Econometrica: Journal of the Econometric Society* 47(3): 641–54.

Comment   Gustavo Manso

Joel Waldfogel's chapter 8 (this volume) studies the impact of digitization on creative products and labor markets. It argues that digitization reduces the costs of creating, distributing, and promoting products, allowing for the introduction of new high-value products. In the context of movies, television, and books, estimated welfare gains are substantial. While labor activity increases with digitization, earnings per worker fall.

Previous research has argued that digitization on product markets increases welfare by giving access to a "long tail" of low-demand products not available in local brick-and-mortar stores (Brynjolffson, Hu, and Smith 2003). The black bars in figure 8.C.1, which represents the sales of products facilitated by digitization, illustrate such welfare gains.

The innovation in chapter 8 is to note that digitization reduces the costs of experimentation, allowing potentially blockbuster products to be discovered. Rather than the conventional long tail depicted in the figures above, Waldfogel argues for a random long tail, represented by the black bars in figure 8.C.2. Digitization produces not only inferior products but also blockbusters that were previously unknown. The welfare gains implied by the random long tail are large compared to the welfare gains implied by the conventional long tail (9 times as large for books, 13 times as large for television, 4 times as large for books).

There are numerous examples of successful artists who likely would have remained unknown if not for digitization. The duo Jack & Jack made it to the top of the iTunes album chart in 2015.[1] Also in 2015, writer Mark

Gustavo Manso is a professor of finance and holds the William A. and Betty H. Hasler Chair in New Enterprise Development at the University of California, Berkeley.

For acknowledgments, sources of research support, and disclosure of the author's material financial relationships, if any, please see https://www.nber.org/books-and-chapters/role-innovation-and-entrepreneurship-economic-growth/comment-digitization-and-its-consequences-creative-industry-product-and-labor-markets-manso.

1. See https://www.forbes.com/sites/natalierobehmed/2015/07/24/how-these-independent-artists-reached-no-1-on-the-itunes-chart/#4a18c16262a0.

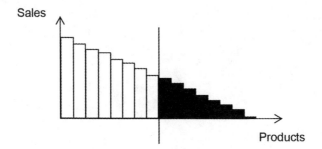

Fig. 8.C.1   Conventional long tail

Note: Open bars represent sales of products that were in the market before digitization, while shaded bars represent sales of products facilitated by digitization. This figure represents the conventional long tail view according to which products facilitated by digitization have lower overall.

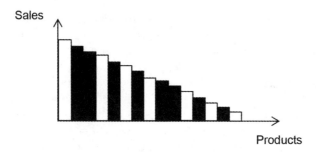

Fig. 8.C.2   Random long tail

Note: Open bars represent sales of products that were in the market before digitization, while shaded bars represent sales of products facilitated by digitization. This figure represents the random long tail view according to which some products facilitated by digitization may be breakthroughs and have higher overall sales.

Dawson was reported to be earning $450,000 a year from the books he self-published at Amazon Kindle Direct Publishing.[2]

Chapter 8 also shows that digitization leads to increased activity in these creative labor markets. However, the abovementioned examples of success are the exception to the rule, as average pay per creative worker decreases with digitization.

My discussion of the chapter revolves around estimation challenges and the relationship to the existing literature. Concerning estimation challenges, I will focus on (1) product success prediction, (2) substitution and cannibalization, and (3) sales vs. total surplus.

2. See https://www.forbes.com/sites/jaymcgregor/2015/04/17/mark-dawson-made-750000-from-self-published-amazon-books/#7dde47a76b5b.

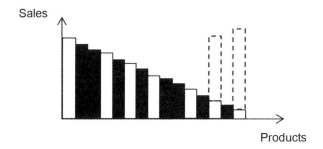

Fig. 8.C.3   Substitution or cannibalization

Note: Open bars represent sales of products that were in the market before digitization, shaded bars represent sales of products facilitated by digitization, and dashed bars represent lost sales of pre-existing products due to the introduction of products facilitated by digitization.

Chapter 8 attempts to estimate the welfare increase implied by the random vs. conventional long tail hypotheses. To predict which products were made possible by digitization, Waldfogel relies on LASSO regressions with sales as the dependent variable and product characteristics as independent variables. Products that have low predicted sales are the ones made possible by digitization, and they are associated with random long tail welfare gains.

One challenge for this approach is that any estimation error in the predictive regression used in chapter 8 tends to overestimate the random long tail welfare gains. If the predictive regression is misspecified (e.g., omitted variable), then we may consider products that would have been around anyway as products made possible by digitization. As a result, our welfare gains may seem to be like the black bars in figure 8.C.2, when in fact, reality is closer to the black bars in figure 8.C.1.

Another challenge is the potential for substitution or cannibalization. What if new products due to digitization are successful at the expense of other traditional products? Figure 8.C.3 illustrates this possibility. The dashed bars represent cannibalization of traditional products. Welfare gains are thus overestimated as they fail to take into account the losses that new products inflict on existing products.

Finally, realized sales may diverge from welfare. For example, digitization may increase competition which leads to lower prices. Sales data would miss a part of the welfare gains. Figure 8.C.4 illustrate this possibility. The dashed bar over the shaded bar represents additional consumer surplus not captured by the sales data.

The "random long tail" hypothesis has parallels in the entrepreneurship and innovation literature. As Waldfogel argues in chapter 8, "no one knows anything" about a product before its launch. This is analogous to the notion that innovation is the result of experimentation with new ideas (Arrow 1969). Weitzman (1979) uses a statistical class of decision problems, called "bandit

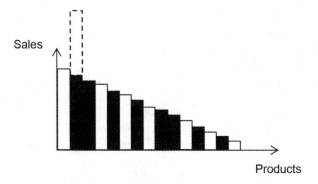

Fig. 8.C.4   Sales price is different from total surplus
Note: Open bars represent sales of products that were in the market before digitization, shaded bars represent sales of products facilitated by digitization, and dashed bars represent additional consumer surplus not captured by the sales data.

problems," to model the experimentation process that results in innovation. Bergemann and Hege (2005) and Manso (2011) consider incentives for innovation in principal-agent models, in which the agent experiments with new ideas in a bandit problem setup.

Digitization reduces the costs of experimentation, since it facilitates product creation, distribution, and promotion of new products. In a related study, Ewens, Nanda, and Rhodes-Kropf (2018) analyze how the introduction of cloud computing services by Amazon in 2006, which reduces the cost of experimentation, affects venture capital (VC) investment strategy. They show that after the introduction of cloud computing, VCs switch to a "spray and pray" strategy, in which they allocate small amounts of funding to many different firms without spending much time on due diligence for each project. Moreover, VCs' new investments tend to be "long-shots," aiming for potential blockbusters. This suggests that the random long tail for VC investments after the introduction of cloud services is large, in line with the results on the effects of digitization for movies, television, and books in chapter 8.

The results that average pay for the creative worker decreases with digitization are related to the literature on the returns to entrepreneurship. Hamilton (2000) and Moskowitz and Vissing-Jørgensen (2002) find that entrepreneurs earn less than salaried workers. Overconfidence, preference for flexibility, and preference for skewness are some of the proposed explanations for why individuals may still choose to become entrepreneurs.

In contrast, Manso (2016) argues that the lower observed cross-sectional payoffs for entrepreneurship do not reflect the lifetime earnings of individuals. Entrepreneurship is the experimentation with new ideas, and many individuals exercise their option to abandon entrepreneurship upon failure, quickly moving back to the salaried workforce. Analyzing panel data, which takes into account the option value of experimentation, I find that entrepreneurship pays off.

Digitization lowers the cost of experimentation for creative workers. At this lower cost, they may write a book, record a song, or make a movie to learn whether they can succeed as creative workers. The average observed worker pay is thus low, because it encompasses all these attempts at subsistence as a creative worker. Most of these want-to-be creative workers will never succeed and will abandon the enterprise. Few can become big hits, such as the two examples at the beginning of this discussion, and will remain as creative workers.

Dominant platforms, such as Amazon Kindle Direct Publishing, iTunes, and Spotify, may facilitate the discovery of unknown creative workers, contributing to the random long tail. However, they may also help perpetuate incumbent artists. Aguiar and Waldfogel (2018) show that being added to Spotify playlists drives streaming traffic, raising the probability of song success. Therefore, platforms have control over the pipeline of new artists, which can create distortions. As argued by Iyer and Manso (2020), these platforms may lack incentives to search for high quality new artists to be included on their playlists and so may tend to prefer recommending status quo artists.

To conclude, Waldfogel (chapter 8, this volume) argues that digitization reduces the cost of experimentation in creative industries. This allows for the discovery of high-quality artists that would have not come to surface without digitization. Rather than a conventional long tail of inferior products, digitization leads to a larger random long tail, implying significant welfare gain. Consistent with this experimentation story, there is increased activity in labor markets, but falling average earnings per creative worker. While digital platforms help publicize the work of new artists, they may reinforce already successful artists through their recommendation systems, actually preventing experimentation. Waldfogel's chapter proves that digital platforms in the creative industry are a fertile ground for the study of all these and other questions.

References

Aguiar, L., and J. Waldfogel. 2018. "Platforms, Promotion, and Product Discovery: Evidence from Spotify Playlists." NBER Working Paper No. 24713. Cambridge, MA: National Bureau of Economic Research.

Arrow, K. 1969. "Classificatory Notes on the Production and Diffusion of Knowledge." *American Economic Review* 59: 29–35.

Bergemann, D., and U. Hege. 2005. "The Financing of Innovation: Learning and Stopping." *RAND Journal of Economics* 36(4):719–52.

Brynjolfsson, E., Y. Hu, and M. D. Smith. 2003. "Consumer Surplus in the Digital Economy: Estimating the Value of Increased Product Variety at Online Booksellers." *Management Science* 49(11): 1580–96.

Ewens, M., R. Nanda, and M. Rhodes-Kropf. 2018. "Cost of Experimentation and the Evolution of Venture Capital." *Journal of Financial Economics* 128(3): 422–42.

Hamilton, B. H. 2000. "Does Entrepreneurship Pay? An Empirical Analysis of the Returns to Self-Employment." *Journal of Political Economy* 108(3): 604–31.

Iyer, G., and G. Manso. 2020. "Recommendation with Feedback." Working paper.

Manso, G. 2011. "Motivating Innovation." *Journal of Finance* 66(5): 1823–60.

———. 2016. "Experimentation and the Returns to Entrepreneurship." *Review of Financial Studies* 29(9): 2319–40.

Moskowitz, Tobias J., and Annette Vissing-Jørgensen. 2002. "The Returns to Entrepreneurial Investment: A Private Equity Premium Puzzle?" *American Economic Review* 92(4): 745–78.

Weitzman, M. L. 1979. "Optimal Search for the Best Alternative." *Econometrica: Journal of the Econometric Society* 47(3): 641–54.

The Cost Disease Sectors

Innovation in the US Government

Joshua R. Bruce and John M. de Figueiredo

9.1 Introduction

In recent years, the US government has spent over $120 billion annually on research and development (R&D).[1] In addition, each OECD country spends the equivalent of billions of dollars every year to support technological infrastructure and advancement to further science and research. The literature on governments' contributions to the worldwide innovation ecosystem has focused on two areas: first, the role of government policy, such as intellectual property rules, tax credits, and infrastructure investments, to support private-sector innovation (e.g., Bloom, Van Reenen, and Williams 2019); and second, the role of government funds targeted to the private and nonprofit sectors to enhance the direction, productivity, and efficiency of R&D (e.g., Azoulay et al. 2019).

Joshua R. Bruce is an assistant professor of business administration at the University of Illinois Urbana-Champaign.

John M. de Figueiredo is the Russell M. Robinson II Professor of Law, Strategy, and Economics at Duke University, and a research associate of the National Bureau of Economic Research.

We thank Michael Andrews, Pierre Azoulay, Ronnie Chatterji, Shane Greenstein, Arti Rai, Scott Stern, Manuel Trajtenberg, and participants at the National Bureau of Economic Research Conference on the Role of Innovation and Entrepreneurship in Economic Growth for very helpful comments. For acknowledgments, sources of research support, and disclosure of the authors' material financial relationships, if any, please see https://www.nber.org /books-and-chapters/role-innovation-and-entrepreneurship-economic-growth/innovation -us-government.

1. For a historical overview of federal R&D spending levels, see the Congressional Research Service's "U.S. Research and Development Funding and Performance: Fact Sheet (Updated January 24, 2020)," available at: https://crsreports.congress.gov/product/pdf/R/R44307 (last accessed March 13, 2020).

While both of these literatures are important for understanding the government's role in innovation, comparatively little academic work has been done examining the direction and effectiveness of government research itself. In fiscal year (FY) 2018, the US government spent over $36 billion on "intramural" R&D—that is, the innovation that the government funds and conducts itself—more than any individual company in the US.[2] In recent years, the federal government has employed approximately 200,000 scientists, just under half of whom engage in R&D. Federal civil service scientists prolifically invent, innovate, patent, and publish. Yet despite the number of personnel and the size of their research budgets, there is almost no systematic or comprehensive scholarship on the US governments' intramural R&D efforts.

Our chapter begins addressing this issue with a look into government innovation. We bring together a variety of data sets to provide an initial comprehensive picture of innovation in government. Some of these data sets, such as those on funding from the National Science Foundation (NSF), are widely available. Others, such as a data set on US government scientists and R&D effort, have rarely been employed and never used in this capacity. Additional data sets, such as those linking US government scientists to patents, have been available but have not been mapped comprehensively in the innovation literature. In this chapter, we bring these and other data together at an aggregate level to understand the inputs and outputs to government intramural innovation (see appendix table 9.A.1 for a complete list). The focus in this chapter is on the US government, but the approaches here are translatable to any government entity for which data are available.

Nearly half of all US government R&D expenditures over the past 50 years went to the Department of Defense (DOD). The Department of Health and Human Services, which contains the National Institutes of Health and Centers for Disease Control and Prevention, was the second largest recipient of federal R&D allocations. The Department of Energy, the National Aeronautics and Space Administration, and the NSF round out the top five R&D-funding agencies, responsible for 90 percent of all federal R&D spending. The concentration of spending on national defense, biomedical science, and physical sciences/engineering is reflected in both the federal scientific workforce, which is predominantly employed in these agencies, and the types of innovations generated with federal dollars, which hew toward these agencies' missions. This leaves comparatively far fewer resources and personnel focused on education, housing, and social science

2. As a point of comparison, Amazon, the top R&D spending company in the US, spent $22.6 billion on R&D in 2017; Alphabet/Google, the next-largest spender, allocated $16.6 billion. See https://www.vox.com/2018/4/9/17204004/amazon-research-development-rd (last accessed March 13, 2020).

research, though innovations in these areas are more difficult to measure, as we discuss below.

This chapter seeks to make four contributions. First, we provide a broad analysis of government intramural innovative inputs and outputs and, we believe, the first comparative analysis of intramural and extramural research efforts. In this capacity, we intend to provide a set of facts and regularities about government innovation. Second, we argue that much of government innovation, broadly defined, is difficult to measure. Innovation has many dimensions, and much of the economics literature is focused on technological innovation. By constraining analyses to government technological innovation, researchers will miss much of the innovation that occurs in government. Third, even if we limit our analysis to technological innovation, traditional output measures of technological innovation will be heavily weighted toward such agencies as the DOD, the National Aeronautics and Space Administration, and the Department of Energy. This is because the nature of innovation in these agencies will be oriented toward engineering and physical science, where innovative outputs are somewhat easier to catalog with patents. However, innovations in agencies that rely on mathematics, social science, and data analytics, for example, will often be missed by this measure. Overall, using traditional measures of patents as a measure of innovative output, while informative, will be biased by the nature and variety of innovations that occur in government. Finally, the data show that while the amount of government funding for R&D has increased substantially over the past few decades, the number of government scientists has not. The government has shifted away from intramural research and toward a more extramural science orientation. In making this shift, the government may increase the diversity and efficiency of innovation, but it risks not developing sufficient internal innovative capability to manage, direct, and develop science and research. We further discuss potential implications of this trend in the conclusion.

The chapter proceeds as follows. In the next section, we provide a brief overview of the US government. In section 9.3, we develop a classification system for different types of government innovation. Section 9.4 discusses inputs into government intramural innovation, with a focus on funding and manpower. Section 9.5 analyzes the outputs from intramural innovation, with a discussion of patents and other measures. In section 9.6, we briefly outline state government contributions to intramural R&D. We conclude in section 9.7 with a brief discussion of implications and future research.

9.2   Overview of the US Government

We begin with an overview of the US government, focusing on money (budget/appropriations) and manpower (human capital) as underlying indicators of government innovative input and capabilities. In fiscal year 2020, US government budgeted expenditures are estimated to total $4.6 trillion.[3] Approximately $2.1 trillion of the budget is allocated to Social Security, Medicare, and interest on the debt. Approximately $1.5 trillion is spent on Medicaid, national defense, and other mandatory programs. Approximately $1 trillion remains for every other function of the government, from land management to foreign relations to agricultural research.

The US government employs approximately 4.3 million full-time equivalent (FTE) workers in 2020. During 1998–2018, US federal employees represented an average of 3.7 percent of the US FTE workforce.[4] As of 2020, about half of these employees are in the uniformed military (1.4 million) and the Post Office (585,000), while the other half are civilians employed in executive branch agencies.[5] In the rest of this chapter, when referring to government personnel, we focus on full-time, nonseasonal executive branch civil servants.

Approximately 70 percent of these federal employees are on the General Schedule (GS) pay plan. This plan has 15 major levels, called "grades," with each movement upward in grade being a promotion in the government.[6] Grade level is a convenient summary statistic for the skill level, education, and expertise of civil servants.[7] Figure 9.1 shows the distribution of federal employees by grade in 1988 and in 2011 along with the median grade in these two fiscal years (Bolton and de Figueiredo 2016). The figure shows a shift from a bimodal distribution of grades of federal workers in 1988 to a more unimodal distribution of workers by 2011. More importantly, the average and median grade increased markedly over that 24-year period, following a substantial upskilling in the federal workforce. Figure 9.2 shows where this upskilling has taken place in the federal workforce by looking at the number of civil servants employed in five occupational categories over time (Bolton and de Figueiredo 2016). Figure 9.2 illustrates the drastic decline in the share of clerical workers in the government (from 24 percent to 7 percent),

---

3. Congressional Budget Office (CBO) projection for FY2020, as of January 28, 2020. See: https://www.cbo.gov/topics/budget. If this spending were entirely production, it would represent around a fifth of the US economy. However, the budget includes substantial transfers. This estimate was created before the COVID-19 pandemic was recognized as a major health threat in the US, which added roughly $1.9 trillion to FY2020 federal spending as of November 30, 2020; for more, see: https://www.usaspending.gov/disaster/covid-19 (last accessed January 25, 2021).

4. See the Bureau of Economic Analysis (BEA) National Accounts (NIPA), "Table 6.4B. Full-Time and Part-Time Employees by Industry" (last accessed February 28, 2020).

5. There are roughly 75,000 FTE individuals employed in the legislative and judicial branches. For more, see the Congressional Research Service's "Federal Workforce Statistics Sources," updated Oct. 24, 2019: https://fas.org/sgp/crs/misc/R43590.pdf.

6. Each grade also has 10 steps. One convenient way to think about grades is as promotions; steps are pay increases for tenure and experience with a job.

7. The starting grade for someone with 4-year college degree, for example, is grade 5; a master's degree is about grade 9; a PhD is grade 12. For more on the GS system, see the Office of Personnel Management's overview at https://www.opm.gov/policy-data-oversight/pay-leave/pay-systems/general-schedule/.

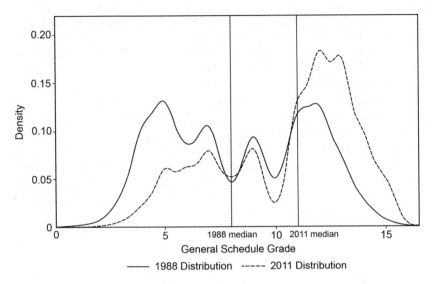

Fig. 9.1 The GS grade distribution, FY1988 vs. FY2011

Source: Bolton and de Figueiredo (2016).

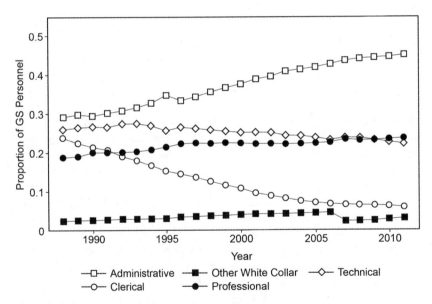

Fig. 9.2 Federal personnel occupation categories, FY1988–2011

Source: Bolton and de Figueiredo (2016).

commensurate with a significant increase in the proportion of more highly skilled "administrators" (from 29 percent to 48 percent).

The literature on public administration has identified (at least) two causes of this upskilling in the workforce. The first is the rise of computers and automation, which has allowed the federal government to remove the large clerical and typing pools that were essential to the operation of the government in the 1960s and 1970s (Rein 2014). Second, there has been a substantial increase in the amount of outsourcing by the government, which has increased the need for more highly skilled procurement specialists, contract managers, accountants, and auditors (Light 2017). This upskilling and outsourcing of the federal workforce has translated into a fourfold increase in the number of budget dollars per employee over this 24-year period (Bolton and de Figueiredo 2016).[8]

9.3   Classification of Government Innovations

The public administration literature has considered a variety of approaches to classifying innovation (e.g., Arundel, Bloch, and Ferguson 2019; Chen, Walker, and Sawhney 2019; Hartley 2005; Vries, Bekkers, and Tummers 2016). Based on these approaches, we developed a four-category classification system that we believe describes most innovation carried out by federal employees and the federal infrastructure. While there is some overlap among these categories, together they describe much of the innovation carried out by the federal government.

The first category of government innovation is technological innovation. These innovations involve technically new and novel inventions and improvements that are consistent with the broader economics literature on technical change. Examples of government innovations in this category include diverse innovations, such as hybrid vehicle control methods, inhibitors of integrase production to combat HIV, and snake repellant identification methods.

A second type of government innovation is organizational innovation. These are innovations that advance the way the government operates and is "organized," often resulting in greater administrative efficiency. Examples of organizational government innovations include the elimination of typing pools and introduction of computers, the implementation of oral proposals for some types of government procurement, novel approaches to managing civil service employees, and the crowdsourcing of citizen science.

A third type of government innovation is regulatory innovation. Unlike the private sector, the federal government's responsibilities include defining and administering the laws of the country through a regulatory apparatus.

---

8. Baumol (1967) theorized that some sectors of the economy, such as governmental services, would see only limited success in innovating because of limitations to labor productivity.

Regulatory innovations include the process of making rules and regulations, enforcing those regulations, and adjudicating them. The government is continually evolving the rule-making process within the rubric of the Administrative Procedures Act of 1946, through such recent innovations as negotiated rulemaking, electronic rulemaking (e-rulemaking), reformation of the drug approval process, and fast-track product recalls.

The fourth type of government innovation is also not found in the private sector: policy innovations. These innovations encompass the new types of regulatory policies and frameworks implemented by the administrative state to achieve desired social welfare and policy objectives. These are the actual policies and regulations themselves that the government has never implemented before, rather than mechanisms of regulatory process. Examples of policy innovations include the cap and trade program to combat air pollution and spectrum auctions to allocate broadcast rights over electromagnetic wave ranges. These policy innovations are not policies implemented by the government to encourage innovation per se, but they may lead to technological innovation in the economy (as a second-order effect, in most cases).

Although the focus of the literature (and the remainder of this chapter) is on technological innovation, such innovations represent only a fraction of all innovation that is conducted by the US government. The Ash Center at the Harvard University Kennedy School of Government has been accepting nominations for its Innovation in American Government Awards since 1985.[9] Over the past 35 years, they have received thousands of nominations for the awards, with nearly all nominations being in the organizational, regulatory, and policy innovation areas. Table 9.1 provides a list of the US agencies and their programs that won this award from 1995 to 1999, illustrating the breadth of programs and government entities engaged in innovation, much of which would not be captured by traditional innovation measures.

One challenge in the statistical literature on government innovation is that no standardized or readily available measure of government innovation applies across all areas of government or all types of innovation. Even in specific agencies, these types of innovations are hard to consistently measure across time. If we are to understand the full scope of innovation in the government, future research should aspire to develop measures that are consistent across agencies and across time, and available in statistically useful ways, to capture the government's true innovative power. Technological innovation is only the tip of the iceberg. Unfortunately, we do not solve this problem in this chapter. Instead, we examine the most readily measurable area of government innovation—technological innovation—about which relatively little is currently known outside the National Institutes of Health (e.g., Li, Azoulay, and Sampat 2017).

9. Federal agencies have been able to apply for the awards since 1995. See: https://ash.harvard .edu/iag-history.

Table 9.1   Innovation in American government award examples, 1995–1999

Agency	Program title	Year
Department of Defense	National Defense on the Offense	1995
US Air Force	Ozone Depleting Chemical Elimination	1995
Bureau of Reclamation	Reinvention of the Bureau of Reclamation	1995
Pension Benefit Guaranty Corporation	Early Warning Program	1995
Immigration and Naturalization Service	Operation Jobs	1995
Federal Emergency Management Agency	Consequence Assessment Tool Set and Operations Concept	1996
Housing and Urban Development	Consolidated Planning/Community Connections	1996
Department of Labor	No Sweat: Eradicating Sweatshops	1996
Food and Drug Administration	Reform of the US Drug Approval Process	1997
Internal Revenue Service	TeleFile	1997
Department of Defense	Best Manufacturing Practices Program	1998
Consumer Product Safety Commission	Fast-Track Product Recall Program	1998
US Forest Service	Northern New Mexico Collaborative Stewardship	1998
Centers for Disease Control	PulseNet	1999
Housing and Urban Development	Continuum of Care	1999

9.4   Inputs to Government Technological Innovation

In this section, we focus on the two main inputs to technological innovation by the government: funding and human capital.

9.4.1   Funding by the Government

The US government spent over $120 billion on R&D in FY2018.[10] Figure 9.3a shows federal spending on R&D for 51 years by major government agencies and demonstrates that the DOD has consumed roughly 50 percent of the R&D spending for most of the past half-century. After the DOD, the Department of Health and Human Services (HHS), which houses the National Institutes of Health (NIH) and the Centers for Disease Control and Prevention (CDC), the Department of Energy (DOE), which conducts a substantial amount of nuclear weapons and energy generation research, the National Aeronautics and Space Administration (NASA), and the National Science Foundation (NSF), in order, possess the next largest government R&D budgets. Together, these agencies comprise over 90 percent of federal R&D dollars appropriated.

Agencies allocate these appropriated funds to researchers, who then perform R&D. Figure 9.3b shows how the money was allocated by the type of entity performing the actual R&D effort. In FY2018, 31 percent ($39.8 billion) was directed to private sector companies; 24 percent ($31.5 billion)

10. A note on federal spending nomenclature: "outlays" represent actual money spent in fulfillment of R&D, whereas "obligations" represent contracted R&D effort backed by Congressional appropriations, which often includes money to be spent in future fiscal years, leading to different amounts, depending on which term is being used.

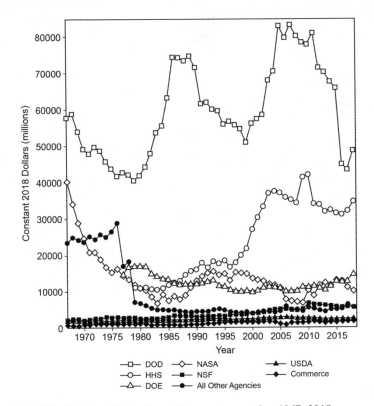

Fig. 9.3a   Distribution of federal spending across agencies, 1967–2018

Source: NSF. Includes research, development, and plant expenditures, in 2018 dollars.

went to higher education and universities; 10 percent ($12.5 billion) went to the operation of federally funded R&D centers (FFRDCs),[11] such as the Jet Propulsion Lab (managed by the California Institute of Technology) or Los Alamos National Lab (managed by the nonprofit and university consortium Triad National Security, LLC); and 28 percent ($36 billion) of federal R&D obligations were allocated to "intramural" research—that is, R&D conducted by federal government civil servant scientists and researchers. The remaining 7 percent of R&D obligations ($9.7 billion) were directed to other nonprofit organizations, state and local governments, and international R&D.

Academic research has spent a substantial amount of energy examin-

11. FFRDCs may be managed by the federal government, universities, private-sector businesses, or other nonprofit organizations. For the purposes of this chapter, all funding directed to the operation of FFRDCs by nongovernmental organizations (also known as GOCOs) has been combined into a single category; government-run FFRDC (also known as GOGOs) obligations are included in the "intramural" category by the NSF.

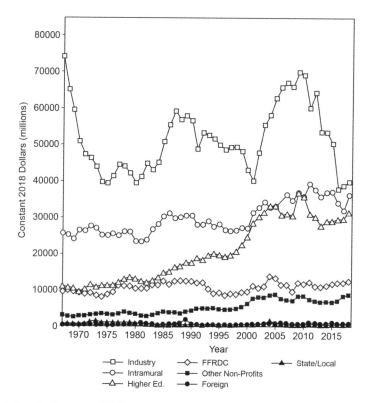

Fig. 9.3b   Performers of Federally Funded R&D, 1967–2018
Source: NSF.
Note: Includes research, development, and plant obligations, in 2018 dollars.

ing the allocation of government money to universities (Lanahan, Graddy-Reed, and Feldman 2016; Mansfield 1995), the private sector (Azoulay et al. 2019; Bruce, de Figueiredo, and Silverman 2019; Howell 2017), and the FFRDCs (Jaffe, Fogarty, and Banks 1998; Jaffe and Lerner 2001; Jaffe and Trajtenberg 1996). These papers have examined both the direct effects of federal funds on scientific effort, as well as the interconnections between federally supported R&D and other sectors' outcomes. However, there have been comparatively few studies of intramural research focused on understanding the work and productivity of government scientists. Therefore, in the remainder of the chapter, unless specifically noted, we examine only intramural science.

9.4.2   Human Capital of the Government

A second key input into government innovation is the manpower that the government dedicates to the task. We have obtained from the Office of Personnel Management (OPM) elements of the Central Personnel Data File, which contains information on every federal government civilian employee

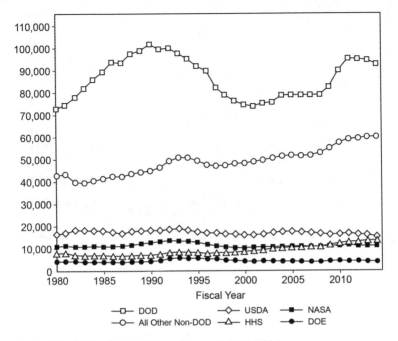

Fig. 9.4a   Total federal scientific employment, 1980–2014

who does not work in a sensitive position or sensitive agency. A detailed personnel data set spans 1988 to 2011; a less detailed data set spans 1980 to 2014. All personnel data presented herein are drawn from one of these two data sets unless otherwise noted.

We begin by examining the number of individuals in 68 distinct scientific occupations, whom we call "scientists."[12] The number of scientists in the government rose from 155,000 in 1980 to just under 200,000 by 2014. These scientists, as illustrated in figure 9.4a, are distributed across agencies, with approximately half of the scientists in the DOD and the remaining gov-

12. The 68 scientific occupations and their categorization in the federal government broadly represent academic scientific disciplines. The occupations included are: (life sciences) microbiology, pharmacology, ecology, zoology, physiology, entomology, toxicology, botany, plant pathology, plant physiology, horticulture, genetics, soil conservation, soil science, agronomy, fish biology, wildlife biology, animal science, general health science, veterinary medical science; (math and statistics) general math and statistics, actuarial science, operations research, mathematics, mathematical statistics, statistics; (engineering and computer science) computer science, general engineering, safety engineering, fire protection engineering, material engineering, architecture, civil engineering, environmental engineering, mechanical engineering, nuclear engineering, electrical engineering, computer engineering, electronics engineering, bioengineering and biomedical engineering, aerospace engineering, mining engineering, petroleum engineering, agricultural engineering, chemical engineering, industrial engineering; (physical sciences) general physical sciences, health physics, physics, geophysics, hydrology, chemistry, metallurgy, astronomy and space science, meteorology, geology, oceanography, cartography, geodesy; (social sciences) social science, economics, workforce research and analysis, geography, history, psychology, sociology, general anthropology, archeology.

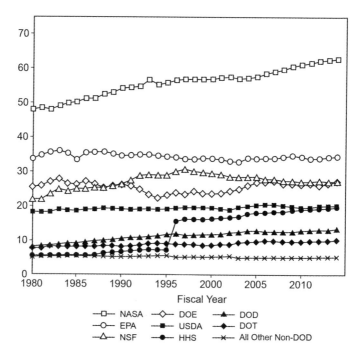

Fig. 9.4b   Percentage of employees in scientific occupations, 1980–2014

Note: Discontinuity in HHS line due to Social Security Administration being re-organized outside HHS in 1995.

ernment scientists being found, in order of prevalence, in the Department of Agriculture (USDA), HHS, NASA, and DOE. Other agencies, such as the Department of Commerce (Commerce), the Department of Veterans Affairs (VA), the Environmental Protection Agency (EPA), the Department of Interior (DOI), and the Department of Transportation (DOT) also possess a notable number of scientists.

Figure 9.4b shows the concentration and intensity of scientific effort in these government agencies by examining the percentage of all agency employees in scientific occupations. Perhaps not surprisingly, NASA has consistently had the highest concentration of scientific personnel, followed by the EPA, NSF, DOE, USDA, and HHS. Many of these agencies' smaller total workforces belie the science intensity in the agencies.

Despite being employed in scientific occupations, not all scientists in the government are primarily engaged in research. OPM classifies each federal scientist in one of 19 different primary activity categories, known as a "functional classification."[13] We focus on a subset of the functional classifications

13. For more, see "Appendix 2: Functional Classification for Scientists and Engineers" in OPM's *Introduction to the Position Classification System*, available at: https://www.opm.gov

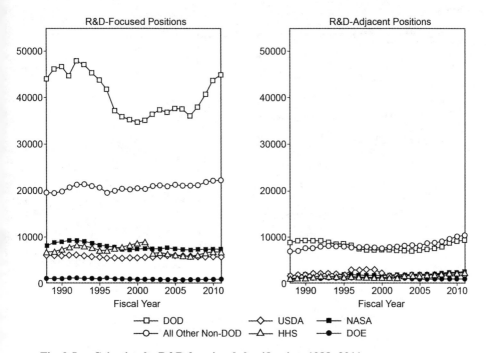

Fig. 9.5a   Scientists by R&D functional classification, 1988–2011

Note: R&D-focused positions are those classified as Research, Development, Data Analysis, or Testing & Evaluation. R&D-adjacent positions are those classified as R&D Grant Administration, Scientific and Technical Information, or Management (of Science).

to identify two groups of scientists: R&D-focused and R&D-adjacent.[14] We classify scientists as being in an R&D-focused position if their primary job is to do research, development, testing and evaluation, or data analysis. We classify scientists as being in an R&D-adjacent position if they are engaged primarily in R&D grant administration, scientific and technical information processing/dissemination, or the management of science.

Figure 9.5a illustrates the distribution of scientists in R&D-focused and R&D-adjacent positions over a 24-year period in major scientific agencies, from which several important patterns emerge. First, about 87,000 government scientists engage in R&D-focused work in the latest years where data are available, while about 26,000 government scientists are engaged

/policy-data-oversight/classification-qualifications/classifying-general-schedule-positions /positionclassificationintro.pdf (last accessed February 15, 2020).

14. There is a third group of scientific personnel whose work is not clearly R&D related, though they are employed in scientific occupations (e.g., a civil engineer with a functional classi-fication of "production," which is focused on building construction). These scientific personnel in non-R&D positions are included in the total scientists employed by the federal government discussed earlier but are not included in this R&D-specific discussion.

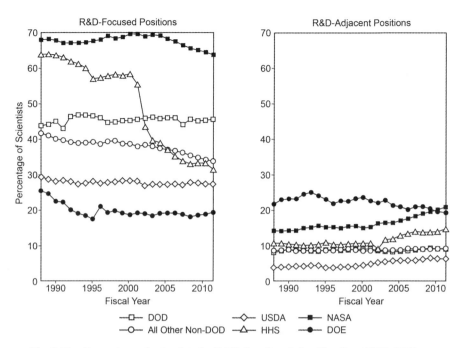

Fig. 9.5b   Percentage of scientists by R&D functional classification, 1988–2011

Note: R&D-focused positions are those classified as Research, Development, Data Analysis, or Testing & Evaluation. R&D-adjacent positions are those classified as R&D Grant Administration, Scientific and Technical Information, or Management (of Science).

in R&D-adjacent activities. The DOD again has the largest share of federal R&D scientists; NASA, HHS, USDA, and DOE have substantial numbers of R&D-focused scientists as well. Figure 9.5b examines the percentage of scientists by R&D area.[15] While the DOD again features prominently, NASA and HHS have comparatively high levels of R&D-focused scientists as well. Figure 9.4b and 9.5b together show that about 40 percent of non-DOD scientists are engaged in R&D, with the exception of NASA, where the number is closer to 85 percent.

To gain traction on the distribution of government scientists across scientific fields, we categorize, in figure 9.6, the percentage of scientists in five broader areas based on OPM classifications. Around 75 percent of the scientists in the DOD work in engineering, and another 10 percent are in physical sciences, such as chemistry and physics. NASA and Energy exhibit similar patterns of scientific personnel being concentrated in engineering and the

15. The decline in HHS R&D-focused personnel is largely the result of a reclassification of a substantial number of scientists at the NIH between FY2001 and FY2002. This occurred because all scientists hired in the excepted service under Title 42 with pay plan AD were converted from the "Research" to the "Other" functional classification with the implementation of the newly acquired human resources information technology system.

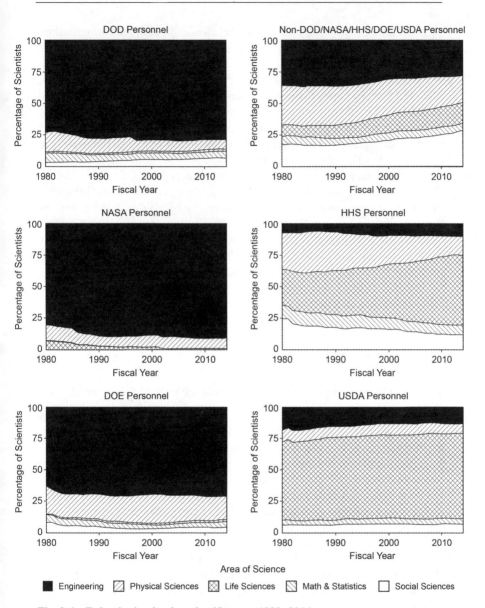

Fig. 9.6   Federal scientists by scientific area, 1980–2014

physical sciences. In contrast, in non-DOD agencies, approximately one quarter of scientists work in engineering and an additional 18 percent in the physical sciences. In the latest years of data, around 30 percent of non-DOD scientists work in social sciences or math and statistics, and an additional 20 percent are in the life sciences. Figure 9.6 also illustrates the concentration of HHS and USDA scientists in the life sciences in conjunction with their health, medical, and agricultural R&D missions, each possessing 56 percent and 68 percent of their scientific workforce in the life sciences, respectively.

We believe there are three takeaway messages from the analysis of federal scientific human capital. First, the nature of innovation being conducted at the DOD is likely very different from that in the non-DOD agencies, based on the composition of its human capital. Second, the DOD is heavily focused on engineering and physical sciences, fields that lend themselves to patenting. Based on the scientific expertise of personnel, non-DOD agencies will tend to innovate in the social sciences, math, statistics, and life sciences. The former three areas do not lend themselves to patenting, and the final area may or may not lend itself to patenting, depending on the nature of the scientific innovation. Our third takeaway is, therefore, that using patents as a measure of innovation in government will tend to overstate the nature of innovations being pursued by the DOD and understate the nature of innovations being conducted by non-DOD agencies, and it will overstate the contribution of the DOD to government innovation (assuming these innovations can be patented without national security concerns) and understate the contribution of the non-DOD agencies to government innovation. These distortions are critical to recognize when analyzing available data for indicators of public-sector innovative success.

9.5   Outputs for Technological Innovation in the Federal Government

The previous sections of this chapter focus on the inputs—human and financial capital—to technological innovation in the government, which are the precursor to government scientific innovation. This section begins by exploring the outputs of technological innovation, beginning with an in-depth analysis of patents followed by a discussion of viable alternative output measures. Although patents are likely to be informative of government technological output, they are unlikely to be comprehensive or necessarily representative measures of the scope, variety, and nature of innovations that occur in the government.

Our analysis of patents is based on US Patent and Trademark Office (USPTO) patent data, which has been processed and made available by PatentsView.org, a collaborative project between USPTO, USDA, the American Institutes for Research, and others.[16] We augment these records with measures made available by the National Bureau of Economic Research (NBER) Patent Data Project.[17]

---

16. See: www.patentsview.org (last accessed February 29, 2020).

17. See: https://sites.google.com/site/patentdataproject/Home (last accessed February 29, 2020).

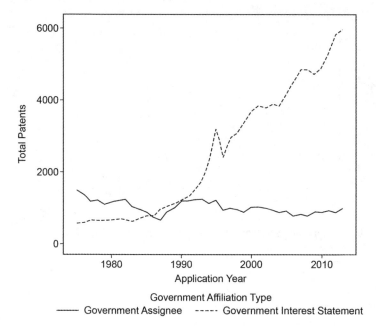

Fig. 9.7   US patents by government assignment and interest, 1975–2013
Note: Data on government affiliation type from PatentsView.org.

9.5.1   Patents

Government involvement in patented innovations takes two primary forms. First, if government scientists create a new invention, the government generally becomes the patent assignee, thereby holding the right to use or license the patented innovation. Second, if the government funds a third party, such as a university, to conduct research leading to a patented innovation, the third party generally takes ownership of the invention and becomes the patent assignee, while the government maintains an "interest" in the patent. That interest is usually composed of a royalty-free license to the invention. All patents generated with government funding are required to report the government's involvement in an interest statement on US patent applications.[18]

Figure 9.7 illustrates the number of US patents in which the government is an assignee and in which the government has an interest. From 1975 to

18. Researchers have found heterogeneity in inventors' disclosure of government interest in their inventions, which may result in underreporting government support for innovation (Rai and Sampat 2012). Patents generated by Cooperative Research and Development Agreements and other scientific procurement mechanisms, especially at the DOD, do not always include an explicit government interest statement or assignment.

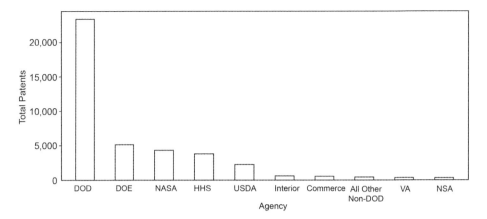

Fig. 9.8a   Total patents assigned to government agencies, 1975–2013
Note: Data from PatentsView.org.

2013, the number of government-assigned patents remained relatively stable at about 1,500 patents per year.[19] Despite the stability of the number of government-assigned patents, the number of government interest patents has increased nearly 12-fold during this time, from roughly 500 patents/year to almost 6,000 patents/year. There are many reasons for this substantial increase in government interest patents (which are beyond the scope of this chapter), including increased government extramural innovation funding, the Bayh Dole Act, career concerns for academic scientists, and numerous other factors (Azoulay et al. 2019; Fleming et al. 2019; Hegde and Mowery 2008; Jaffe and Lerner 2001; Owen-Smith and Powell 2001; Popp Berman 2008).

Figures 9.8a and 9.8b illustrate the total number of patents granted during 1975–2013 with either a federal government assignee or government interest statement tied to a federal agency, respectively. The DOD generates, by far, most of the government-assigned patents (figure 9.8a), while HHS generates most of the government-interest patents (figure 9.8b). These patterns comport with the human capital trends highlighted earlier, as government-assigned patents tend to be most focused on engineering and physical science technologies while government-interest patents are more heavily clustered in the life sciences.

Figure 9.9 shows the top five Cooperative Patent Classification (CPC) technological subsections for government-assigned and government-interest

19. To put this number in a comparative perspective, the time series profile of the number of government-assigned patents is comparable to the time series profile of the number of patents assigned to Texas Instruments Incorporated over a similar time period.

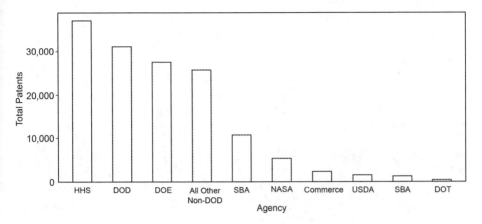

Fig. 9.8b Total patents with government interest statement by agency, 1975–2013
Note: Data from PatentsView.org.

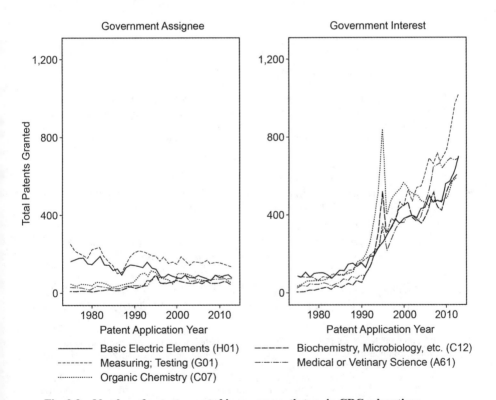

Fig. 9.9 Number of patents granted in government's top six CPC subsections, 1975–2013

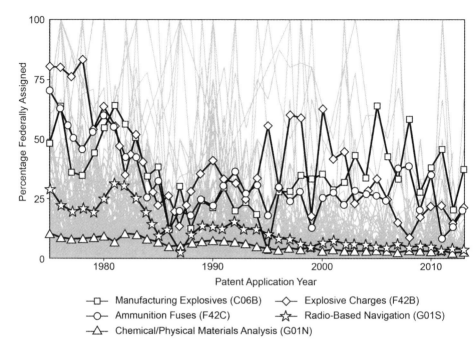

Fig. 9.10   Top CPC patent groups by government assignment, 1975–2013

Note: Top five groups highlighted with highest weighted average percentage; gray lines represent all 631 CPC groups. Denominator is combined patents assigned to US companies and federal government. Annual average weighted by number of federally assigned patents.

patents over nearly 40 years.[20] In addition to the distribution across technologies, we see relative stability in the top CPC subsections for government-assigned patents and the rise of biological and medical-related patents in the government-interest patents.

An alternative way to measure the contribution of government intramural science to technology is to measure the government's patent share in various technological areas. Figure 9.10 shows the share of government-assigned patents relative to all patents from 1975 to 2013 for five CPC groups (tertiary level). These five CPC groups have the highest average weighted percent of

20. The CPC is a classification scheme developed between the USPTO and European Patent Office in an effort to harmonize patent classes around the world. For more, see: https://www.uspto.gov/patents-application-process/patent-search/classification-standards-and-development or https://www.cooperativepatentclassification.org/about (last accessed February 29, 2020). CPC subsections are the second level of specificity in the CPC hierarchy. For example, in the overarching CPC section of "A: Human Necessities" (Level 1), there is a subsection devoted to "A01: Agriculture; Forestry; Animal Husbandry; Hunting; Trapping; Fishing" (Level 2), in which there is a group for patents in "A01D: Harvesting; Mowing" (Level 3). We discuss patents at the second and third levels of the CPC hierarchy (i.e., subsections and groups, following the PatentsView.org labels).

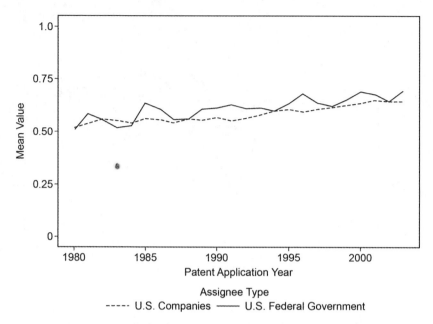

Fig. 9.11a   Average patent originality in Measuring; Testing (G01) patents, 1980–2003

Note: Patent citation records from NBER Patent Data Project.

government patents out of all 671 CPC patent groups.[21] Figure 9.10 highlights the five patent groups in which the government has the largest patent share: Manufacturing Explosives, Ammunition Fuses, Explosive Charges, Radio-Based Navigation, and Chemical/Physical Materials Analysis. This heavy patent share in national defense-related technologies is perhaps not surprising, given the technological focus and magnitude of the DOD intramural R&D effort on what are likely patentable technologies.

Having established the focus of government patenting, we now examine the character and quality of the patents generated by the government. The results we present here were determined for each of the top five patent CPC subsections identified in figure 9.9. Because the results are largely similar for all five of these subsections, we present the results only for the top government-assigned subsection, measuring and testing technologies, in figure 9.11a–c.[22]

We begin with an analysis of patent novelty. In this chapter, we employ

21. The weighted average used to determine which CPC groups have the highest concentration of government patents is calculated by multiplying the annual percent of patents in each group assigned to the federal government by the number of government patents in the group, averaged across all years.

22. Results for the remaining CPC subsections are available from the authors.

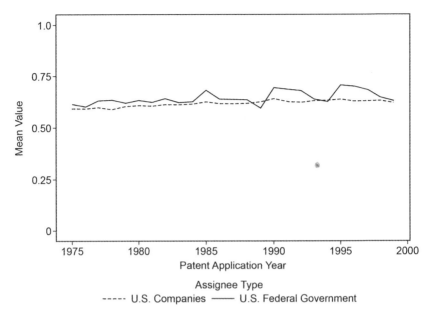

Fig. 9.11b   Average patent generality in Measuring; Testing (G01) patents, 1975–1999

Note: Patent citation records from NBER patent Data Project.

two measures of novelty based on the work of Trajtenberg, Henderson, and Jaffe (1997), which have been made available by the NBER Patent Data Project.[23] The first novelty measure we look at considers the *originality* of patents, which is based on the breadth of patents that the focal patent cites.[24] Figure 9.11a presents the results from 1980 to 2003 for patents in the Measuring and Testing technologies subsection, comparing patents assigned to the federal government with those assigned to US companies. It shows that both the government and corporate inventions are, on average, more original over time, but that over almost the entire period, government-assigned patents are slightly more original than the corporate patents in Measuring and Testing.

As a second measure of novelty, we calculate the Trajtenberg, Henderson, and Jaffe (1997) measure of patent *generality*, which is based on the

23. Researchers have also developed alternative measures of patent novelty (Balsmeier et al. 2018; Fleming and Sorenson 2004; Trajtenberg, Henderson, and Jaffe 1997). We use the Trajtenberg et al. measures because of their scope and ready availability through 2003.

24. $originality_{patent} = 1 - \sum_{1}^{C} c_{cited}^2$, where c^2 is the squared proportion of patents cited by the focal patent from a single patent class, summed across all classes cited, C. Originality is thus a backward-looking measure of novelty, encompassing the breadth of scientific areas that the focal patent incorporates.

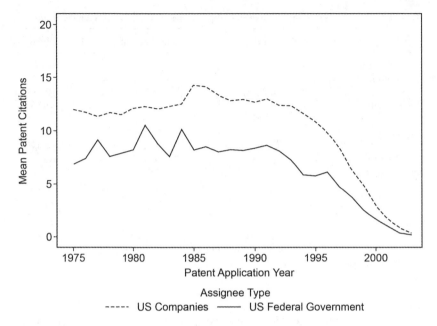

Fig. 9.11c   Average patent citations in Measuring; Testing (G01) patents, 1975–2003

Note: Patent citation records from NBER Patent Data Project.

breadth of later patents citing the focal patent.[25] Figure 9.11b illustrates that both groups of patents are, on average, somewhat more general over time, but again, that government-assigned patents are slightly more general than private company patents.

Finally, we examine the citations to Measuring and Testing patents in figure 9.11c. Some authors have referred to patent citations as a measure of patent quality (Henderson, Jaffe, and Trajtenberg 2005; Trajtenberg 1990). Here, there is a noticeable difference between the two sets of patents. The government assigned patents are substantially less often cited than the private company patents in these patent classes, and that pattern persists for the entire time series of the data. In summary, in the five patent classes we examined, we find that relative to private company patents, the government assigned patents are slightly more original, slightly more general, but substantially less cited.

We conduct a similar analysis comparing government interest patents

---

25. $generality_{patent} = 1 - \Sigma_1^C c_{citing}^2$, where c^2 is the squared proportion of patents citing the focal patent from a single patent class, summed across all classes citing, C. Generality is a forward-looking measure of novelty, illustrating the degree to which the focal patent is later drawn on by patents in numerous other classes.

Table 9.2   OLS regression models of patent originality, generality, and citations

	Patent originality	Patent generality	Patent citations
Assignee type			
Government	0.0484***	0.0462***	−3.3760***
	(0.0025)	(0.0022)	(0.1211)
University	0.0551***	0.0576***	1.8102***
	(0.0018)	(0.0020)	(0.1106)
All others	Reference	Reference	Reference
	Category	Category	Category
Grant year FE	Yes	Yes	Yes
CPC group FE	Yes	Yes	Yes
Constant	0.4502***	0.4911***	16.0662***
	(0.0220)	(0.0212)	(0.5415)
Observations	1,733,166	1,460,715	4,646,540
R^2	0.0956	0.1166	0.1216

Notes: Robust standard errors in parentheses. *** $p < .001$.

with private company patents in the same five CPC subsections. These results show a similar pattern in terms of patent novelty: government interest patents are slightly more original and slightly more general than commercial patents without a government interest statement. However, unlike government assigned patents, government-interest-statements patents are not meaningfully less cited than private-sector patents in the same CPC subsections.[26]

While the examples in figure 9.11 are illustrative of areas of heavy government technology focus, there is no a priori assumption that our findings would hold across all scientific areas. To address the question of how general the pattern of greater originality and generality coupled with lower average citations is, we collect all granted patents in the CPC groups for all years when the federal government has at least one patent in a group. We then use ordinary least squares (OLS) regression to estimate three models describing (1) patent originality, (2) patent generality, and (3) patent citations. Each model includes CPC group (third-level specificity) and patent-grant-year fixed effects to control for differences by area of science and period effects, as well as heteroskedasticity-robust standard errors. In addition to accounting for whether a patent is assigned to the federal government, patents are also categorized as university-assigned if the words "college," "university," "regents," or "fellows" appear in the patent assignee name. Table 9.2 presents the results of these three OLS models that are meant to be merely reduced-form descriptions of the data.

Table 9.2 confirms the patterns identified and discussed from figure 9.11.

26. These results are available from the authors.

Government patents, relative to patents assigned to other entities (excluding universities), are more novel as measured by both originality and generality. Furthermore, government-held patents are less cited that patents held by other assignee types.[27] University patents are more original, general, and frequently cited than commercial patents.

In sum, our analysis of patent novelty and impact suggests two distinct results. First, the government appears to be conducting more original and more general science than the private sector. However, the second pattern of lower citations suggests that other inventors are not building on the government's innovations to the same degree that they build on private sector innovations, or alternatively, that the government is innovating in areas that receive less overall innovative attention.

9.5.2 Alternative Measures of Government Innovation

While patents provide a convenient method for examining a slice of technological innovation by the federal government, there are a host of other potential output metrics that could be explored in future research. In this subsection, we discuss these alternative measures.

The first is the use of academic publications by government scientists. For many innovative ideas and inventions, publications embody or precede the innovative contribution, whether it be a contribution to knowledge or a commercial application of an idea. Indeed, publications and citations thereto are already used in the innovation literature as a measure of output (Angrist et al. 2020; Murray and Stern 2007). With respect to government science, publications are likely to be more representative of innovative output relative to patents in many fields, such as economics, sociology, data analytics, mathematics, management, and parts of the life sciences. Indeed, using publications as a measure of government innovative output would likely increase the proportion of government innovation reported by agencies such as the USDA, Commerce, and the EPA and would allow researchers to obtain a more representative picture of government technical output.

A second potential output measure for government innovation is prizes (Jones 2010; Jones and Weinberg 2011). Agencies in the US government award prizes to government scientists and personnel for innovations that enhance efficiency in the governing process and that contribute to knowledge and invention. These prizes can be for individual or team efforts.[28]

---

27. This result remains consistent when using a negative binomial regression model rather than OLS to estimate the number of citations received. The NBER data containing patent originality and generality measures are based on the USPTO patent class system, not the CPC scheme. Recreating the Trajtenberg, Henderson, and Jaffe (1997) measures with CPC groups replicates the results in table 9.2.

28. There are four types of relevant prizes: individual and group awards, as well as suggestion and invention awards. The former two types distinguish between individual and group efforts, while the latter two distinguish between process improvements and scientific or patentable innovation accomplishments, respectively.

Although prizes cannot be awarded for every innovation, prize data has the advantage of incorporating potentially unobservable information (to the researcher) on the contemporaneous contributions of individuals to innovation in the federal government. While the prize data are not mapped to individual innovations, they are mapped to individual civil servants (Zhang and de Figueiredo 2018), which might also allow researchers to identify "superstar" government innovators and the complementarities and externalities they generate (Zucker and Darby 1996). Likewise, third party prizes, such as the Ash Center prizes for innovativeness in government, might be a vehicle for understanding the contribution of innovations to government efficiency and social welfare.

A third potential method for evaluating the success of government technological innovations is to consider innovations for which the government is a lead user. There is a large literature on user-driven innovation (for a summary, see Franke 2014). Lead users are those who adopt an innovation at the beginning of the innovation's life cycle (von Hippel 1986). Those lead users that stand to capture substantial value from the innovation's success have a high incentive to pursue the innovation themselves (Morrison, Roberts, and von Hippel 2000; Morrison, Roberts, and Midgley 2004). One might rely on this literature to understand when intramural efforts of government innovation are likely to succeed. NASA's development of technologies from rocket propulsion to life-sustaining systems during the Mercury and Apollo programs in the 1960s and 1970s, the government's invention of tabular computing to compile the US Census in the 1940s and 1950s, and the DOD's and NSF's need to connect disparate computing power leading to the Internet are just a handful of examples where the incentives and investments of the US intramural R&D efforts were enhanced because of government as the lead user (Agarwal, Kim, and Moeen 2021; Hacker and Pierson 2016; Mazzucato 2013; Singer 2014).

9.6   State and Local Government Technological Innovation

Throughout this chapter, we have focused on the federal government as the primary public-sector actor in US government technological innovation. However, state-level governments also contribute to intramural R&D efforts. Figure 9.12 illustrates state spending in the seven cumulatively highest-spending states over the decade leading up to 2018 (the faint gray lines in the background of the figure represent the remaining states). New York state spent over $822 million during this period, in 2018 constant dollars, followed by California ($560 million) and Florida ($299 million).

States also indirectly subsidize R&D through many mechanisms. One mechanism is funding the operation of public colleges and universities, which are heavily reliant on state appropriations for their operation. This source

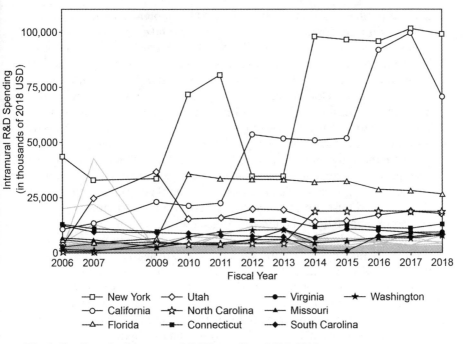

Fig. 9.12   State-level intramural R&D spending, 2006–2018

Source: NSF Survey of State Government Research and Development. Survey not fielded in FY 2008.

Note: Ten highlighted states had the most cumulative spending over the survey period.

of funding declined precipitously after the Great Recession. Although it has been rising since its nadir in 2013, it still remains below pre-recession levels in most states.[29] A second mechanism is through policies, subsidies, and regulations that attract extramural R&D. These and other mechanisms are worthy of further analysis and research.

9.7   Conclusion

Nearly all of the literature on government's role in innovation focuses on either the allocation and productivity of government funds directed to third party research or on various government policies that will enhance private

29. In its 2018 higher education finance report, the State Higher Education Executive Officers Association compared multiple measures of state support for college and university operations, such as per capita spending and allocations as a percentage of state tax revenue. Across multiple measures, nearly all states showed considerable reductions in higher education funding when comparing 2008 to 2016. Report available at: https://sheeo.org/wp-content/uploads/2019/04/SHEEO_SHEF_FY18_Report-2.pdf.

and nonprofit sectors' innovative effort. This chapter examines the nature of intramural government research—the inputs and outputs of government scientists and funding for internal innovation. We believe this analysis of government intramural innovative inputs and outputs is one of the first comparative analyses of the intramural-to-extramural research efforts.

The chapter develops a classification system of innovation in the government, identifying four major types of public-sector innovations: technological, organizational, regulatory, and policy. It is inherently difficult to measure government innovation, because a substantial amount of such innovation occurs in the latter three categories. Therefore, studies that attempt to measure the full government innovative effort are likely to miss much of the nontechnological innovation that occurs in the federal government. We believe that a more robust and comprehensive innovation measurement system is needed to capture the full innovative output of the federal government.

When constraining the analysis to only government technological innovation, we see that inputs (scientists and funding) are heavily weighted toward the DOD, NASA, and DOE. Not surprisingly, output-oriented measures of innovation, such as patents, are also heavily weighted toward these agencies because of the scientific disciplines from which they draw: engineering, the physical sciences, and some parts of the life sciences. Patents will tend to miss innovations in agencies that rely on data analytics, social science, mathematics, and other parts of the life sciences. Thus, patents will give a biased view of the composition of technological innovation in the government. Despite this, the patents that are generated by government scientists are slightly more original, slightly more general, but much less cited than those of the private sector.

One strong trend in the data is that while the amount of government funding for R&D has increased substantially over the past few decades, the number of government scientists has remained relatively stable. The government has shifted toward a more extramural science orientation. This policy may be beneficial if policymakers believe that it enhances the innovativeness and diversity of ideas and inventions, creates more efficient discovery and commercialization, or supports a broader scientific infrastructure of the country. However, these advantages will be mitigated if excessively outsourcing science diminishes the capability of the government to conduct some necessary intramural research, to monitor extramural research, to overcome market failure in the private markets for research, or to develop a socially optimal scientific infrastructure.

Overall, this chapter is only an initial look at the US government's intramural science efforts. It is meant to provide an opening into new research in this field, which could be more fully understood and better mapped. This work attempts to provide a base for future research to understand the role of government innovation and entrepreneurship in economic growth.

Appendix

Table 9.A.1   **Data sources**

Data	Source	Description	Years covered
Innovations in American Government Awards	Harvard Kennedy School Ash Center for Democratic Governance and Innovation	Annual award data on Ash Center's Innovation in American Government Award	1995–1999
Federal Employment Records	Office of Personnel Management (OPM) Central Personnel Data File	Database contains annual employment records for almost all non-national security government employees, including occupation and scientific role, if applicable	1980–2014
Federal R&D Spending by Agency	National Science Foundation (NSF)	Annual R&D spending by government entity, compiled by the NSF using the Survey of Federal Funds for Research and Development	1967–2018
Federal R&D Spending by Performer	National Science Foundation (NSF)	Annual R&D spending allocated to organizations in and outside the federal government, compiled by the NSF using the Survey of Federal Funds for Research and Development	1967–2018
US Patent Records	PatentsView.org	Open-source patent database containing US Patent and Trademark Office-granted patents, supported by USPTO Office of the Chief Economist	1976–2013
US Patent Novelty & Citations	NBER Patent Data Project	Public data files containing originality and generality scores for US patents granted during 1976–2006, based on Trajtenberg, Henderson, and Jaffe (1997); and patent-to-patent citations	1976–2006
State R&D Spending	NSF Survey of State R&D Expenditures	Periodic survey conducted by NSF and US Census Bureau to collect data on state-level R&D spending	2006–2007, 2009–2018

References

Agarwal, Rajshree, Seojin Kim, and Mahka Moeen. 2021. "Catalyzing Incubation: How Does Addressing Mission-Oriented Grand Challenges Enable Industry Inception?" Presented at the Strategy Seminar, January 22, University of Illinois at Urbana-Champaign.

Angrist, Josh, Pierre Azoulay, Glenn Ellison, Ryan Hill, and Susan Feng Lu. 2020. "Inside Job or Deep Impact? Extramural Citations and the Influence of Economic Scholarship." *Journal of Economic Literature* 58(1): 3–52. doi:10.1257/jel.20181508.

Arundel, Anthony, Carter Bloch, and Barry Ferguson. 2019. "Advancing Innovation in the Public Sector: Aligning Innovation Measurement with Policy Goals." *Research Policy* 48(3): 789–98. doi:10.1016/j.respol.2018.12.001.

Azoulay, Pierre, Joshua S. Graff Zivin, Danielle Li, and Bhaven N. Sampat. 2019. "Public R&D Investments and Private-Sector Patenting: Evidence from NIH Funding Rules." *Review of Economic Studies* 86(1): 117–52. doi:10.1093/restud/rdy034.

Balsmeier, Benjamin, Mohamad Assaf, Tyler Chesebro, Gabe Fierro, Kevin Johnson, Scott Johnson, Guan-Cheng Li, Sonja Lück, Doug O'Reagan, Bill Yeh, Guangzheng Zang, and Lee Fleming. 2018. "Machine Learning and Natural Language Processing on the Patent Corpus: Data, Tools, and New Measures." *Journal of Economics & Management Strategy* 27(3): 535–53. doi:10.1111/jems.12259.

Baumol, William J. 1967. "Macroeconomics of Unbalanced Growth: The Anatomy of Urban Crisis." *American Economic Review* 57(3): 415–26.

Bloom, Nicholas, John Van Reenen, and Heidi Williams. 2019. "A Toolkit of Policies to Promote Innovation." *Journal of Economic Perspectives* 33(3): 163–84. doi:10.1257/jep.33.3.163.

Bolton, Alexander, and John M. de Figueiredo. 2016. "Why Have Federal Wages Risen So Rapidly?" Technical report. Duke University Law School, Durham, NC.

Bruce, Joshua R., John M. de Figueiredo, and Brian S. Silverman. 2019. "Public Contracting for Private Innovation: Government Capabilities, Decision Rights, and Performance Outcomes." *Strategic Management Journal* 40(4): 533–55. doi: 10.1002/smj.2973.

Chen, Jiyao, Richard M. Walker, and Mohanbir Sawhney. 2019. "Public Service Innovation: A Typology." *Public Management Review* 22(11): 1674–95. doi:10.1080/14719037.2019.1645874.

Fleming, L., H. Greene, G. Li, M. Marx, and D. Yao. 2019. "Government-Funded Research Increasingly Fuels Innovation." *Science* 364(6446): 1139–41. doi:10.1126/science.aaw2373.

Fleming, Lee, and Olav Sorenson. 2004. "Science as a Map in Technological Search." *Strategic Management Journal* 25(8/9): 909–28.

Franke, Nikolaus. 2014. "User-Driven Innovation." In *The Oxford Handbook of Innovation Management*, edited by M. Dodgson, D. M. Gann, and N. Phillips, 83–101. Oxford: Oxford University Press.

Hacker, Jacob S., and Paul Pierson. 2016. *American Amnesia*. New York: Simon & Schuster.

Hartley, Jean. 2005. "Innovation in Governance and Public Services: Past and Present." *Public Money & Management* 25(1): 27–34. doi:10.1111/j.1467–9302.2005.00447.x.

Hegde, Deepak, and David C. Mowery. 2008. "Politics and Funding in the U.S. Public Biomedical R&D System." *Science* 322(5909): 1797–98. doi:10.1126/science.1158562.

Henderson, Rebecca, Adam Jaffe, and Manuel Trajtenberg. 2005. "Patent Citations and the Geography of Knowledge Spillovers: A Reassessment: Comment." *American Economic Review* 95(1): 461–64. doi:10.1257/0002828053828644.

Howell, Sabrina T. 2017. "Financing Innovation: Evidence from R&D Grants." *American Economic Review* 107(4): 1136–64. doi:10.1257/aer.20150808.

Jaffe, Adam B., and Josh Lerner. 2001. "Reinventing Public R&D: Patent Policy and the Commercialization of National Laboratory Technologies." *RAND Journal of Economics* 32(1): 167–98. doi:10.2307/2696403.

Jaffe, Adam B., and Manuel Trajtenberg. 1996. "Flows of Knowledge from Universities and Federal Laboratories: Modeling the Flow of Patent Citations over Time and across Institutional and Geographic Boundaries." *Proceedings of the National Academy of Sciences* 93(23): 12671–77. doi:10.1073/pnas.93.23.12671.

Jaffe, Adam B., Michael S. Fogarty, and Bruce A. Banks. 1998. "Evidence from Patents and Patent Citations on the Impact of NASA and Other Federal Labs on Commercial Innovation." *Journal of Industrial Economics* 46(2): 183–205.

Jones, Benjamin F. 2010. "Age and Great Invention." *Review of Economics and Statistics* 92(1): 1–14. doi:10.1162/rest.2009.11724.

Jones, Benjamin F., and Bruce A. Weinberg. 2011. "Age Dynamics in Scientific Creativity." *Proceedings of the National Academy of Sciences* 108(47): 18910–14. doi:10.1073/pnas.1102895108.

Lanahan, Lauren, Alexandra Graddy-Reed, and Maryann P. Feldman. 2016. "The Domino Effects of Federal Research Funding." *PLOS ONE* 11(6): e0157325. doi:10.1371/journal.pone.0157325.

Li, Danielle, Pierre Azoulay, and Bhaven N. Sampat. 2017. "The Applied Value of Public Investments in Biomedical Research." *Science* 356(6333): 78–81. doi:10.1126/science.aal0010.

Light, Paul C. 2017. *The True Size of Government Tracking Washington's Blended Workforce, 1984–2015.* New York: The Volcker Alliance.

Mansfield, Edwin. 1995. "Academic Research Underlying Industrial Innovations: Sources, Characteristics, and Financing." *Review of Economics and Statistics* 77(1): 55–65. doi:10.2307/2109992.

Mazzucato, Mariana. 2013. *The Entrepreneurial State: Debunking Public vs. Private Sector Myths.* London: Anthem Press.

Morrison, Pamela D., John H. Roberts, and Eric von Hippel. 2000. "Determinants of User Innovation and Innovation Sharing in a Local Market." *Management Science* 46(12): 1513–27. doi:10.1287/mnsc.46.12.1513.12076.

Morrison, Pamela D., John H. Roberts, and David F. Midgley. 2004. "The Nature of Lead Users and Measurement of Leading Edge Status." *Research Policy* 33(2): 351–62. doi:10.1016/j.respol.2003.09.007.

Murray, Fiona, and Scott Stern. 2007. "Do Formal Intellectual Property Rights Hinder the Free Flow of Scientific Knowledge? An Empirical Test of the Anti-Commons Hypothesis." *Journal of Economic Behavior & Organization* 63(4): 648–87. doi:10.1016/j.jebo.2006.05.017.

Owen-Smith, Jason, and Walter W. Powell. 2001. "To Patent or Not: Faculty Decisions and Institutional Success at Technology Transfer." *Journal of Technology Transfer* 26(1–2): 99–114. doi:10.1023/A:1007892413701.

Popp Berman, Elizabeth. 2008. "Why Did Universities Start Patenting? Institution-Building and the Road to the Bayh-Dole Act." *Social Studies of Science* 38(6): 835–71. doi:10.1177/0306312708098605.

Rai, Arti K., and Bhaven N. Sampat. 2012. "Accountability in Patenting of Federally Funded Research." *Nature Biotechnology* 30(10): 953–56. doi:10.1038/nbt.2382.

Rein, Lisa. 2014. "As Federal Government Evolves, Its Clerical Workers Edge toward Extinction." *Washington Post,* January 14.

Singer, Peter. 2014. *Federally Supported Innovations.* Washington, DC: MIT Washington Office.

Trajtenberg, Manuel. 1990. "A Penny for Your Quotes: Patent Citations and the Value of Innovations." *RAND Journal of Economics* 21(1): 172–87. doi:10.2307 /2555502.

Trajtenberg, Manuel, Rebecca Henderson, and Adam Jaffe. 1997. "University versus Corporate Patents: A Window on the Basicness of Invention." *Economics of Innovation and New Technology* 5(1): 19–50. doi:10.1080/10438599700000006.

von Hippel, Eric. 1986. "Lead Users: A Source of Novel Product Concepts." *Management Science* 32(7): 791–805. doi:10.1287/mnsc.32.7.791.

Vries, Hanna de, Victor Bekkers, and Lars Tummers. 2016. "Innovation in the Public Sector: A Systematic Review and Future Research Agenda." *Public Administration* 94(1): 146–66. doi:10.1111/padm.12209.

Zhang, Congshan, and John M. de Figueiredo. 2018. "Are Recessions Good for Government Hires? The Effect of Unemployment on Public Sector Human Capital." *Economics Letters* 170: 1–5. doi:10.1016/j.econlet.2018.05.008.

Zucker, Lynne G., and Michael R. Darby. 1996. "Star Scientists and Institutional Transformation: Patterns of Invention and Innovation in the Formation of the Biotechnology Industry." *Proceedings of the National Academy of Sciences* 93(23): 12709–16.

Comment   Manuel Trajtenberg

Introduction

Ever since Vannevar Bush's groundbreaking report to President Franklin D. Roosevelt, "Science—The Endless Frontier" (Bush 1945), the US government has played an increasingly prominent role in the realm of research and development (R&D) and innovation. This includes funding of research through the National Science Foundation and the National Institutes of Health (NIH); mission-oriented research in defense, space, and energy; support of commercial R&D by small and medium-size businesses through the SBIR and STTR programs, and the like.

However, the impact of government on innovation goes much further, reflecting the size of government in the economy,[1] procurement policies, the impact of taxation, and the deliberate or unintended effects of regulation. Thus, for example, setting standards for fuel economy or energy conserva-

Manuel Trajtenberg is professor emeritus at the Eitan Berglas School of Economics at Tel Aviv University, a research associate of the National Bureau of Economic Research, and a senior researcher at the Samuel Neaman Institute for National Policy Research at the Technion, Israel.

For acknowledgments, sources of research support, and disclosure of the author's material financial relationships, if any, please see https://www.nber.org/books-and-chapters /role-innovation-and-cntrepreneurship-economic-growth/comment-innovation-us-federal -government-trajtenberg.

1. The average government/GDP ratio for 36 OECD countries stands now at 43 percent, with the US being at the lower end with 38 percent.

tion incentivizes innovation in automobiles and in construction, banning hazardous materials prompts the search for safer substitutes, and immigration policies may affect the extent to which innovations are labor saving. Well before the era of "big government" there are plenty of examples of the unintended impact of government action on innovation: from the invention of the tabulating machine to process data for the 1890 US Census (which eventually gave rise to IBM), to the contribution of government procurement of firearms to the development of the "American System of Manufactures."

Of course, innovation in the provision of public and quasi-public goods, be it in education, health care, or transportation, is directly and indirectly impacted by government policies, and not always for the better. In fact, government inertia, inaction, political meddling, unions, and plain ineptitude often preclude the adoption of innovative methods and procedures. This is also often the case in the realm of housing, zoning, and building codes, and in the delivery of welfare assistance.[2] In view of the growing size and importance of these public goods and services in the economy and for our well-being, the fact that government may play a retarding role in innovation is particularly troubling.

The centrality of innovation for economic growth has been well established long ago, as well as its accelerated pace since World War II. This has happened in tandem with the expanding role and share of government in the economy, and as already suggested, these two parallel and all-important trends are not quite independent. Yet the study of innovation has not paid sufficient attention to the full extent of the interaction between the two, that is, the multiple channels through which government impacts innovation, and the way innovation in turn affects the conduct of government activities and the provision of public goods.

The chapter by Bruce and Figueiredo (chapter 9, this volume) constitutes an important step in that direction, providing an excellent overview of a particular area in that regard: intramural technological innovation done by the US government. More precisely, Bruce and Figueiredo examine both the "inputs" to intramural federal R&D by mapping the scientists employed in R&D by the federal government, and the "outputs" of R&D in the form of patents. To the best of my knowledge, this is the first time that such an endeavor has been undertaken, thus providing a much-needed picture of the extent and type of direct, intramural government innovative activity.

Bruce and Figueiredo are well aware of the limitations of their work, both in terms of the sort of R&D inputs and outputs examined, and the way they are measured. But again, their contribution provides an important piece of

---

2. A great deal has been said about the failures of bureaucracy, but this usually refers to "static inefficiencies," which is what frustrated citizens typically complain about in their encounters with government. Here we shall refer mostly to "dynamic inefficiencies" (i.e., the slowness or failure of government to innovate), which are likely to be even more significant, certainly in the long run.

the wider puzzle, allowing us to push further and examine other areas in the innovation government space, which is my intention here.

The Context: Government and the Emergence of a New GPT

There is increasing evidence that we are witnessing the rise of a new "general purpose technology" (GPT), which I shall refer to as the "digital GPT" (d-GPT).[3] Starting with the steam engine in the late 18th century, electricity a century later, and then semiconductors, computers and the internet, these powerful technological waves impact the economy by fostering transformative innovation in an ever expanding range of adopting sectors. The fundamental role of GPT's in economic growth lies not in the weight of the sector producing the GPT itself, but in the complementary innovations that revolutionize the operations of adopters, old and new.

Government as a sector is no exception: over the past two centuries, we have seen major changes not just in the scope of government activity (an increase of about tenfold), but also in the way governments operate, as they gradually adopt the leading GPT of each era. However, given that we lack measures of productivity of government services,[4] it is hard to gauge the extent to which the GPT drives complementary innovations in government, as it spreads throughout the public sector. Absent such measures, the presumption is that the adoption of GPTs notwithstanding, government remains highly inefficient in its modus operandi, slow in innovating, and not responsive to shifting needs. The widely accepted corollary is that attaining efficiency requires government to outsource its activities as much as possible, downplaying the option of government innovating in and by itself.

I shall argue here that such a sweeping conclusion is unwarranted and even dangerous: the great challenges that we face, ranging from unsettling inequality and climate change, to pandemics and a new wave of technology-induced employment disruption, require more, not less government action and leadership. However, this does not imply moving the dial from "smaller" to "bigger" government along the trite ideological continuum that defined many of the controversies of the past century. Rather, the intention is to move the dial from heavy-handed, slow-moving, and yes, inefficient governments, to smart, d-GPT based, and innovative governments.

As Bruce and Figueiredo explain, beyond technological innovation, which corresponds to notions that we can easily grasp and measure, there are three additional dimensions of innovation in government: organizational, regulatory, and policy related. Organizational innovation pertains

3. For the concept of GPT, see Bresnahan and Trajtenberg (1996); for the new digital GPT, see Brynjolfsson, Rock, and Syverson (2019); Cockburn, Henderson, and Stern (2019); and Goldfarb, Bledi, and Teodoridis (2019).

4 The way the national accounts are constructed does not allow one to compute productivity in the public sector, since neither the "outputs" nor the "prices" are well defined in that context.

to the way government functions in itself, whereas the other two refer to the design and implementation of measures that affect others. In each of these realms, there is vast room for innovation that can be of tremendous consequence to the economy and society. Furthermore, even if government were not to innovate by itself in these dimensions, its actions or its lack of action can be highly consequential for the ability of the business and civic sectors to innovate. Thus, for example, the design and implementation of policies and regulations regarding data privacy issues are already, and will increasingly be, of key importance to the development of the new d-GPT, and the complementary innovations that will stem from it. The following sections elaborate on the key role of government in fostering d-GPT-based innovation in the provision of public or quasi-public goods, particularly in health care, education, and transportation.

d-GPT-Based Innovation in the Provision of Public Goods

Health Care

The health care sector exemplifies as well as any the centrality of government and the need for government-related innovation. The annual budget of the NIH, probably the biggest research agency in the world, stands at about $40 billion, and R&D expenditures by US-based pharmaceutical companies amount to almost twice as much. Not surprisingly, the US is the undisputed leader in biomedical innovation. Yet the US health care system, accounting for a staggering 17 percent of GDP, is one of the most inefficient in the OECD, achieving results well below those of other advanced nations (table 9.C.1).

The point is that innovation in medicine (i.e., in pharma, medical equipment, surgical procedures, etc.) does not necessarily translate into better health outcomes. The intervening factor is obviously the health system itself: the way health care is organized, delivered, and paid for; the extent of access to care, and the like. It is in this context that government plays a key role, in various ways: providing care directly in some countries (as in the United

Table 9.C.1   Health care in the US and the OECD

	US	OECD
Total expenditure on health care (percent of GDP)	17 (highest)	8.8
Life expectancy	78.6	80.7
Diabetes prevalence (percent of adults)	10.8	6.4
Access to care, percent eligible for core services	90.8 (second worse)	98.4

Source: OECD (2019).

Kingdom or Canada); funding and regulating in many others, and in some cases by omission (i.e., abstaining from doing some or any of the above). Managing the health care system so as to attain good health outcomes calls not just for static efficiency but for constant improvement and change (i.e., it requires system-wide innovation, above and beyond medical innovation). What good is, say, innovation in diagnostic imaging (e.g., an improved CT-PET scanner) if access to it is very limited, and the diagnostic results do not lead to improved treatment?

The implications are clear: institutional, organizational, and regulatory innovations in health care are crucial for obtaining better health outcomes, and government has to play a key role in that respect. Furthermore, the emerging d-GPT offers highly promising opportunities for system-wide innovations, precisely in such contexts as health care. The following concrete examples illuminate this contention.

Managing emergency care units (ERs) has become an extremely important aspect of health care, and yet very often demand vastly exceeds capacity, leading to degraded service, long waits, and bad outcomes. Sorting and managing the flow of patients trying to access ERs is thus crucial. In fact, there are three types of admissions to ERs:

1. Those who should not have resorted to ERs in the first place, but should have rather gone to a primary care physician or a local clinic ("false emergencies");

2. Those who could and should have gone earlier for a planned hospital intervention and perhaps hospitalization, before reaching the "emergency" stage; and

3. Those who experience emergencies due to accidents, heart attacks, strokes, and the like.

Using big data and machine learning methods to characterize each category of patients and coupling such categorization with detailed individual data of patients intending to go to ERs, it would be possible to channel these patients in real time to the most appropriate venue. Even if, say, 10 percent of patients were thus steered away from ERs, that can lead to a significant improvement in the functioning of ER units.[5] The development of such organizational innovation based on the intensive use of d-GPT and its system-wide deployment can save precious resources while gaining in efficiency and efficacy in the provision of health care.

Another example is analyzing with machine learning extensive data from electronic medical records to predict gestational diabetes, and using the pre-

5. This is similar to what happens in the context of transportation, whereby even small reductions in the flow of vehicles can greatly reduce traffic congestion   in both cases, the processes are highly nonlinear.

dictions, to do early testing of women at high risk of developing it.[6] Again, such innovation can save resources and bring about better outcomes.

These and similar innovations need not be done by government agencies themselves, and yet the role of government in enabling and supporting system-wide innovations of this nature is likely to be very important and even crucial. One of the reasons is that d-GPT entails and necessitates the intensive use of vast amounts of widely dispersed and varied data pertaining to individuals, which raises difficult issues of privacy, safety, ownership, and intended use, as well as of common protocols. Government intervention is required, since market forces or local authorities cannot by themselves successfully cope with these thorny issues. d-GPT-based innovation in the provision of health care may well occur outside government, but the pace, scope, and reach of it, and the ability to reap system-wide health benefits will strongly depend on proper government action.

Education

Revamping the education system to provide the skills required for the upcoming d-GPT, from early childhood to higher education, is crucial so as allow the young generation to find suitable employment and ensure future growth. Government is a key player in education all over the world, certainly the most powerful, and thus it is bound to play a key role in fostering innovation in education. This is certainly the case for primary and secondary education, which is delivered mostly by public schools, but also for early childhood education, which is increasingly understood to be of paramount importance in the early development of life-long skills.

Furthermore, d-GPT, coupled with big data on pupils, teachers, and schools, offers the possibility to innovate in the direction of "personalize~ducation," moving away from the factory model of education that emerged in the 19th century and is increasingly obsolete. Thus, innovating in education entails these interrelated but distinct channels:

- promoting the skills needed for d-GPT employment,
- taking advantage of d-GTP to reorient the system toward "personalized education," and
- innovating in the delivery and access to education using the capabilities of distant learning, which is a further manifestation of d-GPT.

Regarding the last point, the COVID-19 pandemic forced school closures in 191 countries, affecting at least 1.5 billion students and 63 million primary and secondary teachers (UN 2020). Many of them resorted to studying online (there are no reliable data yet on how many), in what probably will be regarded as the largest educational experiment in history. It is widely

6. Artzi et al. (2020).

assumed that following this dramatic disruption, and the massive exposure to distance learning, some of it will be adopted permanently, but that will require a much more experimentation and innovation.

Transportation

Traffic congestion has become one of the most challenging issues affecting urban life, and it is widely understood that traditional policies entailing the expansion of infrastructure cannot offer lasting improvement. Rather, what is required is smart traffic management based on d-GPT, such as:

- highly differentiated road pricing using real-time data on location, time, and number of passengers in each vehicle;
- the design of efficient shared rides and car-pooling schemes, based on detailed data on the commuting patterns of employees to employment areas; and
- the development of last-mile micro-mobility (scooters, bikes, etc.), and its smart management at the interface between individual and public transportation.

Further Directions to Facilitate Innovation in Government

When it comes to the inner workings of government and the design of policies, there is vast room for improvement, pertaining to the categories of what Bruce and Figueiredo designate as organizational and policy related innovations. There is increasing awareness of the importance of such innovations, as reflected inter alia in the spread of "Moneyball for Government" types of initiatives (Ayotte et al. 2014). The idea, based on Michael Lewis' bestseller (Lewis 2004), is that the long-held conceptions of how to carry out activities in organizations—be they regular businesses, sport clubs, or government agencies—may turn out to be vastly inefficient, and that the intensive use of data and rigorous methods of analysis can point out to far better ways. This is bound to be particularly true in the context of government, due to the lack of competition and of adequate measures of performance. The following suggestions exemplify ways by which government can flush out inefficiencies and pave the way to innovative courses of action:

- Expand the use of fast randomized controlled trials (RCTs) to test the prospective effectiveness of new policy programs. One of the stumbling blocks impeding the wide implementation of RCTs so that they become more relevant for policy making is that they typically take too long (relative to the political clock) and often are too limited in scope. The intensive use of big data to complement that generated by the RCT itself, and of online platforms as well as of machine learning methods, may significantly enhance the effectiveness of RCTs as a viable tool in policy making (Bouguen et al. 2018).

- Revive the application of zero-based budgeting (ZBB) to improve the effectiveness of existing government programs, making use of data-intensive methods. When the yearly government budget is drafted, the discussions typically dwell on the increments or subtractions at the margin, but not on the full budget. Thus, inertia dominates most of public spending, without regard to ex ante intents or to ex post results. ZBB is supposed to help tackle two questions: Are the existing activities that appear in the budget efficient and effective? Should current activities be eliminated or reduced to fund higher-priority new programs or reduce the current budget?

  The ability to address these questions in a timely fashion has greatly improved with the availability of big data and of advanced methods of data analysis. This is so because over time, most government programs generate large amounts of administrative data as they are implemented. These data exist in digital form and can be used to examine their ex-post effectiveness, particularly when combined with further government-owned data. This was not the case in the past. Thus in retrospect, the ZBB approach was introduced prematurely, leading to its abandonment, but now conditions are ripe for its reintroduction.

- Expand the interaction and engagement of government agencies with a wide range of stakeholders to elicit their preferences, pave the way to acceptance of policy reforms, and cultivate public trust. The availability of online, digital platforms has greatly enhanced the ability to reach wide segments of the public in a timely fashion, and to extract from these interactions useful insights and policy implications. The erosion of public trust in government institutions constitutes a serious threat to democracy, and thus deploying *d-GTP* tools to move in the direction of participatory (or deliberative) democracy could be an effective way to restore trust (Fishkin 2011).

Concluding Remarks

Fostering organizational and policy innovation in government encounters many difficulties, prominent among them government inertia, lack of incentives, and the proverbial self-preservation tendency of bureaucracies. This is quite certainly the most formidable hurdle, since innovation entails entrepreneurship, which in turn needs to be elicited by powerful incentives. Measurement of outputs is an accompanying factor, as well as flexibility in rewarding effort, novel ideas, and success. Introducing these key ingredients of innovation to government indeed constitutes a great challenge, but it is one that needs to be tackled in any case: as virtually every aspect of economic activity is being transformed with each new wave of GPTs, the widening divide between government and the rest of the economy will become untenable, and thus is bound to give rise to new government modes of operation.

The point is that reinventing the provision of government services should entail not just moving from one static equilibrium to a temporarily better one, but also creating the conditions for constant innovation.

A second set of obstacles refer to data: as I have repeatedly suggested, d-GPT-based innovations in government entail the massive use of data. For that to happen, it is imperative to link disparate data sources and to ensure the interoperability of different data systems—both are possible but hard to implement. Furthermore, the more government relies on interconnected big data, the more it exposes itself (and thus the public) to cyber threats and privacy hazards. In addition, there is always the lingering concern of abuse, whose utmost manifestation (so far) is the Orwellian "social credit system" being implemented in China. These are very real difficulties, and as with many other side effects of technological progress, we have to learn to confront them, and we must not refrain from embracing progress because of them.

And finally, we economists have our share to contribute to advance government innovation. We need to go much further in the way we define and measure innovation and productivity, so as to be able to quantify them also in the context of government. That is, we need to create new context-dependent performance dimensions, which in turn would allow us to come up with new mechanism designs to incentivize them, including competitive schemes for policy design and experimentation.

In terms of the internal functioning of government, we should consider introducing the routine assessment of the innovative impact of new bills and regulations, conducting "quality rounds" as an integral part of government work, and incentivizing the mobility of personnel. Likewise, we should consider presenting the "grand challenges" that we confront in the 21st century—from climate change to social inclusion—to all government agents on a regular basis, prompting them to contribute their share in responding to the challenges.

To conclude, we should foster innovative government action, both to revamp the provision of 21st century public goods, and to set the stage for the rapid and effective unfolding of the new GPT throughout the economy. For that purpose, we need not "big government" but more effective and *innovative government*, adopting and tailoring d-GPT to policy needs, and in so doing impacting the course of the d-GPT itself.

References

Artzi, Nitzan Shalom, Smadar Shilo, Eran Hadar, Hagai Rossman, Shiri Barbash-Hazan, Avi Ben-Haroush, Ran D. Balicer, Becca Feldman, Arnon Wiznitzer, and Eran Segal. 2020. "Prediction of Gestational Diabetes Based on Nationwide Electronic Health Records." *Nature Medicine* 26: 71–76.
Ayotte, Kelly, Mark Warner, Glenn Hubbard, Gene Sperling, Melody Barnes, John

Bridgeland, Kevin Madden, Howard Wolfson, Jim Nussle, and Peter Orszag. 2014. *Moneyball for Government*. New York: Disruption Books.

Bouguen, Adrien, Yue Huang, Michael Kremer, and Edward Miguel. 2018. "Using RCTs to Estimate Long-Run Impacts in Development Economics." NBER Working Paper No. 25356. Cambridge, MA: National Bureau of Economic Research.

Bresnahan, T., and M. Trajtenberg. 1995. "General Purpose Technologies 'Engines of Growth'?" *Journal of Econometrics* 65: 83–108.

Brynjolfsson, Erik, Daniel Rock, and Chad Syverson. 2019. "Artificial Intelligence and the Modern Productivity Paradox: A Clash of Expectations and Statistics." In *The Economics of Artificial Intelligence: An Agenda*, edited by Ajay Agrawal, Joshua Gans, and Avi Goldfarb, 23–57. Chicago: University of Chicago Press.

Bush, Vannevar. 1945. "Science—The Endless Frontier. A Report to the President." Washington, DC: US Government Printing Office. https://www.nsf.gov/about/history/vbush1945.htm.

Cockburn, Iain, Rebecca Henderson, and Scott Stern. 2019. "The Impact of Artificial Intelligence on Innovation." In *The Economics of Artificial Intelligence: An Agenda*, edited by Ajay Agrawal, Joshua Gans, and Avi Goldfarb, 115–46. Chicago: University of Chicago Press.

Fishkin, James S. 2011. *When the People Speak*. Oxford: Oxford University Press.

Goldfarb, Avi, Bledi Taska, and Florenta Teodoridis. 2019. "Could Machine Learning Be a General-Purpose Technology? Evidence from Online Job Postings." October 12. https://ssrn.com/abstract=3468822.

Lewis, Michael. 2004. *Moneyball: The Art of Winning an Unfair Game*. New York: W. W. Norton.

OECD. 2019. "Health at a Glance." https://www.oecd-ilibrary.org/social-issues-migration-health/health-at-a-glance-2019_4dd50c09-en.

UN. 2020. "Startling Disparities in Digital Learning Emerge as Covid-19 Spreads: UN Education Agency." https://news.un.org/en/story/2020/04/1062232.

10

Venture Capital–Led Entrepreneurship in Health Care

Amitabh Chandra, Cirrus Foroughi,
and Lauren Mostrom

10.1 Introduction

Even though venture capital (VC) funds are generally raised for a limited period of time (usually 10 years) and only account for about $450 billion in assets (compared to several trillion in private equity and $43 trillion in public equity), VCs hold disproportionate influence over financing innovation in all sectors of the economy. Lerner and Nanda (2020) note that among nonfinancial firms that issued an IPO between 1995 and 2018, 47 percent were backed by a VC fund. Of those firms that were still public at the end of 2019, the firms originally backed by VC made up 76.2 percent of the total market capitalization and were responsible for 88.6 percent of total R&D expenditure.

As of 2014, about 37 percent of the healthcare industry's market capitalization was backed by VC, making it the third-most VC-backed industry, behind electronics and software (Gornall and Strebulaev 2015). In 2017, health-care spending in the US made up 17.1 percent of GDP ($3.3 trillion), far exceeding the shares of other developed nations, and per capita health-

Amitabh Chandra is the Henry and Allison McCance Professor of Business Administration at Harvard Business School, the Ethel Zimmerman Wiener Professor of Public Policy and Director of Health Policy Research at the Harvard Kennedy School of Government, and a research associate of the National Bureau of Economic Research.

Cirrus Foroughi is an associate at Analysis Group.

Lauren Mostrom is a research associate at Harvard Business School.

We thank Heidi Williams for helpful comments, and Scott Stern and the editors for very helpful suggestions. The views expressed herein are those of the authors and do not necessarily reflect the views of the National Bureau of Economic Research. For acknowledgments, sources of research support, and disclosure of the authors' material financial relationships, if any, please see https://www.nber.org/books-and-chapters/role-innovation-and-entrepreneurship-economic-growth/venture-capital-led-entrepreneurship-health-care.

care spending has nearly doubled since 1995 (Nunn, Parsons, and Shambaugh 2020). This increase in spending has been partially attributed to Baumol's "cost disease," the phenomenon that service sectors face persistently rising costs and limited opportunities for productivity improvements, and partially to innovations that improve health-care quality but do not reduce costs (Baumol and Bowen 1965; Sheiner and Malinovskaya 2016). Since the future quality and affordability of patient care depends on new medical innovations, the way VC investments shape the treatments, technologies, and delivery systems that come to market are particularly salient in this industry. Put more starkly, if VC investments in a therapeutic area are small relative to the social value of these potential treatments (e.g., a transformational medicine for Alzheimer's or a novel telemedicine platform), then society would forgo the benefits of these discoveries, because commercialization of these ideas depends on the decisions of venture capitalists. These concerns are amplified by the observation that venture capitalists ought to be insulated from public markets given their long time-horizons, but there is some evidence that the quality of research conducted by VC-backed early-stage companies is of lower quality during recessions, which would introduce cyclicality in quality (Howell et al. 2020).

Our model of VC-backed investments in health care is the same as R&D investments outside health care, but with augmented risk and return parameters. Venture capitalists will make R&D investments if the expected net present value (NPV) of a project, discounted at the appropriate cost-of-capital, is positive. Expected NPV will depend on expectations about future revenues—prices and quantities, the risk of failure, and the cost of R&D. These cash flows will be discounted by a cost-of-capital that depends on the correlation between project returns and overall market returns (beta will be low for projects with high scientific and regulatory risk and high for health-care products that are directly sold to consumers, because consumer's willingness to pay is cyclical with the rest of the market). It is important not to conflate uncertainty with the cost of capital—the latter will be lower for pharmaceutical investments than for other investments, but it should be noted that the pharmaceutical investments may still have a low expected NPV because of scientific and regulatory uncertainty.

In this simple model, venture capitalists will want to prioritize projects that are able to move from an idea to a commercialized product in a short time, and this force will—*ceteris paribus*—discourage investments in early-stage pharmaceuticals and biotechnology firms because of the fundamentally long arc of science and regulatory review, and the additional uncertainty stemming from policy uncertainty given government's large role as a purchaser and regulator of health-care services. These additional sources of uncertainty are not present in product markets that have a direct-to-consumer channel for sales, and venture capitalists will seek to overcome these forces by seeking a larger ownership stake in early-stage companies that are particularly risky.

Another concern with the quality of VC-backed investments in health care is that the short time between discovery and commercialization may privilege a set of ideas that are economically viable but less connected to the burden of disease or to the social value of these discoveries. These potential mismatches may be smaller outside the health-care sector, where the regulatory burdens are lower and direct-to-consumer selling is the dominant sales channel. One strategy that reduces the time pressure and uncertainty of innovations is the use of multiple funding rounds in a startup's life, which benefits investors and the entrepreneurs alike by enabling investors to choose the amount of competition and regulatory risk they are exposed to. Multiple funding rounds are likely to be more important for health-care investments, but for this reason, we might expect funding for VC R&D in health care to go to earlier stage companies relative to non-health-care investments, because venture capitalists will have a particular comparative advantage in making sense of these early-stage investments. Another approach used by some specialized venture capitalists to mitigate these challenges, especially in the biotech and pharmaceuticals industries, is to create new startups inside "VC-foundries," to reduce information asymmetry between the venture capitalist and the entrepreneur.

With these motivations, we describe trends in the life cycle of innovation in the health-care sector, starting with a data set from the capital market company Preqin on VC deals in the health-care sector, to develop a more detailed picture of early-stage innovation in health care. We find that VC funding in the health-care sector has grown more slowly and been directed at earlier stage firms than VC funding in other sectors, which suggests that other sectors offer more economically attractive projects. Among VC investments, 60 percent of all money was invested in firms working on drugs, another 20 percent was invested in firms working on a project related to medical devices, and 20 percent was given to firms working on health-care delivery. We also find enormous geographic concentration of health-care deals, which motivates us to explore the "valley of death" hypothesis (the idea that many useful inventions are not explored, because venture capitalists may not know about them). We explore the relationship between patenting and VC funding at the level of cities and find some support for this hypothesis, but we emphasize the need to evaluate it more carefully.

This fact in turn motivates us to consider another way of looking at early-stage entrepreneurship in health care: publications in medical journals and the relative roles of private and public funding of different areas of research in health care (basic science, devices, pharmaceuticals, delivery). Such an analysis would not be possible in other industries, where publication is not a prerequisite for commercialization, but the science and research–intensive nature of innovation in health care means that we can use publications and sources of funding to measure the direction of pre-investment research in health care.

Using publications to measure the development of ideas reveals some additional facts. Two Metropolitan Statistical Areas (MSAs)—Boston and San Francisco—account for a disproportionate share of basic science research, translational research, and clinical research—which may be why they receive the plurality of VC investments. Some evidence, albeit directional evidence, suggests that the National Institutes of Health (NIH) reduces market failure by allocating relatively more dollars for basic science research (research that is fundamental biology and chemistry and not linked to a particular drug or disease) than industry allocates. While we cannot answer the question of whether the NIH should do more or less of this, the allocation that we find is a necessary condition for allocative efficiency of public dollars. Pushing in the other direction is our finding that when it comes to translational research (research that is directly linked to a disease), NIH funded research does not look different than privately funded research—for example, the NIH funded research projects are just as likely to study cancer over infectious diseases as are privately funded research projects. This finding raises questions of whether the government should rethink how it allocates money to projects.

10.2 Venture Capital Deals

We obtain data on VC deals in healthcare from Preqin. Though most existing literature focuses on Preqin's performance data, we focus our attention on the investment deals themselves to develop a fuller understanding of which research ideas and developments are determined a priori to be the most commercializable by venture capitalists. The Venture Capital Deals data set from Preqin includes not only investments by VC funds and angel investors, but also grants from foundations and government agencies (namely, the NIH), which we analyze separately. When we refer to volumes of VC investments or deals throughout this chapter, we are referring to the amounts of money invested by venture capitalists in young companies, not the amounts transacted between venture capitalists and their limited partners. To compare these deal volumes across time, all deal values were converted to 2020 US dollars using the Consumer Price Index for All Urban Consumers.

The Preqin database has been assembled based on voluntary reporting from general partners and limited partners of venture funds and public filings from pension funds. This data set has the advantage of transparency, since general partners are able and willing to submit corrections for inaccurate information about their funds. One potential bias, however, is that the database misses certain high performing VCs, such as Sequoia and Accel, due to the way it collects information.[1] Despite these limitations, Preqin data have been used in recent scholarship to conduct various analyses of perfor-

1. For a more complete discussion of the Preqin data compared to similar sources, see Kaplan and Lerner (2016).

mance.[2] Finally, we feel confident in the suitability of the Preqin data for our analysis, because some of the primary concerns with Preqin data—such as survivorship bias, slow updates, and spotty coverage of cash flow data—impact performance data in Preqin but do not affect the reporting of deals.

In the health care sector, deals are divided by Preqin into one of seven industries: Biotechnology, Biopolymers, Healthcare, Healthcare IT, Healthcare Specialists, Medical Devices & Equipment, and Pharmaceuticals. We simplified this to arrive at five industry groups used in later tables and figures. Given the importance of VCs to biopharmaceutical innovation, we spend some time on this topic and sometimes refer to the Pharmaceuticals and Biotechnology industries collectively as "Drugs." Similarly, we will sometimes refer to Healthcare and Healthcare IT collectively as "Healthcare Delivery," because the most common sub-industries in Healthcare include Diagnostics, Laboratories, and Hospitals, and the top sub-industries of Healthcare IT include Medical Software, Communication Platforms, Diagnostics, and Laboratories. These groupings will facilitate comparison between VC deals and academic publications in these areas.

We also discuss the funding stages at which these deals were made. For ease of explanation, we combine Series E, F, G, H, I, and J, PIPE, Mergers, Pre-IPO, and Secondary Stock Purchases into "Late Stage;" then we combine Series C and D, Venture Debt, Add-On, and Growth Capital into "Expansion;" finally, we combine Series A with Series B and Seed with Angel. The grants from foundations and government agencies mentioned above were tagged as such using the funding stage variable, so the point in the firm's life cycle at which it received the grant is unobservable in this context.

10.3   Three Facts about R&D in Health Care

Our analysis of deal making in this industry reveals three stylized facts about VC involvement in the healthcare sector over the past two decades:

1. VC funding in the health-care sector has grown more slowly and has been directed at earlier stage firms than VC funding in other sectors.

2. VC funding to young and innovative companies is overwhelmingly directed to the development of drugs; this is in fact even truer of grant money from the NIH than of investments by venture capitalists.

3. American firms dominate the VC deals in the Preqin data set on both sides of the transaction, but on the innovation side in particular; the Bay Area and the Greater Boston Area are hubs of both health-care innovation and investment in the US. They are joined by New York City on the investment side and San Diego on the innovation side. We explore this pattern of

2. For example, Gompers and Wang (2017); Harris, Jenkinson, and Kaplan (2014); Korteweg and Nagel (2016).

A. VC Investment Volumes

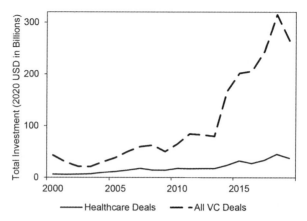

B. Healthcare Share of Venture Capital Invested

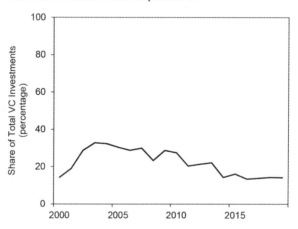

Fig. 10.1   VC deals in health care as a share of all VC deals

allocation in the last section of our chapter, because it is consistent with VC not knowing about health-care innovation from other cities.

1. *VC funding in the health-care sector has grown more slowly and has been directed at slightly less mature firms than VC funding in other sectors.* VC deals in the health-care sector have been increasing fairly steadily over the past 20 years, but they have not grown as rapidly as VC deals in other sectors in the past decade. As a consequence, the health-care share of all VC deals has steadily declined over this period, from 33 percent in 2003 to just 14 percent in 2019 (see figure 10.1). If investments in health care commanded supranormal returns—perhaps because of the guarantee of high drug prices from future launches—then this would not be case.

Table 10.1   **VC Deals by funding stage**

Funding stage	Health-care deals				Non-health-care deals			
	Number of deals	Percent of deals	Deal volume ($ millions)	Percent of deal vol.	Number of deals	Percent of deals	Deal volume ($ millions)	Percent of deal vol.
Seed & angel	3,971	13.00	4,521.43	1.20	42,231	26.57	41,445.84	2.39
Series A & B	9,163	30.00	133,585.76	35.31	42,786	26.92	457,008.58	26.30
Expansion	6,058	19.83	110,100.96	29.11	23,432	14.74	611,918.10	35.22
Late stage	1,271	4.16	38,430.69	10.16	2,868	1.80	215,477.93	12.40
Unspecified	10,085	33.01	91,638.13	24.23	47,614	29.96	411,768.08	23.70
Total	30,548	100.0	378,277.0	100.0	158,931	100.0	1,737,618.5	100.0

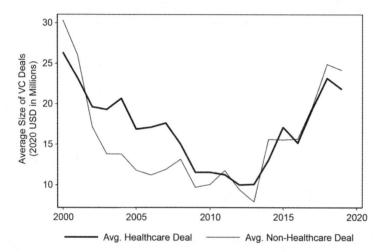

Fig. 10.2   Average deal sizes, health care and non-health care

Health-care deals are more likely to be made to Series A and B firms (35.3 percent) than to Expansion firms (29.1 percent), while firms in other sectors were more likely to receive VC funding during their Expansion stage (34.1 percent) rather than in Series A and B (27.9 percent). R&D in health care, and particularly in biopharmaceuticals, has higher risks earlier in the life cycle of companies, and venture capitalists play an important role in allocating capital to such projects (see table 10.1). Note that the funding stage of the deal is unavailable for about a quarter of VC deals, but nearly all deals with a known funding stage occurred either in the Series A and B stage of a firm's life or in the Expansion stage.

The pattern of VC investments, among health-care deals and non-health-care deals alike, has also been characterized by shrinking average deal sizes between 2000 and 2013, and a gradual return since 2013 to the average deal sizes as they were in 2000 (see figure 10.2). The fact that the trends are very

Table 10.2   VC deals by industry

Primary industry	Number of deals	Percent of deals	Deal volume ($millions)	Percent of deal vol.
Biotechnology	8,500	26.63	$118,086.2	30.94
Pharmaceuticals	6,412	20.09	$112,512.2	29.48
Medical devices & equipment	8,502	26.64	$73,862.4	19.35
Health care	4,182	13.10	$43,394.6	11.37
Health-care IT	4,322	13.54	$33,801.4	8.86
Total	31,918	100.0	$381,656.7	100.0

similar across industries suggests that the explanation is not health-care specific. With the data available to us, we are not able to explore the relationship between deal size and changes in the availability of capital from sources other than VCs.

2. *Funding to young and innovative companies is overwhelmingly directed to the development of drugs; this is in fact even truer for grant money from the NIH than of investments by VCs.* Among VC deals, 60 percent of all money transacted was invested in firms working on drugs, another 20 percent was invested in firms working on a project related to medical devices, and 20 percent was given to firms working on a project related to health-care delivery (see table 10.2). If innovations in the drugs and devices industries allow VCs to capture the value of their investments more than innovations in health-care delivery (perhaps because health-care delivery investments have positive externalities, because of benefiting government payers or network externalities, that are difficult to fully capture), it would be intuitive to expect that private sources of funding favor drugs and devices. Over about the past 7 years, we see the most consistent growth in VC investments in the area of biopharmaceuticals is to firms in the Series A and B stages (see figure 10.3). Expansion investments appear to exhibit less consistent growth, and instead show occasional spikes driven by large deals, most clearly occurring in 2015 and 2018.[3] This is one reason we will spend some time considering VC investments in biotech and pharmaceutical companies.

Interestingly, we find that NIH grants to companies are over-represented in the area of pharmaceuticals—the NIH portfolio of grants is domi-

---

3. The spike in Drugs Expansion investments in 2015 was primarily driven by Horizon Pharma's fundraising efforts to acquire Hyperion Therapeutics and Crealta Holdings, primarily for their orphan drugs (see https://www.nytimes.com/2015/03/31/business/dealbook/horizon-pharma-offers-to-acquire-hyperion-therapeutics-for-1-1-billion.html and https://www.chicagotribune.com/business/ct-horizon-buys-small-drugmaker-1212-biz-20151211-story.html). The spike in 2018 was driven by a large joint venture undertaken by Novartis and Aduro Biotech in the field of immuno-oncology (see https://www.novartis.com/news/media-releases/novartis-accelerates-cancer-immunotherapy-efforts-aduro-biotech-alliance-and-launch-new-immuno-oncology-research-group).

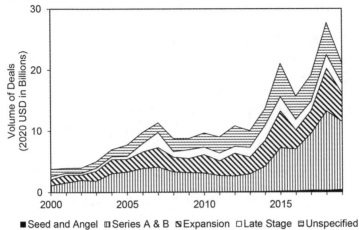

■ Seed and Angel ⊞ Series A & B ◧ Expansion □ Late Stage ◨ Unspecified

Fig. 10.3   Funding stage breakdown of drug investments

nated by contributions to pharmaceuticals firms (see figure 10.4). In total, 76.4 percent of NIH grant money given to startups over the past 20 years has supported the development of drugs, another 13 percent has supported the development of medical devices, and only 10.5 percent supported investments in health-care delivery and infrastructure. Since this money was given in the form of grants, with no claim to future earnings or repayment, these grants should have been allocated based on expected future social good rather than on profitability. One justification for this allocation would be if NIH granted these funds for studying treatments for diseases that primarily affect communities unlikely to be able to pay high drug prices, or for treatments that were just below the threshold for economic viability. Evaluating this claim is beyond the scope of our analysis, but it would be important to know whether NIH grants to early-stage companies induce socially valuable innovation, or whether they are a substitute for private investments.

3. *American firms dominate the VC deals in the Preqin data set on both sides of the transactions, with the Bay Area and the Greater Boston Area serving as hubs for health-care innovation and investment in the US.* In the Preqin data set, 57 percent of VC investments in the health-care sector come from American VCs, and the top 10 investing countries contribute 88 percent of the money invested (see table 10.3). Of the money invested by American venture capitalists, 50 percent was originated from venture capitalists in the Bay Area, New York City, and the Greater Boston Area alone, with the top 10 MSAs contributing 62 percent together. The recipient firms of these investments are even more concentrated at the country level, but slightly less concentrated at the MSA level in the US. American firms receive fully 72.9 percent of the money accounted for in the Preqin deals data set, and

A. NIH Grants to Startups, Share by Number of Grants, 244 Grants Total

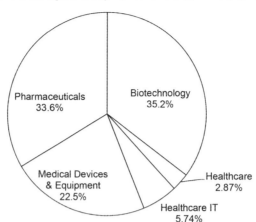

B. NIH Grants to Startups, Share by Grant Volume, $682 Million in Grants Total

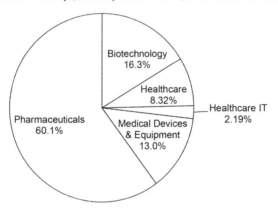

Fig. 10.4   Industry breakdown of NIH grants

the top 10 MSAs received 55 percent of that money. The top three MSAs in terms of received investments were the Bay Area, the Greater Boston Area, and San Diego, which together received 44 percent of the money invested in American firms over the past 20 years.

We find that the top investing MSAs carry diversified portfolios across all five industries in health care (see figure 10.5, top panel). In contrast, Boston and San Diego show a clear specialization in drug development, with an overwhelming proportion of their VC-backed portfolio firms focused on either biotechnology or pharmaceuticals (see figure 10.5, bottom panel). In contrast, the Bay Area has well diversified innovations as well as investments. While at the MSA level investment portfolios appear to be well diversified,

Table 10.3   Geographic dispersion of VC investments

Rank	Top countries	Number of deals	Percent of deals	Deal volume ($millions)	Percent of deal vol.	Top US MSAs	Number of deals	Percent of US deals	Deal volume ($millions)	Percent of US deal vol.
				A. Top recipients of VC funds						
1	US	19,538	61.21	$278,026.80	72.85	Bay Area	3,267	16.82	$63,607.90	23.05
2	China	3,543	11.10	$33,178.60	8.69	Boston	1,675	8.62	$37,376.80	13.55
3	UK	1,714	5.37	$14,961.30	3.92	San Diego	1,131	5.82	$19,815.70	7.18
4	Germany	767	2.40	$6,607.60	1.73	New York	649	3.34	$8,916.10	3.23
5	Canada	805	2.52	$6,529.50	1.71	Los Angeles	457	2.35	$5,392.70	1.95
6	Switzerland	480	1.50	$6,519.80	1.71	Seattle	452	2.33	$5,388.80	1.95
7	France	672	2.11	$6,174.30	1.62	Boulder	167	0.86	$3,015.20	1.09
8	Israel	635	1.99	$5,767.80	1.51	Durham	210	1.08	$2,970.70	1.08
9	Ireland	190	0.60	$2,950.90	0.77	Chicago	137	0.71	$2,937.00	1.06
10	India	592	1.85	$2,712.80	0.71	Austin	250	1.29	$2,305.30	0.84
	Top 10	28,936	90.66	$363,429.34	95.22	Top 10	8,395	43.23	$151,726.33	54.99
				B. Top investors of VC funds						
1	US	14,464	45.27	$185,778.77	56.90	Bay Area	7,778	21.77	$54,680.50	23.30
2	China	3,541	11.08	$27,929.07	8.55	New York	3,494	9.78	$35,910.60	15.30
3	UK	2,562	8.02	$22,642.82	6.93	Boston	3,450	9.66	$26,255.90	11.19
4	Switzerland	1,097	3.43	$12,557.25	3.85	Chicago	812	2.27	$6,529.90	2.78
5	Germany	1,146	3.59	$7,562.86	2.32	Washington, DC	984	2.75	$6,076.70	2.59
6	Hong Kong SAR	480	1.50	$7,260.34	2.22	Houston	305	0.85	$3,630.50	1.55
7	France	1,047	3.28	$6,918.16	2.12	Seattle	557	1.56	$3,554.10	1.51
8	Canada	863	2.70	$6,483.07	1.99	Los Angeles	574	1.61	$3,454.00	1.47
9	Singapore	393	1.23	$5,406.41	1.66	Princeton	767	2.15	$3,332.10	1.42
10	Japan	671	2.10	$5,234.35	1.60	San Diego	458	1.28	$2,238.10	0.95
	Top 10	26,264	82.21	$287,773.11	88.13	Top 10	19,179	53.67	$145,662.34	62.06

A. Top 10 Innovating MSAs

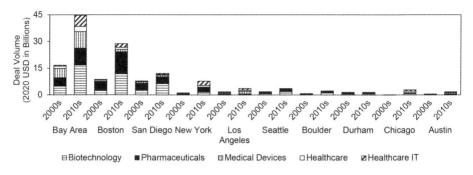

B. Top 10 Investing MSAs

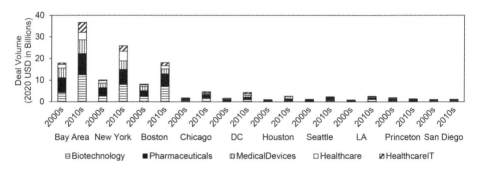

Fig. 10.5   Geographic dispersion and industry specialization of MSAs

at least in the health-care sector, individual VCs appear to focus on one or two industries in particular (namely, biotechnology and pharmaceuticals). This may be an indication that these venture capitalists, while the nature of their work requires some degree of idiosyncratic risk, may be carrying more idiosyncratic risk than necessary. We highlight this observation as a suggestion for further research using other sources.

10.4   Understanding R&D Clusters in Health Care

The above facts on the flow of VC investments by geography motivated us to ask whether the disproportionate allocations of VC investments to San Francisco and Boston would be explained by a larger number of patents originating from these areas. However, some commentators have wondered whether this geographic concentration is a consequence of a phenomenon known as the "valley of death" (Hudson and Khazragui 2013), whereby early stage ventures often fail before commercialization, often as a result of venture capitalists' potential preference for innovation local to themselves. This preference might be rational—search costs are lower for ideas generated by local inventors, and local entrepreneurs might find it easier to establish a better reputation with venture capitalists. In contrast, it could also be the case that innovation stemming from clusters is simply of higher quality than that stemming from non-clusters.

To distinguish between these hypotheses, we sought to understand whether there was a link between VC dollars and the geographic location of patents. This requires us to subset the analysis to VC investments in the biopharma space, because this area relies on patents for innovation.

We obtained data on patenting comes from the US Patent Office's Patents-View—a modern data initiative organized by the USPTO that uses machine learning methods to disambiguate inventors. PatentsView is widely used in studies that require precise data on the location of inventors (Baruffaldi and Simeth 2020; Melero, Palomeras, and Wehrheim 2020). Data were obtained for all granted patents filed from 2000 until 2015 that were classified as "Drugs and Medical," subcategory "Drugs," using the NBER patent classification system. Introduced by Hall, Jaffe, and Trajtenberg (2001), the NBER patent classification system allows for easy identification of pharmaceutical drugs in this setting and lends itself to economic analysis. For certain analyses, chemicals patents were also identified from the PatentsView data using the NBER classification system. We chose 2015 as a cutoff, because it takes a while for patents to be approved.

Inventor locations in PatentsView are provided as latitudes and longitudes, as well as city-state tuples. To create a more usable form of location that takes into account economic clusters (and combines cities in a sensible way), we aggregate these data to the metropolitan statistical area level using the 2015 Census Bureau Shapefiles in conjunction with QGIS 3.1.0.[4] These data were then collapsed to the MSA-year level using inventor weights to prevent double-counting of patents with inventors in multiple locations. To use a stylized example, consider a patent filed in 2011 with three inventors, one from the greater New York City region and two from the Boston metro area. The New York–Newark–Jersey City, NY–NJ–PA MSA would be assigned 1/3 of a patent in 2011, while the Boston–Cambridge–Newton, MA–NH MSA would be assigned 2/3 of a patent in 2011. What remains is an MSA-year-level data set of all US biotech and pharmaceutical drug patenting that is used for all subsequent analyses.

The first fact we present is that innovation in the US, as measured by patenting, is incredibly concentrated across geographies, and that this concentration increases for pharmaceutical and biotech patenting, respectively. Figure 10.6 plots Gini curves for patenting in select industries across MSAs in the US. While Pharmaceutical patenting is roughly as concentrated as patenting in Chemicals, Biotech uniquely stands out as the most concen-

---

4. Shapefiles are publicly accessible at https://catalog.data.gov/.

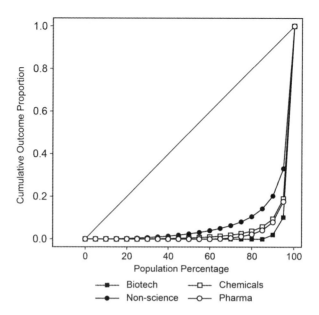

Fig. 10.6   Geographic concentration of patents by industry

Fig. 10.7   Heat-map of biopharma patenting

trated industry in the sense of the origin of biotech patents. The specific geographies driving this concentration can be visualized in figure 10.7, a heat map of pharmaccutical patenting activity across the continental US. The specific geographies that account for the top 10 clusters are visualized in figure 10.8, which reports their contribution to total patenting in pharma

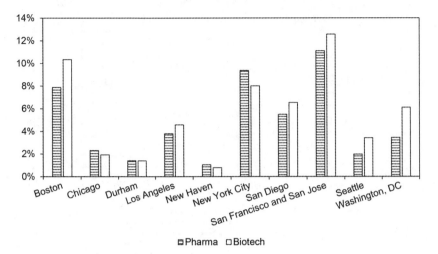

□ Pharma   □ Biotech

Fig. 10.8   Share of pharma and biotech patents in top-10 patenting metropolitical statistical areas (MSAs), 2000–2015

and biotech, respectively. Boston, New York City, and the Bay Area (defined as San Francisco and San Jose, California) are the largest contributors to overall patenting in pharma and biotech from 2000 to 2015.

As a first step in exploring the potential for a "valley of death" phenomena, we examine whether venture capital dollars flow to areas with increased patenting activity—a sign that venture capitalists are responding to increased innovation in geographies. Formally, we regress the log of yearly venture capital flows in pharmaceuticals and biotech on a 1-year lag of logged patenting in those two industries. Results from this exercise can be found in table 10.4, where column 1 includes year fixed effects, and column 2 includes year and MSA (location) fixed effects. Column 1 shows a statistically significant correlation between last year's patenting activity on this year's venture capital flows. When we add MSA fixed effects (column 2), we find that VC funding is no longer correlated with patenting activity, a sign that funding flows are simply a function of geography itself, wherein venture capitalists favor certain locations over others. Columns 3 and 4 use 1- and 2-year lags of patents as instruments to correct for idiosyncratic noise in current-year patent rates; we find similar results in these estimates. To be clear, the IV approach is only to clean up measurement error in the reporting of patents.

These results provide some preliminary evidence that the valley of death phenomenon does exist in this market as it pertains to VC funding flows as a response to innovation. We label our evidence as preliminary, because we cannot reject a model where the quality of patents is fixed across cities but not responsive to changes in the level of patenting (for example, a

Table 10.4   OLS and IV estimates of VC investment elasticity

	Log pharma VC dollars			
Outcome variable	OLS (1)	OLS (2)	IV (3)	IV (4)
Log patents	0.885*	0.149	1.071*	0.147
	(0.118)	(0.135)	(0.146)	(0.853)
Controls:				
Year	Yes	Yes	Yes	Yes
MSA	No	Yes	Yes	Yes
Observations	989	989	563	563
Adjusted R-squared	0.356	0.649	0.371	−0.197

Notes: Standard errors appear in parenthesis and are clustered at the MSA level. Observations are at the MSA-year level. Controls are indicated above and include year and MSA fixed effects. Columns (1) and (2) present OLS estimates, and columns (3) and (4) present IV estimates, where log patents are instrumented by one and two year lags of log patents. $*p < 0.10$, $**p < 0.05$, $***p < 0.01$.

model where patents originating in MSAs like Boston and San Francisco are systematically better than patents from other cities). Evaluating this possibility is a potential area of future research, as the consequences of undiscovered innovation are not just a cost to investors but also a cost to society. In ongoing work, we are using a more formal economic model to assess the presence of the valley of death, by examining one implication of this model—that patients from places that do not receive VC dollars are more successful when funded (which would mean that the marginal project from a city that received fewer VC dollars is better than the marginal project that was funded in Boston or San Francisco).

10.5   Predicting Future Innovations through Research Publications

The above exploration of the potential mismatch between VC investments and patents motivates us to consider another way of looking at early-stage entrepreneurship in health care: publications in medical journals and the relative roles of private and public funding in different areas of research in health care (basic science, devices, pharmaceuticals, delivery). Such an analysis would not be possible in other industries, where publication is not a prerequisite for commercialization. But the science-heavy nature of innovation in new medicines, devices, and the emphasis on clinical trials—not only for regulatory review but also as a standard for evidence—means that we can use publications as another measure of R&D in health care. One challenge with using publications as a measure of research activity is that we are measuring ideas, not dollars, and it is possible that no monotonic relationship exists between research papers and research dollars. Yet research papers may provide a superior prediction of future innovation than research dollars do, because they reflect the size of research support and the realization of that support.

Our data on peer-reviewed research publications were obtained by using the PubMed API to query based on publication characteristics, scrape the unique PubMed Identifiers that identify the papers that fit our criteria, and then group and count those publications by various dimensions. First, we restricted these counts to include only journal articles and clinical trials in phase 2 or 3, published between 1980 and 2019. This step dropped such publications as dissertations, meeting abstracts, lectures, editorials, and newspaper articles. Second, we restricted the counts based on the source of the funding, which can be identified in PubMed based on a combination of publication types and grant codes. PubMed has been tagging publications that received NIH funding by including the string "NIH" in the grant code field since 1980 and has been assigning the paper to the publication types "Research Support, N.I.H., Intramural" or "Research Support, N.I.H., Extramural" since 2005. We included in our counts of NIH publications all those that were tagged in one or both of these ways. We identified a publication as "privately funded" if it did not receive any funding from the NIH, any US government agency other than the NIH, any state or local government in the US, any foreign government, or one of the foundations listed explicitly in PubMed's supporting documentation (including Alzheimer's Association, Susan G. Komen, Wellcome Trust, and 54 others).[5] For this reason, we cannot identify particular big private funding sources of academic publications in the health field, because they are not identified as such in the database. Third, we sometimes restricted publication counts based on the journal in which the publication appeared, in an attempt to adjust for the quality of the paper. For this purpose, we used *British Medical Journal* (BMJ), *Cell*, *Journal of the American Medical Association* (JAMA), *Lancet, Nature, New England Journal of Medicine* (NEJM), and *Science*.

Finally, we classified publications on the basis of the content of each publication, as identified by the Medical Subject Heading (MeSH) classifiers assigned to it. Publications have many MeSH classifiers assigned to them (more than 50 in some cases) by scientists who read the paper and determine what key terms define the topics discussed in it. Some of these classifiers for each publication are marked with an asterisk to denote it as a "major MeSH topic," which is reserved for about 10 or fewer MeSH classifiers that define the most central topics or ideas discussed in the publication. An example of PubMed's display of a paper and its MeSH classifiers, with major topics denoted by asterisks, is included as appendix A for a major review article on

5. The list of foundations explicitly excluded from the counts of privately funded publications in PubMed is available at https://www.nlm.nih.gov/bsd/grant_acronym.html under "Other United States Funding Organizations" and "Non-US Funding Agencies/Organizations."

CRISPR technology. Our grouping of publications is assembled using only those MeSH classifiers marked as major topics.

The two other sets of publication groupings based on content we will be discussing are intended to more closely align with our analysis of VC deals. The first of these groups separates publications about drugs, medical devices, surgery and surgical techniques, health-care delivery, and other forms of science and treatment such as non-drug therapies, non-drug chemicals, and biological phenomena.[6] Publications included in these counts under "Drugs" include papers about prescription drugs, generic drugs, placebos, drug combinations, biotechnology, and related terms, but not about illegal drugs, cannabis, or substance abuse. Publications coded as "Medical Devices" are about devices used both internally and externally, including atmosphere exposure chambers, catheters, diagnostic equipment, tourniquets, and others. Publications coded as "Surgery" include those discussing surgical procedures used either for operating or diagnosing, and structures created inside the body using surgical techniques. Publications coded as "Health Care Delivery" discuss things like administration of health care, access to health care, health-care facilities, disease prevention and outbreak control, and others. Publications coded as "Non-Drug Therapies" include those about various types of treatment that do not involve drugs or medical devices. "Non-Drug Chemicals" include papers about chemical compounds (proteins, amino acids, enzymes, etc.) but not about drugs. In a small set of cases, a publication classified by us as "Non-Drug Chemicals" was in fact about a prescription or over-the-counter drug, but rather than being assigned major MeSH topics related to pharmaceuticals, it was coded only in reference to the chemical composition of the drug (e.g., antihistamine under neurotransmitter agents, or ibuprofen under carboxylic acids). In these cases, the papers were truly about drugs but were misclassified by us as papers about non-drug chemicals. However, these cases are rare, and we do not expect this miscoding to drive our results. Finally, "Biological Phe-

---

6. These groups of publications based on MeSH topics are not mutually exclusive by default, since a publication can discuss many topics. To create groups that were mutually exclusive of one another without dropping a significant number of publications that discuss many aspects of health, these groups had to be prioritized into a hierarchical structure. For the most relevant comparisons between the research in PubMed and the VC deals described below, we first prioritized publications about drugs and medical devices. That is, if a publication was about either drugs or medical devices (or both), it was coded as such, regardless of the publication's other topics. Therefore, the publications in our data set that were coded as surgery or surgical techniques include only papers about surgery *and not* about drugs or medical devices. This is particularly relevant to understanding the overlap between surgery and medical devices, because some medical devices (e.g., stents) are implanted using surgical techniques. While papers about best practices or new innovations in implanting stents are relevant both to discussions of surgical techniques and medical devices, for the purposes of understanding the pushes and pulls for innovations in the health-care sector, we code them here only as medical devices. This prioritization occurs in a similar way for the other groups as well, with publications coded as health-care delivery being those about health-care delivery *and not* about drugs, medical devices, or surgery; non-drug therapies, non-drug chemicals, and biological phenomena are similarly defined by excluding the higher priority topics from their corresponding queries.

nomena" include papers about anatomy, organisms, and other biological processes but none of the topics previously mentioned.

In our third method of categorizing PubMed publications based on their content, we mapped the categories of drugs, devices, surgery, non-drug therapies, non-drug chemicals, and biological phenomena directly to designations of basic science, translational science, and clinical science. Our definitions of these three categories and the MeSH classifiers assigned to each were based on the stages of scientific research as it pertains to medical problem-solving as described by the Dana-Farber Cancer Institute.[7] Here the publications categorized as "basic science" refer to developing knowledge about how body systems and chemical compounds function and interact with one another, and they are defined as publications about biological phenomena, chemicals, and drugs, but not about diseases. Therefore, the publications we group as "basic science" seek to understand the functions and uses of different mechanisms in the body and chemical compounds, even drugs, but not in the context of treating any disease in particular.

We define "translational science" as research that connects the findings of basic science to specific medical issues and challenges. In particular, this group refers to publications about diseases and also chemicals, drugs, biological phenomena, and non-drug therapies, but not surgical or diagnostic techniques. Finally, "clinical science" refers in general to the application of translational science findings to the resolution of medical problems. In particular, we define this group as publications about diseases and also about surgery, diagnostics, anesthesia, analgesia, or medical devices. Basic science, translational science, and clinical science publications counts here include only journal articles that are not clinical studies; that is, they reflect academic research that is still at least one step removed from its implementation in medical problem-solving. Phase 2 and phase 3 clinical trials are included in exhibits as their own separate groups.

With these classifications, we note the extent to which some MSAs appear to be far more specialized in basic science research related to drug discovery at all stages—basic, translational, and clinical (the three panels of figure 10.9 demonstrate the striking degree to which Boston and the Bay area publish papers in basic science, translational science and clinical trials). If basic science research produces better patents because of deeper insights or more novel insights, then the flow of VC dollars to these MSAs may not be surprising, but to truly ascertain this channel, future researchers would have to map quality of downstream patents to the quality of upstream basic and translational science research.

One challenge with basic science research is that it is hard for researchers to expropriate the full social value of their research—because the research may be quite removed from a disease or therapeutic. Recognizing this mar-

---

7. https://blog.dana-farber.org/insight/2017/12/basic-clinical-translational-research-whats -difference/.

A. Basic Science, Top 7 Journals. These Top MSAs Represent 8873 of 35063 (25%) with Affiliation Text

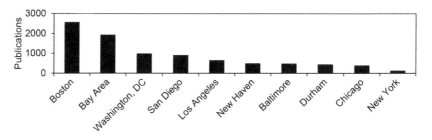

B. Translational Science, Top 7 Journals. These Top MSAs Represent 3941 of 19583 (20%) with Affiliation Text

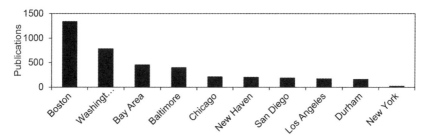

C. Clinical Science, Top 7 Journals
These Top MSAs Represent 2681 of 16086 (17%) with Affiliation Text

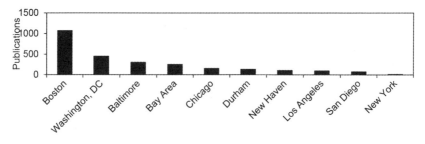

Fig. 10.9   Publications by stage of science research.
Note: Top seven journals are: *BMJ, Cell, JAMA, Lancet, Nature, NEJM, Science*

ket failure is one reason that governments finance basic science research. An open question for new innovations in health care is to understand how well governments fill this gap—governments should, for example, be more willing to finance basic science research and research on topics like health-care delivery than private actors are. One implication is that NIH funded research should skew more toward basic science than it does toward clinical science, in contrast to privately funded research. Figure 10.10 provides

A. Privately Funded Publications, Journal Articles & Clinical Trials (II & III),

Top 7 Journals, Chart Represents 31954 of 88034 Publications

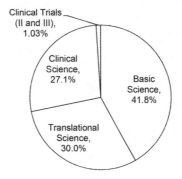

B. NIH-Funded Publications, Journal Articles & Clinical Trials (II & III),

Top 7 Journals, Chart Represents 31961 of 36754 Publications

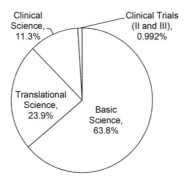

Fig. 10.10   Science publications by stage and funding

some initial evidence of allocative efficiency as measured by the share of NIH funded work that is directed to basic research rather than to clinical or translational science.

10.6   Conclusion

A variety of pull and push forces influence innovation in health care, with venture capitalists playing an extremely important role in marshaling the pull forces that drive innovation. The NIH (or government more generally) is responsible for reducing market failure by subsidizing research that no commercial entity would fund. Our analysis has uncovered several new facts on the operation of these entities. On the VC side, VC dollar allocations have moved away from investment in health care, and a disproportionate share of VC investments—almost 60 percent—are in drugs and devices. While

C. Privately Funded Publications, Journal Articles & Clinical Trials (II & III),

All Journals, Chart Represents 5460920 or 7975858 Publications

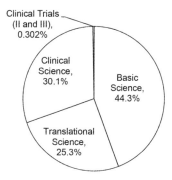

D. NIH-Funded Publications, Journal Articles & Clinical Trials (II & III),

All Journals, Chart Represents 1287102 of 470112 Publications

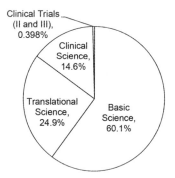

Fig. 10.10   (cont.)

there are many justifications for this allocation, there is also a concern than the VC model will not automatically bring socially valuable innovations to market, because it will emphasize private returns over public ones. Government efforts in health care should therefore try to subsidize socially valuable projects—and while we find that the NIH does do this, we also find that the shape of NIH funded translational research is similar to that of privately funded translational research when it should not be. This deserves further exploration, because the NIH should not follow industry in the desire to show commercial benefit. Public investments should not be a substitute for private investments; instead they should induce complementary investments by the private sector by reducing R&D uncertainty and making these investments more viable for private entities. Another striking fact that deserves further exploration is that three locations account for the plurality of scientific research and also receive the majority of VC investments. Whether this represents higher quality research from these cities, or a "valley of death" is an important question for future research.

The growth prospects of the sector will depend on the answers to these two questions: whether the NIH is overinvesting in clinical and translational research and underinvesting in basic science, and whether the "valley of death" is leading to underinvestment in healthcare innovation outside the investment hubs of Boston and the Bay Area. If these market failures are substantial, remedying them could create sustainable growth in the sector by allocating funding to the marginal invention or research project, which could in turn spur downstream research and innovation. If not, health-care spending will likely continue to grow, but productivity growth in the sector will continue to lag behind that in the economy as a whole. An additional factor at play in the future of the health-care industry will be the lasting impact of the Coronavirus pandemic on health-care delivery infrastructure, particularly in digital health and telehealth resources, for which it is too early to make meaningful projections.

Appendix

Review > Hum Mol Genet. 2014 Sep 15;23(R1):R40-6. doi: 10.1093/hmg/ddu125. Epub 2014 Mar 20.

CRISPR/Cas9 for Genome Editing: Progress, Implications and Challenges

Feng Zhang [1], Yan Wen [1], Xiong Guo [2]

Affiliations + expand
PMID: 24651067   DOI: 10.1093/hmg/ddu125

MeSH terms

> Animals
> Clustered Regularly Interspaced Short Palindromic Repeats / genetics*
> DNA Cleavage
> Gene Expression Regulation
> Gene Transfer Techniques
> Genetic Therapy
> Genome
> Genomics / methods*
> Humans
> Protein Structure, Tertiary
> RNA Editing / genetics*
> Sequence Analysis, DNA

Fig. 10.A.1   Example of PubMed display of a paper with MeSH classifiers

References

Baruffaldi, Stefano H., and Markus Simeth. 2020. "Patents and Knowledge Diffusion: The Effect of Early Disclosure." *Research Policy* 49(4): 103927.
Baumol, W. J., and W. G. Bowen. 1965. "On the Performing Arts: The Anatomy of Their Economic Problems." *American Economic Review* 55(1/2): 495–502.
Gompers, P., and S. Q. Wang. 2017. "And the Children Shall Lead: Gender Diversity and Performance in Venture Capital." NBER Working Paper No. 23454. Cambridge, MA: National Bureau of Economic Research.
Gornall, W., and I. A. Strebulaev. 2015. "The Economic Impact of Venture Capital: Evidence from Public Companies." Stanford GSB Research Paper No. 15-55. https://ssrn.com/abstract=2681841.
Hall, B. H., A. B. Jaffe, and M. Trajtenberg. 2001. "The NBER Patent Citation Data File: Lessons, Insights and Methodological Tools." NBER Working Paper No. 8498. Cambridge, MA: National Bureau of Economic Research.
Harris, R. S., T. Jenkinson, and S. N. Kaplan. 2014. "Private Equity Performance: What Do We Know?" *Journal of Finance* 69(5): 1851–82.
Howell, S., J. Lerner, R. Nanda, and R. Townsend. 2020. "Financial Distancing: How Venture Capital Follows the Economy Down and Curtails Innovation." NBER Working Paper No. 27150. Cambridge, MA: National Bureau of Economic Research.
Hudson, John, and Hanan F. Khazragui. 2013. "Into the Valley of Death: Research to Innovation." *Drug Discovery Today* 18(13–14): 610–13.
Kaplan, S. N., and J. Lerner. 2016. "Venture Capital Data: Opportunities and Challenges." NBER Working Paper No. 22500. Cambridge, MA: National Bureau of Economic Research.
Korteweg, A., and S. Nagel. 2016. "Risk-Adjusting Returns to Venture Capital." *Journal of Finance* 71(3): 1437–70.
Lerner, J., and R. Nanda. 2020. "Venture Capital's Role in Financing Innovation: What We Know and How Much We Still Need to Learn." *Journal of Economic Perspectives* 34(3): 237–61.
Melero, Eduardo, Neus Palomeras, and David Wehrheim. 2020. "The Effect of Patent Protection on Inventor Mobility." *Management Science* 66(12): 5485–504
Nunn, R., J. Parsons, and J. Shambaugh. 2020. "A Dozen Facts about the US Health-Care System." Brookings Institution: The Hamilton Project, Economic Facts, March. https://www.brookings.edu/wp-content/uploads/2020/03/HealthCare_Facts_WEB_FINAL.pdf.
Russell, John. 2015. "Horizon Pharma to Buy Lake Forest Company for $510 Million." *Chicago Tribune*, December 11.
Sheiner, L., and A. Malinovskaya. 2016. *Measuring Productivity in Healthcare: An Analysis of the Literature*. Washington, DC: Brookings Institution, Hutchins Center.

Innovation and Entrepreneurship in Housing

Edward Kung

11.1 Introduction

In this chapter, I discuss innovation and entrepreneurship in housing as it relates to economic growth and productivity. There are two main issues that I seek to address here: (1) What is the impact of innovation and entrepreneurship as a driver of productivity and growth in housing? (2) What are the factors that facilitate or hinder innovation and entrepreneurship in housing? Since housing is such a large and important part of the economy, the answers to these questions have important implications for the impact of innovation and entrepreneurship on overall economic growth and well-being.

11.2 Overview of the Housing Sector

Housing is a large and growing sector of the economy. From 1980 to 2018, personal consumption expenditures on housing rose from 8.6 percent to 10.8 percent of GDP. Of the major household spending categories shown in figure 11.1, only health care grew at a higher rate over the same period.

Because housing is highly durable, most economic activity in housing is related to the leasing, sale, and management of existing housing stock (i.e.,

Edward Kung is an assistant professor of economics at California State University, Northridge.

Prepared for the NBER Growth Conference "Beyond 140 Characters: The Role of Innovation and Entrepreneurship in Economic Growth." I thank the conference organizers Mike Andrews, Ronnie Chatterjie, Josh Lerner, and Scott Stern, my discussant Jessie Handbury, as well as participants at the "Beyond 140 Characters" workshop for their helpful comments. All errors are my own. For acknowledgments, sources of research support, and disclosure of the author's material financial relationships, if any, please see https://www.nber.org/books -and-chapters/role-innovation-and-entrepreneurship-economic-growth/innovation-and -entrepreneurship-housing.

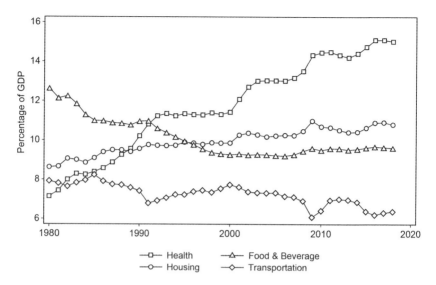

Fig. 11.1   Personal consumption expenditures on selected goods and services as percentage of GDP, 1980–2018

Source: BEA National Income and Product Accounts. Transportation includes vehicles, parts, gasoline, and transportation services.

the real estate industry). A relatively smaller share of the economic activity is related to the actual production of new housing (i.e., the construction industry). Figure 11.2 shows the size of the real estate, construction, and a few other industries in terms of gross output as percentage of GDP, as measured by the Bureau of Economic Analysis (BEA). In 2018, gross output from housing rents was $2.2 trillion, gross output from "other real estate" was $1.4 trillion, and gross output from residential construction was $681 billion.[1]

An important measurement issue that arises in housing is how to value the economic output of owner-occupied housing. A standard thought experiment illustrates the problem: Suppose that Annie and Betty own and live in identical houses next door to each other. Because each owns her own house, no rental payments are made, and no value of housing services is recorded. Now, suppose they switch houses without changing ownership. Instead, Annie pays Betty $1,000 in monthly rent and Betty pays Annie $1,000 in monthly rent. Annie and Betty are each no better or worse off,

---

1. Gross output from housing rents includes both the imputed rents of owner-occupiers and the rents paid by tenants. Gross output from "other real estate" includes all other activities related to residential real estate, including the activities of real estate brokers, appraisers, and property managers. "Other real estate" also includes all commercial real estate activities and rents. The BEA's Industry Economic Accounts do not separate commercial real estate activity from residential real estate activity.

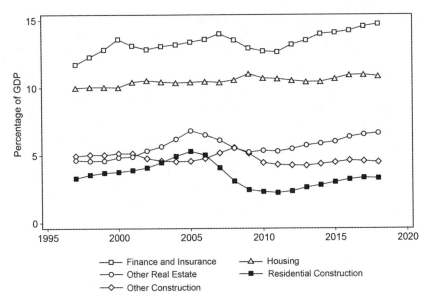

Fig. 11.2   Gross output of selected industries as percentage of GDP, 1997–2018
Source: BEA Industry Economic Accounts.

but economic output appears to have increased by $2,000 a month. Conceptually, economic output should not depend on whether Annie and Betty chose to live in their own homes or chose to rent from each other, and so national income accountants have developed methods for estimating what is known as the imputed rent of owner-occupied housing (BEA 2019). Roughly speaking, the imputed rent can be thought of as the rent that the owner-occupier would have to pay to rent a house of similar quality and characteristics. Imputed rents of owner-occupied housing form a large share of the measured economic output in housing. In 2018, imputed rents from owner-occupied housing were $1.6 trillion, while rents from tenant-occupied housing were $611 billion.

Although the National Income and Product Accounts measure a high level of economic output in housing, most of it does not come from firms. Table 11.1 shows industry statistics from the 2017 Economic Census for selected housing-related subsectors. Despite housing's relative importance in terms of total economic output, residential real estate is comparatively small in terms of firm revenue and employment. The discrepancy arises because most real estate rental payments are either imputed (for owner-occupiers) or paid to individuals not classified as firms.[2] Moreover, both residential real

2. The BEA estimates economic output in housing using all rental payments regardless of who the recipient is (including imputed rents for owner-occupiers). Thus, rental payments made to individual landlords or to firms not primarily engaged in the real estate business would be

Table 11.1   **Statistics for selected industries, 2017**

NAICS	Industry description	Number of firms	Number of establishments	Total revenue ($ billions)	Number of employees
531	Real estate	283,734	350,536	477.2	1,687,621
	Lessors of residential dwellings	52,243	71,552	120.2	361,997
	Offices of real estate agents and brokers	106,548	121,901	113.7	333,854
	Residential property managers	35,668	49,420	45.3	449,176
2361	Construction of residential buildings	170,510	171,901	342.1	690,798

Source: Economic Census.

Notes: Real estate includes both residential and nonresidential real estate. Construction of residential buildings does not include subcontractors (NAICS 2332) due to lack of data.

estate and construction are loosely concentrated industries at the national level, with the average firm earning $2 million or less in annual revenues. The disconnect between total economic output and firm revenues suggests that the social returns to innovation in housing may exceed private returns. I return to this thought later in the chapter.

Finally, it is important to note that housing consists of both structure and land—and related to land, location—hence the old real estate adage, "location, location, location." Innovations that affect the ability to produce structures on land and innovations that affect the ability to derive more value out of the same size or location of land both will affect economic growth and productivity in housing.

Structures and land have very different supply-side characteristics. The supply of structures is affected by the labor market for construction workers, materials costs, and topography. The amount of buildable land in desirable locations, however, is in fixed supply. In theory, the availability of buildable land does not by itself put any hard constraint on the quantity of housing if housing could be built as densely as desired, but in reality, most cities and neighborhoods in the US place restrictions on the density of residential construction. Figure 11.3, which is a reproduction of figure 19.1 from Gyourko and Molloy (2015), shows that growth in house prices has vastly outpaced the growth in the labor and material costs of construction—which has been flat—suggesting that most of the growth in house prices comes from growth in the price of land as opposed to structures. Thus, local land use policy is an important factor when discussing productivity and growth in housing,

counted in gross output (BEA 2009). In contrast, the Economic Census only measures the revenue received by real estate firms and establishments. Individual landlords will typically not be counted as firms in the Economic Census because the Economic Census counts non-employer firms based on business income tax filings, which does not include individuals' real estate rental income reported on 1040 Schedule E (US Census Bureau 2019).

Fig. 11.3   Real construction costs and house prices, 1980–2013

Source: Reproduction of fig. 19.1 from Gyourko and Molloy (2015).

Note: Construction costs are the cost, including labor at union wage rates, of an economy-quality home from RSMeans deflated by the consumer price index. House prices are the repeat-sales index published by CoreLogic deflated by the price index for personal consumption expenditures, excluding housing services.

and it may be that innovations to policy would be more marginally productive than technological innovations in the housing industry. I return to this thought later in the chapter.

The rest of this chapter is organized as follows. In section 11.3, I discuss the existing data on innovation, entrepreneurship, and productivity in residential real estate and construction, and compare to other sectors. Based on R&D spending and patenting statistics, direct innovation inputs and outputs in real estate and construction are shown to be miniscule. However, the amount of venture capital investment in real estate technology companies is growing rapidly, especially from 2013 to 2019. The major waves of innovation in residential real estate from 2000 to 2019 are: (1) the growth of online portals for housing search, (2) the growth of home-sharing platforms that allow homeowners to use their homes as short-term rentals, (3) the growing use of property management software, and (4) the growth of companies using technology to compete directly with residential brokers. The best available statistics on labor productivity show that labor productivity has been roughly flat in single-family residential construction, but it has been growing recently in multifamily residential construction. Labor productivity in real estate has been growing, and this appears to be mostly explained by a deepening of software and information technology (IT) capital, as well as deepening of purchased services. The productivity statistics should be interpreted with caution, however, due to measurement issues that I discuss later in the chapter.

In section 11.4, I review the literature on how the Internet has affected housing search. In theoretical models, the growing use of the Internet in housing search has been modeled as either a decline in search costs or an increase in matching efficiency. The main theoretical prediction of a lowered search cost or increased match efficiency is that buyers and sellers will search more intensely, resulting in a higher number of visited homes and higher average transaction price due to higher surplus between buyer and seller. Empirical evidence is limited by the difficulty of isolating variation in Internet use, but the existing evidence appears to consistently show that Internet use by either the buyer or the seller results in higher prices, but not necessarily shorter search durations. If the main effect of increased search efficiency is higher match quality, but not necessarily shorter search durations or higher rates of sale, then the effect of Internet search on the productivity of housing may be hard to measure, because it is difficult to separate quality from price. The number of homes sold per hour worked in the real estate brokerage industry has not changed much over the past 30 years, and realtor commissions have not been driven down significantly by the growth of Internet search, though this may also be due to anticompetitive practices, which I discuss further in section 11.6.

In section 11.5, I review the literature on how the growth of home-sharing platforms like Airbnb has affected the housing market. Home sharing is one of the largest targets for venture capital investment in residential real estate over the past 10 years. Home-sharing platforms make it easier for homes that are traditionally supplied in the residential housing market to instead be supplied to the short-term rental market (or travel accommodations market). For homeowners, this increases the option value of spare capacity in housing, which should raise the price of housing. Furthermore, if some homeowners switch from supplying the residential market to the short-term rental market, then rental rates in the residential market will increase further. The empirical literature suggests that, in the short-run at least, home-sharing platforms have indeed caused reallocation from the long-term rental market to the short-term rental market, along with a corresponding increase in rental rates and house prices. It is still unclear what the long-run effects of home sharing will be. There could be an increase in the quantity of residential housing and a decrease in the quantity of hotel rooms, and there could be growth in the number of housing units built with spare capacity in mind, such as housing units with attached dwelling units or pieds-à-terre.

In section 11.6, I discuss the future outlook of innovation and entrepreneurship in housing, as well as our study of it. I discuss measurement issues in housing and how better measurement can help us to better understand the full impact of recent technological innovations. I discuss anticompetitive practices in the real estate brokerage industry, and how that may be hindering entrepreneurship and the adoption of new innovations. I discuss how land use regulations may be hindering economic growth—not just in housing but also in the economy as a whole. I discuss how innovations in other sectors can affect housing through their effect on locational preferences, amenities, and transportation costs. And I briefly discuss how housing can influence innovation and entrepreneurship in other sectors. Section 11.7 concludes.

11.3   Key Trends and Cross-Sectoral Metrics

11.3.1   Innovation Inputs and Outputs

Traditionally, residential real estate and construction are considered to be low-innovation industries. Writing for *Forbes*, David Snider and Matt Harris write that "up until a few years ago there were only a handful of significant U.S. real estate tech success stories" (Snider and Harris 2018). They attributed the lack of high-tech success in real estate to difficulties in creating "meaningful client value" and "competitive barriers" in a space that is defined by "real and physical experiences," as well as to landlords and developers who are "reticent to make significant investments." There is likely much truth to this, as the real estate and construction industries are loosely concentrated and dominated by very small firms (table 11.1), indicating perhaps a lack of economies of scale that would make significant investments worthwhile.

Data on actual innovation inputs and outputs seem to confirm this sentiment. Figure 11.4 shows R&D spending as a percentage of revenue for

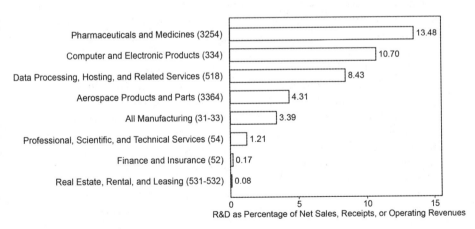

Fig. 11.4   R&D spending for selected industries, 2016
Source: R&D spending is from the NSF Business R&D and Innovation Survey. Manufacturing revenue is from the Quarterly Financial Reports, non-manufacturing revenue is from the Service Annual Survey.

selected industries in 2016. R&D spending in the real estate, rental, and listing industries (NAICS 531–532, the lowest industrial level reported in the Business R&D and Innovation Survey (BRDIS) is less than a tenth of 1 percent, compared to 3.4 percent for the manufacturing sector and 13.5 percent for research-intensive industries like pharmaceuticals. R&D spending is not reported for the construction industry, but it totals less than $930 million, which is again less than a third of 1 percent of construction industry revenues, and probably much smaller.[3] Data on measured innovation output, such as patents, is similarly miniscule. In 2016, the BRDIS reports that companies in the real estate, rental, and leasing industry (NAICS 53) filed for only 87 patents in total, and the number of patents issued was smaller than the disclosure threshold.

11.3.2   Entrepreneurship

The data on measured innovation inputs and outputs paints a picture of low innovation in the housing sector. However, this belies a general sense that the real estate business is being transformed by technology. Everyone is familiar, for example, with how Internet marketing of homes through websites like Zillow and Redfin has transformed the way people buy and sell homes. According to a recent report by the National Association of Realtors, 48 percent of real estate firms cited keeping up with technological change as one of the biggest challenges they currently face (NAR 2018).

Data on venture capital funding shows that there is indeed growing investor interest in real estate technology. Figure 11.5 shows the amount of venture capital funding for real estate and construction related companies, as reported by CrunchBase, a data vendor specializing in tracking startups and innovative companies. I focus on both residential and commercial real estate and construction, because the innovations and technologies driving both sectors appear to be similar, and because it is difficult to accurately distinguish between residential and commercial in the CrunchBase data. The data show that $900 million in venture capital was raised by real estate and construction related companies in 2000, but by November 2019, this number had grown to $5.8 billion. This growth is not an artifact of a shift in the total amount of venture capital funding in all sectors. Nor does it reflect spurious growth in the amount of data that CrunchBase collects: Figure 11.5 shows that venture capital in real estate and construction is growing at a rapid rate even when measured as a percentage of all venture capital funding reported in CrunchBase. Moreover, this growth is not driven by just a handful of superstar companies. WeWork and Airbnb are the two largest fundraisers through this time period, but even if they are excluded from the data, the

---

3. The BRDIS reports that total R&D spending for nonmanufacturing industries (including construction) was $119,690 million, and for the reported sub-industries (not including construction), the total R&D spending was $118,760 million, so R&D spending in construction was at most $930 million.

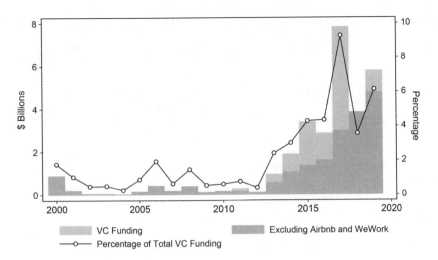

Fig. 11.5 **Venture capital funding of real estate and construction related companies, January 2000–November 2019**

Source: CrunchBase. Only companies headquartered in the US are included. Real estate and construction related companies are companies that CrunchBase has identified with at least one of the following category tags: "Real Estate," "Commercial Real Estate," "Property Management," "Property Development," "Home Improvement," and "Home Renovation." Short-term vacation rental companies like Airbnb were also included.

amount of venture capital funding for real estate and construction related companies still increased markedly after 2013, and it is steadily growing.

It is instructive to look at which of these companies received the most venture capital funding over the past two decades. Table 11.2 shows a selection of major venture capital fundraisers for each half-decade starting from 2000. The first wave of innovation occurred in the early 2000s with the movement toward the online marketing of homes via web portals. Interestingly, the initial wave of web portals were not necessarily the most successful ones in capturing the market. The second wave of online portals, including Zillow and Trulia, now command a larger share of real estate searches, and Zillow is the market leader in residential real estate today. Besides online portals, the 2000s also saw investments in developers of property management software, which suggests capital deepening in the real estate industry, as well as the beginnings of the nascent home-sharing industry with HomeAway.

By the first half of the 2010s, the online portal business appears to have matured, with fewer online portals raising significant amounts of venture investment. Zillow filed for an initial public offering (IPO) in 2011 and acquired Trulia in 2015, solidifying its position as the market leader in residential real estate portals. But the early 2010s saw the emergence of a number of new businesses harnessing technology to directly compete with traditional firms in related markets. Airbnb, a vacation rental platform that

Table 11.2   **Major fundraisers among housing related companies, January 2000–November 2019**

HomeGain.com $53 million raised Online portal	**HomeAway** $477 million raised Vacation rental	**Airbnb** $794 million raised Vacation rental	**Airbnb** $2.6 billion raised Vacation rental
RealPage $52 million raised Property management software	**Zillow** $87 million raised Online portal	**Houzz** $214 million raised Home design	**Compass** $1.5 billion raised Brokerage
Rent.com $47 million raised Online portal	**Trulia** $33 million raised Online portal	**Redfin** $178 million raised Brokerage	**Opendoor** $1.3 billion raised iBuyer
Homes.com $39 million raised Online Portal	**Redfin** $32 million raised Brokerage	**Cityscape Residential** $82 million raised Multifamily developer	**Vacasa** $527 million raised Vacation rental
ZipRealty $35 million raised Brokerage	**Appfolio** $30 million raised Property management software	**Compass** $73 million raised Brokerage	**Knock** $448 million raised iBuyer
2000–2004 $1,299 million raised	2005–2009 $1,349 million raised	2010–2014 $3,492 million raised	2015–2019 $23,755 million raised

Source: Crunchbase.

Notes: The companies are not exactly the five largest fundraisers in each half-decade, but all are in the top 10. The companies were chosen to be representative of innovative trends in housing.

allows homeowners to rent rooms or their entire houses to vacationers, is one of the most highly valued startups in the world and competes directly with the hotel industry. Houzz is an online platform for interior design and home improvement where people can share design ideas and match with contractors. RedFin and Compass bill themselves as technology-driven brokerages, believing that technology will give them a competitive advantage against more traditional brokers. Cityscape Residential is a multifamily residential property developer and is the only company on this list that does not appear to be explicitly technology driven. Its inclusion may highlight a potential trend in multifamily housing development, which I return to discuss later.

The late 2010s saw the emergence of a new type of technology-driven real estate business: the i-Buyer. i-Buyers are companies that want to cut out the middleman in housing transactions and simplify the home-selling process. They use machine learning to estimate the market value of a home, make offers to sellers so that sellers can circumvent the long and complicated selling process and avoid paying realtor fees, and then flip the house for a profit. They also collect fees like realtors, but they believe that sellers are willing to pay the fee for the convenience. i-Buyers have attracted significant investor interest, to the tune of over $1.7 billion in venture capital over the past

3 years. It is still too early to tell what effects this will have on the housing market.

11.3.3   Labor Productivity

The growth of online portals, property management software, and technology-driven brokerages suggests that technological capital and service inputs are becoming increasingly important for the real estate industry. Has this translated to an increase in labor productivity?

Unfortunately, measuring productivity in construction and real estate is a challenging task. The Bureau of Labor Statistics has only recently begun to produce official estimates of labor productivity in the residential construction industry (Sveikauskas, Rowe, and Mildenberger 2018) and still does not produce any official estimates of productivity in the residential real estate industry. One of the main difficulties is that buildings vary widely in their quality and characteristics, making it difficult to construct reliable output price deflators. Another difficulty, especially as it pertains to real estate, is accounting for the depreciation of structures, as well as the treatment of owner-occupied housing and non-firm entities that receive rental payments, as discussed earlier. Nevertheless, it is instructive to look at trends in labor productivity with the measures that are available.

11.3.3.1   Labor Productivity in Residential Construction

In 2018, the BLS began publishing official estimates of gross output-based labor productivity separately for residential and nonresidential construction. The advance is attributed to improved producer price indexes for the separate construction sub-industries, also published by the BLS.[4] Figure 11.6 reports these estimates separately for the single-family residential construction industry and the multifamily residential construction industry. Labor productivity in the manufacturing sector is also shown for comparison. Labor productivity in single-family construction has been roughly flat for the past two decades, consistent with the evidence in Gyourko and Molloy (2015) (figure 11.3) that the real construction cost of single-family housing has not changed much. Labor productivity in multifamily construction is a much different story, with productivity gains that track more closely with the manufacturing sector, especially in the past 15 years. Because data on capital expenditures for multifamily construction is not readily available, it is not immediately clear whether these gains are due to increases in total factor productivity or capital deepening. Another issue is that these measures do not reflect subcontractor hours. Sveikauskas, Rowe, and Mildenberger (2018) show that accounting for subcontractor hours significantly reduces

---

4. The new producer price indexes are not based on the sale prices of actual buildings. Instead, the BLS establishes a building with standardized features and collects cost information from many builders. The cost data is then supplemented with information on profit margins beyond these costs. See Sveikauskas, Rowe, and Mildenberger (2018) for a further discussion.

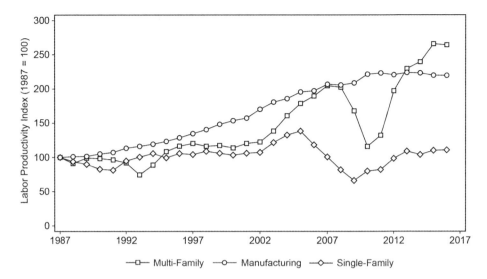

Fig. 11.6   **Labor productivity in residential construction, 1987–2016**
Source: Bureau of Labor Statistics, Office of Productivity and Technology.

the gains in multifamily labor productivity, though the overall trend is still that it is growing at a much faster rate than single-family labor productivity.

11.3.3.2   *Labor Productivity in Real Estate*

Currently, neither the BLS nor the BEA publish official estimates of labor productivity in the residential real estate industry. The BEA does publish an estimate of labor productivity in real estate as a whole (NAICS 531), through its Integrated Industry-Level Production account (KLEMS account).[5] The KLEMS data must be interpreted with caution, however, because of the discrepancy in how gross output is measured and how inputs are measured. In the KLEMS account, gross output in real estate includes all rental payments made, including to firms not primarily classified as real estate and to non-firm landlords. The imputed rents of owner-occupiers are also included. Data on inputs, however, are typically measured from surveys of real estate firms and establishments (see BEA 2009). Thus, there is a difference in the entities from which gross output is measured and from which inputs are measured. It is likely that a significant amount of both labor and capital input goes unmeasured in real estate, such as the amount of time individual landlords and owner-occupiers spend managing their properties, and the equipment, software, and services they employ to help them.

Nevertheless, I present in figure 11.7 labor productivity estimates as

5. Available at https://www.bea.gov/data/special-topics/integrated-industry-level-production-account-klemshttps://www.bea.gov/data/special-topics/integrated-industry-level-production-account-klems. "KLEMS" stands for capital, labor, energy, materials, services.

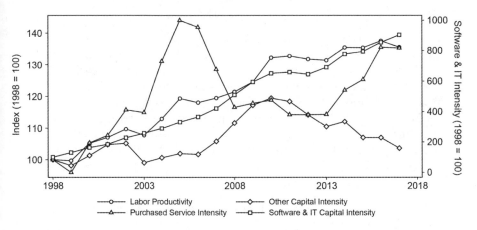

Fig. 11.7   Labor productivity and capital and service intensity in real estate, 1998–2017

Source: BEA-BLS Integrated Industry-Level Production Accounts. Intensity is the quantity of the input divided by the quantity of labor.

reported in the BEA's KLEMS accounts. According to BEA KLEMS data, labor productivity in real estate has been steadily rising since 1998. Over the same period, software and IT capital intensity rose by over 900 percent. By contrast, other non-software and non-IT capital intensity did not rise by nearly as much. The intensity of purchased services also increased, though it exhibits much more cyclicality than the intensity of software and IT capital.

11.3.4   Summary

I now summarize the information presented in this section on sectoral trends and metrics.

1. Real estate and construction firms perform little research and development.
Data from the NSF Business R&D and Innovation Survey shows that real estate and construction firms spend very little on R&D and produce very few patents. This is not surprising and does not imply that real estate and construction firms do not innovate. Instead, whatever innovation does occur is not reported as R&D on the BRDIS, or perhaps the R&D is not conducted by real estate firms themselves but by software and technology companies that service the real estate industry.[6]

2. There is growing investor interest in real estate technology companies.
Venture capital funding for real estate technology companies has increased rapidly since the early 2000s. Investment activity in these companies reveals the major waves of innovation in real estate. In the early 2000s, the focus

6. For example, Zillow, in its SEC filings, is classified with SIC code 7389: "Business Services, Not Elsewhere Defined."

was on online platforms for the digital marketing of homes over the Internet and on software companies that built tools for property management. These companies provide supportive services to traditional firms in real estate, rather than act as direct competitors. The late 2000s to early 2010s saw the growth of more companies harnessing technology to directly compete with traditional firms in multiple areas, such as Airbnb competing in the hotel space and RedFin competing in the brokerage space. A new trend that emerges in the late 2010s is the growth of i-Buyers, companies that aim to buy homes directly from sellers and then sell them for a profit, thus competing directly with brokers but also promising to transform the way real estate is bought and sold.

3. Software and IT capital has been increasing rapidly in real estate, along with labor productivity.
Consistent with the growth in real estate technology companies, data from the BEA KLEMS accounts reveals that software and IT capital intensity has increased very rapidly in real estate, along with labor productivity. By contrast, the intensity of other non-software and non-IT capital has not increased nearly as much.

4. Labor productivity growth in single-family construction has been slow but may have increased recently for multifamily construction.
The best available data for labor productivity in construction shows that labor productivity in single-family residential construction has been mostly flat over the past three decades. This is consistent with previous findings on the real cost of constructing single-family homes (Gyourko and Molloy 2015). On the other hand, labor productivity in multifamily residential construction appears to have increased markedly over the past 15 years. It is not immediately clear what is driving the trend in multifamily construction, and I leave this question to future research.

5. Measurement issues continue to be a problem.
The productivity data need to be interpreted with caution because of measurement issues. One of the difficulties in measurement is the reliability of price deflators when buildings vary widely in their quality and characteristics. Another difficulty, especially as it pertains to real estate, is the discrepancy between how outputs and inputs are measured. I discuss measurement further in section 11.6.

11.4   Internet Search and the Housing Market

One of the major technological trends affecting housing in the past two decades has been the movement of housing search from a primarily offline activity to the Internet. According to the National Association of Realtors, 44 percent of home buyers in 2018 began their search for a home online,

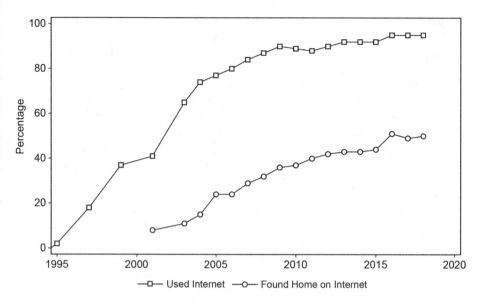

Fig. 11.8   Internet use by home buyers, 1995–2018
Source: National Association of Realtors Profile of Home Buyers and Sellers.

95 percent used the Internet at some point in their search, and 50 percent found the home they ultimately purchased online; 100 percent of home buyers rated online websites as a useful source of information for the home buying process. In contrast, in 2001, only 41 percent of buyers used the Internet at some point in their search, and only 8 percent found their homes online (figure 11.8). The three largest housing-tech IPOs in the past 10 years were RedFin, Zillow, and Trulia, all three of which offer Internet-based search as one of their primary services. Today, prospective home buyers can search for homes anywhere in the US, look at pictures, and take virtual tours, all from the comfort of their own home and without ever speaking to a real estate agent.

11.4.1   Theoretical Effects

How has the Internet affected the efficiency of housing search? Has it made search more efficient, or has old activity simply moved to a new medium? Economic models of housing search follow models of labor market search developed in Diamond (1982), Pissarides (1985), and Mortensen and Pissarides (1994), in which search is modeled as a frictional process through which buyers and sellers meet and learn about match quality.[7] There are

---

7. See Wheaton (1990), Novy-Marx (2009), Genesove and Han (2012), Ngai and Tenreyro (2014), Head, Lloyd-Ellis, and Sun (2014), Guren (2018), and Anenberg and Kung (2018) for some examples of economic housing search models.

three major components to housing search models: (1) search costs—it is costly in terms of time and effort to search, and therefore both buyers and sellers in a housing search market pay costs for each period in which they are searching, (2) match function—the match function is the rate at which buyers and sellers meet in the market and is typically modeled as a reduced-form object,[8] and (3) match quality distribution—once buyers and sellers meet, they find out the quality of their match, which is drawn from a distribution. There is heterogeneity in match quality, because some buyers prefer some features of a home more than others. Match quality is unknown prior to the buyer and seller meeting, because some features of the home are not observed until personally inspected by the buyer. In this way, the traditional home visit or other ways of transmitting information about the home to a prospective buyer is an important part of the search process. If the surplus generated by a match between the buyer and seller exceeds the sum of their reservation values, then the buyer and seller will transact.

The literature has primarily interpreted the effect of the Internet as reducing the cost of searching (Ford, Rutherford, and Yavas 2005) or increasing the match rate (Genesove and Han 2012). The main prediction of either effect is that equilibrium match quality and reservation value will be higher, and therefore equilibrium transaction prices will be higher. Reservation values increase, because a lower search cost and a higher match rate both increase the expected returns to rejecting an offer and continuing to search for a better match. A higher reservation value results in more rejected offers, but the transactions that do happen will have higher surplus on average. The number of offers looked at should increase on average, but the predicted effect on time-on-market is ambiguous, because the Internet may make the time cost of acquiring information lower.

11.4.2   Empirical Evidence

Empirical evidence on the effect of the Internet on housing search is limited due to significant identification challenges. One early study by Ford, Rutherford, and Yavas (2005) used data from a North Texas multiple listing service (MLS) in 1999 to regress price and time-on-market as an indicator for whether or not the property was listed on the Internet in addition to being on the MLS. They found that homes listed on the Internet sold at 1.9 percent higher price and took 6 days longer to sell. A limitation of their results is that the decision of whether to list on the Internet is endogenous, which the paper only controls for using a Heckman selection equation. While helpful, the Heckman procedure may not be valid if the observable controls used to predict Internet listing are related to sale price and time-on-market in non-linear ways. Moreover, only 7 percent of their sample was not listed on the

---

8. There have been attempts to provide microfoundations for the match function. See Petrongolo and Pissarides (2001).

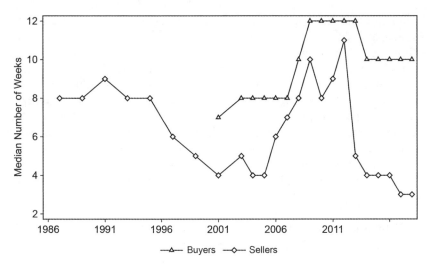

Fig. 11.9   Buyer search duration and seller time on market, 1987–2018
Source: National Association of Realtors Profile of Home Buyers and Sellers.

Internet, which further raises endogenous selection concerns. Nevertheless, this was one of the first attempts to estimate the effect of the Internet on housing search, and it found results consistent with theoretical predictions.

On the buyer side, Zumpano, Johnson, and Anderson (2003) use data from the National Association of Realtors' 2000 Home Buyer and Seller Survey to study the relationship between buyer Internet use and search behavior. They find no effect of Internet use on the total buyer search duration, but they did find a statistically significant increase in search intensity, defined as the number of properties visited per week, which is again consistent with theory. To control for the endogeneity of Internet use, Zumpano, Johnson, and Anderson (2003) also use a Heckman selection equation. An interesting finding in the selection equation was that out-of-town buyers and first-time home buyers were more likely to use the Internet.

Related to these findings are results presented in Genesove and Han (2012). Using National Association of Realtors (NAR) survey data across multiple cities and years, they found that at the city-year level, the fraction of buyers who reported finding their home on the Internet is positively associated with buyer time-on-market and on the number of home visits that buyers conduct; the fraction is negatively associated with seller time-on-market. In the aggregate, buyer search durations have indeed been increasing, while seller search durations have fallen (figure 11.9).

Han and Strange (2014) document a secular increase in the probability of bidding wars (defined as sale price above list price), from 3.5 percent of transactions being a bidding war in 1986 to 10 percent in 2010. To explore whether the Internet may have played a role in increasing the frequency of bidding wars, they use NAR survey data to regress whether a listing was sold in a bidding war on an indicator for whether the buyer found the home through the Internet. They found that the buyer's use of the Internet is associated with a 4.3 percent higher probability of a bidding war. As with Genesove and Han (2012), the focus of Han and Strange (2014) was not specifically on the Internet, and so no further causal analysis was attempted. Still, this finding is consistent with the possibility that the Internet increased the match rate between buyers and sellers, as bidding wars can only happen when multiple buyers vie for the same property. Since bidding wars tend to result in higher prices, the finding is also consistent with the result in Ford, Rutherford, and Yavas (2005) relating Internet listing to higher sale prices.

11.4.3   Implications for Economic Growth and Productivity

If Internet search is increasing equilibrium match quality, then some of the recent observed house price increases may be due to improvements to match quality rather than basic supply and demand factors. Assuming that gross output measures should be adjusted for quality changes, this implies that real growth in the output of housing may be understated due to quality increases being misattributed to the price deflator. Standard hedonic methods for estimating constant-quality price deflators in housing typically only control for the observed physical characteristics of a home; they do not account for unobserved match quality between the buyer and the house.[9]

Is there a limit to the efficiency gains due to reductions in search frictions? After all, search frictions cannot fall below zero. The answer is that it depends on how important learning about match quality is to the search process. If search is primarily "frictional" (meaning that it takes time and effort for buyers and sellers to meet and transact), then an instantaneous match rate would simply reduce the equilibrium vacancy rate to zero without a corresponding increase in the expected surplus of any match.[10] The upper bound on the search efficiency gain would simply be the vacancy rate multiplied by the economic output of occupied homes. Since the current gross output of housing is $2.2 trillion, and the current home vacancy rate (including both rental and owner occupied) is 3.3 percent, this implies an upper bound on search efficiency gains of $73 billion.

If learning about match quality is also important, then the potential efficiency gains due to more efficient search may be much higher. If $\bar{S}$ is the upper bound of the support of the match quality distribution, then as search cost goes to zero or the match rate becomes instantaneous, the vacancy rate goes to zero, and the expected surplus on every match approaches $\bar{S}$.[10] The efficiency gains will be a combination of the increase due to fewer vacancies

9. Unobserved differences in match quality could arise due to commute times, heterogeneous preference for neighborhood amenities, or distance to friends/relatives, among potentially many other things.
10. See the appendix for a derivation.

and the increase due to higher match surplus. Since we do not know how far away current match surpluses are from $\bar{S}$, it is impossible to say what the maximum efficiency gains from search might be. If the support of S has no upper bound, then the gains are potentially unlimited, and the equilibrium vacancy rate may be positive in the limit even as matching becomes instantaneous.

The possibility that efficiency gains are showing up in price increases due to higher quality matches is a broader issue that applies to all search markets, not just housing. Martellini and Menzio (2018) argue that this may explain why the labor market has not experienced significant declines in job vacancy and unemployment rates despite known technological improvements in job search. Martellini and Menzio (2018) showed that if the match quality distribution is Pareto, then unemployment, job vacancy, job-finding, and job-loss rates remain constant even as the efficiency of search grows over time. Improvements in search technology show up in productivity growth. Applied to the housing market, this suggests that improvements in search technology will show up in house price growth, and not necessarily in lower vacancy rates or lower search durations. Accounting for how match quality increases have contributed to the growth in productivity of housing seems like an interesting area for further research.

11.4.4   Impact on Real Estate Agents and Brokers

How has Internet search affected the market structure of the real estate brokerage industry? Early speculation on the effects of the Internet on real estate agents theorized that the Internet would lead to disintermediation by making it easier for buyers and sellers to market their homes without the help of brokers, and that there would be an unbundling of services where listing would be untied from other services that brokers provided (Baen and Guttery 1997). This result was seen as desirable due to a long line of research documenting inefficiencies in the brokerage industry, centering on a lack of price competition due to fixed commission rates (Barwick and Pathak 2015; Han and Hong 2011; Hsieh and Moretti 2003) and incentive misalignment between broker and seller (Bernheim and Meer 2013; Hendel, Nevo, and Ortalo-Magné 2009; Levitt and Syverson 2008).

In the aggregate, it does not appear that growing Internet use has led to disintermediation. Data from the NAR shows that the use of real estate agents has actually gone up over the past two decades, and the percentage of homes sold by the owner without an agent has actually gone down (figure 11.10).

The growing importance of the Internet in housing search does not appear to have affected the productivity of real estate agents. Although the BLS does not publish official estimates of labor productivity in the real estate brokerage industry (NAICS 53121), it does estimate the number of hours worked. This data can be combined with NAR estimates of the number of

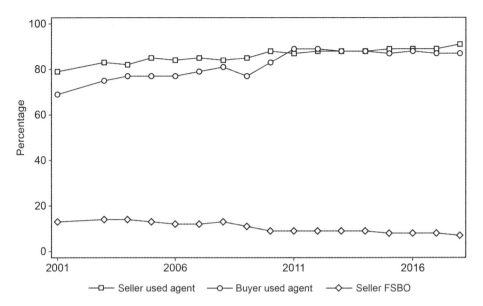

Fig. 11.10   Real estate agent use by home buyers and home sellers, 2001–2018
Source: National Association of Realtors Profile of Home Buyers and Sellers.

existing homes sold each year, and Census estimates of the number of new homes sold each year, to calculate an index of the number of homes sold per hour worked.[11] Clearly, the number of homes sold may not be an accurate measure of the quantity of brokerage services being supplied—for example, the amount of service required to sell a unique, luxury mansion may be very different from the amount of service required to sell a standardized condo in a planned community—but this measure can still give us a sense of productivity trends in the brokerage industry under the assumption that the distribution of services provided per home has remained relatively stable. Figure 11.11 shows the result of this calculation. The number of homes sold and the number of hours worked are highly cyclical, following the house price cycle closely, with the number of hours worked lagging a few years behind, but there does not appear to be any long-run trend in the productivity of real estate agents and brokers, at least by this metric.

Real estate agent commission rates do appear to be falling slightly. Real-Trends reports that between 2012 and 2017, average commission rates fell 20 basis points from 5.32 to 5.12.[12] Investors have made big bets that technology would disrupt the real estate brokerage industry, as seen by the big invest-

11. NAICS 53121 consists of both residential and commercial real estate brokers. NAICS does not separate real estate brokerage by residential and commercial.
12. Source: https://www.realtrends.com/blog/whats-going-on-with-brokerage-profitability /https://www.realtrends.com/blog/whats-going-on-with-brokerage-profitability/.

Fig. 11.11   New and existing homes sold and hours worked in real estate brokerage, 1987–2018
Source: Bureau of Labor Statistics, Census Bureau, and National Association of Realtors. NAICS 53121: Offices of Real Estate Agents and Brokers.

ments in RedFin, a discount brokerage that charges listing commission rates of 1 to 1.5 percent, compared to an average of 2.5 to 3 percent. The advent of i-Buyers promises to disrupt this market further. However, the overall effect of new technologies on the real estate brokerage industry may be currently limited by certain anticompetitive behaviors from the incumbents, which may be limiting the ability of new entrants to gain market share. I discuss these anticompetitive practices further in section 11.6.

11.5   The "Sharing Economy" and the Housing Market

A second major innovation affecting housing markets is the growth of online platforms like Airbnb that allow homeowners to "share" space with travelers by renting out a spare couch, a spare room, or even an entire home when the owner is not present.[13] Since its founding in 2008, Airbnb has experienced remarkable growth. According to data in Barron, Kung, and Proserpio (2019), by 2016, over 1 million listings in the US had been placed on Airbnb across more than 700,000 unique hosts. Investors have surely taken notice, and Airbnb was the second largest venture capital fundraiser among

---

13. A similar phenomenon is happening in commercial real estate, with the growth of shared workspaces and the growth of "pop-up" restaurants, hotels, and other retailers.

real estate related companies in the past 20 years (the largest was WeWork). Other home-sharing and vacation-rental companies like HomeAway and Vacasa have also attracted significant attention from investors. Although these companies most directly compete with hotels and bed and breakfasts in the market for travel accommodations, they also have an impact on the housing market, because they draw some of their supply from residential housing.

11.5.1   Theoretical Effects

Traditionally, the market for short-term accommodations, which serves travelers, and the market for residential housing, which serves local residents, have been strongly segmented. The segmentation arises from the different needs of the consumers in each market (e.g., short-term demanders may only require a bed and a bathroom, while long-term demanders may also require a kitchen and living area) as well as differences in the regulatory environment (e.g., residential tenants are typically afforded rights and protections not available to short-term visitors). Because of these differences, the marketplaces for long-term rentals (housing) and for short-term rentals (accommodations) have historically evolved along separate paths.

The advent of home-sharing platforms has blurred the segmentation on the supply side. It is now much easier than in the past for owners of traditionally residential homes to also supply the short-term rental market.[14] What might we expect the effects to be? First, some owners of residential homes might reallocate from the long-term rental market to the short-term rental market. By "reallocate," I mean an owner who was previously supplying a long-term tenant and now supplies a short-term renter after the advent of home-sharing. The degree to which this reallocation occurs depends on various factors, including relative prices in the long- and short-term markets, relative costs of maintaining a short-term rental property vs. a long-term rental property, and the flexibility of keeping a home primarily for short-term use vs. the stability of having a long-term tenant. The propensity to reallocate also depends on the owner's intended personal use of the home. Owner-occupiers by definition do not reallocate from long- to short-term rental, because they can be considered both the landlord and the tenant in a long-term rental transaction. However, they may still participate in the short-term rental market by selling spare capacity, such as spare rooms, a spare couch, or the entire home when they are not present.[15] Vacation home owners who participate in the short-term rental market would also not be considered as reallocating if the vacation home would not have been rented to a long-term tenant anyway, perhaps due to the restrictiveness of long-

---

14. See Einav, Farronato, and Levin (2016) for a discussion of the technological innovations that reduced transactional frictions and gave rise to these new markets.

15. However, if they were previously renting a spare room to a roommate and then decide to use that room for short-term rental instead, this would constitute a reallocation.

term leases. Landlords of residential renters may therefore be most at risk of reallocating, and this decision depends on their personal preferences as well as relative prices and costs.

Since housing and hotel supply are inelastic in the short run, reallocation reduces the supply of housing units available in the residential market and increases the supply of rooms available in the short-term rental market. This pushes up rental rates and house prices in the housing market, and it drives down prices in the short-term rental market.

In the long run, the supply of housing and of hotels may also be affected. The quantity of homes that can supply both the long- and the short-term rental markets would be expected to increase, and the quantity of hotel rooms that are only able to supply the short-term market would be expected to decrease. The characteristics of the housing stock may change as well. For example, by increasing the option value to having spare capacity, home-sharing may cause future homes to be built with spare capacity in mind. There may be an increase in the supply of homes with accessory dwelling units that are optimized for delivery to short-term renters with the main unit simultaneously being occupied by the owner.

Besides reallocation, the increased option value of spare housing capacity would also be expected to have direct effects on house prices and rents. The increase will depend on the degree to which capacity is currently underutilized due to the frictions that are being resolved by the home-sharing platform. An increase in house prices and rents due to increased option value from home-sharing represents real growth in the productivity of housing.

Finally, home-sharing may entail positive and negative spillovers. On the negative side, neighbors may complain about noisy and unpleasant guests. Concern over neighbors has proven to be a salient point in public debates about home sharing. On the positive side, home sharing may help bring in revenue for local businesses, and it may help tourists discover new destinations and experiences that they had previously not known about.

11.5.2 Empirical Evidence

There is a growing body of literature studying the effects of home sharing on housing market outcomes. Barron, Kung, and Proserpio (2019), Garcia-López et al. (2019), and Horn and Merante (2017) all find that home-sharing drives up rental rates and housing costs, using various research designs and data from various markets. Horn and Merante (2017) examine the effect of Airbnb on rental rates in the Boston housing market from 2015 to 2016. Barron, Kung, and Proserpio (2019) study the effect of Airbnb on house prices and rental rates using data from the entire US from 2011 to 2016. Garcia-López et al. (2019) study the effect of Airbnb on the Barcelona housing market. Estimates of the effect of a one-standard-deviation increase in the number of Airbnb listings on the percentage increase in rental rates range from about 0.4 to 0.6 percent.

Barron, Kung, and Proserpio (2019) present additional evidence on the channels through which home-sharing affects housing markets. They present direct evidence for housing supply reallocation, showing that growth in Airbnb listings is causally associated with a decline in the number of rental housing units and an increase in the number of housing units that are classified as vacant for "seasonal or recreational use" (which is how units held for short-term use would be classified as by the US Census Bureau). They also show that the size of the reallocation depends on the share of owner-occupiers. Zip codes with a greater share of owner-occupiers experience a smaller amount of reallocation and correspondingly a smaller effect on house prices and rents, consistent with the theory that owner-occupiers are less likely to reallocate from the long-term rental market to the short-term rental market.

All these studies estimate only short-run effects. To my knowledge, there is not yet any research on the long-run effects of home sharing on house prices and the housing supply. This is likely because home sharing is a relatively new phenomenon, and is it still too early to look for long-run effects.

Besides the housing market, some papers also study the effect of home sharing on other markets. Zervas, Proserpio, and Byers (2017) and Farronato and Fradkin (2018) study the effects of home sharing on the hotel market. Zervas, Proserpio, and Byers (2017) shows evidence that Airbnb entry drives down hotel revenue, and Farronato and Fradkin (2018) show that Airbnb expands the supply of hotel rooms during times of peak demand, which leads to significant welfare gains for travelers. Alyakoob and Rahman (2018) find a positive relationship between Airbnb entry and restaurant employment. These papers suggest that home sharing may have welfare implications beyond their effects on the housing market.

11.6   Future Outlook

11.6.1   Measurement Issues

In section 11.2, I noted the discrepancy between gross economic output and firm revenues in residential real estate. In 2017, gross output from housing rents alone was $2.1 trillion, $1.5 trillion of which was owner-occupied housing. By comparison, revenue for all real estate firms in 2017 (including both residential and commercial) was only $477 billion. The discrepancy itself is not concerning, as gross output and firm revenues are meant to measure different concepts. However, the discrepancy does suggest that a significant amount of housing services is being supplied by non-firm entities, such as owner-occupiers (who supply themselves), and individual landlords who are not counted as firms. Because data on labor, capital, material, energy, and service inputs come from surveys of firms or establishments, a significant amount of input in real estate may go unmeasured, such as the labor hours that owner-occupiers and landlords spend managing their properties and the labor hours that home buyers and home sellers spend on the search process. More accurate measurement of these inputs would help us better understand the impact of technological innovations on the efficiency of these activities. Questions on the time spent and the cost of managing properties or searching for homes could be included on the American Housing Survey, for example.

Another measurement issue that arises in housing is how increases in the efficiency of search should be measured and accounted for. This may be especially salient, given that the last major wave of technological innovation in real estate was the movement of housing search to the Internet. As discussed in section 11.4, improvements in the efficiency of search will show up in higher prices and higher match quality, but not necessarily in a higher rate of transaction or a reduced vacancy rate. Since an increase in match quality represents growth in the real economic output of housing, attributing gains in match quality entirely to the price deflator may cause us to understate the amount of real output growth in housing. Methods to estimate how much of price gains can be attributed to higher match quality would help us better understand how improvements to search technology are affecting productivity growth in real estate.

11.6.2   Barriers to Innovation and Entrepreneurship

In addition to measurement issues, the relatively small role of firm revenues in the gross economic output of housing suggests that the potential social returns to innovation may be much higher than the private returns. Aghion et al. (2005) have shown evidence of an inverted-U relationship between industry concentration and industry innovation, so low concentration in real estate and construction suggests a possible reason for why direct innovation by real estate and construction firms is low. It may also explain why many of the main innovators in real estate technology, including the initial wave of online portals and software developers, have been primarily upstream firms that supply the real estate industry with software and services, rather than direct providers of real estate services.

Of course, this has not stopped innovative firms from directly competing with industry incumbents. RedFin, for example, offers particularly low listing commission rates relative to the rest of the market. Despite this, commission rates appear to be falling only slightly. As mentioned in section 11.4, RealTrends reports that between 2012 and 2017, average commission rates fell 20 basis points from 5.32 to 5.12. Thus, despite the presence of low commission brokers, they do not seem to have gained significant market share.

The impact of innovation and entrepreneurship on residential brokerage may be limited by certain anticompetitive behaviors. In 2005, the National Association of Realtors was sued by the US Department of Justice over its "virtual office website" (VOW) policy, as Internet-based listings websites were known back then. The VOW policy allowed traditional brokers to discriminate against VOWs by withholding listings information from them, in violation of standard MLS rules governing data sharing between brokers. In 2008, a settlement was reached in which the NAR agreed to repeal its old VOW policy and replace it with a new one that does not discriminate against VOWs.

The new policy applied only to websites operated by actual brokers who participate in a local MLS and not to listing aggregators like Zillow that do not directly provide brokerage services. Thus, non-broker websites that want to provide listings information still need to purchase listings information directly from brokers, MLSs, or national listings syndicators. Speaking at a FTC conference on competition in residential brokerage, industry journalist Brad Inman noted that, "our ability to aggregate a national database of listings is very, very expensive . . . it only costs $2 million to license data and normalize it and publish it, [but] $2 million is a lot of money for an entrepreneur starting out with his or her credit card . . . [and] the reality is $2 million will get you in, but how much do the portals currently spend just schmoozing with MLS executives, not to mention the teams and the maintenance and everything that goes into it" (Inman 2018). Thus, the cost of acquiring and maintaining listings data may still be a significant barrier to entry for firms that want to provide real estate related services but not necessarily be brokers themselves.

In addition to protectiveness over data, real estate brokers may also engage in another anticompetitive practice known as steering. The Department of Justice (DOJ) describes steering as any action taken by a broker or agent to avoid cooperating with a particular competitor (DOJ 2007). For example, a buyer's agent may avoid showing a house listed by a competitor's agent, or by a discount brokerage, despite knowing that the house would be well suited to the buyer's preferences. Barwick, Pathak, and Wong (2017) showed evidence of steering using data from Massachusetts from 1988 to 2011. They showed that properties listed with lower commissions were less likely to sell, and that this was best explained by buyers' agents steering away from low-commission properties, rather than by buyer preferences. This kind of behavior may make it harder for brokers to compete on price, and it may explain why realtor commission rates have not fallen more despite the growing ease of housing search. Of course, this is only possible if significant information asymmetry exists between buyers and their agents, but the empirical evidence strongly suggests that this information gap exists, likely because most people only buy and sell homes a few times in their life.[16] Thus, better education for buyers and sellers of real estate or stronger fiduciary

---

16. See Hsieh and Moretti (2003), Levitt and Syverson (2008), Hendel, Nevo, and Ortalo-Magné (2009), Han and Hong (2011), and Bernheim and Meer (2013) for evidence of information asymmetries in residential brokerage.

requirements on the part of agents may be helpful in boosting the overall impact of innovation and entrepreneurship in housing.

11.6.3   Land Use Regulation

As noted in section 11.2, land use regulations are an important factor to consider when thinking about growth and productivity in housing, especially as it pertains to construction and the housing supply. To what degree are restrictive land use regulations limiting the quantity of housing supply, and what are the implications for economic growth and productivity?

Gyourko and Molloy (2015) provide a comprehensive review of the literature on how land use regulation affects housing supply. To summarize, nearly all studies find a positive correlation between the degree of land use regulation and house prices, and a negative correlation with construction. However, interpreting the magnitudes of the effects is difficult, because land use regulation is a patchwork of laws and regulations, and there is no single well-defined measure of it. Nevertheless, a robust result in many housing studies, as exemplified by Saks (2008), is that house prices respond more vigorously to demand shocks in locations with stricter land use regulations, while construction responds less vigorously, suggesting that tighter regulations reduce the elasticity of the housing supply curve.

An exact quantification of the impact of land use regulation on economic growth and productivity is still an open question. Viewing land as an input to the construction of housing, both Glaeser and Gyourko (2018) and Albouy and Ehrlich (2018) noted the effect of land use regulation as an increase in the cost of housing relative to (non-land) input costs. Glaeser and Gyourko (2018) documented an increase in the price of housing relative to input costs, especially in high-wage urban areas with knowledge-intensive industries. Using a model that also allows land use regulation to potentially have a quality-of-life benefit, Albouy and Ehrlich (2018) estimate that the welfare cost of higher housing costs do not exceed the quality-of-life benefits that land use regulations provide, thus reducing welfare on net.

Hsieh and Moretti (2019) argued that restrictive land use regulations can also deter workers from moving to the most productive locations. Using a structural model, they estimated that inelastic housing supply may have reduced GDP by as much as 9 percent in 2009, and reduced GDP growth by 36 percent from 1964 to 2009. If we roughly estimate the efficiency gains of housing search as at most 3.3 percent of housing output due to the elimination of vacancies, plus 1.9 percent of housing output due to increased match quality (Ford, Rutherford, and Yavas 2005), the result is still less than the potential gain of 9 percent of total output from more efficient labor allocation if we eliminated restrictive housing supply regulations.

A limitation of both the Albouy and Ehrlich (2018) and the Hsieh and Moretti (2019) is that the effect of land use regulations operates through the housing supply curve, but we do not yet have a full understanding of exactly how and which types of regulations translate to reduced housing supply elasticity (again, see the discussion in Gyourko and Molloy 2015). Nevertheless, it is a distinct possibility that innovations to housing policy may currently be more marginally productive in driving growth in the housing sector than even technological innovations. One such policy innovation may be to move control of land use policy from the local level to the state or even federal level, acknowledging that local incumbents often have an incentive to restrict housing production to raise their own asset values. An attempt was made in California to reduce local control of zoning policy (California SB50), but it ultimately failed. It remains to be seen whether other, similar attempts may eventually succeed, and what the impacts might be.

11.6.4   Innovation and Urban Economics

When a house is purchased or leased, part of what is being transacted is the right to occupy the land that the property sits on. This enables the occupants to live in closer proximity to their workplace or to other desirable or productive amenities. Innovation that affects transportation (and thus the demand for proximity) and innovation that affects local productivity or the value of local amenities therefore also affects the housing market. It is therefore important to consider the spatial aspect of housing and how innovations in other sectors may be affecting it.

A well-documented trend is that housing is becoming more expensive nearer city centers (Couture and Handbury 2019), and especially so in cities with intensive knowledge-based industries (Moretti 2013). While some of this price growth is undoubtedly due to restrictive land use regulations, these regulations change much less from year to year than do house prices, and so most of the year-to-year growth in prices can be attributed to growing demand to live near city centers.

Has technological innovation contributed to the growing demand to live near city centers and in major metropolitan areas? The key question is whether these technological innovations are complements or substitutes to urban density. The existing evidence seems to suggest that they are complements. Jaffe, Tratjenberg, and Henderson (1993) showed that patent citations are geographically localized, which means that geographic concentration might be becoming more important as more of the economy moves toward knowledge production. Gaspar and Glaeser (1998) showed that improvements in telecommunication technology, rather than substituting for face-to-face meetings, actually increases the number of face-to-face interactions, thus suggesting that IT complements geographic proximity. Other papers showing evidence for complementarity between urban density and technology include Sinai and Waldfogel (2004), Anenberg and Kung (2015), and Anenberg, Kuang, and Kung (2019). The latter two papers focus on how IT reduces informational uncertainties that may be especially prevalent in urban areas, such as information about traffic and parking conditions, and about the quality of local restaurants when there are too many to learn about by personal experience. Couture and Handbury (2019) also find limited evidence that technology may have contributed to the growing preference among young, high-income households to locate in more urban areas.

The literature on how technology interacts with urban density may have lessons for how we expect near-future technological innovations in transportation to affect housing markets. Normally, one expects innovations that reduce the cost of transportation to reduce the demand for proximity to jobs and amenities, and thus reduce the demand for urban living. However, it may be that the most promising current and forthcoming technologies in transportation, such as self-driving and self-parking cars, and the wide availability of mapping and routing software, have a larger effect on reducing the cost of congestion. Anyone who has driven around in a big city knows how much time finding parking adds to the trip, so the promise of self-driving and self-parking cars includes the ability to no longer have to do that ourselves. If the upcoming innovations in transportation primarily reduce the cost of congestion in dense areas, then this would further increase the demand to live in urban areas, and thus raise house prices in those areas.

11.6.5   Housing's Impact on Innovation and Entrepreneurship

Thus far I have focused on how innovation and entrepreneurship affect housing. Now, I briefly discuss whether housing can affect innovation and entrepreneurship. I already mentioned the paper by Hsieh and Moretti (2019), which showed the impact of supply restrictions on aggregate output. This can also translate to reduced innovation and entrepreneurship, if it leads people to avoid moving to places with the best potential for these activities. House prices themselves can also affect innovation and entrepreneurship. Adelino, Schoar, and Severino (2015) showed that from 1998 to 2010, small business employment grew faster in areas that experienced greater house price increases, and that this effect was more pronounced in industries that need little startup capital and for which lending based on housing collateral is relatively more important. Thus, improvements in the ability of homeowners to borrow against the collateral value of their home (such as through better financial technology) may spur greater entrepreneurship.[17]

11.7   Conclusion

Housing is a large and growing sector of the economy. Economic activity in housing consists of primarily two industries: real estate, which involves the leasing and sale of existing housing, and construction, which involves

[17]. Thus far I have avoided discussing financial technology and other innovations in finance (despite a clear relevance to housing), because I believe that topic is best left to a chapter on innovation and entrepreneurship in finance. Although housing demand and mortgage finance are tightly linked, it is perhaps more appropriate to think of financial innovations that increase household borrowing ability as a demand shock to housing, rather than an increase in the productivity of housing services or of construction per se.

the production of new housing. Because housing is highly durable, the stock of housing is much larger than the flow, and accordingly, the size of the real estate industry is much larger than that of the construction industry. Most productivity in housing therefore comes from better ways to transact and manage existing homes, while improvements to the physical quality and construction of homes will take a longer time to be reflected in the stock.

Both real estate and construction are highly competitive industries and do not appear to invest much in R&D. However, there is growing entrepreneurial interest in companies that provide innovative software and business services to the real estate industry, and in companies that harness technology to directly compete with real estate industry incumbents. Labor productivity appears to be growing in real estate, along with growing intensity of software and IT capital, but caution must be used when interpreting these results due to measurement issues. Labor productivity in single-family housing construction appears to be flat, whereas labor productivity in multifamily residential construction appears to be growing, especially during the past 15 years.

Two recent technological innovations highlight some important issues in how we are measuring economic growth in housing. First, the movement of housing search to the Internet has presumably improved the efficiency of how buyers and sellers find each other. Economic search theory predicts that one of the main effects of an improvement to search efficiency is higher quality matches, which shows up in higher transaction prices. If the most important technological innovation in residential real estate over the past 20 years has its primary effect on increasing match quality, then this would be difficult to detect by methods that do not account for unobserved match quality in the price deflator. Similarly, the introduction of home-sharing platforms may have increased the option value of residential housing, as owners can now use the property either in the housing market or in the travel accommodations market. And they can even use it for both, using part of the space for housing and selling part of it in the short-term rental market. Increases to the option-value of housing would again show up primarily in prices and again be difficult to detect by standard economic accounting methods. The analysis suggests that we need improved methods for measuring output, growth, and productivity in housing if we are to fully understand how recent innovations have impacted the efficiency of housing markets.

The future of housing markets is likely to be shaped by three important factors. First, many economists suspect that stringent land use regulations are responsible for significant inefficiencies in the current level of housing production. Before considering how technology can improve efficiency in housing markets, it may be more useful to first consider how better policy can improve efficiency in housing markets. Second, researchers have documented anticompetitive behaviors in the residential brokerage industry that may limit the impact of innovation and entrepreneurship on making the housing market more efficient. For the impact of new technologies and business practices to have their full effect, barriers to entry and to price competition must be broken down. Finally, new technologies and the movement of the US toward a knowledge-based economy may be rapidly increasing the demand to live in denser, more urban, and more educated areas. This trend has implications for the spatial distribution of housing and house price growth and further emphasizes the need to reexamine land use policy, since many of the most stringent policies are located precisely in the cities that are experiencing the greatest productivity growth.

Appendix

Increasing the Match Rate in Search Models

A standard economic model of housing search is described by two equations:

(1) $$rV_s = -c_s + q(\theta)\beta E[S - y | S \geq y]G(y)$$

(2) $$rV_b = -c_b + \frac{q(\theta)}{\theta}(1 - \beta)E[S - y | S \geq y]G(y)$$

Equation (1) describes the value function of a seller searching for a buyer, and equation (2) describes the value function of a buyer searching for a seller. In these equations, r is the discount rate, and $q(\theta)$ is the match function that describes the instantaneous rate at which sellers meet buyers. It is assumed to depend on θ, which is the *market tightness*, or the ratio of buyers to sellers. If the match rate for sellers is $q(\theta)$, then the match rate for buyers is $q(\theta)/\theta$. The variable y is defined as the sum of reservation values for buyer and seller, and is equal to $y = V_b + V_s$; S is a random variable representing the surplus generated from the match; $G(y)$ is the survivor function for the distribution of S, and thus $G(y)$ is the probability that the match surplus exceeds reservation value y. The rate at which a seller successfully finds a buyer to transact with is therefore $q(\theta)G(y)$, and the rate at which a buyer successfully finds a seller to transact with is $q(\theta)G(y)/\theta$. The net surplus generated is $S - y$, which is split via Nash bargaining, so the sellers get β share of the net surplus, and buyers get $1 - \beta$ share. The search costs for the seller and for the buyer are c_s and c_b, respectively.

Now suppose that instead of $q(\theta)$, we write the match rate as $AQ(\theta)$ to consider the effect of $A \rightarrow \infty$. Equations (1) and (2) then become

(3) $$rV_s = -c_s + Aq(\theta)\beta E[S - y | S \geq y]G(y)$$

(4) $$rV_b = -c_b + \frac{Aq(\theta)}{\theta}(1 - \beta)E[S - y | S \geq y]G(y)$$

To isolate the effect of increasing match efficiency without a change in match quality, I first consider a setting in which all matches give a surplus of $S \geq y$, where S is fixed and is not a random variable. The equations become

$$rV_s = -c_s + Aq(\theta)\beta(S - y)$$

$$rV_b = -c_b + \frac{Aq(\theta)}{\theta}(1 - \beta)(S - y)$$

Combining the two equations gives

$$ry = -c_s - c_b + Aq(\theta)\left[\beta + \frac{1 - \beta}{\theta}\right](S - y)$$

$$S - y = \frac{ry + c_s + c_b}{Aq(\theta)\left[\beta + \dfrac{1 - \beta}{\theta}\right]}$$

Taking the limit as $A \to \infty$ means that $S - y \to 0$.[18] Thus, the reservation value becomes exactly equal to S, and the match rate becomes instantaneous. Therefore no vacancies occur, and every match generates a surplus of S. When $A < \infty$, y is less than S, and the difference depends on the search costs and the match rate.

Now consider a setting in which the upper bound of the support of the match quality distribution is $\bar{S}$. Further, for simplicity, assume that $G(\bar{S}) > 0$ (so there is a positive probability that S is exactly equal to $\bar{S}$). Combining equations (3) and (4) gives

$$E[S - y \,|\, S \geq y]G(y) = \frac{ry + c_s + c_b}{Aq(\theta)\left[\beta + \dfrac{1 - \beta}{\theta}\right]}$$

Taking the limit of $A \to \infty$ means that $E[S - y \,|\, S \geq y]G(y) \to 0$ in the limit. Thus, $y \to \bar{S}$. Since $G(\bar{S}) > 0$, $Aq(\theta)G(y) \to \infty$ as $A \to \infty$, and thus the vacancy rate approaches zero. If $G(y) \to 0$ as $y \to \bar{S}$, then it may be possible for the vacancy rate to remain positive as $A \to \infty$, as not all vacancies are immediately filled.

References

Adelino, Manuel, Antoinette Schoar, and Felipe Severino. 2015. "House Prices, Collateral, and Self-Employment." *Journal of Financial Economics* 117: 288–306.
Aghion, Philippe, Nick Bloom, Richard Blundell, Rachel Griffith, and Peter How-

---

18. Note that it doesn't matter what θ approaches, because $Aq(\theta)[\beta + (1 - \beta)/\theta] \to \infty$ as $A \to \infty$ regardless of whether θ is finite or approaches zero or infinity.

itt. 2005. "Competition and Innovation: An Inverted-U Relationship." *Quarterly Journal of Economics* 120(2): 701–28.

Albouy, David, and Gabriel Ehrlich. 2018. "Housing Productivity and the Social Cost of Land-Use Regulation." *Journal of Urban Economics* 107: 101–20.

Alyakoob, Mohammed, and Mohammad Rahman. 2018. "The Sharing Economy as a Local Economic Engine: The Heterogeneous Impact of Airbnb on Restaurant Employment Growth." Working Paper. West Lafayette, IN: Purdue University.

Anenberg, Elliot, and Edward Kung. 2015. "Information Technology and Product Variety in the City: The Case of Food Trucks." *Journal of Urban Economics* 90: 60–78.

———. 2018. "Interest Rates and Housing Market Dynamics in a Housing Search Model." Working Paper. Washington, DC, and Northridge, CA: Federal Reserve Board and California State University–Northridge.

Anenberg, Elliot, Chun Kuang, and Edward Kung. 2019. "Social Learning and Local Consumption Amenities: Evidence from Yelp." Working Paper. Washington, DC, Beijing, and Northridge, CA: Federal Reserve Board, University of International Business and Economics, and California State University–Northridge.

Baen, John S., and Randall S. Guttery. 1997. "The Coming Downsizing of Real Estate: Implications of Technology." *Journal of Real Estate Portfolio Management* 3(1): 1–18.

Barron, Kyle, Edward Kung, and Davide Proserpio. 2019. "The Effect of Home-Sharing on House Prices and Rents: Evidence from Airbnb." Working Paper. Washington, DC, and Northridge, CA: Federal Reserve Board and California State University–Northridge.

Barwick, Panle Jia, and Parag A. Pathak. 2015. "The Costs of Free Entry: An Empirical Study of Real Estate Agents in Greater Boston." *RAND Journal of Economics* 46(1): 103–45.

Barwick, Panle Jia, Parag A. Pathak, and Maisy Wong. 2017. "Conflicts of Interest and Steering in Residential Brokerage." *American Economic Journal: Applied Economics* 9(3): 191–222.

BEA. 2009. *Concepts and Methods of the Input-Output Accounts*. Washington, DC: US Department of Commerce, Bureau of Economic Analysis.

———. 2019. *Concepts and Methods of the U.S. National Income and Product Accounts*. Washington, DC: US Department of Commerce, Bureau of Economic Analysis.

Bernheim, Douglas, and Jonathan Meer. 2013. "Do Real Estate Brokers Add Value When Listing Services Are Unbundled?" *Economic Inquiry* 51(2): 1166–82.

Couture, Victor, and Jessie Handbury. 2019. "Urban Revival in America." Working Paper. Berkeley, CA, and Philadelphia: University of California–Berkeley and the Wharton School.

Diamond, Peter A. 1982. "Wage Determination and Efficiency in Search Equilibrium." *Review of Economic Studies* 49(2): 217–27.

DOJ. 2007. *Competition in the Real Estate Brokerage Industry*. Washington, DC: US Department of Justice. https://www.justice.gov/atr/competition-real-estate brokerage-industry.

Einav, Liran, Chiara Farronato, and Jonathan Levin. 2016. "Peer-to-Peer Markets." *Annual Review of Economics* 8: 615–35.

Farronato, Chiara, and Andrey Fradkin. 2018. "The Welfare Effects of Peer Entry in the Accommodation Market: The Case of Airbnb." NBER Working Paper No. 24361. Cambridge, MA: National Bureau of Economic Research.

Ford, James Scott, Ronald C. Rutherford, and Abdullah Yavas. 2005. "The Effects of the Internet on Marketing Residential Real Estate." *Journal of Housing Economics* 14: 92–108.

Garcia-López, Miquel-Àngel, Jordi Jofre-Monseny, Rodrigo Martínez Mazza, and Mariona Segú. 2019. "Do Short-Term Rental Platforms Affect Housing Markets? Evidence from Airbnb in Barcelona." IEB Working Paper. Barcelona: Institut d'Economia de Barcelona.

Gaspar, Jess, and Edward Glaeser. 1998. "Information Technology and the Future of Cities." *Journal of Urban Economics* 43: 136–56.

Genesove, Davide, and Lu Han. 2012. "Search and Matching in the Housing Market." *Journal of Urban Economics* 72: 31–45.

Glaeser, Edward, and Joseph Gyourko. 2018. "The Economic Implications of Housing Supply." *Journal of Economic Perspectives* 32(1): 3–30.

Guren, Adam. 2018. "House Price Momentum and Strategic Complementarity." *Journal of Political Economy* 126(3): 1172–1218.

Gyourko, Joseph, and Raven Molloy. 2015. "Regulation and Housing Supply." In *Handbook of Regional and Urban Economics*, vol. 5, edited by Gilles Duranton, J. Vernon Henderson, and William C. Strange, 1289–1337. Amsterdam: Elsevier.

Han, Lu, and Seung-Hyun Hong. 2011. "Testing Cost Inefficiency under Free Entry in the Real Estate Brokerage Industry." *Journal of Business & Economic Statistics* 29(4): 564–78.

Han, Lu, and William C. Strange. 2014. "Bidding Wars for Houses." *Real Estate Economics* 42(1): 1–32.

Head, Allen, Huw Lloyd-Ellis, and Hongfei Sun. 2014. "Search, Liquidity, and the Dynamics of House Prices and Construction." *American Economic Review* 104(4): 1172–1210.

Hendel, Igal, Aviv Nevo, and François Ortalo-Magné. 2009. "The Relative Performance of Real Estate Marketing Platforms: MLS versus FSBOMadison.com." *American Economic Review* 99(5): 1878–98.

Horn, Keren, and Mark Merante. 2017. "Is Home Sharing Driving Up Rents? Evidence from Airbnb in Boston." *Journal of Housing Economics* 38: 14–24.

Hsieh, Chang-Tai, and Enrico Moretti. 2003. "Can Free Entry Be Inefficient? Fixed Commissions and Social Waste in the Real Estate Industry." *Journal of Political Economy* 111(5): 1076–1122.

———. 2019. "Housing Constraints and Spatial Misallocation." *American Economic Journal: Macroeconomics* 11(2): 1–39.

Inman, Brad. 2018. Remarks Made at What's New in Residential Real Estate Brokerage Competition: An FTC-DOJ Workshop, June 5. Transcript at https://www.ftc.gov/news-events/events-calendar/2018/04/whats-new-residential-real-estate-brokerage-competition-ftc-doj.

Jaffe, Adam B., Manuel Tratjenberg, and Rebecca Henderson. 1993. "Geographic Localization of Knowledge Spillovers as Evidenced by Patent Citations." *Quarterly Journal of Economics* 108(3): 577–98.

Levitt, Steven D., and Chad Syverson. 2008. "Market Distortions When Agents Are Better Informed: The Value of Information in Real Estate Transactions." *Review of Economics and Statistics* 90(4): 599–611.

Martellini, Paulo, and Guido Menzio. 2018. "Declining Search Frictions, Unemployment and Growth." Working Paper. Philadelphia and New York: University of Pennsylvania and New York University.

Moretti, Enrico. 2013. *The New Geography of Jobs*. New York: Mariner Books.

Mortensen, Dale T., and Christopher A. Pissarides. 1994. "Job Creation and Job Destruction in the Theory of Unemployment." *Review of Economic Studies* 61(3): 397–415.

NAR. 2018. *Real Estate in a Digital Age 2018 Report*. National Association of Realtors. https://www.nar.realtor/sites/default/files/documents/2018-real-estate-in-a-digital-world-12-12-2018.pdf.

Ngai, L. Rachel, and Silvana Tenreyro. 2014. "Hot and Cold Seasons in the Housing Market." *American Economic Review* 104(12): 3991–4026.

Novy-Marx, Robert. 2009. "Hot and Cold Markets." *Real Estate Economics* 37(1): 1–22.

Petrongolo, Barbara, and Christopher A. Pissarides. 2001. "Looking into the Black Box: A Survey of the Matching Function." *Journal of Economic Literature* 39: 390–431.

Pissarides, Christopher A. 1985. "Short-Run Equilibrium Dynamics of Unemployment, Vacancies, and Real Wages." *American Economic Review* 75(4): 676–90.

Saks, Raven E. 2008. "Job Creation and Housing Construction: Constraints on Metropolitan Area Employment Growth." *Journal of Urban Economics* 64: 178–95.

Sinai, Todd, and Joel Waldfogel. 2004. "Geography and the Internet: Is the Internet a Substitute or a Complement for Cities?" *Journal of Urban Economics* 56: 1–24.

Snider, David, and Matt Harris. 2018. "The Future of Real Estate Tech: How We Got Here and What's Next in an Exploding New Ecosystem." *Forbes.com* https://www.forbes.com/sites/valleyvoices/2018/02/13/futureof-real-estate-tech.

Sveikauskas, Leo, Samuel Rowe, and James D. Mildenberger. 2018. "Measuring Productivity Growth in Construction." *Monthly Labor Review*: 1–34.

US Census Bureau. 2019. *Nonemployer Statistics Technical Documentation: Methodology.* Washington, DC: US Census Bureau. https://www.census.gov/programs-surveys/nonemployerstatistics/technical-documentation/methodology.html.

Wheaton, William C. 1990. "Vacancy, Search, and Prices in a Housing Market Matching Model." *Journal of Political Economy* 98(6): 1270–92.

Zervas, Georgios, Davide Proserpio, and John W. Byers. 2017. "The Rise of the Sharing Economy: Estimating the Impact of Airbnb on the Hotel Industry." *Journal of Marketing Research* 54(5): 687–705.

Zumpano, Leonard V., Ken H. Johnson, and Randy I. Anderson. 2003. "Internet Use and Real Estate Brokerage Market Intermediation." *Journal of Housing Economics* 12(2): 134–50.

Comment   Jessie Handbury

Introduction

Over the past decade, venture capital funding of real estate and construction-related companies in the US has increased dramatically, outpacing growth in other industries and more than doubling its market share. Real estate technology firms, such as WeWork and Airbnb, have seen meteoric growth, and the home search process has been revolutionized with all home purchases reporting that they conducted some of their search online, an option unavailable to them 20 years ago. However, labor productivity

Jessie Handbury is an assistant professor of real estate at the Wharton School at the University of Pennsylvania, and a faculty research fellow of the National Bureau of Economic Research.

For acknowledgments, sources of research support, and disclosure of the author's material financial relationships, if any, please see https://www.nber.org/books-and-chapters/role-innovation-and-entrepreneurship-economic-growth/comment-innovation-and-entrepreneurship-housing-handbury.

in construction of single family homes—by far the most common form of housing—has been flat or has even decreased since the turn of the century. Housing remains unaffordable for many in both the rental market and the owner-occupied market, where real estate brokers continue to command commissions north of 5 percent on home sales. In chapter 11, Kung documents this varied landscape and provides some insight into the market structure that has prevented most of the real estate industry from seeing large gains from innovation. He also discusses why the impact of the technology in the areas where it has become prominent is so hard to decipher.

In this comment, I provide some context for Kung's analysis, highlighting a few key features of US housing markets that might explain why innovation has been limited in scope. The two key areas of innovation have been in the business of trading properties rather than in their production. High take-up of short-term rentals and online listing services suggests that there are gains for participants in those markets. However, the literature Kung reviews indicates that these technologies are, if anything, serving to increase house prices and exacerbate the housing affordability crisis, arguably the central policy issue facing housing markets in the US. Addressing this issue will require that the scope of innovation extend to the construction sector, which seems unlikely without policy intervention to relieve zoning restrictions and building codes.

Examples of Innovation, Unevenly Distributed Gains

Housing is a durable asset. As a result, the scope for innovation is as much in finding efficiencies in the trading and services markets as in its production. Indeed, the two most prolific recent examples of innovation in the housing sector have been focused on the former. Housing assets are also highly differentiated. Information frictions allow for local market power and profitable entry, so while highly entrepreneurial, real estate markets tend to be extremely fragmented, providing little incentive and insufficient scale for profitable R&D investments. It is not surprising, therefore, that innovations have come from an outside sector: tech firms creating platforms to reduce frictions around information sharing (e.g., Zillow's online search platform) and contracting (e.g., Airbnb's short-term rental marketplace). Kung documents high take-up of these services. Despite this, the existing literature has found that the introduction of platforms facilitating online search and short-term rentals has had limited measurable impact on quantities and instead is observed to increase the price of housing and housing services. In a market where supply is constrained by zoning restrictions, these results are not surprising and do not preclude welfare gains from such innovation. The increase in prices that has resulted from improved matches in home sales and more efficient use of real estate with time-sharing of apartments does indicate aggregate welfare gains. But it also implies that these innovations are exacerbating the housing affordability crisis, thereby highlighting the lack of innovation and growth on the construction side of the housing sector. While supply remains constrained, the incidence of the gains from innovation in the housing sector will be enjoyed only by some, with detrimental effects on others. Indeed, recent work studies the incidence of Airbnb using structural estimation in New York (Calder-Wang 2019) and Amsterdam (Almagro and Domínguez-Iino 2019).

Innovation, or Lack Thereof, in Housing Supply

The key constraint on housing supply highlighted by Kung is zoning policy. Restrictive zoning binds especially in gateway markets, like New York and San Francisco, where land is in short supply and accounts for a high share of housing prices and rents. Outside major coastal markets, however, significant progress could be made to reduce housing costs with efficiencies that lower construction costs. Glaeser and Gyourko (2018), for example, estimate that the physical construction costs amount to about 70 percent of the production cost of an economy-quality single-family home, and slightly less than three quarters of homes in the American Housing Survey were priced near or below this in 2013. Schmitz (2020) argues that these physical construction costs are inflated by market power of the labor-intensive stick-built segment of the construction industry. He documents the steep growth of relatively inexpensive modular, or factory-built, housing in the 1960s that was reversed in the 1970s when they were made ineligible for HUD mortgage subsidies and the introduction of strong building code restrictions for modular homes relative to stick-built homes. After accounting for over 50 percent of single-family construction in 1970, factory production accounts for just over 10 percent of the industry today, in spite of significant cost advantages. In 2013, one-piece modular homes cost an average of $38 per square foot, compared to $94 for a single-family home built on-site (Schmitz 2020). These cost advantages cannot be realized in many neighborhoods where modular homes are outlawed by zoning. Relieving these zoning restrictions might go some way toward improving the lagging measured labor productivity that Kung reports for the single-family housing sector.

Innovation in the Multifamily Market

One area where we have seen innovations in the supply, rather than the trading, of housing services is in the multifamily rental market. This market is more concentrated than the single-family market, dominated by large, public firms with sufficient scale to invest profitably in R&D. Examples of this innovation include projects incorporating modular and off-site construction techniques in high-rise development. Though still in its infancy, the modular multifamily construction industry is growing rapidly, with the estimated potential to reduce construction times by 20–50 percent (Bertram et al. 2019). Progress has been made by multifamily landlords in developing pricing algorithms, similar to those used by airlines, and in bundling housing with related amenities provided either internally or by outside service providers, such as Hello Alfred. This pricing and service-oriented R&D in the housing sector is unlikely to be categorized as such in the formal statistics, where it is likely listed as occurring in the FinTech or service sectors, but it will probably be increasingly important for housing markets as the size and scope of rental markets expand. Demographic and labor market shifts have increased the demand for amenitized, high-density housing (Couture and Handbury 2020; Rappaport 2015). The key question here will be whether zoning policies that restrict high-density development are relaxed, but trends indicate that zoning is only becoming more constrained (Gyourko, Hartley, and Krimmel 2019).

References

Almagro, M., and T. Domínguez-Iino. 2019. "Location Sorting and Endogenous Amenities: Evidence from Amsterdam." Unpublished paper.

Bertram, N., S. Fuchs, J. Mischke, R. Palter, G. Strube, and J. Woetzel. 2019. *Capital Projects & Infrastructure: Modular Construction: From Projects to Products*. McKinsey & Company, July. http://modular.org/documents/document_publication/mckinsey-report-2019.pdf.

Calder-Wang, S. 2019. "The Distributional Impact of the Sharing Economy on the Housing Market." Working paper. https://www.sophiecalderwang.com/.

Couture, V., and J. Handbury. 2020. "Urban Revival in America." *Journal of Urban Economics* 119: 103267.

Glaeser, E., and J. Gyourko. 2018. "The Economic Implications of Housing Supply." *Journal of Economic Perspectives* 32(1): 3–30.

Gyourko, J., J. Hartley, and J. Krimmel. 2019. "The Local Residential Land Use Regulatory Environment across US Housing Markets: Evidence from a New Wharton Index." NBER Working Paper No. 26573. Cambridge, MA: National Bureau of Economic Research.

Rappaport, J. 2015. "Millennials, Baby Boomers, and Rebounding Multifamily Home Construction." Working paper. Federal Reserve Bank of Kansas City.

Schmitz, J. A. 2020. "Monopolies Inflict Great Harm on Low-and Middle-Income Americans." Working paper. Federal Reserve Bank of Minneapolis.

12

Education and Innovation

Barbara Biasi, David Deming, and Petra Moser

12.1 Introduction

A vast body of research shows that educational investments yield long-run benefits for students (e.g., Chetty et al. 2014; Deming and Walters 2017; Jackson, Johnson, and Persico 2016). Less is known, however, about the role of education in encouraging entrepreneurship and innovation.

In this chapter, we review the existing literature and attempt to understand the linkages between education and innovation. We first provide a brief review of relevant theoretical frameworks. We then explore the possible impacts of three different types of educational interventions that might have an impact on downstream innovation. We also outline possible avenues for future research.

We draw three main conclusions. First, increasing investment in basic skills would help ensure that all potential future innovators are able to reach

Barbara Biasi is an assistant professor of economics at Yale School of Management, and a faculty research fellow of the National Bureau of Economic Research.

David Deming is a professor of public policy at Harvard University, and a research associate of the National Bureau of Economic Research.

Petra Moser is a professor of economics and Jules I. Backman Faculty Fellow at New York University, and a research associate of the National Bureau of Economic Research.

This chapter was prepared for NBER Growth Conference "Beyond 140 Characters: The Role of Innovation and Entrepreneurship in Economic Growth." We are grateful for valuable comments from Eleanor Dillon, as well as from conference participants and our editors Aaron Chatterji, Josh Lerner, Scott Stern, and Michael J. Andrews. The views expressed herein are those of the authors and do not necessarily reflect the views of the National Bureau of Economic Research. For acknowledgments, sources of research support, and disclosure of the author's or authors' material financial relationships, if any, please see https://www.nber.org/books-and-chapters/role-innovation-and-entrepreneurship-economic-growth/education-and-innovation.

the knowledge frontier and take advantage of their natural talents. Second, since research universities play such an important role in knowledge creation and innovation, democratizing access to them as well as increasing public investment in them would likely yield big benefits in terms of innovation. Third, while technology alone is not a panacea, there is much potential for technology to lower the cost of providing extremely effective personalized education. Software can be used to replace the essential role that a tutor plays in diagnosing specific deficits and meeting learners where they are. Educational innovations, such as computer-assisted learning (CAL), can provide personalized support and feedback at a fraction of the price of a tutor, helping future innovators succeed in the early years of school and widening the talent pipeline.

12.2   Education and Innovation: Theory

The importance of human capital and education for innovation and growth is theoretically grounded in models of endogenous growth, such as Romer (1986, 1990, 1994). Two ingredients of this class of models are critical. First, human capital is factor-augmenting in the production of knowledge (or ideas). Second, ideas are nonrival, implying that they can be used by others who have not developed them, creating positive externalities that fuel growth. The combination of these two ingredients suggests that investments in education, which "create" human capital, not only benefit their original recipients but also encourage growth for the entire economy. A corollary is that, since private individuals do not internalize the social benefits of education, private investments in education are likely to be too low from a social perspective, which calls for public investments in education.

12.3   Defining Human Capital

The concept of human capital is at the core of this class of models. But what exactly is "human capital"? Early research (e.g., Romer 1990) measured differences in human capital by years of education. Subsequent work has tried to better characterize the types of investments that produce valuable knowledge and contribute to innovation and growth. Focusing on the production of knowledge, Scotchmer (1991) argued that the production of innovation is cumulative and that new knowledge builds on existing knowledge. Baumol (2005) emphasized the importance of scientific knowledge for innovation and growth. More recently, macroeconomic models, such as Lucas (2015), Lucas and Moll (2014), and Akcigit et al. (2018), have argued that social learning and interactions play a key role in encouraging growth, while Bell et al. (2019) stressed the importance of mentorship for producing innovators.

How can education produce the type of knowledge that generates innovation and growth? Altonji, Blom, and Meghir (2012) showed substantial differences in the labor market returns to different college majors, which suggests that the content of education matters. In an attempt to create a mapping between higher education, research, and innovation, Biasi and Ma (2020) link the content of college and university courses with that of academic publications and patents and show large differences among and within schools in the extent to which course content is "keeping pace" with the knowledge frontier. Deming and Noray (2018) find that the economic return to technology-intensive jobs and college majors declines with work experience, and they connect this decline to obsolescence of older-vintage skills learned in school. Taken together, this literature suggests that educational institutions foster innovation by teaching skills that keep workers near the technology frontier.

12.4 Growth Accounting

Empirical support for endogenous growth theory comes from exercises of growth accounting, which have shown that differences in human capital can explain differences in rates of growth. Mankiw, Romer, and Weill (1992), Benhabib and Spiegel (1994), Bils and Klenow (2000) as well as Manuelli and Seshadri (2014) use cross-country evidence to establish a link between human capital and growth. Hendricks and Schoellmann (2018) investigate wage gains and wage convergence for immigrants to the US and find that differences in human capital levels in the sending country explain 60 percent of the observed difference in wage gains. Jones (2014) argues that standard growth accounting models estimate a lower bound for the importance of human capital for growth and demonstrates that an alternative method of aggregating human capital in models of endogenous growth can explain all observed cross-country income differences.

In an attempt to better capture human capital, Hanushek and Woessmann (2008) examine the relationship between growth and alternative measures of workers' cognitive skills. They find that countries that increase cognitive skills grow more quickly. Hanushek, Ruhose, and Woessmann (2017) further show that cross-state variation in the US in "knowledge capital" can explain 20–30 percent of state variations in per capita GDP. Relatedly, Schoellmann (2012) uses wage returns to schooling to measure differences in the quality of education across countries and finds that foreign workers from countries with better education experience larger wage gains on moving to the US.

Yet, despite the strong evidence that links human capital with economic growth, there is little direct evidence of a causal effect of human capital on innovation, with a few notable exceptions, such as Bianchi and Giorcelli (2019, discussed below).

12.5   Investing in Basic Skills

Are inventors born or made? Providing an answer to this question requires understanding the production function for innovation. Scotchmer (1991) modeled innovation as a cumulative process, whereby existing knowledge acts as an input in the production of new content. One of the prerequisites for producing high-quality innovative content is therefore the ability to reach the knowledge frontier. As technology progresses, however, this frontier shifts outward (Jones 2009), increasing the "burden of knowledge" on potential inventors.

What does it take to reach the knowledge frontier? Like innovation, education is a cumulative process, and access to higher-level knowledge relies on access to basic education and skills in the very first years of life. Einstein would hardly have been able to invent the theory of general relativity, had he not had access to primary and secondary education. Education alone probably cannot make someone a great innovator. However, a good education is necessary to get potential innovators to the knowledge frontier in the first place. A high-quality education builds cognitive and noncognitive skills, which increase the productivity of future innovators.

12.6   Schooling and Cognitive Abilities

Recent research has emphasized the importance of innate traits of successful inventors and entrepreneurs. Aghion et al. (2017), for example, argue that inventors tend to have higher IQs, which has been interpreted as a signal of high ability and talent. Emphasis on these "innate" traits might suggest that luck is a key factor for becoming a successful inventor.

A closer look at the empirical evidence, however, reveals that education can play an equally important role in determining whether innate traits lead to innovation. Time spent in school, for example, has a causal positive effect on children's cognitive abilities. Ritchie and Tucker-Drob (2018) use a regression-discontinuity design on school entry-age cutoffs to show that an additional year of schooling increases IQ by 1 to 5 points. Moreover, they find that effects persist across the life span. Similarly, Cornelissen and Dustmann (2019) use differences in school-entry rules across regions in England to show that schooling improves literacy and numeracy skills of children aged 5 to 7, as well as noncognitive skills for children aged 11.

The benefits of additional schooling, however, are not confined to the early years. Cascio and Lewis (2006) explore the effects of an additional year of high school on a person's score on the Armed Forces Qualifying Test, and they find large effects, especially for racial minorities. These findings suggest that late investments in schooling can help close racial and ethnic gaps in cognitive skills. Using data from Sweden and exploiting conditionally random variation in test-taking dates, Carlsson et al. (2015) estimate that 10 additional days of high school raise intelligence scores by 1 percent of a standard deviation. Adding to this evidence, Card and Giuliano (2016a,b) show that underrepresented minorities benefit from increased access to gifted and talented programs. Gaining access to these programs in fourth grade leads to a 0.7 standard deviation increase in math test scores for Black students, from 0.8 to 1.5 standard deviations.[1]

Given the relationship between cognitive skill and innovation, gifted and talented programs such as the one studied by Card and Giuliano (2016a,b) could directly create more innovators from underrepresented backgrounds. Comparing their estimates to the relationship between achievement scores and patenting found in Bell et al. (2019) suggests that universal gifted and talented screening might increase the share of inventors (defined as someone who has ever held a patent) from 0.1 to 0.7 per thousand for Black students.[2]

12.7   Schooling and Noncognitive Abilities

Cognitive abilities, however, are not the only innate trait associated with innovation and entrepreneurship. Levine and Rubinstein (2017) find that entrepreneurs have specific personality traits, which make them "smart and illicit." Compared with the unincorporated self-employed, the incorporated self-employed (as a proxy for entrepreneurs) tend to score higher on cognitive tests, show greater self-esteem, and are more likely to have engaged in illicit activities as teenagers. Education can keep "smart and illicit" individuals, especially those coming from less advantaged backgrounds, from falling through the cracks.

Despite these advances, the predictive power of individual traits is fairly low, and there are enormous potential returns to democratizing access to education and to supporting everyone to reach the knowledge frontier.

12.8   Improving the Type and Quality of Education

Beyond simply expanding access to education, improving the type and quality of education might have large effects on innovation, entrepreneurship, and growth. As mentioned earlier, expanding the scale of targeted gifted and talented programs in K–12 schools could greatly widen the pipeline of future innovators (Card and Giuliano 2016a,b). Additionally, certain types of education programs seem to be particularly beneficial for innovation. Bianchi and Giorcelli (2019), for example, show that increased and "democratized" access to STEM (science, technology, engineering, and mathematics) education, through the opening of vocational and technical programs in 1960 Italy, led to increases in patenting. Similarly, Toivanen and

---

1. See Card and Giuliano (2016a), table 3.
2. Bell et al. (2019), figure IV(B).

Vaananen (2016) find large, positive causal effects on patenting of expanding access to Engineering MSc programs in Finland.

Yet despite a possible "democratizing" role of higher education for invention, Bell et al. (2019) show that US inventors (measured through inclusion as patentees) come from a small set of top US schools, which admit very few low-income students. These findings cast doubt on the idea that the current US education system is effective in providing access to the type of innovation that is needed for broad-based and "democratic" invention.

12.9   Universities as a Source of Entrepreneurship and Innovation

If education is important for producing future innovators, what is the role of universities in this process? To answer this question, we first review the existing evidence on linkages between universities, entrepreneurship, and innovation.

Today, universities such as Stanford and the Massachusetts Institute of Technology (MIT) in the US or the Technion in Israel, serve as catalysts for entrepreneurship and innovation. But can entrepreneurship be taught? Many university professors believe that yes, entrepreneurship is a skill that can be trained through exposure and experience. Israel's Technion was one of the first universities to offer a course in entrepreneurship, when Nobel Laureate Dan Shechtman, world renowned for his work in chemistry and material science, set up a course on technological entrepreneurship.[3] Shechtman has been running this course successfully for more than 30 years, and the Technion now pushes to deepen its commitment to teaching entrepreneurship. Ezri Tarazi, a professor of industrial design who is in charge of Technion's program, argues that entrepreneurship can in fact be taught and "talent can be developed."

Focusing on MIT, a major technology-based university, Hsu, Roberts, and Eesley (2007) examine trends in entrepreneurship among MIT alumni since the 1930s to investigate who enters entrepreneurship and how this has changed over time. One of their most striking findings is that rates of company formation by MIT alumni have increased dramatically since the 1930s, suggesting that MIT may have become "better" at encouraging entrepreneurship. Notably, they find that rates of entrepreneurship are generally higher among MIT alumni who are foreign citizens (who might be positively selected) and that women alumnae lag behind their male colleagues in the rate at which they become entrepreneurs. Both these findings suggest that expanding access to university education can encourage entrepreneurship and innovation, especially if they are combined with programs targeting underrepresented minorities and female entrepreneurs.

3. "Technion Fosters Entrepreneurship within Ivory Towers as Startup Nation Calls." *Times of Israel*, December 25, 2019. Available at https://www.timesofisrael.com/technion-fosters-entrepreneurship-within-ivory-towers-as-startup-nation-calls/.

The origins of MIT and other technology-based universities like Cornell and Iowa State can be traced back to the land-grant universities established by the Morrill Acts of 1862 and 1890. Funded initially by granting federally controlled land to colleges, the mission of these colleges was purposefully practical (in stark contrast to the liberal arts curriculum), focusing on agriculture, science, military science, and engineering.

Research on the land grant college system suggests that it played a particularly important role in encouraging local entrepreneurship and innovation. Kantor and Whalley (2019) show that agricultural extension centers that were connected to the US land grant system created important productivity spillovers to the local economy. A working paper by Maloney and Caicedo (2020) shows that the land grant universities, which trained engineers, encouraged county-level economic growth. In addition, research by Andrews (2019) and Valero and Van Reenen (2019) has shown that the establishment of universities increased local invention. Andrews (2019) examines the effects of land grant colleges on agricultural patenting and productivity by exploiting cases in which the location (county) in a state that received a land grant college was chosen through an "as good as random" process and compares outcomes for these 29 universities with runner-up counties that were not chosen. Andrews find that agricultural innovation (both in terms of patents and new crop varieties) increased in these counties relative to the control.

Rosenberg (1994) argued that reliance on local funding has created strong incentives to focus on applied research that has helped create local clusters of innovation. Land grant colleges in particular were good at securing social returns from publicly funded research, and perhaps even superior to the current US system focused on patenting, licensing, and technology transfer (Mowery et al. 2004).

The available evidence suggests that funding plays a major role in determining the rate and direction of technical change. Hvide and Jones (2018), for example, show that a change in funding rules in Norway created dramatic effects on both entrepreneurship and patenting. Until 2003, Norwegian professors benefited from the "professor's privilege," granting full rights to new business ventures and intellectual property. In that year, however, Norway switched to a system of shared rights, similar to the system established by the Bay-Dole Act of 1980, which grants just one-third of these rights to the professor, with two-thirds going to the university (e.g., Lach and Schankerman 2008). Using comprehensive data on Norwegian workers, firms, and patents, Hvide and Jones document a 50 percent decline in entrepreneurship and innovation in response to this change. In earlier research, using alumni presentations on Congressional appropriations committees as an instrument for research funding, Payne and Siow (2003) had shown that an increase of $1 million in federal research funding (in 1996 USD) results in 10 additional articles and 0.2 additional patents.

Analyses of university patenting have shown that the relationship between universities and innovations that surround them is in flux and may be weakening over time (Henderson, Jaffe, and Trajtenberg 2006). Yet the available evidence may underestimate the real benefits of universities for entrepreneurship and innovation if universities develop methods rather than creating specific startups and firms. Cohen, Nelson, and Walsh (2002) find that actual products from academic research are less important than research techniques and tools. Wright (2012) further shows that the way of doing agricultural research that was developed in the land grant system encouraged agricultural innovation that formed the foundation of the Green Revolution. More recently, examining drug development during 1988–2005, Sampat and Lichtenberg (2011) find that public sector labs account directly for about 10 percent of drugs, but may enable two-thirds of marketed drugs. Taken together, these findings suggest that spillovers from universities to the private sectors are difficult to quantify and easy to underestimate.

Another channel by which education can encourage innovation is by improving access to mentors and potential collaborators. Jones, Wuchty, and Uzzi (2008), Wuchty, Jones, and Uzzi (2007), Jones (2009), Deming (2017), and Jaravel, Petkova, and Bell (2018) all show that innovation often happens in teams. Universities and other types of educational institutions may provide the settings in which these teams are formed.

Spillovers in teams and among highly skilled individuals more generally appear to be particularly important in STEM. Azoulay, Graff Zivin, and Wang (2010), for example, document that the death of a superstar in science reduces the productivity of their collaborators. Bell et al. (2019) use tax data linked with patent records to show that mentors matter greatly for invention. Moser, Voena, and Waldinger (2014) show that the arrival of prominent German Jewish émigré chemists resulted in a substantial increase in patenting in the fields of the émigrés. Moser and San (2020) further show that restrictions on immigration in the 1920s, which reduced the number of eastern and southern European-born scientists who were active in the US, caused a persistent decline in invention by US-born inventors. Taken together, this literature suggests that educational institutions are an important source of innovation.

12.10   Effects of Innovation on Education

Our discussion to this point has focused on the potential benefits that improvements in access and in the quality of education can have for innovation, entrepreneurship, and ultimately, growth. Innovation, however, can also directly affect education, for example by reducing costs and improving quality and efficiency.

In recent years, the education sector has adopted new technologies at a much slower rate compared with other sectors (Chatterji 2018). In 2019, only 2.5 percent of the federal Department of Education's budget was earmarked

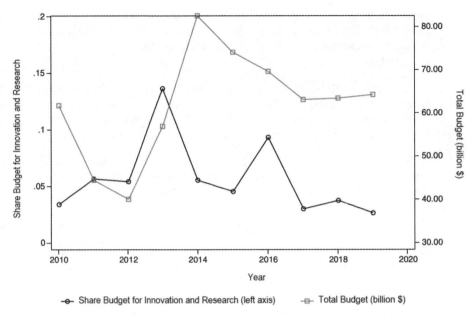

Fig. 12.1   Department of Education's total budget and share earmarked for innovation

Note: The black line shows the total budget of the federal Department of Education. The gray line shows the share of the budget earmarked for *Innovation and Improvement* and for the activities of the *Institute of Education Sciences.* Budget data from https://www2.ed.gov/about /overview/budget/tables.html?src=rt, accessed May 17, 2020.

for research and innovation; this share has been declining from 8.2 percent in 2016 to 3.8 percent in 2019 (figure 12.1). Since 1995, the education sector has been experiencing slow productivity growth (Cutler 2011). A possible reason for this slow growth is that the private benefits from technology adoption are smaller in education than in other sectors due to the structure of the market (Chatterji and Jones 2012). Alternatively, management challenges, which are typical of large organizations in the education sector, may have hindered the adoption of new technologies due to a bias in favor of the status quo and distorted incentives.

One strand of research has used experiments to evaluate the effect of the adoption of new technologies in the classroom on student achievement. In the US, technology adoption has proceeded at a reasonable pace. The ratio of students to computers for 15-year-olds is close to 1 (Bulman and Fairlie 2016), and nearly all students have access to the Internet (Fairlie, Beltran, and Das 2010; Golsbee and Guryan 2006). Barrow, Markman, and Rouse (2009) argue that technology adoption in schools could be beneficial, because it allows for better personalization of the learning experience.

Chatterji (2018) explains:

However, despite the ubiquity of technology in the classroom and various proposed mechanisms of action, rigorous evaluations of the impact of technology on student performance are rare and results are mixed (Bulman and Fairlie 2016). Goolsbee and Guryan (2006) find that while E-Rate increased investments in education technology between 1996–2000 in California public schools, it produced no statistical impact on student performance. This finding is consistent with other studies from the United States and around the world, which find little or no impact of technology on student outcomes (e.g., Angrist and Lavy 2002; Rouse and Krueger 2004). However, some studies have found a positive impact of technology on student performance (Ragosta 1983; Banerjee et al. 2007; Machin et al. 2007; Barrow, Markman and Rouse 2009; Cheung and Slavin 2013). As discussed in Barrow et al. (2009), these benefits must be weighed against the costs of program adoption and ongoing implementation.

There is little evidence that the mere existence of technology in the classroom produces benefits. Teachers and students might not use technology even when it is available (e.g., Cuban, Kirkpatrick, and Peck 2001) or use it in suboptimal ways (Wenglinsky 1998). For example, recent high-profile technology interventions, such as a $1 billion tablet initiative in the Los Angeles Unified School District, have been roundly criticized by journalists and education policy experts due to implementation challenges. In the Los Angeles Unified School District, for example, many students were unable to access the required curriculum due to serious technical issues.

However, one promising way that technology has been applied to enhance learning is through computer-assisted learning (CAL) software. CAL software automatically adapts content and difficulty level based on diagnostic assessment and students' previous responses. This software essentially creates a personalized learning environment for each student that exactly meets his or her needs. Several recent studies have found large benefits of personalized learning through CAL. Muralidharan, Singh, and Ganimian (2019) find that middle-school students in India who randomly receive access to CAL software score 0.37 standard deviations higher in math and 0.23 standard deviations higher in Hindi over only a 4.5 month period. Importantly, they find larger gains for students with lower baseline achievement. CAL essentially replicates the successes of many other interventions that use personalized tutoring and mentoring to teach students "at the right level." We know this approach works, but it is expensive. Thus, one way that innovation might increase productivity in education is by lowering the cost of personalization.

12.11   Conclusion

The research that we have reviewed in this chapter indicates that improvements in access and in the quality of education have immense potential for encouraging entrepreneurship and innovation. Education provides the tools that creative individuals need to succeed as inventors and entrepreneurs. Some of these tools can be measured quantitatively, through improvements in IQ scores, which have been linked to innovation. But many others are intangible, including tools taught in entrepreneurship programs around the world.

These programs encourage innovation at two important margins. First, they help people who would have been innovators anyway to become more successful, either in terms of increased invention or by creating new businesses that are more profitable. Second, they allow creative individuals who would otherwise not have become inventors or entrepreneurs to reach their potential, widening the talent pipeline. Based on the research in this survey, we conclude that this second mechanism is particularly important for encouraging innovation through education.

Many big questions remain, however. For example, to better guide education policy, we need better estimates of the marginal returns to investments in skills for different types of people (such as men vs. women, majority students vs. underrepresented minorities). Moreover, there is a great need for additional research on the stage of life at which investments in education are most effective in encouraging creativity and innovation (e.g., early childhood education vs. universities). Also, no real consensus has been reached on the type of education that is most successful in encouraging innovation (e.g., training in math and science vs. soft skills).

Different approaches to these issues imply radically different policies, ranging from focused investments in the "best and brightest" to concerted efforts at expanding and maintaining a broad pipeline of innovation. Putting aside considerations of inequality for the moment, the approach we take to "access" helps determine the level and the quality of innovation. These considerations heighten the urgency of the issue for education policy.

Technology will become a more important source of educational innovation in the near future, for two reasons. First, advances in machine learning and artificial intelligence tools will lower the cost of personalized instruction, particularly in subjects like math, where learning gaps can be more easily identified and addressed. As these techniques improve, they will become more widespread. Second, growing cost pressures in the education sector will make technological improvements more urgent and necessary. Education is a "people" business, so as people become relatively more expensive, technology becomes a more appealing substitute for some aspects of in-person instruction.

References

Aghion, Philippe, Ufuk Akcigit, Ari Hyytinen, and Otto Toivanenet. 2017. "The Social Origins of Inventors." NBER Working Paper No. 24110. Cambridge, MA: National Bureau of Economic Research.
Akcigit, Ufuk, Santiago Caicedo, Ernest Miguelez, Stefanie Stantcheva, and Vale-

rio Sterziet. 2018. "Dancing with the Stars: Innovation through Interactions." NBER Working Paper No. 24466. Cambridge, MA: National Bureau of Economic Research.

Altonji, Joseph G., Erica Blom, and Costas Meghir. 2012. "Heterogeneity in Human Capital Investments: High School Curriculum, College Major, and Careers." *Annual Review of Economics* 4(1): 185–223.

Andrews, Michael J. 2019. "Local Effects of Land Grant Colleges on Agricultural Innovation and Output." NBER Working Paper No. 26235. Cambridge, MA: National Bureau of Economic Research.

Angrist, Joshua, and Victor Lavy. 2002. "New Evidence on Classroom Computers and Pupil Learning." *Economic Journal* 112(482): 735–65.

Azoulay, Pierre, Joshua S. Graff Zivin, and Jialan Wang. 2010. "Superstar Extinction." *Quarterly Journal of Economics* 125(2): 549–89.

Banerjee, Abhijit V., Shawn Cole, Esther Duflo, and Leigh Linden. 2007. "Remedying Education: Evidence from Two Randomized Experiments in India." *Quarterly Journal of Economics* 122(3): 1235–64.

Barrow, Lisa, Lisa Markman, and Cecilia Elena Rouse. 2009. "Technology's Edge: The Educational Benefits of Computer-Aided Instruction." *American Economic Journal: Economic Policy* 1(1): 52–74.

Baumol, William J. 2005. "Education for Innovation: Entrepreneurial Breakthroughs Versus Corporate Incremental Improvements." *Innovation Policy and the Economy* 5: 33–56.

Bell, Alex, Raj Chetty, Xavier Jaravel, Neviana Petkova, and John Van Reenenet. 2019. "Who Becomes an Inventor in America? The Importance of Exposure to Innovation." *Quarterly Journal of Economics* 134(2): 647–713.

Benhabib, Jess, and Mark M. Spiegel. 1994. "The Role of Human Capital in Economic Development: Evidence from Aggregate Cross-Country Data." *Journal of Monetary Economics* 34(2): 143–73.

Bianchi, Nicola, and Michela Giorcelli. 2019. "Scientific Education and Innovation: From Technical Diplomas to University STEM Degrees." NBER Working Paper No. 25928. Cambridge, MA: National Bureau of Economic Research,

Biasi, Barbara, and Song Ma. 2020. "The Education-Innovation Gap." Working paper. New Haven, CT: Yale University.

Bils, Mark, and Peter J. Klenow. 2000. "Does Schooling Cause Growth?" *American Economic Review* 90(5): 1160–83.

Bulman, George, and Robert W. Fairlie. 2016. "Technology and Education: Computers, Software, and the Internet." *Handbook of the Economics of Education* 5: 239–80.

Card, David, and Laura Giuliano. 2016a. "Can Tracking Raise the Test Scores of High-Ability Minority Students?" *American Economic Review* 106(10): 2783–2816.

———. 2016b. "Universal Screening Increases the Representation of Low-Income and Minority Students in Gifted Education." *Proceedings of the National Academy of Sciences* 113(48): 13678–83.

Carlsson, Magnus, Gordon B. Dahl, Björn Öckert, and Dan-Olof Roothet. 2015. "The Effect of Schooling on Cognitive Skills." *Review of Economics and Statistics* 97(3): 533–47.

Cascio, Elizabeth U., and Ethan G. Lewis. 2006. "Schooling and the Armed Forces Qualifying Test: Evidence from School-Entry Laws." *Journal of Human Resources* 41(2): 294–318.

Chatterji, Aaron K. 2018. "Innovation and American K–12 Education." *Innovation Policy and the Economy* 18: 27–51.

Chatterji, Aaron K., and Benjamin Jones. 2012. "Harnessing Technology to Improve

K–12 Education." Discussion Paper 2012-05. The Hamilton Project. Washington, DC: Brookings Institution.

Chetty, Raj, Nathaniel Hendren, Patrick Kline, and Emmanuel Saez. 2014. "Where Is the Land of Opportunity? The Geography of Intergenerational Mobility in the United States." *Quarterly Journal of Economics* 129(4): 1553–1623.

Cheung, Alan C. K., and Robert E. Slavin. 2013. "The Effectiveness of Educational Technology Applications for Enhancing Mathematics Achievement in K–12 Classrooms: A Meta-analysis." *Educational Research Review* 9: 88–113.

Cohen, Wesley M., Richard R. Nelson, and John P. Walsh. 2002. "Links and Impacts: The Influence of Public Research on Industrial R&D." *Management Science* 48(1): 1–23.

Cornelissen, Thomas, and Christian Dustmann. 2019. "Early School Exposure, Test Scores, and Noncognitive Outcomes." *American Economic Journal: Economic Policy* 11(2): 35–63.

Cuban, Larry, Heather Kirkpatrick, and Craig Peck. 2001. "High Access and Low Use of Technologies in High School Classrooms: Explaining an Apparent Paradox." *American Educational Research Journal* 38(4): 813–34.

Cutler, David M. 2011. "Where Are the Health Care Entrepreneurs? The Failure of Organizational Innovation in Health Care." *Innovation Policy and the Economy* 11: 1–28.

Deming, David J. 2017. "The Growing Importance of Social Skills in the Labor Market." *Quarterly Journal of Economics* 132(4): 1593–1640.

Deming, David J., and Kadeem L. Noray. 2018. "Stem Careers and the Changing Skill Requirements of Work." NBER Working Paper No. 25065. Cambridge, MA: National Bureau of Economic Research.

Deming, David J., and Christopher R. Walters. 2017. "The Impact of Price Caps and Spending Cuts on US Postsecondary Attainment." NBER Working Paper No. 23736. Cambridge, MA: National Bureau of Economic Research.

Fairlie, Robert W., Daniel O. Beltran, and Kuntal K. Das. 2010. "Home Computers and Educational Outcomes: Evidence from the NLSY97 and CPS." *Economic Inquiry* 48(3): 771–792.

Goolsbee, Austan, and Jonathan Guryan. 2006. "The Impact of Internet Subsidies in Public Schools." *Review of Economics and Statistics* 88(2): 336–47.

Hanushek, Eric A., and Ludger Woessmann. 2008. "The Role of Cognitive Skills in Economic Development." *Journal of Economic Literature* 46(3): 607–68.

Hanushek, Eric A., Jens Ruhose, and Ludger Woessmann. 2017. "Knowledge Capital and Aggregate Income Differences: Development Accounting for US States." *American Economic Journal: Macroeconomics* 9(4): 184–224.

Henderson, Rebecca, Adam B. Jaffe, and Manuel Trajtenberg. 2006. "Universities as a Source of Commercial Technology: A Detailed Analysis of University Patenting, 1965–1988." *Review of Economics and Statistics* 80(1): 119–27.

Hendricks, Lutz, and Todd Schoellman. 2018. "Human Capital and Development Accounting: New Evidence from Wage Gains at Migration." *Quarterly Journal of Economics* 133(2): 665–700.

Hsu, David H., Edward B. Roberts, and Charles E. Eesley. 2007. "Entrepreneurs from Technology-Based Universities: Evidence from MIT." *Research Policy* 36(2): 768–88.

Hvide, Hans K., and Benjamin F. Jones. 2018. "University Innovation and the Professor's Privilege." *American Economic Review* 108(7): 1860–98.

Jackson, C. Kirabo, Rucker C. Johnson, and Claudia Persico. 2016. "The Effects of School Spending on Educational and Economic Outcomes: Evidence from School Finance Reforms." *Quarterly Journal of Economics* 131(1): 157–218.

Jaravel, Xavier, Neviana Petkova, and Alex Bell. 2018. "Team-Specific Capital and Innovation." *American Economic Review* 108(4–5): 1034–73.

Jones, Benjamin F. 2009. "The Burden of Knowledge and the 'Death of the Renaissance Man': Is Innovation Getting Harder?" *Review of Economic Studies* 76(1): 283–317.

———. 2014. "The Human Capital Stock: A Generalized Approach." *American Economic Review* 104(11): 3752–77.

Jones, Benjamin F., Stefan Wuchty, and Brian Uzzi. 2008. "Multi-University Research Teams: Shifting Impact, Geography, and Stratification in Science." *Science* 322(5905): 1259–62.

Kantor, Shawn, and Alexander Whalley. 2019. "Research Proximity and Productivity: Long-Term Evidence from Agriculture." *Journal of Political Economy* 127(2). DOI: 10.1086/701035.

Lach, Saul, and Mark Schankerman. 2008. "Incentives and Invention in Universities." *RAND Journal of Economics* 39(2): 403–33.

Levine, Ross, and Yona Rubinstein. 2017. "Smart and Illicit: Who Becomes an Entrepreneur and Do They Earn More?" *Quarterly Journal of Economics* 132(2): 963–1018.

Lucas, Robert E., Jr. 2015. "Human Capital and Growth." *American Economic Review* 105(5): 85–88.

Lucas, Robert E., Jr., and Benjamin Moll. 2014. "Knowledge Growth and the Allocation of Time." *Journal of Political Economy* 122(1): 1–51.

Machin, Stephen, Sandra McNally, and Olmo Silva. 2007. "New Technology in Schools: Is There a Payoff?" *Economic Journal* 117(522): 1145–67.

Maloney, William F., and Felipe Valencia Caicedo. 2020. "Engineering Growth." CEPR Discussion Paper No. DP15144. London: Centre for Economic Policy Research.

Mankiw, N. Gregory, David Romer, and David N. Weil. 1992. "A Contribution to the Empirics of Economic Growth." *Quarterly Journal of Economics* 107(2): 407–37.

Manuelli, Rodolfo E., and Ananth Seshadri. 2014. "Human Capital and the Wealth of Nations." *American Economic Review* 104(9): 2736–62.

Moser, Petra, and Shmuel San. 2020. "Immigration, Science, and Invention. Evidence from the Quota Acts." Working paper. New York University, New York.

Moser, Petra, Alessandra Voena, and Fabian Waldinger. 2014. "German Jewish Émigrés and US Invention." *American Economic Review* 104(10): 3222–55.

Mowery, David C., Richard R. Nelson, Bhaven N. Sampat, and Arvids A. Ziedonis. 2004. *Ivory Tower and Industrial Innovation: University-Industry Technology Transfer before and after the Bayh-Dole Act.* Stanford, CA: Stanford University Press.

Muralidharan, Karthik, Abhijeet Singh, and Alejandro J. Ganimian. 2019. "Disrupting Education? Experimental Evidence on Technology-Aided Instruction in India." *American Economic Review* 109(4): 1426–60.

Payne, Abigail, and Aloysius Siow. 2003. "Does Federal Research Funding Increase University Research Output?" *B.E. Journal of Economic Analysis & Policy* 3(1): 1–24.

Ragosta, Marjorie. 1983. "Computer-Assisted Instruction and Compensatory Education: A Longitudinal Analysis." *Machine-Mediated Learning* 1(1): 97–127.

Ritchie, Stuart J., and Elliot M. Tucker-Drob. 2018. "How Much Does Education Improve Intelligence? A Meta-Analysis." *Psychological Science* 29(8): 1358–69.

Romer, Paul M. 1986. "Increasing Returns and Long-Run Growth." *Journal of Political Economy* 94(5): 1002–37.

———. 1990. "Endogenous Technological Change." *Journal of Political Economy* 98(5, part 2): S71–S102.

————. 1994. "The Origins of Endogenous Growth." *Journal of Economic Perspectives* 8(1): 3–22.

Rosenberg, Nathan, and Richard N. Nelson. 1994. "American Universities and Technical Advance in Industry." University of Illinois at Urbana-Champaign's Academy for Entrepreneurial Leadership Historical Research Reference in Entrepreneurship. https://ssrn.com/abstract=1506333.

Rouse, Cecilia Elena, and Alan B. Krueger. 2004. "Putting Computerized Instruction to the Test: A Randomized Evaluation of a 'Scientifically Based' Reading Program." *Economics of Education Review* 23(4): 323–38.

Sampat, Bhaven N., and Frank R. Lichtenberg. 2011. "What Are the Respective Roles of the Public and Private Sectors in Pharmaceutical Innovation?" *Health Affairs* 30(2): 332–39.

Schoellman, Todd. 2012. "Education Quality and Development Accounting." *Review of Economic Studies* 79(1): 388–417.

Scotchmer, Suzanne. 1991. "Standing on the Shoulders of Giants: Cumulative Research and the Patent Law." *Journal of Economic Perspectives* 5(1): 29–41.

Toivanen, Otto, and Lotta Vaananen. 2016. "Education and Invention." *Review of Economics and Statistics* 98(2): 382–96.

Valero, Anna, and John Van Reenen. 2019. "The Economic Impact of Universities: Evidence from Across the Globe." *Economics of Education Review* 68: 53–67.

Wenglinsky, Harold. 1998. "Does It Compute? The Relationship between Educational Technology and Student Achievement in Mathematics." ETS Policy Information Center Report, Educational Testing Service, Princeton, NJ.

Wright, Brian D. 2012. "Grand Missions of Agricultural Innovation." *Research Policy* 41(10): 1716–28.

Wuchty, Stefan, Benjamin F. Jones, and Brian Uzzi. 2007. "The Increasing Dominance of Teams in Production of Knowledge." *Science* 316(5827): 1036–39.

Comment   Eleanor Wiske Dillon

Many conditions must come together for someone to develop a successful innovation. She, or he, must understand the current base of knowledge in her area to build on it; she must have the spark of a new idea; and she must have the inclination and security to take a risk in developing her idea. Both the content and the structure of educational institutions can be designed to foster these conditions.

In chapter 12, Biasi, Deming, and Moser focus largely on the role of education in providing for the first condition: a base of knowledge from which to innovate. In particular, they emphasize that incomplete and unequal access to quality education leaves some potential entrepreneurs without the base of knowledge they need to develop new ideas. Providing this base of knowledge

Eleanor Wiske Dillon is a principal economist at Microsoft Research New England.

Thanks to the organizers Aaron Chatterji, Josh Lerner, Scott Stern, and Michael J. Andrews and the chapter authors Barbara Biasi, David Deming, and Petra Moser. For acknowledgments, sources of research support, and disclosure of the author's material financial relationships, if any, please see https://www.nber.org/books-and-chapters/role-innovation-and -entrepreneurship-economic-growth/comment-education-and-innovation-dillon.

is undoubtedly the most important role of education in supporting innovation. Failure to provide quality education to all young people will lead to missed opportunities and will lower the overall pace of innovation in the economy. In education systems like that of the US, where access to education varies systematically with parents' income and with race, this failure also reinforces existing inequalities by shutting down a path for economic mobility.

Democratizing access to general education, while valuable for many reasons, is a broad policy and may have limited direct effects on the rates of invention. I focus my discussion on whether the existing economic literature can suggest more targeted interventions that would particularly spark innovation. I follow the authors on focusing mainly on the US context. Universities with strong track records of producing successful innovators share a focus on building mentor relationships, exposing students to real-world open questions, and training in STEM (Science, Technology, Engineering, and Math) fields. Providing curricula with these themes in high school, which nearly all young people now complete in the US, could be another powerful policy for increasing both the representativeness and total level of innovative entrepreneurship.

Access to Training for Innovation

Attendees of a small set of US colleges account for an outsized share of US patents (Bell et al. 2019). Not all innovations generate patents, and not all patents are innovative, but this tight concentration of patenting suggests some colleges and universities are creating environments that nurture invention, beyond simply catching students up to the frontier of knowledge. Biasi, Deming, and Moser emphasize that these most innovative colleges are often small and private (Cal Tech and MIT top the rankings by rates of patenting)[1] and admit relatively few low-income students. Increasing access to these colleges could create more equitable opportunities and reduce the strong relationship between parental income and future innovation in the US.

However, these current centers of innovation make up a tiny fraction of college seats in the United States. Democratizing access to these schools will do little to increase overall innovation unless capacity is simultaneously increased without affecting the quality of instruction. In Bell et al.'s sample, the 10 colleges with the highest rates of patenting among their students produce 90 patent holders per 1,000 attendees, in contrast to 7 per 1,000 in the remaining sample. These 10 colleges had a combined enrollment of

---

1. As part of a larger project using Census data, Bell et al. (2019) match US citizens born between 1980 and 1984 to the college they attended for the longest time and also to US patent records. They then report the share of attendees matched to each college who hold at least one patent.

just over 30,000 undergraduate students in 2018—about the same size as Purdue University.[2]

Policymakers and educators could do more to spur innovation by bringing successful elements of entrepreneurial instruction into more colleges and high schools, reaching a wider audience. Pinpointing what these institutions do to promote invention is difficult to do using observational data, and I have not found any economic studies that attempt it, but profiles of programs like those at Stanford (Read 2019) and Technion (Solomon 2019) suggest a few common practices. Both programs put students in contact with successful entrepreneurs, creating mentorship opportunities. Both also set students to work on current open problems suggested by businesses through class projects and hackathons. Finally, both programs place a specific emphasis on training in STEM fields.

Ingredients of Education for Innovation

Each of these ingredients in training for innovation has at least suggestive support in existing economic studies of innovation and entrepreneurship. Bell et al. (2019) find that young people who grow up in a neighborhood with more inventors are more likely to later become inventors themselves, and they are more likely to innovate in the same fields represented by inventors in their early neighborhoods. Girls are more likely to go on to innovate in the same fields as female inventors in their neighborhoods, but not more likely to follow in the fields of local male inventors. Bell et al. interpret these findings as evidence that neighbors are not just affecting general human capital accumulation (through, for example, higher quality schools), but also sharing specific knowledge and mentorship. Lerner and Malmendier (2013) find that Harvard Business School graduates who interacted with more former entrepreneurs during school were more likely to succeed if they started businesses in the future, providing further support for the importance of learning some soft skills directly from active entrepreneurs.

There is also outside evidence on the importance of exposure to open questions. Chatterji (2009) and many others document that past experience in incumbent firms in the same industry improves entrepreneurial success. While industry experience provides specific skills, helping would-be innovators reach the current frontier of knowledge, it may also surface the kinds of open questions that successful innovations can answer. Koning, Samila, and Ferguson (2020) find that female medical researchers are significantly more likely than male researchers to patent innovative treatments for female diseases and conditions, which may reflect different priorities but

2. Top colleges are from the data that Bell et al. (2019) released with their paper. Counts are full-time undergraduate enrollment in Fall 2018, from the Integrated Postsecondary Education Data System (US Department of Education, National Center for Education Statistics 2018).

again reinforces that innovators must identify an open problem before they can solve it.

As the authors discuss in their chapter, several studies find persuasive evidence that increases in STEM training, such as increased vocational and technical secondary education in Italy (Bianchi and Giorcelli 2020) and expanded engineering training in Finland (Toivanen and Väänänen 2016), generate increases in patenting. The current patent system is better designed to protect innovations in the sciences than in, for example, business operations. These studies may therefore partially capture a transfer of talent and energy from fields where innovations are not captured by patents to fields where they are. However, these are also fields where computerization has rapidly expanded the frontier of what is possible and created entire new fields, with well-documented increases in the demand for workers trained in these areas by incumbent firms. It is reasonable to believe that this training is also particularly valuable for entrepreneurs in this era.

A Role for Vocational Training

Bringing curricula that develop entrepreneurial skills to more colleges, and particularly to secondary schools, would do at least as much to capture more would-be innovators as improving equitable access to the elite, but small, institutions that already target these skills. Technical and vocational curricula, which have declined recently in the US but remain common in many European countries, would seem to be a good environment for this training. Most US high school students follow an academic curriculum, which emphasizes abstract thinking and general knowledge, such as mathematics and writing in preparation for college course work. In contrast, vocational tracks teach applied and often technical skills, providing applied, subject-specific knowledge that is otherwise not available until post-secondary schooling (figure 12.C.1). Increasingly, European vocational tracks emphasize apprenticeships and direct links with active businesses (Hampf and Woessmann 2016). These kinds of curricula could provide all three ingredients for innovation: a focus on technical STEM subjects, mentorship from innovators, and exposure to open questions.

Vocational training lost popularity in the US partially from a perception that multiple tracks would tend to segregate low-income, non-white, and lower-performing students into applied curricula without strong earning prospects while preserving the path to affluence through academic training and college for more privileged students. However, there is growing interest among policymakers, academics, and the public for thoughtfully designed, high-quality technical training in secondary school.[3] Renewal of these pro-

---

3. See Jacob (2017) for a survey of recent academic work, and a cry for more attention, or Belkin's (2018) *Wall Street Journal* article for an example of public interest.

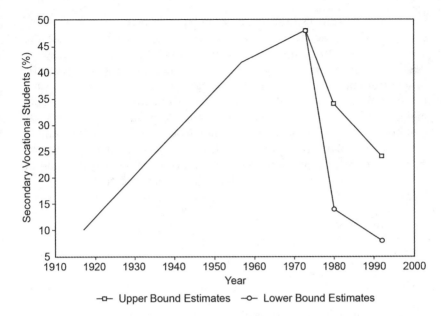

Fig. 12.C.1   Share of US secondary school students in vocational tracks

Source: Alon (2018) "Earning More by Doing Less: Human Capital Specialization and the College Wage Premium." Lower and upper bounds indicate more or less restrictive definitions of vocational curriculums.

grams could include opportunities to switch tracks, commitment to high-quality training, and an awareness of the potential of these programs to reinforce inequalities rather than mitigating them.

I know of no research that estimates the effects of vocational secondary school curricula on business starts or innovation, but several papers find generally positive effects on labor market outcomes (Jacob 2017). In one recent example, Bertrand, Mogstad, and Mountjoy (2019) study a reform in Norway that improved that country's vocational secondary school track, including adding apprenticeships, and led to increased enrollment. They estimate that entering vocational training generates a noticeable increase in post-school earnings, particularly for men, who were more likely to choose the more technical fields of that training. One aspect of the reform allowed students to convert from a vocational track to an academic one, which enabled them to go on to college, but the earnings gains are not a result of men taking this opportunity. This result suggests that vocational training teaches skills that are distinct from those learned in college but still valuable in the labor market.

Bertrand, Mogstad, and Mountjoy (2019) also find that enrollment in Norway's vocational secondary school track reduced criminal charges during students' teenage years, presumably because they were more occupied with school, and modestly increased secondary school completion. Creating strong vocational secondary school options appears to engage students who are otherwise on the margin of dropping out or engaging in illegal activities that would hamper future work. Potential innovators may particularly benefit from these alternative paths through secondary school. Levine and Rubinstein (2017) find that the most successful entrepreneurs have both high cognitive skills and a higher likelihood of having engaged in petty criminal behaviors (i.e., vandalism) in high school. Providing opportunities for creative thinking and applied problem solving early could generate the extra benefit of catching outside-the-box thinkers before they drift out of the system. Exploring the potential for well-designed vocational training to increase innovation would be a valuable area for future research.

References

Alon, Titan. 2018. "Earning More by Doing Less: Human Capital Specialization and the College Wage Premium." Unpublished manuscript.

Belkin, Douglas. 2018. "Why an Honors Student Wants to Skip College and Go to Trade School." *Wall Street Journal*, March 5. https://www.wsj.com/articles/college-or-trade-school-its-a-tough-call-for-many-teens-1520245800.

Bell, Alex, Raj Chetty, Xavier Jaravel, Neviana Petkova, and John Van Reenen. 2019. "Who Becomes an Inventor in America? The Importance of Exposure to Innovation." *Quarterly Journal of Economics* 134(2): 647–713.

Bertrand, Marianne, Magne Mogstad, and Jack Mountjoy. 2019. "Improving Educational Pathways to Social Mobility: Evidence from Norway's 'Reform 94.'" NBER Working Paper No. 25679. Cambridge, MA: National Bureau of Economic Research.

Bianchi, Nicola, and Michela Giorcelli. 2020. "Scientific Education and Innovation: From Technical Diplomas to University STEM Degrees." *Journal of the European Economic Association* 18(5): 2608–46.

Chatterji, Aaron K. 2009. "Spawned with a Silver Spoon? Entrepreneurial Performance and Innovation in the Medical Device Industry." *Strategic Management Journal* 30(2): 185–206.

Hampf, Franziska, and Ludger Woessmann. 2016. "Vocational vs. General Education and Employment over the Life-Cycle: New Evidence from PIAAC." CESifo Working Paper Series No. 6116. Munich: CESifo.

Jacob, Brian. 2017. "What We Know about Career and Technical Education in High School." Technical Report. Washington, DC: Brookings Institution.

Koning, Rembrand, Sampsa Samila, and John-Paul Ferguson. 2020. "Inventor Gender and the Direction of Invention." *AEA Papers and Proceedings* 110: 250–54.

Lerner, Josh, and Ulrike Malmendier. 2013. "With a Little Help from My (Random) Friends: Success and Failure in Post-Business School Entrepreneurship." *Review of Financial Studies* 26(10): 2411–52.

Levine, Ross, and Yona Rubinstein. 2017. "Smart and Illicit: Who Becomes an Entrepreneur and Do They Earn More?" *Quarterly Journal of Economics* 132(2): 963–1018.

Read, Max. 2019. "How to Major in Unicorn." *New York Magazine*, September 4. https://nymag.com/intelligencer/2019/09/how-to-network-through-stanford-university.html.

Solomon, Shoshanna. 2019. "Technion Fosters Entrepreneurship within Ivory Towers as Startup Nation Calls." *Times of Israel*, December 25. https://www.timesofisrael.com/technion-fosters-entrepreneurship-within-ivory-towers-as-startup-nation-calls/.

Toivanen, Otto, and Lotta Väänänen. 2016. "Education and Invention." *Review of Economics and Statistics* 98(2): 382–96.

US Department of Education, National Center for Education Statistics. 2018. Integrated Postsecondary Education Data System (IPEDS). Four-Year Institutions. Accessed June 12, 2020. https://nces.ed.gov/ipeds/.

Panel Remarks
Creating "Smart" Policy to Promote Entrepreneurship and Innovation

Karen G. Mills and Annie V. Dang

Introduction

In 2011, as the US was emerging from the Great Recession, a group of experienced entrepreneurs started a new company seeking to solve the pain points small businesses faced in accessing capital, barriers only exacerbated during the crisis as traditional bank lenders tightened credit to smaller firms. The company, named Kabbage, went on to become one of the most valuable financial technology or "fintech" companies, originating almost $8 billion in loans and attaining unicorn status with a $1.2 billion valuation by the end of 2019. Initially launched as a single loan product for eBay sellers, Kabbage expanded to offer fully automated online financing to small businesses, including a purchasing card, payment-processing solution, and cash flow management tool. Using artificial intelligence, machine learning, and Big Data to power internal loan underwriting algorithms, Kabbage successfully targeted a market segment that had been ill served by the traditional banking industry, while using innovative techniques to speed the lending process, manage risk, and hone the accuracy of its predictive models.

Kabbage's meteoric success story is every entrepreneur's dream, but it

Karen G. Mills is a senior fellow at Harvard Business School, and a member of the board of directors of the National Bureau of Economic Research.

Annie V. Dang was a research associate at Harvard Business School when this paper was written, and is currently a JD candidate at Georgetown University Law Center.

We thank the editors (Mike Andrews, Aaron Chatterji, Josh Lerner, and Scott Stern) for their support and Gabriella Elanbeck for wonderful research assistance. We are grateful to Mercedes Delgado and the participants at the NBER Conference on The Role of Innovation and Entrepreneurship in Economic Growth for their excellent feedback. For acknowledgments, sources of research support, and disclosure of the authors' material financial relationships, if any, please see https://www.nber.org/books-and-chapters/role-innovation-and-entrepreneurship-economic-growth/creating-smart-policy-promote-entrepreneurship-and-innovation.

is not representative of a typical business owner's experience in the US. About half of small businesses fail within 5 years of starting (US Small Business Administration Office of Advocacy 2019). Moreover, the past several decades have witnessed a concerning decrease in startup rates and a general fear that entrepreneurship in America is not what it once was, with the share of US employment accounted for by young firms decreasing by 30 percent over the past 30 years (Decker et al. 2014). Numerous academics, economists, and policymakers have attempted to pinpoint the causes of this unsettling trend, but no definitive answer yet exists.

Why are the numbers so concerning? Research identifies entrepreneurship as key to unlocking innovation and fostering regional and national economic productivity (Acemoglu et al. 2013; Decker et al. 2014; Lerner 2020; Van Praag and Versloot 2007). Although scholars may disagree on the most accurate measures (inputs vs. outputs) of innovation (e.g., proportion of budget spent on research and development vs. patent citations or the introduction of new and meaningful products and technologies), there is general agreement that entrepreneurship has a positive effect on employment, productivity, and growth at the national and local levels.

Extensive studies demonstrate that small and young firms contribute to innovation and employment growth (Almeida and Kogut 1997; Fritsch and Mueller 2004; Haltiwanger, Jarmin, and Miranda 2013; Henrekson and Johansson 2010). The question is: Which businesses are responsible for what kind of contribution? In the US, small businesses form an important part of the national economy, comprising a significant portion of total firms (31.7 million businesses, equaling 99.9 percent of all firms), markedly contributing to employment (47.1 percent of private sector employees), and representing two out of every three net new jobs (US Small Business Administration Office of Advocacy 2020). However, behind these numbers lies a great deal of heterogeneity. As defined by the US Small Business Administration (SBA), a small business is any independent business with fewer than 500 employees. Of the 30 million small businesses, 24.8 million or 81 percent are sole proprietorships—businesses without any employees. Efforts examining the remaining "employer" small businesses underscore the massive variation among small firms in the US (Chatterji 2018; Guzman and Stern 2019; Mills 2019), particularly highlighting the difference between local firms and the fledgling innovative startups that will grow to become the next technology behemoths.

A recent categorization (Delgado and Mills 2020; Mills 2019; see figure P.1) shows that of the 6 million US small businesses with employees, approximately 4 million operate in the local business-to-consumer (B2C) economy, firms conventionally labeled as "Main Street" businesses. These are the restaurants, coffee shops, dry cleaners, and other local businesses that make up the fabric of our communities. Another 1.1 million are supplier businesses, those that operate in the supply chain and traditionally sell

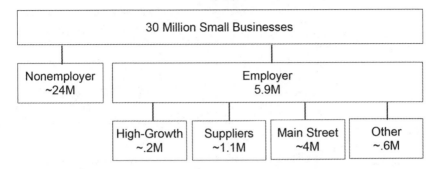

Fig. P.1   Types of small businesses
Source: Mills (2019). Reproduced with permission of Palgrave Macmillan.

to other businesses (B2B) or to the government. Only a small proportion of America's 30 million small businesses—an estimated 200,000—are high-growth startups like Kabbage, generally viewed as the entrepreneurial source of transformative innovation.

The heterogeneity of America's small businesses has led to some confusion and missteps in policy circles regarding the best strategies to promote entrepreneurship and innovation. Many policies that create ideal conditions for large businesses to innovate (such as R&D tax credits) are often less effective for smaller firms. And it has become increasingly evident that small business policies for local Main Street businesses require a different template from actions that support the much smaller number of high-growth innovative firms, such as those that flourish in Silicon Valley and other technology ecosystems. This sliver of high-potential firms requires specially designed, nuanced policies that fuel high-growth entrepreneurship and target innovation (Aulet and Murray 2013).

Policy Playbook for High-Growth Entrepreneurship

In the face of declining startup rates and fears of sinking economic dynamism in the US, both federal and local governments have increased their focus on encouraging entrepreneurship. Some locales have centered their economic development strategies on luring large innovative corporations by offering millions of dollars in tax breaks and other incentives, as seen by Amazon's well publicized and much debated search for a second headquarters (Mills and Rivkin 2018). The hope is that these anchor companies will create an innovation center of gravity and spur other companies to move to or start up in the area. Over the past several decades, state and local governments have pledged significant resources to target these large incumbent firms, with some estimates putting the total amount of incentives at $45 billion annually, tripling in size from 1990 to 2015 (Bartik 2018).

	High-Growth Firms	Main Street Businesses
Access to Capital	• Angel and R&D Tax Credits • Regional VC Support (SBIC) • SBIR/STTR • Scale-Up Capital • Grants/Business Plan Competitions	• Bank Loan Guarantees (SBA) • Fintech/Challenger Banks • Tax Policy
Advice/Education	• Entrepreneurship, education, and mentorship programs • Startup academies	• Small Business Development Centers/SCORE Advisors
Ecosystems	• Accelerators/Incubators • Clusters	• Main Street Associations • Small Business Saturday

Fig. P.2   Policy options to promote different types of entrepreneurship
Source: Examples from authors' analysis.

In recent years, however, this strategy, sometimes called "elephant hunting," has been replaced or supplemented by a series of policies designed to boost innovation and job creation through the direct encouragement of entrepreneurship. These various government policy efforts tend to fall into three main categories: improving access to capital, delivering entrepreneurship advice and education, and creating entrepreneurial ecosystems (see figure P.2). For each category, the policy options differ significantly depending on the type of small business targeted. The majority of efforts to spur innovation are directed at the smaller segment of high-growth firms, which are expected to deliver the most productivity growth.

Access to Capital

Financing is a key determinant of small business growth and success. Entrepreneurs in new and young firms need capital to build their businesses and pay their employees, purchase inventory and startup equipment, and obtain other resources. Depending on the type of small business, access to capital can come from a host of different sources. Traditional Main Street businesses commonly access financing through banks, ranging from large financial institutions—like Bank of America and JPMorgan Chase—to regional banks, community development financial institutions, and community banks. In contrast, high-growth startups seek financing from entirely different capital markets, looking to venture capital and private equity firms for funding.

Venture capital (VC) is structured as high-risk capital that pursues early-stage entrepreneurial opportunities with high potential for dynamic growth and market disruption. The success rate of investments is low for nearly all VC firms, with only one or two out of every ten portfolio companies accounting for the majority of the returns to a particular fund (Kerr, Nanda, and Rhodes-Kropf 2014; Nicholas 2019; Sahlman 2010). Because expertise and relationships are required to access and evaluate VC deals, funding has historically been unevenly distributed, geographically and demographically. In 2020, 85 percent of VC funding in the US went to companies in just three states—California, Massachusetts, and New York (National Venture Capital Association 2019). Similarly, in 2021, only 15.6 percent of venture money went to fund businesses co-founded by women, with an even smaller 2 percent going to businesses founded solely by women (Pitchbook 2019). From 2013 to 2017, only about 23 percent of VC funding went to minority founders (RateMyInvestor 2019). Recently, some VC firms have sought to remedy such disparities and improve their access to this untapped pool of talent and opportunity by funding larger numbers of diverse founders and increasing diversity among their own investors. Other actors, such as academic institutions, private foundations, and pension funds, are also taking steps to increase their investments in women- and minority-owned funds while diversifying their own investment teams.

Several governments have crafted policy initiatives to address market gaps by growing the amount of and points of access to VC. One approach encourages new risk capital formation by stage, such as through angel capital tax credits[1] (Lerner et al. 2015) and R&D tax credits (Becker 2015) in the US and scale-up capital schemes in the United Kingdom.[2] Other policies have focused on geography, such as the SBA's Small Business Investment Company program. This initiative funds over 300 small venture and private equity capital providers in geographies where there is less risk capital available for high-growth firms. Federal set-asides from research budgets fund substantial research and innovation grants to small companies through the Small Business Innovation Research and the Small Business Technology Transfer programs. These activities support new entrepreneurs across multiple industries in their discovery and growth phases. Significant opportunity still exists, however, for additional policies that expand access to risk capital for a larger and more diverse set of investors and entrepreneurs.

1. Section 1202 of the US Internal Revenue Code details an exclusion for both angel investors and entrepreneurs, providing 100 percent of tax-free gains up to $10 million. This angel capital tax credit is designed to incentivize investors to finance promising startups as well as to stimulate entrepreneurship by providing an additional viable source of capital.
2. The UK government provides similar tax credits to promote entrepreneurship and investment, including the Enterprise Investment Scheme and the Seed Enterprise Investment Scheme, both of which seek to incentivize the funding of innovative startups through 30 and 50 percent tax breaks, respectively, and up to a capped amount. In addition, Innovate UK, part of UK Research and Innovation, provides funding to innovative businesses (about 2.5 billion pounds since 2007, matched by industry funding).

Advice and Entrepreneurship Education

The second critical area of support for entrepreneurship is the construction of advising networks that help entrepreneurs navigate the highly uncertain world of starting a business. Entrepreneurship education has come to the fore at numerous universities, business schools, and even high schools and continuing adult education programs. There is an insatiable appetite for counseling and advice, particularly from low-cost or free venues, such as Small Business Development Centers or the SCORE counselor network, both of which are supported by the SBA. The SBA also provides resources to underserved and underrepresented entrepreneurs who may face increased barriers to achieving their business goals, through specially targeted Women's Business Centers and Veterans Business Outreach Centers.

Here again, however, high-growth innovative startups tend to seek counsel via distinct tracks, such as specialized boot camps and startup academies geared toward high-tech and innovation-driven entrepreneurs and teams. Founders of high-growth firms can access tailored advice from VC and private equity partners with intimate knowledge of the particular sector they inhabit. They can also reach out to industry peers and build networks of likeminded entrepreneurs and funders in advance of officially launching their product or service, gaining intangible benefits and lessons in management skills, crisis leadership, and goal setting (Chatterji et al. 2018).

Ecosystems

Entrepreneurs learn from one another, as well as from suppliers, customers, universities, and support organizations in their sector or cluster. Just as in other policy areas, ecosystems conducive to helping innovative high-growth entrepreneurs look quite different from communities designed for businesses on Main Street. For the local mom and pop shops in the town square, Main Street business associations and other types of neighborhood commercial alliances provide a valuable source of business counseling and referrals, and they often serve as conduits to the local and regional governments, with an eye toward the advancement of business owner interests.

For high-growth businesses, innovation ecosystems—clusters, incubators, and accelerators—have gained momentum in recent years. Prior studies show the importance of industry clusters in entrepreneurship and economic performance and growth (Delgado, Porter, and Stern 2010, 2016; Porter 1998; Saxenian 1994). Well-known examples of clusters in the US include information technology in Silicon Valley and biopharmaceuticals and medical devices in Boston. By co-locating with similarly focused companies in a particular field, young firms stand to gain agglomeration benefits and externalities, sharing in the technology, skills, knowledge, and innovations facilitated by both their collaborators and competitors (Chinitz 1961; Delgado, Porter, and Stern 2010; Glaeser and Kerr 2009). Clusters also tend to draw large pools of specialized talent, which is especially important as new innovative service businesses require an increasing number of employees in the fields of science, technology, engineering, and math (Delgado and Mills 2020).

The proven efficacy of industry clusters has not been limited to the traditional coastal cities. For example, strong "fintech" clusters have emerged outside the conventional financial hubs of New York City and San Francisco. Kabbage, highlighted earlier, is headquartered in Atlanta, Georgia, which also serves as home to major American credit reporting agency Equifax, bitcoin payment service BitPay, and international payments giant Global Payments, Inc. The wider Atlanta metropolitan area also boasts a major location for financial systems provider Fiserv and an engineering office for payments processor Square.

Entrepreneurs and early-stage companies also gain significant knowledge and value by participating in mentorship programs designed specifically for high-growth startups. Accelerators and incubators, established by both private and public actors, provide young firms with access to mentorship and potential seed funding to test their business models and refine their innovations. These ecosystems also fuel environments where startups can collaborate with other members of their cohort to gain advice from peers and a broader network of investors and mentors. Research has shown the various beneficial effects of accelerators and incubators on regional entrepreneurship and innovation (Gonzales-Uribe and Leatherbee 2017; Hochberg 2016), leading to many levels of government employing them as tools to promote innovation and economic productivity (e.g., MassChallenge in Boston, LAUNCH accelerator by NASA, USAID, and the Department of State).

Conclusion

Kabbage's journey to success has by no means been a completely smooth ride. Although the long-term effects of COVID-19 and the economic downturn remain to be seen, it is clear that companies like Kabbage are not immune to the shocks created by the pandemic. Soon after the US declared a state of emergency due to coronavirus in mid-March of 2020, Kabbage announced it would furlough a significant number of its employees in America and shut down its Bangalore outpost completely. However, Kabbage reorganized and funneled its resources to help small businesses in a different way, setting up a website where customers could purchase gift cards to support their local businesses. It also repurposed its technology to facilitate loans to small businesses through the Paycheck Protection Program authorized by the CARES Act, ultimately becoming the program's second-largest lender by application volume and approving nearly $7 billion in loans through

August 2020. Kabbage was officially acquired by American Express several months later, in October 2020 (de León 2020; Kabbage Newsroom 2020). As illustrated by the nimble actions of Kabbage and many other financial technology companies responding to the coronavirus pandemic, innovation in times of crisis is a hallmark of entrepreneurship, with benefits that are widely distributed.

*   *   *

America is fortunate to have a strong heritage in both innovation and entrepreneurship. It is part of the national spirit of independence and the belief in economic mobility and the American Dream. Over the past several decades, the US economy has been built on a bedrock of innovations that have dramatically transformed traditional industries, from communications to financial services to Big Tech. However, the preservation of these strengths is far from assured. A relatively small number of high-growth entrepreneurs have been crucial drivers of the nation's innovation and productivity. The continued health of this innovation engine requires supporting a larger and more diverse set of entrepreneurs and investing in targeted ecosystems and policies that close market gaps and give these entrepreneurs the tools they need to grow and prosper.

References

Acemoglu, D., U. Akcigit, H. Alp, N. Bloom, and W. R. Kerr. 2013. "Innovation, Reallocation and Growth." NBER Working Paper No. 18993, revised November 2017. Cambridge, MA: National Bureau of Economic Research.

Almeida, P., and B. Kogut. 1997. "The Exploration of Technological Diversity and the Geographic Localization of Innovation." *Small Business Economics* 9: 21–31.

Aulet, B., and F. Murray. 2013. "A Tale of Two Entrepreneurs: Understanding Differences in the Types of Entrepreneurship in the Economy." Kauffman Foundation Working Paper. Kansas City, MO: Kauffman Foundation.

Bartik, T. J. 2018. "Who Benefits from Economic Development Incentives? How Incentive Effects on Local Incomes and the Income Distribution Vary with Different Assumptions about Incentive Policy and the Local Economy." Upjohn Institute Technical Report No. 18-034. Kalamazoo, MI: Upjohn Institute.

Becker, B. 2015. "Public R&D Policies and Private R&D Investment: A Survey of the Empirical Evidence." *Journal of Economic Surveys* 29(5): 917–42.

Chatterji, A. K. 2018. *The Main Street Fund: Investing in an Entrepreneurial Economy*. Washington, DC: Brookings Institution, The Hamilton Project.

Chatterji, A. K., S. Delecourt, S. Hasan, and R. M. Koning. 2018. "When Does Advice Impact Startup Performance?" NBER Working Paper No. 24789. Cambridge, MA: National Bureau of Economics Research.

Chinitz, B. 1961. "Contrasts in Agglomeration: New York and Pittsburgh." *American Economic Review* 51(2): 279–89.

Decker, R., J. Haltiwanger, R. Jarmin, and J. Miranda. 2014. "The Role of Entrepreneurship in US Job Creation and Economic Dynamism." *Journal of Economic Perspectives* 28(3): 3–24.

de León, R. 2020. "American Express Acquiring Small Business lender Kabbage." CNBC. Accessed January 4, 2021. https://www.cnbc.com/2020/08/17/american -express-acquiring-small-business-lender-kabbage.html.

Delgado, M., and K. G. Mills. 2020. "The Supply Chain Economy: A New Industry Categorization for Understanding Innovation in Services." *Research Policy* 49(8): 104039.

Delgado, M., M. E. Porter, and S. Stern. 2010. "Clusters and Entrepreneurship." *Journal of Economic Geography* 10(4): 495–518.

———. 2016. "Defining Clusters of Related Industries." *Journal of Economic Geography* 16(1): 1–38.

Fritsch, M., and P. Mueller. 2004. "Effects of New Business Formation on Regional Development over Time." *Regional Studies* 38(8): 961–75.

Glaeser, E. L., and W. R. Kerr. 2009. "Local Industrial Conditions and Entrepreneurship: How Much of the Spatial Distribution Can We Explain?" *Journal of Economics & Management Strategy* 18(3): 623–63.

Gonzalez-Uribe, J., and M. Leatherbee 2018. "The Effects of Business Accelerators on Venture Performance: Evidence from Start-Up Chile." *Review of Financial Studies* 31(4): 1566–1603.

Guzman, J., and S. Stern. 2016. "The State of American Entrepreneurship: New Estimates of the Quality and Quantity of Entrepreneurship for 32 US States, 1988–2014." NBER Working Paper No. 22905, revised July 2019. Cambridge, MA: National Bureau of Economic Research.

Haltiwanger, J., R. S. Jarmin, and J. Miranda. 2013. "Who Creates Jobs? Small Versus Large Versus Young." *Review of Economics and Statistics* 95(2): 347–61.

Henrekson, M., and D. Johansson. 2010. "Gazelles as Job Creators: A Survey and Interpretation of the Evidence." *Small Business Economics* 35: 227–44.

Hochberg, Y. V. 2016. "Accelerating Entrepreneurs and Ecosystems: The Seed Accelerator Model." *Innovation Policy and the Economy* 16: 25–51.

Kabbage Newsroom. 2019. "Start Spreading the News: Kabbage Joins American Express." Accessed January 4, 2021. https://newsroom.kabbage.com/news /kabbage-to-join-american-express/.

Kerr, W. R., R. Nanda, and M. Rhodes-Kropf. 2014. "Entrepreneurship as Experimentation." *Journal of Economic Perspectives* 28(3): 25–48.

Lerner, J. 2020. "Government Incentives for Entrepreneurship." Forthcoming in *Innovation and Public Policy*, edited by A. Goolsbee and B. Jones. Chicago: University of Chicago Press.

Lerner, J., A. Schoar, S. Sokolinski, and K. Wilson. 2015. "The Globalization of Angel Investments: Evidence Across Countries." NBER Working Paper No. 21808. Cambridge, MA: National Bureau of Economic Research.

Mills, K. G. 2019. *Fintech, Small Business & the American Dream*. Cham, Switzerland: Palgrave Macmillan.

Mills, K. G., and J. Rivkin. 2018. Amazon's HQ2 (A). Harvard Business School Case 718-494. Revised August 2019. Boston: Harvard Business School.

National Venture Capital Association. 2021. *NVCA 2019 Yearbook*. Washington, DC: National Venture Capital Association.

Nicholas, T. 2019. *VC: An American History*. Cambridge, MA: Harvard University Press.

Pitchbook. 2021. "The VC Female Founders Dashboard." Accessed October 14, 2021. https://pitchbook.com/news/articles/the-vc-female-founders-dashboard.

Porter, M. E. 1998. "Clusters and Competition: New Agendas for Companies, Governments, and Institutions." In *On Competition*, edited by M. E. Porter, 197–299. Boston: Harvard Business School Publishing.

RateMyInvestor, DiversityVC. 2019. "Diversity in U.S. Startups." Accessed May 11, 2020. https://ratemyinvestor.com/DiversityVCReport_Final.pdf.

Sahlman, W. A. 2010. "Risk and Reward in Venture Capital." Background Note 811-036. Boston: Harvard Business School.

Saxenian, A. 1994. *Regional Advantage: Culture and Competition in Silicon Valley and Route 128*. Cambridge, MA: Harvard University Press.

US Small Business Administration Office of Advocacy. 2019. Survival Rates and Firm Age. https://www.sba.gov/sites/default/files/SurvivalRatesAndFirmAge_ADA_0.pdf.

———. 2020. Frequently Asked Questions. https://cdn.advocacy.sba.gov/wp-content/uploads/2020/11/05122043/Small-Business-FAQ-2020.pdf.

Van Praag, M., and P. H. Versloot. 2007. "What Is the Value of Entrepreneurship? A Review of Recent Research." *Small Business Economics* 29: 351–82.

Panel Remarks
Measuring Business Innovation Using a Multidimensional Approach

Lucia Foster

Advancing the US Census Bureau's mission "to serve as the nation's leading provider of quality data about its people and economy" requires a robust and agile research and development (R&D) program working in close collaboration with external experts and Census Bureau programmatic staff. Even straightforward concepts, such as the use of industrial robotics in manufacturing, can require a multidimensional measurement approach. While the Census Bureau is known for its surveys, some of our most innovative work combines survey data with administrative data or combines multiple sources of administrative data.

Here I discuss the multidimensional R&D approach that the Center for Economic Studies (CES) at the Census Bureau takes in attempting to better understand business innovation.[1] Since it is not possible to provide details on these many interrelated efforts, I highlight our multidimensional approach by giving examples of research using administrative data, survey data, and

Lucia Foster is chief of the Center for Economic Studies and chief economist at the US Census Bureau.

Any opinions and conclusions expressed herein are those of the author and do not necessarily represent the views of the US Census Bureau. All results are from existing papers that were reviewed to ensure that no confidential information is disclosed. I thank Emek Basker, John Eltinge, Shawn Klimek, and Nikolas Zolas for helpful comments. For acknowledgments, sources of research support, and disclosure of the author's material financial relationships, if any, please see https://www.nber.org/books-and-chapters/role-innovation-and-entrepreneurship-economic-growth/measuring-business-innovation-using-multi-dimensional-approach.

1. Jarmin (2019) discusses enhancing and improving economic measurement at the Census Bureau.

indirect inference. A more complete view of CES research activities is provided in our annual reports and working paper series.[2]

Context

Census is one of 13 principal statistical agencies in the US. The missions of these other agencies are often complementary to the Census mission and hence one important activity of CES is outreach to other agencies to partner on topics of mutual interest. When the topic is innovation, we often partner with the National Center for Science and Engineering Statistics (NCSES), but we also partner with other federal agencies, state governments, and other institutions (such as universities). Further, we work with individuals, especially academic experts, to help us improve our measures of the US economy and its people. Many of these researchers conduct work through one of the 30 locations in the Federal Statistical Research Data Center (FSRDC) system.[3] Most of the examples given below are based on research conducted with academic experts.

In all this work, we support U.S.C. Title 13, which allows the use of microdata to provide a benefit to the Census Bureau with conditions to protect the confidentiality of our respondents. Operationally, this pledge of confidentiality may constrain the granularity of publicly available information. For research questions that cannot be answered using published data, researchers can apply to use the data through the FSRDC system.

Measuring Business Innovation Using Administrative Data

I start by describing two large R&D projects attempting to measure innovation using administrative data: the Business Dynamics Statistics for Patenting Firms (BDS-PF) and the Innovation Measurement Initiative (IMI). Together they represent the collection and use of administrative data from the federal government, state governments, and universities, and they demonstrate our collaborations with academic researchers.

The Business Dynamics Statistics (BDS) program provides annual information for the US non-farm economy on firm startups and shutdowns, establishment entry and exit, and job creation and destruction. Core data for the BDS come from the Census Bureau's business frame, which relies heavily on federal administrative data.[4] CES has embarked on a multi-year project to enhance the BDS to include a series of indicators enabling us to provide information on business dynamics by firm characteristics, including

---

2. See https://www.census.gov/programs-surveys/ces/research.html.
3. See https://www.census.gov/fsrdc.
4. Researchers at CES developed the Longitudinal Business Database from the business frame (Jarmin and Miranda 2002; Chow et al. 2021), and the BDS is the public product derived from the Longitudinal Business Database.

globalization (exporting, importing, and multinational), human capital (of workers and owners), and innovation (patents, trademarks, R&D expenditures, and other inputs or outcomes of innovative activities). This section focuses on the component of the innovation project identifying firms that patent (BDS-PF).[5]

Multiple research teams have linked patent data to Census business data. An early part of the BDS-PF included a collaboration between the Census Bureau and US Patent and Trademark Office (USPTO). This team improved on the existing linkage (previously done through linking assignee information from patent documents to the business register) by incorporating additional inventor information from the same patent documents linked to the Longitudinal Employer-Household Dynamics (LEHD) data. The LEHD data rely on administrative jobs data from state agencies, federal agencies, and the Quarterly Census of Employment and Wages provided by states (Abowd et al. 2009). The researchers triangulate these two independent sources of information (assignees and inventors) to link granted patents to their firm owners, allowing them to substantially improve match rates over earlier studies (Graham et al. 2018).

The latest research at Census for the BDS-PF focuses on patents related to artificial intelligence (AI) and uses natural language processing and machine learning to conduct this research. While the USPTO classifies the technologies embedded in patents according to preexisting classification systems with hundreds of classes and thousands of subclasses, Alderucci et al. (2019) argue that using these and/or keywords will miss much potential AI use, since AI is becoming a general-purpose technology. Alderucci et al. (2019) train a machine learning algorithm to identify 52,000 AI-related patents (or up to 140,000 patents using a looser definition), which, they note, is about 3 to 10 times the number of AI patents first identified by Cockburn, Henderson, and Stern (2019). The same methodology can potentially be applied across other technology fields.

An entirely different set of metrics comes from the joint IMI, which links Census data to the Institute for Research on Innovation and Science (IRIS) UMETRICS data from universities on federally sponsored research at the project level. The IRIS data include project-level financial transactions, such as payments to internal personnel, payments to outside vendors, and payments to contractors as part of sub-awards. As Lane et al. (2018) note in their overview of the IMI project, the IRIS builds on long-running efforts to demonstrate the innovation flowing from federally funded R&D.

IRIS currently includes over 30 universities with the goal of partnering with 150 universities (IRIS targets every university with at least $100 million in R&D). The data include 392,000 funded awards covering 643,000 research

---

5. Goldschlag and Perlman (2017) provide an overview of the larger project, Business Dynamics of Innovative Firms.

employees, $84 billon in award spending, and $61 billion in vendor and subcontract spending.[6] Dissemination of results from this project currently occurs in three ways: research papers, research datasets for qualified users on approved projects, and two quarterly reports (a vendor report and an employee report) at the campus level for participating universities. Additionally, Census and IRIS are developing other publicly available data products.

Researchers have combined the IMI data with Census datasets to examine such subjects as the gender gaps in science, technology, engineering, and mathematics (STEM) occupations (Buffington et al. 2016), outcomes of PhD recipients (Zolas et al. 2015), and the impact of workers' research experience on new firm outcomes. For the latter, Goldschlag et al. (2021) link the employee data with Census data on startups to look at the link between research experience and young firm outcomes, including survival, growth, and innovation. They find that workers' research experience is correlated with an "up-or-out" firm dynamic (negatively correlated with survival, but conditional on survival, and positively correlated with growth) and with innovative activities (as measured by patent and trademark filings).

Measuring Business Innovation Using Survey Data

To understand technology adoption and diffusion, we turn to survey data. The Annual Business Survey (ABS) is a relatively new survey (starting with reference year 2017) and represents a partnership between Census and NCSES. This firm-level survey covers all sectors of the non-agricultural economy.[7] The ABS 2018 was mailed to about 850,000 firms (about 560,000 firms responded) and includes sections on innovation (16 questions), technology (three questions), and intellectual property (four questions). My focus is on the three questions in the technology section.

These three questions concern the digital share of business activity (digitization), cloud service purchases, and advanced business technologies for reference year 2017. The digitization question asks firms for the extent to which certain information types (such as personnel or financial data) are stored in digital format. Similarly, the cloud services purchases question asks firms about which of their information technology functions in eight different areas (such as servers and data storage) are stored in the cloud. The third question asks directly about the testing or use of nine advanced business technologies (for example, machine learning, natural language processing, and robotics).

The survey results suggest that adoption of digitization is widespread, with the use of cloud computing being less so, and adoption of many of the advanced technologies still in their infancy (Zolas et al. 2020). We find nearly

---

6. For more information, see: https://iris.isr.umich.edu.
7. See also the Business Research and Development and Innovation Survey and the Annual Survey of Entrepreneurs.

70 percent of the firms have adopted some form of digitization (mainly for personnel and financial information), while more than 50 percent of firms report either no cloud purchases or that they are not necessary. Turning to advanced technologies, we find that 2.2 percent of respondents are using machine learning and less than 1 percent are testing its use.

Looking forward, the ABS 2019 has two sections especially relevant for innovation. The "Products and Processes" section has nine questions concerning new or improved goods, services, and business processes. Follow-up questions further distinguish between "new to the business" and "new to the market." The "Technology and Workforce" section has 32 questions about workforce composition and demand, and five advanced technologies (including AI, robotics, and specialized software). Researchers interested in innovation may find the question concerning factors prohibiting technology adoption and utilization in production especially interesting. At the time of this writing, the responses from the 300,000 firms surveyed have been collected and are being processed.

Applying Indirect Inference to Identify Innovative Activities

Given the challenges associated with measuring innovation directly, the last approach relies on indirect inference to identify areas in the economy with innovative activity. Using micro-level data on productivity growth and business entry and exit, Foster et al. (2021) identify patterns in these dynamics that are suggestive of innovative activity. We build on the stages of firm dynamics in response to innovation developed by Gort and Klepper (1982) which we summarize as: innovation leads to a burst of business entry, which is followed by experimentation and adoption, and ultimately a period in which businesses who have successfully responded to the innovation grow while those that have not, shrink and exit.

Foster et al. (2021) apply findings from the literature on the importance of reallocation for aggregate productivity growth to these stages of firm dynamics. Thus, following an innovation, we expect to see business entry, which leads to productivity dispersion as businesses experiment, then rising productivity growth as some businesses become more productive and resources reallocate toward successful businesses. Eventually, productivity dispersion compresses as the sector matures and settles down. Their analysis comparing outcomes of high-tech versus non-high-tech industries suggests that these patterns may be useful guides when looking for industries with innovation.

Conclusion

The Census microdata referenced here are available for qualified researchers on approved projects through the FSRDC system. The CES Working Paper Series and Technical Working Paper series include many papers documenting various Census surveys and research data sets. As these panel remarks have made clear, the Census Bureau leverages its partnership with academic experts to continually improve our measures of our nation's people and economy. Understanding innovation is a critical component in this work, and perhaps these panel remarks will inspire more researchers to utilize the FSRDC network to help us better understand business innovation.

References

Abowd, John M., Bryce E. Stephens, Lars Vilhuber, Fredrik Andersson, Kevin L. McKinney, Marc Roemer, and Simon D. Woodcock. 2009. "The LEHD Infrastructure Files and the Creation of the Quarterly Workforce Indicators." In *Producer Dynamics: New Evidence from Micro Data*, edited by Timothy Dunne, J. Bradford Jensen, and Mark J. Roberts, 149–230. Studies in Income and Wealth Vol. 68. Chicago: University of Chicago Press.

Alderucci, Dean, Lee Branstetter, Eduard Hovy, Andrew Runge, and Nikolas Zolas. 2019. "Quantifying the Impact of AI on Productivity and Labor Demand: Evidence from U.S. Census Microdata." Presented at Poster Session at 2019 NBER Summer Institute on IT and Digitization.

Buffington, Catherine, Benjamin Cerf, Christina Jones, and Bruce Weinberg. 2016. "STEM Training and Early Career Outcomes of Female and Male Graduate Students: Evidence from UMETRICS Data Linked to the 2010 Census." *American Economic Review: Papers and Proceedings* 106: 333–38.

Chow, Melissa, Teresa C. Fort, Christopher Goetz, Nathan Goldschlag, James Lawrence, Elisabeth Ruth Perlman, Martha Stinson, and T. Kirk White. (2021). "Redesigning the Longitudinal Business Database." Working Paper 21-08, Center for Economic Studies, US Census Bureau.

Cockburn, Iain, Rebecca Henderson, and Scott Stern. 2019. "The Impact of Artificial Intelligence on Innovation: An Exploratory Analysis." In *The Economics of Artificial Intelligence: An Agenda*, edited by Ajay Agrawal, Joshua Gans, and Avi Goldfarb, 115–46. Chicago: University of Chicago Press.

Foster, Lucia, Cheryl Grim, John Haltiwanger, and Zoltan Wolf. 2021. "Innovation, Productivity Dispersion, and Productivity Growth." In *Measuring and Accounting for Innovation in the Twenty-First Century*, edited by Carol Corrado, Jonathan Haskel, Javier Miranda, and Daniel Sichel, 103–36. Chicago: University of Chicago Press.

Goldschlag, Nathan, and Elisabeth Perlman. 2017. "Business Dynamics of Innovative Firms." Center for Economic Studies Working Papers 17–72. Washington, DC: US Census Bureau.

Goldschlag, Nathan, Ron Jarmin, Julia Lane, and Nikolas Zolas. 2021. "Research Experience as Human Capital in New Business Outcomes." In *Measuring and Accounting for Innovation in the Twenty-First Century*, edited by Carol Corrado, Jonathan Haskel, Javier Miranda, and Daniel Sichel, 229–54. Chicago: University of Chicago Press.

Gort, Michael, and Steven Klepper. 1982. "Time Paths in the Diffusion of Product Innovations." *Economic Journal* 92(367): 630–53.

Graham, Stuart J., Cheryl Grim, Tariqul Islam, Alan C. Marco, and Javier Miranda.

2018. "Business Dynamics of Innovating Firms: Linking US Patents with Administrative Data on Workers and Firms." *Journal of Economics and Management Strategy* 27(3): 372–402.

Jarmin, Ron S. 2019. "Evolving Measurement for Evolving Economy: Thoughts on 21st Century US Economic Statistics." *Journal of Economic Perspectives* 33(1): 165–84.

Jarmin, Ron, and Javier Miranda. 2002. "The Longitudinal Business Database." Center for Economic Studies, Working Paper 02-17. Washington, DC: US Census Bureau.

Lane, Julia, Jason-Owen Smith, Joseph Staudt, and Bruce Weinberg. 2018. "New Measurement of Innovation." In *Center for Economic Studies and Research Data Centers Research Report: 2017*. Washington, DC: US Census Bureau.

Zolas, Nikolas, Nathan Goldschlag, Ron Jarmin, Paula Stephan, Jason Owen-Smith, Rebecca F. Rosen, Barbara McFadden Allen, Bruce A. Weinberg, and Julia I. Lane. 2015. "Wrapping It Up in a Person: Examining Employment and Earnings Outcomes for Ph.D. Recipients." *Science* 350(6266): 1367–1371.

Zolas, Nikolas, Zachary Kroff, Erik Brynjolfsson, Kristina McElheran, David Beede, Catherine Buffington, Nathan Goldschlag, Lucia Foster, and Emin Dinlersoz. 2020. "Advanced Technologies Adoption and Use by U.S. Firms: Evidence from the Annual Business Survey." Center for Economic Studies Working Paper 20-40, US Census Bureau.

Where Innovation Happens, and Where It Does Not

Benjamin F. Jones

13.1 Introduction

In the US, economic growth rates are remarkably steady. Per capita income has risen at approximately 2 percent per year in real terms since the late nineteenth century (Jones 2016). Innovation—the creation and implementation of new ideas—is typically seen as a primary explanation for this growth (e.g., Mokyr 1990; Romer 1990; Rosenberg 1982; Solow 1956). One measure of innovative effort is research and development (R&D) expenditure, which also appears in aggregate to be a broadly steady activity. For example, aggregate R&D spending in the US has fluctuated between the rather narrow bands of 2.1 percent and 2.8 percent of GDP for the past 60 years, with no apparent trend (National Science Foundation 2020).

This aggregate steadiness, however, masks remarkable underlying sectoral differences and dynamics, where specific industries have experienced extraordinarily different productivity gains and innovation investment. For example, agriculture and manufacturing have seen huge productivity increases, while other areas—such as housing, education, and the energy sector—have seen much less advance and, seemingly, much less innovative

Benjamin F. Jones is the Gordon and Llura Gund Family Professor of Entrepreneurship, a Professor of Strategy, and the faculty director of the Kellogg Innovation and Entrepreneurship Initiative at Northwestern University, and a research associate of the National Bureau of Economic Research.

I thank the conference organizers for helpful comments and gratefully acknowledge support from the AFOSR Minerva award FA9550-19-1-0354. All errors are my own. For acknowledgments, sources of research support, and disclosure of the author's material financial relationships, if any, please see https://www.nber.org/books-and-chapters/role-innovation-and-entrepreneurship-economic-growth/where-innovation-happens-and-where-it-does-not.

effort. Overall, we witness enormous, transformative advances in some sectors of the economy. In others, not so much.

These underlying differences raise fundamental questions. First, why would innovative effort differ so greatly across industries? Second, if the innovation engine operates weakly in some sectors, is this outcome inevitable? Third, what are the implications of these differences for meeting ongoing challenges? For example, as the US economy appears to be caught in an aggregate productivity slowdown, what roles and opportunities can individual sectors play in overcoming this challenge?

This chapter addresses these questions. The discussion integrates across the sector-specific analyses that constitute this book and provide rich and diverse perspectives. The goal here is a synthesis that, while necessarily incomplete and often speculative, provides a framework for thinking about the enormous diversity in innovative effort and productivity gains that we see.

Section 13.2 of this chapter outlines the enormous sectoral differences in innovation, with an emphasis on the sectors examined in this volume. Sections 13.3–13.5 then consider potential explanations for this variation. The analysis is organized around a simple framework for considering the incentives to innovate. Namely, an agent considering an investment in innovation is making some assessment of its value, and effort at innovation should naturally increase when the expected return on an innovation investment is higher. The question then is: Why is the expected return to innovation higher in some industries and lower in others?

The synthesis offered here emphasizes three features that determine the return on innovation investment and that vary across industries. First is demand. Demand incorporates market scale, willingness to pay for a given innovation, and buyer uncertainty. Demand features are the subject of section 13.3. Second is supply. "Supply" here means the fixed costs of creating a productivity-enhancing advance, as well as the ongoing costs of producing, marketing, and distributing this advance. Supply features are the subject of section 13.4. Third is institutions. Institutions here include the standard tools of innovation policy (e.g., patents and public R&D funding) as well as sector-specific regulatory environments and market structure. Institutions are the subject of section 13.5. To the extent possible, this chapter will use this demand-supply-institutions framework to understand the varying efforts at innovation across sectors and the various outcomes that result.

Overall, the picture that develops is multifaceted. The potential explanations for sectoral variation are not easily reduced to a small set, with different sectors often suggesting somewhat different opportunities and challenges. At the same time, an important and relatively contained set of features appear relatively elastic to policy. While fundamental demand and supply features can be rooted deeply in preferences and technological possibilities, institutional features are often, in principle, more malleable. Section 13.5

thus further considers opportunities—through institutions and policy—to accelerate innovation in lagging sectors, such as education, health services, and energy, with applications to diverse challenges, including the productivity slowdown and climate change.

13.2   Industry Variation in Innovation

Innovation differences across industries can be measured through both inputs and outputs. On the input side, a standard approach measures R&D expenditure. One might also look at new venture investment. On the output side, one might look at intellectual property outcomes (i.e., new patents, copyrights, and trademarks), the introduction of new goods and services, productivity growth, market value, or, in a more equilibrium context, market shares. All these approaches have limitations, and one consequently has to keep caveats in mind when studying these data.[1] That said, substantial evidence links these measures in natural ways, and they can paint fairly coherent pictures.[2]

Table 13.1 presents R&D expenditure for various sectors discussed in this volume. The root data source is the National Science Foundation's Business Research and Development and Innovation Survey (BRDIS). BRDIS is a firm-level survey that includes information on R&D and sales, with results reported by industry NAICS code. BRDIS is linked to US Census establishment data and aims to produce a relatively comprehensive picture of R&D for the US and its businesses.

An advantage of BRDIS is that it includes the firms' worldwide sales, which may be more useful than domestic sales or output for thinking about firms' R&D decisions. However, an important caveat with the BRDIS data is that it only includes the sales of firms that report positive R&D expenditures. That is, the survey omits firms that report no R&D. This can make R&D per unit of output look high in a sector, when in fact it is cloistered in a few firms and overall R&D as a share of industry output is very low. R&D-to-sales ratios in the BRDIS data can then lead to odd results, especially for service industries, where most firms report no R&D.[3] For service sectors, table 13.1

1. For example, innovative effort may not be credited explicitly as R&D (e.g., Brouwer and Kleinknecht 1997), patents may apply to a relatively narrow class of product innovations, and total factor productivity measures require production function and input measurement assumptions that are susceptible to error (e.g., Collard-Wexler and De Loecker 2016; B. Jones 2014).

2. For example, firm-level R&D expenditure and patent production are closely linked to the firm's market value and broader productivity gains (e.g., Hall, Jaffe, and Trajtenberg 2005; Hall, Mairesse, and Mohen 2010; Kogan et al. 2017).

3. For example, looking at "real estate and rental leasing" (NAICS code 53), one finds that R&D expenditures amount to 8.84 percent of worldwide sales in BRDIS. This result may seem surprising, as this sector does not obviously appear very engaged in R&D. Digging deeper, one finds that the worldwide sales of these firms is only $5 billion in BRDIS, whereas the US Census's Service Annual Survey (SAS) indicates total sales of $633 billion for employer-firms

Table 13.1   **Variation in R&D intensity: Examples**

Chapter	Industry	NAICS	R&D ($ billions)	Sales ($ billions)	R&D/sales (percent)
Manufacturing (1)	Manufacturing	31–33	306.6	7,484	4.08
Information Technology (2, 7)	Information	51	86.0	1,498[c]	5.74
	Computer and electronic products	334	90.9	1,267	7.18
Energy (3)	Mining, extraction, and support activities	21	3.5	487	0.72
	Utilities	22	0.3	570[c]	0.06
	Engines, turbines, and power transmission equipment	3336	2.3	52	4.40
Agriculture (4)	Agriculture[a]	—	5.6	214	2.63
Education (8)	Education[b]	—	—	—	0.20
Housing (10)	Real estate and rental and leasing	53	0.5	633[c]	0.08
Health care (11)	Health services	621–623	1.0	2,254[c]	0.04
	Pharmaceuticals and medicines	3254	99.3	767	12.94
Transportation (12)	Transportation and warehousing	48–49	0.5	876[c]	0.06
	Automobiles, bodies, trailers, and parts	3361–63	28.2	1,134	2.49
	Aircraft, aircraft engines, and aircraft parts	336411–13	14.1	394	3.58

Notes: R&D expenditure is primarily taken from the Business R&D and Innovation Survey (BRDIS). This R&D is worldwide R&D performed or funded by US private sector companies with at least 5 employees. Worldwide sales are primarily taken from BRDIS. The data year is 2016. Exceptions as noted are (a) agriculture, where data is taken from Alston and Pardey (this volume); (b) education, where the data are from the President's Council of Advisors on Science and Technology (2010): and (c) service industries, where R&D expenditure is still taken from BRDIS but sales are taken from the US Census's Service Annual Survey (2016).

thus replaces sales from BRDIS with the relevant industry-wide sales from the US Census's Service Annual Survey.

The picture of R&D that emerges in table 13.1 is one of enormous variance. Manufacturing sectors typically show large R&D expenditure rates. This is true for manufacturing overall, where the R&D-to-sales ratio is over 4 percent and appears in several subcategories of manufacturing relevant to the chapters in this book, including "computers and electronic products"; "pharmaceuticals and medicines"; "engines, turbines, and power transmission equipment; "automobiles, bodies, trailers, and parts"; and "aircraft, aircraft engines, and aircraft parts." Service industries, by contrast, show much less R&D. The exception is information services, which show an R&D rate (7.18 percent) exceeding that in almost all the manufacturing sectors. The broader story for services is one of very little R&D, with R&D-to-sales ratios often less than 0.1 percent.

It is further notable that the manufacturing versus services distinction tends to operate within related clusters of activity. For example, consider health. We see virtually no recorded R&D in health services, which incorporates ambulatory health care services (NAICS code 621), hospitals (NAICS code 622), and nursing and residential care facilities (NAICS code 623), where the R&D-to-sales ratio overall is 0.04 percent. Yet there is enormous R&D in pharmaceutical and medicines, where R&D rates per dollar of sales are 320 times larger. Similar stories appear for transportation, where transportation and warehousing services exhibit very low reported R&D, whereas relevant transportation manufacturing, including both automobiles and aircraft manufacturing, show R&D-to-sales ratios that are 42 and 60 times greater, respectively. Industries related to the energy sector are once again similar. Utilities show virtually no R&D per unit of sales (0.06 percent), mining and extraction show R&D rates 12 times higher, and relevant energy production machinery shows R&D rates 6 times higher than that.

The remaining sectors displayed in table 13.1 are agriculture, education, and housing. Agriculture presents relatively substantial private R&D-to-sales ratios and is more in line with manufacturing. The agriculture numbers include agricultural machinery as well as chemical and biological R&D investment and are taken from Alston and Pardey (chapter 3, this volume).[4]

---

in this NAICS code. Normalizing the measured R&D expenditure by total sales for this sector reduces R&D expenditure to 0.08 percent of output. The housing analysis by Kung (chapter 11, this volume) makes a similar correction. Another sector where this correction makes a large difference is "health services" (NAICS codes 621–623), where BRDIS shows worldwide sales of R&D-performing firms of $81 billion, while SAS shows that total revenues for all employer firms in this industry are $2.254 trillion. In some service sectors, such as "information" (NAICS code 51), firms typically perform R&D, and the difference in sales between BRDIS ($1.329 trillion) and the SAS ($1.498 trillion) is modest.

4. These numbers do not include public R&D, which is substantial in agriculture and suggests more intensive R&D investment; see Alston and Pardey (chapter 3, this volume) for broader measures.

By contrast, housing services show very little R&D, in line with typical service sectors. Finally, education, while hard to measure, also appears to have very low rates of R&D, even including public R&D (Chatterji and Jones 2012).

Due to data limitations, table 13.1 does not include three areas analyzed in this volume: retail services, creative arts, and the US federal government. But drawing on the relevant book chapters, additional comments on innovation variation are possible. First, Lafontaine and Sivadasan (chapter 6, this volume) show that the retail sales remain dominated by traditional brick and mortar outlets, with e-commerce in 2017 capturing only 7 percent of retail sales and big-box retail (warehouse clubs and supercenters) capturing only 8 percent. Retail services may thus look like other services, with a small number of R&D-intense firms (e.g., in e-commerce) amid a much broader industrial footprint featuring relatively little R&D effort (traditional brick and mortar retail). Second, while the creation of books, music, and movies are not included in BRDIS, Waldfogel (chapter 8, this volume) shows that these industries exhibit increasing innovative effort, measured as a rapidly increasing labor force of creative workers, and expanding production of new material. These creative arts appear to reflect the broader information technology (IT)-enabled booms in many sectors, where production and distribution costs have dramatically fallen amid IT advances and have encouraged entry, as discussed further below. Third, Bruce and Figueiredo (chapter 9, this volume) demonstrate the large scale of intramural research activity in the US government. While government entities are not covered in BRDIS, it is clear that substantial R&D is proceeding in many executive branch agencies, which all told employ over 60,000 R&D-focused scientists. Intramural R&D expenditure (which totals over $30 billion per year or over 2.3 percent of total federal discretionary spending) suggests that US government agencies, including the Department of Defense, Health and Human Services, US Department of Agriculture, and NASA, invest relatively heavily in pushing the frontiers of science and technology.

In terms of overall outcomes, looking to the economy as a whole, one can consider patterns of structural change. Figure 13.1a presents a standard picture, showing how the GDP shares of agriculture and manufacturing have declined dramatically while that for services has risen. A natural interpretation follows Baumol's cost disease (Baumol 1993), where a declining sectoral share is consistent with rapid relative progress of productivity in that sector. For example, relatively rapid advances in manufacturing productivity are associated with declining manufacturing GDP shares not only in the US but also in more global contexts (e.g., Bergoing et al. 2004; Pilat et al. 2006). Conceptually, if demand curves are sufficiently downward sloping, then rapidly advancing productivity in a sector causes its prices to fall sharply as supply shifts outward, and the sector's GDP share declines even as quantity rises. The converse implication is that the lagging sectors will see their GDP shares increase. One could then interpret figure 13.1a as indicating relatively

A. Manufacturing, Agriculture, and Other Private Industries

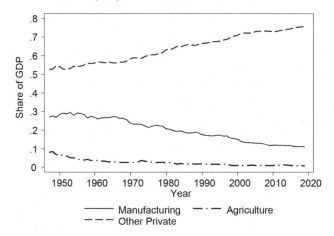

B. Health, Education, and Finance, Insurance, and Real Estate

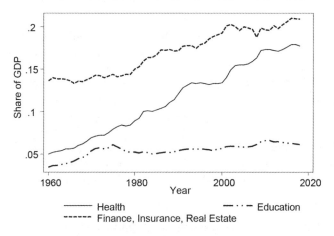

Fig. 13.1   The evolution of sectoral GDP shares

rapid productivity advances in agriculture and manufacturing, leaving the economy stuck with a greater share of activity and resources devoted to the sectors we are not very good at—here, services.

Figure 13.1b extends the services picture. We examine three large sectors that are primarily based on services: health; education; and finance, insurance, and real estate. These sectors represent substantial and increasing shares of the overall economy. These sectors are also areas that appear to see little overall R&D, as shown in table 13.1.[5]

---

5. Note that the Bureau of Economic Analysis's industry-level value-added output series does not match perfectly with the specific NAICS-level organization of R&D expenditures

Overall, we see huge variation in R&D expenditures across sectors. While innovation effort is imperfectly measured by R&D expenditure, outcomes seem to follow related equilibrium output patterns. Service sectors, such as health services and education, see very little measured R&D effort and rising output shares. Manufacturing and agriculture see much larger measured R&D effort and declining output shares.

One can of course track inventive outcomes and productivity gains at more micro levels, but for the purposes of this chapter, the perspective of aggregate output share is useful. In particular, the important equilibrium idea here is that a rising GDP share can be symptomatic of low rates of progress. Moreover, since the overall economy is increasingly made up of the lagging sectors, it suggests that overall progress might slow down if progress in these lagging sectors remains slow. This issue substantially raises the stakes in understanding, and potentially overcoming, the forces that limit innovation in these sectors. The rest of this chapter considers reasons that innovation may proceed faster in some sectors and more slowly in others.

13.3 Demand

The proverb "necessity is the mother of invention" suggests a central role of demand in driving technological advance. That human wants and needs may guide innovative effort is natural, and there is good evidence in the literature that innovation responds to demand. For example, natural experiments regarding pharmaceuticals and vaccines show that expanding demand does indeed drive more innovative activity (e.g., Acemoglu and Linn 2004; Finkelstein 2004). This section uses this lens to consider variation across sectors, drawing on sectoral examples from the book. As we will see, demand-side considerations seem important yet insufficient for understanding the different innovation experiences of different industries.

13.3.1 Scale and Price

From a microeconomic perspective, straightforward logics connect innovative investment to demand. If it is possible for the innovator to appropriate the value of the innovation (e.g., through advantageous market structure or a patent), then the value of such an innovation should be increasing in both the willingness to pay per customer and customer scale, so that more demand will attract more innovative effort. Further, if there is a fixed cost to the creation of the idea, then the innovative process naturally faces increasing returns to scale, again suggesting a key role of demand. These demand-side logics are often explicit in venture capital funding, where the "total addressable market" is a prominent consideration for investment.

---

in BRDIS, so figure 13.1 uses related but somewhat distinct industrial categorizations as in table 13.1.

At a macro level, one may also expect the scale of demand to play a central role. For example, consider endogenous growth models where innovation is getting harder with time (e.g., B. Jones 2009; C. Jones 1995; Kortum 1997), meaning that more people are required to produce a given percentage productivity advance. In this context, rising demand is essential to maintain innovation investment, because while innovation costs are increasing, the value of a given success also increases as the overall market expands. This demand-side expansion maintains incentives to invest in R&D and sustains steady-state growth.

Multiple chapters in this volume speak to these logics. For example, Fuchs et al. (chapter 1, this volume) explore US manufacturing and suggest the importance of scale. A main finding is that US manufacturing firms produce a substantial share of value added outside the US, so that globalization appears to extend the market size for an innovation. With R&D returns substantially realized abroad, this scale logic provides some explanation for high (and sustained) R&D expenditure by US manufacturing firms. Popp et al. (chapter 4, this volume) study the energy sector and suggest the key role of price. Namely, R&D investment in clean energy technologies rises when energy prices are high and falls when they are low. As substitutes for other energy production technologies, a high willingness to pay can then explain clean energy investment, both historically and today.

Further examples come from pharmaceutical R&D. Challenges in drug development for niche diseases, for which there are few consumers, suggest the importance of scale and the need for policy interventions (Drummond et al. 2007). Separately, biomedical firms invest relatively little in diseases like malaria that largely affect lower-income consumers, who have less capacity to pay (Kremer and Glennerster 2004). These demand-side problems further point to the importance of demand-side policy interventions, such as advanced purchase commitments, to pull forth innovations (Kremer 2000).

These examples suggest that one might understand innovative effort in substantial part by considering how scale and willingness to pay affect the market value of an innovation. However, it is also clear when looking at table 13.1 that there are sectors with seemingly enormous demand that see extremely little innovation. For example, all individuals in the US economy experience education and health services, and often spend substantial sums for these services, yet there are appears to be very little innovative effort in these sectors. This suggests that simple price and quantity signals paint a limited picture.

13.3.2   Uncertainty and Salience

A perhaps less obvious but potentially central issue on the demand side concerns consumer uncertainty about the utility of an innovation. That is, consumers may have difficulty assessing whether an innovation is actually worth buying, and this uncertainty may be a fairly fundamental feature of the product or service. If consumers are unable to easily evaluate the good, then reaching the market, even if it is large, may be challenging, lowering the return to innovative effort.

Education services provide a potentially useful example along these lines. While the scales of primary, secondary, and tertiary education are all huge, and costs per student are large, it is often difficult to say what is "better" in this space. The measurement issue is partly one of duration, where important life outcomes from a given educational approach are determined over a long horizon. Proving that any newly innovated approach is better is very difficult in a short period of time. The measurement issue is also one of complex goals and unsettled trade-offs, where the objectives of education are multidimensional and subject to debate. For example, an innovation that improves mathematics scores may be helpful on some dimensions, but what happens if it crowds out historical knowledge, or creativity? If families, as well as teachers and school officials, are unclear about how to assess the benefits from an innovation, selling innovations becomes hard. And if selling such innovations is hard, it may not be surprising that little such innovation investment occurs (Chatterji and Jones 2012). Furthermore, in making choices amid opaque evidence, school systems may end up investing in new technology that may not improve learning. Investment in the "shiny new object" (e.g., computer tablets) may then present a community with a veneer of innovation, while schools fail to create or adopt provably effective pedagogical advances.

Health services appear to face some similar difficulties. It is often difficult to know that a given approach is better in terms of patient outcomes. Patients may recover despite bad care or, conversely, have adverse outcomes despite high-quality care. This noise muddles assessment. Patient selection issues also undermine measurability; for example, attempts at doctor and hospital scorecards are bedeviled by selection issues in the populations served (Dranove et al. 2003). Furthermore, there are difficult balancing issues (somewhat akin to education) across complex endpoints, where success against the diagnosed disease must be weighed against side effects and other quality of life issues.

One sector where we do see enormous innovative effort in health is in pharmaceuticals and medicines. In this case, an explicit (and onerous) process of approval exists through the US Food and Drug Administration (FDA) and similar agencies elsewhere in the world. Side effects are explicitly assessed, and randomized controlled trials are used to prove that an innovative medicine advances the standard of care. Thus, we see that high levels of certainty can be created even where it is hard, and that R&D effort can be enormous when this provability element is created. The FDA example further suggests the importance of institutions in promoting innovation in light of buyer uncertainty, which we return to below.

Coming back to manufactured goods, the qualities of these goods, in contrast to education and health services, may be highly salient. For example, an internal combustion engine, microprocessor, or chemical process that produces the same output but at lower cost will presumably be adopted, as the buyer's self-interest and market forces push in this direction. While quality may not fully be obvious with some manufacturing goods (e.g., the durability of new capital equipment), the uncertainties do seem much more limited compared to things like educational services or hospital services.

Altogether, demand-side considerations—scale, price, and uncertainty—appear to be useful and even powerful ways to think about sectoral variation in innovation. Yet, looking at table 13.1, it is not obvious that these features are anywhere near enough to understand the variation in innovation across sectors. Namely, many sectors account for large amounts of GDP and see extremely little innovation, including sectors like transportation and warehousing services, and real estate, where scale is large, and an uncertainty story does not seem germane. This observation suggests that technological and institutional features may critically important, as we turn to next.

13.4 Supply

The cost side of innovation and associated technological opportunity provide an additional lens for viewing innovation effort (e.g., Jaffe 1986; Scherer 1965). Similar technologies may suggest similar cost-side features, which in turn may push toward broadly similar innovation returns and investment. This cost-side similarity can, in turn, map into sectoral innovation tendencies, if industry classification schemes group sectors in ways that suggest technological affinities. For example, manufacturing processes may in general involve relatively common physical and engineering principles and hence similar technological opportunities, even though the products themselves (e.g., processed foods, printed books, building materials, and aircraft engines) have relatively unrelated sources of demand. Then the observation that manufacturing sectors typically see very high R&D rates and productivity gains may be a statement about common (low) innovation costs as opposed to common (high) demand. In this section, we examine various cost and technology features.

13.4.1 Cost Features

To further articulate costs, we can write the expected present value V of an innovation as

$$V = \Pi(c,s) - F$$

where F is the fixed cost of creating a new product or process, and $\Pi(c,s)$ is the net present value of profits from this innovation once it is created. Other things being equal, the expected value (V) is declining in the fixed cost (F), the per-unit production costs (c) of the new product or service, and the per-unit sales cost (s), which includes sales, marketing, and distribution costs for the new product or service. By this logic, innovation will be relatively high when the cost parameters F, c, and s are relatively low.

An example suggesting the relevance of this cost perspective is the creative arts, where we have witnessed an explosion of movies, television programs, online videos, music production, and new books. As Joel Waldfogel argues (chapter 8, this volume; Waldfogel 2018), this explosion in innovation follows from technological changes in the cost of creating (F), duplicating (c), and distributing (s) new works. For example, musicians today can record at home using sophisticated and inexpensive software. The music can then be duplicated digitally at essentially zero marginal cost and published instantaneously at close to zero cost to followers online. As such costs have declined, it is not surprising that we have witnessed a huge expansion of these creative outputs. Similar cost features appear among other digital products, including in mobile application development, where the Android ecosystem adds over 30,000 new apps in a typical month,[6] further suggesting that innovation effort will be large when the relevant innovation costs are low.

By contrast, consider the energy production sector (Popp et al., chapter 4, this volume). Here innovation costs tend to be high. At one extreme, nuclear fusion has seemingly vast demand-side potential but innovation requires enormous fixed costs for experimentation. In practice, we see relatively few independent innovative efforts in fusion technologies, and these efforts are supported by the public sector. Compared to nuclear power innovations, clean energy technologies like wind and solar power generation see relatively lower innovation costs and have meanwhile seen more rapid technological and market progress.

Uncertainty is also germane (e.g., Arrow 1962; Kerr, Nanda, and Rhodes-Kropf 2014). Beyond the demand-side considerations of consumer uncertainty discussed above, a basic form of uncertainty is that the technological approach will fail, either because the technology doesn't work or, more generally, is not cost effective. Investment portfolio strategies may overcome individual project risk, but this will be difficult for resource-constrained agents when the fixed cost of each innovation bet is high. This feature may suggest why venture capital investment and startup activity in energy technologies has traditionally been relatively low (e.g., Ghosh and Nanda 2010). By contrast, sectors that feature low innovation costs (whether music or mobile apps) may see substantially more innovation attempts and more resulting innovation. Interestingly, Popp et al. (chapter 4, this volume) show that while clean energy patenting and startup activity has been plummeting since 2010, activity is steady or increasing for smaller and more modular energy technologies, which may have cost advantages along these lines.

6. For Android metrics, see https://www.appbrain.com/stats/number-of-android-apps.

13.4.2   Scale and Scalability

Sectors vary in the fixed costs of creating a useful invention. But the costs of producing and distributing the new product or service—the "scalability" of the innovation—may be at least as important. Other things being equal, when the scalability of the product is high, the investment becomes more attractive. These scalability costs often seem essential for understanding innovative effort.[7]

Digitization, and the massive innovation investments therein, seems to hinge significantly on this low-cost scalability. While the fixed costs of developing a new digital product may be high or low—compare enterprise software with a simple mobile application—a common feature of digital products is that they can be duplicated and distributed at very low cost. Returning to services, "information services" see R&D rates that exceed the average in manufacturing (see table 13.1). Information services are a striking outlier among service sectors, and with its expanding set of uses, computing and information approaches are often recognized as a "general purpose technology." At root, closely related technological methods—with common types of (low) scalability costs—are being applied to an ever-expanding range of demands. This phenomenon appears throughout this volume.

Consider, for example, the entrance of digital innovations into housing and transportation services, where measured innovation rates have historically been extremely low (see table 13.1). Kung (chapter 11, this volume) examines the housing sector, including new technology businesses that facilitate real estate transactions (e.g., Redfin, Trulia, and Zillow) and homestays (e.g., Airbnb and HomeAway). These scalable digital platforms connect buyers and sellers, providing key information—locations, reviews, histories, and photographs—to reduce search costs and limit uncertainty. These businesses, which have received substantial venture capital backing, have achieved scalability in dimensions of the real estate and housing sectors that heretofore have been fractured. Interestingly, while real estate R&D is measured to be only 0.08 percent of sales (table 13.1), looking narrowly at the firms in this sector that actually perform R&D in the BRDIS survey, the R&D share of sales rises to 8.84 percent. This looks like a lot like information services in general. It suggests how, when new technology allows for scalability, R&D investment and disruptive business models can enter formerly less-innovative sectors.

Turning to transportation services, we see a similar phenomenon. Choe, Oettl, and Seamans (chapter 5, this volume) discuss the rise of ridesharing as well as efforts to develop autonomous vehicles in the broader context of the transportation sector. Like housing services, transportation and warehous-

7. Business and new venture language is often oriented along these forces, where attractive "unit economics" equates to low costs of producing additional instances of the good or service and attractive "customer acquisition costs" equates to low costs of reaching buyers.

ing services see very low R&D shares of sales (0.06 percent in table 13.1). Yet again like housing services, transportation has recently seen the advent of disruptive, venture-backed business models (e.g., Uber and Lyft) building on digital platforms. While autonomous vehicles are a prominent area of innovative effort, venture capital is also targeting logistics and warehousing, with many bets on IT-enabled approaches.

Finally, Delgado, Kim, and Mills (chapter 7, this volume) explore the "servicification" of the US economy, investigating elements of the transition from manufacturing to services. Abetted by digitization, innovation and the STEM workforce are increasingly located in business-to-business services. This process can be seen in established firms, for example, in the rise of cloud computing services for companies like IBM. More generally, Delgado, Kim, and Mills study 2,000 large incumbent manufacturing firms and see a marked increase in the employment of these firms toward business-to-business service activities.

13.4.3   Nature's Opportunities and Constraints

In tackling the cost side of innovation and its capacity to explain difference across sectors, a fundamental aspect may be the varying technological opportunities that nature provides. For example, digitization and its expanding role are greatly facilitated by Moore's Law, yet gains in engine efficiency are held back by the Carnot maximum.[8] Viewed in terms of the fixed cost of invention, R&D investments in microprocessors can repeatedly produce large percentage gains in performance, while R&D investments in a new engine design, no matter how large, cannot achieve such substantial gains.

To the extent that technological opportunities vary, observers may be tempted to focus on fields and industries where progress has been profound. Looking back through time, sectors where productivity has advanced rapidly have driven economic growth, sectoral dynamics, and social change. Yet this backward-looking perspective is incomplete. For example, rapid computing advances must increasingly be viewed in the context of an apparent productivity slowdown at the aggregate level. Looking forward (and returning to Baumol's cost disease), the harder things take on increasing importance. That is, GDP and future progress depend less and less on the sectors we have found relatively easy to advance (like agriculture, manufacturing, or now digital technologies), and increasingly on the sectors that continue to be hard, which make up a growing share of the economy. Nature's constraints may then ultimately be more important than nature's bounty, and the difficult problems—in energy, transportation, construction, health services, education, and government services—only come to matter more.

---

8. While Moore's Law is partly endogenous to demand and institutions, it also relies on fundamental technological opportunities among computing technologies.

13.5   Institutions

If innovation rates come down to fundamental and largely immutable demand and supply features, then altering the progress of different sectors would be largely out of our hands. However, a substantial part of demand and supply side features may depend not only on basic human preferences and natural laws but also on institutions and policies. This section draws out several institutional roles, with two objectives. First, institutions can help further explain sectoral variation in innovation. Second, institutions can provide explicit mechanisms to advance sectors in which needs may be great but innovation lags.

The institutional parts of the innovation system are manifold: They include intellectual property, R&D tax credits, basic research institutions (e.g., the National Institutes of Health [NIH]), and antitrust policy, among others. While surveying this entire landscape is beyond the scope of this chapter, several institutional features may help explain sectoral variation and are be emphasized here. These include the role of institutions in influencing innovation incentives, advancing basic research, and achieving scalability.

13.5.1   Institutions and Appropriability

A basic issue in innovation incentives is appropriability, which governs the capacity of the innovator to capture a significant share of the innovation's value. In general, appropriability will be low if others can successfully enter and compete using the new idea. The imitator(s) will have a cost advantage over the initial innovator by not having paid the fixed cost of creating the new product or service. With competitive entry reducing post-innovation profits, the initial innovator will see lower returns on the investment and may even face a net loss. Thus, even if the social value of innovations is high, we may expect little innovation if appropriability is low.

Appropriability naturally depends on institutional and market structure features. Consider first intellectual property institutions. Returning to sectoral variation (see table 13.1), one might imagine that patentability could be an important part of the story. New manufacturing products, as tangible goods, seem especially amenable to receiving patent protection, while service industries and various kinds of business model and service innovations seem less so. And trade secrets may provide effective protection for goods with complex manufacturing processes yet do little for service innovations. Low R&D in service industries could then in part be a symptom of weak appropriability in the intellectual property dimension.

Patenting is a complex institution with many trade-offs—for example, between upstream and downstream innovation (e.g., Sampat and Williams 2019; Scotchmer 1991), and its importance for appropriability appears to be mixed and sector dependent (e.g., Levin et al. 1987). But patenting seems to be essential for understanding innovation in some sectors. For example, pharmaceutical innovation typically features very high fixed R&D costs, and recouping these costs would be difficult without patent protection (Mansfield 1986). Separately from patents, trade secrets are important means of appropriability in many manufacturing industries (Cohen, Nelson, and Walsh 2000). Overall, to the extent that patents and trade secrets fit better with manufacturing industries, it is an interesting and open question whether service sector innovation lags in part due to reduced access to these intellectual property institutions.[9]

Separate from intellectual property, market structure can influence appropriability. The relationship between market power and innovation is a deep research topic with diverse theoretical and empirical results (e.g., Arrow 1962; Cohen 2010; Gilbert and Newbery 1982; Schumpeter 1942). The net implications of market structure can be difficult to elucidate generally and appear to be nonlinear (e.g., Aghion et al. 2005). Moreover, many theoretical results frame market power in terms of single-product firms, which may not fit well with actual business structures in many industries. All this suggests that, when seeking to explain cross-industry variation in innovation, market power reasoning may not provide an obvious or simple perspective. At the same time, different sectors have distinct technological and institutional features related to market power that seem relevant to the variation we see.

As one force, market power over a complementary asset may allow a firm to capture value from innovative effort (Teece 1986). One might then expect more innovation from incumbents in sectors where businesses can create market power through complementary assets. For example, for pharmaceutical firms, advantages in regulatory compliance (through FDA trials) and dominant sales networks (to health providers) can be seen as complementary assets that assist value capture, which may further help explain high R&D investment by incumbents—and why entrants tend to sell themselves to the incumbents (e.g., Gans and Stern 2003). In IT, network externalities can lead to dominant firms with substantial market shares and market power. A tendency toward winner-take-all competition for digital platforms may help explain the high level of venture capital devoted to IT businesses (i.e., because winning most of the market is actually possible, and the value of success becomes so high) and also encourage ongoing R&D among the winners (i.e., controlling the winning platform allows ongoing value capture). However, an incumbent's dominance of a necessary complementary input may dissuade entry by others, potentially resulting in less innovation and dynamism in the sector.[10] The sector-wide effect is ultimately unclear. What

9. See also Moser (2005) for historical evidence that the availability of distinct intellectual property forms affects the direction of innovation.

10. The bargaining power advantage of the incumbent firm (with the complementary asset) may dissuade entry. However, in a repeated game, reputational considerations may drive the incumbent firm to avoid taking advantage of any specific entrant, because the incumbent firm benefits by acquiring innovations that are complementary to its business and thus wants to encourage entry. So it is not obvious that innovative entry is discouraged. The broad scale of entry by biotechnology firms and IT firms, and the large scale of acquisitions in these sectors,

is clearer is that certain highly innovative sectors, like pharmaceuticals and IT, feature incumbent firms with dominant complementary assets. Whether variation in innovation efforts across industries can be explained along these lines is an interesting and open research question.

High fixed costs of entry, which support oligopolistic market structure, may also be germane for understanding the locus of innovation effort, including in vertical supply chains. For example, airframes (e.g., Boeing and Airbus) and jet engines (e.g., General Electric, Pratt & Whitney, and Rolls Royce) are industries with large barriers to entry, very few players, and the resulting profitability to support high R&D investment. By contrast, downstream air transportation companies (airlines, air cargo) are more competitive and appear to have less resources to invest in R&D. In automobile transportation (see Choe, Oettl, and Seamans, chapter 5, this volume), note that the advent of ridesharing follows from R&D-intensive upstream oligopolistic players (e.g., Uber and Lyft). Similarly, while farms are extremely competitive, upstream providers of farming inputs (e.g., machinery, seeds) have a more oligopolistic market structure and see high ratios of R&D to sales (Alston and Pardey, chapter 3, this volume). Arguably, the more oligopolistic parts of the supply chain may have favorable R&D conditions, reflecting the inverted-U of innovation effort in market structure that appears in some conceptual models and broader empirical evidence (e.g., Aghion et al. 2005).

As another example linking institutions and appropriability, natural monopolies may face innovation challenges through intermediating regulations. Utilities are natural monopolies that appear to see little R&D (Popp et al., chapter 4, this volume, and table 13.1). Having high fixed costs, electricity distribution, water, and sewage systems (and more classically telecom, cable television, and mail services) do not easily support multiple providers in a single market. Public ownership or price regulation are common institutional responses. However, such institutional intervention can undermine innovation incentives. For example, innovations that lower costs may simply result in lower regulated prices, providing little incentive for the regulated firm to undertake improvements (e.g., Vickers and Yarrow 1995).

Overall, appropriability issues speak to the basic incentives to innovate. They can provide plausible inroads to understanding industry variation in innovation. And appropriability can in part be mapped to institutional features, including intellectual property and market structure (which becomes a potentially malleable institutional feature through antitrust policy and other regulatory mechanisms). In part because such policy features can be revised, this lens on industry variation and laggard sectors seems to be a first-order issue for research.

---

suggests that the entry incentives are substantial, though of course the counterfactual market structures are not observed, and the causal effect of the market structure remains unclear.

13.5.2   Institutions and Basic Research

Basic research can play important roles in advancing marketplace innovations (e.g., Bush 1945), yet the payoffs are often indirect, with market value found in distant and often unexpected downstream applications (e.g., Ahmadpoor and Jones 2017; Azoulay, Graff Zivin, and Li 2019). Basic research thus exhibits another form of the appropriability problem, where virtually all the market returns to basic research are in its spillovers and cannot easily be captured by the researcher. Institutions such as the NIH and the National Science Foundation (NSF) can then play key roles in supporting basic research. Specifically, these institutions implement a policy model in which funding comes ex ante, through grants, rather than ex post, through some market appropriation mechanism.

From an industry point of view, public investment in basic research can be regarded as opening up new technological opportunities. One may then ask whether part of the industry variation in innovation follows from differential public investment in upstream basic research. Bruce and de Figueiredo (chapter 9, this volume) examine the allocation of federal research personnel and R&D expenditures across US executive branch agencies. R&D expenditures are largest in the Department of Defense, followed by Health and Human Services, with substantially lower R&D expenditure by several other agencies, including NASA, the Department of Energy, and NSF, and comparatively tiny R&D expenditure by the remaining agencies. Outside the Department of Defense, US government research funding is heavily tilted toward biomedicine through the NIH, which accounts for 44 percent of federal research funding.[11] NIH-sponsored research is often directly used by the private sector in developing new medicines and with high returns (e.g., Azoulay, Graff Zivin, and Li 2019). The opportunities this publicly funded research provides might then further help explain the high private sector R&D rates in pharmaceuticals and medicines (see table 13.1). By contrast with the biomedical sciences, we see much less government-supported basic research in other fields. For example, the R&D funding for the NIH is approximately 6 times, 36 times, and 144 times larger, respectively, than that for the NSF, Department of Transportation, and Department of Education.

Explaining the low rate of innovation in some sectors through "missing" basic research would be speculative as a primary explanation, but increasing funding for basic research should facilitate progress. And it is striking how little government-funded research occurs for key sectors of the economy. Take education, which is a fundamental force for increasing labor productivity, a key input to the innovative workforce, and a mechanism for intergenerational mobility and individual opportunity (e.g., Biasi, Deming, and

11. This measure is R&D funding to the Department of Health and Human Services (largely NIH) in FY2018, which shows similar tendencies in other years (Sargent 2020).

Moser, chapter 12, this volume; Bell et al. 2019; Card 2001; Hendricks and Schoellman 2018; B. Jones 2014). Yet education is the target of little public R&D. As another example, transportation and warehousing is a larger sector than pharmaceutical and medicines, yet it sees much less federally supported R&D. And in health, basic research in biomedicine is substantial and mirrored by enormously high rates of private-sector R&D, yet R&D targeting the provision of health services in hospitals and nursing homes—a much larger source of expenditure—seems almost absent by comparison.

Another example is energy research, where US federal support is more substantial than in many areas but still small compared to biomedical research. Beyond the social returns logic that applies to supporting basic research in general (e.g., B. Jones and Summers 2020; Stephan 1996), energy generation also calls for public support in other dimensions. First, the private sector will have difficulty marshaling resources for technology areas with substantial uncertainty over success and extraordinary fixed costs for innovation attempts. Nuclear fusion research, both for its high fixed costs and exploratory nature, then naturally relies on public support. Second, energy markets face an additional externality through fossil fuels and climate change, which suggests an even greater importance of basic research in this sector, in this case to advance alternative energy production opportunities. Expanding publicly supported research through the Department of Energy or other institutions thus has a natural logic and may be critical for confronting potentially large damages from climate change (e.g., Acemoglu et al. 2016; Dell, Jones, and Olken 2014).

For sectors that see little basic research support, it may be that basic research and private sector R&D are both low due to limited opportunity. For example, perhaps fundamental technological opportunity factors explain the lack of innovative investment in education or health services. Yet it would be hard to argue that education services or health services in the US could not be improved. The US lags many advanced economics in educational comparisons (e.g., Schleicher 2019). And the US spends twice the share of its GDP on health compared to other advanced economies, even as US citizens live substantially shorter lives.[12] One imagines that research to explain these problems and provide solutions could be endeavors with very high returns.

13.5.3   Institutions and Demand

Government institutions can also play roles on the demand side. Whereas basic research can be seen as part of a "technology push" mechanism, government can also create "demand pull" mechanisms. This can occur through

---

12. The US spent 17 percent of GDP on health in 2019, while the average across OECD countries was 8.8 percent (see OECD Health Statistics 2020, http://www.oecd.org/els/health -systems/health-data.htm).

direct buyer mechanisms (e.g., advanced purchase commitments) or through indirect mechanisms (e.g., tax credits for adopting specific new technologies). Governments can also play a role in certification, reducing buyer uncertainty.

As examples of demand pull policies, one can return to the energy sector, where many policies may have been motivated by direct considerations of negative externalities (from acid rain to greenhouse gases) but where adjusting demand for specific technologies also changes innovation incentives. Notably, for directional technology considerations, broad innovation institutions don't really help: a fossil-fuel innovation (e.g., fracking) can take advantage of patent law or research tax credits just as a clean energy innovation can. Shifting innovation toward technologies with milder negative externalities then requires more specific interventions to tilt innovation effort and incentives (Popp et al., chapter 4, this volume). One approach might be a carbon tax or quota system that asymmetrically raises the price of the more polluting technology. One can also direct energy production technologies with installation credits (e.g., the US Production Tax Credit for wind energy), direct buyer incentives (e.g., the Qualified Plug-In Electric Drive Motor Vehicle Tax Credit), or regulatory mandates (e.g., CAFE standards for automobile efficiency). These approaches are distinct from and can complement technology push approaches.

Institutions can also play first-order roles in certification, working on the uncertainty dimension of demand. Institutional intervention may be especially important where product and service salience is an issue. As discussed above, the FDA helps prove that new drugs are effective and safe. Reducing buyer uncertainty in this way may then be critical for elevating incentives to engage in drug R&D. The education sector appears again here, as a counterexample. While the US Department of Education has implemented the "What Works Clearinghouse" to collect and publicize information about rigorous assessments of innovations, there remains little systematic effort (or requirement) to engage in rigorous assessment of education tools (Chatterji and Jones 2012). One may then observe that many school systems invest in computers, tablets, and software tools but with little or no evidence that these are superior tools for children's learning (Biasi, Deming, and Moser, chapter 12, this volume). The education sector might be well served by the advent of institutions similar to the FDA, providing pathways for innovators to prove the quality of their new products and services. Rigorous certification can facilitate innovative entry and help schools and school systems adopt effective innovations.

13.5.4   Institutions and Scalability

As discussed above, scalability can be a key attractor for innovative investment. The enormous innovative effort and venture capital orientation toward information services seem to hinge on this logic, where new digital goods can scale cheaply, rapidly, and widely to reach new customers. While scalability in digitization depends critically on technology fundamentals, in many contexts, institutional and regulatory mechanisms also seem first order.

For example, health services embed privacy regulations that can inhibit data sharing. Such privacy regulations are well meaning in their own terms, but they also constrain the ability to innovate in health services through information sharing—innovations that could not only reduce costs but also create health benefits (e.g., by reducing diagnostic and treatment errors). Basic information about prices and outcomes is also hard for would-be innovators to ascertain. The balkanized market structure, complex regulatory layers, and intermixture of public and private insurers further inhibits scalability, and the US health system in the context of the COVID-19 pandemic has betrayed further weaknesses in data collection, testing, and coordination for patient care. By contrast, standard-setting organizations in the IT space have developed extremely successful interoperability protocols. The opportunity in health services for improvement seems vast.

Education services also face scalability challenges. Privacy regulations for students, which are again well meaning, can limit the collection of empirical evidence and the ability to assess educational innovations. State and local regulatory variation, and resource differences, further inhibit scalability. With thousands of different school districts, different views on teaching objectives, and weak evidence, selling new products depends enormously on a business's salesforce and its network of relationships with school districts. The Common Core State Standards Initiative may then be important not just for raising standards but also for innovation: It creates high-scale targets for pedagogical innovators. This standard setting effort has faced headwinds, however, and efforts at rigorous evaluations of education tools remain much further behind (Chatterji and Jones 2012).

As a notable contrast, the advance of ridesharing (e.g., Uber) and homestay markets (e.g., Airbnb) developed in the face of existing municipal taxi and hotel regulations. As business models that stood somewhat outside existing regulations, they were able to scale rapidly. Health and education services appear to face stricter restrictions that are hard for innovators to overcome—and an Uber-like approach of asking for forgiveness rather than permission seems less plausible. This suggests that conscious, ex ante regulatory reform and standard setting may be essential for allowing scalability and encouraging innovation. To the extent that regulations inhibiting scalability have benefits (e.g., for safety or privacy), participatory political processes can allow for greater care in how different dimensions of social welfare are balanced.

13.6   Conclusion

The story of growth in advanced economies like the US is one of aggregate steadiness overlaying massive cross-industry differences. This chapter, in tandem with the other chapters in this book, assesses the enormous variation in innovation across industries and presents a range of explanations. The issues at the sectoral level are high stakes. For one, the aggregate steadiness in economic growth has recently met headwinds, with the US economy entering an apparently sustained productivity growth slowdown. This slowdown becomes a sector-level issue not only in the obvious sense that macro outcomes are constructed from sectoral outcomes, but also more acutely because of the dynamics in sectoral GDP shares. Taking the perspective of a Baumol cost disease, the sectors that fail to progress end up occupying greater shares of GDP. Failures to advance these sectors can then become an economic albatross, calling into question the potential for future growth.

Lagging sectors are also high stakes because they directly limit progress at key challenges. One example is innovation in the energy sector and the capacity to avoid damages from climate change. Other examples are education and health services. Education may the greatest of all general-purpose technologies in the sense that it creates human capital, a key input to further innovation across the economy. Education also speaks to inequality, where failure to advance the quality of educational services across the economy undermines individual opportunity. Health services in the US meanwhile manage to be extraordinarily expensive by international comparisons even as the US population faces substantially lower life expectancy.

To assess and organize reasons for the large variation in innovative effort and success across sectors, in this chapter, I have used a three-part framework emphasizing demand, supply, and institutions. Plausibly strong forces exist in each dimension. However, whereas forces rooted in fundamental preferences and natural laws may be important, institutional forces are more elastic to change and therefore of more practical relevance. In this chapter, I have therefore highlighted some institutional roles in furthering innovation. The emphasis has been on institutional features that vary across sectors, from basic research support to regulation to appropriability regimes. While the analysis is necessarily incomplete, the frameworks and sectoral examples suggest fruitful opportunities for policy. Assessing policy options in detail and continuing to unpack the sources of cross-sector innovation differences are critical areas for future research.

Ultimately, innovation comes down to the opportunities and incentives facing individuals, firms, and investors. Naturally, innovative agents gravitate toward sectors with larger opportunities, which today appear especially in biomedicine and IT. But from a social progress point of view, innovators, policymakers, and scholars need to think not just about "the room where it happens" but also about "the rooms where it doesn't happen." If the dearth of innovative activity in some industries is due to a fundamental lack of technological opportunities, then the current allocation of effort across sectors may be appropriate. But innovation is an environment with large spillovers and market failures, and uneven institutions, so that there is little reason to think that we have an efficient allocation. The overarching observation in this chapter is that we need to pay substantial policy and research attention to these "rooms where it doesn't happen," because they matter, and because there are many policy instruments that could elevate innovation and attack the essential problems that these sectors pose.

References

Acemoglu, Daron, and Joshua Linn. 2004. "Market Size in Innovation: Theory and Evidence from the Pharmaceutical Industry." *Quarterly Journal of Economics* 119(3): 1049–90.

Acemoglu, Daron, Ufuk Akcigit, Douglas Hanley, and William Kerr. 2016. "Transition to Clean Technology." *Journal of Political Economy* 124(1): 52–104.

Aghion, Philippe, Nick Bloom, Richard Blundell, Rachel Griffith, and Peter Howitt. 2005. "Competition and Innovation: An Inverted U-Relationship." *Quarterly Journal of Economics* 120(2): 701–28.

Ahmadpoor, M., and B. F. Jones. 2017. "The Dual Frontier: Patented Inventions and Prior Scientific Advance." *Science* 357: 583–87.

Arrow, Kenneth. 1962. "Economic Welfare and the Allocation of Resources for Invention." In *The Rate and Direction of Inventive Activity: Economic and Social Factors*, edited by Universities-National Bureau Committee for Economic Research & Committee on Economic Growth of the Social Science Research Council, 609–25. Princeton, NJ: Princeton University Press.

Azoulay, Pierre, Josh Graff Zivin, and Danielle Li. 2019. "Public R&D Investments and Private-Sector Patenting: Evidence from NIH Funding Rules." *Review of Economic Studies* 86: 117–52.

Baumol, William J. 1993. "Health Care, Education, and the Cost Disease: A Looming Crisis for Public Choice." *Public Choice* 77: 17–28.

Bell, Alex, Raj Chetty, Xavier Jaravel, Neviana Petkova, and John Van Reenen. 2019. "Who Becomes an Inventor in America? The Importance of Exposure to Innovation." *Quarterly Journal of Economics* 134(2): 647–713.

Bergoing, Raphael, Timothy J. Kehoe, Vanessa Strauss-Kahn, and Kei-Mu Yi. 2004. "Why Is Manufacturing Trade Rising Even as Manufacturing Output Is Falling?" *American Economic Review* 94(2): 134–38.

Brouwer, E., and K. Kleinknecht. 1997. "Measuring the Unmeasurable: A Country's Non-R&D Expenditure on Product and Service Innovation." *Research Policy* 25: 1235–42.

Bush, Vannevar. 1945. *Science, The Endless Frontier. A Report to the President*. Washington, DC: US Government Printing Office.

Card, David. 2001. "Estimating the Return to Schooling: Progress on Some Persistent Econometric Problems." *Econometrica* 69(5): 1127–60.

Chatterji, Aaron, and Benjamin Jones. 2012. "Harnessing Technology to Improve K–12 Education." Hamilton Project Discussion Paper 2012-5. Washington, DC: Brookings Institution.

Cohen, Wesley. 2010. "Fifty Years of Empirical Studies of Innovative Activity and Performance." In *Handbook of the Economics of Innovation*, Vol. 1, 129–213. Amsterdam: Elsevier.

Cohen, Wesley, Richard Nelson, and John Walsh. 2000. "Protecting Their Intellectual Assets: Appropriability Conditions and Why U.S. Manufacturing Firms Patent (or Not)." NBER Working Paper No. 7552. Cambridge, MA: National Bureau of Economic Research.

Collard-Wexler, Allan, and Jan De Loecker. 2016. "Production Function Estimation with Measurement Error in Inputs." NBER Working Paper No. 22437. Cambridge, MA: National Bureau of Economic Research.

Dell, Melissa, Benjamin F. Jones, and Benjamin A. Olken. 2014. "What Do We Learn from the Weather? The New Climate-Economy Literature." *Journal of Economic Literature* 52(3): 740–98.

Dranove, David, Daniel Kessler, Mark McClellan, and Mark Satterthwaite. 2003. "Is More Information Better? The Effects of 'Report Cards' on Health Care Providers." *Journal of Political Economy* 111(3): 555–88.

Drummond, Michael F., David A. Wilson, Panos Kanavos, Peter Ubel, and Joan Rovira. 2007. "Assessing the Economic Challenges Posed by Orphan Drugs." *International Journal of Technology Assessment in Health Care* 23(1): 36–42.

Finkelstein, Amy. 2004. "Static and Dynamic Effects of Health Policy: Evidence from the Vaccine Industry." *Quarterly Journal of Economics* 119(2): 527–64.

Gans, Joshua, and Scott Stern. 2003. "The Product Market and the Market for 'Ideas': Commercialization Strategies for Technology Entrepreneurs." *Research Policy* 32(2): 333–50.

Ghosh, Shikhar, and Ramana Nanda. 2010. "Venture Capital Investment in the Clean Energy Sector." Harvard Business School Working Paper 11-020.

Gilbert, Richard, and David Newbery. 1982. "Preemptive Patenting and the Persistence of Monopoly." *American Economic Review* 72(3): 514–26.

Hall, Bronwyn, Adam Jaffe, and Manuel Trajtenberg. 2005. "Market Value and Patent Citations." *RAND Journal of Economics* 36(1): 16–38.

Hall, Bronwyn, Jacques Mairesse, and Pierre Mohnen. 2010. "Measuring the Returns to R&D." In *Handbook of the Economics of Innovation*, Vol. 1, 1033–82. Amsterdam: Elsevier.

Hendricks, Lutz, and Todd Schoellman. 2018. "Human Capital and Development Accounting: New Evidence from Wage Gains at Migration." *Quarterly Journal of Economics* 133(2): 665–700.

Jaffe, Adam. 1986. "Technological Opportunity and Spillovers of R&D." *American Economic Review* 76: 984–1001.

Jones, Benjamin F. 2009. "The Burden of Knowledge and the 'Death of the Renaissance Man': Is Innovation Getting Harder?" *Review of Economic Studies* 7: 283–317.

———. 2014. "The Human Capital Stock: A Generalized Approach." *American Economic Review* 104(11): 3752–77.

Jones, Benjamin F., and Lawrence H. Summers. 2020. "A Calculation of the Social Returns to Innovation." Forthcoming in *Innovation and Public Policy*, edited by Austan Goolsbee and Benjamin F. Jones. Chicago: University of Chicago Press.

Jones, Charles. 1995. "R&D-Based Models of Economic Growth." *Journal of Political Economy* 103: 759–84.

———. 2016. "The Facts of Economic Growth." In *Handbook of Economic Growth*, Vol. 2, edited by John Taylor and Harald Uhlig, 3–69. Amsterdam: Elsevier.

Kerr, William, Ramana Nanda, and Matthew Rhodes-Kropf. 2014. "Entrepreneurship as Experimentation." *Journal of Economic Perspectives* 28: 25–48.

Kogan, Leonid, Dimitris Papanikolaou, Amit Seru, and Noah Stoffman. 2017. "Technological Innovation, Resource Allocation, and Growth." *Quarterly Journal of Economics* 132(2): 665–712.

Kortum, Sam. 1997. "Research, Patenting, and Technological Change." *Econometrica* 65: 1389–1419.

Kremer, Michael. 2000. "Creating Markets for New Vaccines Part I: Rationale." *Innovation Policy and the Economy* 1: 35–72.

Kremer, Michael, and Rachel Glennerster. 2004. *Strong Medicine: Creating Incentives for Pharmaceutical Research on Neglected Diseases.* Princeton, NJ: Princeton University Press.

Levin, Richard, Alvin Klevorick, Richard Nelson, Sidney Winter, Richard Gilbert, and Zvi Griliches. 1987. "Appropriating the Returns from Industrial Research and Development." *Brookings Papers on Economic Activity* 1987(3): 783–831.

Mansfield, Edwin. 1986. "Patents and Innovation: An Empirical Study." *Management Science* 32: 173–81.

Mokyr, Joel. 1990. *The Lever of Riches: Technological Creativity and Economic Progress.* New York: Oxford University Press.

Moser, Petra. 2005. "How Do Patent Laws Influence Innovation? Evidence from Nineteenth-Century World's Fairs." *American Economic Review* 95(4): 1214–36.

National Science Foundation. 2020. "Research and Development: U.S. Trends and International Comparisons." January. Alexandria, VA: National Science Foundation.

Pilat, Dirk, Agnès Cimper, Karsten Olsen, and Colin Webb. 2006. "The Changing Nature of Manufacturing in OECD Economies." OECD Directorate for Science, Technology, and Industry Working Paper 2006/9. Paris.

President's Council of Advisors on Science and Technology. 2010. "Prepare and Inspire: K–12 Science, Technology, Engineering, and Math (STEM) Education for America's Future." https://obamawhitehouse.archives.gov/sites/default/files /microsites/ostp/pcast-stem-ed-final.pdf.

Romer, Paul M. 1990. "Endogenous Technological Change." *Journal of Political Economy* 98: S71–S102.

Rosenberg, Nathan. 1982. *Inside the Black Box: Technology and Economics.* Cambridge: Cambridge University Press.

Sampat, Bhaven, and Heidi L. Williams. 2019. "How Do Patents Affect Follow-On Innovation? Evidence from the Human Genome." *American Economic Review* 109(1): 203–36.

Sargent, John. 2020. "Federal Research and Development (R&D) Funding: FY2020." Report R45715. Washington, DC: Congressional Research Service.

Scherer, Frederick M. 1965. "Firm Size, Market Structure, Opportunity, and the Output of Patented Inventions." *American Economic Review* 55: 1097–1125.

Schleicher, Andreas. 2019. "PISA 2018: Insights and Comparisons." OECD. https:// www.oecd.org/pisa/PISA%202018%20Insights%20and%20Interpretations %20FINAL%20PDF.pdf.

Schumpeter, Joseph. 1942. *Capitalism, Socialism, and Democracy.* New York: Harper & Brothers.

Scotchmer, Suzanne. 1991. "Standing on the Shoulders of Giants: Cumulative Research and the Patent Law." *Journal of Economic Perspectives* 5(1): 29–41.

Solow, Robert M. 1956. "A Contribution to the Theory of Economic Growth." *Quarterly Journal of Economics* 70(1): 65–94.

Stephan, Paula. 1996. "The Economics of Science." *Journal of Economic Literature* 34(3): 1199–1235.

Teece, David J. 1986. "Profiting from Technological Innovation." *Research Policy* 15(6): 285–305.

Vickers, John, and George Yarrow. 1995. *Privatization: An Economic Analysis.* Cambridge, MA: MIT Press.

Waldfogel, Joel. 2018. *Digital Renaissance: What Data and Economics Tell Us about the Future of Popular Culture.* Princeton, NJ: Princeton University Press.

Contributors

Julian M. Alston
Department of Agricultural and
 Resource Economics
University of California
One Shields Avenue
Davis, CA 95616

Michael J. Andrews
Department of Economics
University of Maryland Baltimore
 County
1000 Hilltop Circle
Baltimore, MD 21250

Emek Basker
US Census Bureau
Center for Economic Studies
4600 Silver Hill Road
Washington, DC 20233-9100

Barbara Biasi
Yale School of Management
165 Whitney Avenue
New Haven, CT 06520

Joshua R. Bruce
Gies College of Business
515 East Gregory Drive
University of Illinois
 Urbana-Champaign
Champaign, IL 61820

Amitabh Chandra
John F. Kennedy School of
 Government
Harvard University
79 JFK Street
Cambridge, MA 02138

Aaron K. Chatterji
The Fuqua School of Business
Duke University
100 Fuqua Drive, Box 90120
Durham, NC 27708

Derrick Choe
NYU Stern School of Business
44 West 4th Street
New York, NY 10012

Christophe Combemale
Engineering and Public Policy
Carnegie Mellon University
5000 Forbes Avenue
Pittsburgh, PA 15213

Annie V. Dang
Georgetown University Law Center
600 New Jersey Avenue NW
Washington, DC 20001

John M. de Figueiredo
The Law School and Fuqua School
Duke University
210 Science Drive, Box 90360
Durham, NC 27708

Mercedes Delgado
Copenhagen Business School
Department of Strategy and
    Innovation (SI)
Kilevej 14, 2
2000 Frederiksberg, Denmark

David Deming
Harvard Kennedy School
Malcolm Wiener Center for Social Policy
79 JFK Street
Cambridge, MA 02138

Eleanor Wiske Dillon
Microsoft Research New England
1 Memorial Drive
Cambridge, MA 02142

Gilles Duranton
The Wharton School
University of Pennsylvania
3620 Locust Walk
Philadelphia, PA 19104

Chris Forman
Charles H. Dyson School of Applied
    Economics and Management
Warren Hall
Cornell University
Ithaca, NY 14853-6201

Cirrus Foroughi
Analysis Group
111 Huntington Avenue
Boston, MA 02199

Lucia Foster
US Census Bureau
Center for Economic Studies
4600 Silver Hill Road
Washington, DC 20233-9100

Erica R. H. Fuchs
Department of Engineering and Public
    Policy
Carnegie Mellon University
5000 Forbes Avenue
Pittsburgh, PA 15213

Sharat Ganapati
Walsh School of Foreign Service
Georgetown University
37th and O Streets, NW
Washington, DC 20057

Britta Glennon
The Wharton School
University of Pennsylvania
3620 Locust Walk
Philadelphia, PA 19104

Avi Goldfarb
Rotman School of Management
University of Toronto
105 St. George Street
Toronto, ON M5S 3E6 Canada

Jessie Handbury
The Wharton School
University of Pennsylvania
1463 Steinberg-Dietrich Hall
Philadelphia, PA 19104

Ivan Haščič
Senior Economist, Environment
    Directorate
Organisation for Economic Co-
    operation and Development
2, rue André Pascal
75016 Paris, France

Nick Johnstone
Chief Statistician, Energy Data Centre
International Energy Agency
9 rue de la Fédération
75739 Paris Cedex 15 France

Benjamin F. Jones
Kellogg School of Management
Northwestern University
2211 Campus Drive
Evanston, IL 60208

J. Daniel Kim
University of Pennsylvania
Wharton School
3620 Locust Walk
2029 Steinberg-Dietrich Hall
Philadelphia, PA 19104

Edward Kung
Department of Economics
David Nazarian College of Business
    and Economics
California State University, Northridge
Northridge, CA 91330

Francine Lafontaine
Ross School of Business
University of Michigan
701 Tappan Street
Ann Arbor, MI 48109

Josh Lerner
Harvard Business School
Rock Center 214
Soldiers Field
Boston, MA 02163

Gustavo Manso
Haas School of Business
University of California at Berkeley
545 Student Services Building #1900
Berkeley, CA 94720

Karen G. Mills
Harvard Business School
Soldiers Field
Boston, MA 02163

Petra Moser
Department of Economics
NYU Stern
44 West 4th Street
New York, NY 10012

Lauren Mostrom
Harvard Business School
Soldiers Field
Boston, MA 02163

Alexander Oettl
Scheller College of Business
Georgia Institute of Technology
800 West Peachtree Street NW
Atlanta, GA 30308

Philip G. Pardey
Department of Applied Economics
University of Minnesota
1994 Buford Avenue
St. Paul, MN 55108

Jacquelyn Pless
MIT Sloan School of Management
100 Main Street, E62-479
Cambridge, MA 02142

David Popp
Department of Public Administration
    and International Affairs
Center for Policy Research, The
    Maxwell School
Syracuse University
426 Eggers Hall
Syracuse, NY 13244-1020

Rob Seamans
NYU Stern School of Business
44 West 4th Street, KMC 7-58
New York, NY 10012

Jagadeesh Sivadasan
University of Michigan
Ross School of Business
701 Tappan, Room R4310
Ann Arbor, MI 48103

Scott Stern
MIT Sloan School of Management
100 Main Street, E62-476
Cambridge, MA 02142

Manuel Trajtenberg
Eitan Berglas School of Economics
Tel Aviv University
Tel Aviv 69978 Israel

Joel Waldfogel
3-177 Carlson School of Management
University of Minnesota
321 19th Avenue South
Minneapolis, MN 55455

Kate S. Whitefoot
Engineering and Public Policy
Carnegie Mellon University
5000 Forbes Ave
Pittsburgh, PA 15213

Brian Davern Wright
Agricultural and Resource Economics
University of California, Berkeley
Berkeley, CA 94720-3310

Author Index

Page numbers followed by "f" or "t" refer to figures or tables, respectively.

Subject Index